SIGNS

INTERPRETATION PANELS
HONOURS BOARDS
NOTICE BOARDS

Greenbarnes Ltd.

Unit 7, Barrington Court, Ward Road,
Brackley, Northamptonshire, NN13 7LE
T: 01280 701093 F: 01280 702843
E: sales@greenbarnes.co.uk W: www.greenbarnes.co.uk

God's heart **for the poor hasn't changed.** No one is disposable **to God, so no one is disposable to us. Today's orphans, widows and strangers are** the poor; the powerless; the exploited. **Christian Aid's first priority is fighting for their tomorrow because we believe everyone deserves one.**

The Church of Scotland is committed to this work by sponsoring Christian Aid.

0131 220 1254
www.christianaidscotland.org.uk

We believe in life before death

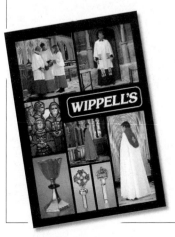

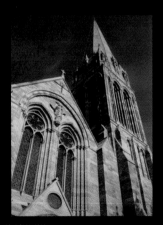

The Right Reverend Sheilagh M. Kesting BA BD

MODERATOR

The Church of Scotland
YEAR BOOK
2007/2008

Editor

Rev. Ronald S. Blakey

MA BD MTh

Published on behalf of
THE CHURCH OF SCOTLAND
by SAINT ANDREW PRESS
121 George Street, Edinburgh EH2 4YN

THE OFFICES OF THE CHURCH

121 George Street
Edinburgh EH2 4YN

Tel: 0131-225 5722
Fax: 0131-220 3113
Internet: http://www.churchofscotland.org.uk/

Office Hours:
Office Manager/Facilities Manager:

Monday–Friday 9:00am–5:00pm
Appointment awaited

MISSION AND DISCIPLESHIP COUNCIL

Edinburgh Office	121 George Street, Edinburgh EH2 4YN	0131-225 5722
Glasgow Office	59 Elmbank Street, Glasgow G2 4PQ	0141-352 6946
Inverness Office	Main Street, North Kessock, Inverness IV1 3XN	01463 731712
Perth Office	Arran House, Arran Road, Perth PH1 3DZ	01738 630514

SOCIAL CARE COUNCIL

Charis House	47 Milton Road East, Edinburgh EH15 2SR	Tel: 0131-657 2000
	[E-mail: info@charis.org.uk]	Fax: 0131-657 5000

SCOTTISH CHARITY NUMBERS

The Church of Scotland	SC011353
The Church of Scotland General Trustees	SC014574
The Church of Scotland Investors Trust	SC022884
The Church of Scotland Trust	SC020269

QUICK DIRECTORY

A.C.T.S.	01259 216980
Bridgeton, St Francis-in-the-East Church House	0141-554 8045
Carberry	0131-665 3135/7604
Christian Aid London	020 7620 4444
Christian Aid Scotland	0131-220 1254
Church of Scotland Insurance Co. Ltd	0131-220 4119
Glasgow Lodging House Mission	0141-552 0285
Kirk Care	0131-225 7246
Netherbow	0131-556 9579/2647
Media Relations Unit (Press Office)	0131-240 2243
Safeguarding Office (item 36 in Assembly Committee list)	0131-240 2256
Scottish Churches House	01786 823588
Scottish Churches Parliamentary Office	0131-558 8137
Year Book Editor	01899 229226

Pulpit Supply: Fee and Expenses
Details of the current fee and related expenses in respect of Pulpit Supply will be found as the last item in number 3 (the Ministries Council) on page 9.

First published in 2007 by SAINT ANDREW PRESS, 121 George Street, Edinburgh EH2 4YN on behalf of the CHURCH of SCOTLAND

Copyright © The CHURCH of SCOTLAND, 2007

ISBN 978 0 86153 384 8

CONTENTS

Prefaces xx

SECTION 1 Assembly Councils, Committees, Departments and Agencies 1

SECTION 2 General Information 43

SECTION 3 Church Procedure 69

SECTION 4 The General Assembly of 2007 97

SECTION 5 Presbytery Lists 105

SECTION 6 Additional Lists of Personnel 283

SECTION 7 Scottish Charity Numbers for Individual Congregations 333

SECTION 8 Congregational Statistics 2006 349

Index of ASSEMBLY COUNCILS, COMMITTEES, DEPARTMENTS
        and AGENCIES 2
Index of MINISTERS 384
Index of PARISHES and PLACES 396
Index of DISCONTINUED PARISH and CONGREGATIONAL NAMES 402
Index of SUBJECTS 423
Index of ADVERTISERS 425

All correspondence regarding the *Year Book* should be sent to
The Editor, *Church of Scotland Year Book*,
Saint Andrew Press, 121 George Street, Edinburgh EH2 4YN
Fax: 0131-220 3113
[E-mail: yearbookeditor@cofscotland.org.uk]

GENERAL ASSEMBLY OF 2008
The General Assembly of 2008 will convene on
Thursday, 15th May 2008

FROM THE MODERATOR

It is a book I have seldom had far from my desk – both as a parish minister and as a secretary in the Church Offices. Even in this electronic age, when databases exist for almost everything, it is often quickest to reach for the *Year Book*. It is a fount of information. How often I have been asked how to contact another church – and I say, as I reach for it, 'It's in the *Year Book*'! It seems that some people are unaware of just how much information there is in this annual volume – and that's before you come to the Presbytery Lists and the lists of those who serve in the various ministries.

We owe a deep debt of gratitude to Ron Blakey for the way he keeps the records up to date and prompts the heads of departments to review the information they submit. The *Year Book* is a significant tool in helping us to be aware of the Church of Scotland beyond our own congregation and our own Presbytery, even to our ecumenical belonging in Scotland, Britain and Ireland, Europe and the world. For behind all the facts and figures lie relationships. For what is the Church about if it is not relationships? Relationships bind us to one another in the community of believers; relationships are the result of our being drawn by the Holy Spirit into that relationship of overflowing love that exists between God and Jesus.

In commending this volume to you, I ask you to use it as a tool to strengthen your relationships of Christian belonging not only within the Church of Scotland but also beyond it.

Sheilagh M. Kesting
July 2007

FROM THE EDITOR

This edition of the *Year Book*, which makes a first foray into colour, includes six new or significantly revised sections:

- Presbytery Clerks have new e-mail addresses; accordingly, their old-style 'akph' addresses have been deleted.
- On the Report of the Legal Questions Committee, this year's General Assembly received a statement regarding the charging of fees (on behalf of ministers) for the conduct of funerals. It was felt that it would be helpful to see this statement included.
- *When all else fails, read the instructions.* This is generally sound advice; indeed, the one exception of which the editor was previously aware related to the DVD recorder in his living room. Over recent weeks, however, several correspondents have remarked that they had trawled in vain through the *Index of Former Parishes and Congregations* for names that they felt should be there. In fact, without exception, they had been looking for names which, in terms of the introduction to that Index, could not be there. The outcome, however, is that that introduction has been reworded to show more precisely what names are and are not included. To clarify matters still further, the title has been changed to the *Index of Discontinued Parish and Congregational Names.*
- A new section lists each congregation's Charity Number. This number indicates that the congregation has been entered on the Scottish Charity Register maintained by the Office of the Scottish Charity Regulator (OSCR) – www.oscr.org.uk. Regulations, to be published by the Scottish Executive, will come into force in the near future requiring charities to disclose their Charity Number on specified documents; and a number of local authorities and funders are now requiring charities to disclose their Charity Number on official forms and applications.

    The acutely observant will note that the Shetland Island parish of Fetlar has no Charity Number. This is not the result of editorial oversight: due processes are being followed, and Fetlar will lose this particular claim to uniqueness ere long. When clarifying this matter, the editor realised to his shame that the only thing he knew about Fetlar was this deficiency. Research was clearly required, and recourse was had to two tried and trusted works of reference. Robin Smith's splendid *The Making of Scotland* pinpoints it as one of Shetland's northern isles lying to the east of the larger Yell. 'For a long time,' he says, 'it has specialised in pony breeding.' Among much else, the *Fasti* reveals that it is not only ponies which have found the Fetlar air conducive to the preservation of the species. Sir John Carnegie appears to have served as minister of Fetlar from around 1694. In the course of his ministry, he succeeded to his father's title, becoming the second baronet of Pitarrow, and fathered 11 children. His successor in 1729, John Bonar, doubtless faced many daunting challenges, not least the achievements of his predecessor. He and his wife, however, did successfully maintain the strong manse family tradition, producing 10 children. By 1990, the population of the island had fallen to less than 100. A Community Council appeal for new residents saw some 20 newcomers arrive. Encouraging as this undoubtedly was, it did not seem that any population explosion of the Carnegie–Bonar type was imminent. Smith reports that the incomers were mainly Franciscan nuns running a retreat for people with problems.
- Until the early 1990s, the *Year Book* included a page giving comparative statistics over a period of years for the whole of the Church of Scotland. Figures shown included the numbers of communicant members, elders and Sunday School scholars. These figures are now published in the 'Blue Book' of Assembly Reports. The editor has received a number of requests that some entry of this kind should again find its way into the *Year Book*. Comparative figures for members and elders over a 40-year period appear this year.

Dr Dan Martin, an internationally renowned mathematician and for more than 50 years an elder in Kirkton Church, Carluke, learned shortly before his death in September 2006 that the *Year Book* might again contain these figures. 'They will suggest', he said, 'that elders today have it easy compared to their predecessors: they will show many fewer members and only slightly fewer elders.' He was right, of course, as far as cold figures go. In 1966, 1,233,808 members were looked after by 47,736 elders (one elder to more than 25 members). In 2006, 504,363 members were cared for by 40,651 elders (one elder to fewer than 13 members). Said Dr Martin: 'such figures positively invite a flawed application of statistics: they do not take account of the fact that in time past there would regularly be three or more communicant members in each household where today there is often only one'. He then amplified his point with typical humour: 'today, the most irresistible elder is regularly met with the steadfastly immovable doorstep response – "she's no' in" '.

• Over the past year, three former Moderators have drawn attention to a lack of consistency in that section of the *Year Book* which lists past Moderators of the General Assembly. In time past, the degrees and decorations recorded alongside the names included only awards and honours received prior to and during the Moderatorial year. More recently, however, at the specific request of individual Moderators, these post-nominal letters have been extended to include later awards. Coincidentally, a representative of one of our national newspapers suggested to the editor that it would help journalists when they come to write obituaries if the *Year Book* did indeed include a comprehensive list, irrespective of when degrees and the like were awarded. The point is taken, and an attempt has been made this year to update this section.

It unfortunately escaped the editor's attention last year that Owain Tudor Hughes, a former minister of Guernsey: St Andrew's in the Grange, celebrated his 100th birthday on 21 April 2006. We offer sincere if belated congratulations. George D. Monro, formerly of Yester, attained his century on 4 June 2007. As we go to press, we note that the Very Rev. Dr W. Roy Sanderson will reach that milestone on 23 September 2007. The 'Father of the Kirk' – the minister who has been ordained longest – is Thomas Mackenzie Donn, formerly of Duthil. He was ordained in Stornoway on 14 August 1932. He is, however, a comparative youngster: he will attain his 100th birthday on 1 October 2007.

Incredible though it must seem to its coterie of aficionados, the occasional voice has been heard venturing the thought that the *Year Book* is overpriced. Purely in the interests of detached academic research, a visit during May to Betty's rightly renowned tea room in Harrogate revealed a wall poster advising that, in pre-decimal 1928, afternoon tea in that establishment cost sixpence; the cost for that day's version of this enduring delectation was £14.50. A copy of the *Year Book* in 1928 cost one shilling and sixpence – three times the cost of an indulgent afternoon in Betty's. The book this year costs a modest £14 even though it includes every congregation's Charity Number (a 'must-know' for the Guild's next trivia quiz evening) and Sheilagh Kesting in full fetching colour.

In the highly competitive world of Internet/website providers and search engines, there are names which, depending on how the mind is working, have interesting connotations. On the telephone about a change of address, a session clerk, who had clearly been having a bad day, asked if the editor could confirm that *TalkTalk* offered concessions to ministers. 'If they do not,' he said, 'they should.' That set running what passes for the editorial mind. *Wanadoo* could make a cut-price offer to frustrated pigeon-fanciers. *Google* would surely appeal to dyslexic cricketers. The scurrilous story continues of the minister who was giving personal details over the telephone when arranging for goods to be delivered to the manse. Said the minister: 'the voice of the woman taking down the particulars was what could be described as "professionally bored" until he disclosed that his e-mail address included "*hotmail*". The bored at once became sultry: "and how", she asked, "would you be spelling that?" '

Ronald S. Blakey
July 2007

SECTION 1

Assembly Councils, Committees, Departments and Agencies

INDEX OF ASSEMBLY COUNCILS, COMMITTEES, DEPARTMENTS AND AGENCIES

Page

Councils

1. The Council of Assembly   3
2. The Church and Society Council   4
3. The Ministries Council   5
4. The Mission and Discipleship Council   10
5. The Social Care Council   15
6. The Support and Services Council   17
7. The World Mission Council   19

Committees, Departments and Agencies

8. Assembly Arrangements Committee   22
9. Central Services Committee   22
10. Chaplains to HM Forces   23
11. Church of Scotland Guild   24
12. Church of Scotland Investors Trust   25
13. Church of Scotland Pension Trustees   26
14. Church of Scotland Trust   26
15. Committee on Church Art and Architecture   27
16. Committee Planning the Church Without Walls Celebration
    (now Church Without Walls Group)   27
17. Ecumenical Relations Committee   27
18. Education and Nurture Task Group   30
19. Facilities Management Department   31
20. General Treasurer's Department   31
21. General Trustees   32
22. Housing and Loan Fund   34
23. Human Resources Department   35
24. Information Technology Department   35
25. Law Department   36
26. Legal Questions Committee   36
27. Mission and Evangelism Task Group   37
28. Nomination Committee   37
29. Panel on Review and Reform   37
30. Parish Appraisal Committee   38
31. Parish Development Fund Committee   38
32. Principal Clerk's Department   38
33. Publishing Committee   39
34. Stewardship and Finance Committee   39
35. Worship and Doctrine Task Group   41
36. Safeguarding Office   41
37. Scottish Churches Parliamentary Office   41

[Note: Years, where given, indicate the year of appointment]

1. THE COUNCIL OF ASSEMBLY

Remit

1. To implement the plan of reorganisation and structural change of the Agencies of the General Assembly as formulated by the Assembly Council and approved by the General Assembly of 2004.
2. To monitor, evaluate and co-ordinate the work of the Agencies of the General Assembly, within the context of policy determined by the Assembly.
3. To advise the General Assembly on the relative importance of work being undertaken by its various Agencies.
4. To receive reports from, offer guidance to and issue instructions to Agencies of the General Assembly as required from time to time on matters of management, organisation and administration.
5. To bring recommendations to the General Assembly concerning the total amount of the Church's Co-ordinated Budget for the following financial year and the disposition thereof among Local Mission, Parish Staffing and the Mission and Renewal Fund.
6. To determine the allocation of the total budgets for the following financial year for Parish Staffing and the Mission and Renewal Fund among the relevant Agencies of the General Assembly and Ecumenical Bodies.
7. To prepare and present to the General Assembly an indicative Rolling Budget for the following five financial years.
8. To receive and distribute unrestricted legacies and donations among the Agencies of the General Assembly with power to specify the use to which the same are to be applied.
9. To consider and decide on proposals from Agencies of the General Assembly to purchase heritable property or any other asset (except investments) valued in excess of £50,000 or lease any heritable property where the annual rental exceeds £10,000 per annum, declaring that no Agency save those referred to in section 19 hereof shall proceed to purchase or lease such property without prior approval from the Council.
10. To consider and decide on proposals from Agencies of the General Assembly, save those referred to in section 19 hereof, to sell or lease for a period in excess of five years or otherwise dispose of any heritable property, or sell or otherwise dispose of any asset (except investments) valued in excess of £50,000, held by or on behalf of that Agency, with power to allocate all or part of the sale or lease proceeds to another Agency or Agencies in terms of section 11 hereof.
11. To reallocate following upon consultation with the Agency or Agencies affected unrestricted funds held by or on behalf of any of the Agencies of the General Assembly to another Agency or Agencies with power to specify the use to which the same are to be applied.
12. To determine staffing and resourcing requirements of Agencies of the General Assembly, including inter-Departmental sharing or transfer of staff, in accordance with policies drawn up by the Council of Assembly in line with priorities approved by the General Assembly, it being declared that the term 'staffing' shall not include those appointed or employed to serve either in particular Parishes or overseas.
13. To consult with the relative Councils and Agencies in their appointment of Council Secretaries to the Church and Society, Ministries, Mission and Discipleship, Social Care and World Mission Councils, to appoint the Ecumenical Officer, the Director of Stewardship, the Head of Media Relations and the Personnel Manager and to nominate individuals to the General Assembly for appointment to the offices of Principal Clerk of the General Assembly,

Depute Clerk of the General Assembly, General Treasurer of the Church and Solicitor of the Church.

14. To keep under review the central administration of the Church, with particular regard to resolving issues of duplication of resources.

15. To provide an Internal Audit function to the General Assembly Councils, Statutory Corporations and Committees (other than the Social Care Council).

16. To attend to the general interests of the Church in matters which are not covered by the remit of any other Agency.

17. To deal with urgent issues arising between meetings of the General Assembly, provided that:
    (a) these do not fall within the jurisdiction of the Commission of Assembly or of any Presbytery or Kirk Session,
    (b) they are not of a legislative or judicial nature and
    (c) any action taken in terms of this clause shall be reported to the next General Assembly.

18. To encourage all Agencies of the General Assembly to work ecumenically wherever possible and to have regard to the international, evangelical and catholic nature of the Church.

19. For the avoidance of doubt, sections 9 and 10 shall not apply to the Church of Scotland General Trustees, the Church of Scotland Housing and Loan Fund for Retired Ministers and Widows and Widowers of Ministers and the New Charge Development Committee and its successor body, all of which may deal with heritable property and other assets without the approval of the Council.

Membership

(a) Convener, Vice-Convener and eight members appointed by the General Assembly; the General Treasurer and the Solicitor of the Church; the Principal Clerk as Secretary to the Council; together with:

(b) the Conveners of the Councils, namely Church and Society, Ministries, Mission and Discipleship, Social Care, Support and Services, and World Mission; the Secretaries of the following Councils, namely Church and Society, Ministries, Mission and Discipleship, Social Care and World Mission.

Convener: Mrs Helen McLeod MA (2004)
Vice-Convener: Rev. Alan Greig BSc BD (2007)
Secretary: The Principal Clerk

---

2. THE CHURCH AND SOCIETY COUNCIL

Remit

The remit of the Church and Society Council is to facilitate the Church of Scotland's engagement with, and comment upon, national, political and social issues through:

• the development of theological, ethical and spiritual perspectives in the formulation of policy on such issues;

• the effective representation of the Church of Scotland in offering on its behalf appropriate and informed comment on political and social issues;

• the building, establishing and maintaining of a series of networks and relationships with leaders and influence-shapers in civic society, and engaging long-term in dialogue and the exchange of ideas with them;

- the support of the local church in its mission and engagement by offering professional and accessible resources on contemporary issues;
- the conducting of an annual review of progress made in discharging the remit and the provision of a written report to the Council of Assembly.

Membership
Convener, Vice-Convener, 28 members appointed by the General Assembly, one of whom will also be appointed to the Ecumenical Relations Committee, and one member appointed from and by the Social Care Council and the Guild. The Nomination Committee will ensure that the Council membership contains at least five individuals with specific expertise in each of the areas of Education, Societal/Political, Science and Technology and Social/Ethical. This number may include the Convener and Vice-Convener of the Council.

Convener:	Mrs Morag Mylne (2005)
Vice-Convener:	Mr David Alexander (2005)
Secretary:	Rev. Dr David I. Sinclair

3. THE MINISTRIES COUNCIL
Tel: 0131-225 5722; Fax: 0131-240 2201
E-mail: ministries@cofscotland.org.uk

Remit
The remit of the Ministries Council is recruitment, training and support of recognised ministries for the mission of the Church, and assessment of patterns of national deployment of parish ministries. In pursuance of this remit, the Council is charged with:
- developing patterns of ministry which allow the Church of Scotland to be effective in its missionary calling and faithful to the one ministry of Jesus Christ;
- recruiting individuals of the highest calibre collaboratively to lead the Church through its ordained ministries;
- providing the Church with a range of ministries including the ministry of word and sacrament, the diaconate, auxiliary ministers, readers and specialist workers;
- developing assessment processes which ensure that those who serve the Church in its various ministries do so in response to God's call on their life;
- providing education, initial training, in-service training and personal-development appraisal of the highest quality to ensure that all those engaged in the various ministries of the Church are equipped to engage in Christ's mission and make the Gospel relevant in a rapidly changing society;
- building good relationships with, and offering quality pastoral support and care to, all the ministries of the Church;
- assisting the whole Church in its responsibility to meet the gospel imperative of giving priority to the poorest and most marginalised in our society;
- undertaking all of its local planning and appraisal work in full co-operation with Presbyteries, local congregations and other denominations, in order to ensure that emerging patterns of church life are effective at a local level and are a viable use of the Church's resources;
- evaluating all developments in ministry in order to ensure their effectiveness and relevance to the life of the Church today;

- working transparently and in collaboration with the other Councils in order to ensure the most effective use of the Church's finance, property and human resources;
- conducting an annual review of progress made in discharging the remit and providing a written report to the Council of Assembly.

Membership

Convener, four Vice-Conveners, 36 members appointed by the General Assembly, one of whom will also be appointed to the Ecumenical Relations Committee, and one member appointed from and by the General Trustees, the Housing and Loan Fund, the Committee on Chaplains to Her Majesty's Forces and the Diaconate Council. For the avoidance of doubt, where a representative of these other bodies is a member of staff, he or she will have no right to vote.

Convener:	Rev. Graham S. Finch MA BD
Vice-Conveners:	Rev. David W. Clark MA BD
	Rev. James S. Dewar MA BD
	Rev. Barry W. Dunsmore MA BD
	Rev. Ian F. Galloway BA BD

Staff

Council Secretary:	Rev. Dr Martin Scott DipMusEd RSAM BD PhD
	(Tel: ext. 389; E-mail: mscott@cofscotland.org.uk)
Pastoral Adviser and Associate Secretary: (Ministries Support and Development)	Rev. John P. Chalmers BD (Tel: ext. 309; E-mail: jchalmers@cofscotland.org.uk)
Associate Secretary: (Planning and Deployment)	Mr John Jackson BSc (Tel: ext. 312; E-mail: jjackson@cofscotland.org.uk)
Associate Secretary: (Priority Areas)	Rev. Dr H. Martin J. Johnstone MA BD MTh PhD (Tel: 0141-248 2905; E-mail: mjohnstone@cofscotland.org.uk)
Associate Secretary: (Vocational Guidance, Education and Training)	Mrs Moira Whyte MA (Tel: ext. 266; E-mail: mwhyte@cofscotland.org.uk)
Ministries Support Officers:	Mrs Elizabeth Chalmers BA (Tel: ext. 348; E-mail: lchalmers@cofscotland.org.uk) Rev. Jane Denniston MA BD (Tel: ext. 204; E-mail: jdenniston@cofscotland.org.uk) Rev. Gavin J. Elliott MA BD (Tel: ext. 255; E-mail: gelliott@cofscotland.org.uk) Mr Garry Leach BD BSc (Tel: ext. 242; E-mail: gleach@cofscotland.org.uk) Rev. Angus R. Mathieson MA BD (Tel: ext. 315; E-mail: amathieson@cofscotland.org.uk) Mrs Suzie Stark (Tel: ext. 225; E-mail: sstark@cofscotland.org.uk) Mr John Thomson (Tel: ext. 248; E-mail: jthomson@cofscotland.org.uk)
Priority Areas Development Worker:	Mr Noel Mathias (Tel: 0141-248 2905; E-mail: nmathias@cofscotland.org.uk)

Ministries Council
Further information about the Council's work and services is obtainable through the Ministries Council at the Church Offices. Information is available on a wide range of matters including the Consolidated Stipend Fund, National Stipend Fund, endowment grants, travelling and other expenses, pulpit supply, study leave, ministry development conferences, pastoral care services (including occupational health), Enquiry and Assessment, Education and Training, Parish Appraisal, Priority Areas, New Charge Development, Area Team Ministry, Interim Ministry, Readership, Chaplaincies, the Diaconate, Parish Staffing, and all aspects of work connected with ministers and the ministry of word and sacrament.

Committees
The policy development and implementation of the work of the Ministries Council is managed under the following committees:

1. Business Committee
Convener: Rev. Graham S. Finch MA BD
The Business Committee is responsible for ordering the business of the Council and ensuring that matters are followed through appropriately. It is empowered to act on behalf of the full Council as an emergency decision-making body, but accountable to it. The Business Committee communicates and liaises with Presbyteries on an ongoing basis on behalf of the Council. It is also responsible for overseeing risk management on behalf of the Council and for monitoring the Council's communications policy.

2. Strategic Advisory Group
Convener: Rev. James S. Dewar MA BD
The Strategic Advisory Group is authorised to act as a 'think tank' for the Council, bringing forward from time to time policy proposals for consideration by the Council in relation to any aspect of its work. The Strategic Advisory Group also considers agenda items relating to policy remitted to it directly by the Council, and through the Council can receive for consideration discussion issues relating to the Council's remit submitted by other bodies such as Presbyteries and other Councils.

3. Assessment Scheme Committee
Convener: Rev. Lezley J. Kennedy BD ThM MTh
The Assessment Scheme Committee is responsible for overseeing and reviewing the Enquiry and Assessment Process for full-time and auxiliary ministers of word and sacrament, deacons and readers, together with the admission and readmission of ministers. The Committee has powers to make final recommendations on suitability for training, to undertake Committee reviews, recruit and train assessors and directors, and liaise with Presbyteries.

4. Candidate Supervision Committee
Convener: Rev. Donald Macleod BD LRAM DRSAM
The Candidate Supervision Committee is responsible for the supervision of those in training for the recognised ministries of the Church, and the production of training reports. It operates with powers to sustain placements, liaise with universities, recruit and train supervisors, arrange placements, deliver residential and conference programmes, liaise with Presbyteries, engage in review of candidature, and oversee the completion of other Church requirements in relation to recognised ministries.

5. Planning and Deployment Committee
Convener: Rev. David W. Clark MA BD
The Planning and Deployment Committee is responsible for the overall planning of the deployment of the Church's ministries, primarily through the ongoing monitoring of the development of Presbytery Plans. The Committee also oversees work on emerging ministries (including New Charge Development work) and deals with all issues relating to policy in respect of employment matters. The Committee receives regular reports from the three Task Groups relating to the above remit.

6. Ministries Support and Development Committee
Convener: Rev. Barry W. Dunsmore MA BD
The Ministries Support and Development Committee is responsible for overseeing the pastoral care of all recognised ministries, which includes the Occupational Health Scheme and Counselling Service: and for the promotion of lifelong learning and development opportunities for these ministries, which includes study leave and accompanied review. Also included is the work of Interim Ministry, Area Team Ministry and all aspects of Chaplaincy.

7. Ministries Finance Committee
Convener: Rev. Jeff A. McCormick BD
The Ministries Finance Committee operates with powers to deal with the Parish Ministries Fund, the National Stipend Scheme, Vacancy Schedules, Maintenance Allowances, Hardship Grants and Bursaries, Stipend Advances, management of investments, writing-off shortfalls and the granting of further endowments. It also maintains an oversight of the budgets for all recognised ministries.

8. Priority Areas Committee
Convener: Rev. Ian F. Galloway BA BD
The Priority Areas Strategy Group implements the policy of the Council in developing, encouraging and overseeing strategy within priority areas parishes. It is empowered to develop resources to enable congregations to make appropriate responses to the needs of people living in poverty in their parishes, and to raise awareness of the effects of poverty on people's lives in Scotland. It also co-ordinates the strategy of the wider Church in its priority to Scotland's poorest parishes.

The Council also has several *ad hoc* Task Groups,which report to the Committees and implement specific policies of the Council, as follows:

Accompanied Review Task Group
Leader: Rev. Karen K. Watson BD MTh

Conference and Development Task Group
Leader: Rev. Joanne Hood MA BD

Interim Ministries Task Group
Leader: Rev. James Reid BD

Chaplaincies Task Group
Leader: Rev. Dorothy Anderson LLB DipLP BD

Communications Task Group
Leader: Rev. Malcolm I.G. Rooney DPE BEd BD

Curriculum Development Task Group
Leader: Rev. Peter White BVMS BD

Pastoral and Spiritual Care Task Group
Leader: Rev. Barry W. Dunsmore MA BD

Employment Issues Task Group
Leader: Mr Grant Gordon

Emerging Ministries Task Group
Leader: Rev. Jared Hay BA MTh DipMin DMin

Presbytery Planning Task Group
Leader: Rev. David W. Clark MA BD

Assessment Issues Task Group
Leader: Rev. Lezley Kennedy BD ThM MTh

Health and Healing Task Group
Leader: Rev. Gordon MacRae BA BD

Other Related Bodies:
Chaplains to HM Forces
See separate entry at number 10.

Housing and Loan Fund
See separate entry at number 22.

Pulpit Supply: Fee and Expenses
The General Assembly of 1995 approved new regulations governing the amount of Supply Fee and Expenses. These were effective from 1 July 1995 and are as follows:
1.   In Charges where there is only one diet of worship, the Pulpit Supply Fee shall be a Standard Fee of £50 (or as from time to time agreed by the Ministries Council).
2.   In Charges where there are additional diets of worship on a Sunday, the person fulfilling the Supply shall be paid £10 for each additional Service (or as from time to time agreed by the Ministries Council).
3.   Where the person is unwilling to conduct more than one diet of worship on a given Sunday, he or she shall receive a pro-rata payment based on the total available Fee shared on the basis of the number of Services conducted.
4.   The Fee thus calculated shall be payable in the case of all persons permitted to conduct Services under Act II 1986.
5.   In all cases, Travelling Expenses shall be paid. Where there is no convenient public conveyance, the use of a private car shall be paid for at the Committee rate of Travelling Expenses. In exceptional circumstances, to be approved in advance, the cost of hiring a car may be met.
6.   Where weekend board and lodging are agreed as necessary, these may be claimed for the weekend at a maximum rate of that allowed when attending the General Assembly. The Fee and Expenses should be paid to the person providing the Supply before he or she leaves on the Sunday.

4. THE MISSION AND DISCIPLESHIP COUNCIL

Remit
The remit of the Mission and Discipleship Council is:
- to take a lead role in developing and maintaining an overall focus for mission in Scotland, and to highlight its fundamental relationships with worship, service, doctrine, education and nurture;
- to take a lead role in developing strategies, resources and services in Christian education and nurture, recognising these as central to both mission and discipleship;
- to offer appropriate servicing and support nationally, regionally and locally in the promotion of nurturing, worshipping and witnessing communities of faith;
- to introduce policy on behalf of the Church in the following areas: adult education and elder training, church art and architecture, congregational mission and development, doctrine, resourcing youth and children's work and worship;
- to establish and support the Mission Forum with representatives of relevant Councils;
- to encourage appropriate awareness of, and response to, the requirements of people with particular needs including physical, sensory and/or learning disabilities;
- to conduct an annual review of progress made in discharging the remit and provide a written report to the Council of Assembly.

Membership
Convener, three Vice-Conveners and 21 members appointed by the General Assembly, one of whom will also be appointed to the Ecumenical Relations Committee, the Director of Stewardship, one member appointed from and by the General Trustees, the Guild, the Parish Development Fund, the 'Church Without Walls' Planning Committee and the Scottish Churches Community Trust, and the Convener or Vice-Convener of the Committee on Church Art and Architecture as that Committee shall determine. The Nomination Committee will ensure that the Council membership contains at least three individuals with specific expertise in each of the areas of Education and Nurture, Mission and Evangelism and Worship and Doctrine.

Convener:	Rev. Angus Morrison MA BD PhD
Vice-Conveners:	Mrs Linda Dunnett BA DCS
	Rev. Peter H. Donald MA PhD BD
	Rev. Jock Stein MA BD

Staff

Council Secretary:	Rev. Douglas A.O. Nicol MA BD
Associate Secretary: (Education and Nurture)	Mr Steve Mallon
Associate Secretary: (Mission and Evangelism)	Rev. Alex. M. Millar MA BD MBA
Associate Secretary: (Worship and Doctrine)	Rev. Nigel J. Robb FCP MA BD ThM MTh

Regional Development Officers
Regional Development Officers work with the Council and Associate Secretaries in developing and delivering quality resources for congregations. Based in Regional Offices in Edinburgh, Inverness, Glasgow and Perth (the addresses of which are on page xviii), the Officers appointed at the time of going to print are:

Mr Graham L. Allison BA	Glasgow
Rev. Andrew B. Campbell BD DPS MTh	Perth

Rev. David E.P. Currie BSc BD	Glasgow
Ms Fiona H. Fidgin BEd	Edinburgh
Rev. Robin J. McAlpine BDS BD	Perth
Rev. Linda Pollock BD MTh	Inverness
Vacant	Inverness
Vacant	Perth

The Netherbow: Scottish Storytelling Centre: The integrated facilities of the **Netherbow Theatre** and the **John Knox House Museum**, together with the outstanding new conference and reception areas, are an important cultural and visitor centre on the Royal Mile in Edinburgh and provide advice and assistance nationally in the use of the arts in mission, education and worship. 'Story Source', 'Scriptaid' and other resources are available. Contact the Director, The Netherbow: Scottish Storytelling Centre, 43–45 High Street, Edinburgh EH1 1SR (Tel: 0131-556 9579; E-mail; donald@scottishstorytellingcentre.com; Website: www.scottishstorytellingcentre.co.uk). The new Centre also houses the **Scottish Churches Parliamentary Office**.

The Well Asian Information and Advice Centre: The Council provides support and funding for the Presbytery of Glasgow's innovative project that serves the south side of Glasgow by assisting with welfare, housing, immigration, asylum and personal problems. The Well has a strong mission basis on the clear principles that sharing the love of Christ has to include accepting people for who they are and respecting the beliefs of others. A regular prayer letter is available. Contact The Well, 48–50 Albert Road, Glasgow G42 8DN (Tel: 0141-424 4523; Fax: 0141-422 1722; E-mail: the.well@btinternet.co.uk). See further under **Mission and Evangelism Task Group**.

Life and Work
(Tel: 0131-225 5722; Fax: 0131-240 2207; E-mail: magazine@lifeandwork.org)
Life and Work is the Church of Scotland's monthly magazine. Its purpose is to keep the Church informed about events in church life at home and abroad and to provide a forum for Christian opinion and debate on a variety of topics. It has an independent editorial policy. Contributions which are relevant to any aspect of the Christian faith are welcome.

The price of *Life and Work* this year is £1.60. With a circulation of around 38,000, it also offers advertisers a first-class opportunity to reach a discerning readership in all parts of Scotland. See further under **Publishing Committee**.

Saint Andrew Press
(Tel: 0131-240 2253; Fax: 0131-220 3113; E-mail: acrawford@cofscotland.org.uk)
Saint Andrew Press is the Church of Scotland's publishing house. Formed in 1954, it publishes Church resources, Church stationery, *The Church of Scotland Year Book* and a wide and varied catalogue of fascinating books. These explore the Christian faith in thought-provoking and inspiring ways.

Saint Andrew Press aims to help engender a closer relationship with God and Jesus Christ by producing a range of books that place the Church of Scotland's publishing programme right at the heart of the community. It aims to promote the Christian voice in a way that is strong, modern and relevant to today's world.

The publishing programme includes the updated series of New Testament commentaries, *The New Daily Study Bible*, by the late Professor William Barclay, which has been read by many millions of people around the world. Best-sellers include *A Glasgow Bible* by Jamie Stuart, *Outside Verdict* by Harry Reid, *Iona* by Kenneth Steven, *My Father: Reith of the BBC* by Marista Leishman and *Silent Heroes* by John Miller. Other popular titles include *Practical Caring* by

Sheilah Steven, *Will You Follow Me?* by Leith Fisher, Beginners' Guides to the Old and New Testament, *Pray Now* and *Common Order* and *Common Ground* from the Church of Scotland Office for Worship and Doctrine.

Saint Andrew Press is compiling a mailing list for all those who would like to receive regular information on its publications. Up-to-date information on all Saint Andrew Press titles can be found at www.churchofscotland.org.uk/standrewpress

All new proposals for publication should be sent to the Head of Publishing in the form of a two-page description of the book and its readership, together with one sample chapter. Saint Andrew Press staff are always happy to offer help and advice. See further under **Publishing Committee**.

Committee on Church Art and Architecture
Membership
The Committee shall comprise a Convener, Vice-Convener and 15 members appointed by the General Assembly.

Remit
This Committee replaces the Committee on Artistic Matters and will take forward that Committee's remit, which is in the following terms:

The Committee advises congregations and Presbyteries regarding the most appropriate way of carrying out renovations, alterations and reordering of interiors, having regard to the architectural quality of Church buildings. It also advises on the installation of stained glass, tapestries, memorials, furniture and furnishings, and keeps a list of accredited artists and craftsworkers.

Any alteration to the exterior or interior of a Church building which affects its appearance must be referred to the Committee for approval, which is given through the General Trustees. Congregations contemplating alterations are urged to consult the Committee at an early stage.

Members of the Committee are prepared, when necessary, to visit churches and meet office-bearers. The Committee's services are given free.

The Committee seeks the conservation of the nation's heritage as expressed in its Church buildings, while at the same time helping to ensure that these buildings continue to serve the worship and witness of the Church in the present day.

In recent years, the General Assembly has conferred these additional duties on the Committee:
1. preparation of reports on the architectural, historical and aesthetic merit of the buildings of congregations involved in questions of readjustment
2. verification of the propriety of repair and renovation work forming the basis of grant applications to public bodies
3. the offering of advice on the maintenance and installation of organs
4. facilitating the transfer of unwanted furnishings from one church to another through the quarterly *Exchange and Transfer*
5. the compilation of a Register of Churches
6. the processing of applications from congregations for permission to dispose of surplus communion plate, and the carrying out of an inventory of sacramental vessels held by congregations.

Education and Nurture Task Group
Individual Christians motivated and equipped for mission and service
This is the aim of the Task Group, and this ideal underpins all that we do. Our task is to create and to encourage learning opportunities in local churches and to provide national events and programmes alongside these that enhance what's going on in the local situation.

We work in the following areas:
- Children's Ministry (Linda Pollock): lpollock@cofscotland.org.uk
- Youth Ministry (Steve Mallon): smallon@cofscotland.org.uk
- Adult Learning (Fiona Fidgin): ffidgin@cofscotland.org.uk
- Elder Training (Sheilah Steven): ssteven@cofscotland.org.uk

In addition, we have the following key areas of concern for which we have established working groups:
- Membership in the Church
- Supporting people with learning difficulties
- Adult learning and spirituality
- Developing educational resources with Saint Andrew Press.

We also seek to continue to support Guild Educational Representatives in their vital role of providing and supporting learning at local Guild meetings around Scotland.

The Task Group is also responsible for the National Youth Assembly which meets each year in September, and supports the Youth Representatives who attend the General Assembly every May. In addition, we work alongside the BB for the Crossover children's and youth event every June.

Recent new programmes include:
- Cosycoffeehouse – a kit for local churches to create an authentic coffee-house experience for younger teenagers
- Digital Witness – new resources created by young people themselves
- Children's and Youth Ministry Trainers – local-resource people to encourage local workers
- Junior Youth Assembly – a forum for 'tweenagers' who want to get involved in the life of the Church of Scotland.

The Task Group is convened by the Rev. Jock Stein. Steve Mallon is the Associate Secretary for Education and Nurture.

Mission and Evangelism Task Group (METAG)
The Mission and Evangelism Task Group, within the Mission and Discipleship Council, operates with the following remit:
- *To encourage* local initiatives;
- *To offer* expertise, research, development and training;
- *To assist* local churches to be mission-focused;
- *To be alert to* new opportunities in today's Scotland; and lastly,
- *To identify* those shifts occurring in theological thinking and reflection that hint at something new, and to consider their appropriateness or otherwise in a Scottish context.

The Convener of the Task Group (Rev. Rosemary Frew) is a Vice-Convener of the Council; its Secretary (Rev. Alex. M. Millar) can be contacted by telephone at 0131-225 5722: ext. 307 or by e-mail at amillar@cofscotland.org.uk

The Task Group has the following priorities:
- **EMERGING CHURCH** (to explore the development of emerging patterns of church in the changing cultural scene that is contemporary Scotland);
- **RURAL CHURCH** (to support rural churches in outreach and community engagement);
- **CONFIDENCE IN SHARING AND SPEAKING ABOUT WHAT WE BELIEVE** (to seek to build confidence in personal witness and faith sharing through resources and training);
- **INTERFAITH** (to promote the development of interfaith relations, supported by The Well Asian Information and Advice Centre in Glasgow); and
- **IMPACT** (to sponsor and recommend the locally based children's and youth work that is undertaken through the programme and to develop it further).

Publishing Committee
Membership
Convener, Vice-Convener and eight members appointed by the General Assembly. The Head of Publishing shall act as Secretary to the Committee, and the Editor of *Life and Work* shall also be in attendance, both on a non-voting basis.

Remit
The remit of the Publishing Committee is:
- to oversee Saint Andrew Press, including the taking of all related commercial decisions, and to receive regular reports on the Press's operation from the Head of Publishing;
- to monitor pricing and delivery of published materials to Councils of the General Assembly and the use by such Councils of Saint Andrew Press;
- to monitor the cost of printing and related activities by Councils and Agencies and to make recommendations to the Council of Assembly's Budget Group on whether any or all of these activities should be outsourced;
- to oversee the publishing of *Life and Work* and to take all relevant commercial decisions affecting the magazine. For the avoidance of doubt, it is expressly declared that, in order to protect the magazine's editorial independence, the *Life and Work* Advisory Committee shall come within the aegis of the Council of Assembly through the Council's Communication Committee;
- to operate within a budget approved by the Council of Assembly and provided by the Mission and Renewal Fund, as augmented by surpluses generated by Saint Andrew Press, and to determine the balance between revenue-earning and subsidised activities within that budget;
- to report quarterly to the Council of Assembly's Budget Group.

Worship and Doctrine Task Group
The Worship and Doctrine Task Group, within the Mission and Discipleship Council, will have responsibility for the remits of the former Panels on Worship and on Doctrine.

The Panel on Worship existed to witness to the importance of worship as a primary function of the Church. In this, the Panel
- was concerned with the provision of worship materials for public use, being responsible for the production of *Common Order* and *Pray Now*;
- encouraged courses and retreats to promote spiritual growth;
- encouraged new developments in church music and the training of musicians;
- was engaged in providing materials for worship in Gaelic;
- was involved in the compilation of new hymn books and supplements;
- published occasional papers on aspects of the practice of public worship.

The Panel on Doctrine was required to:
- fulfil remits from the General Assembly on matters concerning doctrine;
- draw the attention of the Assembly to matters inside the Church of Scotland or elsewhere which might have significant doctrinal implications, with recommendations for action;
- be available for consultation by other Committees of the General Assembly on any matter which might be of doctrinal significance;
- communicate and consult in an ecumenical context on matters involving doctrine.

5. THE SOCIAL CARE COUNCIL
SOCIAL CARE (CrossReach)
Charis House, 47 Milton Road East, Edinburgh EH15 2SR
Tel: 0131-657 2000; Fax: 0131-657 2000
E-mail: info@crossreach.org.uk; Website: www.crossreach.org.uk

The Social Care Council, known as CrossReach, provides social-care services as part of the Christian witness of the Church to the people of Scotland.

Remit
The remit of the Social Care Council is:
• as part of the Church's mission, to offer services in Christ's name to people in need;
• to provide specialist resources to further the caring work of the Church;
• to identify existing and emerging areas of need, to guide the Church in pioneering new approaches to relevant problems and to make responses on issues arising within the area of the Council's concern through appropriate channels such as the Church's Church and Society Council, the Scottish Executive and the like;
• to conduct an annual review of progress made in discharging the remit and provide a written report to the Council of Assembly.

Membership
31 members; 28 appointed by the General Assembly, plus Convener and two Vice-Conveners. They attend meetings of the Council three times a year in February, June and October, and may be asked to serve on one of the two committees.

Convener:	Rev. David L. Court (2005)
Vice-Conveners:	Rev. David I. Souter (2006)
	Rev. Sydney S. Graham (2007)

Staff

Director of Social Care:	Mr Alan Staff
	(E-mail: alan.staff@crossreach.org.uk)
Deputy Director:	Mr James Maguire
	(E-mail: james.maguire@crossreach.org.uk)

Management Structure
The management structure is service-based. There are six Heads of Service, each with specialist areas of responsibility. They are supported by Principal Officers who have lead roles for particular types of service and client groups.

Head of Service (Older People):	Marlene Smith (marlene.smith@crossreach.org.uk)
Principal Officers:	Brenda Fraser (East)
	Allan Logan (West)
	Annie McDonald (North)
	Helen Thomson (Dementia)
Head of Service (Children and Families, Criminal Justice and Learning Disabilities):	Paul Robinson (paul.robinson@crossreach.org.uk)
Principal Officers:	David Clark
	George McNeilly

Head of Service (Addictions, Mental Health, Homelessness and Counselling):	Calum Murray (calum.murray@crossreach.org.uk)
Principal Officers:	Flora Mackenzie
	Gerard Robson
	Dominic Gray (part-time)
Head of Service (Planning and Development):	Jeannette Deacon (jeannette.deacon@crossreach.org.uk)
Principal Officers:	Greg Dougal
	Graham Lumb
Head of Service (Finance):	Robert Nelson (robert.nelson@crossreach.org.uk)
Principal Officers:	Philip Chan
	Alastair Purves
Head of Service (Human Resources):	Peter Bailey (peter.bailey@crossreach.org.uk)
Principal Officers:	Jane Allan
	Mari Rennie
IT Manager:	Yvonne Farrant (yvonne.farrant@crossreach.org.uk)
Estates Manager:	David Reid (david.reid@crossreach.org.uk)
Fundraising, Marketing and Communications Manager:	Pam Taylor (pam.taylor@crossreach.org.uk)

(Heads of Service can be contacted via Charis House on 0131-657 2000. Calum Murray is based at the Regional Office in Perth on 01738 783200.)

List of Services
CrossReach operates over 80 services across Scotland, and a list of these can be obtained from Charis House on 0131-657 2000, or from the CrossReach website: www.crossreach.org.uk

Fundraising, Marketing and Communications

Manager:	Pam Taylor (pam.taylor@crossreach.org.uk)
Publicity, Marketing and Communications Officer:	Hugh Brown (hugh.brown@crossreach.org.uk)
Volunteer Development Co-ordinator:	Maggie Hunt (maggie.hunt@crossreach.org.uk)

The Fundraising, Marketing and Communications department encompasses the functions of fundraising, media and public relations, publicity, congregational liaison and volunteer development. Fundraising aims to increase income development for the Council's work to ensure the long-term sustainability of our valuable care services across Scotland. We want to inform people about our mission, and work with those who are the most needy in our society. We invite people to donate money to support all our work and to volunteer their time – either to fundraise or to help carry out essential tasks of all kinds. We also ask people to pray with us about our services; to help them do that, a free prayer letter is produced three times a year. You can also keep up to date with the latest news about CrossReach by receiving our free newspaper *Circle of Care*, which has a print run of

40,000 copies three times a year. If you would like to know more about any of the above work, or be added to our mailing list, please contact the FM&C team at Charis House on 0131-657 2000.

Congregational Contacts
Congregational Contacts are the link people between CrossReach and local churches. Each church should have an appointed Contact who receives mailings three times a year. There are currently over 1,000 Congregational Contacts. They undertake work in a variety of ways. They provide current, correct and appropriate information to their Church. They often act as distributors for the *Circle of Care* newspaper and act as agents for our calendar, Christmas card and merchandise. Church members are the most important part of the 'Circle of Care' provided by the Church of Scotland. It's the caring work in the communities of Scotland which is our largest area of service provision. Congregational Contacts provide the vital link between the formal services provided by CrossReach and the community work and prayers of the local churches, and we greatly appreciate the work done by these volunteer champions.

Speakers for Guilds and other Groups
Members of CrossReach staff will gladly visit congregations and other Church organisations to talk about our work. To request a speaker, please write to the FM&C team at Charis House, 47 Milton Road East, Edinburgh EH15 2SR.

---

6. THE SUPPORT AND SERVICES COUNCIL

Remit
The Support and Services Council will provide a network for its component Committees which report direct to the General Assembly. The remit of the Council is:
* to provide opportunities for consultation among its component committees with a view to identifying and eliminating areas of overlap and duplication of work and resources;
* to elect a Convener who will represent the Council on the Council of Assembly;
* to receive and consider annual reports from component committees on progress made in discharging their remits and transmit these to the Council of Assembly.

Membership
The Conveners and Vice-Conveners of the following Committees:
* Assembly Arrangements
* Central Services
* Ecumenical Relations
* Legal Questions
* Stewardship and Finance
* Safeguarding

together with (as non-voting members):
* The Principal Clerk
* The Depute Clerk
* The Solicitor of the Church
* The General Treasurer
* The Director of Stewardship
* The Ecumenical Officer
* The Head of the Safeguarding Office.

Staff
Minutes Secretary: Rev. Marjory A. MacLean LLB BD PhD
The Council shall meet annually within two weeks of the close of the General Assembly to elect
a Convener who shall be one of the constituent committee conveners and a Vice-Convener who
may be drawn from the convener or vice-convener members. Secretarial support will be provided
by an appropriate member of administrative staff from within the area. The Convener may serve
for up to a maximum of four years and the Vice-Convener for up to three years, both positions
to be confirmed annually. Other meetings of the Council may be held as required.
Convener: Mrs Vivienne A. Dickson CA
Vice-Convener: Rev. John C. Christie BSc BD

Assembly Arrangements Committee
See separate entry at number 8.

Central Services Committee
See separate entry at number 9.

Ecumenical Relations Committee
See separate entry at number 17.

Facilities Management Department
See separate entry at number 19.

General Treasurer's Department
See separate entry at number 20.

Human Resources Department
See separate entry at number 23.

Information Technology Department
See separate entry at number 24.

Law Department
See separate entry at number 25.

Legal Questions Committee
See separate entry at number 26.

Principal Clerk's Department
See separate entry at number 32.

Stewardship and Finance Committee
See separate entry at number 34.

7. THE WORLD MISSION COUNCIL
Tel: 0131-225 5722; Fax: 0131-226 6121
Answerphone: 0131-240 2231
E-mail: info@world-mission.org
Website: www.world-mission.org

Remit
The remit of the World Mission Council is:
- to give life to the Church of Scotland's understanding that it is part of Jesus Christ's Universal Church committed to the advance of the Kingdom of God throughout the world;
- to discern priorities and form policies to guide the Church of Scotland's ongoing worldwide participation in God's transforming mission, through the Gospel of Jesus Christ;
- to develop and maintain mutually enriching relationships with the Church of Scotland's partner churches overseas through consultation in the two-way sharing of human and material resources;
- to equip and encourage Church of Scotland members at local, Presbytery and national levels to become engaged in the life of the world Church;
- to help the people of Scotland to appreciate the worldwide nature of the Christian faith;
- to keep informed about the cultural, political, social, economic, religious and ecclesiastical issues of relevance to worldwide mission;
- to recruit, train and support paid staff and volunteers to work overseas;
- to direct the work of the Council's centres in Israel;
- to foster and facilitate local partnerships between congregations and Presbyteries and the partner churches;
- to undertake the responsibilities of the former Board of World Mission in regard to the Church's Overseas Charges and the Presbytery of Europe and its congregations as set out in the relevant Assembly legislation;
- to conduct an annual review of progress made in discharging the remit and provide a written report to the Council of Assembly.

Membership
Convener, two Vice-Conveners, 24 members appointed by the General Assembly, one of whom will also be appointed to the Ecumenical Relations Committee, and one member appointed by the Presbytery of Europe.

Convener: Rev. Colin Renwick BMus BD (2006)
Vice-Conveners: Rev. John N. Young MA BD PhD (2007)
                  Mr Leon Marshall CA (2006)

Departmental Staff
Secretary: Rev. Prof. Kenneth R. Ross BA BD PhD
Associate Secretaries: Mr Walter Dunlop ARICS (Israel/Palestine)
                        Mr Sandy Sneddon (Centrally Supported Partnerships)
                        Carol Finlay RGN RMN DipCNE MSc (Local Development)

Finance: Mrs Anne Macintosh BA CA (General Treasurer's Department)

Personnel:

Strategic Commitments: 2006–10
Mission in a New Mode – Local to Local

- **Evangelism** – working with partner churches on new initiatives in evangelism
- **Reconciliation** – working for justice, peace and reconciliation in situations of conflict or threat
- **The Scandal of Poverty** – resourcing the Church to set people free from the oppression of poverty.

Partnership Priorities

Following a consultation with partner churches held in St Andrews in September 1999, the then Board of World Mission identified the following priority areas for partnership in mission:

1. **Theological Education:** developing ministerial and lay training at appropriate levels in all our churches.
2. **Evangelism:** helping one another to create new models and launch new initiatives to take the Gospel to all people.
3. **Holistic Mission:** enabling one another to respond with Christian compassion to human needs in our rapidly changing societies.
4. **Mission in Pluralistic Societies:** strengthening Christian identity in our multi-religious and multi-cultural societies by supporting one another and sharing our experiences.
5. **Prophetic Ministry:** inspiring one another to discern and speak God's Word in relation to critical issues which arise in our times.
6. **Human and Material Resources:** finding new and imaginative ways of sharing our resources at all levels of Church life.

World Mission and World Resources

Sharing in the mission of God worldwide requires a continuing commitment to sharing the Church of Scotland's resources of people and money for mission in six continents as contemporary evidence that it is 'labouring for the advancement of the Kingdom of God throughout the world' (First Article Declaratory). Such resource-sharing remains an urgent matter because most of our overseas work is in the so-called 'Third World', or 'South', in nations where the effects of the widening gap between rich and poor is *the* major issue for the Church. Our partner churches in Africa, most of Asia, the Caribbean and South and Central America are desperately short of financial and technical resources, which we can to some extent meet with personnel and grants. However, they are more than willing to share the resources of their Christian faith with us, including things which the Church in the West often lacks: enthusiasm in worship, hospitality and evangelism, and a readiness to suffer and struggle for righteousness, and in many areas a readiness to sink denominational differences. Mutual sharing in the world Church witnesses to its international nature and has much to offer a divided world, not least in Scotland.

Vacancies Overseas

The Council welcomes enquiries from men and women interested in serving in the Church overseas. Vacancies for mission partner appointments in the Church's centrally supported partnerships, the World Exchange volunteer programme and opportunities with other organisations can all be considered. Those interested in more information are invited to write to the Personnel Manager in the first instance.

HIV/AIDS Project

On the Report of the Board of World Mission, the General Assembly of 2002 adopted an HIV/AIDS Project to run from 2002 to 2007. The 2006 General Assembly extended the Project to 2010. The Project aims to raise awareness in congregations about the impact of HIV/AIDS and seeks to channel urgently needed support to partner churches. For further information, contact the Co-ordinator, HIV/AIDS Project, 121 George Street, Edinburgh EH2 4YN.

Jubilee Scotland

The Council plays an active role in the coalition which works within Scotland for the cancellation of unpayable international debt. For further information, contact the Co-ordinator, Jubilee Scotland, 41 George IV Bridge, Edinburgh EH1 1EL (Tel: 0131-225 4321; Fax: 0131-225 8861; E-mail: mail@jubileescotland.org.uk).

Christian Aid Scotland

Christian Aid is the official relief and development agency of 41 Churches in Britain and Ireland. Christian Aid's mandate is to challenge and enable us to fulfil our responsibilities to the poor of the world. Half a million volunteers and collectors make this possible, with money given by millions of supporters. The Church of Scotland marks its commitment as a Church to this part of its mission through an annual grant from the Mission and Renewal Fund, transmitted through the World Mission Council which keeps in close touch with Christian Aid and its work.

Up-to-date information about projects and current emergency relief work can be obtained from:

* The National Secretary: Mr Gavin McLellan, Christian Aid Scotland, Pentagon Centre, 36 Washington Street, Glasgow G3 8AZ (Tel: 0141-221 7475)
* The Area Co-ordinators:
  Edinburgh: Mrs Shirley Brown, 41 George IV Bridge, Edinburgh EH1 1EL (Tel: 0131-220 1254)
  Glasgow and West of Scotland: Ms Diane Green/Ms Eildon Dyer, Pentagon Centre, 36 Washington Street, Glasgow G3 8AZ (Tel: 0141-221 7475)
  Perth: Miss Marjorie Clark, Perth Christian Centre, 28 Glasgow Road, Perth PH2 0NX (Tel: 01738 643982)
* The Director: Dr Daleep Mukarji, Christian Aid Office, PO Box 100, London SE1 7RT (Tel: 020 7620 4444)

Accommodation in Israel

The Church of Scotland has two Christian Residential Centres in Israel which provide comfortable accommodation for pilgrims and visitors to the Holy Land. Further information is available from:
(a) St Andrew's Guest House, Jerusalem (PO Box 8619, Jerusalem)
    (Tel: 00 972 2 6732401; Fax: 00 972 2 6731711; E-mail: standjer@netvision.net.il)
(b) The Scots Hotel, St Andrew's, Galilee, Tiberias (PO Box 104, Tiberias)
    (Tel: 00 972 4 6710710; Fax: 00 972 4 6710711; E-mail: scottie@netvision.net.il)

A list of Overseas Appointments will be found in List K in Section 6.

A *World Mission Year Book* is available with more details of our partner churches and of people currently serving abroad, including those with ecumenical bodies and para-church bodies.

A list of Retired Missionaries will be found in List L in Section 6.

8. Assembly Arrangements Committee

Membership
Convener, Vice-Convener and ten members appointed by the General Assembly on the Report of the Nomination Committee; the Convener and Vice-Convener also to serve as Convener and Vice-Convener of the General Assembly's Business Committee.

The Clerks are non-voting members of the Assembly Arrangements Committee, and the Moderator and Moderator Designate are members of the Committee.

Convener:	Rev. William C. Hewitt BD DipPS
Vice-Convener:	Rev. A. David K. Arnott MA BD
Secretary:	The Principal Clerk

Remit
The Committee's remit is:
- to make all necessary arrangements for the General Assembly;
- to advise the Moderator on his or her official duties if so required;
- to be responsible to the General Assembly for the care and maintenance of the Assembly Hall and the Moderator's flat;
- to be responsible to the General Assembly for all arrangements in connection with the letting of the General Assembly Hall;
- to conduct an annual review of progress made in discharging the remit and provide a written report to the Support and Services Council.

9. Central Services Committee

Membership
(13 members: nine appointed by the General Assembly, and four *ex officiis* and non-voting, namely the Principal Clerk, the Solicitor of the Church, the General Treasurer and the Human Resources Manager)

Convener:	Rev. Anne R. Lithgow MA BD (2005)
Vice-Conveners:	Mrs Pauline E.D. Weibye MA DPA MCIPD (2006)
	Rev. Douglas S. Paterson MA BD (2006)

Staff

Administrative Secretary:	Mrs Pauline Wilson BA
	(E-mail: pwilson@cofscotland.org.uk)

Remit
- To be responsible for the proper maintenance and insurance of the Church Offices at 117–123 George Street and 21 Young Street, Edinburgh ('the Church Offices');
- To be responsible for matters relating to Health and Safety within the Church Offices;
- To be responsible for matters relating to Data Protection within the Church Offices and with respect to the General Assembly Councils based elsewhere;
- To be responsible for the allocation of accommodation within the Church Offices and the annual determination of rental charges to the Councils and other parties accommodated therein;
- To oversee the delivery of central services to departments within the Church Offices, to Councils of the General Assembly and, where appropriate, to the Statutory Corporations,

Presbyteries and Congregations, namely:
1. Those facilities directly managed by the Office Manager;
2. Information Technology (including the provision of support services to Presbytery Clerks);
3. Insurance;
4. Purchasing;
5. Human Resources;
6. Financial Services (as delivered by the General Treasurer's Department);
7. Legal Services (as delivered by the Law Department and subject to such oversight not infringing principles of 'client/solicitor' confidentiality);
8. Media Relations Services (as delivered by the Media Relations Unit);
9. Design Services (as delivered by the Design Services Unit);
10. Property Services.

- The Committee shall act as one of the employing agencies of the Church and shall, except in so far as specifically herein provided, assume and exercise the whole rights, functions and responsibilities of the former Personnel Committee;
- While the Committee shall *inter alia* have responsibility for determining the terms and conditions of the staff for whom it is the employing agency, any staff who are members of the Committee or who are appointed directly by the General Assembly shall not be present when matters solely relating to their own personal terms and conditions of employment/office are under consideration;
- To conduct an annual review of progress made in discharging this remit and provide a written report to the Support and Services Council.

10. Chaplains to HM Forces

Convener: Rev. James Gibson TD LTh LRAM
Vice-Convener: Rev. Neil N. Gardner MA BD
Secretary: Mr Douglas M. Hunter WS, HBJ Gateley Wareing LLP, Exchange Tower, 19 Canning Street, Edinburgh EH3 8EH

Recruitment
The Chaplains' Committee is entrusted with the task of recruitment of Chaplains for the Regular, Reserve and Auxiliary Forces. Vacancies occur periodically, and the Committee is happy to receive enquiries from all interested ministers.

Forces Registers
The Committee maintains a Register of all those who have been baptised and/or admitted to Communicant Membership by Service Chaplains.

At the present time, registers are being meticulously prepared and maintained. Parish Ministers are asked to take advantage of the facilities by applying for Certificates from the Secretary of the Committee.

Full information may be obtained from the Honorary Secretary, Mr Douglas M. Hunter, HBJ Gateley Wareing LLP, Exchange Tower, 19 Canning Street, Edinburgh EH3 8EH (Tel: 0131-228 2400).

A list of Chaplains may be found in List B in Section 6.

11. Church of Scotland Guild

National Office-bearers and Executive Staff

Convener:	Mrs Ann Bowie
Vice-Convener:	Miss Esme Duncan
General Secretary:	Mrs Alison Twaddle MA JP
	(E-mail: atwaddle@cofscotland.org.uk)
Information Officer:	Mrs Fiona J. Punton MCIPR
	(Tel: 0131-225 5722 ext. 317; 0131-240 2217;
	E-mail: fpunton@cofscotland.org.uk)

The Church of Scotland Guild is a movement within the Church of Scotland whose aim is '**to invite and encourage both women and men to commit their lives to Jesus Christ and to enable them to express their faith in worship, prayer and action**'. Membership of the Guild is open to all who subscribe to that aim.

Groups at congregational level are free to organise themselves under the authority of the Kirk Session, as best suits their own local needs and circumstances. Large groups with frequent meetings and activities continue to operate with a committee or leadership team, while other, smaller groups simply share whatever tasks need to be done among the membership as a whole. Similarly, at Presbyterial Council level, frequency and style of meetings vary according to local needs, as do leadership patterns. Each Council may nominate one person to serve at national level, where five committees take forward the work of the Guild in accordance with the stated Aim.

These committees are:

- Executive
- Finance and General Purposes
- Projects and Topics
- Programmes and Resources
- Marketing and Publicity

There has always been a close relationship between the Guild and other Departments of the Church, and members welcome the opportunity to contribute to the Church's wider mission through the Project Partnership Scheme and other joint ventures. The Guild is represented on both the Church and Society Council and the Mission and Discipleship Council.

The project scheme affords groups at congregational level the opportunity to select a project, or projects, from a range of up to six, selected from proposals submitted by a wide range of Church Departments and other Church-related bodies. A project partner in each group seeks ways of promoting the project locally, increasing awareness of the issues raised by it, and encouraging support of a financial and practical nature. Support is available from the Project Co-ordinator at Council level and the Information Officer based at the Guild Office.

The Guild is very aware of the importance of good communication in any large organisation, and regularly sends mailings to its groups to pass on information and resources to the members. In addition, the Newsletter, sent to members three times per session, is a useful communication tool, as is the website www.cos-guild.org.uk. These are a means of sharing experiences and of communicating something of the wider interest and influence of the Guild, which is represented on other national bodies such as the Network of Ecumenical Women in Scotland and the Scottish Women's Convention.

Each year, the Guild follows a Theme and produces a resources pack covering worship and study material. There is also a related Discussion Topic with supporting material and background information. The theme, topic and projects all relate to a common three-year strategy which, for 2006–9, is '**Let's Live: Body, Mind and Soul**'. Each of the six current projects reflects some aspect of fullness of life. The 2007–8 theme is **'Think of These Things'**, and Guilds are invited to explore the *mind* aspect of the overall strategy by looking at how Jesus teaches, challenges and consoles. The related discussion topic is **'Let's Talk about Learning through Life'**, which explores opportunities for developing new skills and knowledge at every stage of life.

12. Church of Scotland Investors Trust

Membership
(Trustees are appointed by the General Assembly, on the nomination of the Investors Trust)
Chairman: Mr D.M. Simpson BA FFA
Vice-Chairman: Mrs I.J. Hunter MA
Treasurer: Mr I.W. Grimmond BAcc CA
Deputy Treasurer: Mr W.J. McKean BAcc CA
Secretary: Mr F.E. Marsh MCIBS

Remit
The Church of Scotland Investors Trust was established by the Church of Scotland (Properties and Investments) Order Confirmation Act 1994 – Scottish Charity Number SC022884 – and offers investment services to the Church of Scotland and to bodies and trusts within or connected with the Church. It offers simple and economical facilities for investment in its three Funds, and investors receive the benefits of professional management, continuous portfolio supervision, spread of investment risk and economies of scale.
The three Funds are:

1. Deposit Fund
The Deposit Fund is intended for short-term investment and seeks to provide a competitive rate of interest while preserving nominal capital value. It is invested mainly in short-term loans to banks and building societies. Interest is calculated quarterly in arrears and paid gross on 15 May and 15 November. Withdrawals are on demand. The Fund is managed by Thomas Miller Investments Limited, Edinburgh and London.

2. Growth Fund
The Growth Fund is a unitised fund, largely equity-based, intended to provide a growing annual income sufficient to meet the Trustees' target distributions and to provide an increase in the value of capital long term. Units can be purchased or sold within the monthly dealing periods, and income is distributed gross on 15 May and 15 November. The Fund is managed by Newton Investment Management Limited, London.

3. Income Fund
The Income Fund is a unitised fund, invested predominantly in fixed-interest securities, intended to provide consistent high income and to protect the long-term value of capital. Units can be purchased or sold within the monthly dealing periods, and income is distributed gross on 15 March and 15 September. The Fund is managed by Baillie Gifford & Co., Edinburgh.

Further information and application forms for investment can be obtained by writing to the Secretary, The Church of Scotland Investors Trust, 121 George Street, Edinburgh EH2 4YN (E-mail: fmarsh@cofscotland.org.uk).

13. Church of Scotland Pension Trustees

Chairman: Mr D.D. Fotheringham FFA
Vice-Chairman: Mr W.J. McCafferty ACII ASFA CIP
Secretary: Mrs S. Dennison BA

Staff
Pensions Manager: Mrs S. Dennison BA
Assistant Pensions Administrators: Mrs M. Marshall
                                           Mr M. Hannam

Remit
The body acts as Trustees for the Church of Scotland's three Pension Schemes:
1.   The Church of Scotland Pension Scheme for Ministers and Overseas Missionaries
2.   The Church of Scotland Pension Scheme for Staff
3.   The Church of Scotland Pension Scheme for the Board of National Mission.
The Trustees have wide-ranging duties and powers detailed in the Trust Law, Pension Acts and other regulations, but in short the Trustees are responsible for the administration of the Pension Schemes and for the investment of the Scheme Funds. Six Trustees are appointed by the General Assembly, and members nominate up to three Trustees for each Scheme.

The investment of the Funds is delegated to external Investment Managers under the guidelines and investment principles set by the Trustees: Baillie Gifford & Co., Newton Investment Management Ltd and Tilney Fund Management.

The benefits provided by the three Pension Schemes differ in detail, but all provide a pension to the Scheme member and dependants on death of the member, and a lump-sum death benefit on death in service. Scheme members also have the option to improve their benefits by paying additional voluntary contributions (AVCs) to arrangements set up by the Trustees with leading Insurance Companies.

Further information on any of the Church of Scotland Pension Schemes or on individual benefits can be obtained from the Pensions Manager, Mrs S. Dennison, at the Church of Scotland Offices, 121 George Street, Edinburgh EH2 4YN (Tel: 0131-225 5722 ext. 206; Fax: 0131-240 2220; E-mail: sdennison@cofscotland.org.uk).

14. Church of Scotland Trust

Membership
(Members are appointed by the General Assembly, on the nomination of the Trust)
Chairman: Mr Christopher N. Mackay WS
Vice-Chairman: Mr Robert Brodie CB WS
Treasurer: Mr Iain W. Grimmond BAcc CA
Secretary and Clerk: Mrs Jennifer M. Hamilton BA

Remit
The Church of Scotland Trust was established by Act of Parliament in 1932 and has Scottish Charity Number SC020269. The Trust's function since 1 January 1995 has been to hold properties outwith Scotland and to act as Trustee in a number of third-party trusts.

Further information can be obtained from the Secretary and Clerk of the Church of Scotland Trust, 121 George Street, Edinburgh EH2 4YN (Tel: 0131-240 2222; E-mail: jhamilton@cofscotland.org.uk).

15. Committee on Church Art and Architecture

See entry in full under **The Mission and Discipleship Council** (number 4).

16. Committee Planning the Church Without Walls Celebration
(now renamed as Church Without Walls Group)

This group now sits within the Mission and Discipleship Council. Rev. Albert O. Bogle serves as Convener.

17. Ecumenical Relations Committee

Remit
*   to advise the General Assembly on matters of policy affecting ecumenical relations;
*   to ensure that the members on the Committee serving on the other Councils are appropriately informed and resourced so as to be able to represent the ecumenical viewpoint on the Council on which they serve;
*   to ensure appropriate support for the Ecumenical Officer's representative function in the event of his or her absence, whether through illness, holidays or other commitments;
*   to nominate people from across the work of the Church of Scotland to represent the Church in Assemblies and Synods of other churches, ecumenical consultations and delegations to ecumenical assemblies and so on;
*   to call for and receive reports from representatives of the Church of Scotland attending Assemblies and Synods of other churches and those ecumenical conferences and gatherings which are held from time to time;
*   to ensure that appropriate parts of such reports are made available to relevant Councils;
*   to ensure that information is channelled from and to ecumenical bodies of which the Church of Scotland is a member;
*   to ensure that information is channelled from and to other churches in Scotland and beyond;
*   to ensure the continued development of ecumenical relations by means of the Web and other publications;
*   to ensure personal support for the Ecumenical Officer;
*   to approve guidelines for the setting up and oversight of Local Ecumenical Partnerships;
*   to conduct an annual review of progress made in discharging this remit and provide a written report to the Support and Services Council.

Membership

a)   Five members appointed by the General Assembly, each to serve as a member of one of the five Councils of the Church (excluding the Support and Services Council, on which the Convener of the Committee will sit).

b)   Convener who is not a member of any of the other Councils and who will act as a personal support for the Ecumenical Officer, and Vice-Convener, appointed by the General Assembly.

c)   A representative of the United Free Church of Scotland appointed by that Church.

d)   A representative of the Roman Catholic Church in Scotland appointed by the Bishops' Conference and one representative from each of three churches drawn from among the member churches of ACTS and the Baptist Union of Scotland, each to serve for a period of four years.

e)   The Committee may co-opt, as a full voting member, one of the four Church of Scotland representatives on the Scottish Churches' Forum.

f)   The Committee shall co-opt Church of Scotland members elected to the central bodies of Churches Together in Britain and Ireland (CTBI), the Conference of European Churches (CEC), the World Council of Churches (WCC), the World Alliance of Reformed Churches (WARC) and the Community of Protestant Churches in Europe (CPCE, formerly the Leuenberg Fellowship of Churches).

g)   The General Secretary of ACTS shall be invited to attend as a corresponding member.

h)   For the avoidance of doubt, while, for reasons of corporate governance, only Church of Scotland members of the Committee shall be entitled to vote, before any vote is taken the views of members representing other churches shall be ascertained.

Convener:	Rev. William D. Brown BD CQSW (2005)
Vice-Convener:	Rev. Valerie J. Ott BA BD (2002)
Secretary and Ecumenical	
Officer:	Rev. Sheilagh M. Kesting BA BD

Until 1 June 2008, Rev. Douglas Galbraith MA BD BMus MPhil ARSCM will serve as Interim Secretary and Ecumenical Officer.

Administrative Officer:	Miss Rosalind Milne

INTER-CHURCH ORGANISATIONS

World Council of Churches

The Church of Scotland is a founder member of the World Council of Churches, formed in 1948. As its basis declares, it is 'a fellowship of Churches which confess the Lord Jesus Christ as God and Saviour according to the Scriptures, and therefore seek to fulfil their common calling to the Glory of the one God, Father, Son and Holy Spirit'. Its member Churches, which number over 300, are drawn from all continents and include all the major traditions – Eastern and Oriental Orthodox, Reformed, Lutheran, Anglican, Baptist, Disciples, Methodist, Moravian, Friends, Pentecostalist and others. Although the Roman Catholic Church is not a member, there is very close co-operation with the departments in the Vatican.

The World Council holds its Assemblies every seven years. The last, held in Porto Alegre, Brazil in February 2006, had the theme 'God, in your grace, transform the world'. At that Assembly, Mr Graham McGeoch was elected to the new Executive and to the Central Committee of the Council.

The World Council is taking forward the discussion among the churches on global economic justice. In June 2005, it hosted the Conference on World Mission and Evangelism in Athens, Greece. Currently, two documents are with the churches for study: 'The nature and mission of the church' and 'Christian perspectives on theological anthropology'.

The General Secretary is Rev. Dr Sam Kobia, 150 route de Ferney, 1211 Geneva 2, Switzerland (Tel: 00 41 22 791 61 11; Fax: 00 41 22 791 03 61; E-mail: nan@wcc-coe.org; Website: www.wcc-coe.org).

World Alliance of Reformed Churches
The Church of Scotland is a founder member of the World Alliance of Reformed Churches, which began in 1875 as 'The Alliance of the Reformed Churches Throughout the World Holding the Presbyterian System' and which now includes also Churches of the Congregational tradition. Today it is composed of more than 200 Churches in nearly 100 countries, with an increasing number in Asia. It brings together, for mutual help and common action, large Churches which enjoy majority status and small minority Churches. It engages in theological dialogue with other Christian traditions – Orthodox, Roman Catholic, Lutheran, Methodist, Baptist and so on. It is organised in three main departments – Co-operation with Witness, Theology and Partnership. The twenty-fourth General Council was held in Accra, Ghana, from 30 July to 12 August 2004. The theme was 'That all may have life in fullness'. Rev. Sandy Horsburgh was elected to the Executive Committee.

The General Secretary is Rev. Dr Setri Nyomi, 150 route de Ferney, 1211 Geneva 2, Switzerland (Tel: 00 41 22 791 62 38; Fax: 00 41 22 791 65 05; E-mail: sn@warc.ch; Website: www.warc.ch).

Conference of European Churches
The Church of Scotland is a founder member of the Conference of European Churches, formed in 1959 and until recently the only body which involved in common membership representatives of every European country (except Albania) from the Atlantic to the Urals. More than 100 Churches, Orthodox and Protestant, are members. Although the Roman Catholic Church is not a member, there is very close co-operation with the Council of European Catholic Bishops' Conferences. With the removal of the long-standing political barriers in Europe, the Conference has now opportunities and responsibilities to assist the Church throughout the continent to offer united witness and service.

It is currently engaged with the Council of Bishops' Conferences in Europe (CCEE) in a process of consultation and involvement with churches towards the Third European Ecumenical Assembly to be held in Sibiu, Romania in September 2007 under the theme 'The light of Christ shines on all'.

Its General Secretary is the Venerable Colin Williams, 150 route de Ferney, 1211 Geneva 2, Switzerland (Tel: 00 41 22 791 61 11; Fax: 00 41 22 791 03 61; E-mail: cec@cec-kek.org; Website: www.cec-kek.org).

CEC: Church and Society Commission
The Church of Scotland was a founder member of the European Ecumenical Commission for Church and Society (EECCS). The Commission owed its origins to the Christian concern and vision of a group of ministers and European civil servants about the future of Europe. It was established in 1973 by Churches recognising the importance of this venture. Membership included Churches and ecumenical bodies from the European Union. The process of integration with CEC was completed in 2000, and the name, Church and Society Commission (CSC), established. In Brussels, CSC monitors Community activity, maintains contact with MEPs and promotes dialogue between the Churches and the institutions. It plays an educational role and encourages the Churches' social and ethical responsibility in European affairs. It has a General Secretary, a study secretary and an executive secretary in Brussels and a small office in Strasbourg.

The Director is Rev. Rudiger Noll, Ecumenical Centre, 174 rue Joseph II, B-1000 Brussels, Belgium (Tel: 00 32 2 230 17 32; Fax: 00 32 2 231 14 13; E-mail: mo@cec-kek.be).

Churches Together in Britain and Ireland (CTBI)

In September 1990, Churches throughout Britain and Ireland solemnly committed themselves to one another, promising to one another to do everything possible together. To provide frameworks for this commitment to joint action, the Churches established CTBI for the United Kingdom and Ireland, and, for Scotland, ACTS, with sister organisations for Wales and for England.

In 2006, CTBI ceased being a separate ecumenical instrument and became an agency of the four national ecumenical bodies. It is governed by Trustees appointed by the national instruments, is managed by the General Secretaries and has a Forum of Senior Representatives which will incorporate its AGM. It retains two Commissions on Racial Justice and Interfaith Relations. It has three core portfolios – study, church and society, and interfaith – together with a communication officer.

The General Secretary of CTBI is Rev. Canon Bob Fyffe, Third Floor, Bastille Court, 2 Paris Garden, London SE1 8ND (Tel: 020 7654 7254; Fax: 020 7654 7222). The General Secretariat can be contacted by telephoning 020 7654 7211 (E-mail: gensec@ctbi.org.uk; Website: www.ctbi.org.uk).

Action of Churches Together in Scotland (ACTS)

ACTS was restructured at the beginning of 2003. The new structure comprises the Scottish Churches' Forum (replacing the Central Council) composed of Church representatives from trustee member Churches. There are four Networks: Church Life, Faith Studies, Mission, and Church and Society. Contributing to the life of the Networks will be associated ecumenical groups. Such groups are expressions of the Churches' commitment to work together and to bring together key people in a defined field of interest or expertise. ACTS is an expression of the commitment of the Churches to one another.

ACTS is staffed by a General Secretary, an Assistant General Secretary and two Network Officers. Their offices are based in Alloa.

These structures facilitate regular consultation and intensive co-operation among those who frame the policies and deploy the resources of the Churches in Scotland and throughout Britain and Ireland. At the same time, they afford greater opportunity for a wide range of members of different Churches to meet in common prayer and study.

The Assistant General Secretary is Rev. Lindsey Sanderson, 7 Forrester Lodge, Inglewood House, Alloa FK10 2HU (Tel: 01259 216980; Fax: 01259 215964; E-mail: ecumenical@acts-scotland.org; Website: www.acts-scotland.org).

Scottish Churches House

Scottish Churches House is a resource of the churches together in Scotland. It provides space for meetings, conferences and retreats, and offers its own programme of events throughout the year. Set in the attractive town of Dunblane, overlooking the Cathedral, it is a place of refreshment and reflection. The Warden is Alastair Hulbert. For information and bookings, contact the Bookings Secretary, Scottish Churches House, Dunblane FK15 0AJ (Tel: 01786 823588; Fax: 01786 825844; E-mail: reservations@scottishchurcheshouse.org; Website: www.scottishchurcheshouse. org).

---

18. Education and Nurture Task Group

See entry in full under **The Mission and Discipleship Council** (number 4).

19. Facilities Management Department

Staff
Facilities Manager: Appointment awaited

The responsibilities of the Facilities Manager's Department include:
- management of a maintenance budget for the upkeep of the Church Offices at 121 George Street, Edinburgh;
- responsibility for all aspects of health and safety for staff, visitors and contractors working in the building;
- managing a team of staff providing the Offices with security, reception, mail room, print room, switchboard, day-to-day maintenance services and Committee room bookings;
- overseeing all sub-contracted services to include catering, cleaning, boiler-room maintenance, intruder alarm, fire alarms, lifts and water management;
- maintaining building records in accordance with the requirements of statutory legislation;
- overseeing all alterations to the building and ensuring, where applicable, that they meet DDR, Planning and Building Control regulations.

Design Services
Our designers offer a graphic-design service for full-colour promotional literature, display materials and exhibitions to both Councils and organisations of the wider Church. For further information, contact Peter Forrest (Tel: 0131-240 2224; E-mail: pforrest@churchofscotland.co.uk).

20. General Treasurer's Department

Staff

General Treasurer:		Mr Iain W. Grimmond BAcc CA
Deputy Treasurer:		Mr William J. McKean BAcc CA
Assistant Treasurers:	Congregational Support	Mr Archie McDowall BA CA
	World Mission	Mrs Anne F. Macintosh BA CA
	General Trustees	Mr Robert A. Allan CIMA CIPFA
	Ministries	Mrs Pauline E. Willder MA PgDipIS
	Mission and Discipleship	Miss Catherine E. Robertson BAcc CA
Accountants:	Congregational Contributions	Mr Derek W.C. Cant FCCA
	Payroll and VAT	Mr Ross W. Donaldson
	Mission and Discipleship	Mr Steven R. Lane MA MAAT ACCA
	Ministries	Mrs K.C. Hastie BSc CA

Responsibilities of the General Treasurer's Department include:
- payroll processing for the Ministries Council and the Support and Services Council;
- calculating congregational allocations;
- issuing to congregations their annual requirement figures for the Ministries and Mission Allocation;
- receiving payments from congregations towards their central requirements;
- making Gift Aid tax recoveries on behalf of Councils, Committees and Statutory Corporations;

- making VAT returns and tax recoveries on behalf of Councils, Committees and Statutory Corporations and providing support, training and advice on financial matters to congregational treasurers;
- receiving and discharging legacies and bequests on behalf of Councils, Committees and Statutory Corporations;
- providing banking arrangements and operating a central banking system for Councils, Committees and Statutory Corporations;
- providing accountancy systems and services for Councils, Committees and Statutory Corporations and the Trustees of the Church's Pension Schemes;
- providing accounting and financial support for the Councils, Committees and Statutory Corporations.

21. General Trustees

Membership
(New Trustees are appointed, as required, by the General Assembly, on the recommendation of the General Trustees)

Chairman:	Mr W. Findlay Turner CA (2007)
Vice-Chairman:	Rev. James A.P. Jack BSc BArch BD DMin RIBA ARIAS (2007)
Secretary and Clerk:	Mr David D. Robertson LLB NP
Depute Secretary and Clerk:	Mr T.R.W. Parker LLB

Committees:
Fabric Committee
Convener: Rev. James A.P. Jack BSc BArch BD DMin RIBA ARIAS (2004)

Chairman's Committee
Convener: Mr W. Findlay Turner CA (2007)

Glebes Committee
Convener: Rev. William Paterson BD (2003)

Finance Committee
Convener: Mr W. Findlay Turner CA (2004)

Audit Committee
Convener: Dr J. Kenneth Macaldowie LLD CA (2005)

Law Committee
Convener: Mr C. Noel Glen BL NP (2004)

Staff
Secretary and Clerk: Mr. David D. Robertson LLB NP
Depute Secretary and Clerk: Mr T.R.W. Parker LLB

Assistants:	Mr Keith J. Fairweather LLB (Glebes)
	Mr Keith S. Mason LLB NP (Ecclesiastical Buildings)
Treasurer:	Mr Iain W. Grimmond BAcc CA
Deputy Treasurer:	Mr W.J. McKean BAcc CA
Assistant Treasurer:	Mr Robert A. Allan ACMA CPFA

Remit

The General Trustees are a Property Corporation created and incorporated under the Church of Scotland (General Trustees) Order Confirmation Act 1921. They have Scottish Charity Number SC014574. Their duties, powers and responsibilities were greatly extended by the Church of Scotland (Property & Endowments) Acts and Orders 1925 to 1995, and they are also charged with the administration of the Central Fabric Fund (see below) and the Consolidated Fabric Fund and the Consolidated Stipend Fund in which monies held centrally for the benefit of individual congregations are lodged.

The scope of the work of the Trustees is broad, covering all facets of property administration, but particular reference is made to the following matters:

1. **ECCLESIASTICAL BUILDINGS.** The Trustees' Fabric Committee considers proposals for work at buildings, regardless of how they are vested, and plans of new buildings. Details of all such projects should be submitted to the Committee before work is commenced. The Committee also deals with applications for the release of fabric monies held by the General Trustees for individual congregations, and considers applications for assistance from the Central Fabric Fund from which grants and/or loans may be given to assist congregations faced with expenditure on fabric. Application forms relating to consents for work and possible financial assistance from the Central Fabric Fund are available from the Secretary of the Trustees and require to be submitted through Presbytery with its approval. The Committee normally meets on the first or second Tuesday of each month, apart from July, when it meets on the last Tuesday, and August, when there is no meeting.

2. **SALE, PURCHASE AND LETTING OF PROPERTIES.** All sales or lets of properties vested in the General Trustees fall to be carried out by them in consultation with the Financial Board of the congregation concerned, and no steps should be taken towards any sale or let without prior consultation with the Secretary of the Trustees. Where property to be purchased is to be vested in the General Trustees, it is essential that contact be made at the earliest possible stage with the Solicitor to the Trustees, who is responsible for the lodging of offers for such properties and all subsequent legal procedure.

3. **GLEBES.** The Trustees are responsible for the administration of Glebes vested in their ownership. All lets fall to be granted by them in consultation with the minister concerned. It should be noted that neither ministers nor Kirk Sessions may grant lets of Glebe land vested in the General Trustees. As part of their Glebe administration, the Trustees review regularly all Glebe rents.

4. **INSURANCE.** Properties vested in the General Trustees must be insured with the Church of Scotland Insurance Co. Ltd, a company wholly owned by the Church of Scotland whose profits are applied for Church purposes. Insurance enquiries should be sent directly to the Company at 67 George Street, Edinburgh EH2 2JG (Tel: 0131-220 4119; Fax: 0131-220 4120; E-mail: enquiries@cosic.co.uk).

22. The Church of Scotland Housing and Loan Fund for Retired Ministers and Widows and Widowers of Ministers

Membership

The Trustees shall be a maximum of 11 in number, being:

1. four appointed by the General Assembly on the nomination of the Trustees, who, having served a term of three years, shall be eligible for reappointment;
2. three ministers and one member appointed by the Ministries Council;
3. three appointed by the Baird Trust.

Chairman: Mr William McVicar RD CA

Secretary: Miss Lin J. Macmillan MA

Staff

Property Manager: Miss Hilary J. Hardy

Property Assistant: Mr John Lunn

Remit

The Fund, as established by the General Assembly, facilitates the provision of housing accommodation for retired ministers and widows, widowers and separated or divorced spouses of Church of Scotland ministers. When provided, help may take the form of either a house to rent or a house-purchase loan.

The Trustees may grant tenancy of one of their existing houses or they may agree to purchase for rental occupation an appropriate house of an applicant's choosing. Leases are normally on very advantageous terms as regards rental levels. Alternatively, the Trustees may grant a housing loan of up to 70 per cent of a house-purchase price but with an upper limit. Favourable rates of interest are charged.

The Trustees are also prepared to consider assisting those who have managed to house themselves but are seeking to move to more suitable accommodation. Those with a mortgaged home on retirement may be granted a loan to enable them to repay such a mortgage and thereafter to enjoy the favourable rates of interest charged by the Fund.

Ministers making application within five years of retirement, upon their application being approved, will be given a fairly firm commitment that, in due course, either a house will be made available for renting or a house-purchase loan will be offered. Only within nine months of a minister's intended retiral date will the Trustees initiate steps to find a suitable house; only within one year of that date will a loan be advanced. Applications submitted about ten years prior to retirement have the benefit of initial review and, if approved, a place on the preliminary applications list for appropriate decision in due time.

Donations and legacies over the years have been significant in building up this Fund, and the backbone has been provided by congregational contributions.

The Board of Trustees is a completely independent body answerable to the General Assembly, and enquiries and applications are dealt with in the strictest confidence.

Further information can be obtained from the Secretary, Miss Lin J. Macmillan MA, at the Church of Scotland Offices, 121 George Street, Edinburgh EH2 4YN (Tel: 0131-225 5722 ext. 310; Fax: 0131-240 2264; E-mail: lmacmillan@cofscotland.org.uk; Website: www.churchofscotland.org.uk).

23. Human Resources Department

Staff

Head of Human Resources and
   Information Technology: Mr Mike O'Donnell Chartered FCIPD
Human Resources Manager: Mrs Angela Ocak Chartered MCIPD
Human Resources Adviser: Sarah-Jayne McVeigh BA
Human Resources Assistant/
   Personal Assistant: Melanie Sherwood

Remit

The Human Resources Department has responsibility for Recruitment and Selection, Learning and Development, and producing and updating HR Policies and Procedures to ensure that the Central Services Committee is in line with current employment law legislation. The Department produces contracts of employment and advises on any changes to an individual employee's terms and conditions of employment. It also provides professional Human Resource advice to the organisation on Employee Relations matters, Performance Management and Diversity and Equality.

Our main aim is to work closely with Councils within the organisation to influence strategy so that each Council is making best use of its people and its people opportunities. We take a consultancy role that facilitates and supports each Council's own initiatives and help each other share and work together in consultation with Amicus.

24. Information Technology Department

Staff

Information Technology Manager: Alastair Chalmers
Depute Information Technology Manager: Veronica Hay

The Department provides computer facilities to Councils and Departments within 121 George Street and to Presbytery Clerks and other groups within the Councils. It is also responsible for the telephone service within 121 George Street and the provision of assistance and advice on this to other groups.

The facilities provided include:

- the provision and maintenance of data and voice networks
- the purchase and installation of hardware and software
- support for problems and guidance on the use of software
- development of in-house software
- maintenance of data within some central systems.

25. Law Department

Staff

Solicitor of the Church
    and of the General Trustees: Mrs Janette S. Wilson LLB NP
Depute Solicitor: Miss Mary E. Macleod LLB NP
Assistant Solicitors: Mr Ian K. Johnstone MA LLB
    Mrs Jennifer M. Hamilton BA NP
    Mrs Elspeth Annan LLB NP
    Miss Susan Killean LLB NP
    Miss Mairead MacBeath LLB NP
    Mrs Anne Steele LLB NP

The Law Department of the Church was created in 1937/38. The Department acts in legal matters for the Church and all of its Courts, Councils, Committees, the Church of Scotland General Trustees, the Church of Scotland Trust and the Church of Scotland Investors Trust. It also acts for individual congregations and is available to give advice on any legal matter arising.

The Department is under the charge of the Solicitor of the Church, a post created at the same time as the formation of the Department and a post which is now customarily held along with the traditional posts of Law Agent of the General Assembly and the Custodier of former United Free Church titles (E-mail: lawdept@cofscotland.org.uk).

---

26. Legal Questions Committee

Membership

Convener, Vice-Convener and ten members appointed by the General Assembly on the Report of the Nomination Committee.

Convener: Miss Carole Hope LLB WS
Vice-Convener: Rev. Ian A. McLean BSc BD DMin
Secretary: The Depute Clerk

The Convener and Vice-Convener of the Assembly Arrangements Committee are also members of the Legal Questions Committee. The Assembly Clerks, Procurator and Solicitor of the Church are non-voting members of the Legal Questions Committee.

Remit

- to advise the General Assembly on questions of Church Law and of Constitutional Law affecting the relationship between Church and State;
- to advise and assist Agencies of the General Assembly in the preparation of proposed legislation and on questions of interpretation, including interpretation of and proposed changes to remits;
- to compile the statistics of the Church, except Youth and Finance; and to supervise on behalf of the General Assembly all arrangements for care of Church Records and for Presbytery visits;
- to conduct an annual review of progress made in discharging the remit and provide a written report to the Support and Services Council.

27. Mission and Evangelism Task Group

See entry in full under **The Mission and Discipleship Council** (number 4).

28. Nomination Committee

Membership
(44 members)
Convener: Rev. Iain D. Cunningham MA BD (2005)
Vice-Convener: Miss Moira Alexander MBA RGN SCM RNT (2005)
Secretary: The Principal Clerk

Remit
To bring before the General Assembly names of persons to serve on the Boards and Standing Committees of the General Assembly.

29. Panel on Review and Reform

Membership
(10 members appointed by the General Assembly)
Convener: Rev. David S. Cameron BD (2006)
Vice-Convener: Rev. Marina D. Brown MA BD MTh (2007)
(The Ecumenical Officer attends but without the right to vote or make a motion.)

Staff
Administrative Secretary: Mrs Valerie A. Cox MA
                              (Tel: 0131-225 5722 ext. 336;
                              E-mail: vsmith@cofscotland.org.uk)

Remit
The remit of the Panel on Review and Reform, as determined by the General Assembly of 2004, is as follows:
*   To listen to the voices of congregations, Presbyteries, Agencies and those beyond the Church of Scotland.
*   To present a vision of what a Church in need of continual renewal might become and to offer paths by which congregations, Presbyteries and Agencies might travel towards that vision.
*   To consider the changing needs, challenges and responsibilities of the Church.
*   To make recommendations to the Council of Assembly, and, through the report of that Council, to report to the General Assembly.
*   To have particular regard to the Gospel imperative of priority for the poor, needy and marginalised.

30. Parish Appraisal Committee

The Parish Appraisal Committee was discharged with effect from 31 May 2007. Planning and Deployment will remain an area of work for the Ministries Council. (See further under **The Ministries Council.**)

31. Parish Development Fund Committee

Membership
(11 members appointed by the General Assembly. In addition, the Committee has powers to co-opt up to six non-voting advisers with appropriate skills and knowledge.)
Convener: Rev. Dr Martin Fair (2006)
Vice-Convener: Mrs Mary Miller (2006)

Staff
Co-ordinator: Mr Iain Johnston
Administrator: Miss Ruth Boreham
Development Workers: Mrs Jessie Bruce
                        Mrs Susan Smith
Contact details: Tel: 0131-225 5722

Remit
The aim of the Parish Development Fund is to encourage local churches to work for the benefit of the whole community – and to take risks in living and sharing the Gospel in relevant ways.
    The Committee considers applications which are in the spirit of the above aim and the following principles:

* making a positive difference in the lives of people in greatest need in the community
* encouraging partnership work
* helping local people develop their gifts
* encouraging imagination and creativity.

The Committee meets four times each year, with main grant applications considered in April and October. Applications should be submitted by the end of February or the end of August.
    Further information on the types of projects supported by the Fund can be found in the Parish Development Fund section of the Church of Scotland website. Please contact the staff for informal discussion about grant-application enquiries and general advice on funding and project development.

32. Principal Clerk's Department

Staff
Principal Clerk: Very Rev. Finlay A.J. Macdonald MA BD PhD DD
Depute Clerk: Rev. Marjory A. MacLean LLB BD PhD

Personal Assistant to the
  Clerks of Assembly: Mrs Linda Jamieson
Principal Administration Officer: Mrs Alison Murray MA
  (Assembly Arrangements and
  Moderatorial Support)
Principal Administration Officer: Mrs Pauline Wilson BA
  (Council of Assembly, Central
  Services Committee and
  Nomination Committee)

The Principal Clerk's Department has responsibility for the administration of the General Assembly and its Commissions, for supporting the Moderator in preparation for and during his or her year of office and for servicing the Council of Assembly, the Assembly Arrangements Committee, the Legal Questions Committee, the Committee to Nominate the Moderator, the Nomination Committee, the Committee on Overtures and Cases and the Committee on Classifying Returns to Overtures. The Clerks of Assembly are available for consultation on matters of Church law, practice and procedure.

Contact Details
Principal Clerk: 0131-240 2240
Depute Clerk: 0131-240 2232
Linda Jamieson: 0131-240 2240
Alison Murray: 0131-225 5722 (ext. 250)
Pauline Wilson: 0131-240 2229
Office fax number: 0131-240 2239
E-mail: pcoffice@cofscotland.org.uk

---

33. Publishing Committee

See entry in full under **The Mission and Discipleship Council** (number 4).

---

34. Stewardship and Finance Committee

Remit
1. To teach, promote and encourage Christian Stewardship throughout the Church.
2. To provide programmes and training to assist congregations and their office-bearers in teaching, promoting and encouraging Christian Stewardship.
3. To be responsible with Presbyteries for allocating among congregations the expenditure contained in the Co-ordinated Budget approved by the Council of Assembly, and for seeking to ensure that congregations meet their obligations thereto, by transmitting regularly throughout the year to the General Treasurer of the Church contributions towards their allocations.
4. To report annually to the General Assembly on the attestation of Presbytery and

Congregational Accounts, and provide advice or arrange training for Congregational Treasurers and others administering congregational finances.

5. To issue annually to each congregation a Schedule of Congregational Financial Statistics, to be completed and returned by a date determined by the Committee.
6. To set standards of financial management and accounting procedures and to provide financial and accounting services for all Councils and Committees of the General Assembly (except for the Social Care Council).
7. To maintain and update such statistical and financial information as is deemed necessary.
8. To approve and submit annually to the General Assembly the Report and Financial Statements of the Unincorporated Councils and Committees of the General Assembly. In order to enable the Committee to fulfil this part of its remit, the Social Care Council shall provide regular financial reports and such other information as may be required by the Committee.
9. To appoint Auditors for the Financial Statements of the Unincorporated Councils and Committees of the General Assembly.
10. To consider Reports received from the Auditors of the Financial Statements of the Unincorporated Councils and Committees of the General Assembly.
11. To ensure that all funds belonging to Councils and Committees of the General Assembly, which are not contained within the Financial Statements submitted to the General Assembly, are audited or independently examined annually.
12. To exercise custody over funds and to provide bank arrangements.
13. To operate a central banking system for all Councils (except for the Social Care Council), Committees and Statutory Corporations.
14. To consider taxation matters affecting Councils, Committees and Statutory Corporations and congregations of the Church.
15. To determine the types and rates of expenses that may be claimed by members serving Councils, Committees and Statutory Corporations.
16. To carry out such other duties as may be referred to the Committee from time to time by the General Assembly.
17. To conduct an annual review of progress made in discharging the remit and provide a written report for the Support and Services Council.

Membership

The Committee shall consist of a Convener, Vice-Convener and 16 members all appointed by the General Assembly. The General Treasurer and the Head of Stewardship shall be *ex officiis* members of the Committee and of all its Sub-Committees but shall not have voting rights.

Convener: Mrs Vivienne A. Dickson CA (2005)
Vice-Convener: Rev. Richard Baxter MA BD (2007)
General Treasurer: Mr Iain W. Grimmond BAcc CA
Head of Stewardship: Rev. Gordon D. Jamieson MA BD
Administrative Secretary: Mr Fred Marsh MCIBS

Promoting Christian Giving

Stewardship and Finance staff are responsible for promoting Christian giving through stewardship programmes, conferences for office-bearers or members, wider use of Gift Aid, and legacies. Contact the Church Offices to get in touch with the appropriate Stewardship Consultant or to obtain information about stewardship material produced by the Committee (Tel: 0131-225 5722 ext. 273; E-mail: stewardship@cofscotland.org.uk).

35. Worship and Doctrine Task Group

See entry in full under **The Mission and Discipleship Council** (number 4).

---

36. Safeguarding Office
Tel: 0131-240 2256; Fax: 0131-220 3113
E-mail: safeguarding@cofscotland.org.uk

(Reports through the Support and Services Council – see separate item, number 6)

Convener:	Rev. John Christie (2005)
Vice-Convener:	Anne Black (2005)

Staff

National Adviser:	Jennifer McCreanor
Associate National Adviser:	Fiona MacKay
Training Officer:	Andrew Strachan

Remit

The Safeguarding Office, which developed from the Church's Child Protection Unit, plays a major part in the growing and ongoing work of child protection, in particular training and supporting all those who work with children in congregations. This service is shortly to be extended to include all vulnerable groups; the appropriate policies and procedures are currently being developed.

The Safeguarding Office exists to:
• continue the development of the Church of Scotland's Safeguarding Policies and Procedures;
• co-ordinate a national 'safe recruitment' system for all voluntary workers;
• recruit, train and support a team of voluntary trainers in Safeguarding matters across all the Presbyteries;
• facilitate, through the training network, training in Safeguarding matters for all voluntary workers and co-ordinators in congregations;
• develop resources relating to Safeguarding matters;
• provide support, advice and guidance to Presbyteries and congregations and liaise with other church denominations, para-church bodies and other voluntary organisations.

---

37. Scottish Churches Parliamentary Office
Tel: 0131-558 8137
E-mail: graham@actsparl.org

The Scottish Churches Parliamentary Officer is Rev. Graham K. Blount LLB BD PhD. The office is within the Scottish Storytelling Centre, 43–45 High Street, Edinburgh EH1 1SR.

SECTION 2

General Information

(1) OTHER CHURCHES IN THE UNITED KINGDOM

ASSOCIATED PRESBYTERIAN CHURCHES
Clerk of Presbytery: Rev. Archibald N. McPhail, APC Manse, Polvinister Road, Oban PA34 5TN (Tel: 01631 567076).

THE REFORMED PRESBYTERIAN CHURCH OF SCOTLAND
Clerk of Presbytery: Rev. Andrew Quigley, Church Offices, 48 North Bridge Street, Airdrie ML6 6NE (Tel: 01236 620107; E-mail: airdrierpcs@aol.com).

THE FREE CHURCH OF SCOTLAND
Principal Clerk: Rev. James MacIver, The Mound, Edinburgh EH1 2LS (Tel: 0131-226 5286; E-mail: principal.clerk@freechurch.org).

THE FREE PRESBYTERIAN CHURCH OF SCOTLAND
Clerk of Synod: Rev. John Macleod, 133 Woodlands Road, Glasgow G3 6LE (Tel: 0141-332 9283; E-mail: jmac1265@aol.com).

THE UNITED FREE CHURCH OF SCOTLAND
General Secretary: Rev. John Fulton BSc BD, United Free Church Offices, 11 Newton Place, Glasgow G3 7PR (Tel: 0141-332 3435; E-mail: office@ufcos.org.uk).

THE PRESBYTERIAN CHURCH IN IRELAND
Clerk of the General Assembly and General Secretary: Rev. Dr Donald J. Watts, Church House, Fisherwick Place, Belfast BT1 6DW (Tel: 02890 322284; E-mail: clerk@presbyterianireland.org).

THE PRESBYTERIAN CHURCHES OF WALES
General Secretary: Rev. Ifan R.H. Roberts, Tabernacle Chapel, 81 Merthyr Road, Whitchurch, Cardiff CF14 1DD (Tel: 02920 627465; Fax: 02920 616188; E-mail: swyddfa.office@ebcpcw.org.uk).

THE UNITED REFORMED CHURCH
General Secretary: Rev. Dr David Cornick, 86 Tavistock Place, London WC1H 9RT (Tel: 020 7916 2020; Fax: 020 7916 2021; E-mail: david.cornick@urc.org.uk).

UNITED REFORMED CHURCH SCOTLAND SYNOD
Synod Clerk: Dr James Merrilees, Church House, 340 Cathedral Street, Glasgow G1 2BQ (Tel: 0141-332 7667; E-mail: jmerrilees@urcscotland.org.uk).

BAPTIST UNION OF SCOTLAND
General Director: Rev. William G. Slack, 14 Aytoun Road, Glasgow G41 5RT (Tel: 0141-423 6169; E-mail: mary@scottishbaptist.org.uk).

CONGREGATIONAL FEDERATION IN SCOTLAND
Mrs Margaret Cowie, 23 Middleton Crescent, Bridge of Don, Aberdeen AB22 8HY (Tel: 01224 703248; E-mail: secretary@cfscotland.org.uk).

RELIGIOUS SOCIETY OF FRIENDS (QUAKERS)
Clerk to the General Meeting for Scotland: Pamala McDougall, Havana, 3 Teapot Lane, Inverkeilor, Arbroath DD1 5RP (Tel: 01241 830238; E-mail: member@havana.wanadoo.co.uk).

ROMAN CATHOLIC CHURCH
Rev. Paul Conroy, General Secretariat, Bishops' Conference of Scotland, 64 Aitken Street, Airdrie ML6 6LT (Tel: 01236 764061; Fax: 01236 762489; E-mail: gensec@bpsconfscot.com).

THE SALVATION ARMY
Scotland Secretary: Major Robert McIntyre, Scotland Secretariat, 12A Dryden Road, Loanhead EH20 9LZ (Tel: 0131-440 9101; E-mail: robert.mcintyre@salvationarmy.org.uk).

SCOTTISH EPISCOPAL CHURCH
General Secretary: Mr John F. Stuart, 21 Grosvenor Crescent, Edinburgh EH12 5EL (Tel: 0131-225 6357; E-mail: secgen@scotland.anglican.org).

THE SYNOD OF THE METHODIST CHURCH IN SCOTLAND
Secretary: Mrs Janet Murray, Methodist Church Office, Scottish Churches House, Kirk Street, Dunblane FK15 0AJ (Tel/Fax: 01786 820295; E-mail: meth@scottishchurcheshouse.org).

GENERAL SYNOD OF THE CHURCH OF ENGLAND
Secretary General: Mr William Fittall, Church House, Great Smith Street, London SW1P 3NZ (Tel: 020 7898 1000; E-mail: william.fittall@c-of-e.org.uk).

(2) OVERSEAS CHURCHES

PRESBYTERIAN CHURCH IN AMERICA
Stated Clerk: 1700 North Brown Road, Suite 105, Lawrenceville, GA 30043, USA (E-mail: ac@pcanet.org; Website: www.pcanet.org).

PRESBYTERIAN CHURCH IN CANADA
Clerk of Assembly: 50 Wynford Drive, Toronto, Ontario M3C 1J7, Canada (E-mail: pccadmin@presbycan.ca; Website: www.presbycan.ca).

UNITED CHURCH OF CANADA
General Secretary: Suite 300, 3250 Bloor Street West, Toronto, Ontario M8X 2Y4, Canada (E-mail: info@united-church.ca; Website: www.united-church.ca).

PRESBYTERIAN CHURCH (USA)
Stated Clerk: 100 Witherspoon Street, Louisville, KY 40202-1396, USA (E-mail: presbytel@pcusa.org; Website: www.pcusa.org).

REFORMED PRESBYTERIAN CHURCH OF NORTH AMERICA
Stated Clerk: 7408 Penn Avenue, Pittsburgh, PA 15208, USA (Website: www.reformedpresbyterian.org).

CUMBERLAND PRESBYTERIAN CHURCH
General Secretary: 1978 Union Avenue, Memphis, TN 38104, USA (E-mail: assembly@cumberland.org; Website: www.cumberland.org).

REFORMED CHURCH IN AMERICA
General Secretary: 475 Riverside Drive, NY 10115, USA (E-mail: rcamail@rca.org; Website: www.rca.org).

UNITED CHURCH OF CHRIST
General Minister: 700 Prospect Avenue, Cleveland, OH 44115, USA
(Website: www.ucc.org).

UNITING CHURCH IN AUSTRALIA
General Secretary: PO Box A2266, Sydney South, New South Wales 1235, Australia (E-mail: enquiries@nat.uca.org.au; Website: www.uca.org.au).

PRESBYTERIAN CHURCH OF AUSTRALIA
Clerk of Assembly: PO Box 2196, Strawberry Hills, NSW 2012; 168 Chalmers Street, Surry Hills, NSW 2010, Australia (E-mail: general@pcnsw.org.au; Website: www.presbyterian.org.au).

PRESBYTERIAN CHURCH OF AOTEAROA, NEW ZEALAND
Executive Secretary: PO Box 9049, Wellington, New Zealand (E-mail: aes@presbyterian.org.nz; Website: www.presbyterian.org.nz).

EVANGELICAL PRESBYTERIAN CHURCH, GHANA
Synod Clerk: PO Box 18, Ho, Volta Region, Ghana.

PRESBYTERIAN CHURCH OF GHANA
Director of Ecumenical and Social Relations: PO Box 1800, Accra, Ghana.

PRESBYTERIAN CHURCH OF EAST AFRICA
Secretary General: PO Box 27573, 00506 Nairobi, Kenya.

CHURCH OF CENTRAL AFRICA PRESBYTERIAN
Secretary General, General Synod: PO Box 30398, Lilongwe 3, Malawi.
General Secretary, Blantyre Synod: PO Box 413, Blantyre, Malawi.
General Secretary, Livingstonia Synod: PO Box 112, Mzuzu, Malawi.
General Secretary, Nkhoma Synod: PO Box 45, Nkhoma, Malawi.

IGREJA EVANGELICA DE CRISTO EM MOÇAMBIQUE (EVANGELICAL CHURCH OF CHRIST IN MOZAMBIQUE)
(Nampula) General Secretary: Cx. Postale 284, Nampula 70100, Mozambique.
(Zambezia) Superintendente: Cx. Postale 280, Zambezia, Quelimane, Mozambique.

PRESBYTERIAN CHURCH OF NIGERIA
Principal Clerk: 26–29 Ehere Road, Ogbor Hill, PO Box 2635, Aba, Abia State, Nigeria.

UNITING PRESBYTERIAN CHURCH IN SOUTHERN AFRICA (SOUTH AFRICA)
General Secretary: PO Box 96188, Brixton 2019, South Africa.

UNITING PRESBYTERIAN CHURCH IN SOUTHERN AFRICA (ZIMBABWE)
Presbytery Clerk: PO Box CY224, Causeway, Harare, Zimbabwe.

PRESBYTERIAN CHURCH OF SUDAN (A)
Executive Secretary: PO Box 66168, Nairobi, Kenya.

PRESBYTERIAN CHURCH OF SUDAN (M)
General Secretary: PO Box 3421, Khartoum, Sudan.

UNITED CHURCH OF ZAMBIA
General Secretary: Nationalist Road at Burma Road, PO Box 50122, 15101 Ridgeway, Lusaka, Zambia.

CHURCH OF BANGLADESH
Moderator: Synod Office, 54 Johnson Road, Dhaka 1100, Bangladesh.

CHURCH OF NORTH INDIA
General Secretary: Synod Office, 16 Pandit Pant Marg, New Delhi 110 001, India.

CHURCH OF SOUTH INDIA
General Secretary: Synod Office, 5 White's Road, Royapettah, Chennai 600 114, India.

PRESBYTERIAN CHURCH OF KOREA
General Secretary: CPO Box 1125, Seoul 110 611, Korea.

PRESBYTERIAN CHURCH IN THE REPUBLIC OF KOREA
General Secretary: 1501 The Korean Ecumenical Building, 136–156 Yunchi-Dong, Chongno-Ku, Seoul, Korea.

THE UNITED MISSION TO NEPAL
Executive Director: PO Box 126, Kathmandu, Nepal.

CHURCH OF PAKISTAN
General Secretary: c/o St John's Cathedral School, 1 Sir Syed Road, Peshawar 25000, NWFP, Pakistan.

PRESBYTERY OF LANKA
Moderator: 127/1 D S Senanayake Veedyan, Kandy, Sri Lanka.

PRESBYTERIAN CHURCH IN TAIWAN
General Secretary: 3 Lane 269 Roosevelt Road, Sec. 3, Taipei, Taiwan 10763, ROC.

CHURCH OF CHRIST IN THAILAND
General Secretary: 109 CCT (13th Floor), Surawong Road, Khet Bangrak, Bangkok 10500, Thailand.

PRESBYTERY OF GUYANA
Moderator: 169 Thomas Street, Kitty, Georgetown, Guyana.

NATIONAL PRESBYTERIAN CHURCH OF GUATEMALA
Executive Secretary: Av. Simeon Canas 7–13, Zona 2, Aptdo 655, Guatemala City, Guatemala (E-mail: ienpg@terra.com.gt).

UNITED CHURCH IN JAMAICA AND THE CAYMAN ISLANDS
General Secretary: 12 Carlton Crescent, PO Box 359, Kingston 10, Jamaica (E-mail: unitedchurch@colis.com).

PRESBYTERIAN CHURCH IN TRINIDAD AND TOBAGO
General Secretary: Box 92, Paradise Hill, San Fernando, Trinidad (E-mail: pctt@tstt.net.tt).

UNITED PROTESTANT CHURCH OF BELGIUM
Rue de Champ de Mars 5, B-1050 Bruxelles, Belgium (E-mail: epub@epub.be; Website: www.protestanet.be/eput/index.htm).

REFORMED CHRISTIAN CHURCH IN CROATIA
Bishop's Office: Vladimira Nazora 31, HR-32100 Vinkovci, Croatia (E-mail: reformed.church.rcc@vk.htnet.hr).

EVANGELICAL CHURCH OF THE CZECH BRETHREN
Moderator: Jungmannova 9, PO Box 466, CZ-11121 Praha 1, Czech Republic (E-mail: ekumena@srcce.cz; Website: www.srcce.cz).

EGLISE REFORMEE DE FRANCE
General Secretary: 47 rue de Clichy, F-75311 Paris, France (E-mail: erf@unacerf.org; Website: www.eglise-reformee-fr.org).

HUNGARIAN REFORMED CHURCH
General Secretary: PF Box 5, H-1440 Budapest, Hungary (E-mail: zsinat.kulugy@zsinatiiroda.hu; Website: www.reformatus.hu).

WALDENSIAN CHURCH
Moderator: Via Firenze 38, 00184 Rome, Italy (E-mail: moderatore@chiesavaldese.org; Website: www.chiesavaldese.org).

NETHERLANDS REFORMED CHURCH
Landelijk Dienstcentrum Samen op Weg-Kerken, Postbus 8504, NL-3503 RM Utrecht (E-mail: ccs@ngk.nl; Website: www.ngk.nl).

REFORMED CHURCH IN ROMANIA
Bishop's Office: Str. IC Bratianu No. 51, R-3400 Cluj-Napoca, Romania (E-mail: office@reformatus.ro).

REFORMED CHRISTIAN CHURCH IN YUGOSLAVIA
Bishop's Office: Bratstva 26, YU-24323 Feketic, Yugoslavia.

SYNOD OF THE NILE OF THE EVANGELICAL CHURCH
General Secretary: Synod of the Nile of the Evangelical Church, PO Box 1248, Cairo, Egypt (E-mail: epcegypt@yahoo.com).

DIOCESE OF THE EPISCOPAL CHURCH IN JERUSALEM AND THE MIDDLE EAST
Bishop's Office: PO Box 19122, Jerusalem 91191, via Israel (E-mail: ediocese-jer@j-diocese.com; Website: www.jerusalem.anglican.org).

NATIONAL EVANGELICAL SYNOD OF SYRIA AND LEBANON
General Secretary: PO Box 70890, Antelias, Lebanon (E-mail: nessl@minero.net).

[Full information on Churches overseas may be obtained from the World Mission Council.]

(3) SCOTTISH DIVINITY FACULTIES
[* denotes a Minister of the Church of Scotland]
[(R) Reader   (SL) Senior Lecturer   (L) Lecturer]

ABERDEEN
(School of Divinity, History and Philosophy)
King's College, Old Aberdeen AB24 3UB
(Tel: 01224 272380; Fax: 01224 273750;
E-mail: divinity@abdn.ac.uk)

Master of Christ's College: Rev. J.H.A. Dick* MA MSc BD
(E-mail: christs-college@abdn.ac.uk)

Head of School: Professor Robert Frost MA PhD FRHistS

Professors: Robert Segal BA MA PhD (Religious Studies)
Joachim Schaper DipTheol PhD (Old Testament)
Rev. John Swinton* BD PhD RNM RNMD (Practical Theology and Pastoral Care)
Francis Watson MA DPhil LRAM (New Testament)
John Webster MA PhD DD (Systematic Theology)

Readers: Francesca Murphy BA MA PhD (Systematic Theology)

Senior Lecturers: Andrew Clarke BA MA PhD (New Testament)
Martin Mills MA PhD (Religious Studies)

Lecturers: Kenneth Aitken BD PhD (Hebrew Bible)
Christopher Brittain BA MDiv PhD (Practical Theology)
Brian Brock BS MA DipTheol DPhil (Moral and Practical Theology)
Gabriele Maranci BA MA PhD (Religious Studies)
Nick Thompson BA MA MTh PhD (Church History)
Lena-Sofia Tiemeyer BA MA MPhil (Old Testament/Hebrew Bible)
Will Tuladhar-Douglas BA MA MPhil (Religious Studies)
Donald Wood BA MA MPhil DPhil (Systematic Theology)
Philip Ziegler BA MA MDiv ThD (Systematic Theology)

ST ANDREWS
(University College of St Mary)
St Mary's College, St Andrews, Fife KY16 9JU
(Tel: 01334 462850/1; Fax: 01334 462852)

Principal, Dean and Head of School: J.R. Davila BA MA UCLA PhD

Chairs: M.I. Aguilar BA MA STB PhD
(Religion and Politics)
P.F. Esler BA LLB LLM DPhil (Biblical Criticism)
T.A. Hart BA PhD (Divinity)
R.A. Piper BA BD PhD (Christian Origins)
A.J. Torrance* MA BD DrTheol
(Systematic Theology)

Readerships, Senior Lectureships, Lectureships:

I.C. Bradley* BA MA BD DPhil (R) (Practical Theology)
J.R. Davila BA MA UCLA PhD (Early Jewish Studies)
M. Elliott BA BD PhD (Church History)
S.R. Holmes BA MA MTh PGDip PhD (Theology)
G. Hopps BA MPhil PhD
G. Macaskill BSc DipTh PhD
N. MacDonald MA MPhil (Old Testament and Hebrew)
E.D. Reed BA PhD (SL) (Theology and Ethics)
E. Stoddart BD PhD

EDINBURGH
(School of Divinity and New College)
New College, Mound Place, Edinburgh EH1 2LX
(Tel: 0131-650 8900; Fax: 0131-650 7952; E-mail: divinity.faculty@ed.ac.uk)

Head of School: Rev. Professor David A.S. Fergusson* MA BD DPhil FRSE
Principal of New College: Rev. Professor A. Graeme Auld* MA BD PhD DLitt FSAScot
FRSE
Chairs: Rev. Professor A. Graeme Auld* MA BD PhD DLitt FSAScot
FRSE (Hebrew Bible)
Professor Hans Barstad DrTheol (Hebrew and Old Testament)
Professor Stewart J. Brown BA MA PhD FRHistS
(Ecclesiastical History)
Professor James L. Cox BA MDiv PhD (Religious Studies)
Rev. Professor David A.S. Fergusson* MA BD DPhil FRSE
(Divinity)
Professor Larry W. Hurtado BA MA PhD
(New Testament Language, Literature and Theology)

Professor Timothy Lim BA MPhil DPhil (Biblical Studies)
Rev. Professor Oliver O'Donovan MA DPhil (Christian Ethics)
Professor Marcella Althaus Reid BTh PhD
(Contextual Theology)

Readers, Senior Lecturers and Lecturers:

Biblical Studies:	David J. Reimer BTh BA MA MA (SL)
	Graham Paul Foster PhD MSt BD
	Helen K. Bond MTheol PhD (SL)
Theology and Ethics:	Jolyon Mitchell BA MA (SL)
	Michael S. Northcott MA PhD (R)
	Cecelia Clegg BD MSc PhD (L)
	Rev. Ewan Kelly* MB ChB BD PhD (L) (part-time)
	Nicholas S. Adams BA PhD (L)
	John C. McDowell BD PhD (L)
	Michael Purcell MA PhD PhL PhB (SL)
	Sara Parvis BA PhD (L)
Ecclesiastical History:	Jane E.A. Dawson BA PhD DipEd (SL)
	Jack Thompson BA PhD (SL)
	Susan Hardman Moore MA PhD (L)
Religious Studies:	Jeanne Openshaw BA MA PhD (SL)
	Elizabeth Kopping MA PhD DipSocSci MTh (L)
	Steven Sutcliffe BA MPhil PhD
	Hannah Holtschneider MPhil PhD (L)
	Afeosemime U. Adogame BA MA PhD (L)
	Christian Lange BA MA PhD (L)

Fulton Lecturer in Speech and Communication:
Richard Ellis BSc MEd LGSM

Hope Trust Post-Doctoral Fellow:
Rev. Alison Jack* MA BD PhD

GLASGOW
(School of Divinity and Trinity College)
4 The Square, University of Glasgow, Glasgow G12 8QQ
(Tel: 0141-330 6526; Fax: 0141-330 4943; E-mail: divinity@arts.gla.ac.uk)

Head of Department:	Professor W. Ian P. Hazlett
Principal of Trinity College:	Professor W. Ian P. Hazlett

Chairs: W. Ian P. Hazlett BA BD Dr theol DLitt DD (Ecclesiastical History)
                     Rev. David Jasper MA PhD BD DD TeolD FRSE (Literature and Theology)
                     Werner Jeanrond Mag theol PhD (Divinity)
                     Rev. George M. Newlands* MA BD PhD DLitt FRSA (Divinity)
                     Perry Schmidt-Leukel Dipl theol MA Dr theol Dr theol habil
                        (Systematic Theology and World Religions).
                     Mona Siddiqui MA PhD DLitt FRSE (Public Understanding of Islam)

Honorary Professorships: Rev. Donald Macleod MA
                                Rev. John K. Riches MA

Senior Lecturers and Lecturers:
  Biblical Studies: Ward W. Blanton BA MDiv PhD (L)
                           Paul A. Holloway AB MA PhD (L)
                           Rev. Alastair G. Hunter* MSc BD PhD (SL)
                           Sarah Nicholson MTheol PhD (L)
                           Yvonne M. Sherwood BA PhD DipJS (SL)

  Catholic Theology and Ethics:
                           Julie P. Clague BSc PGCE PGDip MTh (L)

  Practical Theology: Douglas Gay MA BD PhD (L)
                           Heather E. Walton BA MA(Econ) PhD (SL)

  Islamic Studies: Lloyd V.J. Ridgeon BA MA PhD (SL)

Honorary Lecturer in Church History:
                           Rev. John R. McIntosh BA BD MLitt PhD

Centre for Advanced Studies in Christian Ministry:
Director: Dr Heather E. Walton

Centre for Literature, Theology and the Arts:
Co-Director: Dr Heather E. Walton

Centre for the Study of Islam:
Director: Professor Mona Siddiqui

Divinity Graduate School:
Director: Rev. Professor David Jasper

Centre for Inter-faith Studies:
Director: Professor P. Schmidt-Leukel

HIGHLAND THEOLOGICAL COLLEGE
High Street, Dingwall IV15 9HA
(Tel: 01349 780000; Fax: 01349 780201;
E-mail: htc@uhi.ac.uk)

Principal of HTC:	Rev. Professor Andrew McGowan* BD STM PhD
Vice-Principal of HTC:	Rev. Hector Morrison BSc BD MTh ILTM

Lecturers: Hector Morrison BSc BD MTh ILTM (Old Testament and Hebrew)
Jamie Grant PhD MA LLB (Biblical Studies)
Michael Bird BMin BA PhD (New Testament)
Innes Visagie MA BTh BA PhD (Pastoral Theology)
Nick Needham BD PhD (Church History)
Robert Shillaker BSc BA PhD (Systematic Theology)

---

(4) SOCIETIES AND ASSOCIATIONS

The undernoted list shows the name of the Association, along with the name and address of the Secretary.

INTER-CHURCH ASSOCIATIONS

THE FELLOWSHIP OF ST ANDREW: The fellowship promotes dialogue between Churches of the east and the west in Scotland. Further information available from the Secretary, Rev. Robert Pickles, The Manse, 3 Perth Road, Milnathort, Kinross KY13 9XU (Tel: 01577 863461; E-mail: robert.pickles1@btopenworld.com).

THE FELLOWSHIP OF ST THOMAS: An ecumenical association formed to promote informed interest in and learn from the experience of Churches in South Asia (India, Pakistan, Bangladesh, Nepal, Sri Lanka). Secretary: Dr R.L. Robinson, 43 Underwood Road, Burnside, Rutherglen, Glasgow G73 3TE (Tel: 0141-643 0612; E-mail: robinson.burnside @surefish.co.uk).

THE SCOTTISH ORDER OF CHRISTIAN UNITY: Secretary: Rev. William D. Brown MA, 9/3 Craigend Park, Edinburgh EH16 5XY (Tel: 0131-672 2936; E-mail: wdbrown@ surefish.co.uk; Website: www.socu.org.uk).

CHURCH PASTORAL AID SOCIETY (CPAS): Consultant for Scotland: Rev. Richard W. Higginbottom, 2 Highfield Place, Bankfoot, Perth PH1 4AX (Tel: 01738 787429). A home mission agency working cross-denominationally through consultancy, training and resources to encourage Churches in local evangelism: accredited officially to the Mission and Discipleship Council.

FRONTIER YOUTH TRUST: Encourages and resources those engaged in youth work, particularly with disadvantaged young people. Co-ordinator: Matt Hall, 8 Dalswinton Street, Glasgow G34 0PS (Tel: 0141-771 9151).

IONA COMMUNITY: Leader: Rev. Kathy Galloway, Fourth Floor, Savoy House, 140 Sauchiehall Street, Glasgow G2 3DH (Tel: 0141-332 6343; Fax: 0141-332 1090; E-mail: admin@iona.org.uk; Website: www.iona.org.uk); Warden: Richard Sharples, Iona Abbey, Isle of Iona, Argyll PA76 6SN (Tel: 01681 700404).

SCOTTISH CHURCHES HOUSING ACTION: Provides the Churches with information, education, advice and support concerning homelessness. Chief Executive: Alastair Cameron, 28 Albany Street, Edinburgh EH1 3QH (Tel: 0131-477 4500; Fax: 0131-477 2710; E-mail: info@churches-housing.org; Website: www.churches-housing.org).

WORLD EXCHANGE: Volunteers can help turn the world upside down, in Scotland and in the developing world. When it comes to making the world a better place, there are no limits to what's possible. Teachers, ministers, managers, accountants, joiners, engineers, musicians, artists and others are all invited to explore the possibility of working with World Exchange.
• Consultancies and work camps (4–6 weeks)
• Six-month 'gap' projects for school-leavers and younger volunteers
• One-year programme (in Scotland or overseas)
Church-based community projects in Scotland, Africa, South Asia, Europe and the Caribbean (Tel: 0131-315 4444; Website: www.worldexchange.org.uk). Your potential is boundless. Now may be the time to unleash it.

ST COLM'S INTERNATIONAL HOUSE: Available for ministers and church conferences: an excellent place to stay and an opportunity to support an important ecumenical project. English-language and Capacity-Building Courses for community leaders from the developing world. A place to meet in the heart of the Capital on the perimeter of the Royal Botanic Gardens (Tel: 0131-315 4444).

FRIENDS OF ST COLM'S: An association for all from any denomination who have trained, studied or been resident in St Colm's or have an interest in its work and life. There is an annual retreat, an annual lecture and some local associations for more regular meetings. It offers support to St Colm's International House. Secretary: c/o St Colm's International House, 23 Inverleith Terrace, Edinburgh EH3 5NS (Tel: 0131-315 4444).

SCOTTISH JOINT COMMITTEE ON RELIGIOUS AND MORAL EDUCATION: Mr Rob Whiteman, 121 George Street, Edinburgh EH2 4YN (Tel: 0131-225 5722), and Mr Lachlan Bradley, 6 Clairmont Gardens, Glasgow G3 7LW (Tel: 0141-353 3595).

SCOTTISH NATIONAL COUNCIL OF YMCAs: National General Secretary: Mr Peter Crory, James Love House, 11 Rutland Street, Edinburgh EH1 2DQ (Tel: 0131-228 1464; E-mail: info@ymcascotland.org; Website: www.ymcascotland.org).

INTERSERVE SCOTLAND: Part of Interserve International, an international, evangelical and interdenominational organisation with over 150 years of Christian service. Interserve internationally supports over 700 partners in cross-cultural ministry, and works in the Arab world and across Asia. Interserve's mission is to serve the Church and share Jesus Christ in all aspects of life, and Interserve workers are therefore involved in a wide range of work including children and youth, the environment, evangelism, Bible training, engineering, agriculture, business, development and so on. We rely on supporters in Scotland and throughout the UK to join us. Join the adventure with Interserve. Director: Grace Penney, 12 Elm Avenue, Lenzie, Glasgow G66 4HJ (Tel: 0141-578 0207; Fax: 0141-578 0208; E-mail: info@isscott.org; Website: www.interservescotland.org.uk).

SCRIPTURE UNION SCOTLAND: 70 Milton Street, Glasgow G4 0HR (Tel: 0141-332 1162; Fax: 0141-352 7600; E-mail: info@suscotland.org.uk; Website: www.suscotland.org.uk).

STUDENT CHRISTIAN MOVEMENT: Co-ordinator: Mr Liam Purcell, SCM Office, Unit 308F, The Big Peg, 120 Vyse Street, The Jewellery Quarter, Birmingham B18 6NF (Tel: 0121-200 3355; E-mail: scm@movement.org.uk; Website: www.movement.org.uk). See also Christian Action and Thought.

CHRISTIAN ACTION AND THOUGHT (Edinburgh SCM): Ms Amy Mormino, CAT, Chaplaincy Centre, 1 Bristo Square, Edinburgh EH8 9AL (E-mail: amymormino@ hotmail.com; Website: www.eusa.ed.ac.uk/societies/euscm).

UNIVERSITIES AND COLLEGES CHRISTIAN FELLOWSHIP: Pod Bhogal, 38 De Montfort Street, Leicester LE1 7GP (Tel: 0116-255 1700; E-mail: pbhogal@uccf.org.uk).

WORLD DAY OF PRAYER: SCOTTISH COMMITTEE: Convener: Christian Williams, 61 McCallum Gardens, Strathview Estate, Bellshill ML4 2SR. Secretary: Morag Hannah, 8 Dovecote View, Kirkintilloch, Glasgow G66 3HY (Tel: 0141-776 2432; E-mail: morag.hannah.wdp@virgin.net; Website: www.wdpscotland.org.uk).

CHURCH OF SCOTLAND SOCIETIES

AROS (Association of Returned Overseas Staff of the Church of Scotland World Mission Council): Hon. Secretary: Rev. Kenneth J. Pattison, 2 Castle Way, St Madoes, Glencarse, Perth PH2 7NY (Tel: 01738 860340).

FORUM OF GENERAL ASSEMBLY AND PRESBYTERY CLERKS: Rev. David W. Lunan MA BD, 260 Bath Street, Glasgow G2 4JP (Tel: 0141-332 6606).

FORWARD TOGETHER: An organisation for evangelicals within the Church of Scotland. Secretary: Rev. Ian M. Watson LLB DipLP BD, The Manse, 2 Lanark Road, Kirkmuirhill, Lanark ML11 9RB (Tel: 01555 892409; Website: www.forwardtogether.org.uk).

FRIENDS OF ST COLM'S: Secretary: c/o St Colm's International House, 23 Inverleith Terrace, Edinburgh EH3 5NS (Tel: 0131-315 4444).

SCOTTISH CHURCH SOCIETY: Secretary: Rev. W. Gerald Jones MA BD MTh, The Manse, Kirkmichael, Maybole KA19 7PJ (Tel: 01655 750286).

SCOTTISH CHURCH THEOLOGY SOCIETY: Rev. Gordon R. Mackenzie BSc(Agr) BD, The Manse of Dyke, Brodie, Forres IV36 2TD (Tel: 01309 641239; E-mail: rev.g.mackenzie@btopenworld.com). The Society encourages theological exploration and discussion of the main issues confronting the Church in the twenty-first century.

SOCIETY OF FRIENDS OF ST ANDREW'S JERUSALEM: Hon. Secretary: Major J.M.K. Erskine MBE, World Mission Council, 121 George Street, Edinburgh EH2 4YN. Hon. Treasurer: Mrs Anne Macintosh BA CA, Assistant Treasurer, The Church of Scotland, 121 George Street, Edinburgh EH2 4YN (Tel: 0131-225 5722).

THE CHURCH OF SCOTLAND CHAPLAINS' ASSOCIATION: Hon. Secretary: Rev. Donald M. Stephen TD MA BD ThM, 10 Hawkhead Crescent, Edinburgh EH16 6LR (Tel: 0131-658 1216).

THE CHURCH OF SCOTLAND RETIRED MINISTERS' ASSOCIATION: Hon. Secretary: Rev. Elspeth G. Dougall MA BD, 60B Craigmillar Park, Edinburgh EH16 5PU (Tel: 0131-668 1342).

THE CHURCH SERVICE SOCIETY: Secretary: Rev. Neil N. Gardner MA BD, The Manse of Canongate, Edinburgh EH8 8BR (Tel: 0131-556 3515).

THE IRISH MINISTERS' FRATERNAL: Secretary: Rev. Eric G. McKimmon BA BD MTh, The Manse, St Andrews Road, Ceres, Cupar KY15 5NQ (Tel: 01334 829466).

THE NATIONAL CHURCH ASSOCIATION: Secretary: Miss Margaret P. Milne, 10 Balfron Crescent, Hamilton ML3 9UH.

BIBLE SOCIETIES

THE SCOTTISH BIBLE SOCIETY: Director of Programmes: Mr Colin S. Hay, 7 Hampton Terrace, Edinburgh EH12 5XU (Tel: 0131-347 9809).

WEST OF SCOTLAND BIBLE SOCIETY: Secretary: Rev. Finlay MacKenzie, 51 Rowallan Gardens, Glasgow G11 7LH (Tel: 0141-563 5276; E-mail: f.c.mack51@ntlworld.com).

GENERAL

THE BOYS' BRIGADE: Scottish Headquarters, Carronvale House, Carronvale Road, Larbert FK5 3LH (Tel: 01324 562008; Fax: 01324 552323; E-mail: carronvale@boys-brigade.org.uk).

THE GIRLS' BRIGADE SCOTLAND: 11A Woodside Crescent, Glasgow G3 7UL (Tel: 0141-332 1765; E-mail: enquiries@girls-brigade-scotland.org.uk; Website: www.girls-brigade-scotland.org.uk).

GIRLGUIDING SCOTLAND: 16 Coates Crescent, Edinburgh EH3 7AH (Tel: 0131-226 4511; Fax: 0131-220 4828; E-mail: administrator@girlguiding-scot.org.uk).

THE SCOUT ASSOCIATION: Scottish Headquarters, Fordell Firs, Hillend, Dunfermline KY11 7HQ (Tel: 01383 419073; E-mail: shq@scouts-scotland.org.uk).

BOYS' AND GIRLS' CLUBS OF SCOTLAND: 88 Giles Street, Edinburgh EH6 6BZ (Tel: 0131-555 1729; E-mail: secretary@bgcs.co.uk).

YOUTH SCOTLAND: Balfour House, 19 Bonnington Grove, Edinburgh EH6 4BL (Tel: 0131-554 2561; Fax: 0131-454 3438; E-mail: office@youthscotland.org.uk).

CHRISTIAN AID SCOTLAND: National Secretary: The Pentagon Centre, 36 Washington Street, Glasgow G3 8AZ (Tel: 0141-221 7475; Fax: 0141-241 6145; E-mail: glasgow@christian-aid.org). Edinburgh Office: Tel: 0131-220 1254.

FEED THE MINDS: 36 Causton Street, London SW1P 4AU (Tel: 08451 212102).

LADIES' GAELIC SCHOOLS AND HIGHLAND BURSARY ASSOCIATION: Mr Donald J. Macdonald, 9 Hatton Place, Edinburgh EH9 1UD (Tel: 0131-667 1740).

RELATE SCOTLAND: Chief Executive: Mrs Hilary Campbell, 18 York Place, Edinburgh EH1 3EP (Tel: 0845 119 6088; Fax: 0845 119 6089; E-mail: enquiries@relatescotland.org.uk; Website: www.relatescotland.org.uk).

RUTHERFORD HOUSE: Warden: Rev. Robert Fyall MA BD PhD, 17 Claremont Park, Edinburgh EH6 7PJ (Tel: 0131-554 1206; Fax: 0131-555 1002).

SCOTTISH CHURCH HISTORY SOCIETY: Hon. Secretary: Rev. William D. Graham MA BD, 48 Corbiehill Crescent, Edinburgh EH4 5BD (Tel: 0131-336 4071; E-mail: w.d.graham@btinternet.com).

SCOTTISH EVANGELICAL THEOLOGY SOCIETY: Secretary: Rev. David J.C. Easton MA BD, 'Rowanbank', Cormiston Road, Quothquan, Biggar ML12 6ND (Tel: 01899 308459; E-mail: deaston@btinternet.com; Website: www.setsonline.org.uk).

CHRISTIAN ENDEAVOUR IN SCOTLAND: Winning, Teaching and Training Youngsters for Christ and the Church: The Murray Library, 8 Shore Street, Anstruther KY10 3EA (Tel: 01333 310345 Monday, Wednesday and Friday mornings; E-mail: christine@ ce-in-scotland.fsnet.co.uk; Website: www.cescotland.org.uk).

TEARFUND: 100 Church Road, Teddington TW11 8QE (Tel: 0845 355 8355). Manager: Peter Chirnside, Tearfund Scotland, Challenge House, 29 Canal Street, Glasgow G4 0AD (Tel: 0141-332 3621; E-mail: scotland@tearfund.org; Website: www.tearfund.org).

THE LEPROSY MISSION: Suite 2, Earlsgate Lodge, Livilands Lane, Stirling FK8 2BG (Tel: 01786 449266; Fax: 01786 449766). National Director: Miss Linda Todd. Area Co-ordinator, Scotland Central and South: Mr Stuart McAra. Area Co-ordinator: Scotland North and Islands: Mr Jim Clark (Tel: 01343 843837; E-mail: contactus@tlmscotland.org.uk and meetings@tlmscotland.org.uk; Website: www.tlmscotland.org.uk).

DAYONE CHRISTIAN MINISTRIES (THE LORD'S DAY OBSERVANCE SOCIETY): Ryelands Road, Leominster, Herefordshire HR6 8NZ (Tel: 01568 613740).

THE SCOTTISH REFORMATION SOCIETY: Secretary: Rev. A. Sinclair Horne, The Magdalen Chapel, 41 Cowgate, Edinburgh EH1 1JR (Tel: 0131-220 1450; E-mail: ashbethany43@ hotmail.co.uk; Website: www.scottishreformation.co.uk).

THE SOCIETY IN SCOTLAND FOR PROPAGATING CHRISTIAN KNOWLEDGE: J. Gordon Cunningham WS, Tods Murray LLP, Edinburgh Quay, 133 Fountainbridge, Edinburgh EH3 9AG (Tel: 0131-656 2000).

THE WALDENSIAN MISSIONS AID SOCIETY FOR WORK IN ITALY: David A. Lamb SSC, 36 Liberton Drive, Edinburgh EH16 6NN (Tel: 0131-664 3059; E-mail: david@dlamb.co.uk).

YWCA SCOTLAND: Chief Executive: Elaine Samson, 7B Randolph Crescent, Edinburgh EH3 7TH (Tel: 0131-225 7592; E-mail: info@ywcascotland.org; Website: www.ywcascotland.org).

(5) TRUSTS AND FUNDS

THE SOCIETY FOR THE BENEFIT OF THE SONS AND DAUGHTERS OF THE CLERGY OF THE CHURCH OF SCOTLAND

Secretary and Treasurer: R. Graeme Thom FCA
17 Melville Street
Edinburgh EH3 7PH (Tel: 0131-473 3500;
E-mail: charity@scott-moncrieff.com)

Annual grants are made to assist in the education of the children (normally between the ages of 12 and 25 years) of ministers of the Church of Scotland. The Society also gives grants to aged and infirm daughters of ministers and ministers' unmarried daughters and sisters who are in need. Applications are to be lodged by 31 May in each year.

THE GLASGOW SOCIETY OF THE SONS AND DAUGHTERS OF MINISTERS OF THE CHURCH OF SCOTLAND

Secretary and Treasurer: R. Graeme Thom FCA
17 Melville Street
Edinburgh EH3 7PH (Tel: 0131-473 3500;
E-mail: charity@scott-moncrieff.com)

The Society's primary purpose is to grant financial assistance to children (no matter what age) of deceased ministers of the Church of Scotland. Applications are to be submitted by 1 February in each year. To the extent that funds are available, grants are also given for the children of ministers or retired ministers, although such grants are normally restricted to university and college students. These latter grants are considered in conjunction with the Edinburgh-based Society. Limited funds are also available for individual application for special needs or projects. Applications are to be submitted by 31 May in each year. Emergency applications can be dealt with at any time when need arises. Application forms may be obtained from the Secretary.

ESDAILE TRUST:
Clerk and Treasurer: R. Graeme Thom FCA
17 Melville Street
Edinburgh EH3 7PH (Tel: 0131-473 3500;
E-mail: charity@scott-moncrieff.com)

Assists education and advancement of daughters of ministers, missionaries and widowed deaconesses of the Church of Scotland between 12 and 25 years of age. Applications are to be lodged by 31 May in each year.

HOLIDAYS FOR MINISTERS

The undernoted hotels provide special terms for ministers and their families. Fuller information may be obtained from the establishments:

CRIEFF HYDRO HOTEL and MURRAYPARK HOTEL: The William Meikle Trust Fund and Paton Fund make provision whereby active ministers and their spouses, members of the Diaconate and other full-time employees of the Church of Scotland may enjoy hotel and self-catering accommodation at certain times of the year. Crieff Hydro offers a wide range of leisure facilities such as the Lagoon swimming pool, in-house cinema, entertainment and over thirty-five activities both indoors and outside. Crieff Hydro has a registered children's club that provides expert childcare for children of 0 to 12 years of age. For reservations, please contact the Accommodation Sales Team (Crieff Hydro, Ferntower Road, Crieff PH7 3LQ) on 01764 651670 or by e-mail: enquiries@crieffhydro.com

THE CINTRA BEQUEST: The Trust provides financial assistance towards the cost of accommodation in Scotland for missionaries on leave, or for ministers on temporary holiday, or on rest. In addition, due to additional funds generously donated by the Tod Endowment Trust, grants can be given to defray the cost of obtaining rest and recuperation in Scotland. In appropriate cases, therefore, the cost of travel within Scotland may also be met. Applications should be made to Mrs J.S. Wilson, Solicitor, 121 George Street, Edinburgh EH2 4YN.

TOD ENDOWMENT TRUST: CINTRA BEQUEST: MINISTRY BENEVOLENT FUND: The Trustees of the Cintra Bequest and of the Church of Scotland Ministry Benevolent Fund can consider an application for a grant from the Tod Endowment funds from any ordained or commissioned minister or deacon in Scotland of at least two years' standing before the date of application, to assist with the cost of the beneficiary and his or her spouse or partner and dependants obtaining rest and recuperation in Scotland. The Trustees of the Church of Scotland Ministry Benevolent Fund can also consider an application from an ordained or commissioned minister or deacon who has retired. Application forms are available from Mrs J.S. Wilson, Solicitor (for the Cintra Bequest), and from Mrs P. Willder, Assistant Treasurer (Ministries) (for the Ministry Benevolent Fund). The address in both cases is 121 George Street, Edinburgh EH2 4YN (Tel: 0131-225 5722). (Attention is drawn to separate individual entries for both the Cintra Bequest and the Church of Scotland Ministry Benevolent Fund.)

THE LYALL BEQUEST: Makes available the following benefits to ministers of the Church of Scotland:
1. A grant towards the cost of holiday accommodation in or close to the town of St Andrews may be paid to any minister and to his or her spouse at the rate of £100 per week each for a stay of one week or longer. Grants for a stay of less than one week may also be paid, at the rate of £14 per day each. Due to the number of applications which the Trustees now receive, an applicant will not be considered to be eligible if he or she has received a grant from the Bequest during the three years prior to the holiday for which the application is made. Applications prior to the holiday should be made to the Secretaries. Retired ministers are not eligible for grants.
2. Grants towards costs of sickness and convalescence so far as not covered by the National Health Service or otherwise may be available to applicants, who should apply to the Secretaries giving relevant details.
All communications should be addressed to Pagan Osborne, Solicitors, Secretaries to the Lyall Bequest, 106 South Street, St Andrews KY16 9QD (Tel: 01334 475001; E-mail: elcalderwood@pagan.co.uk).

MARGARET AND JOHN ROSS TRAVELLING FUND: Offers grants to ministers and their spouses for travelling and other expenses for trips to the Holy Land where the purpose is recuperation or relaxation. Applications should be made to the Secretary and Clerk, Church of Scotland Trust, 121 George Street, Edinburgh EH2 4YN (Tel: 0131-240 2222; E-mail: jhamilton@cofscotland.org.uk).

The undernoted represents a list of the more important trusts available for ministers, students and congregations. A brief indication is given of the trust purposes, but application should be made in each case to the person named for full particulars and forms of application.

THE ABERNETHY TRUST: Offers residential accommodation and outdoor activities for Youth Fellowships, Church family weekends, Bible Classes and so on at four outdoor centres in Scotland. Further details from the Executive Director, Abernethy Trust, Nethy Bridge PH25 3ED (Tel/Fax: 01479 821279; Website: www.abernethytrust.org.uk).

THE ARROL TRUST: The Arrol Trust gives small grants to young people between the ages of 16 and 25 for the purposes of travel which will provide education or work experience. Potential recipients would be young people with disabilities or who would for financial reasons be otherwise unable to undertake projects. It is expected that projects would be beneficial not only to applicants but also to the wider community. Application forms are available from Callum S. Kennedy WS, Lindsays WS, Caledonian Exchange, 19a Canning Street, Edinburgh EH3 8HE (Tel: 0131-656 5663).

THE BAIRD TRUST: Assists in the building and repair of churches and halls, endows Parishes and generally assists the work of the Church of Scotland. Apply to Ronald D. Oakes CA ACMA, 182 Bath Street, Glasgow G2 4HG (Tel: 0141-332 0476; Fax: 0141-331 0874; E-mail: baird.trust@btconnect.com).

THE REV. ALEXANDER BARCLAY BEQUEST: Assists mother, daughter, sister or niece of deceased minister of the Church of Scotland who at the time of his death was acting as his housekeeper and who is in needy circumstances. Apply to Robert Hugh Allan LLB DipLP NP, Pomphreys, 79 Quarry Street, Hamilton ML3 7AG (Tel: 01698 891616).

BELLAHOUSTON BEQUEST FUND: Gives grants to Protestant evangelical denominations in the City of Glasgow and certain areas within five miles of the city boundary for building and repairing churches and halls and the promotion of religion. Apply to Mr Donald B. Reid, Mitchells Roberton, 36 North Hanover Street, Glasgow G1 2AD.

BEQUEST FUND FOR MINISTERS: Assists ministers in outlying districts with manse furnishings, pastoral efficiency aids, educational or medical costs. Apply to A. Linda Parkhill CA, 60 Wellington Street, Glasgow G2 6HJ (Tel: 0141-226 4994).

CARNEGIE TRUST FOR THE UNIVERSITIES OF SCOTLAND: In cases of hardship, the Carnegie Trust is prepared to consider applications by students of Scottish birth or extraction (at least one parent born in Scotland), or who have had at least three years' education at a secondary school in Scotland, for financial assistance with the payment of their fees for a first degree at a Scottish university. For further details, students should apply to the Secretary, Carnegie Trust for the Universities of Scotland, Cameron House, Abbey Park Place, Dunfermline, Fife KY12 7PZ (Tel: 01383 622148; E-mail: jgray@carnegie-trust.org; Website: www.carnegie-trust.org).

CHURCH OF SCOTLAND INSURANCE CO. LTD: Undertakes insurance of Church property and pays surplus profits to Church schemes. It is authorised and regulated by the Financial Services Authority. The company can also arrange household insurance for members and adherents of the Church of Scotland. At 67 George Street, Edinburgh EH2 2JG (Tel: 0131-220 4119; Fax: 0131-220 4120; E-mail: enquiries@cosic.co.uk).

CHURCH OF SCOTLAND MINISTRY BENEVOLENT FUND: Makes grants to retired men and women who have been ordained or commissioned for the ministry of the Church of Scotland and to widows, widowers, orphans, spouses or children of such, who are in need. Apply to the Assistant Treasurer (Ministries), 121 George Street, Edinburgh EH2 4YN (Tel: 0131-225 5722).

CLARK BURSARY: Awarded to accepted candidate(s) for the ministry of the Church of Scotland whose studies for the ministry are pursued at the University of Aberdeen. Applications or recommendations for the Bursary to the Clerk to the Presbytery of Aberdeen, Mastrick Church, Greenfern Road, Aberdeen AB16 6TR by 16 October annually.

CRAIGCROOK MORTIFICATION:
Clerk and Factor: R. Graeme Thom FCA
                                     17 Melville Street
                                     Edinburgh EH3 7PH (Tel: 0131-473 3500;
                                     E-mail: charity@scott-moncrieff.com)

Pensions are paid to poor men and women over 60 years old, born in Scotland or who have resided in Scotland for not less than ten years. At present, pensions amount to £850–£1,000 p.a.
    Ministers are invited to notify the Clerk and Factor of deserving persons and should be prepared to act as a referee on the application form.

THE ALASTAIR CRERAR TRUST FOR SINGLE POOR: Provides churches, Christian organisations and individual Christians with grants to help single adults and groups of single people, who live on low incomes and have little capital, to improve their quality of life. Apply to the Secretary, Michael I.D. Sturrock, Garden Flat, 34 Mayfield Terrace, Edinburgh EH9 1RZ (Tel: 0131-668 3524; E-mail: actrust@uwclub.net).

CROMBIE SCHOLARSHIP: Provides grants annually on the nomination of the Deans of Faculty of Divinity of the Universities of St Andrews, Glasgow, Aberdeen and Edinburgh, who each nominate one matriculated student who has taken a University course in Greek (Classical or Hellenistic) and Hebrew. Award by recommendation only.

THE DRUMMOND TRUST: Makes grants towards the cost of publication of books of 'sound Christian doctrine and outreach'. The Trustees are also willing to receive grant requests towards the cost of audio-visual programme material, but not equipment. Requests for application forms should be made to the Secretaries, Hill and Robb, 3 Pitt Terrace, Stirling FK8 2EY (Tel: 01786 450985; E-mail: douglaswhyte@hillandrobb.co.uk). Manuscripts should *not* be sent.

THE DUNCAN TRUST: Makes grants annually to students for the ministry in the Faculties of Arts and Divinity. Preference is given to those born or educated within the bounds of the former Presbytery of Arbroath. Applications not later than 31 October to G.J.M. Dunlop, Brothockbank House, Arbroath DD11 1NE (Tel: 01241 872683).

FERGUSON BEQUEST FUND: For the maintenance and promotion of religious ordinances and education and missionary operations in the first instance in the Counties of Ayr, Kirkcudbright, Wigtown, Lanark, Renfrew and Dunbarton. Apply to Ronald D. Oakes CA ACMA, 182 Bath Street, Glasgow G2 4HG (Tel: 0141-332 0476; Fax: 0141-331 0874).

GEIKIE BEQUEST: Makes small grants to students for the ministry, including students studying for entry to the University, preference being given to those not eligible for SAAS awards. Apply to the Assistant Treasurer (Ministries), 121 George Street, Edinburgh EH2 4YN by September for distribution in November each year.

JAMES GILLAN'S BURSARY FUND: Bursaries are available for students for the ministry who were born or whose parents or parent have resided and had their home for not less than three years continually in the old counties (not Districts) of Moray or Nairn. Apply to R. and R. Urquhart, 117–121 High Street, Forres IV36 1AB.

HAMILTON BURSARY TRUST: Awarded, subject to the intention to serve overseas under the Church of Scotland World Mission Council or to serve with some other Overseas Mission Agency approved by the Council, to a student at the University of Aberdeen. Preference is given to a student born or residing in (1) Parish of Skene, (2) Parish of Echt, (3) the Presbytery of Aberdeen, Kincardine and Deeside, or Gordon; failing which to Accepted Candidate(s) for the Ministry of the Church of Scotland whose studies for the Ministry are pursued at Aberdeen University. Applications or recommendations for the Bursary to the Clerk to the Presbytery of Aberdeen by 16 October annually.

MARTIN HARCUS BEQUEST: Makes annual grants to candidates for the ministry resident within the City of Edinburgh. Applications to the Clerk to the Presbytery of Edinburgh, 10/1 Palmerston Place, Edinburgh EH12 5AA by 15 October (E-mail: akph50@uk.uumail.com).

THE HOPE TRUST: Gives some support to organisations involved in combating drink and drugs, and has as its main purpose the promotion of the Reformed Faith throughout the world. There is also a Scholarship programme for Postgraduate Theology Study in Scotland. Apply to Robert P. Miller SSC LLB, 31 Moray Place, Edinburgh EH3 6BY (Tel: 0131-226 5151).

KEAY THOM TRUST: The principal purposes of the Keay Thom Trust are:
1.   To benefit the widows, daughters or other dependent female relatives of deceased ministers, or wives of ministers who are now divorced or separated, all of whom have supported the minister in the fulfilment of his duties and who, by reason of death, divorce or separation, have been required to leave the manse. The Trust can assist them in the purchase of a house or by providing financial or material assistance whether it be for the provision of accommodation or not.
2.   To assist in the education or training of the above female relatives or any other children of deceased ministers.
Further information and application forms are available from Miller Hendry, Solicitors, 10 Blackfriars Street, Perth PH1 5NS (Tel: 01738 637311).

GILLIAN MACLAINE BURSARY FUND: Open to candidates for the ministry of the Church of Scotland of Scottish or Canadian nationality. Preference is given to Gaelic-speakers. Information and terms of award from Rev. George G. Cringles BD, Depute Clerk of the Presbytery of Argyll, St Oran's Manse, Connel, Oban PA37 1PJ.

THE E. McLAREN FUND: The persons intended to be benefited are widows and unmarried ladies, preference being given to ladies above 40 years of age in the following order:
(a) Widows and daughters of Officers in the Highland Regiment, and
(b) Widows and daughters of Scotsmen.
Further details from the Secretary, The E. McLaren Fund, Apsley House, 29 Wellington Street, Glasgow G2 6JA (Tel: 0141-221 8004; Fax: 0141-221 2407; E-mail: rrs@bmkwilson.co.uk).

THE MISSES ANN AND MARGARET McMILLAN'S BEQUEST: Makes grants to ministers of the Free and United Free Churches, and of the Church of Scotland, in charges within the Synod of Argyll, with income not exceeding the minimum stipend of the Church of Scotland. Apply by 30 June in each year to Rev. Samuel McC. Harris, Trinity Manse, 12 Crichton Road, Rothesay, Isle of Bute PA20 9JR.

MORGAN BURSARY FUND: Makes grants to candidates for the Church of Scotland ministry studying at the University of Glasgow. Apply to Rev. David W. Lunan MA BD, 260 Bath Street, Glasgow G2 4JP (Tel/Fax: 0141-332 6606).

NOVUM TRUST: Provides small short-term grants – typically between £200 and £2,500 – to initiate projects in Christian research and action which cannot readily be financed from other sources. Special consideration is given to proposals aimed at the welfare of young people, investment in training, new ways of communicating the faith, and work in association with overseas churches or on behalf of immigrants in Scotland. The Trust cannot support large building projects or individuals applying for maintenance during courses or training. Application forms and guidance notes from Rev. Alex. M. Millar, 121 George Street, Edinburgh EH2 4YN (E-mail: amillar@cofscotland.org.uk).

PARK MEMORIAL BURSARY FUND: Provides grants for the benefit of candidates for the ministry of the Church of Scotland from the Presbytery of Glasgow under full-time training. Apply to Rev. David W. Lunan MA BD, Presbytery of Glasgow, 260 Bath Street, Glasgow G2 4JP (Tel: 0141-332 6606).

PATON TRUST: Assists ministers in ill health to have a recuperative holiday outwith, and free from the cares of, their parishes. Apply to Iain A.T. Mowat CA, Alexander Sloan, Chartered Accountants, 144 West George Street, Glasgow G2 2HG (Tel: 0141-354 0354; Fax: 0141-354 0355; E-mail iatm@alexandersloan.co.uk).

RENFIELD STREET TRUST: Assists in the building and repair of churches and halls. Apply to Ronald D. Oakes CA ACMA, 182 Bath Street, Glasgow G2 4HG (Tel: 0141-332 0476; Fax: 0141-331 0874).

SCOTTISH CHURCHES ARCHITECTURAL HERITAGE TRUST: Assists congregations of any denomination in the preservation of the fabric of buildings in regular use for public worship. Apply to the Grants Administrator, Scottish Churches Architectural Heritage Trust, 15 North Bank Street, The Mound, Edinburgh EH1 2LP (Tel: 0131-225 8644; E-mail: info@scaht.org.uk).

MISS M.E. SWINTON PATERSON'S CHARITABLE TRUST: The Trust can give modest grants to support smaller congregations in urban or rural areas who require to fund essential maintenance or improvement works at their buildings. Apply to Mr Callum S. Kennedy WS, Messrs Lindsays WS, Caledonian Exchange, 19a Canning Street, Edinburgh EH3 8HE (Tel: 0131-229 1212).

SMIETON FUND: Makes small holiday grants to ministers. Administered at the discretion of the pastoral staff, who will give priority in cases of need. Applications to the Associate Secretary (Support and Development), Ministries Council, 121 George Street, Edinburgh EH2 4YN.

MARY DAVIDSON SMITH CLERICAL AND EDUCATIONAL FUND FOR ABERDEENSHIRE: Assists ministers who have been ordained for five years or over and are in full charge of a congregation in Aberdeen, Aberdeenshire and the north, to purchase books, or to travel for educational purposes, and assists their children with scholarships for further education or vocational training. Apply to Alan J. Innes MA LLB, 100 Union Street, Aberdeen AB10 1QR.

THE NAN STEVENSON CHARITABLE TRUST FOR RETIRED MINISTERS: Provides houses, or loans to purchase houses, for retired ministers or missionaries on similar terms to the Housing and Loan Fund, with preference given to those with a North Ayrshire connection. Secretary: Rev. Johnston R. McKay, Upper Burnfoot, 27 Stanlane Place, Largs KA30 8DD.

PRESBYTERY OF ARGYLL BURSARY FUND: Open to students who have been accepted as candidates for the ministry and the readership of the Church of Scotland. Preference is given to applicants who are natives of the bounds of the Presbytery, or are resident within the bounds of the Presbytery, or who have a strong connection with the bounds of the Presbytery. Information and terms of award from Rev. George G. Cringles BD, Depute Clerk of the Presbytery of Argyll, St Oran's Manse, Connel, Oban PA37 1PJ.

SYNOD OF GRAMPIAN CHILDREN OF THE CLERGY FUND: Makes annual grants to children of deceased ministers. Apply to Rev. Iain U. Thomson, Clerk and Treasurer, The Manse, Skene, Westhill AB32 6LX.

SYNOD OF GRAMPIAN WIDOWS FUND: Makes annual grants (currently £225 p.a.) to widows or widowers of deceased ministers who have served in a charge in the former Synod. Apply to Rev. Iain U. Thomson, Clerk and Treasurer, The Manse, Skene, Westhill AB32 6LX.

YOUNG MINISTERS' FURNISHING LOAN FUND: Makes loans (of £1,000) to ministers in their first charge to assist with furnishing the manse. Apply to the Assistant Treasurer (Ministries), 121 George Street, Edinburgh EH2 4YN.

(6) RECENT LORD HIGH COMMISSIONERS
TO THE GENERAL ASSEMBLY

1967/68	The Rt Hon. Lord Reith of Stonehaven GCVO GBE CB TD
1969	Her Majesty the Queen attended in person
1970	The Rt Hon. Margaret Herbison PC
1971/72	The Rt Hon. Lord Clydesmuir of Braidwood CB MBE TD
1973/74	The Rt Hon. Lord Ballantrae of Auchairne and the Bay of Islands GCMG GCVO DSO OBE
1975/76	Sir Hector MacLennan KT FRCPGLAS FRCOG
1977	Francis David Charteris, Earl of Wemyss and March KT LLD
1978/79	The Rt Hon. William Ross MBE LLD
1980/81	Andrew Douglas Alexander Thomas Bruce, Earl of Elgin and Kincardine KT DL JP
1982/83	Colonel Sir John Edward Gilmour BT DSO TD
1984/85	Charles Hector Fitzroy Maclean, Baron Maclean of Duart and Morvern KT GCVO KBE

1986/87	John Campbell Arbuthnott, Viscount of Arbuthnott CBE DSC FRSE FRSA
1988/89	Sir Iain Mark Tennant KT FRSA
1990/91	The Rt Hon. Donald MacArthur Ross FRSE
1992/93	The Rt Hon. Lord Macfarlane of Bearsden
1994/95	Lady Marion Fraser
1996	Her Royal Highness the Princess Royal LG GCVO
1997	The Rt Hon. Lord Macfarlane of Bearsden
1998/99	The Rt Hon. Lord Hogg of Cumbernauld
2000	His Royal Highness the Prince Charles, Duke of Rothesay
2001/02	The Rt Hon. Viscount Younger of Leckie
	Her Majesty the Queen attended the opening of the General Assembly of 2002
2003/04	The Rt Hon. Lord Steel of Aikwood
2005/06	The Rt Hon. Lord Mackay of Clashfern KT
2007	His Royal Highness the Prince Andrew, Duke of York KG KCVO

(7) RECENT MODERATORS
OF THE GENERAL ASSEMBLY

1967	W. Roy Sanderson DD, Stenton with Whittingehame
1968	J.B. Longmuir TD DD, Principal Clerk of Assembly
1969	T.M. Murchison MA DD, Glasgow: St Columba Summertown
1970	Hugh O. Douglas CBE DD LLD, Dundee: St Mary's
1971	Andrew Herron MA BD LLB LLD DD, Clerk to the Presbytery of Glasgow
1972	R.W.V. Selby Wright JP CVO TD DD FRSE, Edinburgh: Canongate
1973	George T.H. Reid MC MA BD DD, Aberdeen: Langstane
1974	David Steel MA BD DD, Linlithgow: St Michael's
1975	James G. Matheson MA BD DD, Portree
1976	Thomas F. Torrance MBE DLitt DD FRSE, University of Edinburgh
1977	John R. Gray VRD MA BD ThM DD, Dunblane: Cathedral
1978	Peter P. Brodie MA BD LLB DD, Alloa: St Mungo's
1979	Robert A.S. Barbour KCVO MC MA BD STM DD, University of Aberdeen
1980	William B. Johnston MA BD DD DLitt, Edinburgh: Colinton
1981	Andrew B. Doig BD STM DD, National Bible Society of Scotland
1982	John McIntyre CVO DD DLitt FRSE, University of Edinburgh
1983	J. Fraser McLuskey MC DD, London: St Columba's
1984	John M.K. Paterson MA ACII BD DD, Milngavie: St Paul's
1985	David M.B.A. Smith MA BD DUniv, Logie
1986	Robert Craig CBE DLitt LLD DD, Emeritus of Jerusalem
1987	Duncan Shaw *Bundesverdienstkreuz* Drhc PhD ThDr JP, Edinburgh: Craigentinny St Christopher's
1988	James A. Whyte MA LLD DUniv DD, University of St Andrews
1989	William J.G. McDonald MA BD DD, Edinburgh: Mayfield
1990	Robert Davidson MA BD DD FRSE, University of Glasgow
1991	William B.R. Macmillan MA BD LLD DD, Dundee: St Mary's
1992	Hugh R. Wyllie MA MCIBS DD FCIBS, Hamilton: Old Parish Church
1993	James L. Weatherhead CBE MA LLB DD, Principal Clerk of Assembly
1994	James A. Simpson BSc BD STM DD, Dornoch Cathedral

1995	James Harkness KCVO CB OBE MA DD, Chaplain General (Emeritus)
1996	John H. McIndoe MA BD STM DD, London: St Columba's linked with Newcastle: St Andrew's
1997	Alexander McDonald BA CMIWSc DUniv, General Secretary, Department of Ministry
1998	Alan Main TD MA BD STM PhD DD, Professor of Practical Theology at Christ's College, University of Aberdeen
1999	John B. Cairns LTh LLB LLD DD, Dumbarton: Riverside
2000	Andrew R.C. McLellan MA BD STM DD, Edinburgh: St Andrew's and St George's
2001	John D. Miller BA BD DD, Glasgow: Castlemilk East
2002	Finlay A.J. Macdonald MA BD PhD DD, Principal Clerk of Assembly
2003	Iain R. Torrance TD DPhil DD DTheol LHD CorrFRSE, University of Aberdeen
2004	Alison Elliot OBE MA MSc PhD LLD DD, Associate Director CTPI
2005	David W. Lacy BA BD DLitt, Kilmarnock: Henderson
2006	Alan D. McDonald LLB BD MTh, Cameron linked with St Andrews: St Leonard's
2007	Sheilagh M. Kesting BA BD, Secretary of Ecumenical Relations Committee

MATTER OF PRECEDENCE

The Lord High Commissioner to the General Assembly of the Church of Scotland (while the Assembly is sitting) ranks next to the Sovereign and the Duke of Edinburgh and before the rest of the Royal Family.

The Moderator of the General Assembly of the Church of Scotland ranks next to the Lord Chancellor of Great Britain and before the Prime Minister and the Dukes.

(8) HER MAJESTY'S HOUSEHOLD IN SCOTLAND
ECCLESIASTICAL

Dean of the Chapel Royal:	Very Rev. John B. Cairns LTh LLB LLD DD
Dean of the Order of the Thistle:	Very Rev. Gilleasbuig Macmillan CVO MA BD Drhc DD

Chaplains in Ordinary:	Very Rev. Gilleasbuig Macmillan CVO MA BD Drhc DD
	Rev. Charles Robertson MA JP
	Rev. Norman W. Drummond MA BD
	Rev. John L. Paterson MA BD STM
	Rev. Alastair H. Symington MA BD
	Very Rev. Prof. Iain R. Torrance TD DPhil DD DTheol LHD CorrFRSE
	Very Rev. Finlay A.J. Macdonald MA BD PhD DD

Rev. James M. Gibson TD LTh LRAM
Rev. Angus Morrison MA BD PhD

Extra Chaplains: Very Rev. W. Roy Sanderson DD
Rev. Kenneth MacVicar MBE DFC TD MA
Very Rev. Prof. Robert A.S. Barbour
   KCVO MC BD STM DD
Rev. Alwyn Macfarlane MA
Rev. Mary I. Levison BA BD DD
Very Rev. William J. Morris KCVO PhD LLD DD JP
Rev. John MacLeod MA
Rev. A. Stewart Todd MA BD DD
Very Rev. James L. Weatherhead CBE MA LLB DD
Rev. Maxwell D. Craig MA BD ThM
Very Rev. James A. Simpson BSc BD STM DD
Very Rev. James Harkness
   KCVO CB OBE MA DD

---

(9) LONG SERVICE CERTIFICATES

Long Service Certificates, signed by the Moderator, are available for presentation to elders and others in respect of not less than thirty years of service. It should be noted that the period is years of *service*, not (for example) years of ordination in the case of an elder.

In the case of Sunday School teachers and Bible Class leaders, the qualifying period is twenty-one years of service.

Certificates are not issued posthumously, nor is it possible to make exceptions to the rules, for example by recognising quality of service in order to reduce the qualifying period, or by reducing the qualifying period on compassionate grounds, such as serious illness.

A Certificate will be issued only once to any particular individual.

Applications for Long Service Certificates should be made in writing to the Principal Clerk at 121 George Street, Edinburgh EH2 4YN by the parish minister, or by the session clerk on behalf of the Kirk Session. Certificates are not issued from this office to the individual recipients, nor should individuals make application themselves.

---

(10) LIBRARIES OF THE CHURCH

GENERAL ASSEMBLY LIBRARY AND RECORD ROOM

Most of the books contained in the General Assembly Library have been transferred to the New College Library. Records of the General Assembly, Synods, Presbyteries and Kirk Sessions are now in HM Register House, Edinburgh.

CHURCH MUSIC
The Library of New College contains a selection of works on Church music.

(11) RECORDS OF THE CHURCH OF SCOTLAND

Church records more than fifty years old, unless still in use, should be sent or delivered to the Principal Clerk for onward transmission to the Scottish Record Office. Where ministers or session clerks are approached by a local repository seeking a transfer of their records, they should inform the Principal Clerk, who will take the matter up with the National Archives of Scotland.

Where a temporary retransmission of records is sought, it is extremely helpful if notice can be given three months in advance so that appropriate procedures can be carried out satisfactorily.

SECTION 3

Church Procedure

(1) THE MINISTER AND BAPTISM

The administration of Baptism to infants is governed by Act V 2000 as amended by Act IX 2003. A Statement and Exposition of the Doctrine of Baptism may be found at page 13/8 in the published volume of Reports to the General Assembly of 2003.

The Act itself is as follows:

3.   Baptism signifies the action and love of God in Christ, through the Holy Spirit, and is a seal upon the gift of grace and the response of faith.
   (a)   Baptism shall be administered in the name of the Father and of the Son and of the Holy Spirit, with water, by sprinkling, pouring, or immersion.
   (b)   Baptism shall be administered to a person only once.
4.   Baptism may be administered to a person upon profession of faith.
   (a)   The minister and Kirk Session shall judge whether the person is of sufficient maturity to make personal profession of faith, where necessary in consultation with the parent(s) or legal guardian(s).
   (b)   Baptism may be administered only after the person has received such instruction in its meaning as the minister and Kirk Session consider necessary, according to such basis of instruction as may be authorised by the General Assembly.
   (c)   In cases of uncertainty as to whether a person has been baptised or validly baptised, baptism shall be administered conditionally.
5.   Baptism may be administered to a person with learning difficulties who makes an appropriate profession of faith, where the minister and Kirk Session are satisfied that the person shall be nurtured within the life and worship of the Church.
6.   Baptism may be administered to a child:
   (a)   where at least one parent, or other family member (with parental consent), having been baptised and being on the communion roll of the congregation, will undertake the Christian upbringing of the child;
   (b)   where at least one parent, or other family member (with parental consent), having been baptised but not on the communion roll of the congregation, satisfies the minister and Kirk Session that he or she is an adherent of the congregation and will undertake the Christian upbringing of the child;
   (c)   where at least one parent, or other family member (with parental consent), having been baptised, professes the Christian faith, undertakes to ensure that the child grows up in the life and worship of the Church and expresses the desire to seek admission to the communion roll of the congregation;
   (d)   where the child is under legal guardianship, and the minister and Kirk Session are satisfied that the child shall be nurtured within the life and worship of the congregation;
   and, in each of the above cases, only after the parent(s), or other family member, has received such instruction in its meaning as the minister and Kirk Session consider necessary, according to such basis of instruction as may be authorised by the General Assembly.
7.   Baptism shall normally be administered during the public worship of the congregation in which the person makes profession of faith, or of which the parent or other family member is on the communion roll, or is an adherent. In exceptional circumstances, baptism may be administered elsewhere (e.g. at home or in hospital). Further, a minister may administer baptism to a person resident outwith the minister's parish, and who is not otherwise

connected with the congregation, only with the consent of the minister of the parish in which the person would normally reside, or of the Presbytery.

8. In all cases, an entry shall be made in the Kirk Session's Baptismal Register and a Certificate of Baptism given by the minister. Where baptism is administered in a chaplaincy context, it shall be recorded in the Baptismal Register there, and, where possible, reported to the minister of the parish in which the person resides.

9. Baptism shall normally be administered by an ordained minister. In situations of emergency,

   (a) a minister may, exceptionally, notwithstanding the preceding provisions of the Act, respond to a request for baptism in accordance with his or her pastoral judgement, and

   (b) baptism may be validly administered by a person who is not ordained, always providing that it is administered in the name of the Father and of the Son and of the Holy Spirit, with water.

   In every occurrence of the latter case, of which a minister or chaplain becomes aware, an entry shall be made in the appropriate Baptismal Register and where possible reported to the Clerk of the Presbytery within which the baptism was administered.

10. Each Presbytery shall form, or designate, a committee to which reference may be made in cases where there is a dispute as to the interpretation of this Act. Without the consent of the Presbytery, no minister may administer baptism in a case where to his or her knowledge another minister has declined to do so.

11. The Church of Scotland, as part of the Universal Church, affirms the validity of the sacrament of baptism administered in the name of the Father and of the Son and of the Holy Spirit, with water, in accordance with the discipline of other members of the Universal Church.

---

(2) THE MINISTER AND MARRIAGE

1. BACKGROUND

Prior to 1939, every marriage in Scotland fell into one or other of two classes: regular or irregular. The former was marriage by a minister of religion after due notice of intention had been given; the latter could be effected in one of three ways: (1) declaration *de presenti*, (2) by promise *subsequente copula*, or (3) by co-habitation with habit and repute.

The Marriage (Scotland) Act of 1939 put an end to (1) and (2) and provided for a new classification of marriage as either religious or civil. Marriage by co-habitation with habit and repute was abolished by the Family Law (Scotland) Act 2006.

The law of marriage as it was thus established in 1939 had two important limitations to the celebration of marriage: (1) certain preliminaries had to be observed; and (2) in respect of religious marriage, the service had to be conducted according to the forms of either the Christian or the Jewish faith.

2. THE MARRIAGE (SCOTLAND) ACT 1977

These two conditions were radically altered by the Marriage (Scotland) Act 1977.

Since 1 January 1978, in conformity with the demands of a multi-racial society, the benefits of religious marriage have been extended to adherents of other faiths, the only requirements being the observance of monogamy and the satisfaction of the authorities with the forms of the vows imposed.

Since 1978, the calling of banns has also been discontinued. The couple themselves must each complete a Marriage Notice form and return this to the District Registrar for the area in which they are to be married, irrespective of where they live, at least fifteen days before the ceremony is due to take place. The form details the documents which require to be produced with it.

If everything is in order, the District Registrar will issue, not more than seven days before the date of the ceremony, a Marriage Schedule. This must be in the hands of the minister officiating at the marriage ceremony before the service begins. Under no circumstances must the minister deviate from this rule. To do so is an offence under the Act.

Ministers should note the advice given by the Procurator of the Church in 1962, that they should not officiate at any marriage until at least one day after the 16th birthday of the younger party.

3. THE MARRIAGE (SCOTLAND) ACT 2002

Although there have never been any limitations as to the place where a religious marriage can be celebrated, civil marriage originally could take place only in the Office of a Registrar. The Marriage (Scotland) Act 2002 permits the solemnisation of civil marriages at places approved by Local Authorities. Regulations have been made to specify the kinds of place which may be 'approved' with a view to ensuring that the places approved will not compromise the solemnity and dignity of civil marriage and will have no recent or continuing connection with any religion so as to undermine the distinction between religious and civil ceremonies.

4. PROCLAMATION OF BANNS

Proclamation of banns is no longer required in Scotland; but, in the Church of England, marriage is governed by the provisions of the Marriage Act 1949, which requires that the parties' intention to marry has to have been proclaimed and which provides that in the case of a party residing in Scotland a Certificate of Proclamation given according to the law or custom prevailing in Scotland shall be sufficient for the purpose. In the event that a minister is asked to call banns for a person resident within the registration district where his or her church is situated, the proclamation needs only to be made on one Sunday if the parties are known to the minister. If they are not, it should be made on two Sundays. In all cases, the Minister should, of course, have no reason to believe that there is any impediment to the marriage.

Proclamation should be made at the principal service of worship in this form:

There is a purpose of marriage between AB (Bachelor/Widower/Divorced), residing at .... in this Registration District, and CD (Spinster/Widow/Divorced), residing at .... in the Registration District of ...., of which proclamation is hereby made for the first and only (second and last) time.

Immediately after the second reading, or not less than forty-eight hours after the first and only reading, a Certificate of Proclamation signed by either the minister or the Session Clerk should be issued in the following terms:

At .... the ...... day of ...... 20 ....
It is hereby certified that AB, residing at ...., and CD, residing at ...., have been duly proclaimed in order to marriage in the Church of .... according to the custom of the Church of Scotland, and that no objections have been offered.
Signed .... minister or
Signed .... Session Clerk

5. MARRIAGE OF FOREIGNERS

Marriages in Scotland of foreigners, or of foreigners with British subjects, are, if they satisfy the requirements of Scots Law, valid within the United Kingdom and the various British overseas territories; but they will not necessarily be valid in the country to which the foreigner belongs. This will be so only if the requirements of the law of his or her country have also been complied with. It is therefore most important that, before the marriage, steps should be taken to obtain from the Consul, or other diplomatic representative of the country concerned, a satisfactory assurance that the marriage will be accepted as valid in the country concerned.

6. REMARRIAGE OF DIVORCED PERSONS

By virtue of Act XXVI 1959, a minister of the Church of Scotland may lawfully solemnise the marriage of a person whose former marriage has been dissolved by divorce and whose former spouse is still alive. The minister, however, must carefully adhere to the requirements of the Act which, as slightly altered in 1985, are briefly as follows:

1. The minister should not accede as a matter of routine to a request to solemnise such a marriage. To enable a decision to be made, he or she should take all reasonable steps to obtain relevant information, which should normally include the following:
    (a) Adequate information concerning the life and character of the parties. The Act enjoins the greatest caution in cases where no pastoral relationship exists between the minister and either or both of the parties concerned.
    (b) The grounds and circumstances of the divorce case.
    (c) Facts bearing upon the future well-being of any children concerned.
    (d) Whether any other minister has declined to solemnise the proposed marriage.
    (e) The denomination to which the parties belong. The Act enjoins that special care should be taken where one or more parties belong to a denomination whose discipline in this matter may differ from that of the Church of Scotland.
2. The minister should consider whether there is danger of scandal arising if he or she should solemnise the remarriage, at the same time taking into careful consideration before refusing to do so the moral and spiritual effect of a refusal on the parties concerned.
3. As a determinative factor, the minister should do all he or she can to be assured that there has been sincere repentance where guilt has existed on the part of any divorced person seeking remarriage. He or she should also give instruction, where needed, in the nature and requirements of a Christian marriage.
4. A minister is not required to solemnise a remarriage against his or her conscience. Every Presbytery is required to appoint certain individuals with one of whom ministers in doubt as to the correct course of action may consult if they so desire. The final decision, however, rests with the minister who has been asked to officiate.

(3) CONDUCT OF MARRIAGE SERVICES
(CODE OF GOOD PRACTICE)

The code which follows was submitted to the General Assembly in 1997. It appears, on page 1/10, in the Volume of Assembly Reports for that year within the Report of the Board of Practice and Procedure.

1. *Marriage in the Church of Scotland is solemnised by an ordained minister in a religious ceremony wherein, before God, and in the presence of the minister and at least two competent witnesses, the parties covenant together to take each other as husband and wife as long as they both shall live, and the minister declares the parties to be husband and wife. Before solemnising a marriage, a minister must be assured that the necessary legal requirements are being complied with and that the parties know of no legal impediment to their marriage, and he or she must afterwards ensure that the Marriage Schedule is duly completed.* (Act I 1977)
2. Any ordained minister of the Church of Scotland who is a member of Presbytery or who holds a current Ministerial Certificate may officiate at a marriage service (see Act II 1987).
3. While the marriage service should normally take place in church, a minister may, at his or her discretion, officiate at a marriage service outwith church premises. Wherever conducted, the ceremony will be such as to reflect appropriately both the joy and the solemnity of the occasion. In particular, a minister shall ensure that nothing is done which would bring the Church and its teaching into disrepute.
4. A minister agreeing to conduct a wedding should endeavour to establish a pastoral relationship with the couple within which adequate pre-marriage preparation and subsequent pastoral care may be given.
5. 'A minister should not refuse to perform ministerial functions for a person who is resident in his or her parish without sufficient reason' (Cox, *Practice and Procedure in the Church of Scotland*, sixth edition, page 55). Where either party to the proposed marriage has been divorced and the former spouse is still alive, the minister invited to officiate may solemnise such a marriage, having regard to the guidelines in the Act anent the Remarriage of Divorced Persons (Act XXVI 1959 as amended by Act II 1985).
6. A minister is acting as an agent of the National Church which is committed to bringing the ordinances of religion to the people of Scotland through a territorial ministry. As such, he or she shall not be entitled to charge a fee or allow a fee to be charged for conducting a marriage service. When a gift is spontaneously offered to a minister as a token of appreciation, the above consideration should not be taken to mean that he or she should not accept such an unsolicited gift. The Financial Board of a congregation is at liberty to set fees to cover such costs as heat and light, and in addition Organists and Church Officers are entitled to a fee in respect of their services at weddings.
7. A minister should not allow his or her name to be associated with any commercial enterprise that provides facilities for weddings.
8. A minister is not at liberty to enter the bounds of another minister's parish to perform ministerial functions without the previous consent of the minister of that parish. In terms of Act VIII 1933, a minister may 'officiate at a marriage or funeral by private invitation', but, for the avoidance of doubt, an invitation conveyed through a commercial enterprise shall not be regarded as a 'private invitation' within the meaning of that Act.
9. A minister invited to officiate at a Marriage Service where neither party is a member of his or her congregation or is resident within his or her own parish or has any connection with the parish within which the service is to take place should observe the following courtesies:
    (a) he or she should ascertain from the parties whether either of them has a Church of Scotland connection or has approached the appropriate parish minister(s);
    (b) if it transpires that a ministerial colleague has declined to officiate, then he or she (the invited minister) should ascertain the reasons therefor and shall take these and all other relevant factors into account in deciding whether or not to officiate.

(4) CONDUCT OF FUNERAL SERVICES: FEES

The General Assembly of 2007 received the Report of the Legal Questions Committee which included a statement regarding fees for funerals. That statement had been prepared in the light of approaches from two Presbyteries seeking guidance on the question of the charging of fees (on behalf of ministers) for the conduct of funerals. It had seemed to the Presbyteries that expectations and practice were unacceptably varied across the country, and that the question was complicated by the fact that, quite naturally and legitimately, ministers other than parish ministers occasionally conduct funeral services.

The full text of that statement was engrossed in the Minutes of the General Assembly, and it was felt that it would be helpful to include it also in the *Year Book*.

The statement
The (Legal Questions) Committee believes that the question is two-fold, relating firstly to parish ministers (including associate and assistant ministers, deacons and the like) within their regular ministry, and secondly to ministers and others taking an occasional funeral, for instance by private invitation or in the course of pastoral cover of another parish.

Ministers in receipt of a living
The Committee believes that the position of the minister of a parish, and of other paid staff on the ministry team of a parish, is clear. The Third Declaratory Article affirms the responsibility of the Church of Scotland to provide the ordinances of religion through its territorial ministry, while the stipend system (and, for other staff members, the salary) provides a living that enables that ministry to be exercised without charging fees for services conducted. The implication of this principle is that no family in Scotland should ever be charged for the services of a Church of Scotland minister at the time of bereavement. Clearly, therefore, no minister in receipt of a living should be charging separately (effectively being paid doubly) for any such service. The Committee is conscious that the position of congregations outside Scotland may be different, and is aware that the relevant Presbyteries will offer appropriate superintendence of these matters.

A related question is raised about the highly varied culture of gift-giving in different parts of the country. The Committee believes it would be unwise to seek to regulate this. In some places, an attempt to quash a universal and long-established practice would seem ungracious, while in other places there is no such practice, and encouragement in that direction would seem indelicate.

A second related question was raised about Funeral Directors charging for the services of the minister. The Committee believes that Presbyteries should make it clear to Funeral Directors that, in the case of Church of Scotland funerals, such a charge should not be made.

Ministers conducting occasional services
Turning to the position of ministers who do not receive a living that enables them to conduct funerals without charge, the Committee's starting point is the principle articulated above that no bereaved person should have to pay for the services of a minister. The territorial ministry and the parish system of this Church mean that a bereaved family should not find itself being contingently charged because the parish minister happens to be unavailable, or because the parish is vacant.

Where a funeral is being conducted as part of the ministry of the local parish, but where for any reason another minister is taking it and not otherwise being paid, it is the responsibility of the congregation (through its financial body) to ensure that appropriate fees and expenses are met.

Where that imposes a financial burden upon a congregation because of the weight of pastoral need, the need should be taken into account in calculating the resource-needs of that parish in the course of updating the Presbytery Plan.

It is beyond the remit of the Legal Questions Committee to make judgements about the appropriate level of payment. The Committee suggests that the Ministries Council should give the relevant advice on this aspect of the issue.

The Committee believes that these principles could be applied to the conduct of weddings and are perfectly compatible with the Guidelines on that subject which are reproduced in the *Year Book* at item 3 of section 3 dealing with Church Procedure.

(5) THE MINISTER AND WILLS

The Requirements of Writing (Scotland) Act 1995, which came into force on 1 August 1995, has removed the power of a minister to execute wills notarially. Further clarification, if required, may be obtained from the Solicitor of the Church.

(6) PROCEDURE IN A VACANCY

Procedure in a vacancy is regulated by Act VIII 2003 as amended by Acts IX and X 2004, II 2005 and V 2006. The text of the most immediately relevant sections is given here for general information. Schedules of Intimation referred to are also included. The full text of the Act and subsequent amendments can be obtained from the Principal Clerk.

1. Vacancy Procedure Committee
(1)   Each Presbytery shall appoint a number of its members to be available to serve on Vacancy Procedure Committees and shall provide information and training as required for those so appointed.
(2)   As soon as the Presbytery Clerk is aware that a vacancy has arisen or is anticipated, he or she shall consult the Moderator of the Presbytery and they shall appoint a Vacancy Procedure Committee of five persons from among those appointed in terms of subsection (1), which Committee shall (a) include at least one minister and at least one elder and (b) exclude any communicant member or former minister of the vacant charge or of any constituent congregation thereof. The Vacancy Procedure Committee shall include a Convener and Clerk, the latter of whom need not be a member of the Committee but may be the Presbytery Clerk. The same Vacancy Procedure Committee may serve for more than one vacancy at a time.
(3)   The Vacancy Procedure Committee shall have a quorum of three for its meetings.
(4)   The Convener of the Vacancy Procedure Committee may, where he or she reasonably believes a matter to be non-contentious, consult members individually, provided that reasonable efforts are made to consult all members of the Committee. A meeting shall be held at the request of any member of the Committee.

(5)   Every decision made by the Vacancy Procedure Committee shall be reported to the next meeting of Presbytery, but may not be recalled by Presbytery where the decision was subject to the provisions of section 2 below.

2. Request for Consideration by Presbytery

Where in this Act any decision by the Vacancy Procedure Committee is subject to the provisions of this section, the following rules shall apply:

(1)   The Presbytery Clerk shall intimate to all members of the Presbytery by mailing or at a Presbytery meeting the course of action or permission proposed, and shall arrange for one Sunday's pulpit intimation of the same to be made to the congregation or congregations concerned, in terms of Schedule A. The intimation having been made, it shall be displayed as prominently as possible at the church building for seven days.

(2)   Any four individuals, being communicant members of the congregation or full members of the Presbytery, may give written notice requesting that action be taken in terms of subsection (3) below, giving reasons for the request, within seven days after the pulpit intimation.

(3)   Upon receiving notice in terms of subsection (2), the Presbytery Clerk shall sist the process or permission referred to in subsection (1), which shall then require the approval of the Presbytery.

(4)   The Moderator of the Presbytery shall in such circumstances consider whether a meeting *pro re nata* of the Presbytery should be called in order to avoid prejudicial delay in the vacancy process.

(5)   The Presbytery Clerk shall cause to have served upon the congregation or congregations an edict in terms of Schedule B citing them to attend the meeting of Presbytery for their interest.

(6)   The consideration by Presbytery of any matter under this section shall not constitute an appeal or a Petition, and the decision of Presbytery shall be deemed to be a decision at first instance subject to the normal rights of appeal or dissent-and-complaint.

3. Causes of Vacancy

The causes of vacancy shall normally include:

(a)   the death of the minister of the charge;

(b)   the removal of status of the minister of the charge or the suspension of the minister in terms of section 20(2) of Act III 2001;

(c)   the dissolution of the pastoral tie in terms of Act I 1988 or Act XV 2002;

(d)   the demission of the charge and/or status of the minister of the charge;

(e)   the translation of the minister of the charge to another charge;

(f)   the termination of the tenure of the minister of the charge in terms of Act VI 1984.

4. Release of Departing Minister

The Presbytery Clerk shall be informed as soon as circumstances have occurred that cause a vacancy to arise or make it likely that a vacancy shall arise. Where the circumstances pertain to section 3(d) or (e) above, the Vacancy Procedure Committee shall

(1)   except in cases governed by subsection (2) below, decide whether to release the minister from his or her charge and, in any case involving translation to another charge or introduction to an appointment, instruct him or her to await the instructions of the Presbytery or another Presbytery;

(2)   in the case of a minister in the first five years of his or her first charge, decide whether there are exceptional circumstances to justify releasing him or her from his or her charge and proceeding in terms of subsection (1) above;

(3)   determine whether a vacancy has arisen or is anticipated and, as soon as possible, determine the date upon which the charge becomes actually vacant, and

(4)   inform the congregation or congregations by one Sunday's pulpit intimation as soon as convenient.

(5)   The provisions of section 2 above shall apply to the decisions of the Vacancy Procedure Committee in terms of subsections (1) and (2) above.

5. Demission of Charge

(1)   Subject to the provisions of subsection (2) below, when a vacancy has occurred in terms of section 3(c), (d) or (f) above, the Presbytery shall determine whether the minister is, in the circumstances, entitled to a seat in the Presbytery in terms of section 16 of Act III 2000 (as amended).

(2)   In the case where it is a condition of any basis of adjustment that a minister shall demit his or her charge to facilitate union or linking, and the minister has agreed in writing in terms of the appropriate regulations governing adjustments, formal application shall not be made to the Presbytery for permission to demit. The minister concerned shall be regarded as retiring in the interest of adjustment, and he or she shall retain a seat in Presbytery unless in terms of Act III 2000 (as amended) he or she elects to resign it.

(3)   A minister who demits his or her charge without retaining a seat in the Presbytery shall, if he or she retains status as a minister, be subject to the provisions of sections 5 to 15 of Act II 2000 (as amended).

6. Appointment of Interim Moderator

At the same time as the Vacancy Procedure Committee makes a decision in terms of section 4 above, or where circumstances pertain to section 3(a), (b), (c) or (f) above, the Vacancy Procedure Committee shall appoint an Interim Moderator for the charge and make intimation thereof to the congregation subject to the provisions of section 2 above. The Interim Moderator shall be either a ministerial member of the Presbytery in terms of Act III 2000 or Act V 2001 or a member of the Presbytery selected from a list of those who have received such preparation for the task as the Ministries Council shall from time to time recommend or provide, and he or she shall not be a member in the vacant charge nor a member of the Vacancy Procedure Committee. The name of the Interim Moderator shall be forwarded to the Ministries Council.

7. Duties of Interim Moderator

(1)   It shall be the duty of the Interim Moderator to preside at all meetings of the Kirk Session (or of the Kirk Sessions in the case of a linked charge) and to preside at all congregational meetings in connection with the vacancy, or at which the minister would have presided had the charge been full. In the case of a congregational meeting called by the Presbytery in connection with adjustment, the Interim Moderator, having constituted the meeting, shall relinquish the chair in favour of the representative of the Presbytery, but he or she shall be at liberty to speak at such a meeting. In consultation with the Kirk Session and the Financial Court, he or she shall make arrangements for the supply of the vacant pulpit.

(2)   The Interim Moderator appointed in a prospective vacancy may call and preside at meetings of the Kirk Session and of the congregation for the transaction of business relating to the said prospective vacancy. He or she shall be associated with the minister until the date of the actual vacancy; after that date, he or she shall take full charge.

(3)   The Interim Moderator shall act as an assessor to the Nominating Committee, being available to offer guidance and advice. If the Committee so desire, he or she may act as their Convener, but in no case shall he or she have a vote.

(4) In the event of the absence of the Interim Moderator, the Vacancy Procedure Committee shall appoint a member of the Presbytery who is not a member of the vacant congregation to fulfil any of the rights and duties of the Interim Moderator in terms of this section.

(5) The Interim Moderator shall have the same duties and responsibilities towards all members of ministry teams referred to in section 16 of Act VII 2003 as if he or she were the parish minister, both in terms of this Act and in respect of the terms and conditions of such individuals.

8. Permission to Call

When the decision to release the minister from the charge has been made and the Interim Moderator appointed, the Vacancy Procedure Committee shall consider whether it may give permission to call a minister in terms of Act VII 2003, and may proceed subject to the provisions of section 2 above. The Vacancy Procedure Committee must refer the question of permission to call to the Presbytery if:

(a) shortfalls exist which in the opinion of the Committee require consideration in terms of section 9 hereunder;

(b) the Committee has reason to believe that the vacancy schedule referred to in section 10 below will not be approved;

(c) the Committee has reason to believe that the Presbytery will, in terms of section 11 below, instruct work to be carried out on the manse before a call can be sustained, and judges that the likely extent of such work warrants a delay in the granting of permission to call, or

(d) the Committee has reason to believe that the Presbytery may wish to delay or refuse the granting of permission for any reason.

Any decision by Presbytery to refuse permission to call shall be subject to appeal or dissent-and-complaint.

9. Shortfalls

(1) As soon as possible after intimation of a vacancy or anticipated vacancy reaches the Presbytery Clerk, the Presbytery shall ascertain whether the charge has current or accumulated shortfalls in contributions to central funds, and shall determine whether and to what extent any shortfalls that exist are justified.

(2) If the vacancy is in a charge in which the Presbytery has determined that shortfalls are to any extent unjustified, it shall not resolve to allow a call of any kind until:

(a) the shortfalls have been met to the extent to which the Presbytery determined that they were unjustified, or

(b) a scheme for the payment of the unjustified shortfall has been agreed between the congregation and the Presbytery and receives the concurrence of the Ministries Council and/or the Stewardship and Finance Committee for their respective interests, or

(c) a fresh appraisal of the charge in terms of Act VII 2003 has been carried out, regardless of the status of the charge in the current Presbytery plan.

(i) During such appraisal, no further steps may be taken in respect of filling the vacancy, and the Presbytery shall make final determination of what constitutes such steps.

(ii) Following such appraisal and any consequent adjustment or deferred adjustment, the shortfalls shall be met or declared justifiable or a scheme shall be agreed in terms of subsection (b) above; the Presbytery shall inform the Ministries Council and the Stewardship and Finance Committee of its decisions in terms of this section; and the Presbytery shall remove the suspension-of-vacancy process referred to in sub-paragraph (i).

10. Vacancy Schedule

(1)   When in terms of sections 4 and 6 above the decision to release the minister from the charge has been made and the interim Moderator appointed, there shall be issued by the Ministries Council a Schedule or Schedules for completion by the responsible Financial Board(s) of the vacant congregation(s) in consultation with representatives of the Presbytery, setting forth the proposed arrangements for payment of ministerial expenses and for provision of a manse, showing the ministry requirements and details of any endowment income. The Schedule, along with an Extract Minute from each relevant Kirk Session containing a commitment fully and adequately to support the ministry, shall be forwarded to the Presbytery Clerk.

(2)   The Schedule shall be considered by the Vacancy Procedure Committee and, if approved, transmitted to the Ministries Council by the Presbytery Clerk. The Vacancy Procedure Committee or Presbytery must not sustain an appointment and call until the Schedule has been approved by them and by the Ministries Council, which shall intimate its decision within six weeks of receiving the schedule from the Presbytery.

(3)   The accuracy of the Vacancy Schedule shall be kept under review by the Vacancy Procedure Committee.

(4)   The provisions of section 2 above shall apply to the decisions of the Vacancy Procedure Committee.

11. Manse

As soon as possible after the manse becomes vacant, the Presbytery Property Committee shall inspect the manse and come to a view on what work, if any, must be carried out to render it suitable for a new incumbent. The views of the Property Committee should then be communicated to the Presbytery, which should, subject to any modifications which might be agreed by that Court, instruct the Financial Board of the congregation to have the work carried out. No induction date shall be fixed until the Presbytery Property Committee has again inspected the manse and confirmed that the work has been undertaken satisfactorily.

12. Advisory Committee

(1)   As soon as possible after intimation of a vacancy or anticipated vacancy reaches the Presbytery Clerk, the Vacancy Procedure Committee shall appoint an Advisory Committee of three, subject to the following conditions:

(a)   at least one member shall be an elder and at least one shall be a minister;

(b)   the Advisory Committee shall contain no more than two members of the Vacancy Procedure Committee;

(c)   the Advisory Committee may contain individuals who are not members of the Presbytery;

(d)   the appointment shall be subject to section 2 above.

(2)   The Advisory Committee shall meet:

(a)   before the election of the Nominating Committee, with the Kirk Session (or Kirk Sessions both separately and together) of the vacant charge, to consider together in the light of the whole circumstances of the parish or parishes (i) what kind of ministry would be best suited to their needs and (ii) which system of election of the Nominating Committee described in paragraph 14(2)(d) hereunder shall be used;

(b)   with the Nominating Committee before it has taken any steps to fill the vacancy, to consider how it should proceed;

(c)   with the Nominating Committee before it reports to the Kirk Session and Presbytery the identity of the nominee, to review the process followed and give any further advice it deems necessary;

(d)   with the Nominating Committee at any other time by request of either the Nominating Committee or the Advisory Committee.

In the case of charges which are in the opinion of the Presbytery remote, it will be adequate if the Interim Moderator (accompanied if possible by a member of the Nominating Committee) meets with the Advisory Committee for the purposes listed in paragraphs (a) to (c) above.

13. Electoral Register

(1)   It shall be the duty of the Kirk Session of a vacant congregation to proceed to make up the Electoral Register of the congregation. This shall contain (1) as communicants the names of those persons (a) whose names are on the communion roll of the congregation as at the date on which it is made up and who are not under Church discipline, (b) whose names have been added or restored to the communion roll on revision by the Kirk Session subsequently to the occurrence of the vacancy, and (c) who have given in valid Certificates of Transference by the date specified in terms of Schedule C hereto; and (2) as adherents the names of those persons who, being parishioners or regular worshippers in the congregation at the date when the vacancy occurred, and not being members of any other congregation, have claimed (in writing in the form prescribed in Schedule D and within the time specified in Schedule C) to be placed on the Electoral Register, the Kirk Session being satisfied that they desire to be permanently connected with the congregation and knowing of no adequate reasons why they should not be admitted as communicants should they so apply.

(2)   At a meeting to be held not later than fourteen days after intimation has been made in terms of Schedule C hereto, the Kirk Session shall decide on the claims of persons to be placed on the Electoral Register, such claims to be sent to the Session Clerk before the meeting. At this meeting, the Kirk Session may hear parties claiming to have an interest. The Kirk Session shall thereupon prepare the lists of names and addresses of communicants and of adherents which it is proposed shall be the Electoral Register of the congregation, the names being arranged in alphabetical order and numbered consecutively throughout. The decision of the Kirk Session in respect of any matter affecting the preparation of the Electoral Register shall be final.

(3)   The proposed Electoral Register having been prepared, the Interim Moderator shall cause intimation to be made on the first convenient Sunday in terms of Schedule E hereto that on that day an opportunity will be given for inspecting the Register after service, and that it will lie for inspection at such times and such places as the Kirk Session shall have determined; and further shall specify a day when the Kirk Session will meet to hear parties claiming an interest and will finally revise and adjust the Register. At this meeting, the list, having been revised, numbered and adjusted, shall on the authority of the court be attested by the Interim Moderator and the Clerk as the Electoral Register of the congregation.

(4)   This Register, along with a duplicate copy, shall without delay be transmitted to the Presbytery Clerk, who, in name of the Presbytery, shall attest and return the principal copy, retaining the duplicate copy in his or her own possession. For all purposes connected with this Act, the congregation shall be deemed to be those persons whose names are on the Electoral Register, and no other.

(5)   If after the attestation of the Register any communicant is given a Certificate of Transference, the Session Clerk shall delete that person's name from the Register and initial the deletion. Such a Certificate shall be granted only when application for it has been made in writing, and the said written application shall be retained until the vacancy is ended.

(6)   When a period of more than six months has elapsed between the Electoral Register being attested and the congregation being given permission to call, the Kirk Session shall have power, if it so desires, to revise and update the Electoral Register. Intimation of this intention shall be given in terms of Schedule F hereto. Additional names shall be added to the Register in the form of an Addendum which shall also contain authority for the deletions which have been made; two copies of this Addendum, duly attested, shall be lodged with the Presbytery Clerk, who, in name of the Presbytery, shall attest and return the principal copy, retaining the duplicate copy in his or her own possession.

14. Appointment of Nominating Committee

(1)   When permission to call has been given and the Electoral Register has been attested, intimation in terms of Schedule G shall be made that a meeting of the congregation is to be held to appoint a Committee of its own number for the purpose of nominating one person to the congregation with a view to the appointment of a minister.

(2)   (a)   The Interim Moderator shall preside at this meeting, and the Session Clerk, or in his or her absence a person appointed by the meeting, shall act as Clerk.

      (b)   The Interim Moderator shall remind the congregation of the number of members it is required to appoint in terms of this section and shall call for Nominations. To constitute a valid Nomination, the name of a person on the Electoral Register has to be proposed and seconded, and assurance given by the proposer that the person is prepared to act on the Committee. The Clerk shall take a note of all Nominations in the order in which they are made.

      (c)   When it appears to the Interim Moderator that the Nominations are complete, they shall be read to the congregation and an opportunity given for any withdrawals. If the number of persons nominated does not exceed the maximum fixed in terms of subsection (4) below, there is no need for a vote, and the Interim Moderator shall declare that these persons constitute a Nominating Committee.

      (d)   If the number exceeds the maximum, the election shall proceed by one of the following means, chosen in advance by the Kirk Session, and being either (i) the submission of the names by the Interim Moderator, one by one as they appear on the list, to the vote of the congregation, each member having the right to vote for up to the maximum number fixed for the Committee, and voting being by standing up, or (ii) a system of written ballot devised by the Kirk Session to suit the size of the congregation and approved by the Vacancy Procedure Committee or the Presbytery. In either case, in the event of a tie for the last place, a further vote shall be taken between or among those tying.

      (e)   The Interim Moderator shall, at the same meeting or as soon thereafter as the result of any ballot has been determined, announce the names of those thus elected to serve on the Nominating Committee, and intimate to them the time and place of their first meeting, which may be immediately after the congregational meeting provided that has been intimated along with the intimation of the congregational meeting.

(3)   Where there is an agreement between the Presbytery and the congregation or congregations that the minister to be inducted shall serve either in a team ministry involving another congregation or congregations, or in a designated post such as a chaplaincy, it shall be

competent for the agreement to specify that the Presbytery shall appoint up to two representatives to serve on the Nominating Committee.

(4)   The Vacancy Procedure Committee shall, subject to the provisions of section 2 above, determine the number who will act on the Nominating Committee, being an odd number up to a maximum of thirteen.

(5)   When the vacancy is in a linked charge, or when a union or linking of congregations has been agreed but not yet effected, or when there is agreement to a deferred union or a deferred linking, or where the appointment is to more than one post, the Vacancy Procedure Committee shall, subject to the provisions of section 2 above, determine how the number who will act on the Nominating Committee will be allocated among the congregations involved, unless provision for this has already been made in the Basis of Union or Basis of Linking as the case may be.

(6)   The Nominating Committee shall not have power to co-opt additional members, but the relevant Kirk Session shall have power when necessary to appoint a replacement for any of its appointees who ceases, by death or resignation, to be a member of the Nominating Committee, or who, by falling ill or by moving away from the area, is unable to serve as a member of it.

15. Constitution of the Nominating Committee
It shall be the duty of the Interim Moderator to summon and preside at the first meeting of the Nominating Committee, which may be held at the close of the congregational meeting at which it is appointed and at which the Committee shall appoint a Convener and a Clerk. The Clerk, who need not be a member of the Committee, shall keep regular minutes of all proceedings. The Convener shall have a deliberative vote (if he or she is not the Interim Moderator) but shall in no case have a casting vote. If the Clerk is not a member of the Committee, he or she shall have no vote. At all meetings of the Committee, only those present shall be entitled to vote.

16. Task of the Nominating Committee
(1)   The Nominating Committee shall have the duty of nominating one person to the congregation with a view to the election and appointment of a minister. It shall proceed by a process of announcement in a monthly vacancy list, application and interview, and may also advertise, receive recommendations and pursue enquiries in other ways.

(2)   The Committee shall give due weight to any guidelines which may from time to time be issued by the Ministries Council or the General Assembly.

(3)   The Committee shall make themselves aware of the roles of the other members of any ministry team as described in section 16 of Act VII 2003 and may meet with them for this purpose, but shall not acquire responsibility or authority for the negotiation or alteration of their terms and conditions.

17. Eligibility for Election
The following categories of persons, and no others, are eligible to be nominated, elected and called as ministers of parishes in the Church of Scotland, but always subject, where appropriate, to the provisions of Act IX 2002:

(1)   A minister of a parish of the Church, a minister holding some other appointment that entitles him or her to a seat in Presbytery or a minister holding a current Practising Certificate in terms of Section 5 of Act II 2000 (as amended).

(2)   A minister of the Church of Scotland who has retired from a parish or appointment as above, provided he or she has not reached his or her 65th birthday.

(3) (a)   A licentiate of the Church of Scotland who has satisfactorily completed, or has been granted exemption from, his or her period of probationary service.

(b)   A graduate candidate in terms of section 22 of Act X 2004.

(4)   A minister, licentiate or graduate candidate of the Church of Scotland who, with the approval of the World Mission Council, has entered the courts of an overseas Church as a full member, provided he or she has ceased to be such a member.

(5)   A minister, licentiate or graduate candidate of the Church of Scotland who has neither relinquished nor been judicially deprived of the status he or she possessed and who has served, or is serving, furth of Scotland in any Church which is a member of the World Alliance of Reformed Churches.

(6)   The holder of a Certificate of Eligibility in terms of Act IX 2002.

18. Ministers of a Team
Ministers occupying positions within a team ministry in the charge, or larger area including the charge, and former holders of such positions, shall be eligible to apply and shall not by virtue of office be deemed to have exercised undue influence in securing the call. A *locum tenens* in the vacant charge shall not by virtue of office be deemed to have exercised undue influence in securing the call. Any Interim Moderator in the current vacancy shall not be eligible to apply.

19. Ministers of Other Churches
(1)   Where a minister of a church furth of Scotland, who holds a certificate of eligibility in terms of Act IX 2002, is nominated, the nominee, Kirk Session and Presbytery may agree that he or she shall be inducted for a period of three years only and shall retain status as a minister of his or her denomination of origin.

(2)   Upon induction, such a minister shall be accountable to the Presbytery for the exercise of his or her ministry and to his or her own church for matters of life and doctrine. He or she shall be awarded corresponding membership of the Presbytery.

(3)   With the concurrence of the Presbytery and the Ministries Council, and at the request of the congregation, the period may be extended for one further period of not more than three years.

20. Nomination
(1)   Before the candidate is asked to accept Nomination, the Interim Moderator shall ensure that the candidate is given an adequate opportunity to see the whole ecclesiastical buildings (including the manse) pertaining to the congregation, and to meet privately with all members of staff of the charge or of any wider ministry team, and shall be provided with a copy of the constitution of the congregation, a copy of the current Presbytery Plan and of any current Basis of Adjustment or Basis of Reviewable Tenure, and the most recent audited accounts and statement of funds, and the candidate shall acknowledge receipt in writing to the Interim Moderator.

(2)   Before any Nomination is intimated to the Kirk Session and Presbytery Clerk, the Clerk to the Nominating Committee shall secure the written consent thereto of the nominee.

(3)   Before reporting the Nomination to the Vacancy Procedure Committee, the Presbytery Clerk shall obtain from the nominee or Interim Moderator evidence of the eligibility of the nominee to be appointed to the charge.

(a)   In the case of a minister not being a member of any Presbytery of the Church of Scotland, this shall normally constitute an Exit Certificate in terms of Act X 2004, or evidence of status from the Ministries Council, or a current practising certificate, or certification from the Ministries Council of eligibility in terms of Act IX 2002.

(b)   In the case of a minister in the first five years of his or her first charge, this shall consist of an extract minute either from the Vacancy Procedure Committee of his or her current Presbytery, or from that Presbytery, exceptionally releasing the minister.

21. Preaching by Nominee

(1) The Interim Moderator, on receiving notice of the Committee's Nomination, shall arrange that the nominee conduct public worship in the vacant church or churches, normally within four Sundays, and that the ballot take place immediately after each such service.

(2) The Interim Moderator shall thereupon cause intimation to be made on two Sundays regarding the arrangements made in connection with the preaching by the nominee and the ballot thereafter, all in terms of Schedule H hereto.

22. Election of Minister

(1) The Interim Moderator shall normally preside at all congregational meetings connected with the election, which shall be in all cases by ballot. The Interim Moderator shall be in charge of the ballot.

(2) The Interim Moderator may invite one or more persons (not being persons whose names are on the Electoral Register of the vacant congregation) to assist him or her in the conduct of a ballot vote when he or she judges this desirable.

(3) When a linking or a deferred union or deferred linking is involved, the Interim Moderator shall consult and reach agreement with the minister or Interim Moderator of the other congregation regarding the arrangements for the conduct of public worship in these congregations by the nominee as in section 21(1) above. The Interim Moderator shall in writing appoint a member of Presbytery to take full charge of the ballot vote for the other congregation. In the case of a deferred union or deferred linking, the minister already inducted shall not be so appointed, nor shall he or she be in any way involved in the conduct of the election.

23. Ballot Procedure

(1) The Kirk Session shall arrange to have available at the time of election a sufficient supply of voting-papers printed in the form of Schedule I hereto, and these shall be put into the custody of the Interim Moderator who shall preside at the election, assisted as in section 22 above. He or she shall issue on request to any person whose name is on the Electoral Register a voting-paper, noting on the Register that this has been done. Facilities shall be provided whereby the voter may mark the paper in secrecy, and a ballot-box shall be available wherein the paper is to be deposited when marked. The Interim Moderator may assist any person who asks for help in respect of completing the voting-paper, but no other person whatever shall communicate with the voter at this stage. The Interim Moderator, or the deputy appointed by him or her, shall be responsible for the safe custody of ballot-box, papers and Electoral Register.

(2) As soon as practicable, and at latest within twenty-four hours after the close of the voting, the Interim Moderator shall constitute the Kirk Session, or the joint Kirk Sessions when more than one congregation is involved, and in presence of the Kirk Session shall proceed with the counting of the votes, in which he or she may be assisted as provided in section 22 above. When more than one ballot-box has been used and when the votes of more than one congregation are involved, all ballot-boxes shall be emptied and the voting-papers shall be mixed together before counting begins so that the preponderance of votes in one area or in one congregation shall not be disclosed.

(3) If the number voting For exceeds the number voting Against, the nominee shall be declared elected and the Nominating Committee shall be deemed to be discharged.

(4)   If the number voting For is equal to or less than the number voting Against, the Interim Moderator shall declare that there has been failure to elect and that the Nominating Committee is deemed to have been discharged. He or she shall proceed in terms of section 26(b) without further reference to the Presbytery.

(5)   After the counting has been completed, the Interim Moderator shall sign a declaration in one of the forms of Schedule J hereto, and this shall be recorded in the minute of the Kirk Session or of the Kirk Sessions. An extract shall be affixed to the notice-board of the church, or of each of the churches, concerned. In presence of the Kirk Session, the Interim Moderator shall then seal up the voting-papers along with the marked copy of the Electoral Register, and these shall be transmitted to the Presbytery Clerk in due course along with the other documents specified in section 27 below.

24. Withdrawal of Nominee

(1)   Should a nominee intimate withdrawal before he or she has preached as nominee, the Nominating Committee shall continue its task and seek to nominate another nominee.

(2)   Should a nominee intimate withdrawal after he or she has been elected, the Interim Moderator shall proceed in terms of sections 23(4) above and 26(b) below without further reference to the Presbytery.

25. The Call

(1)   The Interim Moderator shall, along with the intimation regarding the result of the voting, intimate the arrangements made for members of the congregation over a period of not less than eight days to subscribe the Call (Schedule K). Intimation shall be in the form of Schedule L hereto.

(2)   The Call may be subscribed on behalf of a member not present to sign in person, provided a mandate authorising such subscription is produced as in Schedule M. All such entries shall be initialled by the Interim Moderator or by the member of the Kirk Session appending them.

(3)   Those eligible to sign the call shall be all those whose names appear on the Electoral Register. A paper of concurrence in the Call may be signed by regular worshippers in the congregation and by adherents whose names have not been entered on the Electoral Register.

26. Failure to Nominate

The exercise by a congregation of its right to call a minister shall be subject to a time-limit of one year; this period shall be calculated from the date when intimation is given of the agreement to grant leave to call. If it appears that an appointment is not to be made within the allotted time (allowing one further calendar month for intimation to the Presbytery), the congregation may make application to the Presbytery for an extension, which will normally be for a further three months. In exceptional circumstances, and for clear cause shown, a further extension of three months may be granted. If no election has been made and intimated to the Presbytery by the expiry of that time, the permission to call shall be regarded as having lapsed. The Presbytery may thereupon look afresh at the question of adjustment. If the Presbytery is still satisfied that a minister should be appointed, it shall itself take steps to make such an appointment, proceeding in one of the following ways:

(a)   (i)   The Presbytery may discharge the Nominating Committee, strengthen the Advisory Committee which had been involved in the case by the appointment of an additional minister and elder, instruct that Committee to bring forward to a subsequent meeting the name of an eligible individual for appointment to the charge and intimate this instruction to the congregation. If satisfied with the recommendation brought by the Advisory Committee, the Presbytery shall thereupon make the appointment.

(ii) The Presbytery Clerk shall thereupon intimate to the person concerned the fact of his or her appointment, shall request him or her to forward a letter of acceptance along with appropriate Certificates if these are required in terms of section 27 below, and shall arrange with him or her to conduct public worship in the vacant church or churches on an early Sunday.

(iii) The Presbytery Clerk shall cause intimation to be made in the form of Schedule N that the person appointed will conduct public worship on the day specified and that a Call in the usual form will lie with the Session Clerk or other suitable person for not less than eight free days to receive the signatures of the congregation. The conditions governing the signing of the Call shall be as in section 25 above.

(iv) At the expiry of the time allowed, the Call shall be transmitted by the Session Clerk to the Presbytery Clerk who shall lay it, along with the documents referred to in sub-paragraph (ii) above, before the Presbytery at its first ordinary meeting or at a meeting *in hunc effectum.*

(b) Otherwise, the Presbytery shall instruct that a fresh Nominating Committee be elected in terms of section 14 above. The process shall then be followed in terms of this Act from the point of the election of the Nominating Committee.

27. Transmission of Documents

(1) After an election has been made, the Interim Moderator shall secure from the person appointed a letter of acceptance of the appointment.

(2) The Interim Moderator shall then without delay transmit the relevant documents to the Presbytery Clerk. These are: the minute of Nomination by the Nominating Committee, all intimations made to the congregation thereafter, the declaration of the election and appointment, the voting-papers, the marked copy of the Register and the letter of acceptance. He or she shall also inform the Clerk of the steps taken in connection with the signing of the Call, and shall arrange that, at the expiry of the period allowed for subscription, the Call shall be transmitted by the Session Clerk to the Presbytery Clerk.

(3) After the person elected has been inducted to the charge, the Presbytery Clerk shall:

(a) deliver to him or her the approved copy of the Vacancy Schedule referred to in section 10(2) above, and

(b) destroy the intimations and voting-papers lodged with him or her in terms of subsection (2) above and ensure that confidential documents and correspondence held locally are destroyed.

28. Sustaining the Call

(1) All of the documents listed in section 27 above shall be laid before the Vacancy Procedure Committee, which may resolve to sustain the call and determine arrangements for the induction of the new minister, subject to (a) a request for the release, if appropriate, of the minister from his or her current charge in terms of this Act and (b) the provisions of section 2 above. The Moderator of the Presbytery shall, if no ordinary meeting of the Presbytery falls before the proposed induction date, call a meeting *pro re nata* for the induction.

(2) In the event that the matter comes before the Presbytery in terms of section 2 above, the procedure shall be as follows:

(a) The Call and other relevant documents having been laid on the table, the Presbytery shall hear any person whom it considers to have an interest. In particular, the Advisory Committee shall be entitled to be heard if it so desires, or the Presbytery may ask for a report from it. The Presbytery shall then decide whether to sustain the appointment in terms of subsection (1) above, and in doing so shall give consideration to the number of signatures on the Call. It may delay reaching a decision and return the Call to the Kirk Session to give further opportunity for it to be subscribed.

(b)   If the Presbytery sustain an appointment and Call to a Graduate Candidate, and there be no appeal tendered in due form against its judgement, it shall appoint the day and hour and place at which the ordination and induction will take place.

(c)   If the Presbytery sustain an appointment and Call to a minister of the Church of Scotland not being a minister of a parish, or to a minister of another denomination, and there be no ecclesiastical impediment, the Presbytery shall appoint the day and hour and place at which the induction will take place.

(3)   In the event that the Call is not sustained, the Presbytery shall determine either (a) to give more time for it to be signed in terms of section 25 above or (b) to proceed in terms of subsection (a) or (b) of section 26 above.

29. Admission to a Charge

(1)   When the Presbytery has appointed a day for the ordination and induction of a Graduate Candidate, or for the induction of a minister already ordained, the Clerk shall arrange for an edict in the form of Schedule O to be read to the congregation on the two Sundays preceding the day appointed.

(2)   At the time and place named in the edict, the Presbytery having been constituted, the Moderator shall call for the return of the edict attested as having been duly served. If the minister is being translated from another Presbytery, the relevant minute of that Presbytery or of its Vacancy Procedure Committee agreeing to translation shall also be laid on the table. Any objection, to be valid at this stage, must have been intimated to the Presbytery Clerk at the objector's earliest opportunity, must be strictly directed to life or doctrine and must be substantiated immediately to the satisfaction of the Presbytery, in which case procedure shall be sisted and the Presbytery shall take appropriate steps to deal with the situation that has arisen. Otherwise, the Presbytery shall proceed with the ordination and induction, or with the induction, as hereunder.

(3)   The Presbytery shall proceed to the church where public worship shall be conducted by those appointed for the purpose. The Clerk shall read a brief narrative of the cause of the vacancy and of the steps taken for the settlement. The Moderator, having read the Preamble, shall, addressing him or her by name, put to the person to be inducted the questions prescribed (*see the Ordinal of the Church as authorised from time to time by the General Assembly*). Satisfactory answers having been given, the person to be inducted shall sign the Formula. If he or she has not already been ordained, the person to be inducted shall then kneel, and the Moderator by prayer and the imposition of hands, in which members of the Presbytery, appointed by the Presbytery for the purpose, and other ordained persons associated with it, if invited to share in such imposition of hands, shall join, shall ordain him or her to the office of the Holy Ministry. Prayer being ended, the Moderator shall say: 'I now declare you to have been ordained to the office of the Holy Ministry, and in name of the Lord Jesus Christ, the King and Head of the Church, and by authority of this Presbytery, I induct you to this charge, and in token thereof we give you the right hand of fellowship'. The Moderator with all other members of Presbytery present and those associated with it shall then give the right hand of fellowship. The Moderator shall then put the prescribed question to the members of the congregation. Suitable charges to the new minister and to the congregation shall then be given by the Moderator or by a minister appointed for the purpose.

(4)   When an ordained minister is being inducted to a charge, the act of ordination shall not be repeated, and the relevant words shall be omitted from the declaration. In other respects, the procedure shall be as in subsection (3) above.

(5)   When the appointment is for a limited or potentially limited period (including Reviewable Tenure, or an appointment in terms of section 19 above), the service shall proceed as in subsections (3) or (4) above, except that in the declaration the Moderator shall say: 'I induct you to this charge on the Basis of [specific Act and Section] and in terms of Minute of Presbytery of date . . .'.

(6)   After the service, the Presbytery shall resume its session, when the name of the new minister shall be added to the Roll of Presbytery, and the Clerk shall be instructed to send certified intimation of the induction to the Session Clerk to be engrossed in the minutes of the first meeting of Kirk Session thereafter, and, in the case of a translation from another Presbytery or where the minister was prior to the induction subject to the supervision of another Presbytery, to the Clerk of that Presbytery.

30. Service of Introduction

(1)   When a minister has been appointed to a linked charge, the Presbytery shall determine in which of the churches of the linking the induction is to take place. This shall be a service of induction to the charge, in consequence of which the person inducted shall become minister of each of the congregations embraced in the linking. The edict regarding the induction, which shall be in terms of Schedule O, shall be read in all of the churches concerned. There shall be no other service of induction; but, if the churches are far distant from one another, or for other good reason, the Presbytery may appoint a service of introduction to be held in the other church or churches. Intimation shall be given of such service, but not in edictal form.

(2)   In any case of deferred union or deferred linking, the minister elected and appointed shall be inducted 'to the vacant congregation of A in deferred union (or linking) with the congregation of B' and there shall be no need for any further act to establish his or her position as minister of the united congregation or of the linked congregation as the case may be. The Presbytery, however, shall in such a case arrange a service of introduction to the newly united congregation of AB or the newly linked congregation of B. Intimation shall be given of such service, but not in edictal form.

(3)   When an appointment has been made to an extra-parochial office wholly or mainly under control of the Church (community ministry, full-time chaplaincy in hospital, industry, prison or university, full-time clerkship and so on), the Presbytery may deem it appropriate to arrange a service of introduction to take place in a church or chapel suitable to the occasion.

(4)   When an appointment has been made to a parochial appointment other than that of an inducted minister, the Presbytery may arrange a service of introduction to take place within the parish. If ordination is involved, suitable arrangements shall be made and edictal intimation shall be given in terms of Schedule P.

(5)   A service of introduction not involving ordination shall follow the lines of an induction except that, instead of putting the normal questions to the minister, the Moderator shall ask him or her to affirm the vows taken at his or her ordination. Where the service, in terms of subsection (3) or (4) above, includes the ordination of the minister, the vows shall be put in full. In either case, in the declaration, the Moderator in place of 'I induct you to . . .' shall say: 'I welcome you as . . .'.

31. Demission of Status
If a minister seeks to demit his or her status as a minister of the Church of Scotland, any accompanying demission of a charge will be dealt with by the Vacancy Procedure Committee in terms of section 4 of this Act without further delay, but the question of demission of status shall be considered by the Presbytery itself. The Moderator of Presbytery, or a deputy appointed by him or her, shall first confer with the minister regarding his or her reasons and shall report to the Presbytery if there appears to be any reason not to grant permission to demit status. Any decision to grant permission to demit status shall be immediately reported to the Ministries Council.

32. Miscellaneous
For the purposes of this Act, intimations to congregations may be made (a) verbally during every act of worship or (b) in written intimations distributed to the whole congregation provided that the congregation's attention is specifically drawn to the presence of an intimation there in terms of this Act.

For the purposes of this Act, attestation of all intimations to congregations shall consist of certification thereof by the Session Clerk as follows:

(a)   Certification that all intimations received have been duly made on the correct number of Sundays shall be sent to the Presbytery Clerk before the service of induction or introduction.

(b)   Certification that any particular intimation received has been duly made on the correct number of Sundays shall be furnished on demand to the Vacancy Procedure Committee or the Presbytery Clerk.

(c)   Intimation shall be made immediately to the Presbytery Clerk in the event that intimation has not been duly made on the appropriate Sunday.

SCHEDULES

A INTIMATION OF ACTION OR DECISION OF VACANCY PROCEDURE COMMITTEE – Section 2(1)

To be read on one Sunday

The Vacancy Procedure Committee of the Presbytery of .... proposes [here insert action or permission proposed]....... Any communicant member of the congregation(s) of A [and B] may submit to the Presbytery Clerk a request for this proposal to be considered at the next meeting of the Presbytery: where such requests are received from four individuals, being communicant members of the congregation(s) or full members of the Presbytery, the request shall be met. Such request should be submitted in writing to [name and postal address of Presbytery Clerk] by [date seven days after intimation].

A .... B ....   Presbytery Clerk

B EDICT CITING A CONGREGATION TO ATTEND – Section 2(5)

To be read on one Sunday

Intimation is hereby given that, in connection with the [anticipated] vacancy in this congregation, a valid request has been made for the matter of [here insert action or permission which had been proposed] to be considered by the Presbytery. [The proposed course of action] is in the meantime sisted.

Intimation is hereby further given that the Presbytery will meet to consider this matter at ....
on .... the .... day of .... at .... o'clock and that the congregation are hereby
cited to attend for their interests.

A .... B ....   Presbytery Clerk

C PREPARATION OF ELECTORAL REGISTER – Section 13(1) and (2)

To be read on two Sundays

Intimation is hereby given that in view of the [1]anticipated vacancy, the Kirk Session is about to
make up an Electoral Register of this congregation. Any communicant whose name is not already
on the Communion Roll as a member should hand in to the Session Clerk a Certificate of
Transference, and anyone wishing his or her name added to the Register as an adherent should
obtain from the Session Clerk, and complete and return to him or her, a Form of Adherent's
Claim. All such papers should be in the hands of the Session Clerk not later than .... The
Kirk Session will meet in .... on .... at .... to make up the Electoral Register,
when anyone wishing to support his or her claim in person should attend.

C .... D ....   Interim Moderator

[1] This word to be included where appropriate – otherwise to be deleted

D FORM OF ADHERENT'S CLAIM – Section 13(1)

I, [1] .... of [2] ...., being a parishioner or regular worshipper in the Church of .... and
not being a member of any other congregation in Scotland, claim to have my name put on the
Electoral Register of the parish of .... as an adherent.

Date ....   (Signed).......................

[1] Here enter full name in block capitals
[2] Here enter address in full

E INSPECTION OF ELECTORAL REGISTER – Section 13(3)

To be read on one Sunday

Intimation is hereby given that the proposed Electoral Register of this congregation has now
been prepared and that an opportunity of inspecting it will be given today in .... at the
close of this service, and that it will be open for inspection at .... on .... between the
hours of .... and .... each day. Any questions regarding entries in the Register should
be brought to the notice of the Kirk Session which is to meet in .... on .... at ....
o'clock, when it will finally make up the Electoral Register.

C .... D ....   Interim Moderator

F REVISION OF ELECTORAL REGISTER – Section 13(6)

To be read on two Sundays

Intimation is hereby given that, more than six months having elapsed since the Electoral Register of this congregation was finally made up, it is now proposed that it should be revised. An opportunity of inspecting the Register will be given in ………. at the close of this service, and also at ………. on ………. between the hours of ………. and ………. each day. Anyone wishing his or her name added to the Electoral Register as a member should give in a Transference Certificate, or as an adherent should give in a Form of Adherent's Claim (copies of which may be had from the Session Clerk) not later than ………. The Kirk Session will meet in ………. on ………. at ………. o'clock, when it will finally make up the Revised Register.

C ………. D ……….   Interim Moderator

G INTIMATION OF ELECTION OF NOMINATING COMMITTEE – Section 14(1)

To be read on two Sundays

Intimation is hereby given that a meeting of this congregation will be held in the Church [or other arrangement may be given here] on Sunday ……. at the close of morning worship for the purpose of appointing a Nominating Committee which will nominate one person to the congregation with a view to the appointment of a minister.

C ………. D ……….   Interim Moderator

H MINUTE OF NOMINATION BY NOMINATING COMMITTEE – Section 21

To be read on two Sundays

(1)   The Committee chosen by this congregation to nominate a person with a view to the election and appointment of a minister, at a meeting held at ………. on ……….., resolved to name and propose [1] ………., and they accordingly do name and propose the said ……….

Date ………………..

E ………. F ……….   Convener of Committee

[1] The name and designation of the person should at this point be entered in full

(2)   Intimation is therefore hereby given that the Nominating Committee having, as by minute now read, named and proposed [Name], arrangements have been made whereby public worship will be conducted in this Church by him or her on Sunday the ………. day of ………. at ………. o'clock; and that a vote will be taken by voting-papers immediately thereafter; and that electors may vote For or Against electing and appointing the said [Name] as minister of this vacant charge.

C ………. D ……….   Interim Moderator

I VOTING-PAPER – Section 23

FOR Electing [Name]
AGAINST Electing [Name]

Directions to Voters: If you are in favour of electing [Name], put a cross (x) on the upper space. If you are not in favour of electing [Name], put a cross (x) in the lower space. Do not put a tick or any other mark upon the paper; if you do, it will be regarded as spoilt and will not be counted.

Note: The Directions to Voters must be printed prominently on the face of the voting-paper

J DECLARATION OF ELECTION RESULT – Section 23(5)

First Form (Successful Election)

I hereby declare that the following are the results of the voting for the election and appointment of a minister to the vacant charge of [1] .... and that the said [Name] has accordingly been elected and appointed subject to the judgement of the courts of the Church.

Date ....   C .... D ....   Interim Moderator

[1] Here enter details

FOR Electing [Name]
AGAINST Electing [Name]

Second Form (Failure to Elect)

I hereby declare that the following are the results of the voting for the election and appointment of a minister to the vacant charge of [1] .... and that in consequence of this vote there has been a failure to elect, and the Nominating Committee is deemed to have been discharged. [Continue in terms of Schedule G if appropriate.]

Date ....   C .... D ....   Interim Moderator

[1] Here enter details

FOR Electing [Name]
AGAINST Electing [Name]

K THE CALL – Section 25(1)

Form of Call

We, members of the Church of Scotland and of the congregation known as ...., being without a minister, address this Call to be our minister to you, ..., of whose gifts and qualities we have been assured, and we warmly invite you to accept this Call, promising that we shall devote ourselves with you to worship, witness, mission and service in this parish, and also to the furtherance of these in the world, to the glory of God and for the advancement of His Kingdom.

Paper of Concurrence

We, regular worshippers in the congregation of the Church of Scotland known as ...., concur in the Call addressed by that congregation to .... to be their minister.

Note: The Call and Paper of Concurrence should be dated and attested by the Interim Moderator before they are transmitted to the Clerk of the Presbytery.

L SUBSCRIBING THE CALL – Section 25(1)

To be read on at least one Sunday

Intimation is hereby given that this congregation having elected [Name] to be their minister, a Call to the said [Name] has been prepared and will lie in .... on .... the .... day of .... between the hours of .... and ...., when those whose names are on the Electoral Register of the congregation may sign in person or by means of mandates. Forms of mandate may be obtained from the Session Clerk.

A Paper of Concurrence will also be available for signature by persons who are connected with the congregation but whose names are not on the Electoral Register of the congregation.

C .... D ....   Interim Moderator

M MANDATE TO SIGN CALL – Section 25(2)

I, ... of ...., being a person whose name is on the Electoral Register of the congregation, hereby authorise the Session Clerk, or other member of Session, to add my name to the Call addressed to [Name] to be our minister.

(Signed) ....…….

N CITATION IN CASE OF NOMINATION BY PRESBYTERY – Section 26(a)(iii)

To be read on one Sunday

Intimation is hereby given that [Name], whom the Presbytery has appointed to be minister of this congregation, will conduct public worship in the Church on Sunday the .... day of .... at .... o'clock.

Intimation is hereby further given that a Call addressed to the said [Name] will lie in .... on .... the .... day of .... between the hours of .... and .... during the day and between the hours of .... and .... in the evening, when members may sign in person or by means of mandates, forms of which may be had from the Session Clerk.

Intimation is hereby further given that the Presbytery will meet to deal with the appointment and Call at .... on .... the .... day of .... at .... o'clock and that the congregation are hereby cited to attend for their interests.

A .... B ....   Presbytery Clerk

O EDICTAL INTIMATION OF ADMISSION – Section 29(1)

To be read on two Sundays

- Whereas the Presbytery of .... has received a Call from this congregation addressed to [Name] to be their minister, and the said Call has been sustained as a regular Call, and has been accepted by him/her[1];
- And whereas the said Presbytery, having judged the said [Name] qualified[2] for the ministry of the Gospel and for this charge, has resolved to proceed to his or her[3] ordination and induction on .... the .... day of .... at .... o'clock unless something occur which may reasonably impede it:

Notice is hereby given to all concerned that if they, or any of them, have anything to object to in the life or doctrine of the said [Name], they may appear at the Presbytery which is to meet at .... on .... the .... day of .... at .... o'clock; with certification that if no relevant objection be then made and immediately substantiated, the Presbytery will proceed without further delay.

By order of the Presbytery

A .... B .... Presbytery Clerk

[1] add, where appropriate, 'and his or her translation has been agreed to by the Presbytery of ....'
[2] omit 'for the ministry of the Gospel and' if the minister to be inducted has been ordained previously
[3] omit, where appropriate, 'ordination and'

P EDICTAL INTIMATION OF ORDINATION IN CASE OF INTRODUCTION – Section 30(1)

To be read on two Sundays

- Whereas [narrate circumstances requiring service of introduction]
- And whereas the Presbytery, having found the said [Name] to have been regularly appointed and to be qualified for the ministry of the Gospel and for the said appointment, has resolved to proceed to his or her ordination to the Holy Ministry and to his or her introduction as [specify appointment] on .... the .... day of .... at .... o'clock unless something occur which may reasonably impede it:

Notice is hereby given to all concerned that if they, or any of them, have anything to object to in the life or doctrine of the said [Name], they may appear at the Presbytery which is to meet at .... on .... the .... day of .... at .... o'clock; with certification that if no relevant objection be then made and immediately substantiated, the Presbytery will proceed without further delay.

By order of the Presbytery

A .... B ....   Presbytery Clerk

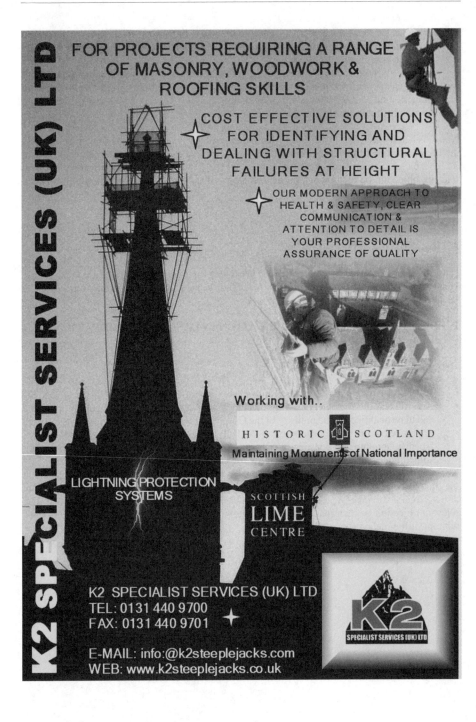

SECTION 4

The General Assembly of 2007

(1) THE GENERAL ASSEMBLY

The Lord High Commissioner:	His Royal Highness the Prince Andrew, Duke of York KG KCVO
Moderator:	Right Rev. Sheilagh Kesting BA BD
Chaplains to the Moderator:	Rev. Sheila Maxey BA BD Rev. Colin G. McIntosh BSc BD
Principal Clerk:	Very Rev. Finlay A.J. Macdonald MA BD PhD DD
Depute Clerk:	Rev. Marjory A. MacLean LLB BD PhD
Procurator:	Miss Laura Dunlop QC
Law Agent:	Mrs Janette S. Wilson LLB NP
Convener of the Business Committee:	Rev. William C. Hewitt BD DipPS
Vice-Convener of the Business Committee:	Rev. A. David K. Arnott MA BD
Precentor:	Rev. Douglas Galbraith MA BD BMus MPhil ARSCM
Assembly Officer:	Mr David McColl
Assistant Assembly Officer:	Mr Craig Marshall

(2) THE MODERATOR

The Right Reverend Sheilagh M. Kesting BA BD

The saying 'still waters run deep' is a good one when considering the particular kind of leadership that Sheilagh Kesting will give to the Church of Scotland during her year of office. Her quiet and gentle manner hides a formidable intelligence, a passionate commitment to an inclusive Christianity, and a deep personal faith. She is known as an excellent, thoughtful preacher; but many local parishes and Presbyteries in Scotland also know her as the careful listener and experienced adviser on all things ecumenical. Those qualities of careful listening, passionate commitment and formidable intelligence are well known and appreciated in the various councils of her own Church, by other churches in Scotland, and well beyond Scotland, in European and world bodies.

Sheilagh grew up in Stornoway, becoming a member of St Columba's Old Parish Church at 16, teaching in Sunday School and singing in the choir. Already she was troubled by a surrounding culture of hostility towards Roman Catholics; and, in later years, she occasionally worshipped in the Episcopal Church. During her years of study at Edinburgh University, she continued her ecumenical exploration, worshipping in different congregations ranging from conservative evangelical to high Episcopalian.

Meanwhile, she explored faith academically, following her general BA degree with a BD with first-class honours in philosophy of religion – a formidable intelligence indeed! During her first year at New College, she was encouraged to attend Selection School to test the sense of call which was beginning to come to the surface of those 'still waters'.

After a two-year probationary period at St John's Renfield in Glasgow, Sheilagh had two significant ministries in Overtown parish, Lanarkshire and in St Andrew's High, Musselburgh. In both, in very different ways, helping people to face and manage change was a significant part of the ministry. In Overtown, the challenge was the closure of the steel works and the community depression which followed. In St Andrew's High, it was the uniting of two congregations and the development of a new worship space. Both called for and developed Sheilagh's careful listening skills and the attention to detail which also characterises her style of ministry. In Musselburgh, she began to find the ecumenical colleagueship which has become such a feature of her particular ministry.

Within a year of ordination, Sheilagh became a member of the Panel on Doctrine. Her keen theological mind had been recognised and would go on to be invaluable as she served the Church of Scotland locally, in Presbytery, at a national level and, in due course, at an international level.

In 1993, Sheilagh became the Church of Scotland's first Secretary of the new Committee for Ecumenical Relations, and in the years since then this role has moved from the edges to the centre of the life of the Kirk. This is, of course, partly because of changing times but is also in no small measure due to the quiet, persistent, intelligent way in which Sheilagh has built up relationships and overcome anxieties and prejudices. In ecumenical situations, whether in Livingston, London, Geneva or Brazil, Sheilagh's preferred role is as the servant of the meeting – taking the minutes, writing the report, quietly and unobtrusively influencing the meeting through a few well-chosen contributions – the still waters running deep!

During her year as Moderator, the Church will see Sheilagh emerging from her chosen background role and finding her public voice. But she will still be the same person, bringing to this leadership role her formidable intelligence, her passionate commitment to an inclusive Christianity and her deep faith. The many, many people in the Church of Scotland who are looking forward to her leadership with eager expectation will be joined by another 'cloud of witnesses' from other churches and other countries who will be cheering her on her way.

Sheila Maxey and Colin G. McIntosh, Chaplains

---

(3) DIGEST OF ASSEMBLY DECISIONS

Following the practice of recent years, this section of the *Year Book* contains the editor's personal selection of the decisions of the most recent General Assembly which, in his view at the time of writing, seemed likely to be of most immediate or practical interest to those likely to read it.

It is readily recognised that there will be those whose selection would be somewhat different: there will doubtless be some surprise that this decision rather than that decision has been highlighted. With the brief headline approach which this section necessarily employs, full justice cannot be done to every topic that was raised. As always, however, those who wish to explore in more detail the editor's 'sins of omission' can obtain from the office of the Principal Clerk the full published volume of Assembly Reports. In due course, copies of that volume, including in addition the approved Deliverances on each Report, will be available from the same source.

REPORTS OF COUNCILS, COMMITTEES AND OTHER AGENCIES

Assembly Arrangements Committee:
With effect from 2008, the General Assembly will meet on the third Thursday of May. The Committee was authorised to determine the duration of the 2008 Assembly.

Chaplains to HM Forces Committee:
The Assembly recorded 'particular thanks' to the Chaplains of the Royal Navy, Army and Royal Air Force for their moral and spiritual leadership during service in Iraq and Afghanistan.

Church and Society Council:
Recognising the courage of British servicemen and women and the endurance of their families, yet believing that the continued presence of UK forces in Iraq can no longer be seen to be a positive contribution to resolving the situation of that country, the Assembly called on HM Government to withdraw its troops in as short a time as possible.

The Assembly called on HM Government, the Scottish Parliament and Executive and local authorities to set clear and radical long-term targets for greenhouse gas reductions, by the implementation of stringent and specific environmental legislation, in recognition that we all have a duty of care for the world and its people beyond present market considerations.

The Assembly expressed the Church's grave concern at the proliferation of gambling opportunities and advertising and invited HM Government to take more seriously its responsibility for the more vulnerable in our society. The Assembly further encouraged Church members actively to oppose the growth of the gambling culture in our country and to expose the false hope of gambling as a route out of poverty.

Church of Scotland Guild:
The Assembly commended the Guild for its work in raising awareness in the Church of human trafficking and for its contribution to the resource pack for use in congregations. The Assembly urged the Guild to work, as far as possible in consultation with appropriate Councils and Presbyteries, to investigate methods of alerting potential brothel clients to the evils of human trafficking and to communicate these widely through their networks.

Council of Assembly:
The Assembly resolved that congregations should continue to be separate registered Charities and agreed that any pressure from the Office of the Scottish Charity Regulator to require consolidated accounts should be resisted.

Ecumenical Relations Committee:
The Assembly invited Presbyteries to appoint Ecumenical Facilitators as a means of resourcing the implementation of the ecumenical policy at local level.

The Assembly endorsed the joint statement with the Free Church of Scotland.

General Trustees:
The Assembly noted with concern the proposed withdrawal by the Scottish Executive of the exemption enjoyed by congregations from Water and Sewerage charges after 2010, and urged congregations and Presbyteries to make representations to their local MSPs.

The Assembly instructed the Trustees to consider a grant/loan system for Renewable Energy projects in Church properties and to report to the General Assembly of 2008.

HIV/AIDS Project:
The Assembly renewed its call to all people of faith in Scotland to work to address issues of HIV stigma and discrimination.

Iona Community Board:
The Assembly welcomed the current co-operation between the Community and Historic Scotland on the site of Iona Abbey and looked forward to a positive landlord–tenant relationship in the future.

The Assembly welcomed the developing link between Camas (the Community's outdoor education centre on Mull) and the Young Offenders' Institution, Polmont, and the much-appreciated assistance provided for the "Jacob Project" for young ex-offenders by the Parish Development Fund.

Legal Questions Committee:
The Assembly received the Committee's Report which included a statement regarding fees for funerals. The full text of that statement is printed in the *Year Book* in item 4 of section 3 dealing with Church Procedure.

Ministries Council:
The Assembly instructed the Ministries Council, in partnership with the Mission and Discipleship Council, to consult with Presbyteries, Readers and Auxiliary Ministers regarding the proposals outlined in the Ministries Council's Report for more flexible structures for Ministry of Word and Sacrament and for a Local Ordained Ministry to replace in future the Readership and the Auxiliary Ministry.

The Council was instructed to investigate the possibility of allowing retired ministers to serve in parishes without ministers on a reviewable basis.

In view of the recent and disproportionately low number of women candidates for full-time ministry, the Council was instructed to report on this matter to the General Assembly of 2008.

The Assembly instructed the Council to bring a report to the General Assembly of 2008 on the principle of an independent seminary-style institution outwith the context of a university as a suitable environment for training candidates for the Ministry of Word and Sacrament.

Mission and Discipleship Council:
The Assembly encouraged every Presbytery to send a representative aged 10 to 12 to the National Children's Assembly to be held in Gartmore House during September 2007.

The Assembly urged every Presbytery to nominate at least one person to become a Presbytery Youth and Children's Trainer so that best practice may continue to be observed in our ministry to and with young people and children.

The Assembly welcomed the Report on promoting the inclusion of people with learning disabilities in the local church and urged congregations to be aware of people with learning disabilities within the parish and to take all steps to welcome them into the life of the Church.

The Assembly instructed the Council, in collaboration with the Ministries Council, to undertake an investigation into the present standing of Gaelic in the Church of Scotland with a view to reporting to the 2008 General Assembly on the strategic development of the use of the language in the Kirk.

Panel on Review and Reform:
The Assembly instructed the Panel to review the effectiveness of change resulting from the Church Without Walls Re-Energise conferences and encouraged the Panel to undertake a review of how the Church has taken forward the recommendations of the Church Without Walls report. The Panel is to report to the General Assembly of 2008.

Parish Appraisal Committee:
The Assembly noted with thanks the work of the Parish Appraisal Committee, discharged it with effect from 31 May 2007 and, with effect from 1 June 2007, approved the transfer of responsibilities for overseeing ongoing planning work in Presbyteries to the Ministries Council's Planning and Deployment Committee and its associated Presbytery Planning Task Group.

The Assembly instructed the Ministries Council, in consultation with the Mission and Discipleship Council, to assess the implications for rural congregations of the Presbytery Planning process.

Parish Development Fund:
The Assembly encouraged congregations applying to the Fund for youth-work development to ensure that the voices of young people are placed firmly at the heart of the design, delivery and review process of proposed applications and projects.

Returns to Overtures:
At the invitation of the Assembly, the Principal Clerk provided an interpretation of the legal implications of the non-approval of the Overture anent Civil Partnerships. The Assembly agreed that that interpretation, which was in the following terms, should be engrossed in the Minutes: 'There were two proposals before last year's General Assembly. The Legal Questions Committee asked the Assembly to declare that "a minister or deacon who conducts any service marking a civil partnership does not commit a disciplinary offence in terms of Act III, 2001 (as amended)". The proposal also made explicit that "no minister or deacon shall be compelled to or obliged to conduct such a service against his or her conscience". A counter-proposal asked the General Assembly to instruct that "no minister or deacon shall conduct any service marking a civil partnership". Before putting the matter to a vote, the General Assembly agreed that, whichever proposal was successful, the matter would be referred to Presbyteries under the Barrier Act. When a vote was taken, the Legal Questions Committee's proposal carried.

'However, the proposal did not receive the consent of a majority of Presbyteries. This means that Presbyteries have failed positively to affirm that "a minister or deacon who conducts any service marking a civil partnership does not commit a disciplinary offence in terms of Act III, 2001 (as amended)". However, it does not follow from that failure that a minister or deacon who so acts does commit a disciplinary offence. For that to have become the position, it would have been necessary for the unsuccessful Overture from last year's Assembly to have prevailed, gone down under the Barrier Act, received the support of a majority of Presbyteries and been converted into a standing law of the Church this year. In effect, the Church is back where it was before last year's General Assembly, with the uncertainty highlighted by the Legal Questions Committee remaining. There is no law of the Church specifically authorising ministers to mark civil partnerships, and no law specifically forbidding it.'

Safeguarding Committee:
The Assembly instructed the Committee to seek discussion with members of the Worship and Doctrine Task Group to discover a theology of forgiveness and proportionality relating to sex offenders seeking to return to worship in congregations.

The Assembly instructed the Committee, in consultation with appropriate agencies, to establish a policy and procedures for the effective vetting of those who have recently come from abroad and who apply to work on a paid or voluntary basis with vulnerable groups.

The Assembly noted and approved the guidelines on managing Safeguarding-related complaints, instructed kirk sessions to establish a written policy (using the information in the Appendix to the Report) and instructed the Committee to prepare a template to enable them to carry out this task.

Social Care Council:
The Assembly urged the Council to investigate continuing collaborative working with Social Care wings of other Christian denominations in Scotland for the benefit of all service-users.

Stewardship and Finance Committee:
The Assembly welcomed the challenging opportunity of the Council of Assembly's decision to support stewardship programmes in all congregations in two Presbyteries with a view to a national stewardship programme at a future date.

World Mission Council:
The Assembly instructed the Council to keep the reconciling character of the Gospel central to all its work and to offer meaningful solidarity to partner churches which witness in situations of division and conflict.

*'Arrive for your perfect wedding day
in exquisite luxury,
a car to complement your special day'*

Zenith Executive Drive is driven to provide you with the best service possible, giving you the best experience possible. We also consider that our business should be morally responsible and not preoccupied with profits at all costs. For this reason we vow to give 25 percent of the profits from the second car on any booking using two cars or more, to the Hope School in Bethlehem working with young people of all faiths in order to achieve peace and reconciliation.

Our Jaguar cars are available for weddings, shopping trips, anniversaries, golf tours, sight-seeing trips and travel to and from corporate meetings.

find us at: www.zenithdrive.co.uk, and contact us at enquiries@zenithdrive.co.uk
or telephone us on 01506 852877

SECTION 5

Presbytery Lists

SECTION 5 – PRESBYTERY LISTS

In each Presbytery list, the congregations are listed in alphabetical order. In a linked charge, the names appear under the first named congregation. Under the name of the congregation will be found the name of the minister and, where applicable, that of an associate minister, auxiliary minister and member of the Diaconate. The years indicated after a minister's name in the congregational section of each Presbytery list are the year of ordination (column 1) and the year of current appointment (column 2). Where only one date is given, it is both the year of ordination and the year of appointment.

In the second part of each Presbytery list, those named are listed alphabetically. The first date is the year of ordination, and the following date is the year of appointment or retirement. If the person concerned is retired, then the appointment last held will be shown in brackets.

KEY TO ABBREVIATIONS

(E)   Indicates a Church Extension charge. New Charge Developments are separately indicated.
(GD) Indicates a charge where it is desirable that the minister should have a knowledge of Gaelic.
(GE) Indicates a charge where public worship must be regularly conducted in Gaelic.
(H)   Indicates that a Hearing Aid Loop system has been installed. In Linked charges, the (H) is placed beside the appropriate building as far as possible.
(L)   Indicates that a Chair Lift has been installed.
(T)   Indicates that the minister has been appointed on the basis of Terminable Tenure.

PRESBYTERY NUMBERS

1 Edinburgh	18 Dumbarton	35 Moray
2 West Lothian	19 Argyll	36 Abernethy
3 Lothian	20	37 Inverness
4 Melrose and Peebles	21	38 Lochaber
5 Duns	22 Falkirk	39 Ross
6 Jedburgh	23 Stirling	40 Sutherland
7 Annandale and Eskdale	24 Dunfermline	41 Caithness
8 Dumfries and Kirkcudbright	25 Kirkcaldy	42 Lochcarron–Skye
9 Wigtown and Stranraer	26 St Andrews	43 Uist
10 Ayr	27 Dunkeld and Meigle	44 Lewis
11 Irvine and Kilmarnock	28 Perth	45 Orkney
12 Ardrossan	29 Dundee	46 Shetland
13 Lanark	30 Angus	47 England
14 Greenock and Paisley	31 Aberdeen	48 Europe
15	32 Kincardine and Deeside	49 Jerusalem
16 Glasgow	33 Gordon	
17 Hamilton	34 Buchan	

(1) EDINBURGH

Meets at Palmerston Place Church, Edinburgh, on the first Tuesday of October, November, December, February, March, April and May and on the second Tuesday in September and on the last Tuesday of June. When the first Tuesday of April falls in Holy Week, the meeting is on the second Tuesday.

Clerk: REV. W. PETER GRAHAM MA BD   10/1 Palmerston Place, Edinburgh EH12 5AA   0131-225 9137
[E-mail: edinburgh@cofscotland.org.uk]

1 **Edinburgh: Albany Deaf Church of Edinburgh (H)**
Alistair F. Kelly BL (Locum)   1961   19 Avon Place, Edinburgh EH4 6RE   0131-317 9877
[E-mail: alistairkelly@tiscali.co.uk]

2 **Edinburgh: Balerno (H)**
Jared W. Hay BA MTh DipMin DMin   1987   2001   3 Johnsburn Road, Balerno EH14 7DN   0131-449 3830
[E-mail: jared.hay@blueyonder.co.uk]

3 **Edinburgh: Barclay (0131-229 6810) (E-mail: admin@barclaychurch.org.uk)**
Samuel A.R. Torrens BD   1995   2005   113 Meadowspot, Edinburgh EH10 5UY   0131-478 2376
[E-mail: samtorrens@blueyonder.co.uk]

4 **Edinburgh: Blackhall St Columba's (0131-332 4431) (E-mail: secretary@blackhallstcolumba.org.uk)**
Alexander B. Douglas BD   1979   1991   5 Blinkbonny Crescent, Edinburgh EH4 3NB   0131-343 3708
[E-mail: alexandjill@douglas.net]

5 **Edinburgh: Bristo Memorial Craigmillar**
James Patterson BSc BD   2003   2006   72 Blackchapel Close, Edinburgh EH15 3SL   0131-657 3266
[E-mail: patterson@jimandmegan.force9.co.uk]
Agnes M. Rennie (Miss) DCS   3/1 Craigmillar Court, Edinburgh EH16 4AD   0131-661 8475

6 **Edinburgh: Broughton St Mary's (H) (0131-556 4786)**
Joanne C. Hood (Miss) MA BD   2003   103 East Claremont Street, Edinburgh EH7 4JA   0131-556 7313
[E-mail: hood137@btinternet.com]

7 **Edinburgh: Canongate (H)**
Neil N. Gardner MA BD   1991   2006   Manse of Canongate, Edinburgh EH8 8BR   0131-556 3515
[E-mail: nng@btinternet.com]

8 **Edinburgh: Carrick Knowe (H) (0131-334 1505) (E-mail: carrickknowechurch@btinternet.com)**
Fiona M. Mathieson (Mrs) BEd BD   1988   2001   21 Traquair Park West, Edinburgh EH12 7AN   0131-334 9774
[E-mail: fiona.mathieson@ukgateway.net]

9   Edinburgh: Colinton (H) (0131-441 2232) (E-mail: church.office@colinton-parish.com)
George J. Whyte BSc BD DMin   1981 1992   The Manse, Colinton, Edinburgh EH13 0JR   0131-441 2315
                                                        [E-mail: george.whyte@colinton-parish.com]
Christine M. Clark (Mrs) BA BD MTh   2006   32 Dreghorn Loan, Edinburgh EH13 0DE   0131-466 4353
(Assoc)

10 Edinburgh: Colinton Mains (H)
Ian A. McQuarrie BD   1993   17 Swanston Green, Edinburgh EH10 7EW   0131-445 3451
                                                        [E-mail: ian.mcquarrie1@btinternet.com]

11 Edinburgh: Corstorphine Craigsbank (H) (0131-334 6365)
Stewart M. McPherson BD CertMin   1991 2003   17 Craigs Bank, Edinburgh EH12 8HD   0131-467 6826
                                                        [E-mail: smcpherson@blueyonder.co.uk]   07814 901429 (Mbl)

12 Edinburgh: Corstorphine Old (H) (0131-334 7864) (E-mail: corold@aol.com)
Moira McDonald MA BD   1997 2005   23 Manse Road, Edinburgh EH12 7SW   0131-476 5893
                                                        [E-mail: moira.mc@tesco.net]

13 Edinburgh: Corstorphine St Anne's (0131-316 4740) (E-mail: stannesoffice@surefish.co.uk)
MaryAnn R. Rennie (Mrs) BD MTh   1998 2002   23 Belgrave Road, Edinburgh EH12 6NG   0131-334 3188
                                                        [E-mail: maryann.rennie@blueyonder.co.uk]

14 Edinburgh: Corstorphine St Ninian's (H) (0131-539 6204) (E-mail: office@st-ninians.co.uk)
Alexander T. Stewart MA BD FSAScot   1975 1995   17 Templeland Road, Edinburgh EH12 8RZ   0131-334 2978
                                                        [E-mail: alextstewart@blueyonder.co.uk]
Margaret Gordon (Mrs) DCS   92 Lanark Road West, Currie EH14 5LA   0131-449 2554

15 Edinburgh: Craigentinny St Christopher's
Vacant   61 Milton Crescent, Edinburgh EH15 3PQ   0131-669 2429

16 Edinburgh: Craiglockhart (H) (E-mail: office@craiglockhartchurch.org.uk)
Andrew Ritchie BD DipMin DMin   1984 1991   202 Colinton Road, Edinburgh EH14 1BP   0131-443 2020
                                                        [E-mail: andrewritchie@talk21.com]

17 Edinburgh: Craigmillar Park (H) (0131-667 5862)
Sarah E.C. Nicol (Mrs) BSc BD   1985 1994   14 Hallhead Road, Edinburgh EH16 5QJ   0131-667 1623

18 Edinburgh: Cramond (H) (E-mail: cramond.kirk@blueyonder.co.uk)
G. Russell Barr BA BD MTh DMin   1979 1993   Manse of Cramond, Edinburgh EH4 6NS   0131-336 2036
                                                        [E-mail: rev.r.barr@blueyonder.co.uk]

19 Edinburgh: Currie (H) (0131-451 5141) (E-mail: currie_kirk@btconnect.com)
Vacant   43 Lanark Road West, Currie EH14 5JX   0131-449 4719

20 Edinburgh: Dalmeny linked with Edinburgh: Queensferry
John G. Carrie BSc BD   1971   2006   1 Station Road, South Queensferry EH30 9HY   0131-331 1100
                                                          [E-mail: john.carrie@virgin.net]

21 Edinburgh: Davidson's Mains (H) (0131-312 6282) (E-mail: life@dmainschurch.plus.com)
Jeremy R.H. Middleton LLB BD   1981   1988   1 Hillpark Terrace, Edinburgh EH4 7SX   0131-336 3078
                                                          [E-mail: life@dmainschurch.plus.com]

22 Edinburgh: Dean (H)
Mark M. Foster BSc BD   1998   1 Ravelston Terrace, Edinburgh EH4 3EF   0131-332 5736
                                                          [E-mail: markmfoster@mac.com]

23 Edinburgh: Drylaw (0131-343 6643)
Patricia Watson (Mrs) BD   2005   15 House o' Hill Gardens, Edinburgh EH4 2AR   0131-343 1441
                                                          [E-mail: patricia@patriciawatson.wanadoo.co.uk]   07969 942627 (Mbl)

24 Edinburgh: Duddingston (H) (E-mail: dodinskirk@aol.com)
James A.P. Jack DMin BSc BArch BD   1989   2001   Manse of Duddingston, Old Church Lane, Edinburgh EH15 3PX   0131-661 4240
                                                          [E-mail: jamesapjack@aol.com]

25 Edinburgh: Fairmilehead (H) (0131-445 2374) (E-mail: fairmilehead_p.c@btconnect.com)
John R. Munro BD   1976   1992   6 Braid Crescent, Edinburgh EH10 6AU   0131-446 9363
                                                          [E-mail: revjohnmunro@hotmail.com]

26 Edinburgh: Gilmerton (New Charge Development)
Paul H. Beautyman MA BD   1993   2002   43 Ravenscroft Street, Edinburgh EH17 8QJ   0131-664 7538
                                                          [E-mail: ncdgilmerton@uk.uumail.com]

27 Edinburgh: Gorgie (H) (0131-337 7936)
Peter I. Barber MA BD   1984   1995   90 Myreside Road, Edinburgh EH10 5BZ   0131-337 2284
                                                          [E-mail: pibarber@toucansurf.com]

28 Edinburgh: Granton (H) (0131-552 3033)
Norman A. Smith MA BD   1997   2005   8 Wardie Crescent, Edinburgh EH5 1AG   0131-551 2159
                                                          [E-mail: norm@smith1971.fsnet.co.uk]
Marilynn Steele (Mrs) DCS   2 Northfield Gardens, Prestonpans EH32 9LQ   01875   811497
                                                          [E-mail: marilynmsteele@aol.com]

29 Edinburgh: Greenbank (H) (0131-447 9969) (E-mail: greenbankchurch@btconnect.com)
Alison J. Swindells (Mrs) LLB BD   1998   2007   112 Greenbank Crescent, Edinburgh EH10 5SZ   0131-447 4032
                                                          [E-mail: alisonswindells@aol.com]

30 Edinburgh: Greenside (H) (0131-556 5588)
Andrew F. Anderson MA BD 1981 80 Pilrig Street, Edinburgh EH6 5AS [E-mail: andrew@pilrig.fsnet.co.uk] 0131-554 3277 (Tel/Fax)

31 Edinburgh: Greyfriars Tolbooth and Highland Kirk (GE) (H) (0131-225 1900) (E-mail: enquiries@greyfriarskirk.com)
Richard E. Frazer BA BD DMin 1986 2003 12 Tantallon Place, Edinburgh EH9 1NZ [E-mail: tantallon@ukonline.co.uk] 0131-667 6610

32 Edinburgh: High (St Giles') (0131-225 4363) (E-mail: stgilescathedral@btconnect.com)
Gilleasbuig Macmillan CVO MA BD Drhc DD 1969 1973 St Giles' Cathedral, Edinburgh EH1 1RE [E-mail: minister.stgiles@btconnect.com] 0131-225 4363
Hilary W. Smith (Miss) BD DipMin MTh PhD (Assistant) 1999 2003 11 South Lauder Road, Edinburgh EH9 2NB [E-mail: heloise.smith@virgin.net] 0131-667 6539

33 Edinburgh: Holyrood Abbey (H) (0131-661 4883)
Philip R. Hair BD 1980 1998 100 Willowbrae Avenue, Edinburgh EH8 7HU [E-mail: phil@holyroodabbey.f2s.com] 0131-652 0640

34 Edinburgh: Holy Trinity (H) (0131-442 3304)
Kenneth S. Borthwick MA BD 1983 2005 16 Thorburn Road, Edinburgh EH13 0BQ [E-mail: kennysamuel@aol.com] 0131-441 1403
Ian MacDonald (Assoc) 2005 12 Sighthill Crescent, Edinburgh EH11 4QE 0131-453 6279
Joyce Mitchell (Mrs) DCS 16/4 Murrayburn Place, Edinburgh EH14 2RR 0131-453 6548
Oliver M. Clegg BD (Youth Minister) 2003 256/5 Lanark Road, Edinburgh EH14 2LR 0131-443 0825

35 Edinburgh: Inverleith (H)
D. Hugh Davidson MA 1965 1975 43 Inverleith Gardens, Edinburgh EH3 5PR [E-mail: hdavidson@freeuk.com] 0131-552 3874

36 Edinburgh: Juniper Green (H)
James S. Dewar MA BD 1983 2000 476 Lanark Road, Juniper Green, Edinburgh EH14 5BQ [E-mail: jim.dewar@blueyonder.co.uk] 0131-453 3494

37 Edinburgh: Kaimes Lockhart Memorial
Iain D. Penman BD 1977 1995 76 Lasswade Road, Edinburgh EH16 6SF [E-mail: iainpenmanklm@aol.com] 0131-664 2287

38 Edinburgh: Kirkliston
Glenda J. Keating (Mrs) MTh 1996 43 Main Street, Kirkliston EH29 9AF [E-mail: kirkglen@aol.com] 0131-333 3298

39 Edinburgh: Kirk o' Field (T) (H)
Ian D. Maxwell MA BD PhD 1977 1996 31 Hatton Place, Edinburgh EH9 1UA [E-mail: i.d.maxwell@quista.net] 0131-667 7954

40   Edinburgh: Leith North (H) (0131-553 7378) (E-mail: nlpc-office@btinternet.com)
Kenneth S. Baird   1998   2003   6 Craighall Gardens, Edinburgh EH6 4RJ   0131-552 4411
  MSc PhD BD CEng MIMarEST

41   Edinburgh: Leith St Andrew's (H)
Elizabeth J.B. Youngson BD   1996   2006   30 Lochend Road, Edinburgh EH6 8BS   0131-554 7695
                                           [E-mail: elizabeth.youngson@virgin.net]

42   Edinburgh: Leith St Serf's (T) (H)
Sara R. Embleton (Mrs) BA BD MTh   1987   1999   20 Wilton Road, Edinburgh EH16 5NX   0131-478 1624
                                                 [E-mail: sara.embleton@blueyonder.co.uk]

43   Edinburgh: Leith St Thomas' Junction Road (T)
George C. Shand MA BD   1981   2003   107 Easter Warriston, Edinburgh EH7 4QZ   0131-467 7789
                                          [E-mail: georgeshand@blueyonder.co.uk]

44   Edinburgh: Leith South (H) (0131-554 2578) (E-mail: slpc@dial.pipex.com)
Ian Y. Gilmour BD   1985   1995   37 Claremont Road, Edinburgh EH6 7NN   0131-554 3062
                                         [E-mail: IanYG@blueyonder.co.uk]
Louise Duncan (Mrs) BD (Assoc)   2005   25 Elmwood Terrace, Edinburgh EH6 8DF   0131-538 0243

45   Edinburgh: Leith Wardie (H) (0131-551 3847) (E-mail: churchoffice@wardie.org.uk)
Brian C. Hilsley LLB BD   1990   35 Lomond Road, Edinburgh EH5 3JN   0131-552 3328
                                         [E-mail: brian@wardie10.freeserve.co.uk]

46   Edinburgh: Liberton (H)
John N. Young MA BD PhD   1996   7 Kirk Park, Edinburgh EH16 6HZ   0131-664 3067
                                         [E-mail: LLLjyoung@btinternet.com]

47   Edinburgh: Liberton Northfield (H) (0131-551 3847)
John M. McPake LTh   2000   9 Claverhouse Drive, Edinburgh EH16 6BR   0131-658 1754
                                         [E-mail: john_mcpake9@yahoo.co.uk]

48   Edinburgh: London Road (H) (0131-661 1149)
Sigrid Marten   1997   2006   26 Inchview Terrace, Edinburgh EH7 6TQ   0131-669 5311
                                         [E-mail: minister.lrpc@phonecoop.coop]

49   Edinburgh: Marchmont St Giles' (H) (0131-447 4359)
Karen K. Watson BD MTh   1997   2002   19 Hope Terrace, Edinburgh EH9 2AP   0131-447 2834
                                         [E-mail: kkw@btinternet.com]

50   Edinburgh: Mayfield Salisbury (0131-667 1522)
Scott S. McKenna BA BD MTh   1994   2000   26 Seton Place, Edinburgh EH9 2JT   0131-667 1286
                                           [E-mail: scottsmckenna@aol.com]

51 **Edinburgh: Morningside (H) (0131-447 6745) (E-mail: office@morningsideparishchurch.net)**
Derek Browning MA BD DMin   1987   2003   20 Braidburn Crescent, Edinburgh EH10 6EN   0131-447 1617 (Tel/Fax)
                                                          [E-mail: derek.browning@btinternet.com]   07050 133876 (Mbl)

52 **Edinburgh: Morningside United (H) (0131-447 3152)**
John R. Smith MA BD   1973   1998   1 Midmar Avenue, Edinburgh EH10 6BS   0131-447 8724
                                                          [E-mail: jrs@blueyonder.co.uk]

53 **Edinburgh: Muirhouse St Andrew's (E)**
R. Russell McLarty MA BD   1985   2006   9 Sanderson's Wynd, Tranent EH33 1DA   01875 614496
(Interim Minister)
Brenda Robson PhD (Auxiliary Minister)   Old School House, 2 Baird Road, Ratho, Newbridge EH28 8RA   0131-333 2746
                                                          [E-mail: brendarobson@tiscali.co.uk]

54 **Edinburgh: Murrayfield (H) (0131-337 1091) (E-mail: mpchurch@btconnect.com)**
William D. Brown BD CQSW   1987   2001   45 Murrayfield Gardens, Edinburgh EH12 6DH   0131-337 5431
                                                          [E-mail: wdb@fish.co.uk]

55 **Edinburgh: Newhaven (H)**
Vacant   158 Granton Road, Edinburgh EH5 3RF   0131-552 8906

56 **Edinburgh: New Restalrig (H) (0131-661 5676)**
David L. Court BSc BD   1989   2000   19 Abercorn Road, Edinburgh EH8 7DP   0131-661 4045
                                                          [E-mail: david@dlc.org.uk]

57 **Edinburgh: Old Kirk (H) (0131-332 4354) (E-mail: minister.oldkirk@btinternet.com)**
Tony McLean-Foreman   1987   2007   24 Pennywell Road, Edinburgh EH4 4HD   0131-332 4354
                                                          [E-mail: tony@foreman.org.uk]

58 **Edinburgh: Palmerston Place (H) (0131-220 1690) (E-mail: admin@palmerstonplacechurch.com)**
Colin A.M. Sinclair BA BD   1981   1996   30B Cluny Gardens, Edinburgh EH10 6BJ   0131-447 9598
                                                          [E-mail: colins.ppc@virgin.net]   0131-225 3312 (Fax)

59 **Edinburgh: Pilrig St Paul's (0131-553 1876)**
John M. Tait BSc BD   1985   78 Pilrig Street, Edinburgh EH6 5AS   0131-554 1842
                                                          [E-mail: john.m.tait@blueyonder.co.uk]

60 **Edinburgh: Polwarth (H) (0131-346 2711) (E-mail: polwarthchurch@tiscali.co.uk)**
Linda J. Dunbar BSc BA BD PhD FRHS   2000   2005   88 Craiglockhart Road, Edinburgh EH14 1EP   0131-441 5335
                                                          [E-mail: polwarthminister@ouvip.com]

61 **Edinburgh: Portobello Old (H)**
Andrew R.M. Patterson MA BD   1985   2006   6 Hamilton Terrace, Edinburgh EH15 1NB   0131-657 5545

62 Edinburgh: Portobello St James' (H)
Peter Webster BD   1977 2002   34 Brighton Place, Edinburgh EH15 1LT   0131-669 1767
[E-mail: peterwebster101@hotmail.com]

63 Edinburgh: Portobello St Philip's Joppa (H) (0131-669 3641)
Stewart G. Weaver BA BD PhD   2003   6 St Mary's Place, Edinburgh EH15 2QF   0131-669 2410
[E-mail: stewartweaver@beeb.net]

64 Edinburgh: Priestfield (H) (0131-667 5644)
Thomas N. Johnston LTh   1972 1990   13 Lady Road, Edinburgh EH16 5PA   0131-668 1620
[E-mail: tomjohnston@blueyonder.co.uk]

65 Edinburgh: Queensferry (H) See Edinburgh: Dalmeny

66 Edinburgh: Ratho
Ian J. Wells BD   1999   2 Freelands Road, Ratho, Newbridge EH28 8NP   0131-333 1346
[E-mail: ianjwells@btinternet.com]

67 Edinburgh: Reid Memorial (H) (0131-662 1203) (E-mail: reid.memorial@btinternet.com)
Brian M. Embleton BD   1976 1985   20 Wilton Road, Edinburgh EH16 5NX   0131-667 3981
[E-mail: brianembleton@btinternet.com]

68 Edinburgh: Richmond Craigmillar (H) (0131-661 6561)
Elizabeth M. Henderson (Miss)   1985 1997   13 Wisp Green, Edinburgh EH15 3QX   0131-669 1133
MA BD MTh
[E-mail: lizhende@tiscali.co.uk]

69 Edinburgh: St Andrew's and St George's (H) (0131-225 3847) (E-mail: info@standrewsandstgeorges.org.uk)
Roderick D.M. Campbell TD BD FSAScot   1975 2003   25 Comely Bank, Edinburgh EH4 1AJ   0131-332 5324
[E-mail: rdmcampbell@aol.com]
Dorothy U. Anderson LLB DipLP BD   2006   5 West Castle Road, Edinburgh EH10 5AT   0131-229 5862
(Outreach Minister)

70 Edinburgh: St Andrew's Clermiston
Alistair H. Keil BD DipMin   1989   87 Drum Brae South, Edinburgh EH12 8TD   0131-339 4149
[E-mail: ahkeil@blueyonder.co.uk]

71 Edinburgh: St Catherine's Argyle (H) (0131-667 7220)
Victor W.N. Laidlaw BD   1975   5 Palmerston Road, Edinburgh EH9 1TL   0131-667 9344
[E-mail: viclaid@aol.com]

72 Edinburgh: St Colm's (T) (H)
Douglas S. Paterson MA BD   1976 2005   5 Groathill Loan, Edinburgh EH4 2WL   0131-315 4541
[E-mail: dostpa@aol.com]

73 Edinburgh: St Cuthbert's (H) (0131-229 1142) (E-mail: office@stcuthberts.net)
Vacant
34A Murrayfield Road, Edinburgh EH12 6ER
0131-337 6637

74 Edinburgh: St David's Broomhouse (H) (0131-443 9851)
Robert A. Mackenzie LLB BD   1993   2005
33 Traquair Park West, Edinburgh EH12 7AN
[E-mail: rob.anne@blueyonder.co.uk]
0131-334 1730

Liz Crocker (Mrs) DipComEd DCS
77C Craigcrook Road, Edinburgh EH4 3PH
0131-332 0227

75 Edinburgh: St George's West (H) (0131-225 7001) (E-mail: st-georges-west@btconnect.com)
Peter J. Macdonald BD DipMin   1986   1998
6 Wardie Avenue, Edinburgh EH5 2AB
[E-mail: peter@stgeorgeswest.com]
0131-552 4333

76 Edinburgh: St John's Oxgangs
Gillean P. Maclean (Mrs) BD   1994   2003
2 Caiystane Terrace, Edinburgh EH10 6SR
[E-mail: gmaclean@fish.co.uk]
0131-445 1688

77 Edinburgh: St Margaret's (H) (0131-554 7400) (E-mail: stm.parish@virgin.net)
Carol H.M. Ford DSD RSAMD BD   2003
43 Moira Terrace, Edinburgh EH7 6TD
[E-mail: fordcar@fish.co.uk]
0131-669 7329

Pauline Rycroft-Sadi (Mrs) DCS   2006
6 Ashville Terrace, Edinburgh EH6 8DD
0131-554 6564

78 Edinburgh: St Martin's
Vacant
5 Duddingston Crescent, Edinburgh EH15 3AS
0131-657 9894

79 Edinburgh: St Michael's (H) (E-mail: office@stmichaels-kirk.co.uk)
James D. Aitken BD   2002   2005
9 Merchiston Gardens, Edinburgh EH10 5DD
[E-mail: james.aitken2@btinternet.com]
0131-346 1970

80 Edinburgh: St Nicholas' Sighthill
Vacant
122 Sighthill Loan, Edinburgh EH11 4NT
0131-453 6921

81 Edinburgh: St Stephen's Comely Bank (0131-315 4616)
Jonathan de Groot BD MTh CPS   2007
8 Blinkbonny Crescent, Edinburgh EH4 3NB
[E-mail: jdeg@blueyonder.co.uk]
0131-332 3364

82 Edinburgh: Slateford Longstone
Michael W. Frew BSc BD   1978   2005
50 Kingsknowe Road South, Edinburgh EH14 2JW
[E-mail: mwfrew@blueyonder.co.uk]
0131-466 5308

83 Edinburgh: Stenhouse St Aidan's
Vacant
65 Balgreen Road, Edinburgh EH12 5UA
0131-337 7711

84 Edinburgh: Stockbridge (H) (0131-332 0122)

| Anne T. Logan (Mrs) MA BD MTh DMin | 1981 | 1993 | 19 Eildon Street, Edinburgh EH3 5JU | 0131-557 6052 |

[E-mail: annetlogan@blueyonder.co.uk]

85 Edinburgh: Tron Moredun

| Scott C. Blythe BSc BD MBA | 1997 | 2006 | 467 Gilmerton Road, Edinburgh EH17 7JG | 0131-666 2584 |

[E-mail: blythescott@yahoo.co.uk]

86 Edinburgh: Viewforth (T) (H) (0131-229 1917)

| Anthony P. Thornthwaite MTh | | 1995 | 91 Morningside Drive, Edinburgh EH10 5NN | 0131-447 6684 |

[E-mail: tony.thornthwaite@blueyonder.co.uk]

Name			Charge/Position	Address	Telephone
Aitken, Alexander R. MA	1965	1997	(Newhaven)	36 King's Meadow, Edinburgh EH16 5JW	0131-667 1404
Aitken, Ewan R. BA BD	1992	2002	City of Edinburgh Council	159 Restalrig Avenue, Edinburgh EH7 6PJ	0131-467 1660
Anderson, Robert S. BD	1988	1997	Scottish Churches World Exchange	St Colm's International House, 23 Inverleith Terrace, Edinburgh EH3 5NS	0131-315 4444
Armitage, William L. BSc BD	1976	2006	(Edinburgh: London Road)	27 West Windygoul Gardens, Tranent EH33 2LB [E-mail: bill@billarm.plus.com]	01875 612047
Auld, A. Graeme MA BD PhD DLitt FSAScot FRSE	1973	1973	University of Edinburgh	Nether Swanshiel, Hobkirk, Bonchester Bridge, Hawick TD9 8JU	
Baigrie, R.A. MA	1945	1985	(Kirkurd with Newlands)	32 Inchcolm Terrace, South Queensferry EH30 9NA	0131-331 4311
Barrington, Charles W.H. MA BD	1997	2007	(Associate: Edinburgh: Balerno)	502 Lanark Road, Edinburgh EH14 5DH	0131-453 4826
Baxter, Richard F. OBE MA BD	1954	1990	(Assistant at St Andrew's and St George's)	138 Braid Road, Edinburgh EH10 6JB	0131-447 7735
Beckett, David M. BA BD	1964	2002	(Greyfriars, Tolbooth and Highland Kirk)	1FI, 31 Sciennes Road, Edinburgh EH9 1NT [E-mail: davidbeckett3@aol.com]	0131-667 2672
Blakey, Ronald S. MA BD MTh	1962	2000	Editor: *The Year Book*	5 Moss Side Road, Biggar ML12 6GF	01899 229226
Booth, Jennifer (Mrs) BD	1996	2004	(Associate: Leith South)	39 Lilyhill Terrace, Edinburgh EH8 7DR	0131-661 3813
Boyd, Kenneth M. MA BD PhD FRCPE	1970	1996	University of Edinburgh: Medical Ethics	1 Doune Terrace, Edinburgh EH3 6DY	0131-225 6485
Brady, Ian D. BSc ARCST BD	1967	2001	(Edinburgh: Corstorphine Old)	28 Frankfield Crescent, Dalgety Bay, Dunfermline KY11 9LW [E-mail: pidb@dbay28.fsnet.co.uk]	01383 825104
Brown, William D. MA	1963	1989	(Wishaw: Thornlie)	9/3 Craigend Park, Edinburgh EH16 5XY [E-mail: wdbrown@surefish.co.uk]	0131-672 2936
Bruce, Lilian M. (Miss) BD MTh	1971	2001	(Daviot and Dunlichity with Moy, Dalarossie and Tomatin)	33 Falcon Court, Edinburgh EH10 4AF	
Cameron, G. Gordon MA BD STM	1957	1997	(Juniper Green)	4 Ladywell Grove, Clackmannan FK10 4JQ	01259 723769
Cameron, John W.M. MA BD	1957	1996	(Liberton)	10 Plewlands Gardens, Edinburgh EH10 5JP	0131-447 1277
Chalmers, John P. BD	1979	1995	Ministries Council	10 Liggars Place, Dunfermline KY12 7XZ	01383 739130
Chalmers, Murray MA	1965	2006	(Hospital Chaplain)	8 Easter Warriston, Edinburgh EH7 4QX	0131-552 4211
Clinkenbeard, William W. BSc BD STM	1966	2000	(Edinburgh: Carrick Knowe)	4 Aline Court, Dalgety Bay, Dunfermline KY11 5GP [E-mail: bjclinks@compuserve.com]	01383 824011
Cook, John MA BD	1967	2005	(Edinburgh: Leith St Andrew's)	26 Silverknowes Court, Edinburgh EH4 5NR	0131-312 8447
Cook, John Weir MA BD	1962	2002	(Edinburgh: Portobello St Philip's Joppa)	74 Pinkie Road, Musselburgh EH21 7QT [E-mail: jwc@freeuk.com]	0131-653 0992
Crichton, Thomas JP ChStJ MA	1965	2004	(Hospital Chaplain)	18 Carlton Terrace, Edinburgh EH7 5DD	0131-557 0009
Cross, Brian F. MA	1961	1998	(Coalburn)	1474 High Road, Whetstone, London N20 9QD	0208 492 9313

Name			Position	Address	Tel.
Cuthell, Tom C. MA BD MTh	1965	2007	(Edinburgh: St Cuthbert's)	Flat 10, 2 Kingsburgh Crescent, Waterfront, Edinburgh EH5 1JS	0131-664 0074
Davidson, Ian M.P. MBE MA BD	1957	1994	(Stirling: Allan Park South with Church of the Holy Rude)	13/8 Craigend Park, Edinburgh EH16 5XX	
Dawson, Michael S. BTech BD	1979	2005	(Associate: Edinburgh: Holy Trinity)	9 The Broich, Alva FK12 5NR [E-mail: mixpen.dawson@btinternet.com]	01259 769309
Dilbey, Mary D. (Miss) BD	1997	2002	(West Kirk of Calder)	41 Bonaly Rise, Edinburgh EH13 0QU	0131-441 9092
Dougall, Elspeth G. (Mrs) MA BD	1989	2001	(Edinburgh: Marchmont St Giles')	60B Craigmillar Park, Edinburgh EH16 5PU	0131-668 1342
Douglas, Colin R. MA BD STM	1969	2007	(Livingston Ecumenical Parish)	34 West Pilton Gardens, Edinburgh EH4 4EQ [E-mail: colinrdouglas@btinternet.com]	0131-551 3808
Doyle, Ian B. MA BD PhD	1946	1991	(Department of National Mission)	21 Lygon Road, Edinburgh EH16 5QD	0131-667 2697
Drummond, Rhoda (Miss) DCS			(Deaconess)	Flat K, 23 Grange Loan, Edinburgh EH9 2ER	0131-668 3631
Dunn, W. Iain C. DA LTh	1983	1998	(Pilrig and Dalmeny Street)	10 Fox Covert Avenue, Edinburgh EH12 6UQ	0131-334 1665
Elliott, Gavin J. MA BD	1976	2004	(Ministries Council)	c/o 121 George Street, Edinburgh EH2 4YN	0131-225 5722
Farquharson, Gordon MA BD DipEd	1998	2007	(Stonehaven: Dunnottar)	26 Learmonth Court, Edinburgh EH4 1PB [E-mail: gfarqu@talktalk.net]	0131-343 1047
Faulds, Norman L. MA BD FSAScot	1968	2000	(Aberlady with Gullane)	10 West Fenton Court, West Fenton, North Berwick EH39 5AE	01620 842331
Fergusson, David A.S. MA BD DPhil FRSE	1984	2000	University of Edinburgh	23 Riselaw Crescent, Edinburgh EH10 6HN	0131-447 4022
Forrester, Duncan B. MA BD DPhil DD FRSE	1962	1978	(University of Edinburgh)	25 Kingsburgh Road, Edinburgh EH12 6DZ	0131-337 5646
Forrester, Margaret R. (Mrs) MA BD	1974	2003	(Edinburgh: St Michael's)	25 Kingsburgh Road, Edinburgh EH12 6DZ [E-mail: margaret@theforesters.fsnet.co.uk]	0131-337 5646
Fraser, Shirley A. (Miss) MA BD	1992	2001	Scottish Field Director: Friends International	30 Parkhead Avenue, Edinburgh EH11 4SG	0131-443 7268
Fyall, Robert S. MA BD PhD	1986	1989	Warden: Rutherford House	Rutherford House, 17 Claremont Park, Edinburgh EH6 7PJ	0131-554 1206
Galbraith, Douglas MA BD BMus MPhil ARSCM	1965	2005	(Office for Worship, Doctrine and Artistic Matters)	c/o 121 George Street, Edinburgh EH2 4YN [E-mail: dgalbraith@cofscotland.org.uk]	0131-240 2233
Gardner, John V.	1997	2003	(Glamis, Inverarity and Kinnettles)	104 Comiston Drive, Edinburgh EH10 5QU [E-mail: jvg66@hotmail.com]	0131-447 6859
Gibson, John C.L. MA BD DPhil	1959	1994	(University of Edinburgh)	Cairnbank, Morton Street South, Edinburgh EH15 2NB	0131-669 3635
Gordon, Tom MA BD	1974	1994	Chaplain: Fairmile Marie Curie Centre	22 Gosford Road, Port Seton, Prestonpans EH32 0HF	01875 812262
Graham, W. Peter MA BD	1967	1993	Presbytery Clerk	23/6 East Comiston, Edinburgh EH10 6RZ [E-mail: edinburgh@cofscotland.org.uk]	0131-445 5763
Harkness, James CB OBE QHC MA DD	1961	1995	(Chaplain General: Army)	13 Saxe Coburg Place, Edinburgh EH3 5BR	0131-343 1297
Hill, J. William BA BD	1967	2001	(Corstorphine St Anne's)	33/9 Murrayfield Road, Edinburgh EH12 6EP	0131-332 8020
Hutchison, Maureen (Mrs) DCS	1985	2005	(Deaconess)	23 Drylaw Crescent, Edinburgh EH4 2AU	0131-441 3384
Irving, William D. LTh			(Golspie)	122 Swanston Muir, Edinburgh EH10 7HY	
Jamieson, Gordon D. MA BD	1974	2000	Director of Stewardship	41 Goldpark Place, Livingston EH54 6LW	01506 412020
Jeffrey, Eric W.S. JP MA	1954	1994	(Edinburgh Bristo Memorial)	18 Gillespie Crescent, Edinburgh EH10 4HT	0131-229 7815
Kant, Everard FVCM MTh	1953	1988	(Kinghorn)	10/1 Maxwell Street, Edinburgh EH10 5GZ	0131-466 2607
Kelly, Ewan R. MB ChB BD PhD	1994	2006	Chaplain: St Columba's Hospice	15 Boswall Road, Edinburgh EH5 3RW	0131-551 7706
Lawson, Kenneth C. MA BD	1963	1999	(Adviser in Adult Education)	56 Easter Drylaw View, Edinburgh EH4 2QP	0131-539 3311
Lyon, D.H.S. MA BD STM	1952	1986	(Board of World Mission and Unity)	7 Marchbank Gardens, Balerno EH14 7ET	0131-449 5031
McCaskill, George I.L. MA BD	1953	1990	(Religious Education)	19 Tyler's Acre Road, Edinburgh EH12 7HY	0131-334 7451
Macdonald, Finlay A.J. MA BD PhD DD	1971	1996	Principal Clerk	c/o 121 George Street, Edinburgh EH2 4YN	0131-225 5722

Name			Position	Address	Tel
Macdonald, William J. BD	1976	2002	(Board of National Mission: New Charge Development)	1/13 North Werber Park, Edinburgh EH4 1SY	0131-332 0254
McGillivray, A. Gordon MA BD STM	1951	1993	(Presbytery Clerk)	7 Greenfield Crescent, Balerno EH14 7HD	0131-449 4747
MacGregor, Margaret S. (Miss) MA BD DipEd	1985	1994	(Calcutta)	16 Learmonth Court, Edinburgh EH4 1PB	0131-332 1089
McGregor, Alistair G.C. QC BD	1987	2002	(Edinburgh: Leith North)	22 Primrose Bank Road, Edinburgh EH5 3JG	0131-551 2802
McGregor, T. Stewart MBE MA BD	1957	1998	(Chaplain: Edinburgh Royal Infirmary)	19 Lonsdale Terrace, Edinburgh EH3 9HL [E-mail: cetsm@dircon.uk]	0131-229 5332
Maclean, Ailsa G. (Mrs) BD DipCE LLB BD PhD	1979	1988	Chaplain: George Heriot's School	28 Swan Spring Avenue, Edinburgh EH10 6NJ	0131-445 1320
MacLean, Marjory A. (Miss) LLB BD PhD	1991	1998	Depute Clerk: General Assembly	c/o 121 George Street, Edinburgh EH2 4YN	0131-225 5722
McLellan, Andrew R.C. MA BD STM DD	1970	2002	HM Inspector of Prisons	4 Liggars Place, Dunfermline KY12 7XZ	01383 725959
McLeod, Roderick MA BD	1951	1990	(Lochwinnoch)	2 East Savile Road, Edinburgh EH16 5ND	0131-667 1475
McMahon, John K.S. MA BD	1998	2006	Lead Chaplain: NHS Lothian Primary Care and Mental Health	Department of Spiritual Care, Royal Edinburgh Hospital, Morningside Terrace, Edinburgh EH10 5HF [E-mail: john.mcmahon@1pct.scot.nhs.uk]	0131-220 5150
MacMurchie, F. Lynne LLB BD	1998	2003	Health Care Chaplain	Edinburgh Community Mental Health Chaplaincy, 41 George IV Bridge, Edinburgh EH1 1EL	
McPheat, Elspeth DCS	1953	1993	Deaconess: CrossReach	11/5 New Orchardfield, Edinburgh EH6 5ET	0131-554 4143
McPhee, Duncan C. MA BD	1967	1993	(Department of National Mission)	8 Belvedere Park, Edinburgh EH6 4LR	0131-552 6784
Macpherson, Allan S. MA	1958	1996	Merchiston Castle School	36 Craigmillar Castle Road, Edinburgh EH16 4AR	0131-667 1456
Macpherson, Colin C.R. MA BD			(Dunfermline St Margaret's)	7 Eva Place, Edinburgh EH9 3ET	0131-620 0589
Manners, Stephen MA BD	1989		(Edinburgh: Tron Moredun)	124 Fernieside Crescent, Edinburgh EH17 7DH	
Mathieson, Angus R. MA BD	1988	1998	Ministries Council	21 Traquair Park West, Edinburgh EH12 7AN	0131-334 9774
Middleton, Paul BMus BD ThM PhD	2000	2005	University of Wales: Lampeter	Department of Theology and Religious Studies, University of Wales, Lampeter, Ceredigion SA48 7ED [E-mail: p.middleton@lamp.ac.uk]	01570 424801
Moir, Ian A. MA BD	1962	2000	(Adviser for Urban Priority Areas)	28/6 Comely Bank Avenue, Edinburgh EH4 1EL	0131-332 2748
Monteith, W. Graham BD PhD	1974	1994	(Flotta and Fara with Hoy and Walls)	20/3 Grandfield, Edinburgh EH6 4TL	0131-552 2564
Morrice, William G. MA BD STM PhD	1957	1991	(St John's College Durham)	Flat 37, The Cedars, 2 Manse Road, Edinburgh EH12 7SN [E-mail: w.g.morrice@btinternet.com]	0131-316 4845
Morrison, Mary B. (Mrs) MA BD DipEd	1978	2000	(Edinburgh: Stenhouse St Aidan's)	14 Eildon Terrace, Edinburgh EH3 5LU	0131-556 1962
Morton, Andrew R. MA BD DD	1956	1994	(Board of World Mission and Unity)	11 Oxford Terrace, Edinburgh EH4 1PX	0131-332 6592
Morton, R. Colin BA BD	1960	1998	(Jerusalem)	313 Lanark Road West, Currie EH14 5RS	0131-449 7359
Moyes, Sheila A. (Miss) DCS			(Deaconess)	158 Pilton Avenue, Edinburgh EH5 2JZ	0131-551 1731
Mulligan, Anne MA DCS			Deaconess: Hospital Chaplain	27A Craigour Avenue, Edinburgh EH17 1NH	0131-664 3426
Munro, George A.M.	1968	2000	(Edinburgh: Cluny)	108 Caiyside, Edinburgh EH10 7HR	0131-445 5829
Murison, William G.	1951	1990	(Department of World Mission and Unity)	21 Hailes Gardens, Edinburgh EH13 0JL	0131-441 2460
Murrie, John BD	1953	1996	(Kirkliston)	31 Nicol Road, The Whins, Broxburn EH52 6JJ	01506 852464
Musgrave, Clarence W. BA BD ThM	1966	2006	(Jerusalem: St Andrew's)	4 Ravelston Heights, Edinburgh EH4 3LX [E-mail: cwm_edinburgh@biopenworld.com]	0131-332 6337
Neilson, Peter MA BD MTh	1975	2006	Mission Consultant	12 Strathalmond Court, Edinburgh EH4 8AE	0131-339 4536
Nicol, Douglas A.O. MA BD	1974	1991	Mission and Discipleship Council	24 Corbiehill Avenue, Edinburgh EH4 5DR	0131-336 1965
Page, Ruth MA BD DPhil	1976	2000	(University of Edinburgh)	22/5 West Mill Bank, West Mill Road, Edinburgh EH13 0QT	0131-441 3740
Paterson, J.M.K. MA ACII BD DD	1964	1987	(Milngavie: St Paul's)	58 Orchard Drive, Edinburgh EH4 2DZ	
Patterson, John M.	1976	1987	(Blackbraes and Shieldhill)	Flat 20, Murrayfield House, 66 Murrayfield Avenue, Edinburgh EH12 6AY	0131-332 5876

Name	Position			Address	Telephone
Philip, James MA	(Holyrood Abbey)	1948	1997	3 Ferguson Gardens, Musselburgh EH21 6XF	0131-653 2310
Philp, Connie (Miss) BD	(Arbuthnott with Bervie)	1980	1995	Oaklands, 35 Canaan Lane, Edinburgh EH10 4SG	0131-339 8539
Plate, Maria A.G. (Miss) LTh BA	(South Ronaldsay and Burray)	1983	2000	Flat 29, 77 Barnton Park View, Edinburgh EH4 6EL	0131-557 2144
Potts, Jean (Miss) DCS	(Deaconess)	1950	1990	28B East Claremont Street, Edinburgh EH7 4JP	0131-447 7642
Reid, W. Scott BD MA DipPS PhD	(St Colm's)	1958	1990	14/37 Ethel Terrace, Edinburgh EH10 5NA	0131-447 0601
Renton, Ian P.	(London Road)	1982	2000	98 Homeross House, Strathearn Road, Edinburgh EH9 2QY	0131-333 2711
Ridland, Alistair K. MA BD	(Chaplain: Western General Hospital)	1965	2005	13 Stewart Place, Kirkliston EH29 0BQ	0131-662 9025
Robertson, Charles LVO MA	(Edinburgh: Canongate)			3 Ross Gardens, Edinburgh EH9 3BS	0131-334 8736
Ronald, Norma A. (Miss) MBE DCS	(Deaconess)	1958	1998	2B Saughton Road North, Edinburgh EH12 7HG	0131-228 8984
Ross, Andrew C. MA BD STM PhD	(University of Edinburgh)	1982	1999	20 Forbes Road, Edinburgh EH10 4ED	0131-225 5722
Ross, Kenneth R. BA BD PhD	(World Mission Council)	1960	2000	c/o 121 George Street, Edinburgh EH2 4YN	0131-449 4745
Schofield, Melville F. MA	(Chaplain: Western General Hospitals)	1965	2006	25 Rowantree Grove, Currie EH14 5AT	01875 612907
Scott, Ian G. BSc BD STM	(Edinburgh: Greenbank)			50 Forthview Walk, Tranent EH33 1FE [E-mail: iandascott@tiscali.co.uk]	
Scott, Martin DipMusEd RSAM BD PhD	(Ministries Council)	1986	2000	18 Covenanters Rise, Dunfermline KY11 8QS	01383 722328
Shewan, Frederick D. MA BD	(Edinburgh: Muirhouse St Andrew's)	1970	2005	38 Tremayne Place, Dunfermline KY12 9YH	01383 734354
Sim, John G. MA	(Kirkcaldy: Old)	1946	1987	7 Grosvenor Crescent, Edinburgh EH12 5EP	0131-226 3190
Skinner, Donald M. MBE JP FIES	(Edinburgh: Gilmerton)	1962	2000	12 Sraid-a-Cnoc, Clynder, Helensburgh G84 0QX	01436 831795
Slorach, Alexander CA BD	(Kirk of Lammermuir with Langton and Polwarth)	1970	2002	61 Inverleith Row, Edinburgh EH3 5PX	
Stephen, Donald M. TD MA BD ThM	(Edinburgh: Marchmont St Giles')	1962	2001	10 Hawkhead Crescent, Edinburgh EH16 6LR	0131-658 1216
Stevenson, John MA BD PhD	(Department of Education)	1963	2001	12 Swanston Gardens, Edinburgh EH10 7DL	0131-445 3960
Stirling, A. Douglas BSc	(Rhu and Shandon)	1956	1994	162 Avontoun Park, Linlithgow EH49 6QH	01506 845021
Stiven, Iain K. MA BD	(Strachur and Strathlachlan)	1960	1997	7 Gloucester Place, Edinburgh EH3 6EE	0131-225 8177
Taylor, Howard G. BSc BD MTh	(Chaplain: Heriot Watt University)	1971	1998	The Chaplaincy, Heriot Watt University, Riccarton, Currie EH14 4AS	0131-449 5111 (ext 4508)
Taylor, William R. MA BD	(Chaplaincy Co-ordinator: Scottish Prison Service)	1983	2003	33 Kingsknowe Drive, Edinburgh EH14 2JY	
Teague, Yvonne (Mrs) DCS	(Board of Ministry)			46 Craigcrook Avenue, Edinburgh EH4 3PX	0131-336 3113
Telfer, Iain J.M. BD DPS	(Chaplain: Royal Infirmary)	1978	2001	Royal Infirmary of Edinburgh, 51 Little France Crescent, Edinburgh EH16 4SA	0131-242 1997
Thom, Helen (Miss) DCS	(Deaconess)			84 Great King Street, Edinburgh EH3 6QU	0131-556 5687
Torrance, Thomas F. MBE DLitt DD DSc DrTheol DrfTeol FBA FRSE	(University of Edinburgh)	1940	1979	37 Braid Farm Road, Edinburgh EH10 6LE	
Whyte, Iain A. BA BD STM PhD	(Community Mental Health Chaplain)	1968	2001	14 Carlingnose Point, North Queensferry, Inverkeithing KY11 1ER [E-mail: iainisabel@whytes28.fsnet.co.uk]	01383 410732
Wigglesworth, J. Christopher MBE BSc PhD BD	(St Andrew's College, Selly Oak)	1968	1999	12 Leven Terrace, Edinburgh EH3 9LW	0131-228 6335
Wilkie, James L. MA BD	(Board of World Mission)	1959	1998	7 Comely Bank Avenue, Edinburgh EH4 1EW [E-mail: jl.wilkie@btinternet.com]	0131-343 1552
Wilkinson, John BD MD FRCP DTM&H	(Kikuyu)	1946	1975	70 Craigleith Hill Gardens, Edinburgh EH4 2JH	0131-332 2994
Williams, Jenny M. (Miss) BSc CQSW BD	(Christian Fellowship of Healing)	1996	1997	16 Blantyre Terrace, Edinburgh EH10 5AE	0131-447 0050
Wilson, John M. MA	(Adviser in Religious Education)	1964	1995	27 Bellfield Street, Edinburgh EH15 2BR	0131-669 5257
Young, Alexander W. BD DipMin	(Chaplain: Royal Infirmary)	1988	1999	32 Lindsay Circus, The Hawthorns, Rosewell EH24 9EP	(Work) 0131-242 1997

EDINBURGH ADDRESSES

Albany	At Greenside
Balerno	Johnsburn Road, Balerno
Barclay	Barclay Place
Blackhall St Columba's	Queensferry Road
Bristo Memorial	Peffermill Road, Craigmillar
Broughton St Mary's	Bellevue Crescent
Canongate	Canongate
Carrick Knowe	North Saughton Road
Colinton	Dell Road
Colinton Mains	Oxgangs Road North
Corstorphine	
Craigsbank	Craig's Crescent
Old	Kirk Loan
St Anne's	Kaimes Road
St Ninian's	St John's Road
Craigentinny	
St Christopher's	Craigentinny Road
Craiglockhart	Craiglockhart Avenue
Craigmillar Park	Craigmillar Park
Cramond	Cramond Glebe Road
Currie	Kirkgate, Currie
Davidson's Mains	Quality Street
Dean	Dean Path
Drylaw	Groathill Road North
Duddingston	Old Church Lane, Duddingston
Fairmilehead	Frogston Road West, Fairmilehead
Gilmerton	Ravenscroft Street
Gorgie	Gorgie Road
Granton	Boswall Parkway
Greenbank	Braidburn Terrace
Greenside	Royal Terrace
Greyfriars Tolbooth and Highland Kirk	Greyfriars Place
High (St Giles')	High Street
Holyrood Abbey	Dalziel Place x London Road
Holy Trinity	Hailesland Place, Wester Hailes
Inverleith	Inverleith Gardens
Juniper Green	Lanark Road, Juniper Green
Kaimes Lockhart Memorial	Gracemount Drive
Kirkliston	The Square, Kirkliston
Kirk o' Field	Pleasance
Leith	
North	Madeira Street off Ferry Road
St Andrew's	Easter Road
St Serf's	Ferry Road
St Thomas', Junction Road	
South	Great Junction Street
Wardie	Kirkgate, Leith
Liberton	Primrosebank Road
Northfield	Kirkgate, Liberton
London Road	Gilmerton Road, Liberton
Marchmont St Giles'	London Road
Mayfield Salisbury	Kilgraston Road
Morningside	Mayfield Road x West Mayfield
Morningside United	Cluny Gardens
Muirhouse St Andrew's	Bruntsfield Place x Chamberlain Road
Murrayfield	Pennywell Gardens
Newhaven	Abinger Gardens
New Restalrig	Craighall Road
	Willowbrae Road
Old Kirk	Pennywell Road
Palmerston Place	Palmerston Place
Pilrig St Paul's	Pilrig Street
Polwarth	Polwarth Terrace x Harrison Road
Portobello	
Old	Bellfield Street
St James'	Rosefield Place
St Philip's Joppa	Abercorn Terrace
Priestfield	Dalkeith Road x Marchhall Place
Queensferry	The Loan, South Queensferry
Ratho	Baird Road, Ratho
Reid Memorial	West Savile Terrace
Richmond Craigmillar	Niddrie Mains Road
St Andrew's and St George's	George Street
St Andrew's Clermiston	Clermiston View
St Catherine's Argyle	Grange Road x Chalmers Crescent
St Colm's	Dalry Road x Cathcart Place
St Cuthbert's	Lothian Road
St David's Broomhouse	Broomhouse Crescent
St George's West	Shandwick Place
St John's Oxgangs	Oxgangs Road
St Margaret's	Restalrig Road South
St Martin's	Magdalene Drive
St Michael's	Slateford Road
St Nicholas' Sighthill	Calder Road
St Stephen's Comely Bank	Comely Bank
Slateford Longstone	Kingsknowe Road North
Stenhouse St Aidan's	Chesser Avenue
Stockbridge	Saxe Coburg Street
Tron Moredun	Fernieside Drive
Viewforth	Gilmore Place

(2) WEST LOTHIAN

Meets in the church of the incoming Moderator on the first Tuesday of September and in St John's Church Hall, Bathgate, on the first Tuesday of every other month, except December, when the meeting is on the second Tuesday, and in January, July and August, when there is no meeting.

Clerk: REV. DUNCAN SHAW BD MTh   St John's Manse, Mid Street, Bathgate **EH48 1QD**   01506 653146
[E-mail: westlothian@cofscotland.org.uk]

Abercorn (H) linked with Pardovan, Kingscavil (H) and Winchburgh (H)
A. Scott Marshall DipComm BD   1984 1998   The Manse, Winchburgh, Broxburn EH52 6TT   01506 890919
[E-mail: pkwla@aol.com]

Armadale (H)
Vacant

70 Mount Pleasant, Armadale, Bathgate EH48 3HB

01501 730358

Avonbridge (H) linked with Torphichen (H)
Clifford R. Acklam BD MTh   1997   2000
Manse Road, Torphichen, Bathgate EH48 4LT
[E-mail: cliff@torphichen.org]
01506 652794

Bathgate: Boghall (H)
Dennis S. Rose LTh   1996   2004
1 Manse Place, Ash Grove, Bathgate EH48 1NJ
[E-mail: dsrosekirk@aol.com]
01506 652940

Bathgate: High (H)
Ronald G. Greig MA BD   1987   1998
19 Hunter Grove, Bathgate EH48 1NN
[E-mail: rongreig@tiscali.co.uk]
01506 652654

Bathgate: St David's
Vacant
70 Marjoribanks Street, Bathgate EH48 1AL
01506 653177

Bathgate: St John's (H)
Duncan Shaw BD MTh   1975   1978
St John's Manse, Mid Street, Bathgate EH48 1QD
[E-mail: duncanshaw@uk.uumail.com]
01506 653146

Blackridge and Seafield (H)
Robert A. Anderson MA BD DPhil   1980   1998
The Manse, 5 MacDonald Gardens, Blackburn, Bathgate EH47 7RE
[E-mail: robertanderson307@btinternet.com]
01506 652825

Blackridge (H) linked with Harthill: St Andrew's (H)
Robert B. Gehrke BSc BD CEng MIEE   1994   2006
East Main Street, Harthill, Shotts ML7 5QW
[E-mail: bob.gehrke@gmail.com]
01501 751239

Breich Valley
Thomas Preston BD   1978   2001
Stoneyburn, Bathgate EH47 8AU
01501 762018

Broxburn (H)
Terry Taylor BA MTh   2005
2 Church Street, Broxburn EH52 5EL
[E-mail: revtaylor@tiscali.co.uk]
01506 852825

Fauldhouse: St Andrew's (H)
Elizabeth Smith (Mrs) BD   1996   2000
7 Glebe Court, Fauldhouse, Bathgate EH47 9DX
[E-mail: smithrevb@btinternet.com]
01501 771190

Harthill: St Andrew's See Blackridge

Kirknewton (H) and East Calder (H)
Ann M. Ballentine (Miss) MA BD 1981 1993 8 Manse Court, East Calder, Livingston EH53 0HF   01506 880802
[E-mail: annballentine@tiscali.co.uk]

Kirk of Calder (H)
John M. Povey MA BD 1981 19 Maryfield Park, Mid Calder, Livingston EH53 0SB   01506 882495
[E-mail: revjpovey@aol.com]
Phyllis Thomson (Miss) DCS 2003 63 Caroline Park, Mid Calder, Livingston EH53 0SJ   01506 883207

Linlithgow: St Michael's (H) (E-mail: info@stmichaels-parish.org.uk)
D. Stewart Gillan BSc MDiv PhD 1985 2004 St Michael's Manse, Kirkgate, Linlithgow EH49 7AL   01506 842195
[E-mail: stewart@stmichaels-parish.org.uk]
Thomas S. Riddell BSc (Aux) 1993 1994 4 The Maltings, Linlithgow EH49 6DS   01506 843251
[E-mail: tsriddell@blueyonder.co.uk]

Linlithgow: St Ninian's Craigmailen (H)
W. Richard Houston BSc BD 1998 2004 29 Philip Avenue, Linlithgow EH49 7BH   01506 202246
[E-mail: wrichardhouston@blueyonder.co.uk]

Livingston Ecumenical Parish
Incorporating the Worship Centres at:
Carmondean (H) and Knightsridge
Suzanna Bates BTh 13 Eastcroft Court, Livingston EH54 7ET   01506 464567
(The Methodist Church) [E-mail: rev.suzanna@btinternet.com]
Craigshill (St Columba's) and Ladywell (St Paul's)
Appointment awaited 27 Heatherbank, Ladywell, Livingston EH54 6EE   01506 432326
Dedridge and Murieston
Eileen Thompson BD MTh 53 Garry Walk, Craigshill, Livingston EH54 5AS   01506 433451
(Scottish Episcopal Church) [E-mail: eileenthompson@blueyonder.co.uk]

Livingston: Old (H)
Graham W. Smith BA BD FSAScot 1995 Manse of Livingston, Charlesfield Lane, Livingston EH54 7AJ   01506 420227
[E-mail: gws@livoldpar.org.uk]

Pardovan, Kingscavil and Winchburgh See Abercorn

Polbeth Harwood linked with West Kirk of Calder (H)
David A. Albon BA MCS 1991 2004 27 Learmonth Crescent, West Calder EH55 8AF   01506 870460
[E-mail: albon@onetel.com]

Strathbrock (H)
David W. Black BSc BD 1968 1984 1 Manse Park, Uphall, Broxburn EH52 6NX   01506 852550

Torphichen See Avonbridge

Uphall: South (H)

Margaret Steele (Miss) BSc BD	2000	8 Fernlea, Uphall, Broxburn EH52 6DF [E-mail: mdsteele@tiscali.co.uk]	01506 852788

West Kirk of Calder (H) See Polbeth Harwood

Whitburn: Brucefield (H)

Richard J.G. Darroch BD MTh	1993 2003	Brucefield Manse, Whitburn, Bathgate EH47 8NU [E-mail: richdarr@aol.com]	01501 740263

Whitburn: South (H)

Christine Houghton (Mrs) BD	1997 2004	5 Mansewood Crescent, Whitburn, Bathgate EH47 8HA [E-mail: c.houghton1@btinternet.com]	01501 740333

Name	Dates	(Previous charge)	Address	Telephone
Cameron, Ian MA BD	1953 1981	(Kilbrandon and Kilchattan)	Craigellen, West George Street, Blairgowrie PH10 6DZ	01250 872087
Dundas, Thomas B.S. LTh	1969 1996	(West Kirk of Calder)	35 Coolkill, Sandyford, Dublin 18, Republic of Ireland	00353 12953061
Mackay, Kenneth J. MA BD	1971 2007	(Edinburgh: St Nicholas' Sighthill)	46 Chuckethall Road, Livingston EH54 8FB [E-mail: knnth_mackay@yahoo.co.uk]	01506 410884
MacRae, Norman I. LTh	1966 2003	(Inverness: Trinity)	144 Hope Park Gardens, Bathgate EH48 2QX	01506 635254
Manson, Robert L. MA DPS	1956 1991	(Chaplain: Royal Edinburgh Hospital)	4 Murieston Drive, Livingston EH54 9AU [E-mail: roy@manson25.freeserve.co.uk]	01506 434746
Moore, J.W. MA	1950 1983	(Daviot with Rayne)	31 Lennox Gardens, Linlithgow EH49 7PZ	01506 842534
Morrice, Charles S. MA BD PhD	1959 1997	(Kenya)	104 Baron's Hill Avenue, Linlithgow EH49 7JG [E-mail: cs.morrice@blueyonder.co.uk]	01506 847167
Morrison, Iain C. BA BD	1990 2003	(Linlithgow: St Ninian's Craigmailen)	Whaligoe, 53 Eastcroft Drive, Polmont, Falkirk FK2 0SU [E-mail: iain@kirkweb.org]	01324 713249
Murray, Ronald N.G. MA	1946 1986	(Pardovan and Kingscavil with Winchburgh)	Linlithgow Nursing Home, 45 St Ninian's Road, Linlithgow EH49 7BW	
Nelson, Georgina (Mrs) MA BD PhD DipEd	1990 1995	(Hospital Chaplain)	63 Hawthorn Bank, Seafield, Bathgate EH47 7EB	
Nicol, Robert M.	1984 1996	(Jersey: St Columba's)	59 Kinloch View, Blackness Road, Linlithgow EH49 7HT	01506 670391
Russell, Archibald MA	1949 1991	(Duror with Glencoe)	The Chamberlain Nursing Home, 7–9 Chamberlain Road, Edinburgh EH10 4DJ	
Smith, W. Ewing BSc	1962 1994	(Livingston: Old)	8 Hardy Gardens, Bathgate EH48 1NH [E-mail: wesmith@hardygdns.freeserve.co.uk]	01506 652028
Trimble, Robert DCS	1973 2007	(Deacon)	5 Templar Rise, Dedridge, Livingston EH54 6PJ	01506 412504
Walker, Ian BD MEd DipMS		(Rutherglen: Wardlawhill)	92 Carseknowe, Linlithgow EH49 7LG [E-mail: walk102822@aol.com]	01506 844412
Whitson, William S. MA	1959 1999	(Cumbernauld: St Mungo's)	2 Chapman's Brae, Bathgate EH48 4LH [E-mail: william_whitson@tiscali.co.uk]	01506 650027

(3) LOTHIAN

Meets at Musselburgh: St Andrew's High Parish Church on the last Thursday of January and June and the first Thursday of March, April, May, September, October, November and December. (Alternative arrangements are made to avoid meeting on Maundy Thursday.)

Clerk: MR JOHN D. McCULLOCH DL   Auchindinny House, Penicuik EH26 8PE   01968 676300 (Tel/Fax)
[E-mail: lothian@cofscotland.org.uk]

Aberlady (H) linked with Gullane (H)
John B. Cairns LTh LLB LLD DD   1974   2001   The Manse, Hummel Road, Gullane EH31 2BG   01620 843192
[E-mail: johncairns@mail.com]

Athelstaneford linked with Whitekirk and Tyninghame
Kenneth D.F. Walker MA BD PhD   1976   The Manse, Athelstaneford, North Berwick EH39 5BE   01620 880378
[E-mail: kandy-walker@connectfree.co.uk]

Belhaven (H) linked with Spott
Laurence H. Twaddle MA BD MTh   1977   1978   The Manse, Belhaven Road, Dunbar EH42 1NH   01368 863098
[E-mail: revtwaddle@aol.com]

Bilston linked with Glencorse (H) linked with Roslin (H)
John R. Wells BD DipMin   1991   2005   31A Manse Road, Roslin EH25 9LG   0131-440 2012
[E-mail: wellsjr3@aol.com]

Bolton and Saltoun linked with Humbie linked with Yester (H)
Vacant   The Manse, Tweeddale Avenue, Gifford, Haddington EH41 4QN   01620 810515

Bonnyrigg (H)
John Mitchell LTh CMin   1991   9 Viewbank View, Bonnyrigg EH19 2HU   0131-663 8287 (Tel/Fax)
[E-mail: jmitchell241@tiscali.co.uk]

Borthwick (H) linked with Cranstoun, Crichton and Ford (H) linked with Fala and Soutra (H)
D. Graham Leitch MA BD   1974   2003   Cranstoun Cottage, Ford, Pathhead EH37 5RE   01875 320314
[E-mail: leitch@cranscott.fsnet.co.uk]
Andrew Don BD (Aux)   2006   5 Eskvale Court, Penicuik EH26 8HT   01968 675766
[E-mail: andrew.don@lineone.net]

Cockenzie and Port Seton: Chalmers Memorial (H)
Robert L. Glover BMus BD MTh ARCO   1971   1997   Braemar Villa, 2 Links Road, Port Seton, Prestonpans EH32 0HA   01875 812481
[E-mail: rlglover@btinternet.com]

Cockenzie and Port Seton: Old (H)
Continued Vacancy   1 Links Road, Port Seton, Prestonpans EH32 0HA   01875 812310

Cockpen and Carrington (H) linked with Lasswade (H) linked with Rosewell (H)
Wendy F. Drake (Mrs) BD   1978 1992   11 Pendreich Terrace, Bonnyrigg EH19 2DT   0131-663 6884
[E-mail: revwdrake@hotmail.co.uk]

Cranstoun, Crichton and Ford (H) See Borthwick

Dalkeith: St John's and King's Park (H)
Keith L. Mack BD MTh DPS   2002   13 Weir Crescent, Dalkeith EH22 3JN   0131-454 0206
[E-mail: kthmacker@aol.com]

Dalkeith: St Nicholas' Buccleuch (H)
Alexander G. Horsburgh MA BD   1995 2004   116 Bonnyrig Road, Dalkeith EH22 3HZ   0131-663 3036
[E-mail: alexanderhorsburgh@googlemail.com]

Dirleton (H) (E-mail: dirletonkirk@hotmail.com) linked with North Berwick: Abbey (H) (01620 890110) (E-mail: abbeychurch@hotmail.com)
David J. Graham BSc BD PhD   1982 1998   20 Westgate, North Berwick EH39 4AF   01620 890110
[E-mail: abbeychurch@hotmail.com]

Dunbar (H)
Eric W. Foggitt MA BSc BD   1991 2000   The Manse, Bayswell Road, Dunbar EH42 1AB   01368 863749 (Tel/Fax)
[E-mail: ericleric3@btopenworld.com]

Dunglass
Anne R. Lithgow (Mrs) MA BD   1992 1994   The Manse, Cockburnspath TD13 5XZ   01368 830713
[E-mail: anne.lithgow@btinternet.com]

Fala and Soutra See Borthwick

Garvald and Morham linked with Haddington: West (H)
Cameron Mackenzie BD   1997   15 West Road, Haddington EH41 3RD   01620 822213
[E-mail: mackenz550@aol.com]

Gladsmuir linked with Longniddry (H)
Robin E. Hill LLB BD PhD   2004   The Manse, Elcho Road, Longniddry EH32 0LB   01875 853195
[E-mail: robin.hill@homecall.co.uk]

Glencorse (H) See Bilston

Gorebridge (H)
Mark S. Nicholas MA BD   1999   100 Hunterfield Road, Gorebridge EH23 4TT   01875 820387
[E-mail: mark@nicholasfamily.wanadoo.co.uk]

Gullane See Aberlady

Haddington: St Mary's (H)
Vacant — 1 Nungate Gardens, Haddington EH41 4EE — 01620 823109

Haddington: West See Garvald and Morham

Howgate (H) linked with Penicuik: South (H)
Ian A. Cathcart BSc BD — 1994 — 15 Stevenson Road, Glencorse, Penicuik EH26 0LU — 01968 674692
[E-mail: iacjoc@tiscali.co.uk]

Humbie See Bolton and Saltoun
Lasswade See Cockpen and Carrington

Loanhead
Graham L. Duffin BSc BD DipEd — 1989 2001 — 120 The Loan, Loanhead EH20 9AJ — 0131-448 2459
[E-mail: gduffin@loanheadparishchurch.co.uk]
Frances M. Henderson BA BD (Associate) — 2006 — 14 (1F2) Viewforth Gardens, Edinburgh EH10 4EU — 0131-478 1384
[E-mail: frances.henderson@blueyonder.co.uk]

Longniddry See Gladsmuir

Musselburgh: Northesk (H)
Alison P. McDonald MA BD — 1991 1998 — 16 New Street, Musselburgh EH21 6JP — 0131-665 2128
[E-mail: alisonpmcdonald@btinternet.com]

Musselburgh: St Andrew's High (H) (0131-665 7239)
Yvonne E.S. Atkins (Mrs) BD — 1997 2004 — 8 Ferguson Drive, Musselburgh EH21 6XA — 0131-665 1124
[E-mail: yesatkins@yahoo.co.uk]

Musselburgh: St Clement's and St Ninian's
Muriel Willoughby (Mrs) MA BD — 2006 — The Manse, Wallyford Loan Road, Wallyford, Musselburgh EH21 8BU — 0131-653 6588
[E-mail: stcmanse@btinternet.com]
John Buchanan DCS — 2004 — 19 Gillespie Crescent, Edinburgh EH10 4HU — 0131-229 0794

Musselburgh: St Michael's Inveresk
Andrew B. Dick BD DipMin — 1986 1999 — 8 Hope Place, Musselburgh EH21 7QE — 0131-665 0545
[E-mail: dixbit@aol.com]

Newbattle (H) (Website: http://freespace.virgin.net/newbattle.focus)
Monika R.W. Redman (Mrs) BA BD — 2003 — 70 Newbattle Abbey Crescent, Dalkeith EH22 3LW — 0131-663 3245
[E-mail: monika.walker@ukgateway.net]
Gordon R. Steven BD DCS — 2004 — 51 Nantwich Drive, Edinburgh EH7 6RB — 0131-669 2054 / 07904 385256 (Mbl)
[E-mail: grsteven@btinternet.com]

Congregation / Minister	Ordained	Inducted	Address	Telephone
Newton Vacant			The Manse, Newton, Dalkeith EH22 1SR	0131-663 3845
North Berwick: Abbey See Dirleton				
North Berwick: St Andrew Blackadder (H) (E-mail: admin@standrewblackadder.org.uk) (Website: www.standrewblackadder.org.uk) Neil J. Dougall BD	1991	2003	7 Marine Parade, North Berwick EH39 4LD [E-mail: neil@standrewblackadder.org.uk]	01620 892132
Ormiston linked with Pencaitland Mark Malcolm MA BD	1999		The Manse, Pencaitland, Tranent EH34 5DL [E-mail: mark.minister@virgin.net]	01875 340208
Pencaitland See Ormiston				
Penicuik: North (H) John W. Fraser MA BD	1974	1982	93 John Street, Penicuik EH26 8AG [E-mail: revpnk@tiscali.co.uk]	01968 672213
Penicuik: St Mungo's (H) Ronald W. Smith BA BEd BD	1979	2004	31A Kirkhill Road, Penicuik EH26 8JB	01968 672916
Penicuik: South See Howgate				
Prestonpans: Prestongrange Robert R. Simpson BA BD	1994		The Manse, East Loan, Prestonpans EH32 9ED [E-mail: robert@pansmanse.co.uk]	01875 810308
Rosewell See Cockpen and Carrington **Roslin** See Bilston **Spott** See Belhaven				
Tranent Thomas M. Hogg BD	1986		244 Church Street, Tranent EH33 1BW [E-mail: tom@hoggtran.freeserve.co.uk]	01875 610210
Traprain Howard J. Haslett BA BD	1972	2000	The Manse, Preston Road, East Linton EH40 3DS [E-mail: howard.haslett@btinternet.com]	01620 860227 (Tel/Fax)
Whitekirk and Tyninghame See Athelstaneford **Yester** See Bolton and Saltoun				

Name			Charge	Address	Tel
Andrews, J. Edward MA BD DipCG FSAScot	1985	2005	(Armadale)	1A Meadowpark, Haddington EH41 4DS [E-mail: edward.andrews@btinternet.com]	(Tel/Fax) 01620 829804 (Mbl) 07808 720708
Bayne, Angus L. LTh BEd MTh	1969	2005	(Edinburgh: Bristo Memorial Craigmillar)	14 Myredale, Bonnyrigg EH19 3NW [E-mail: angus@mccookies.com]	0131-663 6871
Black, A. Graham MA	1964	2003	(Gladsmuir with Longniddry)	26 Hamilton Crescent, Gullane EH31 2HR [E-mail: grablack@aol.com]	01620 843899
Brown, Ronald H.	1974	1998	(Musselburgh: Northesk)	6 Monktonhall Farm Cottages, Musselburgh EH21 6RZ	0131-653 2531
Brown, William BD	1972	1997	(Edinburgh: Polwarth)	13 Thornyhall, Dalkeith EH22 2ND [E-mail: william@brown1826.fsnet.co.uk]	0131-654 0929
Chalmers, William R. MA BD STM	1953	1992	(Dunbar)	18 Forest Road, Burghead, Elgin IV30 5XL	01343 835674
Forbes, Iain M. BSc BD	1964	2005	(Aberdeen: Beechgrove)	6 Auld Orchard, Lothian Street, Bonnyrigg EH19 3BR [E-mail: panama.forbes@tiscali.co.uk]	0131-454 0717
Fraser, John W. BEM MA BD PhD	1950	1983	(Farnell)	The Elms Nursing Home, 148 Whitehouse Loan, Edinburgh EH9 2EZ	
Gilfillan, James LTh	1968	1997	(East Kilbride: Old)	15 Long Cram, Haddington EH41 4NS	01620 824843
Hill, Arthur T.	1940	1981	(Ormiston with Prestonpans: Grange)	8A Hamilton Road, North Berwick EH39 4NA	01620 893961
Hutchison, Alan E.W.			(Deacon)	132 Lochbridge Road, North Berwick EH39 4DR	01620 894077
Jones, Anne M. (Mrs) BD	1998	2002	(Hospital Chaplain)	7 North Elphinstone Farm, Tranent EH33 2ND [E-mail: revamjones@aol.com]	01875 614442
Levison, L. David MA BD	1943	1982	(Ormiston with Pencaitland)	Westdene Conservatory Flat, 506 Perth Road, Dundee DD2 1LS	01382 630460
Macdonell, Alasdair W. MA BD	1955	1992	(Haddington: St Mary's)	St Andrews Cottage, Duns Road, Gifford, Haddington EH41 4QW [E-mail: alasdair.macdonell@btinternet.com]	01620 810341
Macrae, Norman C. MA DipEd	1942	1985	(Loanhead)	49 Lixmount Avenue, Edinburgh EH5 3EW [E-mail: nandcmacrae@onetel.com]	0131-552 2428
Manson, James A. LTh	1981	2004	(Glencorse with Roslin)	31 Nursery Gardens, Kilmarnock KA1 3JA [E-mail: jamanson@supanet.com]	01563 535430
Pirie, Donald LTh	1975	2006	(Bolton and Saltoun with Humbie with Yester)	46 Caiystane Avenue, Edinburgh EH10 6SH	0131-445 2654
Ritchie, James McL. MA BD MPhil	1950	1985	(Coalsnaughton)	Flat 2/25, Croft-an-Righ, Edinburgh EH8 8EG [E-mail: jasritch_77@msn.com]	0131-557 1084
Robertson, James LTh	1970	2000	(Newton)	11 Southfield Square, Edinburgh EH15 1QS	0131-657 5661
Sanderson, W. Roy DD	1933	1973	(Stenton with Whittingehame)	1 Waterside Drive, Newton Mearns, Glasgow G77 6TL	041-638 8025
Swan, Andrew F. BD	1983	2000	(Loanhead)	3 Mackenzie Gardens, Dolphinton, West Linton EH46 7HS	01968 682247
Thomson, William H.	1964	1999	(Edinburgh: Liberton Northfield)	3 Baird's Way, Bonnyrigg EH19 3NS [E-mail: wh.thomson@tiscali.co.uk]	0131-654 9799
Torrance, David W. MA BD	1955	1991	(Earlston)	38 Forth Street, North Berwick EH39 4IQ [E-mail: dwtmet@connectfree.co.uk]	(Tel/Fax) 01620 895109
Underwood, Florence A. (Mrs) BD	1992	2006	(Assistant: Gladsmuir with Longniddry)	The Shieling, Main Street, Stenton, Dunbar EH42 1TE [E-mail: geoffrey.underwood@homecall.co.uk]	01368 850629
Underwood, Geoffrey H. BD DipTh FPhS	1964	1992	(Cockenzie and Port Seton: Chalmers Memorial)	The Shieling, Main Street, Stenton, Dunbar EH42 1TE [E-mail: geoffrey.underwood@homecall.co.uk]	01368 850629
Whiteford, David H. CBE MA BD PhD	1943	1985	(Gullane)	3 Old Dean Road, Longniddry EH32 0QY	01875 852980

(4) MELROSE AND PEEBLES

Meets at Innerleithen on the first Tuesday of February, March, May, October, November and December, and on the fourth Tuesday of June, and in places to be appointed on the first Tuesday of September.

Clerk: MR JACK STEWART   3 St Cuthbert's Drive, St Boswells, Melrose TD6 0DF   01835 822600
[E-mail: melrosepeebles@cofscotland.org.uk]

Ashkirk linked with Selkirk (H)
James W. Campbell BD   1995   1 Loanside, Selkirk TD7 4DJ   01750 22833
[E-mail: revjimashkirk@aol.com]

Bowden (H) and Melrose (H)
Alistair G. Bennett BSc BD   1978   1984   Tweedmount Road, Melrose TD6 9ST   01896 822217
[E-mail: agbennettmelrose@aol.com]
(Charge formed by the union of Bowden and Melrose)

Broughton, Glenholm and Kilbucho (H) linked with Stobo and Drumelzier linked with Tweedsmuir (H)
Rachel J.W. Dobie (Mrs) LTh   1991   1996   The Manse, Broughton, Biggar ML12 6HQ   01899 830331
[E-mail: revracheldobie@aol.com]

Caddonfoot (H) linked with Galashiels: Trinity (H)
Morag A. Dawson BD   1999   2005   8 Mossilee Road, Galashiels TD1 1NF   01896 752420
[E-mail: moragdawson@st-aidans.wanadoo.co.uk]

Carlops linked with Kirkurd and Newlands (H) linked with West Linton: St Andrew's (H)
Thomas W. Burt BD   1982   1985   The Manse, West Linton EH46 7EN   01968 660221
[E-mail: tomburt@westlinton.com]

Channelkirk and Lauder
Vacant   Brownsmuir Park, Lauder TD2 6QD   01578 722320

Earlston
Michael D. Scouler MBE BSc BD   1988   1992   The Manse, High Street, Earlston TD4 6DE   01896 849236

Eddleston (H) linked with Peebles: Old (H)
Malcolm M. Macdougall BD   1981   2001   The Old Manse, Innerleithen Road, Peebles EH45 8BD   01721 720568
[E-mail: calum.macdougall@btopenworld.com]

Ettrick and Yarrow
Samuel Siroky BA MTh   2003   Yarrow Manse, Yarrow, Selkirk TD7 5LA   01750 82336
[E-mail: sesiroky@onetel.com]

Galashiels: Old and St Paul's (H) (Website: www.oldparishandstpauls.org.uk)
Leslie M. Steele MA BD 1973 1988 Barr Road, Galashiels TD1 3HX
[E-mail: lmslms@tiscali.co.uk] 01896 752320

Galashiels: St John's (H)
Jane M. Howitt (Miss) MA BD 1996 2006 St John's Manse, Hawthorn Road, Galashiels TD1 2JZ
[E-mail: jane_m_howitt@yahoo.co.uk] 01896 752573

Galashiels: Trinity (H) See Caddonfoot

Innerleithen (H), Traquair and Walkerburn
Janice M. Faris (Mrs) BSc BD 1991 2001 The Manse, 1 Millwell Park, Innerleithen, Peebles EH44 6JF
[E-mail: revjfaris@hotmail.com] 01896 830309

Kirkurd and Newlands See Carlops

Lyne and Manor
Nancy M. Norman (Miss) BA MDiv MTh 1988 1998 25 March Street, Peebles EH45 8EP
[E-mail: nancy.norman@btopenworld.com] 01721 721699

Maxton and Mertoun linked with Newtown linked with St Boswells
Vacant St Modans Manse, Main Street, St Boswells, Melrose TD6 0BB 01835 822255

Newtown See Maxton and Mertoun
Peebles: Old See Eddleston

Peebles: St Andrew's Leckie (H) (01721 723121) 1973
James H. Wallace MA BD 1983 Mansfield, Innerleithen Road, Peebles EH45 8BE
[E-mail: jimwallace@freeola.com] 01721 721749 (Tel/Fax)

St Boswells See Maxton and Mertoun
Selkirk See Ashkirk
Skirling See Broughton, Glenholm and Kilbucho
Stobo and Drumelzier See Broughton, Glenholm and Kilbucho

Stow: St Mary of Wedale and Heriot
Catherine A. Buchan (Mrs) MA MDiv 2002 The Manse, 209 Galashiels Road, Stow, Galashiels TD1 2RE
[E-mail: buchan@alan-cath.freeserve.co.uk] 01578 730237

Tweedsmuir See Broughton, Glenholm and Kilbucho
West Linton: St Andrew's See Carlops

Name			Parish / Position	Address	Telephone
Bowie, Adam McC.	1976	1996	(Cavers and Kirkton with Hobkirk and Southdean)	Glenbield, Redpath, Earlston TD4 6AD	01896 848173
Brown, Robert BSc	1962	1997	(Kilbrandon and Kilchattan)	11 Thornfield Terrace, Selkirk TD7 4DU [E-mail: ruwcb@tiscali.co.uk]	01750 20311
Cashman, P. Hamilton BSc	1985	1998	(Dirleton with North Berwick: Abbey)	38 Abbotsford Road, Galashiels TD1 3HR [E-mail: mcashman@tiscali.co.uk]	01896 752711
Devenny, Robert P.	2002		Borders Health Board	Blakeburn Cottage, Wester Housebyres, Melrose TD6 9BW	01896 822350
Dick, J. Ronald BD	1973	1996	Hospital Chaplain	5 Georgefield Farm Cottages, Earlston TD4 6BH	01896 848956
Donald, Thomas W. LTh CA	1977	1987	(Bowden with Lilliesleaf)	The Quest, Huntly Road, Melrose TD6 9SB	01896 822345
Duncan, Charles A. MA	1956	1992	(Heriot with Stow: St Mary of Wedale)	10 Elm Grove, Galashiels TD1 3JA	01896 753261
Hardie, H. Warner BD	1979	2005	(Blackridge with Harthill: St Andrew's)	Keswick Cottage, Kingsmuir Drive, Peebles EH45 9AA [E-mail: hardies@bigfoot.com]	01721 724003
Kellet, John M. MA	1962	1995	(Leith: South)	4 High Cottages, Walkerburn EH43 6AZ	01896 870351
Kennon, Stanley BA BD	1992	2000	Chaplain: Navy	The Chaplaincy, HMS Raleigh, Tor Point, Cornwall PL2 2PD	
Laing, William F. DSC VRD MA	1952	1986	(Selkirk: St Mary's West)	10 The Glebe, Selkirk TD7 5AB	01750 21210
MacFarlane, David C. MA	1957	1997	(Eddleston with Peebles: Old)	11 Station Bank, Peebles EH45 8EJ	01721 720639
Moore, W. Haisley MA	1966	1996	(Secretary: The Boys' Brigade)	26 Tweedbank Avenue, Tweedbank, Galashiels TD1 3SP	01896 668577
Munson, Winnie (Ms) BD	1996	2006	(Delting with Northmavine)	6 St Cuthbert's Drive, St Boswells, Melrose TD6 0DF	01835 823375
Neill, Bruce F. MA BD	1966	2007	(Maxton and Mertoun with St Boswells)	18 Brierydean, St Abbs, Eyemouth TD14 5PQ	01890 771569
Rae, Andrew W.	1951	1987	(Annan: St Andrew's Greenknowe Erskine)	Roseneuk, Tweedside Road, Newtown St Boswells TD6 0PQ	01835 823783
Riddell, John A. MA BD	1967	2006	(Jedburgh: Trinity)	Orchid Cottage, Gingham Row, Earlston TD4 6ET	01896 848784
Shields, John M. MBE LTh	1972	2007	(Channelkirk and Lauder)	12 Eden Park, Ednam, Kelso TD5 7RG	
Taverner, Glyn R. MA BD	1957	1995	(Maxton and Mertoun with St Boswells)	Woodcot Cottage, Waverley Road, Innerleithen EH44 6QW	01896 830156
Thomson, George F.M. MA	1956	1988	(Dollar Associate)	6 Abbotsford Terrace, Darnick, Melrose TD6 9AD	01896 823112

(5) DUNS

Meets at Duns, in the Old Parish Church Hall, normally on the first Tuesday of February, March, April, May, October, November, December, on the last Tuesday in June, and in places to be appointed on the first Tuesday of September.

Clerk: MR PETER JOHNSON MBE MPhil   Todlaw, Duns TD11 3EJ   **01361 883724**
[E-mail: duns@cofscotland.org.uk]

Ayton (H) and Burnmouth linked with Grantshouse and Houndwood and Reston
Norman R. Whyte BD DipMin   1982   2006   The Manse, Beanburn, Ayton, Eyemouth TD14 5QY   01890 781333

Berwick-upon-Tweed: St Andrew's Wallace Green (H) and Lowick
Paul M.N. Sewell MA BD   1970   2003   3 Meadow Grange, Berwick-upon-Tweed TD15 1NW   01289 303304

Bonkyl and Preston linked with Chirnside (H) linked with Edrom: Allanton (H)
Duncan E. Murray BA BD   1970   2005   Parish Church Manse, The Glebe, Chirnside, Duns TD11 3XL   01890 819109
[E-mail: duncanemurray@tiscali.co.uk]

Chirnside   See Bonkyl and Preston

Coldingham and St Abb's linked with Eyemouth
Daniel G. Lindsay BD   1978   1979   Victoria Road, Eyemouth TD14 5JD   01890 750327

Coldstream (H) linked with Eccles
James B. Watson BSc   1968   2004   36 Bennecourt Drive, Coldstream TD12 1BY   01890 883149
[E-mail: jimwatson007@hotmail.com]

Duns (H)
Andrew A. Morrice MA BD   1999   The Manse, Duns TD11 3DG   01361 883755
[E-mail: andrew@morrice5.wanadoo.co.uk]

Eccles   See Coldstream
Edrom: Allanton   See Bonkyl and Preston
Eyemouth   See Coldingham and St Abb's

Fogo and Swinton linked with Ladykirk linked with Leitholm linked with Whitsome (H)
Alan C.D. Cartwright BSc BD   1976   Swinton, Duns TD11 3JJ   01890 860228

Foulden and Mordington linked with Hutton and Fishwick and Paxton
Vacant   Hutton, Berwick-upon-Tweed TD15 1TS   01289 386396

Gordon: St Michael's linked with Greenlaw (H) linked with Legerwood linked with Westruther
Thomas S. Nicholson BD DPS   1982   1995   The Manse, Todholes, Greenlaw, Duns TD10 6XD   01361 810316

Grantshouse and Houndwood and Reston   See Ayton and Burnmouth
Greenlaw   See Gordon: St Michael's
Hutton and Fishwick and Paxton   See Foulden and Mordington

Kirk of Lammermuir and Langton and Polwarth
Ann Inglis (Mrs) LLB BD   1986   2003   The Manse, Cranshaws, Duns TD11 3SJ   01361 890289
(Charge formed by the union of Kirk of Lammermuir with Langton and Polwarth)

Ladykirk   See Fogo and Swinton
Legerwood   See Gordon: St Michael's
Leitholm   See Fogo and Swinton
Westruther   See Gordon: St Michael's
Whitsome   See Fogo and Swinton

Name			(Charge)	Address	Tel
Gaddes, Donald R.	1961	1994	(Kelso: North and Ednam)	35 Winterfield Gardens, Duns TD11 3EZ [E-mail: donga@winterfield.fslife.co.uk]	01361 883172
Gale, Ronald A.A. LTh	1982	1995	(Dunoon: Old and St Cuthbert's)	55 Lennel Mount, Coldstream TD12 4NS	01890 883699
Hay, Bruce J.L.	1957	1997	(Makerstoun and Smailholm with Stichill, Hume and Nenthorn)		
Higham, Robert D. BD	1985	2002	(Tiree)	Assynt, 1 East Ord Gardens, Berwick-upon-Tweed TD15 2LS	01289 303171
				36 Low Greens, Berwick-upon-Tweed TD15 1LZ	01289 302392
Hope, Geraldine H. (Mrs) MA BD	1986	2007	(Foulden and Mordington with Hutton and Fishwick and Paxton)	4 Well Court, Chirnside, Duns TD11 3UD [E-mail: geraldine.hope@virgin.net]	01890 818134
Kerr, Andrew MA BLitt	1948	1991	(Kilbarchan: West)	Meikle Harelaw, Westruther, Gordon TD10 6XT	01578 740263
Landale, William S.	2004		Auxiliary Minister	Green Hope Guest House, Green Hope, Duns TD11	01361 890242
Ledgard, J. Christopher BA	1969	2004	(Ayton and Burnmouth with Grantshouse and Houndwood and Reston)	Streonshalh, 8 David Hume View, Chirnside, Duns TD11 3SX	01890 817105
Macleod, Allan M. MA	1945	1985	(Gordon: St Michael's with Legerwood with Westruther)	Silverlea, Machrihanish, Argyll PA28 6PZ	
Paterson, William BD	1977	2001	(Bonkyl and Preston with Chirnside with Edrom: Allanton)	Benachie, Gavinton, Duns TD11 3QT	01361 882727

(6) JEDBURGH

Meets at Jedburgh on the first Wednesday of February, March, May, October, November and December and on the last Wednesday of June. Meets in the Moderator's church on the first Wednesday of September.

Clerk	REV. FRANK CAMPBELL			22 The Glebe, Ancrum, Jedburgh TD8 6UX [E-mail: jedburgh@cofscotland.org.uk]	01835 830318 01835 830262 (Fax)

Ale and Teviot United (H)

Frank Campbell	1989	1991	22 The Glebe, Ancrum, Jedburgh TD8 6UX [E-mail: jedburgh@cofscotland.org.uk]	01835 830318 (Tel) 01835 830262 (Fax)

Cavers and Kirkton linked with Hawick: Trinity

E.P. Lindsay Thomson MA	1964	1972	Fenwick Park, Hawick TD9 9PA [E-mail: eplindsayt@aol.com]	01450 372705

Hawick: Burnfoot

Charles J. Finnie LTh DPS	1991	1997	29 Wilton Hill, Hawick TD9 8BA [E-mail: charles@finnierev.freeserve.co.uk]	01450 373181

Hawick: St Mary's and Old (H)
Marina D. Brown (Mrs) MA BD MTh   2000   2007   The Manse of St Mary's and Old, Braid Road, Hawick TD9 9LZ   01450 378163
[E-mail: smop@btinternet.com]

Hawick: Teviot (H) and Roberton
Neil R. Combe BSc MSc BD   1984   Teviot Manse, Buccleuch Road, Hawick TD9 0EL   01450 372150
[E-mail: neil.combe@btinternet.com]

Hawick: Trinity (H) See Cavers and Kirkton

Hawick: Wilton linked with Teviothead
Lisa-Jane Rankin (Miss) BD CPS   2003   4 Wilton Hill Terrace, Hawick TD9 8BE   01450 370744 (Tel/Fax)
[E-mail: lisajane20@tiscali.co.uk]

Hobkirk and Southdean linked with Ruberslaw
Anthony M. Jones   1994   2003   The Manse, Denholm, Hawick TD9 8NB   01450 870268 (Tel/Fax)
BD DPS DipTheol CertMin FRSA
[E-mail: revanthonymjones@amserve.com]

Jedburgh: Old and Trinity
Vacant   Honeyfield Drive, Jedburgh TD8 6LQ   01835 863417
(Charge formed by the union of Jedburgh: Old and Edgerston with Jedburgh: Trinity)

Kelso Country Churches
Jenny Earl MA BD   2007   The Manse, 1 The Meadow, Stichill, Kelso TD5 7TG   01573 470607
[E-mail: earl_jenny@hotmail.com]

Kelso: North (H) and Ednam (H) (01573 224154) (E-mail: office@kelsonorthandednam.org.uk) (Website: www.kelsonorthandednam.org.uk)
Tom McDonald BD   1994   20 Forestfield, Kelso TD5 7BX   01573 224677
[E-mail: revtom@20thepearlygates.co.uk]

Kelso: Old (H) and Sprouston
Marion E. Dodd (Miss) MA BD LRAM   1988   1989   Glebe Lane, Kelso TD5 7AU   01573 226254
[E-mail: mariondodd@btinternet.com]

Linton, Morebattle, Hownam and Yetholm (H)
Robin D. McHaffie BD   1979   1991   The Manse, Main Street, Kirk Yetholm, Kelso TD5 8PF   01573 420308
[E-mail: robinmchaffie@f2s.com]

Oxnam
Continued Vacancy

Ruberslaw See Hobkirk and Southdean
Teviothead See Hawick: Wilton

Brown, Joseph MA	1954 1991	(Linton with Hownam and Morebattle with Yetholm)	The Orchard, Hermitage Lane, Shedden Park Road, Kelso TD5 7AN	01573 223481
Fox, G. Dudley A.	1972 1988	(Kelso Old)	14 Pinnacle Hill Farm, Kelso TD5 8HD	01573 223335
Hamilton, Robert MA BD	1938 1979	(Kelso Old)	Ridge Cottage, 391 Totnes Road, Collaton St Mary, Paignton TQ4 7PW	01803 526440
Longmuir, William LTh	1984 2001	(Bedrule with Denholm with Minto)	Viewfield, South Street, Gavinton, Duns TD11 3QT	01361 882728
McNicol, Bruce	1967 2006	(Jedburgh: Old and Edgerston)	42 Dounehill, Jedburgh TD8 6LJ [E-mail: mcnicol95@btinternet.com]	01835 862991
Ritchie, Garden W.M.	1961 1995	(Ardersier with Petty)	23 Croft Road, Kelso TD5 7EP	01573 224419
Thompson, W.M.D. MA	1950 1997	(Crailing and Eckford with Oxnam with Roxburgh)	Beech House, Etal, Cornhill-on-Tweed TD12 4TL	01890 820621

HAWICK ADDRESSES

Burnfoot	Fraser Avenue
St Mary's and Old	Kirk Wynd
Teviot	off Buccleuch Road
Trinity	Central Square
Wilton	Princes Street

(7) ANNANDALE AND ESKDALE

Meets on the first Tuesday of February, May, September and December; and the third Tuesday of March, June and October, in a venue to be determined by Presbytery.

Clerk:	**REV. C. BRYAN HASTON LTh**	**The Manse, Gretna Green, Gretna DG16 5DU** **[E-mail: annandaleeskdale@cofscotland.org.uk]** **[E-mail: cbhaston@cofs.demon.co.uk]**	**01461 338313 (Tel)** **08701 640119 (Fax)**

Annan: Old (H) linked with Dornock

Hugh D. Steele LTh DipMin	1994	2004	12 Plumdon Park Avenue, Annan DG12 6EY [E-mail: hugdebra@aol.com]	01461 201405
Alexander Falconer (Pastoral Assistant)			23 Summergate Road, Annan DG12 6EX	01461 202943

Annan: St Andrew's (H) linked with Brydekirk

George K. Lind BD MCIBS	1998	1 Annerley Road, Annan DG12 6HE [E-mail: gklind@onetel.com]	01461 202626
Alexander Falconer (Pastoral Assistant)		23 Summergate Road, Annan DG12 6EX	01461 202943

Applegarth, Sibbaldbie (H) and Johnstone linked with Lochmaben (H)

Jack M. Brown BSc BD	1977	2002	The Manse, Barrashead, Lochmaben, Lockerbie DG11 1QF [E-mail: jackm.brown@tiscali.co.uk]	01387 810066

Brydekirk See Annan: St Andrew's

Canonbie United (H) linked with Liddesdale (H)   1989
Alan D. Reid MA BD   23 Langholm Street, Newcastleton TD9 0QX   01387 375242
[E-mail: canonbie.liddesdale@talktalk.net]

Dalton linked with Hightae linked with St Mungo
Alexander C. Stoddart BD   2001   The Manse, Hightae, Lockerbie DG11 1JL   01387 811499
[E-mail: sandystoddart@supanet.com]

Dornock See Annan: Old

Gretna: Old (H), Gretna: St Andrew's (H) and Half Morton and Kirkpatrick Fleming
C. Bryan Haston LTh   1975   The Manse, Gretna Green, Gretna DG16 5DU   01461 338313 (Tel)
[E-mail: cbhaston@cofs.demon.co.uk]   08701 640119 (Fax)
Alexander Falconer (Pastoral Assistant)   23 Summergate Road, Annan DG12 6EX   01461 202943

Hightae See Dalton

Hoddam linked with Kirtle-Eaglesfield linked with Middlebie linked with Waterbeck
Vacant

Hutton and Corrie linked with Tundergarth
Vacant

Kirkpatrick Juxta linked with Moffat: St Andrew's (H) linked with Wamphray
David M. McKay MA BD   1979   2001   The Manse, 1 Meadowbank, Moffat DG10 9LR   01683 220128
[E-mail: demacmin@ukgateway.net]

Kirtle-Eaglesfield See Hoddam

Langholm Eskdalemuir Ewes and Westerkirk
Robert B. Milne BTh   1999   1999   The Manse, Langholm DG13 0BL   01387 380252 (Tel)
[E-mail: rbmilne@aol.com]   01387 381399 (Fax)
(Charge formed by the union of Eskdalemuir with Langholm, Ewes and Westerkirk)

Liddesdale (H) See Canonbie United
Lochmaben See Applegarth, Sibbaldbie and Johnstone

Lockerbie: Dryfesdale
Vacant   The Manse, 5 Carlisle Road, Lockerbie DG11 2DW   01576 202361

Middlebie See Hoddam
Moffat: St Andrew's (H) See Kirkpatrick Juxta
St Mungo See Dalton

The Border Kirk
Vacant

Tundergarth See Eskdalemuir
Wamphray See Kirkpatrick Juxta
Waterbeck See Hoddam

Name	Charge	Dates	Address	Phone
Annand, James M. MA BD	(Lockerbie: Dryfesdale)	1955 1995	48 Main Street, Newstead, Melrose TD6 9DX	0131-225 3393
Beveridge, S. Edwin P. BA	(Brydekirk with Hoddam)	1959 2004	19 Rothesay Terrace, Edinburgh EH3 7RY	
Byers, Alan J.	(Gamrie with King Edward)	1959 1992	Meadowbank, Plumdon Road, Annan DG12 6SJ	01461 206512
Byers, Mairi (Mrs) BTh CPS	(Jura)	1992 1998	Meadowbank, Plumdon Road, Annan DG12 6SJ	01461 206512
Fisher, D. Noel MA BD	(Glasgow: Sherbrooke St Gilbert's)	1939 1979	Sheraig Cottage, Killochries Fold, Kilmacolm PA13 4TE	
Gibb, James Daniel MacGhee BA LTh	(Aberfoyle with Port of Menteith)	1994 2006	21 Victoria Gardens, Eastriggs, Dumfries DG12 6TW [E-mail: dannygibb@hotmail.co.uk]	01461 40560
MacMillan, William M. LTh	(Kilmory with Lamlash)	1980 1998	Balskia, 61 Queen Street, Lochmaben DG11 1PP	01387 811528
Macpherson, Duncan J. BSc BD	Chaplain: Army	1993 2002	Household Cavalry Regiment, Combermere Barracks, Windsor, Berkshire SL4 3DN	
Rennie, John D. MA	(Broughton, Glenholm and Kilbucho with Skirling with Stobo and Drumelzier with Tweedsmuir)	1962 1996	Dundoran, Ballplay Road, Moffat DG10 9JX [E-mail: tworennies@talktalk.net]	01683 220223
Ross Alan C. CA BD	(Eskdalemuir with Hutton and Corrie with Tundergarth)	1988 2007	Yarra, Ettrickbridge, Selkirk TD7 5JN [E-mail: alkaross@aol.com]	01750 52324
Seaman, Ronald S. MA	(Dornock)	1967 2007	1 Springfield Farm Court, Main Street, Springfield, Gretna DG16 5EH	01461 337228
Swinburne, Norman BA	(Sauchie)	1960 1993	Damerosehay, Birch Hill Lane, Kirkbride, Wigton CA7 5HZ	01697 351497
Vivers, Katherine A.	Auxiliary Minister	2004	Blacket House, Eaglesfield, Lockerbie DG11 3AA [E-mail: katevivers@yahoo.co.uk]	01461 500412
Williams, Trevor C. LTh	(Hoddam with Kirtle-Eaglesfield with Middlebie with Waterbeck)	1990 2007	2 Trinity Way, Littlehampton, West Sussex BN17 5SS	

(8) DUMFRIES AND KIRKCUDBRIGHT

Meets at Dumfries on the first Wednesday of February, March, April, May, September, October, November and December, and the fourth Wednesday of June.

Clerk:	REV. GORDON M.A. SAVAGE MA BD	11 Laurieknowe, Dumfries DG2 7AH [E-mail: dumfrieskirkcudbright@ofscotland.org.uk]	01387 252929
Depute Clerk:	REV. WILLIAM T. HOGG MA BD	The Manse, Glasgow Road, Sanquhar DG4 6BZ [E-mail: wthogg@yahoo.com]	01659 50247

Auchencairn (H) and Rerrick linked with Buittle (H) and Kelton (H)
Alistair J. MacKichan MA BD   1984   2005   Auchencairn, Castle Douglas DG7 1QS   01556 640041

Balmaclellan and Kells (H) linked with Carsphairn (H) linked with Dalry (H)
David S. Bartholomew BSc MSc PhD BD   1994   The Manse, Dalry, Castle Douglas DG7 3PJ   01644 430380
[E-mail: dhbart@care4free.net]

Balmaghie linked with Tarff and Twynholm (H)
Christopher Wallace BD DipMin   1988   Manse Road, Twynholm, Kirkcudbright DG6 4NY   01557 860381
[E-mail: cwallaceuk@hotmail.com]

Borgue linked with Gatehouse of Fleet
Valerie J. Ott (Mrs) BA BD   2002   The Manse, Planetree Park, Gatehouse of Fleet, Castle Douglas DG7 2EQ   01557 814233
[E-mail: dandvott@aol.com]

Buittle and Kelton See Auchencairn and Rerrick

Caerlaverock linked with Dumfries: St Mary's-Greyfriars
Jamie Milliken BD   2005   4 Georgetown Crescent, Dumfries DG1 4EQ   01387 257045
[E-mail: minister@stmarysgreyfriars.org.uk]

Carsphairn See Balmaclellan and Kells

Castle Douglas (H)
Robert J. Malloch BD   1987   2001   1 Castle View, Castle Douglas DG7 1BG   01556 502171
[E-mail: robert@scotnish.freeserve.co.uk]

Closeburn linked with Durisdeer
James W. Scott MA CDA   1952   1953   The Manse, Durisdeer, Thornhill DG3 5BJ   01848 500231

Colvend, Southwick and Kirkbean
James F. Gatherer BD   1984   2003   The Manse, Colvend, Dalbeattie DG5 4QN   01556 630255
[E-mail: james@gatherer.net]

Corsock and Kirkpatrick Durham linked with Crossmichael and Parton
Sally Marsh BTh MTh   2006   Knockdrocket, Clarebrand, Castle Douglas DG7 3AH   01556 503645
[E-mail: rev.sal@btinternet.com]

Crossmichael and Parton See Corsock and Kirkpatrick Durham

Cummertrees linked with Mouswald linked with Ruthwell (H)
James Williamson BA BD   1986   1991   The Manse, Ruthwell, Dumfries DG1 4NP   01387 870217
[E-mail: jimwill@rcmkirk.fsnet.co.uk]

Dalbeattie (H) linked with Urr (H) Norman M. Hutcheson MA BD	1973	1988	36 Mill Street, Dalbeattie DG5 4HE [E-mail: norman.hutcheson@virgin.net]	01556 610029
Dalry See Balmaclellan and Kells				
Dumfries: Lincluden and Holywood linked with Dumfries: Lochside Neil G. Campbell BA BD	1988	2006	27 St Anne's Road, Dumfries DG2 9HZ [E-mail: mail@neilgcampbell.co.uk]	01387 249964
Dumfries: Lochside See Dumfries: Lincluden and Holywood				
Dumfries: Maxwelltown West (H) Gordon M.A. Savage MA BD	1977	1984	Maxwelltown West Manse, 11 Laurieknowe, Dumfries DG2 7AH [E-mail: gordonsavage@uk.uumail.com]	01387 252929
Dumfries: St George's (H) Donald Campbell BD	1997		9 Nunholm Park, Dumfries DG1 1JP [E-mail: saint-georges@ukonline.co.uk]	01387 252965
Dumfries: St Mary's-Greyfriars (H) See Caerlaverock				
Dumfries: St Michael's and South Maurice S. Bond MTh BA DipEd PhD	1981	1999	39 Cardoness Street, Dumfries DG1 3AL [E-mail: maurice.bond3@tiscali.co.uk]	01387 253849
Dumfries: Troqueer (H) William W. Kelly BSc BD	1994		Troqueer Manse, Troqueer Road, Dumfries DG2 7DF [E-mail: ww.kelly@btinternet.com]	01387 253043
Dunscore linked with Glencairn and Moniaive Christine Sime (Miss) BSc BD	1994		Wallaceton, Auldgirth, Dumfries DG2 0TJ [E-mail: revsime@aol.com]	01387 820245
Durisdeer See Closeburn **Gatehouse of Fleet** See Borgue **Glencairn and Moniaive** See Dunscore				
Irongray, Lochrutton and Terregles Vacant			Shawhead Road, Dumfries DG2 9SJ	01387 730287

Kirkconnel (H)
David D. Melville BD · 1989 · 1999 · The Manse, 31 Kingsway, Kirkconnel, Sanquhar DG4 6PN [E-mail: ddm@kirkconnel.org] · 01659 67241

Kirkcudbright (H)
Douglas R. Irving LLB BD WS · 1984 · 1998 · 6 Bourtree Avenue, Kirkcudbright DG6 4AU [E-mail: douglasirving05@tiscali.co.uk] · 01557 330489

Kirkgunzeon
Continued Vacancy

Kirkmahoe
Vacant · Kirkmahoe, Dumfries DG1 1ST · 01387 710572

Kirkmichael, Tinwald and Torthorwald
Louis C. Bezuidenhout MA DD · 1978 · 2000 · Manse of Tinwald, Tinwald, Dumfries DG1 3PL [E-mail: macbez@btinternet.com] · 01387 710246
Elizabeth A. Mack (Miss) DipPEd (Aux) · 1994 · 2006 · 24 Roberts Crescent, Dumfries DG2 7RS · 01387 264847

Lochend and New Abbey
William Holland MA · 1967 · 1971 · The Manse, 28 Main Street, New Abbey, Dumfries DG2 8BY [E-mail: bilholland@aol.com] · 01387 850232

Mouswald See Cummertrees

Penpont, Keir and Tynron linked with Thornhill (H)
Donald Keith MA BD · 1971 · 2002 · The Manse, Manse Park, Thornhill DG3 5ER [E-mail: dnkdonald@aol.com] · 01848 331191

Ruthwell (H) See Cummertrees

Sanquhar: St Bride's (H)
William T. Hogg MA BD · 1979 · 2000 · St Bride's Manse, Glasgow Road, Sanquhar DG6 6BZ [E-mail: wthogg@yahoo.com] · 01659 50247

Tarff and Twynholm See Balmaghie
Thornhill (H) See Penpont, Keir and Tynron
Urr See Dalbeattie

Baillie, David R.	1979	1990	(Crawford with Lowther)	4 Southwick Drive, Dalbeattie DG5 4HW	01556 610871
Bennett, David K.P. BA	1974	2000	(Kirkpatrick Irongray with Lochrutton with Terregles)	53 Anne Arundel Court, Heathhall, Dumfries DG1 3SL	01387 257755
Craig, N. Douglas MA BD	1947	1987	(Dalbeattie: Craignair with Urr)	33 Albert Road, Dumfries DG2 9DN	01387 252187

Name			Charge	Address	Phone
Elder, Albert B. MA	1960	1998	(Dumfries: St Michael's and South)	Charnwood Lodge, 18 Annan Road, Dumfries DG1 3AD	01387 252287
Geddes, Alexander J. MA BD	1960	1998	(Stewarton: St Columba's)	166 Georgetown Road, Dumfries DG1 4DT [E-mail: sandy.elizabeth@virgin.net]	
Gillespie, Ann M. (Miss) DCS	1956	1996	(Deaconess)	Barlochan House, Palnackie, Castle Douglas DG7 1PF	01556 600378
Greer, A. David C. LLB DMin DipAdultEd			(Barra)	10 Watling Street, Dumfries DG1 1HF [E-mail: kandadc@greer10.fsnet.co.uk]	01387 256113
Hamill, Robert BA	1956	1989	(Castle Douglas: St Ringan's)	11 St Andrew Drive, Castle Douglas DG7 1EW	01556 502962
Hammond, Richard J. BA BD	1993	2007	(Kirkmahoe)	3 Marchfield Mount, Marchfield, Dumfries DG1 1SE [E-mail: libby.hammond@virgin.net]	(Mbl) 07764 465783
Kirk, W. Logan MA BD MTh	1988	2000	(Dalton with Hightae with St Mungo)	2 Raecroft Avenue, Collin, Dumfries DG1 4LP	01387 750489
Leishman, James S. LTh BD MA(Div)	1969	1999	(Kirkmichael with Tinwald with Torthorwald)	11 Hunter Avenue, Heathhall, Dumfries DG1 3UX	01387 249241
McKenzie, William M. DA	1958	1993	(Dumfries: Troqueer)	41 Kingholm Road, Dumfries DG1 4SR [E-mail: mckenzie.dumfries@virgin.net]	01387 253688
Miller, John G. BEd BD MTh	1983	2005	(Port Glasgow: St Martin's)	22 Lime Grove, Georgetown, Dumfries DG1 4SQ [E-mail: johnmiller22@hotmail.co.uk]	01387 272502
Miller, John R. MA BD	1958	1992	(Carsphairn with Dalry)	4 Fairgreen Court, Rhonehouse, Castle Douglas DG7 1SA	01556 680428
Morrison, James G. MBE MA	1942	1980	(Rotterdam)	1 Woodvale Lodge, Midsummer Meadows, Cambridge CB4 1HL	07812 148161
Owen, John J.C. LTh	1967	2001	(Applegarth and Sibbaldbie with Lochmaben)	5 Galla Avenue, Dalbeattie DG5 4JZ [E-mail: jj.owen@onetel.net]	01556 612125
Robertson, Ian W. MA BD	1956	1995	(Colvend, Southwick and Kirkbean)	10 Marjoriebanks, Lochmaben, Lockerbie DG11 1QH	01387 810541
Smith, Richmond OBE MA BD	1952	1983	(World Alliance of Reformed Churches)	Aignish, Merse Way, Kippford, Dalbeattie DG5 4LH	01556 620624
Strachan, Alexander E. MA BD	1974	1999	(Dumfries Health Care Chaplain)	2 Leafield Road, Dumfries DG1 2DS [E-mail: aestrachan@aol.com]	01387 279460
Vincent, C. Raymond MA FSAScot	1952	1992	(Stonehouse)	Rosebank, Newton Stewart Road, New Galloway, Castle Douglas DG7 3RT	01644 420451
Wilkie, James R. MA MTh	1957	1993	(Penpont, Keir and Tynron)	31 West Morton Street, Thornhill DG3 5NF	01848 331028
Wotherspoon, Robert C. LTh	1976	1998	(Corsock and Kirkpatrick Durham with Crossmichael and Parton)	7 Hillowton Drive, Castle Douglas DG7 1LL [E-mail: robert@wotherspoon11.wanadoo.co.uk]	01556 502267
Young, John MTh DipMin	1963	1999	(Airdrie: Broomknoll)	Craigview, North Street, Moniaive, Thornhill DG3 4HR	01848 200318

DUMFRIES ADDRESSES

Lincluden	Stewartry Road		
Lochside	Lochside Road	St Mary's-Greyfriars	St Mary's Street
Maxwelltown West	Laurieknowe	St Michael's and South	St Michael's Street
St George's	George Street	Troqueer	Troqueer Road

(9) WIGTOWN AND STRANRAER

Meets at Glenluce, in the church hall, on the first Tuesday of March, October and December for ordinary business; on the first Tuesday of September for formal business followed by meetings of committees; on the first Tuesday of November, February and May for worship followed by meetings of committees; and at a church designated by the Moderator on the first Tuesday of June for Holy Communion followed by ordinary business.

Clerk: REV. DAVID W. DUTTON BA   High Kirk Manse, Leswalt High Road, Stranraer DG9 0AA   **01776 703268**
[E-mail: wigtownstranraer@cofscotland.org.uk]

Ervie Kirkcolm linked with Leswalt
Michael J. Sheppard BD   1997   Ervie Manse, Stranraer DG9 0QZ   01776 854225
[E-mail: mjs@uwclub.net]

Glasserton and Isle of Whithorn linked with Whithorn: St Ninian's Priory
Alexander I. Currie BD CPS   1990   The Manse, Whithorn, Newton Stewart DG8 8PT   01988 500267

Inch linked with Stranraer: Town Kirk (H)
John H. Burns BSc BD   1985 1988   Bayview Road, Stranraer DG9 8BE   01776 702383

Kirkcowan (H) linked with Wigtown (H)
Eric Boyle BA MTh   2006   The Manse, Church Lane, Wigtown, Newton Stewart DG8 9HT   01988 402314
[E-mail: ecthered@aol.com]

Kirkinner linked with Sorbie (H)
Jeffrey M. Mead BD   1978 1986   The Manse, Kirkinner, Newton Stewart DG8 9AL   01988 840643

Kirkmabreck linked with Monigaff (H)
Peter W.I. Aiken   1996 2005   Creebridge, Newton Stewart DG8 6NR   01671 403361
[E-mail: aikenp@btinternet.com]

Kirkmaiden (H) linked with Stoneykirk
Vacant   2007   Church Street, Sandhead, Stranraer DG9 9JJ   01776 830337
Mike Binks (Aux)   Holly Bank, Corsbie Road, Newton Stewart DG8 6JD   01671 402201
[E-mail: mike@hollybank.net]

Leswalt See Ervie Kirkcolm

Mochrum (H)
Vacant   Manse of Mochrum, Port William, Newton Stewart DG8 9QP   01988 700257

Monigaff (H) See Kirkmabreck

New Luce (H) linked with Old Luce (H)
Thomas M. McWhirter MA MSc BD   1992 1997   Glenluce, Newton Stewart DG8 0PU   01581 300319

Old Luce See New Luce

Penninghame (H)
Edward D. Lyons BD MTh   2007   The Manse, 1A Corvisel Road, Newton Stewart DG8 6LW   01671 404425
[E-mail: edwardlyons@hotmail.com]

Portpatrick linked with Stranraer: St Ninian's (H)
Gordon Kennedy BSc BD MTh   1993 2000   2 Albert Terrace, London Road, Stranraer DG9 8AB   01776 702443
[E-mail: gordon.k1@btinternet.com]

Sorbie See Kirkinner
Stoneykirk See Kirkmaiden

Stranraer: High Kirk (H)
David W. Dutton BA   1973 1986   High Kirk Manse, Leswalt High Road, Stranraer DG9 0AA   01776 703268
[E-mail: akph79@uk.uumail.com]

Stranraer: St Ninian's See Portpatrick
Stranraer: Town Kirk See Inch
Whithorn: St Ninian's Priory See Glasserton and Isle of Whithorn
Wigtown See Kirkcowan

Cairns, Alexander B. MA   1957 1997   (Ervie Kirkcolm with Leswalt)   Beechwood, Main Street, Sandhead, Stranraer DG9 9JG   01776 830389
[E-mail: sandy.cairns@btinternet.com]
Crawford, Joseph F. BA   1970 2006   (Bowden with Newtown)   21 South Street, Port William, Newton Stewart DG8 9SH   01988 700761
Dean, Roger A.F. LTh   1983 2004   (Mochrum)   Albion Cottage, 59 Main Street, Kirkinner, Newton Stewart DG8 9AN   01988 840621
[E-mail: roger.dean4@btopenworld.com]
Harkes, George   1962 1988   (Cumbernauld: Old)   11 Main Street, Sorbie, Newton Stewart DG8 8EG   01988 850255
McGill, Thomas W.   1972 1990   (Portpatrick with Stranraer: St Ninian's)   Ravenstone Moor, Dranrae, Whithorn, Newton Stewart DG8 8DS   01988 700449
Munro, Mary (Mrs) BA   1993 2004   (Auxiliary Minister)   14 Auchneil Crescent, Stranraer DG9 0JH   01776 702305
Ogilvy, Oliver M.   1959 1985   (Leswalt)   8 Dale Crescent, Stranraer DG9 0HG   01776 706285

(10) AYR

Meets on the first Tuesday of every month from September to May, excluding January, and on the fourth Tuesday of June. The June meeting will be held in the Moderator's Church. One meeting will be held in a venue to be determined by the Business Committee. Other meetings will be held in Alloway Church Hall.

Clerk: REV. JAMES CRICHTON MA BD MTh   30 Garden Street, Dalrymple KA6 6DG
[E-mail: ayr@cofscotland.org.uk]

01292 560263 (Fax)
01292 560574
01292 611117 (Tel/Fax)

Alloway (H)
Neil A. McNaught BD MA   1987 1999   1A Parkview, Alloway, Ayr KA7 4QG
[E-mail: neil@mcnaught3427.freeserve.co.uk]   01292 441252

Annbank (H) linked with Tarbolton
Alexander Shuttleworth MA BD   2004   1 Kirkport, Tarbolton, Mauchline KA5 5QJ
[E-mail: revshuttleworth@aol.com]   01292 541236

Auchinleck (H) linked with Catrine
Stephen F. Clipston MA BD   1982 2006   28 Mauchline Road, Auchinleck KA18 2BN   01290 424776

Ayr: Auld Kirk of Ayr (St John the Baptist) (H)
David R. Gemmell MA BD   1991 1999   58 Monument Road, Ayr KA7 2UB
[E-mail: drgemmell@aol.com]   01292 262580 (Tel/Fax)

Ayr: Castlehill (H)
Peter B. Park BD MCIBS   1997 2003   3 Old Hillfoot Road, Ayr KA7 3LF
[E-mail: peterpark9@btinternet.com]   01292 267332

Ayr: Newton on Ayr (H)
G. Stewart Birse CA BD BSc   1980 1989   9 Nursery Grove, Ayr KA7 3PH
[E-mail: gstewart@birse21.freeserve.co.uk]   01292 264251

Ayr: St Andrew's (H)
Harry B. Mealyea BArch BD   1984 2000   31 Bellevue Crescent, Ayr KA7 2DP
[E-mail: mealyea@tiscali.co.uk]   01292 261126

Ayr: St Columba (H)
Fraser R. Aitken MA BD   1978 1991   2 Hazelwood Road, Ayr KA7 2PY
[E-mail: frasercolumba@msn.com]   01292 284177

Ayr: St James' (H)
Robert McCrum BSc BD   1982 2005   1 Prestwick Road, Ayr KA8 8LD
[E-mail: robert@stjamesayr.org.uk]   01292 262420

Ayr: St Leonard's (H)
Robert Lynn MA BD
1984 1989
7 Shawfield Avenue, Ayr KA7 4RE
[E-mail: robert@shawfield200.fsnet.co.uk]
01292 442109

Ayr: St Quivox (H)
David T. Ness LTh
1972 1988
11 Springfield Avenue, Prestwick KA9 2HA
[E-mail: dtness@tiscali.co.uk]
01292 478306

Ayr: Wallacetown (H)
Mary C. McLauchlan (Mrs) LTh
1997 2003
87 Forehill Road, Ayr KA7 3JR
[E-mail: mary@revmother.co.uk]
01292 263878

Ballantrae (H)
Vacant
Ballantrae, Girvan KA26 0NH
01465 831252

Barr linked with Dailly linked with Girvan South
Ian K. McLachlan MA BD
1999
30 Henrietta Street, Girvan KA26 9AL
[E-mail: iankmclachlan@yetiville.freeserve.co.uk]
01465 713370

Catrine See Auchinleck

Coylton linked with Drongan: The Schaw Kirk
Vacant
4 Hamilton Place, Coylton, Ayr KA6 6JQ
01292 570272

Craigie linked with Symington
Vacant
16 Kerrix Road, Symington, Kilmarnock KA1 5QD
01563 830205

Crosshill (H) linked with Dalrymple (H)
James Crichton MA BD MTh
1969
30 Garden Street, Dalrymple KA6 6DG
[E-mail: ayr@cofscotland.org.uk]
01292 560263 (Tel)
01292 560574 (Fax)

Dailly See Barr

Dalmellington linked with Patna: Waterside
Kenneth B. Yorke BD DipEd
1982 1999
4 Carsphairn Road, Dalmellington, Ayr KA6 7RE
[E-mail: kennethyorke@tiscali.co.uk]
01292 550353

Muriel Wilson (Ms) DCS BD
28 Bellevue Crescent, Ayr KA7 2DR
[E-mail: muriel.wilson4@btinternet.com]
01292 264939

Dalrymple See Crosshill
Drongan: The Schaw Kirk See Coylton

Dundonald (H) Robert Mayes BD	1982	1988	64 Main Street, Dundonald, Kilmarnock KA2 9HG [E-mail: bobmayes@fsmail.net]	01563 850243
Fisherton (H) linked with Kirkoswald Arrick D. Wilkinson BSc BD	2000	2003	The Manse, Kirkoswald, Maybole KA19 8HZ [E-mail: arrick@clergy.net]	01655 760210
Girvan: North (Old and St Andrew's) (H) Douglas G. McNab BA BD	1999		38 The Avenue, Girvan KA26 9DS [E-mail: dougmcnab@aol.com]	01465 713203
Girvan: South See Barr linked with Dailly				
Kirkmichael linked with Straiton: St Cuthbert's W. Gerald Jones MA BD MTh	1984	1985	Patna Road, Kirkmichael, Maybole KA19 7PJ [E-mail: revgerald@jonesg99.freeserve.co.uk]	01655 750286
Kirkoswald (H) See Fisherton				
Lugar linked with Old Cumnock: Old (H) John W. Paterson BSc BD DipEd	1994		33 Barrhill Road, Cumnock KA18 1PJ [E-mail: ocochurchwow@hotmail.com]	01290 420769
Mauchline (H) Alan B. Telfer BA BD	1983	1991	4 Westside Gardens, Mauchline KA5 5DJ [E-mail: telferab@tiscali.co.uk]	01290 550386
Maybole David Whiteman BD	1998		64 Culzean Road, Maybole KA19 8AH [E-mail: soohsw@aol.com]	01655 889456
Douglas T. Moore (Aux)	2003		9 Midton Avenue, Prestwick KA9 1PU [E-mail: douglastmoore@hotmail.com]	01292 671352
Monkton and Prestwick: North (H) Arthur A. Christie BD	1997	2000	40 Monkton Road, Prestwick KA9 1AR [E-mail: revaac@btinternet.com]	01292 477499
Muirkirk (H) linked with Sorn Vacant			2 Smallburn Road, Muirkirk, Cumnock KA18 3RF	01290 661157
New Cumnock (H) Rona M. Young (Mrs) BD DipEd	1991	2001	37 Castle, New Cumnock, Cumnock KA18 4AG [E-mail: revronyoung@hotmail.com]	01290 338296

Ochiltree linked with Stair
Carolyn M. Baker (Mrs) BD — 1997 — 10 Mauchline Road, Ochiltree, Cumnock KA18 2PZ [E-mail: cncbaker@btinternet.com] — 01290 700365

Old Cumnock: Old See Lugar

Old Cumnock: Trinity
Vacant — 46 Ayr Road, Cumnock KA18 1DW — 01290 422145

Patna: Waterside See Dalmellington

Prestwick: Kingcase (H) (E-mail: office@kingcase.freeserve.co.uk)
T. David Watson BSc BD — 1988 1997 — 15 Bellrock Avenue, Prestwick KA9 1SQ [E-mail: tdavidwatson@btinternet.com] — 01292 479571

Prestwick: St Nicholas' (H)
George R. Fiddes BD — 1979 1985 — 3 Bellevue Road, Prestwick KA9 1NW [E-mail: george@gfiddes.freeserve.co.uk] — 01292 477613

Prestwick: South (H)
Kenneth C. Elliott BD BA CertMin — 1989 — 68 St Quivox Road, Prestwick KA9 1JF [E-mail: kennethc@revelliott.freeserve.co.uk] — 01292 478788

St Colmon (Arnsheen Barrhill and Colmonell)
John S. Lochrie BSc BD MTh PhD — 1967 1999 — Manse Road, Colmonell, Girvan KA26 0SA — 01465 881224
(Charge formed by the union of Arnsheen Barrhill and Colmonell)

Sorn See Muirkirk
Stair See Ochiltree
Straiton: St Cuthbert's See Kirkmichael
Symington See Craigie
Tarbolton See Annbank

Troon: Old (H)
Alastair H. Symington MA BD — 1972 1998 — 85 Bentinck Drive, Troon KA10 6HZ [E-mail: revahs@tiscali.co.uk] — 01292 313644

Troon: Portland (H)
Ronald M.H. Boyd BD DipTh — 1995 1999 — 89 South Beach, Troon KA10 6EQ [E-mail: rmhboyd@wightcablenorth.net] — 01292 313285

Troon: St Meddan's (H) (E-mail: st.meddan@virgin.net)
David L. Harper BSc BD   1972 1979   27 Bentinck Drive, Troon KA10 6HX   01292 311784
[E-mail: d.l.harper@btinternet.com]

Name	Dates	Position	Address	Phone
Andrew, R.J.M. MA	1955 1994	(Uddingston: Old)	6A Ronaldshaw Park, Ayr KA7 2TS	01292 263430
Banks, John BD	1968 2001	(Hospital Chaplain)	19 Victoria Drive, Troon KA10 6JF	01292 317758
Bell, Robert P. BSc	1968 2007	(Ballantrae)	14 Templeton Crescent, Prestwick KA9 1JA	01292 476504
			[E-mail: bobandirenebell@btinternet.com]	
Blyth, James G.S. BSc BD	1963 1986	(Glenmuick)	40 Robsland Avenue, Ayr KA7 2RW	01292 261276
Bogle, Thomas C. BD	1983 2003	(Fisherton with Maybole: West)	38 McEwan Crescent, Mossblown, Ayr KA6 5DR	01292 521215
Campbell, Effie C. (Mrs) BD	1981 1991	(Old Cumnock: Crichton West with St Ninian's)		
Cranston, George BD	1976 2001	(Rutherglen: Wardlawhill)	7 Lansdowne Road, Ayr KA8 8LS	01292 264282
Dickie, Michael M. BSc	1955 1994	(Ayr: Castlehill)	20 Capperview, Prestwick KA9 1BH	01292 476627
Garrity, T. Alan W. BSc BD MTh	1969 1999	Christ Church, Warwick, Bermuda	8 Noltmire Road, Ayr KA8 9ES	01292 618512
			PO Box PG88, Paget PG BX, Bermuda	
			[E-mail: revtawg@logic.bm]	
Glencross, William M. LTh	1968 1999	(Bellshill: Macdonald Memorial)	1 Lochay Place, Troon KA10 7HH	01292 317097
Grant, J. Gordon MA BD	1957 1997	(Edinburgh: Dean)	33 Fullarton Drive, Troon KA10 6LE	01292 311852
Guthrie, James A.	1969 2005	(Corsock and Kirkpatrick Durham with Crossmichael and Parton)	2 Barrhill Road, Pinwherry, Girvan KA26 0QE	01465 841236
			[E-mail: revjguth@fish.co.uk]	
Hannah, William BD MCAM MIPR	1987 2001	(Muirkirk)	8 Dovecote View, Kirkintilloch, Glasgow G66 3HY	0141-776 1337
Helon, George G. BA BD	1984 2000	(Barr linked with Dailly)	9 Park Road, Maxwelltown, Dumfries DG2 7PW	01387 259255
Johnston, Kenneth L. BA LTh	1969 2001	(Annbank)	2 Rylands, Prestwick KA9 2DX	01292 471980
			[E-mail: ken@kenston.co.uk]	
Kent, Arthur F.S.	1966 1999	(Monkton and Prestwick: North)	17 St David's Drive, Evesham, Worcs WR11 6AS	01386 421562
King, Chris (Mrs) MA BD DCS	1991 2006	Deaconess	28 Kilnford Drive, Dundonald, Kilmarnock KA2 9ET	01563 851197
Lennox, Lawrie I. MA BD DipEd	1965 1999	(Cromar)	7 Carwinshoch View, Ayr KA7 4AY	
McCrorie, William		(Free Church Chaplain: Royal Brompton Hospital)		
Macdonald, Ian U.	1960 1997	(Tarbolton)	12 Shieling Park, Ayr KA7 2UR	01292 288854
McNidder, Roderick H. BD	1987 1997	Chaplain: NHS Ayrshire and Arran Trust	18 Belmont Road, Ayr KA7 2PF	01292 283085
McPhail, Andrew M. BA	1968 2002	(Ayr: Wallacetown)	6 Hollow Park, Alloway, Ayr KA7 4SR	01292 442554
Mills, Ian A.M.	2006	Auxiliary Minister	25 Maybole Road, Ayr KA7 2QA	01292 282108
Mitchell, Sheila M. (Miss) BD MTh	1995 2002	Chaplain: NHS Ayrshire and Arran Trust	4 Farden Place, Prestwick KA9 2HS	01292 475212
Russell, Paul R. MA BD	1984 2006	Chaplain: NHS Ayrshire and Arran Trust	Ailsa Hospital, Ayr KA6 6BQ	01292 610556
Sanderson, Alastair M. BA LTh	1971 2007	(Craigie with Symington)	23 Nursery Wynd, Ayr KA7 3NZ	01292 618020
			26 Main Street, Monkton, Prestwick KA9 2QL	
			[E-mail: alel@sanderson29.fsnet.co.uk]	
Saunders, Campbell M. MA BD	1952 1989	(Ayr: St Leonard's)	42 Marle Park, Ayr KA7 4RN	01292 441673
Stirling, Ian R. BSc BD	1990 2002	Chaplain: The Ayrshire Hospice	Ayrshire Hospice, 35–37 Racecourse Road, Ayr KA7 2TG	01292 269200

AYR ADDRESSES

Ayr
Auld Kirk — Kirkport (116 High Street)
Castlehill — Castlehill Road x Hillfoot Road
Newton on Ayr — Main Street
St Andrew's — Park Circus
St Columba — Midton Road x Carrick Park
St James' — Prestwick Road x Falkland Park Road

St Leonard's — St Leonard's Road x Monument Road
Wallacetown — John Street x Church Street

Girvan
North — Montgomerie Street
South — Stair Park

Prestwick
Kingcase — Waterloo Road
Monkton and Prestwick North — Monkton Road
St Nicholas — Main Street
South — Main Street

Troon
Old — Ayr Street
Portland — St Meddan's Street
St Meddan's — St Meddan's Street

(11) IRVINE AND KILMARNOCK

The Presbytery meets ordinarily at 6:30pm in the Hall of Howard St Andrew's Church, Kilmarnock, on the first Tuesday of each month from September to May (except January and April), and on the fourth Tuesday in June. The September meeting begins with the celebration of Holy Communion.

Clerk:	REV. COLIN G.F. BROCKIE BSc(Eng) BD SOSc	51 Portland Road, Kilmarnock KA1 2EQ [E-mail: irvinekilmarnock@cofscotland.org.uk]	01563 525311
Depute Clerk:	I. STEUART DEY LLB NP	72 Dundonald Road, Kilmarnock KA1 1RZ [E-mail: steuart.dey@btinternet.com]	01563 521686
Treasurer:	JAMES McINTOSH BA CA	15 Dundonald Road, Kilmarnock KA1 1RU	01563 523552

The Presbytery office is manned each Tuesday, Wednesday and Thursday from 9am until 12:45pm. The office telephone number is 01563 526295.

Crosshouse
| T. Edward Marshall BD | 1987 | 2007 | 27 Kilmarnock Road, Crosshouse, Kilmarnock KA2 0EZ [E-mail: marshall1654@hotmail.com] | 01563 521035 |

Darvel (01560 722924)
| Charles M. Cameron BA BD PhD | 1980 | 2001 | 46 West Main Street, Darvel KA17 0AQ | 01560 322924 |

Dreghorn and Springside
| Gary E. Horsburgh BA | 1976 | 1983 | 96A Townfoot, Dreghorn, Irvine KA11 4EZ | 01294 217770 |

Dunlop Maureen M. Duncan (Mrs) BD	1996	4 Dampark, Dunlop, Kilmarnock KA3 4BZ	01560 484083
Fenwick (H) Geoffrey Redmayne BSc BD MPhil	2000	2 Kirkton Place, Fenwick, Kilmarnock KA3 6DW [E-mail: geoff@gredmayne.fsnet.co.uk]	01560 600217
Galston (H) (01563 820136) Graeme R. Wilson MCIBS BD ThM	2006	60 Brewland Street, Galston KA4 8DX [E-mail: graeme.wilson@gmail.com]	01563 820246
John H.B. Taylor MA BD DipEd FEIS (Assoc)	1952 1990	62 Woodlands Grove, Kilmarnock KA3 1TZ	01563 526698
Hurlford (H) James D. McCulloch BD MIOP MIPJ	1996	12 Main Road, Crookedholm, Kilmarnock KA3 6JT	01563 535673
Irvine: Fullarton (H) (Website: www.fullartonchurch.co.uk) Neil Urquhart BD DipMin	1989	48 Waterside, Irvine KA12 8QJ [E-mail: neilurquhart@beeb.net]	01294 279909
Irvine: Girdle Toll (E) (H) (Website: www.girdletoll.fsbusiness.co.uk) Clare B. Sutcliffe BSc BD	2000	2 Littlestane Rise, Irvine KA11 2BJ [E-mail: revclare@tesco.net]	01294 213565
Irvine: Mure (H) Hugh M. Adamson BD	1976	West Road, Irvine KA12 8RE	01294 279916
Irvine: Old (H) (01294 273503) Robert Travers BA BD	1993 1999	22 Kirk Vennel, Irvine KA12 0DQ [E-mail: robert@travers46.freeserve.co.uk]	01294 279265
Irvine: Relief Bourtreehill (H) Andrew R. Black BD	1987 2003	4 Kames Court, Irvine KA11 1RT [E-mail: andrewblack@tiscali.co.uk]	01294 216939
Irvine: St Andrew's (H) (01294 276051) Vacant		206 Bank Street, Irvine KA12 0YD	01294 211403
Kilmarnock: Grange (H) (07818 550606) (Website: www.grangechurch.org.uk) Colin G.F. Brockie BSc(Eng) BD SOSc	1967 1978	51 Portland Road, Kilmarnock KA1 2EQ [E-mail: revcol@revcol.demon.co.uk]	01563 525311
Kilmarnock: Henderson (H) (01563 541302) (Website: www.hendersonchurch.org.uk) David W. Lacy BA BD DLitt	1976 1989	52 London Road, Kilmarnock KA3 7AJ [E-mail: thelacys@tinyworld.co.uk]	01563 523113 (Tel/Fax)

Kilmarnock: Howard St Andrew's (H) (Website: www.kirk.il2.com)
Vacant — 1 Evelyn Villas, Holehouse Road, Kilmarnock KA3 7AX — 01563 522278

Kilmarnock: Laigh West High (H)
David S. Cameron BD — 2001 — 1 Holmes Farm Road, Kilmarnock KA1 1TP [E-mail: dvdcam5@msn.com] — 01563 525416

Kilmarnock: Old High Kirk (H)
William M. Hall BD — 1972 1979 — 107 Dundonald Road, Kilmarnock KA1 1UP [E-mail: revwillie@tiscali.co.uk] — 01563 525608

Kilmarnock: Riccarton (H)
Colin A. Strong BSc BD — 1989 2007 — 2 Jasmine Road, Kilmarnock KA1 2HD [E-mail: colinastrong@aol.com] — 01563 549490

Kilmarnock: St John's Onthank (H)
Susan M. Anderson (Mrs) — 1997 — 84 Wardneuk Drive, Kilmarnock KA3 2EX [E-mail: stjohnthank@yahoo.co.uk] — 01563 521815

Kilmarnock: St Kentigern's (Website: www.stkentigern.org.uk)
S. Grant Barclay LLB BD — 1995 — 1 Thirdpart Place, Kilmarnock KA1 1UL [E-mail: grant.barclay@bigfoot.com] — 01563 571280

Kilmarnock: St Marnock's (H) (01563 541337)
James McNaughtan BD DipMin — 1983 1989 — 35 South Gargieston Drive, Kilmarnock KA1 1TB [E-mail: jim@mcnaughtan.demon.co.uk] — 01563 521665

Kilmarnock: St Ninian's Bellfield (01563 524705) linked with Kilmarnock: Shortlees
H. Taylor Brown BD CertMin — 1997 2002 — 14 McLelland Drive, Kilmarnock KA1 1SF [E-mail: htaylorbrown@hotmail.com] — 01563 529920

Kilmarnock: Shortlees See Kilmarnock: St Ninian's Bellfield

Kilmaurs: St Maur's Glencairn (H) (Website: www.jimcorbett.freeserve.co.uk/page2.html)
John A. Urquhart BD — 1993 — 9 Standalane, Kilmaurs, Kilmarnock KA3 2NB — 01563 538289

Newmilns: Loudoun (H)
John Macleod MA BD — 2000 — Loudoun Manse, 116A Loudoun Road, Newmilns KA16 9HH — 01560 320174

Stewarton: John Knox
Vacant — 27 Avenue Street, Stewarton, Kilmarnock KA3 5AP — 01560 482418

Stewarton: St Columba's (H)
Vacant
1 Kirk Glebe, Stewarton, Kilmarnock KA3 5BJ   01560 482453

Ayrshire Mission to the Deaf
S. Grant Barclay LLB BD (Chaplain)   1991   1998   89 Mure Avenue, Kilmarnock KA3 1TT   01563 571280
[E-mail: grant.barclay@bigfoot.com]

Name	Ord	Ind	Charge	Address	Phone
Campbell, George H.	1957	1992	(Stewarton: John Knox)	20 Woodlands Grove, Kilmarnock KA3 1TZ [E-mail: geen@ecampbell5.fsnet.co.uk]	01563 536365
Campbell, John A. JP FIEM	1984	1998	(Irvine: St Andrew's)	Flowerdale, Balmoral Lane, Blairgowrie PH10 7AF	01250 872795
Cant, Thomas M. MA BD	1964	2004	(Paisley: Laigh Kirk)	3 Meikle Cutstraw Farm, Stewarton, Kilmarnock KA3 5HU [E-mail: revtmcant@aol.com]	01560 480566
Christie, Robert S. MA BD ThM	1964	2001	(Kilmarnock: West High)	24 Homeroyal House, 2 Chalmers Crescent, Edinburgh EH9 1TP	
Davidson, James BD DipAFH	1989	2002	(Wishaw: Old)	13 Redburn Place, Irvine KA12 9BQ	01294 312515
Gillon, C. Blair BD	1980	2007	(Glasgow: Ibrox)	East Muirshield Farmhouse, by Dunlop, Kilmarnock KA3 4EJ	01560 483778
Hare, Malcolm M.W. BA BD	1956	1994	(Kilmarnock: St Kentigern's)	21 Raith Road, Fenwick, Kilmarnock KA3 6DB	01560 600388
Hay, W.J.R. MA BD	1959	1995	(Buchanan with Drymen)	18 Jamieson Place, Stewarton, Kilmarnock KA3 3AY	01560 482799
Hosain, Samuel BD MTh PhD	1979	2006	(Stewarton: John Knox)	7 Dalwhinnie Crescent, Kilmarnock KA3 1QS [E-mail: samuel.h2@ukonline.co.uk]	01563 551717
Huggett, Judith A. (Miss) BA BD	1990	1998	Hospital Chaplain	4 Westmoor Crescent, Kilmarnock KA1 1TX	01563 526314
Jarvie, Thomas W. BD	1953	2005	(Kilmarnock: Riccarton)	3 Heston Place, Kilmarnock KA3 2JR	01563 573994
Kelly, Thomas A. Davidson MA BD FSAScot	1975	2002	(Glasgow: Govan Old)	2 Springhill Stables, Portland Road, Kilmarnock KA1 2EJ [E-mail: dks@springhillstables.freeserve.co.uk]	
McAlpine, Richard H.M. BA FSAScot	1968	2000	(Lochgoilhead and Kilmorich)	7 Kingsford Place, Kilmarnock KA3 6FG	01563 572075
MacDonald, James M.	1964	1987	(Kilmarnock: St John's Onthank)	29 Carmel Place, Kilmaurs, Kilmarnock KA3 2QU	01563 525254
Morrison, Alistair H. BTh DipYCS	1985	2004	(Paisley: St Mark's Oldhall)	92 St Leonard's Road, Ayr KA7 2PU [E-mail: alistairmorrison@supanet.com]	01292 266021
O'Leary, Thomas BD	1983	1998	(Lochwinnoch)	1 Carter's Place, Irvine KA12 0BU	01294 313274
Rae, Scott M. MBE BD CPS	1976	2007	(Principal Chaplain: Royal Navy)	12 Primrose Place, Kilmarnock KA1 2RR [E-mail: catherine.rae1@btopenworld.com]	
Roy, James BA	1967	1982	(Irvine: Girdle Toll)	23 Bowes Rigg, Stewarton, Kilmarnock KA3 5EL [E-mail: jimroy@fountainmag.fsnet.co.uk]	01560 482185
Scott, Thomas T.	1968	1989	(Kilmarnock: St Marnock's)	6 North Hamilton Place, Kilmarnock KA1 2QN [E-mail: tomtscott@btinternet.com]	01563 531415
Shaw, Catherine A.M. MA	1998	2006	(Auxiliary Minister)	40 Merrygreen Place, Stewarton, Kilmarnock KA3 5EP [E-mail: catherine.shaw@tesco.net]	01560 483352
Urquhart, Barbara (Mrs) DCS			Deaconess and Presbytery S.S. Adviser	9 Standalane, Kilmaurs, Kilmarnock KA3 2NB	01563 538289
Welsh, Alex M. MA BD	1979	2007	Hospital Chaplain	8 Greenside Avenue, Prestwick KA9 2HB	01292 475341

IRVINE and KILMARNOCK ADDRESSES

Irvine

Dreghorn and Springside	Townfoot x Station Brae
Fullarton	Marress Road x Church Street
Girdle Toll	Bryce Knox Court
Mure	West Road
Old	Kirkgate
Relief Bourtreehill	Crofthead, Bourtreehill
St Andrew's	Caldon Road x Oaklands Ave

Kilmarnock

Ayrshire Mission to the Deaf	10 Clark Street	Riccarton	Old Street
Grange	Woodstock Street	St Andrew's Glencairn	St Andrew's Street
Henderson	London Road	St John's Onthank	84 Wardneuk Street
Howard	5 Portland Road	St Marnock's	St Marnock's Street
Laigh	John Dickie Street	St Ninian's Bellfield	Whatriggs Road
Old High Kirk	Church Street x Soulis Street	Shortlees	Central Avenue
		West High	Portland Street

01475 568802
07885 876021 (Mbl)
01475 687217

(12) ARDROSSAN

Meets at Saltcoats, New Trinity, on the first Tuesday of February, March, April, May, September, October, November and December, and on the second Tuesday of June.

Clerk: REV. JOHNSTON R. McKAY MA BA   15 Montgomerie Avenue, Fairlie, Largs KA29 0EE
[E-mail: ardrossan@cofscotland.org.uk]

Depute Clerk: MR ALAN K. SAUNDERSON   17 Union Street, Largs KA30 8DG

Ardrossan: Barony St John's (H) (01294 465009)
Vacant   10 Seafield Drive, Ardrossan KA22 8NU   01294 463868

Ardrossan: Park (01294 463711)
William R. Johnston BD   1998   35 Ardneil Court, Ardrossan KA22 7NQ   01294 471808
Marion L.K. Howie (Mrs) MA ACRS (Aux)   1992   51 High Road, Stevenston KA20 3DY   01294 466571
[E-mail: marion.howie@ndirect.co.uk]

Beith: High (H) (01505 502686) linked with Beith: Trinity (H)
Roderick I.T. MacDonald BD CertMin   1992   2005   2 Glebe Court, Beith KA15 1ET   01505 503858
Valerie G.C. Watson MA BD STM (Assoc)   1987   2007   14B Gladstone Road, Saltcoats KA21 5LD   01294 470030
[E-mail: vgcwatson@tiscali.co.uk]

Beith: Trinity (H) See Beith: High

Brodick linked with Corrie linked with Lochranza and Pirnmill linked with Shiskine (H)
Angus Adamson BD   2006   4 Manse Crescent, Brodick, Isle of Arran KA27 8AS   01770 302334
[E-mail: s-adamson@corriecraviehome.fsnet.co.uk]

Corrie See Brodick

Cumbrae
Marjory H. Mackay (Mrs) BD DipEd CCE   1998   Marine Parade, Millport, Isle of Cumbrae KA28 0ED   01475 530416
[E-mail: mmackay@fish.co.uk]

Dalry: St Margaret's
Vacant   Bridgend, Dalry KA24 4DA   01294 832234

Dalry: Trinity (H)
Martin Thomson BSc DipEd BD   1988   2004   Trinity Manse, West Kilbride Road, Dalry KA24 5DX   01294 832363
[E-mail: martin@thomsonm40.freeserve.co.uk]

Fairlie (H)
James Whyte BD   1981   2006   14 Fairlieburne Gardens, Fairlie, Largs KA29 0ER   01475 568342
[E-mail: jameswhyte89@btinternet.com]

Fergushill
Vacant

Kilbirnie: Auld Kirk (H)
Ian W. Benzie BD   1999   49 Holmhead, Kilbirnie KA25 6BS   01505 682348
[E-mail: revian@btopenworld.com]

Kilbirnie: St Columba's (H) (01505 685239)
Fiona C. Ross (Miss) BD DipMin   1996   2004   Manse of St Columba's, Dipple Road, Kilbirnie KA25 7JU   01505 683342
[E-mail: fionaross@calvin78.freeserve.co.uk]

Kilmory
Vacant

Kilwinning: Mansefield Trinity (E) (01294 550746)
Vacant   27 Treesbank, Kilwinning KA13 6LY   01294 558746

Kilwinning: Old
Alison Davidge MA BD   1990   2006   54 Dalry Road, Kilwinning KA13 7HE   01294 552606

Lamlash
Vacant

Largs: Clark Memorial (H) (01475 675186)
Stephen J. Smith BSc BD   1993   1998   31 Douglas Street, Largs KA30 8PT   01475 672370
[E-mail: stephenrevsteve@aol.com]

Largs: St Columba's (01475 686212) Roderick J. Grahame BD CPS	1991	2002	17 Beachway, Largs KA30 8QH [E-mail: rjgrahame@supanet.com]	01475 673107
Largs: St John's (H) (01475 674468) Andrew F. McGurk BD	1983	1993	1 Newhaven Grove, Largs KA30 8NS [E-mail: afmcg.largs@talk21.co.uk]	01475 676123
Lochranza and Pirnmill See Brodick				
Saltcoats: New Trinity (H) (01294 472001) Elaine W. McKinnon MA BD	1988	2006	1 Montgomerie Crescent, Saltcoats KA21 5BX [E-mail: elaine@newtrinity.co.uk]	01294 461143
Saltcoats: North (01294 464679) Alexander B. Noble MA BD ThM	1982	2003	25 Longfield Avenue, Saltcoats KA21 6DR	01294 604923
Saltcoats: St Cuthbert's (H) Brian H. Oxburgh BSc BD	1980	1988	10 Kennedy Road, Saltcoats KA21 5SF [E-mail: oxburgh9@aol.com]	01294 602674
Shiskine (H) See Brodick				
Stevenston: Ardeer linked with Stevenston: Livingstone (H) John M.M. Lafferty BD		1999	32 High Road, Stevenston KA20 3DR	01294 464180
Stevenston: High (H) (Website: www.highkirk.com) M. Scott Cameron MA BD		2002	Glencairn Street, Stevenston KA20 3DL [E-mail: scottie_cameron@ukonline.co.uk]	01294 463356
Stevenston: Livingstone (H) See Stevenston: Ardeer				
West Kilbride: Overton (H) Vacant			Goldenberry Avenue, West Kilbride KA23 9LJ	01294 823186
West Kilbride: St Andrew's (H) (01294 829902) Vacant			7 Overton Drive, West Kilbride KA23 9LQ	01294 823142
Whiting Bay and Kildonan Elizabeth R.L. Watson (Miss) BA BD	1981	1982	Whiting Bay, Brodick, Isle of Arran KA27 8RE [E-mail: revewatson@surefish.co.uk]	01770 700289

Name	Charge / Role	Ord.	Ind.	Address & E-mail	Telephone
Bristow, Irene A. (Mrs) BD	(Lochgelly: Macainsh)	1989	2005	20 Montgomerie Road, Saltcoats KA21 5DP [E-mail: ibristow@btinternet.com]	01294 601537
Coogan, J. Melvyn LTh	(Carstairs with Carstairs Junction)	1992	2004	Flat E, 9 Silverdale Gardens, Largs KA30 9LT	01475 675955
Cruickshank, Norman BA BD	(West Kilbride: Overton)	1983	2006	24D Faulds Wynd, Seamill, West Kilbride KA23 9FA	01294 822239
Dailly, J.R. BD DipPS	(Staff Chaplain: Army)	1979	1979	DACG, HQ 42 (NW) Bde, Fulwood Barracks, Preston PR2 8AA	
Downie, Alexander S.	(Ardrossan: Park)	1975	1997	14 Korsankel Wynd, Saltcoats KA21 6HY	01294 464097
Drysdale, James H. LTh	(Blackbraes and Shieldhill)	1987	2006	10 John Clark Street, Largs KA30 9AH	01475 674870
Gordon, David C.	(Gigha and Cara)	1953	1988	Quoys of Barnhouse, Stenness, Orkney KW16 3JY	
Harbison, David J.H.	(Beith: High with Beith: Trinity)	1958	1998	42 Mill Park, Dalry KA24 5BB [E-mail: djh@harbi.fsnet.co.uk]	01294 834092
Hebenton, David J. MA BD	(Ayton and Burnmouth linked with Grantshouse and Houndwood and Reston)	1958	2002	22B Faulds Wynd, Seamill, West Kilbride KA23 9FA	01294 829228
Leask, Rebecca M. (Mrs)	(Callander: St Bride's)	1977	1985	20 Strathclyde House, 31 Shore Road, Skelmorlie PA17 5AN	01475 520765
McCallum, Alexander D. BD	(Saltcoats: New Trinity)	1987	2005	33 Greeto Falls Avenue, Largs KA30 9HJ [E-mail: sandyandjose@madasafish.com]	01475 670133
McCance, Andrew M. BSc	(Coatbridge: Middle)	1986	1995	6A Douglas Place, Largs KA30 8PU	01475 673303
McKay, Johnston R. MA BA	(Religious Broadcasting: BBC)	1969	1987	15 Montgomerie Avenue, Fairlie, Largs KA29 0EE [E-mail: johnston.mckay@btopenworld.com]	01475 568802
MacLeod, Ian LTh BA MTh PhD	(Brodick with Corrie)	1969	2006	Cromla Cottage, Corrie, Isle of Arran KA27 8JB [E-mail: i.macleod829@btinternet.com]	01770 810237
Mitchell, D. Ross BA BD	(West Kilbride: St Andrew's)	1972	2007	11 Dunbar Gardens, Saltcoats KA21 6GJ [E-mail: ross.mitchell@virgin.net]	
Paterson, John H. BD	(Kirkintilloch: St David's Memorial Park)	1977	2000	Creag Bhan, Golf Course Road, Whiting Bay, Isle of Arran KA27 8QT	01770 700569
Roy, Iain M. MA BD	(Stevenston: Livingstone)	1960	1997	2 The Fieldings, Dunlop, Kilmarnock KA3 4AU	01560 483072
Selfridge, John BTh BREd	(Eddrachillis)	1969	1991	Strathclyde House, Apt 1, Shore Road, Skelmorlie PA17 5AN	01475 529514
Taylor, Andrew S. BTh FPhS	(Greenock Union)	1959	1992	9 Raillies Avenue, Largs KA30 8QY [E-mail: andrew@taylorlargs.fsnet.co.uk]	01475 674709
Thomson, Margaret (Mrs)	(Saltcoats: Erskine)	1988	1993	72 Knockrivoch Place, Ardrossan KA22 7PZ	01294 468685
Walker, David S. MA	(Makerstoun with Smailholm with Stichill, Hume and Nenthorn)	1939	1978	The Anchorage, Baycroft, Strachur, Argyll PA27 8BY	

(13) LANARK

Meets on the first Tuesday of February, March, April, May, September, October, November and December, and on the third Tuesday of June.

Clerk: REV. JAMES S.H. CUTLER BD CEng MIStructE   17 Mercat Loan, Biggar ML12 6DG   01899 220625
[E-mail: lanark@cofscotland.org.uk]

Biggar (H) (E-mail: j.francis@lanarkpresbytery.org)
James Francis BD PhD   2002   2005   61 High Street, Biggar ML12 6DA   01899 220227
[E-mail: revjim.francis@btinternet.com]

Black Mount linked with Cutler linked with Libberton and Quothquan (E-mail: j.cutler@lanarkpresbytery.org)
James S.H. Cutler BD CEng MIStructE   1986   2004   17 Mercat Loan, Biggar ML12 6DG   01899 220625
[E-mail: jim.cutler1@virgin.net]

Cairngryffe linked with Symington (E-mail: g.houston@lanarkpresbytery.org)
Graham R. Houston BSc BD MTh PhD   1978   2001   16 Abington Road, Symington, Biggar ML12 6JX   01899 308838
[E-mail: gandih@onetel.net]

Carluke: Kirkton (H) (01555 750778) (E-mail: i.cunningham@lanarkpresbytery.org)
Iain D. Cunningham MA BD   1979   1987   9 Station Road, Carluke ML8 5AA   01555 771262
[E-mail: iaindc@btconnect.com]

Carluke: St Andrew's (H) (E-mail: h.jamieson@lanarkpresbytery.org)
Helen E. Jamieson (Mrs) BD DipED   1989   120 Clyde Street, Carluke ML8 5BG   01555 771218
[E-mail: helen@hjamieson.wanadoo.co.uk]

Carluke: St John's (H) (Website: www.carluke-stjohns.org.uk)
Roy J. Cowieson BD   1979   2007   18 Old Bridgend, Carluke ML8 4HN   01555 752519
[E-mail: roy.cowieson@btinternet.com]

Carnwath (H) (E-mail: b.gauld@lanarkpresbytery.org)
Beverly G.D.D. Gauld MA BD   1972   1978   The Manse, Carnwath, Lanark ML11 8JY   01555 840259
[E-mail: bevrev.gauld@southlanarkshire.gov.uk]

Carstairs and Carstairs Junction, The United Church of
Vacant   80 Lanark Road, Carstairs, Lanark ML11 8QH   01555 870250

Coalburn linked with Lesmahagow: Old (Church office: 01555 892425)
Aileen Robson BD   2003   9 Elm Bank, Lesmahagow, Lanark ML11 0EA   01555 895325
[E-mail: a.robson@lanarkpresbytery.org]

Crossford linked with Kirkfieldbank (E-mail: s.reid@lanarkpresbytery.org)
Steven Reid BAcc CA BD   1989   1997   74 Lanark Road, Crossford, Carluke ML8 5RE   01555 860415
[E-mail: steven.reid@sky.com]

Cutler See Black Mount

Forth: St Paul's (H) (E-mail: s.ross@lanarkpresbytery.org)
Sarah L. Ross (Mrs) BD MTh PGDip   2004   22 Lea Rig, Forth, Lanark ML11 8EA   01555 812832
[E-mail: rev_sross@btinternet.com]

Glencaple linked with Lowther
Margaret A. Muir (Miss) MA LLB BD   1989   2001   66 Carlisle Road, Crawford, Biggar ML12 6TW   01864 502625

Kirkfieldbank See Crossford

Kirkmuirhill (H) (E-mail: i.watson@lanarkpresbytery.org)
Ian M. Watson LLB DipLP BD   1998 2003   The Manse, 2 Lanark Road, Kirkmuirhill, Lanark ML11 9RB   01555 892409
[E-mail: ian.watson21@btopenworld.com]

Lanark: Greyfriars (Church office: 01555 661510) (E-mail: b.kerr@lanarkpresbytery.org) (Website: www.lanarkgreyfriars.com)
Bryan Kerr BA BD   2002 2007   Greyfriars Manse, 3 Bellefield Way, Lanark ML11 7NW   01555 663363
[E-mail: bryan@lanarkgreyfriars.com]   08700 518795 (Fax)

Lanark: St Nicholas' (E-mail: a.meikle@lanarkpresbytery.org)
Alison A. Meikle (Mrs) BD   1999 2002   2 Kaimhill Court, Lanark ML11 9HU   01555 662600
[E-mail: alison@lanarkstnichs.fsnet.co.uk]

Law (E-mail: a.mcivor@lanarkpresbytery.org)
Anne McIvor (Miss) SRD BD   1996 2003   The Manse, 53 Lawhill Road, Law, Carluke ML8 5EZ   01698 373180
[E-mail: annemcivor@btinternet.com]

Lesmahagow: Abbeygreen (E-mail: d.carmichael@lanarkpresbytery.org)
David S. Carmichael   1982   Abbeygreen Manse, Lesmahagow, Lanark ML11 0DB   01555 893384
[E-mail: david.carmichael@abbeygreen.org.uk]

Lesmahagow: Old (H) See Coalburn
Libberton and Quothquan See Black Mount
Lowther See Glencaple
Symington See Cairngryffe

The Douglas Valley Church (Church office: Tel/Fax: 01555 850000) (Website: www.douglasvalleychurch.org)
Vacant   The Manse, Douglas, Lanark ML11 0RB   01555 851213

Name			(Former charge)	Address	Tel
Cowell, Susan G. (Miss) BA BD	1986	1998	(Budapest)	3 Gavel Lane, Regency Gardens, Lanark ML11 9FB	01555 665509
Craig, William BA LTh	1974	1997	(Cambusbarron: The Bruce Memorial)	31 Heathfield Drive, Blackwood, Lanark ML11 9SR	01555 893710
Easton, David J.C. MA BD	1965	2005	(Glasgow: Burnside-Blairbeth)	Rowanbank, Cormiston Road, Quothquan, Biggar ML12 6ND [E-mail: deaston@btinternet.com]	01899 308459
Findlay, Henry J.W. MA BD	1965	2005	(Wishaw: St Mark's)	2 Alva Gardens, Carluke ML8 5UY	01555 759995
Fox, George H.	1959	1977	(Coalsnaughton)	Brahead House, Crossford, Carluke ML8 5NQ	01555 860716
Jones, Philip H.	1968	1987	(Bishopbriggs: Kenmure)	39 Bankhouse, 62 Abbeygreen, Lesmahagow, Lanark ML11 0JS	
McCormick, W. Cadzow MA BD	1943	1983	(Glasgow: Maryhill Old)	82 Main Street, Symington, Biggar ML12 6LJ	01899 308221
McMahon, Robert J. BD	1959	1997	(Crossford with Kirkfieldbank)	7 Ridgepark Drive, Lanark ML11 9PG	01555 663844
Paciti, Stephen A. MA	1963	2003	(Black Mount with Culter with Libberton and Quothquan)	157 Nithsdale Road, Glasgow G41 5RD	0141-423 5792
Seath, Thomas J.G.	1980	1992	(Motherwell: Manse Road)	Flat 11, Wallace Court, South Vennel, Lanark ML11 7LL	01555 665399

Stewart, John M. MA BD	1964 2001	(Johnstone with Kirkpatrick Juxta)	5 Rathmor Road, Biggar ML12 6QG	01899 220398
Turnbull, John LTh	1994 2006	(Balfron with Fintry)	4 Rathmor Road, Biggar ML12 6QG	01899 221502
Young, David A.	1972 2003	(Kirkmuirhill)	15 Mannachie Rise, Forres IV36 2US [E-mail: youngdavid@aol.com]	01309 672849

(14) GREENOCK AND PAISLEY

Meets on the second Tuesday of September, October, November, December, February, March, April and May, and on the third Tuesday of June.

| Clerk: | REV. ALAN H. WARD MA BD | The Presbytery Office as detailed below [E-mail: greenockpaisley@cofscotland.org.uk] [E-mail: akph69@uk.uumail.com] | |
| Presbytery Office: | | 'Homelea', Faith Avenue, Quarrier's Village, Bridge of Weir PA11 3SX | 01505 615033 (Tel) 01505 615088 (Fax) |

Barrhead: Arthurlie (H) (0141-881 8442)

| James S.A. Cowan BD DipMin | 1986 | 1998 | 10 Arthurlie Avenue, Barrhead, Glasgow G78 2BU [E-mail: jim_cowan@ntlworld.com] | 0141-881 3457 |

Barrhead: Bourock (H) (0141-881 9813)

| Maureen Leitch (Mrs) BA BD | 1995 | | 14 Maxton Avenue, Barrhead, Glasgow G78 1DY [E-mail: maureen.leitch@ntlworld.com] | 0141-881 1462 |

Barrhead: South and Levern (H) (0141-881 7825)

| Morris M. Dutch BD BA | 1998 | 2002 | 3 Colinbar Circle, Barrhead, Glasgow G78 2BE [E-mail: mmdutch@yahoo.co.uk] | 0141-571 4059 |

Bishopton (H)

| Gayle J.A. Taylor (Mrs) MA BD | 1999 | | The Manse, Newton Road, Bishopton PA7 5JP [E-mail: gayletaylor@btinternet.com] | 01505 862161 |

Bridge of Weir: Freeland (H) (01505 612610)

| Kenneth N. Gray BA BD | 1988 | | 15 Lawmarnock Crescent, Bridge of Weir PA11 3AS [E-mail: aandkgray@btinternet.com] | 01505 690918 |

Bridge of Weir: St Machar's Ranfurly (01505 614364)

| Suzanne Dunleavy (Miss) BD DipEd | 1990 | 1992 | 9 Glen Brae, Bridge of Weir PA11 3BH [E-mail: suzanne.dunleavy@btinternet.com] | 01505 612975 |

Caldwell John Campbell MA BA BSc	1973	2000	The Manse of Caldwell, Uplawmoor, Glasgow G78 4AL [E-mail: campbelljohn@talktalk.net]	01505 850215
Elderslie Kirk (H) (01505 323348) Robin N. Allison BD DipMin	1994	2005	282 Main Road, Elderslie, Johnstone PA5 9EF [E-mail: robin@mansemob.org]	01505 321767
Erskine (0141-812 4620) Ian W. Bell LTh	1990	1998	The Manse, 7 Leven Place, Linburn, Erskine PA8 6AS [E-mail: rviwbepc@ntlworld.com]	0141-581 0955
Gourock: Old Gourock and Ashton (H) Vacant			90 Albert Road, Gourock PA19 1NN	01475 631516
Gourock: St John's (H) P. Jill Clancy (Mrs) BD	2000		6 Barrhill Road, Gourock PA19 1JX [E-mail: jgibson@totalise.co.uk]	01475 632143
Greenock: Ardgowan Alan H. Ward MA BD	1978	2002	72 Forsyth Street, Greenock PA16 8SX [E-mail: alanhward@ntlworld.com]	01475 790849
Greenock: East End David J. McCarthy BSc BD	1985	2003	29 Denholm Street, Greenock PA16 8RH [E-mail: ncdgreenockeast@uk.uumail.com]	01475 722111
Eileen Manson (Mrs) DipCE (Aux)	1994	2005	1 Cambridge Avenue, Gourock PA19 1XT [E-mail: rev.eileen@ntlworld.com]	01475 632401
Greenock: Finnart St Paul's (H) David Mill KJSJ MA BD	1978	1979	105 Newark Street, Greenock PA16 7TW [E-mail: minister@finnart-stpauls-church.org]	01475 639602
Greenock: Mount Kirk Francis E. Murphy BEng DipDSE BD	2006		76 Finnart Street, Greenock PA16 8HJ [E-mail: francis_e_murphy@hotmail.com]	01475 722338
Greenock: Old West Kirk C. Ian W. Johnson MA BD	1997		39 Fox Street, Greenock PA16 8PD [E-mail: ian.ciw.johnson@btinternet.com]	01475 888277
Greenock: St Margaret's (01475 781953) Isobel J.M. Kelly (Miss) MA BD DipEd	1974	1998	105 Finnart Street, Greenock PA16 8HN	01475 786590

Greenock: St Ninian's
Allan G. McIntyre BD
1985
5 Auchmead Road, Greenock PA16 0PY
[E-mail: agmcintyre@lineone.net]
01475 631878

Greenock: Wellpark Mid Kirk
Alan K. Sorensen BD MTh DipMin FSAScot
1983   2000
101 Brisbane Street, Greenock PA16 8PA
[E-mail: alansorensen@beeb.net]
01475 721741

Greenock: Westburn
W. Douglas Hamilton BD
1975   1986
67 Forsyth Street, Greenock PA16 8SX
[E-mail: revwdhamilton@hotmail.com]
01475 724003

William C. Hewitt BD DipPS
1977   1994
50 Ardgowan Street, Greenock PA16 8EP
[E-mail: william.hewitt@ntlworld.com]
01475 721048

(Charge formed by the union of Greenock: St George's North and Greenock: St Luke's)

Houston and Killellan (H)
Donald Campbell BD
1998   2007
The Manse of Houston, Main Street, Houston, Johnstone PA6 7EL
[E-mail: houstonmanse@btinternet.com]
01505 612569

Howwood
David Stewart MA DipEd BD MTh
1977   2001
The Manse, Beith Road, Howwood, Johnstone PA9 1AS
[E-mail: revdavidst@aol.com]
01505 703678

Inchinnan (H) (0141-812 1263)
Marilyn MacLaine (Mrs) LTh
1995
The Manse, Inchinnan, Renfrew PA4 9PH
0141-812 1688

Inverkip (H)
Elizabeth A. Crumlish (Mrs) BD
1995   2002
The Manse, Langhouse Road, Inverkip, Greenock PA16 0BJ
[E-mail: lizcrumlish@aol.com]
01475 521207

Johnstone: High (H) (01505 336303)
Ann C. McCool (Mrs) BD DSD IPA ALCM
1989   2001
76 North Road, Johnstone PA5 8NF
[E-mail: ann.mccool@ntlworld.com]
01505 320006

Johnstone: St Andrew's Trinity
May Bell (Mrs) LTh
1998   2002
The Manse, 7 Leven Place, Linburn, Erskine PA8 6AS
[E-mail: may.bell@ntlbusiness.com]
0141-581 7352

Johnstone: St Paul's (H) (01505 321632)
Alistair N. Shaw MA BD
1982   2003
9 Stanley Drive, Brookfield, Johnstone PA5 8UF
[E-mail: ans2006@talktalk.net]
01505 320060

Kilbarchan: East John Owain Jones MA BD FSAScot	1981	2002	East Manse, Church Street, Kilbarchan, Johnstone PA10 2JQ [E-mail: johnowainjones@ntlworld.com]	01505 702621
Kilbarchan: West Arthur Sherratt BD	1994		West Manse, Shuttle Street, Kilbarchan, Johnstone PA10 2JR [E-mail: arthur.sherratt@ntlworld.com]	01505 342930
Kilmacolm: Old (H) (01505 8739911) Peter McEnhill BD PhD	1992	2007	The Old Kirk Manse, Glencairn Road, Kilmacolm PA13 4NJ	01505 873174
Kilmacolm: St Columba (H) R. Douglas Cranston MA BD	1986	1992	6 Churchill Road, Kilmacolm PA13 4LH [E-mail: robert.cranston@tiscali.co.uk]	01505 873271
Langbank (T) William G. McKaig BD	1979	2007	The Manse, Main Road, Langbank, Port Glasgow PA14 6XP	01475 540252
Linwood (H) (01505 328802) Vacant			49 Napier Street, Linwood, Paisley PA3 3AJ	01505 325131
Lochwinnoch (T) Christine Murdoch	1999	2007	1 Station Rise, Lochwinnoch PA12 4NA [E-mail: rev.christine@btinternet.com]	01505 843484
Neilston (0141-881 9445) Vacant			The Manse, Neilston Road, Neilston, Glasgow G78 3NP	0141-881 1958
Paisley: Abbey (H) (Tel: 0141-889 7654; Fax: 0141-887 3929) Alan D. Birss MA BD	1979	1988	15 Main Road, Castlehead, Paisley PA2 6AJ [E-mail: alan.birss@paisleyabbey.com]	0141-889 3587
Paisley: Castlehead Esther J. Ninian (Miss) MA BD	1993	1998	28 Fulbar Crescent, Paisley PA2 9AS [E-mail: esther.ninian@ntlworld.com]	01505 812304
Paisley: Glenburn (0141-884 2602) Graham Nash MA BD	2006		10 Hawick Avenue, Paisley PA2 9LD [E-mail: gpnash@btopenworld.com]	0141-884 4903
Paisley: Laigh Kirk (H) (0141-889 7700) David J. Thom BD	2000	2005	25 John Neilson Avenue, Paisley PA1 2SX [E-mail: david@thelaigh.co.uk]	0141-887 8191

Paisley: Lylesland (H) (0141-561 7139)
Vacant
Greta Gray (Miss) DCS
36 Potterhill Avenue, Paisley PA2 8BA — 0141-884 2882
67 Crags Avenue, Paisley PA3 6SG — 0141-884 6178

Paisley: Martyrs' (0141-889 6603)
Kenneth A.L. Mayne BA MSc CertEd   1976
21 John Neilson Avenue, Paisley PA1 2SX — 0141-889 2182

Paisley: Oakshaw Trinity (H) (Tel: 0141-889 4010; Fax: 0141-848 5139)
G. Hutton B. Steel MA BD   1982   2006
16 Golf Drive, Paisley PA1 3LA — 0141-887 0884
[E-mail: hutton@oakshawtrinity.org.uk]

Paisley: St Columba Foxbar (H) (01505 812377)
Vacant
13 Corsebar Drive, Paisley PA2 9QD

Paisley: St James' (0141-889 2422)
Eleanor J. McMahon (Miss) BEd BD   1994
38 Woodland Avenue, Paisley PA2 8BH — 0141-884 3246
[E-mail: eleanor.mcmahon@ntlworld.com]

Paisley: St Luke's (H)
D. Ritchie M. Gillon BD DipMin   1994
31 Southfield Avenue, Paisley PA2 8BX — 0141-884 6215
[E-mail: revgillon@hotmail.com]

Paisley: St Mark's Oldhall (H) (0141-882 2755)
Robert G. McFarlane BD   2001   2005
36 Newtyle Road, Paisley PA1 3JX — 0141-889 4279
[E-mail: robertmcf@hotmail.com]

Paisley: St Ninian's Ferguslie (E) (0141-887 9436) (New Charge Development)
William Wishart DCS
10 Stanely Drive, Paisley PA2 6HE — 0141-884 4177
[E-mail: bill@saintninians.co.uk]

Paisley: Sandyford (Thread Street) (0141-889 5078)
David Kay BA BD MTh   1974
6 Southfield Avenue, Paisley PA2 8BY — 0141-884 3600
[E-mail: davidkay@ntlworld.com]

Paisley: Sherwood Greenlaw (H) (0141-889 7060)
Alasdair F. Cameron BD CA   1986
5 Greenlaw Drive, Paisley PA1 3RX — 0141-889 3057
[E-mail: alcamron@lineone.net]

Paisley: Wallneuk North (0141-889 9265)
Vacant

Port Glasgow: Hamilton Bardrainney James A. Munro BA BD DMS	1979 2002	80 Bardrainney Avenue, Port Glasgow PA14 6HD [E-mail: james@jmunro33.wanadoo.co.uk]	01475 701213
Port Glasgow: St Andrew's (H) Andrew T. MacLean BA BD	1980 1993	St Andrew's Manse, Barr's Brae, Port Glasgow PA14 5QA [E-mail: standrews.pg@mac.com]	01475 741486
Port Glasgow: St Martin's Archibald Speirs BD	1995 2006	Clunebraehead, Clune Brae, Port Glasgow PA14 5SL [E-mail: archiespeirs1@aol.com]	01475 704115
Renfrew: North (0141-885 2154) E. Lorna Hood (Mrs) MA BD	1978 1979	1 Alexandra Drive, Renfrew PA4 8UB [E-mail: lorna.hood@ntlworld.com]	0141-886 2074
Renfrew: Old Alexander C. Wark MA BD STM	1982 1998	31 Gibson Road, Renfrew PA4 0RH [E-mail: alecwark@yahoo.co.uk]	0141-886 2005
Renfrew: Trinity (H) (0141-885 2129) Stuart C. Steell BD CertMin	1992	25 Paisley Road, Renfrew PA4 8JH [E-mail: ssren@tiscali.co.uk]	0141-886 2131
Skelmorlie and Wemyss Bay William R. Armstrong BD	1979	3A Montgomerie Terrace, Skelmorlie PA17 5TD [E-mail: warmstrong17@tiscali.co.uk]	01475 520703

Name			Position	Address	Tel
Abeledo, Benjamin J.A. BTh DipTh PTh	1991	2000	Army Chaplain	40 Rawlinson Road, Catterick Garrison DL9 3AP [E-mail: benjamin.abeledo@btinternet.com]	01748 833816
Alexander, Douglas N. MA BD	1961	1999	(Bishopton)	West Morningside, Main Road, Langbank, Port Glasgow PA4 6XP	01475 540249
Black, Janette M.K. (Mrs) BD	1993	2006	(Assistant: Paisley: Oakshaw Trinity)	5 Craigiehall Avenue, Erskine PA8 7DB	0141-812 0794
Bruce, A. William MA	1942	1981	(Fortingall and Glenlyon)	75 Union Street, Greenock PA16 8BG	01475 787534
Cameron, Margaret (Miss) DCS			(Deaconess)	2 Rowans Gate, Paisley PA2 6RD	0141-840 2479
Chestnut, Alexander MBE BA	1948	1987	(Greenock: St Mark's Greenbank)	5 Douglas Street, Largs KA30 8PS	01475 674168
Copland, Agnes M. (Mrs) MBE DCS			(Deacon)	3 Craigmuschat Road, Gourock PA19 1SE	01475 631870
Cubie, John P. MA BD	1961	1999	(Caldwell)	36 Winram Place, St Andrews KY16 8XH	01334 474708
Forrest, Kenneth P. CBE BSc PhD		2006	Auxiliary Minister	5 Carruth Road, Bridge of Weir PA11 3HQ [E-mail: kenpforrest@hotmail.com]	01505 615033
Gardner, Frank J. MA	1966	2007	(Gourock: Old Gourock and Ashton)	1 Levanne Place, Gourock PA16 1AX	(Tel/Fax) 01475 630187
Hetherington, Robert M. MA BD	1966	2002	(Barrhead South and Levern)	31 Brodie Park Crescent, Paisley PA2 6EU [E-mail: r-hetherington@sky.com]	0141-848 6560
Johnston, Mary (Miss) DCS			(Deaconess)	19 Lounsdale Drive, Paisley PA2 9ED	0141-849 1615

Name			Charge	Address	Telephone
Lowe, Edwin MA BD	1950	1988	(Caldwell)	45 Duncarnock Crescent, Neilston, Glasgow G78 3HH [E-mail: edwin.lowe50@ntlworld.com]	0141-580 5726
McBain, Margaret (Miss) DCS				33 Quarry Road, Paisley PA2 7RD	0141-884 2920
MacColl, James C. BSc BD	1966	2002	(Johnstone: St Andrew's Trinity)	Greenways, Winton, Kirkby Stephen, Cumbria CA17 4HL	01768 372290
MacColl, John BD DipMin	1989	2001	Teacher: Religious Education	1 Birch Avenue, Johnstone PA5 0DD	01505 326506
McCully, M. Isobel (Miss) DCS			(Deacon)	10 Broadstone Avenue, Port Glasgow PA14 5BB [E-mail: mi.mccully@tesco.net]	01475 742240
Macdonald, Alexander MA BD	1966	2006	(Neilston)	35 Lochore Avenue, Paisley PA3 4BY [E-mail: alexmacdonald42@aol.com]	0141-889 0066
McDonald, Alexander BA CMIWSC DUniv	1968	1988	Department of Ministry	36 Alloway Grove, Paisley PA2 7DQ [E-mail: amcdonald1 @ntlworld.com]	0141-560 1937
Macfarlane, Thomas G. BSc PhD BD	1956	1992	(Glasgow: South Shawlands)	12 Elphinstone Court, Lochwinnoch Road, Kilmacolm PA13 4DW	01505 874962
McLachlan, Fergus C. BD	1982	2002	Hospital Chaplain: Inverclyde Royal	46 Queen Square, Glasgow G41 2AZ [E-mail: fergus.mclachlan@irh.scot.nhs.uk]	(Home) 0141-423 3830 (Work) 01475 633777
Marshall, Fred J. BA	1946	1992	(Bermuda)	Flat 4, Varrich House, 7 Church Hill, Edinburgh EH10 4BG	0131-446 0205
Moffett, James R. BA	1942	1979	(Paisley: St Matthew's)	32 Eglinton Suite, Buckreddan Care Centre, Kilwinning KA13 7PF	
Montgomery, Robert A. MA	1955	1992	(Quarrier's Village: Mount Zion)	11 Myreton Avenue, Kilmacolm PA13 4LJ	01505 872028
Nicol, Joyce M. (Mrs) BA DCS			(Deacon)	93 Brisbane Street, Greenock PA16 8NY [E-mail: joycenicol@hotmail.co.uk]	01475 723235
Page, John R. BD DipMin	1988	2003	(Gibraltar)	Flat 0/1 'Toward', The Lighthouses, Greenock Road, Wemyss Bay PA18 6DT	01475 520281
Palmer, S.W. BD	1980	1991	(Kilbarchan: East)	4 Bream Place, Houston PA6 7ZJ	01505 615280
Prentice, George BA BTh	1964	1997	(Paisley: Martyrs)	46 Victoria Gardens, Corsebar Road, Paisley PA2 9AQ [E-mail: g.prentice04@virgin.net]	0141-842 1585
Pyper, J. Stewart BA	1951	1986	(Greenock: St George's North)	39 Brisbane Street, Greenock PA16 8NR	01475 793234
Scott, Ernest M. MA	1957	1992	(Port Glasgow: St Andrew's)	17 Bruearce Road, Wemyss Bay PA18 6ER [E-mail: ernie.scott@ernes70.fsnet.co.uk]	01475 522267
Simpson, James H. BD LLB	1964	2004	(Greenock: Mount Kirk)	82 Harbourside, Inverkip, Greenock PA16 0BF [E-mail: jameshsimpson@yahoo.co.uk]	01475 520582
Smillie, Andrew M. LTh	1990	2005	(Langbank)	7 Turnbull Avenue, West Freeland, Erskine PA8 7DL [E-mail: andrewsmillie@talktalk.net]	0141-812 7030
Stone, W. Vernon MA BD	1949	1985	(Langbank)	36 Woodrow Court, Port Glasgow Road, Kilmacolm KA13 4QA [E-mail: stone@kilmacolm.fsnet.co.uk]	01505 872644
Whyte, John H. MA	1946	1986	(Gourock: Ashton)	6 Castle Levan Manor, Cloch Road, Gourock PA19 1AY	01475 636788

GREENOCK ADDRESSES

Gourock
Old Gourock
and Ashton   41 Royal Street
St John's   Bath Street x St John's Road

Greenock
Ardgowan   31 Union Street

Finnart St Paul's
Mount Kirk
Old West Kirk
St Margaret's
St Ninian's
Wellpark Mid Kirk
Westburn

Newark Street x Bentinck Street
Dempster Street at Murdieston Park
Esplanade x Campbell Street
Finch Road x Kestrel Crescent
Warwick Road, Larkfield
Cathcart Square
9 Nelson Street

Port Glasgow
Hamilton   Bardrainney

St Andrew's
St Martin's

Bardrainney Avenue x
  Auchenbothie Road
Princes Street
Mansion Avenue

PAISLEY ADDRESSES

Abbey   Town Centre
Castlehead   Canal Street
Glenburn   Nethercraigs Drive off Glenburn Road
Laigh Kirk   Causeyside Street

Lylesland
Martyrs'
Oakshaw Trinity
St Columba Foxbar
St James'
St Luke's

Rowan Street off Neilston Road
Broomlands
Churchill
Amochrie Road, Foxbar
Underwood Road
Neilston Road

St Mark's Oldhall
St Ninian's Ferguslie
Sandyford (Thread St)
Sherwood Greenlaw
Wallneuk North

Glasgow Road, Ralston
Blackstoun Road
Gallowhill
Glasgow Road
off Renfrew Road

(16) GLASGOW

Meets at New Govan Church, Govan Cross, Glasgow, on the second Tuesday of each month, except June when the meeting takes place on the second last Tuesday.
In January, July and August there is no meeting.

Clerk: REV. DAVID W. LUNAN MA BD   260 Bath Street, Glasgow G2 4JP   0141-332 6606 (Tel/Fax)
                                                [E-mail: glasgow@cofscotland.org.uk]
                                                [E-mail: glasgowpresbytery@yahoo.co.uk]
                                                [E-mail: glasgowpres@yahoo.co.uk]
Hon. Treasurer: DOUGLAS BLANEY   Text Phone: 18002 0141-331 2962

1 **Banton linked with Twechar**
   Alexandra Farrington LTh   2003   Manse of Banton, Kilsyth, Glasgow G65 0QL   01236 826129
                                                [E-mail: sandra.farrington@virgin.net]

2 **Bishopbriggs: Kenmure**
   Iain A. Laing MA BD   1971   5 Marchfield, Bishopbriggs, Glasgow G64 3PP   0141-772 1468
                                                [E-mail: iain@ilaing.fsnet.co.uk]

3 **Bishopbriggs: Springfield**
   Ian Taylor BD ThM   1995 2006 64 Miller Drive, Bishopbriggs, Glasgow G64 1FB   0141-772 1540
                                                [E-mail: taylorian@btinternet.com]

No.	Charge / Name	Ord.	Ind.	Address	Telephone
4	**Broom (0141-639 3528)**				
	James A.S. Boag BD	1992	2007	3 Laigh Road, Newton Mearns, Glasgow G77 5EX	0141-639 2916 (Tel) / 0141-639 3528 (Fax) / 0141-639 6853
	Margaret McLellan (Mrs) DCS			18 Broom Road East, Newton Mearns, Glasgow G77 5SD	
5	**Burnside Blairbeth (0141-634 4130)**				
	William T.S. Wilson BSc BD	1999	2006	59 Blairbeth Road, Burnside, Glasgow G73 4JD [E-mail: william.wilson@burnsideblairbethchurch.org.uk]	0141-583 6470
	Colin Ogilvie DCS			32 Upper Bourtree Court, Glasgow G73 4HT	0141-569 2750
6	**Busby (0141-644 2073)**				
	Jeremy C. Eve BSc BD	1998		17A Carmunnock Road, Busby, Glasgow G76 8SZ [E-mail: jerry.eve@btinternet.com]	0141-644 3670
7	**Cadder (0141-772 7436)**				
	Graham S. Finch MA BD	1977	1999	6 Balmuildy Road, Bishopbriggs, Glasgow G64 3BS [E-mail: gsf1957@ntlworld.com]	0141-772 1363
8	**Cambuslang; Flemington Hallside**				
	Neil Glover BD BSc	2005		103 Overton Road, Cambuslang, Glasgow G72 7XA [E-mail: neil@naglover.plus.com]	0141-641 1049 / 07779 280074 (Mbl)
9	**Cambuslang: Old**				
	Lee Messeder BD PgDipMin	2003		74 Stewarton Drive, Cambuslang, Glasgow G72 8DG [E-mail: messeder.74@tiscali.co.uk]	0141-641 3261
10	**Cambuslang: St Andrew's**				
	Vacant			37 Brownside Road, Cambuslang, Glasgow G72 8NH	0141-641 3847
11	**Cambuslang: Trinity St Paul's**				
	Eileen M. Ross (Mrs) BD MTh	2005		4 Glasgow Road, Cambuslang, Glasgow G72 7BW [E-mail: revemr@yahoo.co.uk]	0141-641 1699
12	**Campsie (01360 310939)**				
	David J. Torrance BD DipMin	1993		19 Redhills View, Lennoxtown, Glasgow G66 7BL [E-mail: torrance@fish.co.uk]	01360 312527
13	**Chryston (H)**				
	Martin A.W. Allen MA BD ThM	1977		Main Street, Chryston, Glasgow G69 9LA [E-mail: allensall@hotmail.com]	0141-779 1436
	David J. McAdam BSc BD (Assoc)	1990	2000	12 Dunellan Crescent, Moodiesburn, Glasgow G69 0GA [E-mail: dmca29@hotmail.co.uk]	01236 870472

No.	Congregation / Minister	Ordained	Inducted	Address	Telephone
14	**Eaglesham (01355 302047)** Lynn M. McChlery BA BD	2005		The Manse, Cheapside Street, Eaglesham, Glasgow G76 0NS [E-mail: lsmcchlery@btinternet.com]	01355 303495
15	**Fernhill and Cathkin** Margaret McArthur BD DipMin	1995	2002	82 Blairbeth Road, Rutherglen, Glasgow G73 4JA	0141-634 1508
16	**Gartcosh (H) (01236 873770) linked with Glenboig (01236 875625)** Alexander M. Fraser BD DipMin	1985		26 Inchknock Avenue, Gartcosh, Glasgow G69 8EA [E-mail: sandyfraser2@hotmail.com]	01236 872274
17	**Giffnock: Orchardhill (0141-638 3604)** Chris Vermeulen DipLT BTh MA	1986	2005	23 Huntly Avenue, Giffnock, Glasgow G46 6LW [E-mail: chris@orchardhill.org.uk]	0141-620 3734
	Daniel Frank BA MDiv DMin (Assoc)	2003	2006	106 Ormonde Crescent, Glasgow G44 3SW	0141-586 0875
18	**Giffnock: South (0141-638 2599)** Edward V. Simpson BSc BD	1972	1983	5 Langtree Avenue, Whitecraigs, Glasgow G46 7LN [E-mail: eddie.simpson3@ntlworld.com]	0141-638 8767 (Tel) 0141-620 0605 (Fax)
19	**Giffnock: The Park** Calum D. Macdonald BD	1993	2001	41 Rouken Glen Road, Thornliebank, Glasgow G46 7JD [E-mail: parkhoose@msn.com]	0141-638 3023
20	**Glenboig** See Gartcosh				
21	**Greenbank (H) (0141-644 1841)** Jeanne Roddick BD	2003		Greenbank Manse, 38 Eaglesham Road, Clarkston, Glasgow G76 7DJ [E-mail: jeanne.roddick@ntlworld.com]	0141-644 1395
22	**Kilsyth: Anderson** Charles M. MacKinnon BD	1989	1999	Anderson Manse, Kingston Road, Kilsyth, Glasgow G65 0HR [E-mail: cm.ccmackinnon@tiscali.co.uk]	01236 822345
23	**Kilsyth: Burns and Old** Robert Sloan BD	1997	2005	The Grange, Glasgow Road, Kilsyth, Glasgow G65 9AE [E-mail: robertsloan@scotnet.co.uk]	01236 823116
24	**Kirkintilloch: Hillhead** Vacant			64 Waverley Park, Kensington Gate, Kirkintilloch, Glasgow G66 2BP	0141-775 0395

25	**Kirkintilloch: St Columba's (H)** David M. White BA BD	1988	1992	14 Crossdykes, Kirkintilloch, Glasgow G66 3EU [E-mail: david.m.white@ntlworld.com]	0141-578 4357
26	**Kirkintilloch: St David's Memorial Park (H)** Bryce Calder MA BD	1995	2001	2 Roman Road, Kirkintilloch, Glasgow G66 1EA [E-mail: ministry100@aol.com]	0141-776 1434
27	**Kirkintilloch: St Mary's** Mark E. Johnstone MA BD	1993	2001	St Mary's Manse, 60 Union Street, Kirkintilloch, Glasgow G66 1DH [E-mail: mark.johnstone2@ntlworld.com]	0141-776 1252
28	**Lenzie: Old (H)** Douglas W. Clark LTh	1993	2000	41 Kirkintilloch Road, Lenzie, Glasgow G66 4LB [E-mail: douglaswclark@hotmail.com]	0141-776 2184
29	**Lenzie: Union (H)** Daniel J.M. Carmichael MA BD	1994	2003	1 Larch Avenue, Lenzie, Glasgow G66 4HX [E-mail: djm@carmichael39.fsnet.co.uk]	0141-776 3831
30	**Maxwell Mearns Castle (Tel/Fax: 0141-639 5169)** David C. Cameron BD CertMin	1993		122 Broomfield Avenue, Newton Mearns, Glasgow G77 5JR [E-mail: maxwellmearns@hotmail.com]	0141-616 0642
31	**Mearns (H) (0141-639 6555)** Joseph A. Kavanagh BD DipPTh MTh	1992	1998	Manse of Mearns, Newton Mearns, Glasgow G77 5DE [E-mail: mearnskirk@hotmail.com]	0141-616 2410 (Tel/Fax)
32	**Milton of Campsie (H)** Julie H.C. Wilson BA BD	2006		Dunkeld, 33 Birdston Road, Milton of Campsie, Glasgow G66 8BX [E-mail: jhcwilson@msn.com]	01360 310548 07787 184800 (Mbl)
33	**Netherlee (H)** Thomas Nelson BSc BD	1992	2002	25 Ormonde Avenue, Glasgow G44 3QY [E-mail: tomnelson@ntlworld.com]	0141-585 7502 (Tel/Fax)
34	**Newton Mearns (H) (0141-639 7373)** Angus Kerr BD CertMin ThM DMin	1983	1994	28 Waterside Avenue, Newton Mearns, Glasgow G77 6TJ [E-mail: office@churchatthecross.org.uk]	0141-616 2079
35	**Rutherglen: Old (H)** Alexander Thomson BSc BD MPhil PhD	1973	1985	31 Highburgh Drive, Rutherglen, Glasgow G73 3RR [E-mail: alexander.thomson6@btopenworld.com]	0141-647 6178

36	**Rutherglen: Stonelaw (0141-647 5113)**			
	Alistair S. May LLB BD PhD	2002	80 Blairbeth Road, Rutherglen, Glasgow G73 4JA [E-mail: alistair.may@ntlworld.com]	0141-583 0157
37	**Rutherglen: West and Wardlawhill**			
	John W. Drummond MA BD	1971	1986	12 Albert Drive, Rutherglen, Glasgow G73 3RT	0141-569 8547
	(Charge formed by the union of Rutherglen: West and Rutherglen: Wardlawhill)			
38	**Stamperland (0141-637 4999) (H)**			
	George C. MacKay BD CertMin	1994	2004	109 Ormonde Avenue, Glasgow G44 3SN [E-mail: g.mackay3@btinternet.com]	0141-637 4976 (Tel/Fax)
39	**Stepps (H)**			
	Neil Buchanan BD	1991	2005	2 Lenzie Road, Stepps, Glasgow G33 6DX [E-mail: neil.buchanan@talk21.com]	0141-779 5746
40	**Thornliebank (H)**			
	Robert M. Silver BA BD	1995		19 Arthurlie Drive, Giffnock, Glasgow G46 6UR	0141-620 2133
41	**Torrance (T) (01360 620970)**			
	Nigel L. Barge BSc BD	1991		27 Campbell Place, Meadow Rise, Torrance, Glasgow G64 4HR [E-mail: nigel@nbarge.freeserve.co.uk]	01360 622379
42	**Twechar** See Banton			
43	**Williamwood**			
	Iain M.A. Reid MA BD	1990	2007	125 Greenwood Road, Clarkston, Glasgow G76 7LL	0141-571 7949
44	**Glasgow: Anderston Kelvingrove (0141-221 9408)**			
	John A. Coutts BTh	1984	2004	16 Royal Terrace, Glasgow G3 7NY [E-mail: john@jmcoutts.org.uk]	0141-332 7704
45	**Glasgow: Baillieston Mure Memorial (0141-773 1216)**			
	Allan S. Vint BSc BD	1989	1996	28 Beech Avenue, Baillieston, Glasgow G69 6LF [E-mail: allan@vint.co.uk]	0141-771 1217
46	**Glasgow: Baillieston St Andrew's (0141-771 6629)**			
	Alisdair T. MacLeod-Mair MEd DipTheol	2001	2007	55 Station Park, Baillieston, Glasgow G69 7XY [E-mail: revalisdair@hotmail.com]	0141-771 1791
47	**Glasgow: Balshagray Victoria Park**			
	Campbell Mackinnon BSc BD	1982	2001	20 St Kilda Drive, Glasgow G14 9JN [E-mail: cmackinnon@ntlworld.com]	0141-954 9780

48	**Glasgow: Barlanark Greyfriars** David I.W. Locke MA MSc BD	2000	4 Rhindmuir Grove, Glasgow G69 6NE [E-mail: revdavidlocke@ntlworld.com]	0141-771 1240
49	**Glasgow: Battlefield East (H) (0141-632 4206)** Alan C. Raeburn MA BD	1971 1977	110 Mount Annan Drive, Glasgow G44 4RZ [E-mail: acraeburn@hotmail.com]	0141-632 1514
50	**Glasgow: Blawarthill** Ian M.S. McInnes BD DipMin	1995 1997	46 Earlbank Avenue, Glasgow G14 9HL [E-mail: ian.liz1@ntlworld.com]	0141-579 6521
51	**Glasgow: Bridgeton St Francis in the East (H) (L) (Church House: Tel: 0141-554 8045)** Howard R. Hudson MA BD	1982 1984	10 Albany Drive, Rutherglen, Glasgow G73 3QN [E-mail: howard.hudson@ntlworld.com]	0141-587 8667
	Margaret S. Beaton (Miss) DCS		64 Gardenside Grove, Fernlee Meadows, Carmyle, Glasgow G32 8EZ	0141-646 2297
52	**Glasgow: Broomhill (0141-334 2540)** William B. Ferguson BA BD	1971 1987	27 St Kilda Drive, Glasgow G14 9LN [E-mail: revferg@aol.com]	0141-959 3204
53	**Glasgow: Calton Parkhead (0141-554 3866)** Vacant		98 Drumover Drive, Glasgow G31 5RP	0141-556 2520
54	**Glasgow: Cardonald (0141-882 6264)** Malcolm MacLeod BA BD	1979 2007	133 Newtyle Road, Paisley PA1 3LB	0141-561 1891
55	**Glasgow: Carmunnock** G. Gray Fletcher BSc BD	1989 2001	The Manse, 161 Waterside Road, Carmunnock, Glasgow G76 9AJ [E-mail: gray.fletcher@virgin.net]	0141-644 1578 (Tel/Fax)
56	**Glasgow: Carmyle linked with Kenmuir Mount Vernon** Murdo Maclean BD CertMin	1997 1999	3 Meryon Road, Glasgow G32 9NW [E-mail: murdo.maclean@ntlworld.com]	0141-778 2625
57	**Glasgow: Carnwadric (E)** Graeme K. Bell BA BD	1983	62 Loganswell Road, Glasgow G46 8AX [E-mail: slbellmrs@yahoo.co.uk]	0141-638 5884
58	**Glasgow: Castlemilk East (H) (0141-634 2444)** Vacant		15 Castlemilk Drive, Glasgow G45 9TL	0141-631 1244
	Duncan Ross DCS	2006	4 Glasgow Road, Cambuslang, Glasgow G72 7BW	0141-641 1699

No.	Charge / Minister	Dates	Address	Telephone
59	**Glasgow: Castlemilk West (H) (0141-634 1480)** Vacant		156 Old Castle Road, Glasgow G44 5TW	0141-637 5451
60	**Glasgow: Cathcart Old** Neil W. Galbraith BD CertMin	1987 1996	21 Courthill Avenue, Cathcart, Glasgow G44 5AA [E-mail: revneilgalbraith@hotmail.com]	0141-633 5248 (Tel/Fax)
61	**Glasgow: Cathcart Trinity (H) (0141-637 6658)** Ian Morrison BD	1991 2003	82 Merrylee Road, Glasgow G43 2QZ [E-mail: iain77@tiscali.co.uk]	0141-633 3744
	Wilma Pearson (Mrs) BD (Assoc)	2004	90 Newlands Road, Glasgow G43 2JR	0141-632 2491
62	**Glasgow: Cathedral (High or St Mungo's)** Laurence A.B. Whitley MA BD PhD	1975 2007	23 Laurel Park Close, Glasgow G13 1RD [E-mail: labwhitley@btinternet.com]	0141-954 0216
63	**Glasgow: Colston Milton (0141-772 1922)** Vacant		118 Birsay Road, Glasgow G22 7QP	0141-772 1958
64	**Glasgow: Colston Wellpark (H)** Christine M. Goldie (Miss) LLB BD MTh	1984 1999	16 Bishop's Gate Gardens, Colston, Glasgow G21 1XS [E-mail: christine.goldie@ntlworld.com]	0141-589 8866
65	**Glasgow: Cranhill (H) (0141-774 3344)** Muriel B. Pearson (Ms) MA BD	2004	31 Lethamhill Crescent, Glasgow G33 2SH [E-mail: murielpearson@btinternet.com]	0141-770 6873 07951 888860 (Mbl)
66	**Glasgow: Croftfoot (H) (0141-637 3913)** John M. Lloyd BD CertMin	1984 1986	20 Victoria Road, Burnside, Rutherglen, Glasgow G73 3QG [E-mail: johnLloyd@croftfootparish.co.uk]	0141-647 5524
67	**Glasgow: Dennistoun New (H)** Gordon A. McCracken BD CertMin DMin	1988 2006	31 Pencaitland Drive, Glasgow G32 8RL (Charge formed by the union of Dennistoun Blackfriars and Dennistoun Central)	0141-763 0000
68	**Glasgow: Drumchapel Drumry St Mary's (0141-944 1998)** Brian S. Sheret MA BD DPhil	1982 2002	8 Fruin Road, Glasgow G15 6SQ	0141-944 4493
69	**Glasgow: Drumchapel St Andrew's (0141-944 3758)** John S. Purves LLB BD	1983 1984	6 Firdon Crescent, Glasgow G15 6QQ [E-mail: john.s.purves@talk21.com]	0141-944 4566
70	**Glasgow: Drumchapel St Mark's** Audrey Jamieson BD MTh	2004 2007	146 Garscadden Road, Glasgow G15 6PR [E-mail: audrey.jamieson2@btinternet.com]	0141-944 5440

71 Glasgow: Easterhouse St George's and St Peter's (E) (0141-771 8810)
Malcolm Cuthbertson BA BD   1984   3 Barony Gardens, Baillieston, Glasgow G69 6TS   0141-573 8200 (Tel)
[E-mail: malcuth@aol.com]   0141-773 4878 (Fax)

72 Glasgow: Eastwood
Moyna McGlynn (Mrs) BD PhD   1999   54 Mansewood Road, Glasgow G43 1TL   0141-632 0724
[E-mail: moyna_mcglynn@hotmail.com]

73 Glasgow: Gairbraid (H)
Vacant   1515 Maryhill Road, Glasgow G20 9AB   0141-946 1568

74 Glasgow: Gardner Street (GE)
Roderick Morrison MA BD   1974   1994   148 Beechwood Drive, Glasgow G11 7DX   0141-563 2638

75 Glasgow: Garthamlock and Craigend East (E)
Valerie J. Duff (Miss) DMin   1993   1996   175 Tillycairn Drive, Garthamlock, Glasgow G33 5HS   0141-774 6364
[E-mail: valduff@tiscali.co.uk]
Marion Buchanan (Mrs) MA DCS   2 Lenzie Road, Stepps, Glasgow G33 6DX   0141-779 5746

76 Glasgow: Gorbals
Ian F. Galloway BA BD   1976   1996   44 Riverside Road, Glasgow G43 2EF   0141-649 5250
[E-mail: ianfgalloway@msn.com]

77 Glasgow: Govan Old (Tel/Fax: 0141-440 2466)
Vacant

78 Glasgow: Govanhill Trinity
Lily F. McKinnon MA BD   1993   2006   12 Carleton Gate, Giffnock, Glasgow G46 6NU   0141-637 8399

79 Glasgow: High Carntyne (0141-778 4186)
Joan Ross (Miss) BSc BD PhD   1999   2005   163 Lethamhill Road, Glasgow G33 2SQ   0141-770 9247

80 Glasgow: Hillington Park (H)
John B. MacGregor BD   1999   2004   61 Ralston Avenue, Glasgow G52 3NB   0141-882 7000
[E-mail: johnmacgregor494@msn.com]

81 Glasgow: Househillwood St Christopher's
May M. Allison (Mrs) BD   1988   2001   12 Leverndale Court, Crookston, Glasgow G53 7SJ   0141-810 5953
[E-mail: revmayallison@hotmail.com]

82 **Glasgow: Hyndland (H) (Website: www.hyndlandparishchurch.org)**
Craig Lancaster MA BD   2004
24 Hughenden Gardens, Glasgow G12 9YH
[E-mail: craig@hyndlandparishchurch.org]
0141-334 1002

83 **Glasgow: Ibrox (H) (0141-427 0896)**
Vacant
3 Dargarvel Avenue, Glasgow G41 5LD
0141-427 1282 (Tel/Fax)

84 **Glasgow: John Ross Memorial Church for Deaf People**
(Voice Text: 0141-420 1759; Text Only: 0141-429 6682; Fax: 0141-429 6860; ISDN Video Phone: 0141-418 0579)
Richard C. Durno DSW CQSW (Aux)   1989   1998
31 Springfield Road, Bishopbriggs, Glasgow G64 1PJ   (Voice/Text) 0141-772 1052
[E-mail: richard.durno@ntlworld.com]
[Website: www.deafconnections.co.uk]

85 **Glasgow: Jordanhill (Tel: 0141-959 2496)**
Colin C. Renwick BMus BD   1989   1996
96 Southbrae Drive, Glasgow G13 1TZ
[E-mail: jordchurch@btconnect.com]
0141-959 1310

86 **Glasgow: Kelvin Stevenson Memorial (0141-339 1750)**
Gordon Kirkwood BSc BD   1987   2003
94 Hyndland Road, Glasgow G12 9PZ
[E-mail: gordonkirkwood@tiscali.co.uk]
0141-334 5352

87 **Glasgow: Kelvinside Hillhead**
Jennifer Macrae (Mrs) MA BD   1998   2000
39 Athole Gardens, Glasgow G12 9BQ
[E-mail: minister@kelvinside-hillhead.org.uk]
0141-339 2865

88 **Glasgow: Kenmuir Mount Vernon** See Carmyle

89 **Glasgow: King's Park (H) (0141-632 1131)**
Vacant
1101 Aikenhead Road, Glasgow G44 5SL
0141-637 2803

90 **Glasgow: Kinning Park (0141-427 3063)**
Margaret H. Johnston BD   1988   2000
168 Arbroath Avenue, Cardonald, Glasgow G52 3HH
0141-810 3782

91 **Glasgow: Knightswood St Margaret's (H)**
Adam Dillon BD ThM   2003
26 Airthrey Avenue, Glasgow G14 9LJ
[E-mail: adamdillon@ntlworld.com]
0141-959 7075

92 **Glasgow: Langside (0141-632 7520)**
David N. McLachlan BD   1985   2004
36 Madison Avenue, Glasgow G44 5AQ
[E-mail: dmclachlan77@hotmail.com]
0141-637 0797

93 **Glasgow: Lansdowne**
Roy J.M. Henderson MA BD DipMin   1987   1992
18 Woodlands Drive, Glasgow G4 9EH
[E-mail: roy.henderson7@ntlworld.com]
0141-339 2794

No.	Charge / Minister	Year	Address / E-mail	Telephone
94	**Glasgow: Linthouse St Kenneth's** Vacant			
95	**Glasgow: Lochwood (H) (0141-771 2649)** Stuart M. Duff BA	1997	42 Rhindmuir Road, Swinton, Glasgow G69 6AZ [E-mail: stuart.duff@gmail.com]	0141-773 2756
96	**Glasgow: Martyrs', The** Ewen MacLean BA BD	1995	30 Louden Hill Road, Robroyston, Glasgow G33 1GA [E-mail: revewenmaclean@tiscali.co.uk]	0141-558 7451
97	**Glasgow: Maryhill (H) (0141-946 3512)** Anthony J.D. Craig BD	1987	111 Maxwell Avenue, Glasgow G61 1HT [E-mail: craig.glasgow@ntlworld.com]	0141-570 0642
	Stuart C. Matthews BD MA (Assoc) James Hamilton DCS	2006	15 Currie Place, Glasgow 6 Beckfield Gate, Robroyston, Glasgow G33 1SW	0141-946 0497 0141-558 3195
98	**Glasgow: Merrylea (0141-637 2009)** David P. Hood BD CertMin DipIOB(Scot)	1997	4 Pilmuir Avenue, Glasgow G44 3HX [E-mail: dphood3@ntlworld.com]	0141-637 6700
99	**Glasgow: Mosspark (H) (0141-882 2240)** Alan H. MacKay BD	1974	396 Kilmarnock Road, Glasgow G43 2DJ [E-mail: alanhmackay@aol.com]	0141-632 1247
100	**Glasgow: Mount Florida (H) (0141-561 0307)** Vacant		90 Mount Annan Drive, Glasgow G44 4RZ	0141-589 5381
101	**Glasgow: New Govan (H)** Vacant		19 Dumbreck Road, Glasgow G41 5LJ	0141-427 3197
102	**Glasgow: Newlands South (H) (0141-632 3055)** John D. Whiteford MA BD	1989	24 Monreith Road, Glasgow G43 2NY [E-mail: jwhiteford@hotmail.com]	0141-632 2588
103	**Glasgow: North Kelvinside** William G. Alston	1961	41 Mitre Road, Glasgow G14 9LE [E-mail: williamalston@hotmail.com]	0141-954 8250
104	**Glasgow: Partick South (H)** Alan L. Dunnett LLB BD	1994	3 Branklyn Crescent, Glasgow G13 1GJ [E-mail: dustydunnett@prtck2.freeserve.co.uk]	0141-959 3732

105 Glasgow: Partick Trinity (H)
Stuart J. Smith BEng BD — 1994 — 99 Balshagray Avenue, Glasgow G11 7EQ
[E-mail: ssmith99@ntlworld.com] — 0141-576 7149

106 Glasgow: Penilee St Andrew's (H) (0141-882 2691)
Alastair J. Cherry BA BD — 1982 2003 — 80 Tweedsmuir Road, Glasgow G52 2RX
[E-mail: alastair.j.cherry@btopenworld.com] — 0141-882 2460

107 Glasgow: Pollokshaws
Margaret Whyte (Mrs) BA BD — 1988 2000 — 33 Mannering Road, Glasgow G41 3SW
[E-mail: whytes@fish.co.uk] — 0141-649 0458

108 Glasgow: Pollokshields (H)
David R. Black MA BD — 1986 1997 — 36 Glencairn Drive, Glasgow G41 4PW
[E-mail: minister@pollokshieldschurch.org.uk] — 0141-423 4000

109 Glasgow: Possilpark
W.C. Campbell-Jack BD MTh PhD — 1979 2003 — 108 Erradale Street, Lambhill, Glasgow G22 6PT
[E-mail: c.c-j@homecall.co.uk] — 0141-336 6909

110 Glasgow: Priesthill and Nitshill
Douglas M. Nicol BD CA — 1987 1996 — 36 Springkell Drive, Glasgow G41 4EZ
[E-mail: dougiemnicol@aol.com] — 0141-427 7877

111 Glasgow: Queen's Park (0141-423 3654)
T. Malcolm F. Duff MA BD — 1985 2000 — 5 Alder Road, Glasgow G43 2UY
[E-mail: malcolm.duff@ntlworld.com] — 0141-637 5491

112 Glasgow: Renfield St Stephen's (Tel: 0141-332 4293; Fax: 0141-332 8482)
Peter M. Gardner MA BD — 1988 2002 — 101 Hill Street, Glasgow G3 6TY
[E-mail: pmg1@renfieldststephens.org] — 0141-353 0349

113 Glasgow: Robroyston (New Charge Development)
Hilary McDougall MA BD — 2004 — 86 Stewarton Drive, Cambuslang, Glasgow G72 8DJ
[E-mail: ncdrobroyston@uk.uumail.com] — 0141-586 4310

Jean Clark (Ms) DCS — 2006 — 1/1, 15 Colston Grove, Bishopbriggs, Glasgow G64 1BF — 0141-762 5684

114 Glasgow: Ruchazie (0141-774 2759)
William F. Hunter MA BD — 1986 1999 — 18 Borthwick Street, Glasgow G33 3UU
[E-mail: billhunter@dsl.pipex.com] — 0141-774 6860

115 Glasgow: Ruchill (0141-946 0466)
John C. Matthews MA BD — 1992 — 9 Kirklee Road, Glasgow G12 0RQ
[E-mail: jmatthews@kirklee9.fsnet.co.uk] — 0141-357 3249

116 Glasgow: St Andrew's East (0141-554 1485)
Janette G. Reid (Miss) BD   1991
43 Broompark Drive, Glasgow G31 2JB
[E-mail: JANETTEGREID@aol.com]
0141-554 3620

117 Glasgow: St Columba (GE) (0141-221 3305)
Donald Michael MacInnes BD   2002
1 Reelick Avenue, Peterson Park, Glasgow G13 4NF
[E-mail: minister@highlandcathedral.org]
0141-952 0948

118 Glasgow: St David's Knightswood (0141-959 1024) (E-mail: dringlis@stdavidschurch.freeserve.co.uk)
Graham M. Thain LLB BD   1988   1999
60 Southbrae Drive, Glasgow G13 1QD
[E-mail: graham_thain@btopenworld.com]
0141-959 2904

119 Glasgow: St Enoch's Hogganfield (H) (Tel: 0141-770 5694; Fax: 0870 284 0084) (E-mail: church@st-enoch.org.uk) (Website: www.st-enoch.org.uk)
Vacant
43 Smithycroft Road, Glasgow G33 2RH
0141-770 7593
0870 284 0085 (Fax)

120 Glasgow: St George's Tron (0141-221 2141)
William J.U. Philip MB ChB MRCP BD   2004
12 Dargarvel Avenue, Glasgow G41 5LU
[E-mail: wp@wphilip.com]
0141-427 1402

121 Glasgow: St James' (Pollok) (0141-882 4984)
John Mann BSc MDiv DMin   2004
30 Ralston Avenue, Glasgow G52 3NA
[E-mail: drjohnmann@hotmail.com]
0141-883 7405
0141-883 2488

122 Glasgow: St John's Renfield (0141-339 7021) (Website: www.stjohns-renfield.org.uk)
Vacant
26 Leicester Avenue, Glasgow G12 0LU
0141-339 4637

123 Glasgow: St Luke's and St Andrew's
Ian C. Fraser BA BD   1983   1995
10 Chalmers Street, Glasgow G40 2HA
[E-mail: stluke@cqm.co.uk]
0141-556 3883

124 Glasgow: St Margaret's Tollcross Park
George M. Murray LTh   1995
31 Kenmuir Avenue, Sandyhills, Glasgow G32 9LE
[E-mail: george.murray@ntlworld.com]
0141-778 5060

125 Glasgow: St Nicholas' Cardonald
Sandi McGill (Ms) BD   2002   2007
104 Lamington Road, Glasgow G52 2SE
[E-mail: smcgillbox-mail@yahoo.co.uk]
0141-882 2065

126 Glasgow: St Paul's (0141-770 8559)
Vacant
38 Lochview Drive, Glasgow G33 1QF
0141-770 9611

127 Glasgow: St Rollox
James K. Torrens MB ChB BD 2005 42 Melville Gardens, Bishopbriggs, Glasgow G64 3DE 0141-562 6296
[E-mail: james.torrens@ntlworld.com]

128 Glasgow: St Thomas' Gallowgate
Peter R. Davidge BD MTh 2003 8 Helenvale Court, Glasgow G31 4LB 07765 096599 (Mbl)
[E-mail: rev.davidge@virgin.net]

129 Glasgow: Sandyford Henderson Memorial (H) (L)
C. Peter White BVMS BD 1974 1997 66 Woodend Drive, Glasgow G13 1TG 0141-954 9013
[E-mail: revcpw@ntlworld.com]

130 Glasgow: Sandyhills
Graham T. Atkinson MA BD 2006 60 Wester Road, Glasgow G32 9JJ 0141-778 2174
[E-mail: gtatkinson@btopenworld.com]

131 Glasgow: Scotstoun (T)
Richard Cameron BD DipMin 2000 15 Northland Drive, Glasgow G14 9BE 0141-959 4637
[E-mail: rev.rickycam@virgin.net]

132 Glasgow: Shawlands (0141-649 1773)
Stephen A. Blakey BSc BD 1977 2005 29 St Ronan's Drive, Glasgow G41 3SQ 0141-649 2034
[E-mail: shawlandskirk@aol.com]

133 Glasgow: Sherbrooke St Gilbert's (H) (0141-427 1968)
Thomas L. Pollock BA BD MTh FSAScot JP 1982 2003 114 Springkell Avenue, Glasgow G41 4EW 0141-427 2094
[E-mail: tompollock06@aol.com]

134 Glasgow: Shettleston New
Ronald A.S. Craig BAcc BD 1983 2007 211 Sandyhills Road, Glasgow G32 9NB 0141-778 1286
(Charge formed by the union of Glasgow: Carntyne Old and Glasgow: Eastbank)

135 Glasgow: Shettleston Old (T) (H) (0141-778 2484)
Vacant 57 Mansionhouse Road, Mount Vernon, Glasgow G32 0RP 0141-778 8904

136 Glasgow: South Carntyne (H) (0141-778 1343)
Vacant 47 Broompark Drive, Glasgow G31 2JB 0141-554 3275

137 Glasgow: South Shawlands (T) (0141-649 4656)
Fiona Gardner (Mrs) BD MA MLitt 2000 391 Kilmarnock Road, Glasgow G43 2NU 0141-632 0013
[E-mail: fionaandcolin@hotmail.com]

No. / Congregation / Minister	Ordained	Appointed	Address	Telephone
138 Glasgow: Springburn (H) (0141-557 2345)				
Alan A. Ford BD AIBScot	1977	2000	3 Tofthill Avenue, Bishopbriggs, Glasgow G64 3PA [E-mail: springburnchurch@dsl.pipex.com]	0141-762 1844 / 07710 455737 (Mbl)
Helen Hughes (Miss) DCS			2/2 Burnbank Terrace, Glasgow G20 6UQ	0141-333 9459
139 Glasgow: Temple Anniesland (0141-959 1814)				
John Wilson BD	1985	2000	76 Victoria Park Drive North, Glasgow G14 9PJ [E-mail: revjwilson@btinternet.com]	0141-959 5835
140 Glasgow: Toryglen (H)				
Sandra Black (Mrs) BSc BD	1988	2003	36 Glencairn Drive, Glasgow G41 4PW [E-mail: sandra@blacksandra.wanadoo.co.uk]	0141-423 0867
141 Glasgow: Trinity Possil and Henry Drummond				
Richard G. Buckley BD MTh	1990	1995	50 Highfield Drive, Glasgow G12 0HL [E-mail: richardbuckley@hotmail.com]	0141-339 2870
142 Glasgow: Tron St Mary's				
Vacant			3 Hurly Hawkin', Bishopbriggs, Glasgow G64 1YL	0141-772 8555
143 Glasgow: Victoria Tollcross				
Monica Michelin Salomon BD	1999	2007	228 Hamilton Road, Glasgow G32 9QU [E-mail: monica@michelin-salomon.freeserve.co.uk]	0141-778 2413
144 Glasgow: Wallacewell				
Ian C. MacKenzie MA BD	1970	2005	21 Wilson Street, Motherwell ML1 INP [E-mail: iancmackenzie@ntlworld.com]	01698 301230
145 Glasgow: Wellington (H) (0141-339 0454)				
Vacant			27 Kingsborough Gardens, Glasgow G12 9NH	0141-339 3627
146 Glasgow: Whiteinch (New Charge Development) (Website: www.whiteinchcofs.co.uk)				
Alan McWilliam BD	1993	2000	65 Victoria Park Drive South, Glasgow G14 9NX [E-mail: alan@whiteinchcofs.co.uk]	0141-576 9020
147 Glasgow: Yoker (T)				
Karen E. Hendry BSc BD	2005		15 Coldingham Avenue, Glasgow G14 0PX [E-mail: karen@hendry-k.fsnet.co.uk]	0141-952 3620

Name			Charge	Address	Telephone
Aitken, Andrew J. BD APhS MTh PhD	1951	1981	(Tollcross Central with Park)	18 Dorchester Avenue, Glasgow G12 0EE	0141-357 1617
Alexander, Eric J. MA BD	1958	1997	(St George's Tron)	77 Norwood Park, Bearsden, Glasgow G61 2RZ	0141-942 4404
Allan, A.G.	1959	1989	(Candlish Polmadie)	30 Dalrymple Drive, East Mains, East Kilbride, Glasgow G74 4LF	01355 226190

Name	Charge / Position			Address	Tel
Anderson, Colin M. BA BD STM MPhil	(Inverness: St Stephen's with The Old High)	1968	2003	83 Marlborough Avenue, Glasgow G11 7BT	0141-357 2838
Barr, Alexander C. MA BD	(St Nicholas' Cardonald)	1950	1992	25 Fisher Drive, Phoenix Park, Paisley PA1 2TP	0141-848 5941
Barr, John BSc PhD BD	(Kilmacolm: Old)	1958	1979	31 Kelvin Court, Glasgow G12 0AD	0141-357 4338
Beattie, John A.	(Dalmuir Overtoun)	1951	1984	c/o 15 Kelvindale Gardens, Glasgow G20 8DW	0141-946 5978
Bell, John L. MA BD FRSCM DUniv	Iona Community	1978	1988	Flat 2/1, 31 Lansdowne Crescent, Glasgow G20 6NH	0141-334 0688
Birch, James PgDip FRSA FIOC	(Auxiliary Minister)	2001	2007	1 Kirkhill Grove, Cambuslang, Glasgow G72 8EH	0141-583 1722
Bradley, Andrew W. BD	(Paisley: Lylesland)	1975	2007	Flat 1/1, 38 Cairnhill View, Bearsden, Glasgow G61 1RP	0141-931 5344
Brain, Ernest J.	(Liverpool: St Andrew's)	1955	1985	14 Chesterfield Court, 1240 Great Western Road, Glasgow G12 0BJ	0141-357 2249
Brain, Isobel J. (Mrs) MA	(Ballantrae)	1987	1997	14 Chesterfield Court, 1240 Great Western Road, Glasgow G12 0BJ	0141-357 2249
Brice, Dennis G. BSc BD	(Taiwan)	1981		18 Hermitage Avenue, Benfleet, Essex E57 1TQ	01702 555333
Brough, Robin BA	(Whitburn: Brucefield)	1968	2002	'Kildavanan', 10 Printers Lea, Lennoxtown, Glasgow G66 7GF	01360 310223
Bryden, William A. BD	(Yoker: Old with St Matthew's)	1977	1984	145 Bearsden Road, Glasgow G13 1BS	0141-959 5213
Bull, Alister W. BD DipMin	Head of Chaplaincy Service	1994	2001	Chaplaincy Centre Office, First Floor, Queen Mother's Hospital, Yorkhill Division, Dalnair Street, Glasgow G3 8SJ [E-mail: alister.bull@yorkhill.scot.nhs.uk]	0141-201 0000
Campbell, A. Iain MA DipEd	(Busby)	1961	1997	430 Clarkston Road, Glasgow G44 3QF [E-mail: bellmac@sagainternet.co.uk]	0141-637 7460
Cartlidge, G.R.G. MA BD STM	Religious Education RE Teacher.	1977	1993	5 Briar Grove, Newlands, Glasgow G43 2TG	0141-637 3228
Chester, Stephen J. BA BD	International Christian College	1999		42 Drumlochy Road, Ruchazie, Glasgow G33 3RE	0141-774 4666
Coley, Richard LTh	(Glasgow: Victoria Tollcross)	1971	2004	146 Hamilton Road, Glasgow G32 9QR	0141-764 1259
Collard, John K. MA BD	Presbytery Congregational Facilitator	1986	2003	1 Nelson Terrace, East Kilbride, Glasgow G74 2EY	01355 520093
Coull, Morris C. BD	(Stirling: Allan Park South with the Church of the Holy Rude)	1974	2006	112 Greenock Road, Largs KA30 8PF	01475 686838
Cunningham, Alexander MA BD	(Presbytery Clerk)	1961	2002	The Glen, 103 Glenmavis Road, Airdrie ML6 0PQ	01236 763012
Cunningham, James S.A. MA BD BLit PhD	(Glasgow: Barlanark Greyfriars)	1992	2000	'Kirkland', 5 Inveresk Place, Coatbridge ML5 2DA	01236 421541
Currie, Robert MA	(Community Minister)	1955	1990	Flat 3/2, 13 Redlands Road, Glasgow G12 0SJ	0141-334 5111
Dunnett, Linda (Mrs) DCS	Urban Mission Co-ordinator	1972	2002	International Christian College, 110 St James Road, Glasgow G4 0PS (Office); 3 Branklyn Crescent, Glasgow G13 1GJ (Home)	0141-959 3732
Ferguson, James B. LTh	(Lenzie: Union)	1969	2000	3 Bridgeway Place, Kirkintilloch, Glasgow G66 3HW	0141-588 5868
Finlay, William P. MA BD	(Glasgow: Townhead Blochairn)	1967	2006	High Corrie, Brodick, Isle of Arran KA27 8JB	01770 810689
Fisher, M. Leith MA BD	(Glasgow: Wellington)	1977	2002	31 Millburn Avenue, Clydebank G81 1EP [E-mail: fleith@fish.co.uk]	0141-952 3023
Galloway, Kathy (Mrs) BD	Leader: Iona Community	1957	1996	20 Hamilton Park Avenue, Glasgow G12 8UU	0141-357 4079
Gibson, H. Marshall MA BD	(St Thomas' Gallowgate)	1974	2001	39 Burnbroom Drive, Glasgow G69 7XG	0141-771 0749
Gibson, Michael BD STM	(Giffnock: The Park)	1975	1998	12 Mile End Park, Pocklington, York YO42 2TH	
Goss, Alister BD	Industrial Chaplain	1969	2003	79 Weymouth Crescent, Gourock PA19 1HR	01475 638944
Grant, David I.M. MA BD	(Dalry: Trinity)	1996	2001	8 Mossbank Drive, Glasgow G33 1LS	0141-770 7186
Gray, Christine (Mrs)	(Deaconess)			11 Woodside Avenue, Thornliebank, Glasgow G46 7HR	0141-571 1008
Gregson, Elizabeth M. (Mrs) BD	(Drumchapel: St Andrew's)	1949	1986	17 Westfields, Bishopbriggs, Glasgow G64 3PL	0141-563 1918
Grimstone, A. Frank MA	(Calton Parkhead)	1960	1999	144C Howth Drive, Parkview Estate, Anniesland, Glasgow G13 1RL	0141-954 1009
Haley, Derek BD DPS	(Chaplain: Gartnavel Royal)			9 Kinnaird Crescent, Bearsden, Glasgow G61 2BN	0141-942 9281

Name and Qualifications		Charge / Position	Address	Tel.
Harper, Anne J.M. (Miss) BD STM MTh CertSocPsych	1979 1990	Hospital Chaplain	122 Greenock Road, Bishopton PA7 5AS	01505 862466
Harvey, W. John BA BD	1965 2002	(Edinburgh: Corstorphine Craigsbank)	501 Shields Road, Glasgow G41 2RF	0141-429 3774
Haughton, Frank MA BD	1942 2000	(Kirkintilloch: St Mary's)	64 Regent Street, Kirkintilloch, Glasgow G66 1JF	0141-777 6802
Hope, Evelyn P. (Miss) BA BD	1990 1998	(Wishaw: Thornlie)	Flat 0/1, 48 Moss-side Road, Glasgow G41 3UA	0141-649 1522
Houston, Thomas C.	1975 2004	(Glasgow: Priesthill and Nitshill)	110 Elder Crescent, Drumsagart, Glasgow G72 7GL	0141-641 1117
Hunter, Alastair G. MSc BD	1976 1980	University of Glasgow	487 Shields Road, Glasgow G41 2RG	0141-429 1687
Hutcheson, J. Murray MA	1943 1987	(Possilpark)	88 Ainslie Road, Kildrum, Cumbernauld, Glasgow G67 2ED	01236 631168
Hutchison, Henry MA BEd BD MLitt PhD LLCM AMusLCM	1948 1993	(Carmunnock)	4A Briar Grove, Newlands, Glasgow G43 2TG	0141-637 2766
Irvine, Euphemia H.C. (Mrs) BD	1972 1988	(Milton of Campsie)	32 Baird Drive, Bargarran, Erskine PA8 6BB	0141-812 2777
Johnston, Robert W.M. MA BD STM	1964 1999	(Temple Anniesland)	13 Kilmardinny Crescent, Bearsden, Glasgow G61 3NP	0141-931 5862
Johnstone, H. Martin J. MA BD MTh PhD	1989 2000	Urban Priority Areas Adviser	3/1, 952 Pollokshaws Road, Glasgow G41 2ET [E-mail: priorityareas@uk.uumail.com]	0141-636 5819
Keddie, David A. MA BD	1966 2005	(Glasgow: Linthouse St Kenneth's)	21 Ilay Road, Bearsden, Glasgow G61 1QG [E-mail: revked@hotmail.com]	0141-577 1408
Lang, I. Pat (Miss) BSc	1996 2003	(Dunoon: The High Kirk)	37 Crawford Drive, Glasgow G15 6TW	0141-944 2240
Langlands, Cameron H. BD MTh ThM	1995 1999	Hospital Chaplain	G1/28 Plantation Park Gardens, Glasgow G51 1NW	(Mbl) 07890 752877
Levison, C.L. MA BD	1972 1998	Health Care Chaplaincy Training and Development Officer	5 Deaconsbank Avenue, Stewarton Road, Glasgow G46 7UN	0141-620 3492
Lewis, E.M.H. MA	1962 1993	(Drumchapel St Andrew's)	7 Cleveden Place, Glasgow G12 0HG	0141-334 5411
Liddell, Matthew MA BD	1943 1982	(St Paul's (Outer High) and St David's (Ramshorn))		
Lodge, Bernard P. BD	1967 2004	(Glasgow: Govanhill Trinity)	17 Traquair Drive, Glasgow G52 2TB	0141-810 3776
Lunan, David W. MA BD	1970 2002	Presbytery Clerk	6 Darluith Park, Brookfield, Johnstone PA5 8DD	01505 320378
Lyall, Ann (Miss) DCS	1950 2001	Chaplain: Lodging House Mission	142 Hill Street, Glasgow G3 6UA	0141-353 3687
			117 Barlia Drive, Glasgow G45 0AY	0141-631 3643
McAreavey, William BA	1990 1998	(Kelvin Stevenson Memorial)	c/o Bisset, Heronbrook, Ladeside, Newmilns KA16 9BE	
Macaskill, Marjory (Mrs) LLB BD	1971 1993	Chaplain: University of Strathclyde	44 Forfar Avenue, Cardonald, Glasgow G52 3JQ	0141-883 5956
MacBain, Ian BD	2001 2006	(Coatbridge: Coatdyke)	24 Thornyburn Drive, Baillieston, Glasgow G69 7ER	0141-771 7030
MacDonald, Anne (Miss) BA DCS	1995	Healthcare Chaplain: Leverndale Hospital	c/o Leverndale Hospital, Glasgow G53 7TU	0141-840 1875
Macdonald, Kenneth MA BD	1978 2005	(Auxiliary Minister)	5 Henderland Road, Glasgow G61 1AH	0141-943 1103
MacFadyen, Anne M. (Mrs) BSc BD FSAScot	1971 2001	(Auxiliary Minister)	295 Mearns Road, Glasgow G77 5LT	0141-639 3605
McLachlan, Eric BD MTh	1989 2004	(Cardonald)	268 Dyke Road, Knightswood, Glasgow G13 4QX [E-mail: eric.mclachlan@ntlworld.com]	0141-954 1574
McLaren, D. Muir MA BD MTh PhD	1949 1989	(Mosspark)	House 44, 145 Shawhill Road, Glasgow G43 1SX	0141-569 5503
McLay, Alastair D. BSc BD	1984 2001	(Glasgow: Shawlands)	183 King's Park Avenue, Glasgow G44 4HZ	0141-339 1294
Macnaughton, J.A. MA BD	1988	(Hyndland)	62 Lauderdale Gardens, Glasgow G12 9QW	0141-616 6468
MacPherson, James B. DCS	1994 2005	(Deacon)	0/1, 104 Cartside Street, Glasgow G42 9TQ	
MacQuarrie, Stuart BD BSc JP		Chaplain: Glasgow University	The Chaplaincy Centre, University of Glasgow, Glasgow G12 8QQ	0141-330 5419
MacQuien, Duncan DCS		(Deacon)	35 Criffel Road, Mount Vernon, Glasgow G32 9JE	
Martindale, John P.F. BD		(Glasgow: Sandyhills)	50 Springfield Park Road, Burnside, Glasgow G73 3RG	0141-575 1137

Name	Years	Role	Address	Tel
Miller, John D. BA BD DD	1971 2007	(Glasgow: Castlemilk East)	98 Kirkcaldy Road, Glasgow G41 4LD [E-mail: john@miller15.freeserve.co.uk]	
Moore, William B.	1968 2002	Prison Chaplain: Low Moss	10 South Dumbreck Road, Kilsyth, Glasgow G65 9LX	01236 821918
Morrice, Alastair M. MA BD		(Rutherglen: Stonelaw)	5 Brechin Road, Kirriemuir DD8 4BX	
Morris, William J. KCVO PhD LLD DD JP	1951 2005	(Glasgow: Cathedral)	1 Whitehill Grove, Newton Mearns, Glasgow G77 5DH	0141-639 6327
Morton, Thomas MA BD LGSM	1945 1986	(Rutherglen: Stonelaw)	54 Greystone Avenue, Burnside, Rutherglen, Glasgow G73 3SW	0141-647 2682
Muir, Fred C. MA BD ThM ARCM	1961 1997	(Stepps)	20 Alexandra Avenue, Stepps, Glasgow G33 6BP	0141-779 2504
Myers, Frank BA	1952 1978	(Springburn)	18 Birmingham Close, Grantham NG31 8SD	0476 574430
Newlands, George M. MA BD PhD	1970 1986	University of Glasgow	12 Jamaica Street North Lane, Edinburgh EH3 6HQ	0141-339 8855 (Work) / 0141-942 1327
Philp, George M. MA	1953 1996	(Sandyford Henderson Memorial)	44 Beech Avenue, Bearsden, Glasgow G61 3EX	
Philp, Robert A. BA BD	1937 1981	(Stepps: St Andrew's)	Bybrook Nursing Home, Middlehill, Box, Wiltshire SN13 8QP	0141-629 2887
Porter, Richard MA	1953 1988	(Govanhill)	47 Braemar Court, Hazelden Gardens, Glasgow G44 3HF	0141-776 2915
Ramsay, W.G.	1967 1999	(Springburn)	53 Kelvinvale, Kirkintilloch, Glasgow G66 1RD [E-mail: billram@biopenworld.com]	
Robertson, Archibald MA BD	1957 1999	(Eastwood)	19 Canberra Court, Braidpark Drive, Glasgow G46 6NS	0141-637 7572
Robertson, Blair MA BD ThM	1990 1998	Chaplain: Southern General Hospital	c/o Chaplain's Office, Southern General Hospital, 1345 Govan Road, Glasgow G51 4TF	0141-201 2357
Ross, Donald M. MA	1953 1994	(Industrial Mission Organiser)	14 Cartsbridge Road, Busby, Glasgow G76 8DH	0141-644 2220
Ross, James MA BD	1968 1998	(Kilsyth: Anderson)	53 Turnberry Gardens, Westerwood, Cumbernauld, Glasgow G68 0AY	01236 730501
Saunders, Keith BD	1983 1999	Hospital Chaplain	Western Infirmary, Dumbarton Road, Glasgow G11 6NT	0141-211 2000
Shackleton, William	1960 1996	(Greenock: Wellpark West)	3 Tynwald Avenue, Burnside, Glasgow G73 4RN	0141-569 9407
Shanks, Norman J. MA BD DD	1983 2007	(Glasgow: Govan Old)	1 Marchmont Terrace, Glasgow G12 9LT [E-mail: mshnks@shanks1942.freeserve.co.uk]	0141-339 4421
Simpson, Neil A. BA BD PhD	1992 2001	(Glasgow: Yoker Old with Yoker St Matthew's)	c/o Glasgow Presbytery Office	
Smith, G. Stewart MA BD STM	1966 2006	(Glasgow: King's Park)	33 Brent Road, Stewartfield, East Kilbride, Glasgow G74 4RA [E-mail: stewart.smith@tinyworld.co.uk]	(Tel/Fax) 01355 226718
Smith, James S.A.	1956 1991	(Drongan: The Schaw Kirk)	146 Aros Drive, Glasgow G52 1TJ	0141-883 9666
Spence, Elisabeth G.B. (Miss) BD DipEd	1995 2000	Industrial Missioner: Glasgow Area	76 Rylees Crescent, Glasgow G52 4BY [E-mail: elisabeth.spence@btinternet.com]	0141-883 8973
Spencer, John MA BD	1962 2001	(Dumfries: Lincluden with Holywood)	10 Kinkell Gardens, Kirkintilloch, Glasgow G66 2HJ	0141-777 8935
Spiers, John M. LTh MTh	1972 2004	(Giffnock: Orchardhill)	58 Woodlands Road, Thornliebank, Glasgow G46 7JQ	(Tel/Fax) 0141-638 0632
Stevenson, John LTh	1998 2006	(Cambuslang: St Andrew's)	20 Cawowehead Gardens, Uddingston, Glasgow G71 7PY [E-mail: therev20@sky.com]	01698 817582
Stewart, Diane E. BD	1988 2006	(Milton of Campsie)	4 Miller Gardens, Bishopbriggs, Glasgow G64 1FG [E-mail: destewar@fish.co.uk]	0141-762 1358
Stewart, Norma D. (Miss) MA MEd BD	1977 2000	(Glasgow: Strathbungo Queens Park)	127 Nether Auldhouse Road, Glasgow G43 2YS	0141-637 6956
Sutherland, Denis I.	1963 1995	(Hutchesontown)	56 Lime Crescent, Cumbernauld, Glasgow G67 3PQ	01236 731723
Sutherland, Elizabeth W. (Miss) BD	1972 1996	(Balornock North with Barmulloch)	20 Kirkland Avenue, Blanefield, Glasgow G63 9BZ [E-mail: ewsutherland@aol.com]	01360 770154
Tait, Alexander	1967 1995	(St Enoch's Hogganfield)	129 Lochview Drive, Hogganfield, Glasgow G33 1LN	0141-770 6027
Turner, Angus BD	1976 1998	(Industrial Chaplain)	46 Keir Street, Pollokshields, Glasgow G41 2LA	0141-424 0493
Tuton, Robert M. MA	1957 1995	(Shettleston: Old)	6 Holmwood Gardens, Uddingston, Glasgow G71 7BH	01698 321108
Walker, A.L.	1955 1988	(Trinity Possil and Henry Drummond)	11 Dundas Avenue, Torrance, Glasgow G64 4BD	01360 622281

Walton, Ainslie MA MEd   1954 1995   (University of Aberdeen)   501 Shields Road, Glasgow G41 2RF   0141-420 3327
                                                                                       [E-mail: revainslie@aol.com]
White, Elizabeth (Miss) DCS   (Deaconess)   Woodside House, Rodger Avenue, Rutherglen, Glasgow G73 3QZ
Younger, Adah (Mrs) BD   1978 2004   (Glasgow: Dennistoun Central)   Flat 0/1, 101 Greenhead Street, Glasgow G40 1HR   0141-550 0878

GLASGOW ADDRESSES

Banton — Kelvinhead Road, Banton
Bishopbriggs
  Kenmure — Viewfield Road, Bishopbriggs
  Springfield — Springfield Road
Broom — Mearns Road, Newton Mearns
Burnside Blairbeth — Church Avenue, Burnside
  Kirkriggs Avenue, Blairbeth
Busby — Church Road, Busby

Cadder — Cadder Road, Glasgow
Cambuslang
  Flemington Hallside — 265 Hamilton Road
  Old — Cairns Road
St Andrew's — Main Street x Clydeford Road
  Trinity St Paul's — Main Street
Campsie — Main Street, Lennoxtown
Chryston — Main Street, Chryston

Eaglesham — Montgomery Street, Eaglesham

Fernhill and Cathkin — Neilvaig Drive

Gartcosh — 113 Lochend Road, Gartcosh
Giffnock
  Orchardhill — Church Road
  South — Eastwood Toll
  The Park — Ravenscliffe Drive
Glenboig — 138 Main Street, Glenboig
Greenbank — Eaglesham Road, Clarkston

Kilsyth
  Anderson — Kingston Road
  Burns and Old — Church Street
Kirkintilloch
  Hillhead — Newdyke Road
  St Columba's — Waterside Road nr Old Aisle Road
  St David's Mem Pk — Alexander Street
  St Mary's — Cowgate

Lenzie
  Old — Kirkintilloch Road x Garngaber Ave
  Union — Moncrieff Ave x Kirkintilloch Road
Maxwell
  Mearns Castle — Waterfoot Road
  Mearns — Mearns Road, Newton Mearns
Netherlee — Ormonde Drive x Ormonde Avenue
Newton Mearns — Ayr Road, Newton Mearns

Rutherglen
  Old — Main Street at Queen Street
  Stonelaw — Stonelaw Road x Dryburgh Avenue
  Wardlawhill — Hamilton Road
  West — Glasgow Road nr Main Street
Stamperland — Stamperland Gardens, Clarkston
Stepps — Whitehill Avenue

Thornliebank — 61 Spiersbridge Road
Torrance — School Road, Torrance
Twechar — Main Street, Twechar

Williamwood — Vardar Avenue x Seres Ave, Clarkston

Glasgow

Anderston Kelvingrove — Argyle Street x Elderslie Street

Baillieston
  Mure Memorial — Beech Avenue, Garrowhill
  St Andrew's — Bredisholm Road
Balshagray Victoria Pk — Broomhill Cross
Barlanark Greyfriars — Edinburgh Road x Hallhill Road
Battlefield East — 1216 Cathcart Road
Blawarthill — Millbrix Avenue
Bridgeton St Francis
  in the East — 26 Queen Mary Street
Broomhill — Randolph Rd x Marlborough Ave

Calton Parkhead — 122 Helenvale Street
Cardonald — 2155 Paisley Road West
Carmunnock — Kirk Road, Carmunnock
Carmyle — South Carmyle Avenue
Carnwadric — 556 Boydstone Road, Thornliebank
Castlemilk
  East — Barlia Terrace
  West — Carmunnock Road
Cathcart
  Old — 119 Carmunnock Road
  Trinity — 92 Clarkston Road
Cathedral — Cathedral Square
Colston Milton — Egilsay Crescent
Colston Wellpark — 1378 Springburn Road
Cranhill — Bellrock Crescent x Bellrock Street
Croftfoot — Croftpark Ave x Crofthill Road

Dennistoun New — Whitehill Street and Armadale Street

Drumchapel
  Drumry St Mary's — Drumry Road East
  St Andrew's — Garscadden Road
  St Mark's — Kinfauns Drive

Easterhouse St George's
  and St Peter's — Boyndie Street
Eastwood — Mansewood Road

Gairbraid — 1517 Maryhill Road
Gardner Street — Gardner Street x Muirpark Street
Garthamlock and
  Craigend East — Porchester Street x Balveny Street
Gorbals — Eglinton Street x Cumberland Street
Govan Old — 866 Govan Road
Govanhill Trinity — Daisy Street nr Allison Street

High Carntyne — 358 Carntynehall Road
Hillington Park — 24 Berryknowes Road
Househillwood
  St Christopher's — Meikle Road
Hyndland — Hyndland Road, opp Novar Drive

Ibrox	Carillon Road x Clifford Street
John Ross Memorial	100 Norfolk Street
Jordanhill	Woodend Drive x Munro Road
Kelvin Stevenson Mem	Belmont Street at Belmont Bridge
Kelvinside Hillhead	Huntly Gardens
Kenmuir Mount Vernon	London Road, Mount Vernon
King's Park	242 Castlemilk Road
Kinning Park	Eaglesham Place
Knightswood St Margaret's	Knightswood Cross
Langside	Ledard Road x Lochleven Road
Lansdowne	Gt Western Road at Kelvin Bridge
Linthouse St Kenneth's	9 Skipness Drive
Lochwood	Liff Place
Martyrs', The	St Mungo Avenue
Maryhill	1990 Maryhill Road
Merrylea	78 Merrylee Road
Mosspark	149 Ashkirk Drive
Mount Florida	1123 Cathcart Road
New Govan	Govan Cross
Newlands South	Riverside Road x Langside Drive
North Kelvinside	153 Queen Margaret Drive
Partick South	Dumbarton Road
Penilee St Andrew's Trinity	20 Lawrence Street
Pollokshaws	Bowfield Cres x Bowfield Avenue
Pollokshields	223 Shawbridge Street
Possilpark	Albert Drive x Shields Road
Priesthill	124 Saracen Street
and Nitshill	Priesthill Road x Muirshiel Cresc
	Dove Street
Queen's Park	170 Queen's Drive
Renfield St Stephen's	260 Bath Street
Robroyston	34 Saughs Road
Ruchazie	Elibank Street x Milncroft Road
Ruchill	Shakespeare Street nr Maryhill Rd
St Andrew's East	681 Alexandra Parade
St Columba	300 St Vincent Street
St David's Knightswood	Boreland Drive nr Lincoln Avenue
St Enoch's Hogganfield	860 Cumbernauld Road
St George's Tron	163 Buchanan Street
St James' (Pollok)	Lyoncross Road x Byrebush Road
St John's Renfield	22 Beaconsfield Road
St Luke's and St Andrew's	Bain Square at Bain Street
St Margaret's Tollcross Pk	179 Braidfauld Street
St Nicholas' Cardonald	Hartlaw Crescent nr Gladsmuir Road
St Paul's	Langdale Street x Greenrig Street
St Rollox	Fountainwell Road
St Thomas' Gallowgate	Gallowgate opp Bluevale Street
Sandyford Henderson Memorial	Kelvinhaugh Street at Argyle Street
Sandyhills	28 Baillieston Rd nr Sandyhills Rd
Scotstoun	Earlbank Avenue x Ormiston Avenue
Shawlands	Shawlands Cross
Sherbrooke St Gilbert's	Nithsdale Rd x Sherbrooke Avenue
Shettleston New	679 Old Shettleston Road
Shettleston Old	99–111 Killin Street
South Carntyne	538 Carntyne Road
South Shawlands	Regwood Street x Deanston Drive
Springburn	Springburn Road x Atlas Street
Temple Anniesland	869 Crow Road
Toryglen	Glenmore Ave nr Prospecthill Road
Trinity Possil and Henry Drummond	Crowhill Street x Broadholm Street
Tron St Mary's	128 Red Road
Victoria Tollcross	1134 Tollcross Road
Wallacewell	57 Northgate Road
	Ryehill Road x Quarrywood Rd
Wellington	University Ave x Southpark Avenue
Whiteinch	St Paul's R.C. Primary School, Primrose Street
Yoker	Dumbarton Road at Hawick Street

(17) HAMILTON

Meets at Motherwell: Dalziel St Andrew's Parish Church Halls, on the first Tuesday of February, March, May, September, October, November and December; and on the third Tuesday of June.

Presbytery Office: 353 Orbiston Street, Motherwell ML1 1QW 01698 259135
[E-mail: hamilton@cofscotland.org.uk]

Clerk: REV. SHAW J. PATERSON BSc BD MSc [E-mail: clerk@presbyteryofhamilton.co.uk]
c/o The Presbytery Office

Depute Clerk: REV. NORMAN B. McKEE BD c/o The Presbytery Office

Presbytery Treasurer: MR ROBERT A. ALLAN 7 Graham Place, Ashgill, Larkhall ML9 3BA 01698 883246
[E-mail: Fallan3246@aol.com]

1   **Airdrie: Broomknoll (H) (Tel: 01236 762101) (E-mail: airdrie-broomknoll@presbyteryofhamilton.co.uk)**
    linked with Calderbank (E-mail: calderbank@presbyteryofhamilton.co.uk)
    Vacant   38 Commonhead Street, Airdrie   ML6 6NS   01236 602538

2   **Airdrie: Clarkston (E-mail: airdrie-clarkston@presbyteryofhamilton.co.uk)**
    Vacant   Clarkston Manse, Forrest Street, Airdrie   ML6 7BE   01236 769676

3   **Airdrie: Flowerhill (H) (E-mail: airdrie-flowerhill@presbyteryofhamilton.co.uk)**
    Vacant   31 Victoria Place, Airdrie   ML6 9BX   01236 763025

4   **Airdrie: High (E-mail: airdrie-high@presbyteryofhamilton.co.uk)**
    Ian R. W. McDonald BSc BD PhD   2007   17 Etive Drive, Airdrie   ML6 9QL   01236 760023
                                             [E-mail: Ian@spingetastic.freeserve.co.uk]

5   **Airdrie: Jackson (Tel: 01236 733508) (E-mail: airdrie-jackson@presbyteryofhamilton.co.uk)**
    Sharon E.F. Colvin (Mrs)   1985   1998   48 Dunrobin Road, Airdrie   ML6 8LR   01236 763154
    BD LRAM LTCL   [E-mail: dibley@hotmail.com]

6   **Airdrie: New Monkland (H) (E-mail: airdrie-newmonkland@presbyteryofhamilton.co.uk)**
    linked with Greengairs (E-mail: greengairs@presbyteryofhamilton.co.uk)
    Vacant   3 Dykehead Crescent, Airdrie   ML6 6PU   01236 763554

7   **Airdrie: St Columba's (E-mail: airdrie-stcolumbas@presbyteryofhamilton.co.uk)**
    Margaret F. Currie BEd BD   1980   1987   52 Kennedy Drive, Airdrie   ML6 9AW   01236 763173
                                             [E-mail: margaretfcurrie@btinternet.com]

8   **Airdrie: The New Wellwynd (E-mail: airdrie-newwellwynd@presbyteryofhamilton.co.uk)**
    Robert A. Hamilton BA BD   1995   2001   20 Arthur Avenue, Airdrie   ML6 9EZ   01236 763022
                                             [E-mail: revrob13@blueyonder.co.uk]

9   **Bargeddie (H) (E-mail: bargeddie@presbyteryofhamilton.co.uk)**
    John Fairful BD   1994   2001   The Manse, Manse Road, Bargeddie, Baillieston, Glasgow   G69 6UB   0141-771 1322

10 **Bellshill: Macdonald Memorial (E-mail: bellshill-macdonald@presbyteryofhamilton.co.uk) linked with Bellshill: Orbiston**
    Alan McKenzie BSc BD   1988   2001   32 Adamson Street, Bellshill   ML4 1DT   01698 849114
                                             [E-mail: rev.a.mckenzie@btopenworld.com]

11 **Bellshill: Orbiston (E-mail: bellshill-orbiston@presbyteryofhamilton.co.uk)** See Bellshill: Macdonald Memorial

12 **Bellshill: West (H) (01698 747581) (E-mail: bellshill-west@presbyteryofhamilton.co.uk)**
    Agnes A. Moore (Miss) BD   1987   2001   16 Croftpark Street, Bellshill   ML4 1EY   01698 842877
                                             [E-mail: revamoore@tiscali.co.uk]

13 Blantyre: Livingstone Memorial (E-mail: blantyre-livingstone@presbyteryofhamilton.co.uk)
Colin A. Sutherland LTh   1995   2003   286 Glasgow Road, Blantyre, Glasgow G72 9DB   01698 823794
[E-mail: colin.csutherland@btinternet.com]

14 Blantyre: Old (H) (E-mail: blantyre-old@presbyteryofhamilton.co.uk)
Rosemary A. Smith (Ms) BD   1997   The Manse, Craigmuir Road, High Blantyre, Glasgow G72 9UA   01698 823130
[E-mail: revrosieanne@btopenworld.com]

15 Blantyre: St Andrew's (E-mail: blantyre-standrews@presbyteryofhamilton.co.uk)
J. Peter N. Johnston BSc BD   2001   332 Glasgow Road, Blantyre, Glasgow G72 9LQ   01698 828633
[E-mail: peter.johnston@standrewsblantyre.com]

16 Bothwell (H) (E-mail: bothwell@presbyteryofhamilton.co.uk)
James M. Gibson TD LTh LRAM   1978   1989   Manse Avenue, Bothwell, Glasgow G71 8PQ   01698 853189 (Tel)
[E-mail: jamesmgibson@msn.com]   01698 854903 (Fax)

17 Calderbank See Airdrie: Broomknoll

18 Caldercruix and Longriggend (H) (E-mail: caldercruix@presbyteryofhamilton.co.uk)
George M. Donaldson MA BD   1984   2005   Main Street, Caldercruix, Airdrie ML6 7RF   01236 842279
[E-mail: gmdonaldson@gmdonaldson.force9.co.uk]

19 Carfin (E-mail: carfin@presbyteryofhamilton.co.uk) linked with Newarthill (E-mail: newarthill@presbyteryofhamilton.co.uk)
Vacant   Church Street, Newarthill, Motherwell ML1 5HS   01698 860316

20 Chapelhall (H) (E-mail: chapelhall@presbyteryofhamilton.co.uk)
Vacant   Russell Street, Chapelhall, Airdrie ML6 8SG   01236 763439

21 Chapelton (E-mail: chapelton@presbyteryofhamilton.co.uk)
linked with Strathaven: Rankin (H) (E-mail: strathaven-rankin@presbyteryofhamilton.co.uk)
Shaw J. Paterson BSc BD MSc   1991   15 Lethame Road, Strathaven ML10 6AD   01357 520019 (Tel)
[E-mail: shaw@patersonsj.freeserve.co.uk]   01357 529316 (Fax)

22 Cleland (H) (E-mail: cleland@presbyteryofhamilton.co.uk)
John A. Jackson BD   1997   The Manse, Bellside Road, Cleland, Motherwell ML1 5NP   01698 860260
[E-mail: johnjackson@uk2.net]

23 Coatbridge: Blairhill Dundyvan (H) (E-mail: coatbridge-blairhill@presbyteryofhamilton.co.uk)
Patricia A. Carruth (Mrs) BD   1998   2004   18 Blairhill Street, Coatbridge ML5 1PG   01236 432304

24 Coatbridge: Calder (H) (E-mail: coatbridge-calder@presbyteryofhamilton.co.uk)
Amelia Davidson (Mrs) BD   2004   26 Bute Street, Coatbridge ML5 4HF   01236 421516
[E-mail: amelia@davidson1293.freeserve.co.uk]

25 Coatbridge: Clifton (H) (E-mail: coatbridge-clifton@presbyteryofhamilton.co.uk)
Vacant   132 Muiryhall Street, Coatbridge ML5 3NH   01236 421181

26 Coatbridge: Middle (E-mail: coatbridge-middle@presbyteryofhamilton.co.uk)
Vacant   47 Blair Road, Coatbridge ML5 1JQ   01236 432427

27 Coatbridge: Old Monkland (E-mail: coatbridge-oldmonkland@presbyteryofhamilton.co.uk)
Scott Raby LTh   1991   2003   2 Brandon Way, Coatbridge ML5 5QT   01236 423788
                            [E-mail: revscott@rabyfamily28.freeserve.co.uk]

28 Coatbridge: St Andrew's (E-mail: coatbridge-standrews@presbyteryofhamilton.co.uk)
Fiona Nicolson BA BD   1996   2005   77 Eglinton Street, Coatbridge ML5 3JF   01236 437271

29 Coatbridge: Townhead (H) (E-mail: coatbridge-townhead@presbyteryofhamilton.co.uk)
Ecilo Selemani LTh MTh   1993   2004   Crinan Crescent, Coatbridge ML5 2LH   01236 702914
                            [E-mail: eciloselemani@msn.com]

30 Dalserf (E-mail: dalserf@presbyteryofhamilton.co.uk)
D. Cameron McPherson BSc BD DMin   1982   Manse Brae, Dalserf, Larkhall ML9 3BN 01698 882195
                            [E-mail: dCameronMc@aol.com]

31 East Kilbride: Claremont (H) (Tel: 01355 238088) (E-mail: ek-claremont@presbyteryofhamilton.co.uk)
Gordon R. Palmer MA BD STM   1986   2003   17 Deveron Road, East Kilbride, Glasgow G74 2HR   01355 248526
                            [E-mail: gkrspalmer@blueyonder.co.uk]
Paul Cathcart DCS   59 Glen Isla, St Leonards, East Kilbride, Glasgow G74 3TG   0141-569 6865
                            [E-mail: paulcathcart@msn.com]

32 East Kilbride: Greenhills (E) (Tel: 01355 221746) (E-mail: ek-greenhills@presbyteryofhamilton.co.uk)
John Brewster MA BD DipEd   1988   21 Turnberry Place, East Kilbride, Glasgow G75 8TB   01355 242564
                            [E-mail: johnbrewster@blueyonder.co.uk]

33 East Kilbride: Moncreiff (H) (Tel: 01355 223328) (E-mail: ek-moncreiff@presbyteryofhamilton.co.uk)
Alastair S. Lusk BD   1974   1983   16 Almond Drive, East Kilbride, Glasgow G74 2HX   01355 238639

34 East Kilbride: Mossneuk (E) (Tel: 01355 260954) (E-mail: ek-mossneuk@presbyteryofhamilton.co.uk)
John L. McPake BA BD PhD   1987   2000   30 Eden Grove, Mossneuk, East Kilbride, Glasgow G75 8XU   01355 234196

35 East Kilbride: Old (H) (E-mail: ek-old@presbyteryofhamilton.co.uk)
Anne S. Paton BA BD   2001   40 Maxwell Drive, East Kilbride, Glasgow G74 4HJ   01355 220732
                            [E-mail: annepaton@fsmail.net]

36 **East Kilbride: South (H) (E-mail: ek-south@presbyteryofhamilton.co.uk)**
John C. Sharp BSc BD PhD   1980   7 Clamps Wood, East Kilbride, Glasgow G74 2HB   01355 247993

37 **East Kilbride: Stewartfield (New Charge Development)**
Douglas W. Wallace MA BD   1981 2001   8 Thistle Place, Stewartfield, East Kilbride, Glasgow G74 4RH   01355 260879

38 **East Kilbride: West (H) (E-mail: ek-west@presbyteryofhamilton.co.uk)**
Vacant   4 East Milton Grove, East Kilbride, Glasgow G75 8FN   01355 236639

39 **East Kilbride: Westwood (H) (Tel: 01355 245657) (E-mail: ek-westwood@presbyteryofhamilton.co.uk)**
Kevin Mackenzie BD DPS   1989 1996   16 Inglewood Crescent, East Kilbride, Glasgow G75 8QD   01355 223992
[E-mail: kevin@westwoodmanse.freeserve.co.uk]

40 **Glasford (E-mail: glassford@presbyteryofhamilton.co.uk) linked with Strathaven: East (E-mail: strathaven-east@presbyteryofhamilton.co.uk)**
William T. Stewart BD   1980   68 Townhead Street, Strathaven ML10 6DJ   01357 521138

41 **Greengairs** See Airdrie: New Monkland

42 **Hamilton: Burnbank (E-mail: hamilton-burnbank@presbyteryofhamilton.co.uk)
linked with Hamilton: North (H) (E-mail: hamilton-north@presbyteryofhamilton.co.uk)**
Raymond D. McKenzie BD   1978 1987   9 South Park Road, Hamilton ML3 6PJ   01698 424609

43 **Hamilton: Cadzow (H) (Tel: 01698 428695) (E-mail: hamilton-cadzow@presbyteryofhamilton.co.uk)**
Arthur P. Barrie LTh   1973 1979   3 Carlisle Road, Hamilton ML3 7BZ   01698 421664 (Tel)
[E-mail: elizabeth@elsiebarrie.wanadoo.co.uk]   01698 891126 (Fax)

44 **Hamilton: Gilmour and Whitehill (H) (E-mail: hamilton-gilmourwhitehill@presbyteryofhamilton.co.uk)**
Ronald J. Maxwell Stitt   1977 2000   86 Burnbank Centre, Burnbank, Hamilton ML3 0NA   01698 284201
LTh BA ThM BREd DMin FSAScot

45 **Hamilton: Hillhouse (E-mail: hamilton-hillhouse@presbyteryofhamilton.co.uk)**
David W.G. Burt BD DipMin   1989 1998   66 Wellhall Road, Hamilton ML3 9BY   01698 422300
[E-mail: dwgburt@blueyonder.co.uk]

46 **Hamilton: North** See Hamilton: Burnbank

47 **Hamilton: Old (H) (Tel: 01698 281905) (E-mail: hamilton-old@presbyteryofhamilton.co.uk)**
John M.A. Thomson TD JP BD ThM   1978 2001   1 Chateau Grove, Hamilton ML3 7DS   01698 422511
[E-mail: jt@john1949.plus.com]

48 **Hamilton: St Andrew's (T) (E-mail: hamilton-standrews@presbyteryofhamilton.co.uk)**
Norman MacLeod BTh   1999 2005   15 Bent Road, Hamilton ML3 6QB   01698 283264
[E-mail: normanmacleod@btopenworld.com]

49 Hamilton: St John's (H) (Tel: 01698 283492) (E-mail: hamilton-stjohns@presbyteryofhamilton.co.uk)
Robert M. Kent MA BD   1973   1981   12 Castlehill Crescent, Hamilton ML3 7DG   01698 425002
[E-mail: robertmkent@btinternet.com]

50 Hamilton: South (H) (Tel: 01698 281014) (E-mail: hamilton-south@presbyteryofhamilton.co.uk)
linked with Quarter (E-mail: quarter@presbyteryofhamilton.co.uk)
George MacDonald BTh   2004   The Manse, Limekilnburn Road, Quarter, Hamilton ML3 7XA   01698 424511
[E-mail: george.macdonald1@btinternet.com]

51 Hamilton: Trinity (Tel: 01698 284254) (E-mail: hamilton-trinity@presbyteryofhamilton.co.uk)
Karen E. Harbison (Mrs) MA BD   1991   69 Buchan Street, Hamilton ML3 8JY   01698 425326

52 Hamilton: West (H) (Tel: 01698 284670) (E-mail: hamilton-west@presbyteryofhamilton.co.uk)
Elizabeth A. Waddell (Mrs) BD   1999   2005   43 Bothwell Road, Hamilton ML3 0BB   01698 458770

53 Holytown (E-mail: holytown@presbyteryofhamilton.co.uk) linked with New Stevenston: Wrangholm Kirk
Iain M. Goring BSc BD   1976   2006   The Manse, 260 Edinburgh Road, Holytown, Motherwell ML1 5RU   01698 832622
[E-mail: imgoring@tiscali.co.uk]

54 Kirk o' Shotts (H) (E-mail: kirk-o-shotts@presbyteryofhamilton.co.uk)
Sheila M. Spence (Mrs) MA BD   1979   The Manse, Kirk o' Shotts, Salsburgh, Shotts ML7 4NS   01698 870208
[E-mail: sm_spence@hotmail.com]

55 Larkhall: Chalmers (H) (E-mail: larkhall-chalmers@presbyteryofhamilton.co.uk)
James S.G. Hastie CA BD   1990   Quarry Road, Larkhall ML9 1HH   01698 882238
[E-mail: jHastie@chalmers0.demon.co.uk]   08700 562133 (Fax)

56 Larkhall: St Machan's (H) (E-mail: larkhall-stmachans@presbyteryofhamilton.co.uk)
Alastair McKillop BD DipMin   1995   2004   2 Orchard Gate, Larkhall ML9 1HG   01698 321976

57 Larkhall: Trinity (E-mail: larkhall-trinity@presbyteryofhamilton.co.uk)
Lindsay Schluter (Miss) ThE CertMin   1995   13 Machan Avenue, Larkhall ML9 2HE   01698 881401

58 Motherwell: Crosshill (H) (E-mail: mwell-crosshill@presbyteryofhamilton.co.uk)
Gavin W.G. Black BD   2006   15 Orchard Street, Motherwell ML1 3JE   01698 263410
[E-mail: gavin.black12@blueyonder.co.uk]

59 Motherwell: Dalziel St Andrew's (H) (Tel: 01698 264097) (E-mail: mwell-dalzielstandrews@presbyteryofhamilton.co.uk)
Derek W. Hughes BSc BD DipEd   1990   1996   4 Pollock Street, Motherwell ML1 1LP   01698 263414
[E-mail: derekthecleric@btinternet.com]

60 **Motherwell: North (E-mail: mwell-north@presbyteryofhamilton.co.uk)**
Derek H.N. Pope BD   1987   1995   35 Birrens Road, Motherwell ML1 3NS   01698 266716
                                             [E-mail: derekpopemotherwell@hotmail.com]

61 **Motherwell: St Margaret's (E-mail: mwell-stmargarets@presbyteryofhamilton.co.uk)**
Andrew M. Campbell BD   1984   70 Baron's Road, Motherwell ML1 2NB   01698 263803
                                             [E-mail: drewdorca@hotmail.com]

62 **Motherwell: St Mary's (H) (E-mail: mwell-stmarys@presbyteryofhamilton.co.uk)**
David W. Doyle MA BD   1977   1987   19 Orchard Street, Motherwell ML1 3JE   01698 263472

63 **Motherwell: South (H)**
Vacant

       (Charge formed by the union of Motherwell: Manse Road and Motherwell: South Dalziel)

64 **Newarthill** See Carfin

65 **Newmains: Bonkle (H) (E-mail: bonkle@presbyteryofhamilton.co.uk)**
linked with **Newmains: Coltness Memorial (H) (E-mail: coltness@presbyteryofhamilton.co.uk)**
Graham Raeburn MTh   2004   5 Kirkgate, Newmains, Wishaw ML2 9BT   01698 383858
                                             [E-mail: grahamraeburn@tiscali.co.uk]

66 **Newmains: Coltness Memorial** See Newmains: Bonkle
67 **New Stevenston: Wrangholm Kirk (E-mail: wrangholm@presbyteryofhamilton.co.uk)** See Holytown

68 **Overtown (E-mail: overtown@presbyteryofhamilton.co.uk)**
Nan Low (Mrs) BD   2002   The Manse, Main Street, Overtown, Wishaw ML2 0QP   01698 372330
                                             [E-mail: nanlow@supanet.com]

69 **Quarter** See Hamilton: South

70 **Shotts: Calderhead Erskine (E-mail: calderhead-erskine@presbyteryofhamilton.co.uk)**
Ian G. Thom BSc PhD BD   1990   2000   The Manse, 9 Kirk Road, Shotts ML7 5ET   01501 820042
                                             [E-mail: the.thoms@btinternet.com]

71 **Stonehouse: St Ninian's (H) (E-mail: stonehouse@presbyteryofhamilton.co.uk)**
Paul G.R. Grant BD MTh   2003   4 Hamilton Way, Stonehouse, Larkhall ML9 3PU   01698 792947
                                             [E-mail: agpg@surefish.co.uk]

72 **Strathaven: Avendale Old and Drumclog (H) (Tel: 01357 529748) (E-mail: strathaven-avendaleold@presbyteryofhamilton.co.uk and
       E-mail: drumclog@presbyteryofhamilton.co.uk)**
Alan W. Gibson BA BD   2001   Kirk Street, Strathaven ML10 6BA   01357 520077
                                             [E-mail: awgibson82@hotmail.com]

73 **Strathaven: East** See Glasford
74 **Strathaven: Rankin** See Chapelton

75 **Strathaven: West (E-mail: strathaven-west@presbyteryofhamilton.co.uk)**
Una B. Stewart (Ms) BD DipEd   1995   2002   6 Avenel Crescent, Strathaven ML10 6JF   01357 529086
[E-mail: rev.ubs@virgin.net]

76 **Uddingston: Burnhead (H) (E-mail: uddingston-burnhead@presbyteryofhamilton.co.uk)**
Vacant   90 Laburnum Road, Uddingston, Glasgow G71 5DB   01698 813716
Karen Hamilton (Mrs) DCS   6 Beckfield Gate, Glasgow G33 1SW   0141-558 3195

77 **Uddingston: Old (H) (Tel: 01698 814015) (E-mail: uddingston-old@presbyteryofhamilton.co.uk)**
Norman B. McKee BD   1987   1994   1 Belmont Avenue, Uddingston, Glasgow G71 7AX   01698 814757
[E-mail: n.mckee1@btinternet.com]

78 **Uddingston: Viewpark (H) (E-mail: uddingston-viewpark@presbyteryofhamilton.co.uk)**
Michael G. Lyall BD   1993   2001   14 Holmbrae Road, Uddingston, Glasgow G71 6AP   01698 813113
[E-mail: michaellyall@blueyonder.co.uk]

79 **Wishaw: Cambusnethan North (H) (E-mail: wishaw-cambusnethannorth@presbyteryofhamilton.co.uk)**
Mhorag Macdonald (Ms) MA BD   1989   350 Kirk Road, Wishaw ML2 8LH   01698 381305
[E-mail: mhorag.force9.co.uk]

80 **Wishaw: Cambusnethan Old (E-mail: wishaw-cambusnethanold@presbyteryofhamilton.co.uk)**
and Morningside (E-mail: wishaw-morningside@presbyteryofhamilton.co.uk)
Iain C. Murdoch MA LLB DipEd BD   1995   22 Coronation Street, Wishaw ML2 8LF   01698 384235
[E-mail: iaincmurdoch@btopenworld.com]

81 **Wishaw: Craigneuk and Belhaven (H) (E-mail: wishaw-craigneukbelhaven@presbyteryofhamilton.co.uk) linked with Wishaw: Old**
Vacant   100 Glen Road, Wishaw ML2 7NP   01698 372495

82 **Wishaw: Old (H) (Tel: 01698 376080) (E-mail: wishaw-old@presbyteryofhamilton.co.uk)** See Wishaw: Craigneuk and Belhaven

83 **Wishaw: St Mark's (E-mail: wishaw-stmarks@presbyteryofhamilton.co.uk)**
Vacant   Coltness Road, Wishaw ML2 7EX   01698 384596

84 **Wishaw: South Wishaw (H)**
Klaus O.F. Buwert LLB BD   1984   1999   Wishaw South Manse, 16 West Thornlie Street, Wishaw ML2 7AR   01698 372356
[E-mail: k.buwert@btinternet.com]

Name	Ord.	Ind.	Charge / Position	Address	Tel
Anderson, Catherine B. (Mrs) DCS	1951	1986	(Deaconess)	13 Mosshill Road, Bellshill ML4 1NQ	01698 745907
Beattie, William G. BD BSc	1963	2002	(Hamilton: St Andrew's)	33 Dungavel Gardens, Hamilton ML3 7PE	01698 423804
Black, John M. MA BD	1995	2003	(Coatbridge: Blairhill Dundyvan)	3 Grantown Avenue, Airdrie ML6 8HH	01236 750638
Brown, Allan B. BD MTh			Chaplain: Shotts Prison	HMP Shotts, Scott Drive, Shotts ML7 4LE [E-mail: alan.brown3@sps.gov.uk]	01501 824071
Cook, J. Stanley BD Dip PSS	1974	2001	(Hamilton: West)	Mansend, 137A Old Manse Road, Netherton, Wishaw ML2 0EW [E-mail: stancook@blueyonder.co.uk]	01698 299600
Cullen, William T. BA LTh	1984	1996	(Kilmarnock: St John's Onthank)	6 Laurel Wynd, Cambuslang, Glasgow G72 7BA	0141-641 4337
Currie, David E.P. BSc BD	1983	2000	Congregational Development Consultant	21 Rosa Burn Avenue, Lindsayfield, East Kilbride, Glasgow G75 9DE	01355 248510
Currie, R. David BSc BD	1984	2004	(Cambuslang: Flemington Hallside)	69 Kethers Street, Motherwell ML1 3HN	01698 323424
Dunn, W. Stuart LTh	1970	2006	(Motherwell: Crosshill)	10 Macrostie Gardens, Crieff PH7 4LP	01764 655178
Easton, Lilly C. (Mrs)	1999	2007	(Airdrie: Clarkston)	Flat 2, 90 Beith Street, Glasgow G11 6DQ	0141-586 7628
Fraser, James P.	1951	1988	(Strathaven: Avendale Old and Drumclog)		
Gilchrist, Kay (Miss) BD	1996	1999	Part-time Chaplain: Polmont Young Offenders Institution	26 Hamilton Road, Strathaven ML10 6JA	01357 522758
Grier, James BD	1991	2005	(Coatbridge: Middle)	45 Hawthorn Drive, Craigneuk, Airdrie ML6 8AP	01698 742545
Handley, John	1954	1993	(Motherwell: Clason Memorial)	14 Love Drive, Bellshill ML4 1BY	01698 262733
Hunter, James E. LTh	1974	1997	(Blantyre: Livingstone Memorial)	12 Airbles Crescent, Motherwell ML1 3AR	01698 826177
King, Crawford S. MA	1958	1984	(Glenboig)	57 Dalwhinnie Avenue, Blantyre, Glasgow G72 9NQ	
McAlpine, John BSc	1998	2004	(Auxiliary Minister)	Rawyards House, Motherwell Street, Airdrie ML6 7HP	
McCabe, George	1963	1996	(Airdrie: High)	201 Bonkle Road, Newmains, Wishaw ML2 9AA	01698 384610
McDonald, John A. MA BD	1978	1997	(Cumbernauld: Condorrat)	Flat 8, Park Court, 2 Craighouse Park, Edinburgh EH10 5LD	0131-447 9522
Mackenzie, James G. BA BD	1980	2005	(Jersey: St Columba's)	17 Thomson Drive, Bellshill ML4 3ND	
Martin, James MA BD DD	1946	1987	(Glasgow: High Carntyne)	10 Sandpiper Crescent, Carnbroe, Coatbridge ML5 4UW	01698 385825
Melrose, J.H. Loudon MA BD MEd	1955	1996	(Gourock: Old Gourock and Ashton [Assoc])	9 Magnolia Street, Wishaw ML2 7EQ; 1 Laverock Avenue, Hamilton ML3 7DD	01698 427958
Munton, James G. BA	1969	2002	(Coatbridge: Old Monkland)	2 Moorcroft Drive, Airdrie ML6 8ES [E-mail: jacjim@supanet.com]	01236 754848
Price, Peter O. CBE QHC BA FPhS	1960	1996	(Blantyre: Old)	22 Old Bothwell Road, Bothwell, Glasgow G71 8AW [E-mail: peteroprice@aol.com]	01698 854032
Rogerson, Stuart D. BSc BD	1980	2001	(Strathaven: West)	17 Westfield Park, Strathaven ML10 6XH [E-mail: srogerson@cnetwork.co.uk]	01357 523321
Ross, Keith W.	1984	2007	Congregational Development Officer for the Presbytery of Hamilton	Easter Bavlaw Farm, Balerno EH14	(Mbl) 07855 163449
Salmond, James S. BA BD MTh ThD	1979	2003	(Holytown)	165 Torbothie Road, Shotts ML7 5NE	
Thomson, Andrew BA	1976	2006	(Airdrie: Broomknoll with Calderbank)	3 Laurel Wynd, Drumfargard Village, Cambuslang, Glasgow G72 7BH [E-mail: andrewthomson@hotmail.com]	0141-641 2936
Thorne, Leslie W. BA LTh	1987	2001	(Coatbridge: Clifton)	'Hatherleigh', 9 Chatton Walk, Coatbridge ML5 4FH [E-mail: lesthorne@tiscali.co.uk]	01236 432241
Wilson, James H. LTh	1970	1996	(Cleland)	21 Austine Drive, Hamilton ML3 7YE [E-mail: wilsonjh@blueyonder.co.uk]	(Mbl) 07963 199921; 01698 457042
Wyllie, Hugh R. MA DD FCIBS	1962	2000	(Hamilton: Old)	18 Chantinghall Road, Hamilton ML3 8NP	01698 420002
Zambonini, James LIADip		1997	Auxiliary Minister	100 Old Manse Road, Wishaw ML2 0EP	01698 350887

HAMILTON ADDRESSES

Airdrie
Broomknoll — Broomknoll Street
Clarkston — Forrest Street
Flowerhill — 89 Graham Street
High — North Bridge Street
Jackson — Glen Road
New Monkland — Glenmavis
St Columba's — Thrashbush Road
The New Wellwynd — Wellwynd

Coatbridge
Blairhill Dundyvan — Blairhill Street
Calder — Calder Street
Clifton — Muiryhall Street x Jackson Street
Middle — Bank Street
Old Monkland — Woodside Street
St Andrew's — Church Street
Townhead — Crinan Crescent

East Kilbride
Claremont — High Common Road, St Leonard's
Greenhills — Greenhills Centre
Moncreiff — Calderwood Road
Mossneuk — Eden Drive
Old — Montgomery Street
South — Baird Hill, Murray
West — Kittoch Street
Westwood — Belmont Drive, Westwood

Hamilton
Burnbank — High Blantyre Road
Cadzow — Woodside Walk
Gilmour and Whitehill — Glasgow Road, Burnbank
Hillhouse — Abbotsford Road, Whitehill
North — Clerkwell Road
Old — Windmill Road
St Andrew's — Leechlee Road
St John's — Avon Street
South — Duke Street
Trinity — Strathaven Road
West — Neilsland Square off North Road
— Burnbank Road

Motherwell
Crosshill — Windmillhill Street x Airbles Street
Dalziel St Andrew's — Merry Street and Muir Street
North — Chesters Crescent
St Margaret's — Shields Road
St Mary's — Avon Street
South — Gavin Street

Uddingston
Burnhead — Laburnum Road
Old — Old Glasgow Road
Viewpark — Old Edinburgh Road

Wishaw
Cambusnethan North — Kirk Road
Old — Kirk Road
Chalmers — East Academy Street
Craigneuk and Belhaven — Craigneuk Street
Old — Main Street
St Mark's — Coltness Road
Thornlie — West Thornlie Street

(18) DUMBARTON

Meets at Dumbarton, in Riverside Church Halls, on the first Tuesday of February, March, April, May, October, November and December, on the second Tuesday of June and September (and April when the first Tuesday falls in Holy Week), and at the incoming Moderator's church on the first Tuesday of June for the installation of the Moderator.

Clerk:	REV. J. COLIN CASKIE BA BD			11 Ardenconnel Way, Rhu, Helensburgh G84 8LX	01436 820213
				[E-mail: dumbarton@cofscotland.org.uk]	

Alexandria

Elizabeth W. Houston (Miss) MA BD DipEd	1985	1995	32 Ledrish Avenue, Balloch, Alexandria G83 8JB	01389 751933

Arrochar linked with Luss

H. Dane Sherrard BD DMin	1971	1998	The Manse, Luss, Alexandria G83 8NZ	01436 860240
			[E-mail: dane@cadder.demon.co.uk]	07801 939138 (Mbl)

Baldernock (H)
Andrew P. Lees BD — 1984 2002 — The Manse, Bardowie, Milngavie, Glasgow G62 6ES [E-mail: thereverend@alees.fsnet.co.uk] — 01360 620471

Bearsden: Baljaffray (H)
Vacant — 5 Fintry Gardens, Bearsden, Glasgow G61 4RJ — 0141-942 0366

Bearsden: Cross (H)
John W.F. Harris MA — 1967 2006 — 61 Drymen Road, Bearsden, Glasgow G61 2SU [E-mail: jwfh@bearsdencross.org] — 0141-942 0507 / 07711 573877 (Mbl)
(Charge formed by the union of Bearsden: North and Bearsden: South)

Bearsden: Killermont (H)
Alan J. Hamilton LLB BD — 2003 — 8 Clathic Avenue, Bearsden, Glasgow G61 2HF [E-mail: alanj@hamilton63.freeserve.co.uk] — 0141-942 0021

Bearsden: New Kilpatrick (H) (0141-942 8827) (E-mail: mail@nkchurch.org.uk)
David D. Scott BSc BD — 1981 1999 — 51 Manse Road, Bearsden, Glasgow G61 3PN [E-mail: mail@nkchurch.org.uk] — 0141-942 0035

Bearsden: Westerton Fairlie Memorial (H) (0141-942 6960)
Vacant — 3 Canniesburn Road, Bearsden, Glasgow G61 1PW — 0141-942 2672

Bonhill (H) (01389 756516)
Ian H. Miller BA BD — 1975 — 1 Glebe Gardens, Bonhill, Alexandria G83 9NZ [E-mail: ianmiller@bonhillchurch.freeserve.co.uk] — 01389 753039

Cardross (H) (01389 841322)
Andrew J. Scobie MA BD — 1963 1965 — The Manse, Main Road, Cardross, Dumbarton G82 5LB [E-mail: ascobie55@cardross.dunbartonshire.co.uk] — 01389 841289 / 07889 670252 (Mbl)

Clydebank: Abbotsford (E-mail: abbotsford@lineone.net) (Website: www.abbotsford.org.uk)
Roderick G. Hamilton MA BD — 1992 1996 — 35 Montrose Street, Clydebank G81 2PA [E-mail: rghamilton@ntlworld.com] — 0141-952 5151

Clydebank: Faifley
Gregor McIntyre BSc BD — 1991 — Kirklea, Cochno Road, Hardgate, Clydebank G81 6PT [E-mail: mail@gregormcintyre.com] — 01389 876836

Clydebank: Kilbowie St Andrew's
Peggy Roberts (Mrs) BA BD — 2003 — 5 Melfort Avenue, Clydebank G81 2HX [E-mail: peggy.r@ntlworld.com] — 0141-951 2455

Clydebank: Radnor Park (H)
Margaret J.B. Yule (Mrs) BD 1992 Church Manse, Spencer Street, Clydebank G81 3AS [E-mail: mjbyule@yahoo.co.uk] 0141-951 1007

Clydebank: St Cuthbert's (T) linked with Duntocher (H)
David Donaldson MA BD DMin 1969 2002 The Manse, Roman Road, Duntocher, Clydebank G81 6BT [E-mail: david.donaldson3@btopenworld.com] 01389 873471

Craigrownie linked with Rosneath: St Modan's (H)
Vacant Edenkiln, Argyll Road, Kilcreggan, Helensburgh G84 0JW 01436 842274

Dalmuir: Barclay (0141-941 3988)
Fiona E. Maxwell BA BD 2004 16 Parkhall Road, Dalmuir, Clydebank G81 3RJ [E-mail: fionamaxi@btinternet.com] 0141-941 3317

Dumbarton: Riverside (H) (01389 742551)
Robert J. Watt BD 1994 2002 5 Kirkton Road, Dumbarton G82 4AS [E-mail: robertjwatt@blueyonder.co.uk] 01389 762512

Dumbarton: St Andrew's (H)
Vacant 17 Mansewood Drive, Dumbarton G82 3EU 01389 604259

Dumbarton: West Kirk (H)
Vacant 3 Havoc Road, Dumbarton G82 4JW 01389 604840

Duntocher (H) See Clydebank: St Cuthbert's

Garelochhead (01436 810589)
Alastair S. Duncan MA BD 1989 Old School Road, Garelochhead, Helensburgh G84 0AT [E-mail: gpc@churchuk.fsnet.co.uk] 01436 810022

Helensburgh: Park (H) (01436 674825)
Gavin McFadyen BEng BD 2006 Park Manse, 35 East Argyle Street, Helensburgh G84 7EL [E-mail: parkchurchminister@tiscali.co.uk] 01436 679970

Helensburgh: St Columba (H)
George Vidits BD MTh 2000 2006 46 Suffolk Street, Helensburgh G84 9QZ [E-mail: george.vidits@btinternet.com] 01436 672054

Helensburgh: The West Kirk (H) (01436 676880)
David W. Clark MA BD 1975 1986 37 Campbell Street, Helensburgh G84 9NH [E-mail: clarkdw@lineone.net] 01436 674063

Jamestown (H)
Norma Moore (Ms) MA BD   1995   26 Kessog's Gardens, Balloch, Alexandria G83 8QJ   01389 756447
[E-mail: norma.moore5@btinternet.com]

Kilmaronock Gartocharn
Janet P.H. MacMahon (Mrs) MSc BD   1992 2006   Kilmaronock Manse, Alexandria G83 8SB   01360 660295
[E-mail: janetmacmahon@yahoo.co.uk]

Luss See Arrochar

Milngavie: Cairns (H) (0141-956 4868)
Andrew Frater BA BD MTh   1987 1994   4 Cairns Drive, Milngavie, Glasgow G62 8AJ   0141-956 1717
[E-mail: office@cairnschurch.org.uk]

Milngavie: St Luke's (0141-956 4226)
Ramsay B. Shields BA BD   1990 1997   70 Hunter Road, Milngavie, Glasgow G62 7BY   0141-577 9171 (Tel)
[E-mail: rbs@minister.com]   0141-577 9181 (Fax)

Milngavie: St Paul's (H) (0141-956 4405)
Fergus C. Buchanan MA BD MTh   1982 1988   8 Buchanan Street, Milngavie, Glasgow G62 8DD   0141-956 1043
[E-mail: f.c.buchanan@ntlworld.com]

Old Kilpatrick Bowling
Jeanette Whitecross (Mrs) BD   2002   The Manse, 175 Dumbarton Road, Old Kilpatrick, Glasgow G60 5JQ   01389 873130
[E-mail: jeanettewx@yahoo.com]

Renton: Trinity (H)
Vacant   38 Main Street, Renton, Dumbarton G82 4PU   01389 752017

Rhu and Shandon (H)
J. Colin Caskie BA BD   1977 2002   11 Ardenconnel Way, Rhu, Helensburgh G84 8LX   01436 820213
[E-mail: colin@jcaskie.eclipse.co.uk]

Rosneath: St Modan's See Craigrownie

Booth, Frederick M. LTh   1970 2005   (Helensburgh: St Columba)   Achnashie Coach House, Clynder, Helensburgh G84 0QD   01436 831522
Crombie, William D. MA BD   1947 1987   (Calton New with St Andrew's)   32 Westbourne Drive, Bearsden, Glasgow G61 4BH   0141-943 0235
Davidson, Professor Robert   1956 1991   (University of Glasgow)
MA BD DD FRSE   30 Dumgoyne Drive, Bearsden, Glasgow G61 3AP   0141-942 1810
Donaghy, Leslie G.
BD DipMin PGCE FSAScot   1990 2004   (Dumbarton: St Andrew's)   130 Dumbuck Road, Dumbarton G82 3LZ   01389 604251
Easton, I.A.G. MA FIPM   1945 1988   Lecturer   6 Edgehill Road, Bearsden, Glasgow G61 3AD   0141-942 4214

Name	Dates	Role	Address	Telephone
Ferguson, Archibald M. MSc PhD CEng FRINA	1989 2004	Auxiliary Minister with Clerk	The Whins, Barrowfield, Cardross, Dumbarton G82 5NL [E-mail: archiefferguson@supanet.com]	01389 841517
Houston, Peter M. FPhS	1952 1997	(Renfrew: Old)	25 Honeysuckle Lane, Jamestown, Alexandria G83 8PL	01389 721165 (Mbl) 07770 390936
Hudson, Eric V. LTh	1971 2007	(Bearsden: Westerton Fairlie Memorial)	2 Murrayfield Drive, Bearsden, Glasgow G61 1JE	0141-942 6110
Jack, Robert MA BD	1950 1996	(Bearsden: Killermont)	142 Turnhill Drive, Erskine PA8 7AH	0141-812 8370
Kemp, Tina MA	2005	Auxiliary Minister	12 Oaktree Gardens, Dumbarton G82 1EU	01389 730477
Lawson, Alexander H. ThM ThD FPhS	1950 1988	(Clydebank: Kilbowie)		
McIntyre, J. Ainslie MA BD	1963 1984	(University of Glasgow)	60 Bonnaughton Road, Bearsden, Glasgow G61 4DB [E-mail: jamcintyre@hotmail.com]	0141-942 5143 (Mbl) 07050 295103
Munro, David P. MA BD STM	1953 1996	(Bearsden: North)	14 Birch Road, Killearn, Glasgow G63 9SQ	01360 550098
Murdoch, William M. BSc PhD BD STM	1980 2007	(Craigrownie with Rosneath: St Modan's)	19 Annesley Grove, Torphins AB31 4HZ	
Ramage, Alistair E. BA ADB CertEd	1996 2004	Auxiliary Minister with Clerk	6 Claremont Gardens, Milngavie, Glasgow G62 6PG [E-mail: ara3@waitrose.com]	0141-956 2897
Shackleton, Scott J.S. BA BD PhD	1993 1993	Chaplain: Royal Navy	HMS Neptune, HMNB Clyde, Faslane, Helensburgh G84 8HL	
Spence, C.K.O. MC TD MA BD	1949 1983	(Craigrownie)	8B Cairndhu Gardens, Helensburgh G84 8PG	01436 678838
Steven, Harold A.M. LTh FSA Scot	1970 2001	(Baldernock)	9 Cairnhill Road, Bearsden, Glasgow G61 1AT	0141-942 1598
Wright, Malcolm LTh	1970 2003	(Craigrownie with Rosneath: St Modan's)	30 Clairinsh, Drunkinnon Gate, Balloch, Alexandria G83 8SE	01389 720338

DUMBARTON ADDRESSES

Clydebank
Abbotsford — Town Centre
Faifley — Faifley Road
Kilbowie St Andrew's — Kilbowie Road
Radnor Park — Radnor Street
St Cuthbert's — Linnvale

Dumbarton
Riverside — High Street
St Andrew's — Aitkenbar Circle
West Kirk — West Bridgend

Helensburgh
Park — Charlotte Street
St Columba — Sinclair Street
The West Kirk — Colquhoun Square

(19) ARGYLL

Meets at various locations in Argyll on the first Tuesday or Wednesday of March, June, September and December. For details, contact the Presbytery Clerk.

Clerk:	MR IAN MACLAGAN LLB FSAScot	Carmonadh, Eastlands Road, Rothesay, Isle of Bute PA20 9JZ [E-mail: argyll@cofscotland.org.uk]	01700 503015
Depute Clerk:	REV. GEORGE G. CRINGLES BD	St Oran's Manse, Connel, Oban PA37 1PJ [E-mail: george.cringles@btinternet.com]	01631 710242
Treasurer:	MRS PAMELA A. GIBSON	Allt Ban, Portsonachan, Dalmally PA33 1BJ [E-mail: macgills1234@aol.com]	01866 833344

Appin linked with Lismore

Vacant		The Manse, Appin PA38 4DD	01631 730206

Ardchattan (H)

Jeffrey A. McCormick BD	1984	Ardchattan Manse, North Connel, Oban PA37 1RG [E-mail: jeff.mcc@virgin.net]	01631 710364

Ardrishaig (H) linked with South Knapdale

David Carruthers BD	1998	The Manse, Park Road, Ardrishaig, Lochgilphead PA30 8HE	01546 603269

Campbeltown: Highland (H)

Michael J. Lind LLB BD	1984 1997	Highland Church Manse, Kirk Street, Campbeltown PA28 6BN [E-mail: myknan@tiscali.co.uk]	01586 551146

Campbeltown: Lorne and Lowland (H)

Philip D. Burroughs BSc BTh DTS	1998 2004	Lorne and Lowland Manse, Castlehill, Campbeltown PA28 6AN [E-mail: burroughs@btinternet.com]	01586 552468
Kirsty-Ann Burroughs (Mrs) BA BD CertTheol DRM PhD (Aux)	2007	Lorne and Lowland Manse, Castlehill, Campbeltown PA28 6AN [E-mail: burroughs@btinternet.com]	01586 552468

Coll linked with Connel

George G. Cringles BD	1981 2002	St Oran's Manse, Connel, Oban PA37 1PJ [E-mail: george.cringles@btinternet.com]	(Connel) 01631 710242 (Coll) 01879 230366

Colonsay and Oronsay (Website: www.islandchurches.org.uk)

Vacant

Connel See Coll

Craignish linked with Kilbrandon and Kilchattan linked with Kilninver and Kilmelford

T. Alastair McLachlan BSc	1972 2004	The Manse, Kilmelford, Oban PA34 4XA [E-mail: talastair@tesco.net]	01852 200565

Cumlodden, Lochfyneside and Lochgair

Roderick MacLeod MA BD PhD(Edin) PhD(Open)	1966 1985	Cumlodden Manse, Furnace, Inveraray PA32 8XU [E-mail: revroddy@yahoo.co.uk]	01499 500288

Dunoon: St John's linked with Sandbank (H)

Joseph Stewart LTh	1979 1989	23 Bullwood Road, Dunoon PA23 7QJ	01369 702128
Glenda M. Wilson (Mrs) DCS	1990 2006	Charity Cottage, Blairmore, Dunoon PA23 8TP [E-mail: GlendaMWilson@aol.com]	01369 810397

Dunoon: The High Kirk (H) linked with Innellan linked with Toward

Vacant		7A Matheson Lane, Innellan, Dunoon PA23 7SH	01369 830276
Ruth I. Griffiths (Mrs) (Aux)	2004	Kirkwood, Matheson Lane, Innellan, Dunoon PA23 7TA [E-mail: ruthigriffiths@googlemail.com]	01369 830145

Gigha and Cara (H) (GD)

Vacant		The Manse, Isle of Gigha PA41 7AA	01583 505245

Glassary, Kilmartin and Ford linked with North Knapdale

Richard B. West	1994 2005	The Manse, Kilmichael Glassary, Lochgilphead PA31 8QA [E-mail: richard.west999@btinternet.com]	01546 606926

Glenaray and Inveraray

Vacant		The Manse, Inveraray PA32 8XT	01499 302060

Glenorchy and Innishael linked with Strathfillan

Vacant		The Manse, Dalmally PA33 1AA	01838 200386

Innellan (H) See Dunoon: The High Kirk

Iona linked with Kilfinichen and Kilvickeon and the Ross of Mull

Sydney S. Graham BD DipYL MPhil	1987 2004	The Manse, Bunessan, Isle of Mull PA67 6DW [E-mail: syd@sydgraham.force9.co.uk]	01681 700227

Jura (GD)

Vacant		Church of Scotland Manse, Craighouse, Isle of Jura PA60 7XG	01496 820384

Kilarrow (H)

Vacant		The Manse, Bowmore, Isle of Islay PA43 7LH	01496 810271

Kilberry linked with Tarbert (H)
Vacant   The Manse, Tarbert, Argyll PA29

Kilbrandon and Kilchattan See Craignish

Kilcalmonell linked with Killean and Kilchenzie (H)
Vacant   The Manse, Muasdale, Tarbert, Argyll PA29 6XD   01583 421249

Kilchoman (GD) linked with Kilmeny linked with Portnahaven (GD)
Stephen Fulcher BA MA   1993   2003   The Manse, Port Charlotte, Isle of Islay PA48 7TW   01496 850241
                                                   [E-mail: scr@fish.co.uk]

Kilchrenan and Dalavich linked with Muckairn
Margaret R.M. Millar (Miss) BTh   1977   1996   Muckairn Manse, Taynuilt PA35 1HW   01866 822204
                                                         [E-mail: macoje@aol.com]

Kildalton and Oa (GD) (H)
Vacant   The Manse, Port Ellen, Isle of Islay PA42 7DB   01496 302447

Kilfinan linked with Kilmodan and Colintraive linked with Kyles (H)
David Mitchell BD DipPTheol MSc   1988   2006   West Cowal Manse, Kames, Tighnabruaich PA21 2AD   01700 811045
                                                    [E-mail: revdmitchell@yahoo.co.uk]

Kilfinichen and Kilvickeon and the Ross of Mull See Iona
Killean and Kilchenzie (H) See Kilcalmonell
Kilmeny See Kilchoman
Kilmodan and Colintraive See Kilfinan

Kilmore (GD) and Oban (E-mail: obancofs@btinternet.com)
Dugald J.R. Cameron BD DipMin MTh   1990   2007   Kilmore and Oban Manse, Ganavan Road, Oban PA34 5TU   01631 566253
                                                      [E-mail: dugald.cameron@ntlworld.com]
Elizabeth Gibson (Mrs) MA MLitt BD (Assoc) 2003   Rudha-na-Cloiche, Esplanade, Oban PA34 5AQ   01631 562759
                                                      [E-mail: lizgibson@phonecoop.coop]

Kilmun (St Munn's) (H) linked with Strone (H) and Ardentinny
Franklin G. Wyatt MA MDiv DMin   1974   2004   The Manse, Blairmore, Dunoon PA23 8TE   01369 840313
                                                   [E-mail: shorechurches@btinternet.com]

Kilninver and Kilmelford See Craignish

Kirn (H)
Grahame M. Henderson BD | 1974 | 2004 | Kirn Manse, 13 Dhailling Park, Hunter Street, Kirn, Dunoon PA23 8FK [E-mail: ghende5884@aol.com] | 01369 702256

Glenda M. Wilson (Mrs) DCS | 1990 | 2006 | Charity Cottage, Blairmore, Dunoon PA23 8TP [E-mail: GlendaMWilson@aol.com] | 01369 810397

Kyles See Kilfinan
Lismore See Appin

Lochgilphead
Hilda C. Smith (Miss) MA BD MSc | 1992 | 2005 | Parish Church Manse, Manse Brae, Lochgilphead PA31 8QZ [E-mail: hilda.smith2@btinternet.com] | 01546 602238

Lochgoilhead (H) and Kilmorich
James Macfarlane PhD | 1991 | 2000 | The Manse, Lochgoilhead, Cairndow PA24 8AA [E-mail: jmacfarlane@stmac.demon.co.uk] | 01301 703059

Muckairn See Kilchrenan

Mull, Isle of, Kilninian and Kilmore linked with Salen (H) and Ulva linked with Tobermory (GD) (H) linked with Torosay (H) and Kinlochspelvie
Robert C. Nelson BA BD | 1980 | 2003 | The Manse, Gruline Road, Salen, Aros, Isle of Mull PA72 6JF [E-mail: robertnelson@onetel.net] | 01680 300001

North Knapdale See Glassary, Kilmartin and Ford
Portnahaven See Kilchoman

Rothesay: Trinity (H)
Samuel McC. Harris BA BD | 1974 | 2004 | 12 Crichton Road, Rothesay, Isle of Bute PA20 9JR | 01700 503010

Saddell and Carradale (H) linked with Skipness
John Vischer | 1993 | 2006 | The Manse, Carradale, Campbeltown PA28 6QG [E-mail: j_vischer@yahoo.co.uk] | 01583 431253

Salen and Ulva See Mull
Sandbank See Dunoon: St John's
Skipness See Saddell and Carradale
South Knapdale See Ardrishaig

Southend (H)

Martin R. Forrest BA MA BD	1988	2001	St Blaans Manse, Southend, Campbeltown PA28 6RQ [E-mail: jmr.forrest@btopenworld.com]	01586 830274

Strachur and Strathlachlan

Robert K. Mackenzie MA BD PhD	1976	1998	The Manse, Strachur, Cairndow PA27 8DG [E-mail: rkmackenzie@strachurmanse.fsnet.co.uk]	01369 860246

Strathfillan See Glenorchy
Strone (H) and Ardentinny See Kilmun
Tarbert See Kilberry

The United Church of Bute

Ian S. Currie MBE BD	1975	2005	10 Bishop Terrace, Rothesay, Isle of Bute PA20 9HF [E-mail: ianscurrie@tiscali.co.uk]	01700 504502
Raymond Deans DCS	1994	2003	60 Ardmory Road, Rothesay, Isle of Bute PA20 0PG [E-mail: deans@fish.co.uk]	01700 504893

Tiree (GD)

Vacant			The Manse, Scarinish, Isle of Tiree PA77 6TN	01879 220377

Tobermory See Mull
Torosay and Kinlochspelvie See Mull
Toward (H) See Dunoon: The High Kirk

Anderson, David P.	2002	2007	Chaplain: Army	3 Bn The Royal Regiment of Scotland (Black Watch), BFPO 806	
Bell, Douglas W. MA LLB BD	1975	1993	(Alexandria: North)	3 Cairnbaan Lea, Cairnbaan, Lochgilphead PA31 8BA	01546 606815
Bristow, W.H.G. BEd HDipRE DipSpecEd	1951	2002	Part-time Hospital Chaplain: Campbeltown	Laith Cottage, Southend, Campbeltown PA28 6RU	01586 830667
Dunlop, Alistair J. MA FSAScot	1965	2004	(Saddell and Carradale)	8 Pipers Road, Cairnbaan, Lochgilphead PA31 8UF [E-mail: dunrevn@btinternet.com]	01546 600316
Erskine, Austin U.	1986	2001	(Anwoth and Girthon with Borgue)	'Anwoth', 8 Dunloskin View, Kirn, Dunoon PA23 8HW	01369 701295
Fenemore, John H.C.	1980	1993	(Edinburgh: Colinton Mains)	Seaford Cottage, 74E Shore Road, Innellan, Dunoon PA23 7TR	01369 830678
Forrest, Alan B. MA	1956	1993	(Uphall: South)	126 Shore Road, Innellan, Dunoon PA23 7SX	01369 830424
Forrest, Janice (Mrs) DCS			Part-time Hospital Chaplain: Campbeltown	St Blaans Manse, Southend, Campbeltown PA28 6RQ	01586 830274
Gibson, Frank S. BL BD STM DSWA DD	1963	1995	(Kilarrow with Kilmeny)	163 Gilbertstoun, Edinburgh EH15 2RG	0131-657 5208
Grainger, Ian G.	1985	1991	(Maxton with Newtown)	Seaview, Ardtun, Bunessan, Isle of Mull PA67 6DH	01681 700457
Gray, William LTh	1971	2006	(Kilberry with Tarbert)	Lochnagar, Longsdale Road, Oban PA34 5DZ [E-mail: gray98@hotmail.com]	01631 567471
Henderson, Charles M.	1952	1989	(Campbeltown: Highland)	Springbank House, Askomill Walk, Campbeltown PA28 6EP	01586 552759
Hood, Catriona A.	2006		Auxiliary Minister	2 Bellmhor Court, Campbeltown PA28 6AN	01586 552065
Hood, H. Stanley C. MA BD	1966	2000	(London: Crown Court)	10 Dalriada Place, Kilmichael Glassary, Lochgilphead PA31 8QA	01546 606168

Name			Charge	Address	Tel
Inglis, Donald B.C. MA MEd BD	1975	2000	(Turriff: St Andrew's)	'Lindores', 11 Bullwood Road, Dunoon PA23 7QJ	01369 701334
Lamont, Archibald	1952	1994	(Kilcalmonell with Skipness)	8 Achlonan, Taynuilt PA35 1JJ	01866 822385
MacKechnie, J.M. MBE MA	1938	1978	(Kilchrenan and Dalavich)	c/o Montgomery, 185 Mill Road, Hamilton ML3 8PE	
Marshall, Freda (Mrs) BD FCII	1993	2005	(Colonsay and Oronsay with Kilbrandon and Kilchattan)	All Mhaluidh, Glenview, Dalmally PA33 1BE [E-mail: mail@freda.org.uk]	01838 200693
Miller, Harry Galbraith MA BD	1941	1985	(Iona and Ross of Mull)	16 Lobnitz Avenue, Renfrew PA4 0TG	0141-886 2147
Morrison, Angus W. MA BD	1959	1999	(Kildalton and Oa)	1 Livingstone Way, Port Ellen, Isle of Islay PA42 7EP	01496 300043
Paton, John H. BSc BD	1983	2006	(Killean and Kilchenzie)	Lower Flat, Seabank, Low Askomil Walk, Campbeltown PA28 6EP [E-mail: jonymar@globalnet.co.uk]	01586 553904
Pollock, William MA BD PhD	1987	2002	(Isle of Mull Parishes)	Correay, Salen, Aros, Isle of Mull PA72 6JF	01680 300507
Ritchie, Malcolm A.	1955	1990	(Kilbrandon and Kilchattan)	Roadside Cottage, Tayvallich, Lochgilphead PA31 8PN	01546 870616
Ritchie, Walter M.	1973	1999	(Uphall: South)	Hazel Cottage, Barr Mor View, Kilmartin, Lochgilphead PA31 8UN	01546 510343
Stewart, Jean E. (Mrs)	1983	1989	(Kildalton and Oa)	Tigh-na-Truain, Port Ellen, Isle of Islay PA42 7AH	01496 302068
Taylor, Alan T. BD	1980	2005	(Isle of Mull Parishes)	Erray Road, Tobermory, Isle of Mull PA75 6PS	01688 302496
Troup, Harold J.G. MA	1951	1980	(Garelochhead)	Tighshee, Isle of Iona PA76 6SP	01681 700309
Watson, James LTh	1968	1994	(Bowden with Lilliesleaf)	7 Lochan Avenue, Kirn, Dunoon PA23 8HT	01369 702851
Wilkinson, W. Brian MA BD	1968	2007	(Glenaray and Inveraray)	3 Achlonan, Taynuilt PA35 1JJ [E-mail: brianwilkinson@f2s.com]	01866 822036

Communion Sundays

Congregation	Communion Sundays
Ardrishaig	4th Apr, 1st Nov
Campbeltown	
Highland	1st May, Nov
Lorne and Lowland	1st May, Nov
Craignish	1st Jun, Nov
Cumlodden, Lochfyneside and Lochgair	1st May, 3rd Nov
Dunoon	
St John's	1st Mar, Jun, Nov
The High Kirk	1st Feb, Jun, Oct
Gigha and Cara	1st May, Nov
Glassary, Kilmartin and Ford	1st Apr, Sep
Glenaray and Inveraray	1st Apr, Jul, Oct, Dec
Innellan	1st Mar, Jun, Sep, Dec
Inverlussa and Bellanoch	2nd May, Nov
Jura	Passion Sun., 2nd Jul, 3rd Nov
Kilarrow	1st Mar, Jun, Sep, Dec
Kilberry with Tarbert	1st May, Oct
Kilcalmonell	1st Jul, 3rd Nov
Kilchoman	1st Jul, 2nd Dec, Easter
Kildalton	Last Jan, Jun, Oct, Easter
Kilfinan	Last Apr, Oct
Killean and Kilchenzie	1st Mar, Jul, Oct
Kilmeny	2nd May, 3rd Nov
Kilmodan and Colintraive	1st Apr, Sep
Kilmun	Last Jun, Nov
Kilninver and Kilmelford	Last Feb, Jun, Oct
Kirn	2nd Jun, Oct
Kyles	1st May, Nov
Lochgair	Last Apr, Oct
Lochgilphead	2nd Oct (Gaelic), 1st Apr, Nov
Lochgoilhead and Kilmorich	2nd Mar, Jun, Sep, Nov
North Knapdale	1st Aug, Easter
Portnahaven	3rd Oct, 2nd May
Rothesay Trinity	3rd Jul
Saddell and Carradale	1st Feb, May, Nov
Sandbank	2nd May, 1st Nov
Skipness	1st Jan, May, Nov
Southend	2nd May, Nov
South Knapdale	1st Jun, Dec
Strachur and Strathlachlan	4th Apr, 1st Nov
Strone and Ardentinny	1st Mar, Jun, Nov
Tayvallich	Last Feb, Jun, Oct
The United Church of Bute	2nd May, Nov
Toward	1st Feb, May, Nov
	Last Feb, May, Aug, Nov

(22) FALKIRK

Meets at St Andrew's West, Falkirk, on the first Tuesday of September, October, November, December and March, on the fourth Tuesday of January and on the third Tuesday of June; and in Kildrum Church, Cumbernauld on the first Tuesday in May.

Clerk:	REV. JEROME O'BRIEN BA LLB BTh	3 Orchard Grove, Polmont, Falkirk FK2 0XE [E-mail: falkirk@cofscotland.org.uk]	01324 718677 01324 471656 (Presby)
Associate Clerk:	REV. IAN W. BLACK MA BD	Zetland Manse, Ronaldshay Crescent, Grangemouth FK3 9JH	01324 472868
Treasurer:	MR. IAN MACDONALD	1 Jones Avenue, Larbert FK5 3ER [E-mail: ian_macdonald1938@hotmail.com]	01324 553603

Airth (H)
Vacant
The Manse, Airth, Falkirk FK2 8LS
01324 831474

Blackbraes and Shieldhill linked with Muiravonside
Vacant
81 Stevenson Drive, Polmont, Falkirk FK2 0GU

Bo'ness: Old (H)
David S. Randall BA BD   2003
10 Dundas Street, Bo'ness EH51 0DG
[E-mail: dsrandall@blueyonder.co.uk]
01506 822206

Bo'ness: St Andrew's (Website: www.standonline.org.uk)
Albert O. Bogle BD MTh   1981
St Andrew's Manse, 11 Erngath Road, Bo'ness EH51 9DP
[E-mail: a.bogle@blueyonder.co.uk]
01506 822195

Bonnybridge: St Helen's (H) (01324 815756)
Vacant
133 Falkirk Road, Bonnybridge FK4 1BA
01324 812621 (Tel/Fax)

Bothkennar and Carronshore
Vacant
11 Hunter Place, Greenmount Park, Carronshore, Falkirk FK2 8QS
01324 570525

Brightons (H)
Murdo M. Campbell BD DipMin   1997 2007
The Manse, Maddiston Road, Brightons, Falkirk FK2 0JP
[E-mail: murdocampbell@hotmail.com]
01324 712062

Carriden (H)
R. Gordon Reid BSc BD MIEE   1993
The Spires, Foredale Terrace, Carriden, Bo'ness EH51 9LW
01506 822141

Cumbernauld: Abronhill (H)
Joyce A. Keyes (Mrs) BD   1996 2003
26 Ash Road, Cumbernauld, Glasgow G67 3ED
01236 723833
Linda Black (Miss) BSc DCS
148 Rowan Road, Cumbernauld, Glasgow G67 3DA
01236 786265

Cumbernauld: Condorrat (H)
William Jackson BD CertMin — 1994 2004 — 11 Rosehill Drive, Cumbernauld, Glasgow G67 4EQ [E-mail: wiljcksn4@aol.com] — 01236 721464

Janette McNaughton (Miss) DCS — 4 Dunellan Avenue, Moodiesburn, Glasgow G69 0GB — 01236 870180

Cumbernauld: Kildrum (H)
Elinor J. Gordon (Miss) BD — 1988 2004 — 64 Southfield Road, Balloch, Cumbernauld, Glasgow G68 9DZ [E-mail: elinorgordon@aol.com] — 01236 723204

David Nicholson DCS — 2D Doon Side, Kildrum, Cumbernauld, Glasgow G67 2HX [E-mail: deacdave@btopenworld.com] — 01236 732260

Cumbernauld: Old (H) (Website: cumbernauldold.org.uk)
Catriona Ogilvie (Mrs) MA BD — 1999 — The Manse, 23 Baronhill, Cumbernauld, Glasgow G67 2SD — 01236 721912

Valerie Cuthbertson (Miss) DCS — 105 Bellshill Road, Motherwell ML1 3SJ — 01698 259001

Cumbernauld: St Mungo's
Neil MacKinnon BD — 1990 1999 — 18 Fergusson Road, Cumbernauld, Glasgow G67 1LS [E-mail: neil.mackinnon@homecall.co.uk] — 01236 721513

Ronald M. Mackinnon DCS — 71 Cromarty Road, Cairnhill, Airdrie ML6 9RL — 01236 762024

Denny: Dunipace (H)
Jean W. Gallacher (Miss)
BD CMin CTheol DMin — 1989 — Dunipace Manse, Denny FK6 6QJ — 01324 824540

Denny: Old
John Murning BD — 1988 2002 — 31 Duke Street, Denny FK6 6NR [E-mail: bridgebuilder@supanet.com] — 01324 824508

Denny: Westpark (H) (Website: www.westparkchurch.org.uk)
Andrew Barrie BSc BD — 1984 2000 — 13 Baxter Crescent, Denny FK6 5EZ [E-mail: andrew.barrie@blueyonder.co.uk] — 01324 876224

David Wandrum (Aux) — 1993 2005 — 5 Cawder View, Carrickstone Meadows, Cumbernauld, Glasgow G68 0BN — 01236 723288

Falkirk: Bainsford
Michael R. Philip BD — 1978 2001 — 1 Valleyview Place, Newcarron Village, Falkirk FK2 7JB [E-mail: mrphilip@btinternet.com] — 01324 621087

Falkirk: Camelon (Church office: 01324 870011)
Stuart Sharp MTheol DipPA — 2001 — 30 Cotland Drive, Falkirk FK2 7GE — 01324 623631

Margaret Corrie (Miss) DCS — 44 Sunnyside Street, Falkirk FK1 4BH — 01324 670656

Falkirk: Erskine (H) Glen D. Macaulay BD	1999	Burnbrae Road, Falkirk FK1 5SD [E-mail: gd.macaulay@blueyonder.co.uk]	01324 623701
Falkirk: Grahamston United (H) Ian Wilkie BD PGCE	2001 2007	16 Cromwell Road, Falkirk FK1 1SF [E-mail: yanbluejeans@aol.com]	01324 624461 07877 803280 (Mbl)
Falkirk: Laurieston linked with Redding and Westquarter Geoffrey H. Smart LTh	1994 2002	11 Polmont Road, Laurieston, Falkirk FK2 9QQ	01324 621196
Falkirk: Old and St Modan's (H) Robert S.T. Allan LLB DipLP BD	1991 2003	9 Major's Loan, Falkirk FK1 5QF	01324 625124
Falkirk: St Andrew's West (H) Alastair M. Horne BSc BD	1989 1997	1 Maggiewood's Loan, Falkirk FK1 5SJ	01324 623308
Falkirk: St James' Vacant		13 Wallace Place, Falkirk FK2 7EN	01324 622757
Grangemouth: Abbotsgrange Vacant		8 Naismith Court, Grangemouth FK3 9BQ	01324 482109
Grangemouth: Kirk of the Holy Rood David J. Smith BD DipMin	1992 2003	The Manse, Bowhouse Road, Grangemouth FK3 0EX [E-mail: davidkhrood@tiscali.co.uk]	01324 471595
Grangemouth: Zetland (H) Ian W. Black MA BD	1976 1991	Ronaldshay Crescent, Grangemouth FK3 9JH	01324 472868
Haggs (H) Helen F. Christie (Mrs) BD	1998	5 Watson Place, Dennyloanhead, Bonnybridge FK4 2BG	01324 813786
Larbert: East Melville D. Crosthwaite BD DipEd DipMin Lorna A. MacDougall (Miss) MA (Aux)	1984 1995 2003	1 Cortachy Avenue, Carron, Falkirk FK2 8DH 34 Millar Place, Carron, Falkirk FK2 8QB	01324 562402 01324 552739
Larbert: Old (H) Clifford A.J. Rennie MA BD	1973 1985	The Manse, 38 South Broomage Avenue, Larbert FK5 3ED	01324 562868
Larbert: West (H) Gavin Boswell BTheol	1993 1999	11 Carronvale Road, Larbert FK5 3LZ	01324 562878

Muiravonside See Blackbraes and Shieldhill

Polmont: Old
Jerome O'Brien BA LLB BTh   2001   2005   3 Orchard Grove, Polmont, Falkirk FK2 0XE   01324 718677

Redding and Westquarter See Falkirk: Laurieston

Slamannan
Raymond Thomson BD DipMin   1992   Slamannan, Falkirk FK1 3EN   01324 851307

Stenhouse and Carron (H)
William Thomson BD   2001   2007   The Manse, 21 Tipperary Place, Stenhousemuir,   01324 416628
Larbert FK5 4SX

Name			(Charge/role)	Address	Telephone
Barclay, Neil W. BSc BEd BD	1986	2006	(Falkirk: Grahamston United)	4 Gibsongray Street, Falkirk FK2 7LN	01324 874681
Blair, Douglas B. LTh	1969	2004	(Grangemouth: Dundas)	Flat 6, Hanover Grange, Forth Street, Grangemouth FK3 8LF	01324 484414
Brown, James BA BD DipHSW DipPsychol	1973	2001	(Abercorn with Dalmeny)	Fern Cottage, 3 Philpingstone Lane, Bo'ness EH51 9JP	01506 822454
Chalmers, George A. MA BD MLitt	1962	2002	(Catrine with Sorn)	3 Cricket Place, Brightons, Falkirk FK2 0HZ	01324 712030
Goodman, Richard A.	1976	1986	(Isle of Mull Associate)	Carrowdale Nursing Home, Beaufort Drive, Falkirk FK2 8SN	01324 551788
Gunn, F. Derek BD	1986	1997	(Falkirk: Bainsford)	6 Yardley Place, Falkirk FK2 7FH	01324 624938
Hardie, Robert K. MA BD	1968	2005	(Stenhouse and Carron)	33 Palace Street, Berwick-upon-Tweed TD15 1HN	01324 711352
Heriot, Charles R. JP BA	1962	1996	(Brightons)	20 Eastcroft Drive, Polmont, Falkirk FK2 0SU	01324 634483
Hill, Stanley LTh	1967	1998	(Muiravonside)	28 Creteil Court, Falkirk FK1 1UL	01324 880109
Holland, John C.	1976	1985	(Strone and Ardentinny)	7 Polmont Park, Polmont, Falkirk FK2 0XT	01324 671489
Kesting, Sheilagh M. (Miss) BA BD	1980	1993	(Ecumenical Relations)	12 Glenview Drive, Falkirk FK1 5JU	001 242 373 2568
Kirkland, Scott R.McL. BD MAR	1996	2005	(Lucaya Presbyterian Kirk, Bahamas)	PO Box F-40777, Freeport, Bahamas	001 242 373 4961 (Fax)
McCallum, John	1962	1998	(Falkirk: Irving Camelon)	11 Burnbrae Gardens, Falkirk FK1 5SB	01324 619766
McDonald, William G. MA BD	1959	1975	(Falkirk: Grahamston United)	38 St Mary Street, St Andrews KY16 8AZ	01334 470481
McDowall, Ronald J. BD	1980	2001	(Falkirk: Laurieston with Redding and Westquarter)		
McMullin, J. Andrew MA	1960	1996	(Blackbraes and Shieldhill)	'Kailas', Windsor Road, Falkirk FK1 5EJ	01324 871947
Martin, Neil DCS			(Deacon)	33 Eastcroft Drive, Polmont, Falkirk FK2 0SU	01324 624938
Mathers, Daniel L. BD	1982	2001	(Grangemouth: Charing Cross and West)	3 Strathmiglo Place, Stenhousemuir, Larbert FK5 4UQ	01324 551362
Maxton, Ronald M. MA	1955	1995	(Dollar: Associate)	10 Ercall Road, Brightons, Falkirk FK2 0RS	01324 872253
Miller, Elsie M. (Miss) DCS			(Deaconess)	5 Rulley View, Denny FK6 6QQ	01324 825441
Munro, Henry BA LTh LTI	1971	1988	(Denny: Dunipace North with Old)	30 Swinton Avenue, Rowansbank, Baillieston, Glasgow G69 6JR	0141-771 0857
Paul, Iain BSc PhD BD PhD	1976	1991	(Wishaw: Craigneuk and Belhaven)	Viewforth, High Road, Maddiston, Falkirk FK2 0BL	01324 712446
Ross, Evan J. LTh	1986	1998	(Cowdenbeath: West with Mossgreen and Crossgates)	11 Hope Park Terrace, Larbert Road, Bonnybridge FK4 1DY	
Scott, Donald H. BA BD	1987	2002	Prison Chaplain	5 Arneil Place, Brightons, Falkirk FK2 0NJ	01324 719936
				Polmont Young Offenders' Institution, Newlands Road, Brightons, Falkirk FK2 0DE	01324 722241

| Smith, Richard BD | 1976 2002 | (Denny: Old) | Easter Wayside, 46 Kennedy Way, Airth, Falkirk FK2 8GB | 01324 831386 |

[E-mail: richards@uklinux.net]

Talman, Hugh MA	1943 1987	(Polmont: Old)	Niagara, 70 Lawers Crescent, Polmont, Falkirk FK2 0QU	01324 711240
Whiteford, Robert S. MA	1945 1986	(Shapinsay)	3 Wellside Court, Wellside Place, Falkirk FK1 5RG	01324 610562
Wilson, Phyllis M. (Mrs) DipCom DipRE	1985 2006	(Motherwell: South Dalziel)	'Landemer', 17 Sneddon Place, Airth, Falkirk FK2 8GH	01324 832257

[E-mail: thomas.wilson38@btinternet.com]

FALKIRK ADDRESSES

Falkirk				Grangemouth	
Bainsford	Hendry Street, Bainsford	Laurieston	Main Falkirk Road	Abbotsgrange	Abbot's Road
Camelon	Dorrator Road	Old and St Modan's	Kirk Wynd	Kirk of the Holy Rood	Bowhouse Road
Erskine	Cockburn Street x Hodge Street	St Andrew's West	Newmarket Street	Zetland	Ronaldshay Crescent
Grahamston	Bute Street	St James'	Thornhill Road x Firs Street		

(23) STIRLING

Meets at the Moderator's Church on the second Thursday of September, and at Stirling: Allan Park South Church on the second Thursday of every other month except January, July and August, when there is no meeting.

| Clerk: | MOIRA G. MacCORMICK BA LTh | Presbytery Office, St Columba's Church, Park Terrace, Stirling FK8 2NA | 01786 449522 (Tel) (Mon–Fri: 9:30am–12 noon) |

[E-mail: stirling@cofscotland.org.uk]

| Treasurer: | MR GILMOUR CUTHBERTSON | 'Denovan', 1 Doune Road, Dunblane FK15 9AR | 01786 823487 |

Aberfoyle (H) linked with Port of Menteith (H)

| Vacant | | | The Manse, Loch Ard Road, Aberfoyle, Stirling FK8 3SZ | 01877 382391 |

Alloa: North (H)

| Elizabeth Clelland (Mrs) BD | 2002 | 30 Claremont, Alloa FK10 2DF | 01259 210403 |

Alloa: St Mungo's (H)

| Alan F.M. Downie MA BD | 1977 1996 | 37A Claremont, Alloa FK10 2DG | 01259 213872 |

[E-mail: alan@stmungos.freeserve.co.uk]

Alloa: West

| Vacant | | | 29 Claremont, Alloa FK10 2DF | 01259 214204 |

Alva James N.R. McNeil BSc BD	1990	1997	The Manse, 34 Ochil Road, Alva FK12 5JT	01259 760262
Balfron linked with Fintry (H) Willem J. Bezuidenhout	2007		7 Station Road, Balfron, Glasgow G63 0SX	01360 440285
Balquhidder linked with Killin and Ardeonaig (H) John Lincoln MPhil BD	1986	1997	The Manse, Killin FK21 8TN [E-mail: gm0jol@zetnet.co.uk]	01567 820247
Bannockburn: Allan (H) (Website: www.allanchurch.org.uk) Jim Landels BD CertMin	1990		The Manse, Bogend Road, Bannockburn, Stirling FK7 8NP [E-mail: revjimlandels@btinternet.com]	01786 814692
Bannockburn: Ladywell (H) Elizabeth M.D. Robertson (Miss) BD CertMin	1997		57 The Firs, Bannockburn FK7 0EG [E-mail: lizr@tinyonline.uk]	01786 812467
Bridge of Allan (H) (01786 834155) Gillian Weighton (Mrs) BD STM	1992	2004	19 Keir Street, Bridge of Allan, Stirling FK9 4QJ [E-mail: gillweighton@aol.com]	01786 832753
Buchanan linked with Drymen Alexander J. MacPherson BD	1986	1997	Buchanan Manse, Drymen, Glasgow G63 0AQ	01360 870212
Buchlyvie (H) linked with Gartmore (H) Elaine H. MacRae (Mrs) BD	1985	2004	The Manse, Kippen, Stirling FK8 3DN	01786 871170
Callander (H) (Tel/Fax: 01877 331409) Stanley A. Brook BD MTh	1977	2004	3 Aveland Park Road, Callander FK17 8FD [E-mail: stan_brook@hotmail.com]	01877 330097
Cambusbarron: The Bruce Memorial (H) Brian G. Webster BSc BD	1998		14 Woodside Court, Cambusbarron, Stirling FK7 9PH [E-mail: revwebby@aol.com]	01786 450579
Clackmannan (H) Vacant			The Manse, Port Street, Clackmannan FK10 4JH	01259 211255
Cowie (H) and Plean linked with Fallin Vacant			The Manse, Plean, Stirling FK7 8BX	01786 813287

Dollar (H) linked with Glendevon linked with Muckhart (Website: www.dollarparishchurch.org.uk)
Suzanne G. Fletcher (Mrs) BA MDiv MA 2001 2004 2 Manse Road, Dollar FK14 7AJ 01259 743432
[E-mail: revfletcher@btinternet.com]

J. Mary Henderson (Miss) 1990 2005 Glebe House, Muckhart, Dollar FK14 7JN
  MA BD DipEd PhD (Assoc)

Drymen See Buchanan

Dunblane: Cathedral (H)
Colin G. McIntosh BSc BD 1976 1988 Cathedral Manse, The Cross, Dunblane FK15 0AQ 01786 822205
Sally Foster-Fulton (Mrs) BA BD (Assoc) 1999 2007 21 Craiglea, Causewayhead, Stirling FK9 5EE 01786 463060

Dunblane: St Blane's (H)
Alexander B. Mitchell 1981 2003 49 Roman Way, Dunblane FK15 9DJ 01786 822268
[E-mail: alex.mitchell6@btopenworld.com]

Fallin See Cowie and Plean
Fintry See Balfron

Gargunnock linked with Kilmadock linked with Kincardine-in-Menteith
Richard S. Campbell LTh 1993 2001 The Manse, Gargunnock, Stirling FK8 3BQ 01786 860678

Gartmore See Buchlyvie
Glendevon See Dollar

Killearn (H)
Philip R.M. Malloch LLB BD 1970 1993 2 The Oaks, Killearn, Glasgow G63 9SF 01360 550045
[E-mail: minister@killearnkirk.org.uk]

Killin and Ardeonaig (H) See Balquhidder
Kilmadock See Gargunnock
Kincardine-in-Menteith See Gargunnock

Kippen (H) linked with Norrieston
Gordon MacRae BA BD 1985 1998 The Manse, Kippen, Stirling FK8 3DN 01786 870229

Lecropt (H)
William M. Gilmour MA BD 1969 1983 5 Henderson Street, Bridge of Allan, Stirling FK9 4NA 01786 832382

Logie (H)
R. Stuart M. Fulton BA BD 1991 2006 21 Craiglea, Causewayhead, Stirling FK9 5EE 01786 463060

Menstrie (H)
Mairi F. Lovett BSc BA DipPS MTh 2005 The Manse, 7 Long Row, Menstrie FK11 7BA 01259 761461
[E-mail: mairi.lovett@kanyo.co.uk]

Muckhart See Dollar
Norrieston See Kippen
Port of Menteith See Aberfoyle

Sauchie and Coalsnaughton
Alan T. McKean BD   1982   2003   19 Graygoran, Sauchie, Alloa FK10 3ET   01259 212037
[E-mail: almack@freeuk.com]

Stirling: Allan Park South (H) linked with Church of the Holy Rude (H)
Vacant   22 Laurelhill Place, Stirling FK8 2JH   01786 473999

Stirling: Church of the Holy Rude (H) See Stirling: Allan Park South

Stirling: North (H) (01786 463376) (Website: www.northparishchurch.com)
Calum Jack BSc BD   2004   18 Shirra's Brae Road, Stirling FK7 0BA   01786 475378
[E-mail: info@northparishchurch.com]

Stirling: St Columba's (H) (01786 449516)
Kenneth G. Russell BD CCE   1986   2001   5 Clifford Road, Stirling FK8 2AQ   01786 475802
[E-mail: kenrussell1000@hotmail.com]

Stirling: St Mark's
Vacant   176 Drip Road, Stirling FK8 1RR   01786 473716

Stirling: St Ninians Old (H)
Gary J. McIntyre BD DipMin   1993   1998   7 Randolph Road, Stirling FK8 2AJ   01786 474421
[E-mail: garymcintyre@btinternet.com]

Stirling: Viewfield (T) (H)
Vacant   7 Windsor Place, Stirling FK8 2HY   01786 474534

Strathblane (H)
Alex H. Green MA BD   1986   1995   The Manse, Strathblane, Glasgow G63 9AB   01360 770226

Tillicoultry (H)
James Cochrane LTh   1994   2000   The Manse, Dollar Road, Tillicoultry FK13 6PD   01259 750340
[E-mail: jc@cochranemail.co.uk]   01259 752951 (Fax)

Tullibody: St Serf's (H)
Vacant   16 Menstrie Road, Tullibody, Alloa FK10 2RG   01259 213236

Name	Ord.	Ret.	Charge	Address	Phone
Aitken, E. Douglas MA	1961	1998	(Clackmannan)	1 Dolan Grove, Saline, Dunfermline KY12 9UP	01383 852730
Benson, James W. BA BD DipEd	1975	1996	(Balquhidder)	1 Sunnyside, Dunblane FK15 9HA	01786 822624
Blackley, Jean R.M. (Mrs) BD	1989	2001	(Banton with Twechar)	8 Rodders Grove, Alva FK12 5RR	01259 760198
Brown, James H. BD	1977	2005	(Helensburgh: Park)	14 Gullipen View, Callander FK17 8HN	01877 339425
Brown, T. John MA BD	1995	2006	(Tullibody: St Serf's)	1 Callendar Park Walk, Callendar Grange, Falkirk FK1 1TA	01324 617352
Cloggie, June (Mrs)	1997	2006	(Auxiliary Minister: Callander)	11A Tulipan Crescent, Callander FK17 8AR	01877 331021
Craig, Maxwell D. BD ThM	1966	2000	(Jerusalem: St Andrew's: Locum)	3 Queen's Road, Stirling FK8 2QY	01259 472319
Cruickshank, Alistair A.B. MA	1991	2004	(Auxiliary Minister)	2A Chapel Place, Dollar FK14 7DW	01259 742549
Doherty, Arthur James DipTh	1957	1993	(Fintry)	1 Murdiston Avenue, Callander FK17 8AY	
Fleming, Alexander F. MA BD	1966	1995	(Strathblane)	4 Horsburgh Avenue, Kilsyth, Glasgow G65 9BZ	01236 821461
Gillespie, Irene C. (Mrs) BD	1991	2007	(Tiree)	39 King O'Muirs Drive, Tullibody, Alloa FK10 3AY	01259 723937
				[E-mail: revicg@btinternet.com]	
Izett, William A.F.	1968	2000	(Law)	1 Duke Street, Clackmannan FK10 4EF	01259 724203
MacCormick, Moira G. BA LTh	1986	2003	(Buchlyvie with Gartmore)	12 Rankine Wynd, Tullibody, Alloa FK10 2UW	01259 724619
McCreadie, David W.	1961	1995	(Kirkmabreck)	23 Willoughby Place, Callander PH17 8DG	01877 330785
McIntosh, Hamish N.M. MA	1949	1987	(Fintry)	1 Forth Crescent, Stirling FK8 1LE	01786 470453
Murray, Douglas R. MA BD	1994	2004	(Lausanne)	32 Forth Park, Bridge of Allan, Stirling FK9 5NT	01786 831081
Nicol, John C. MA BD	1965	2002	(Bridge of Allan: Holy Trinity)	37 King O'Muirs Drive, Tullibody, Alloa FK10 3AY	01259 212305
Ovens, Samuel B. BD	1982	1993	(Slamannan)	21 Bevan Drive, Alva FK12 5PD	01259 222723
Paterson, John L. MA BD STM	1964	2003	(Linlithgow: St Michael's)	'Kirkmichael', 22 Waterfront Way, Stirling FK9 5GH	01786 447165
				[E-mail: lornandian.paterson@virgin.net]	
Pryce, Stuart F.A.	1963	1997	(Dumfries: St George's)	36 Forth Park, Bridge of Allan, Stirling FK9 5NT	01786 831026
Rennie, James B. MA	1959	1992	(Leochel Cushnie and Lynturk with Tough)	17 Oliphant Court, Riverside, Stirling FK8 1US	01786 841894
Robertson, Alex	1974	1993	(Baldernock)	4 Moray Park, Moray Street, Doune FK16 6DJ	
Sangster, Ernest G. BD ThM	1958	1997	(Alva)	6 Law Hill Road, Dollar FK14 7BG	01877 330565
Scott, James F.	1957	1997	(Dyce)	5 Gullipen View, Callander FK17 8HN	01786 825976
Scoular, J. Marshall	1954	1996	(Kippen)	2H Buccleuch Court, Dunblane FK15 0AH	01259 220665
Sherry, George T. LTh	1977	2004	(Menstrie)	37 Moubray Gardens, Silver Meadows, Cambus, Alloa FK10 2NQ	
Silcox, John R. BD DipPhilEd CPP CF TD	1976	1984	(School Chaplain)	Queen Victoria School, Dunblane FK15 0JY	01786 824944
Sinclair, James H. MA BD	1966	2004	(Auchencairn and Rerrick with Buittle and Kelton)	16 Delaney Court, Alloa FK10 1RB	01259 729001
Stewart, Angus T. MA BD PhD	1962	1999	(Glasgow: Greenbank)	Mansefield, Station Road, Buchlyvie, Stirling FK8 3NE	01360 850117
Todd, A. Stewart MA BD DD	1952	1993	(Aberdeen: St Machar's Cathedral)	Ferntoun House, 11 Bedford Place, Alloa FK10 1LJ	01259 212737
Watson, Jean S. (Miss) MA	1993	2004	(Auxiliary Minister)	29 Strachan Crescent, Dollar FK14 7HL	01259 742872
Watt, Robert MA BD	1943	1982	(Aberdeen: Woodside South)	1 Coldstream Avenue, Dunblane FK15 9JN	01786 823632
Wright, John P. BD	1977	2000	(Glasgow: New Govan)	Plane Castle, Airth, Falkirk FK2 8SF	01786 480840

STIRLING ADDRESSES

Allan Park South	Dumbarton Road	St Columba's	Park Terrace	Viewfield	Barnton Street
Holy Rude	St John Street	St Mark's	Drip Road		
North	Springfield Road	St Ninians Old	Kirk Wynd, St Ninians		

(24) DUNFERMLINE

Meets at Dunfermline in the Abbey Church Hall, Abbey Park Place, on the first Thursday of each month, except January, July and August when there is no meeting, and June when it meets on the last Thursday.

Clerk:	REV. ELIZABETH S.S. KENNY BD RGN SCM	The Manse, Carnock, Dunfermline KY12 9JG [E-mail: dunfermline@cofscotland.org.uk]	01383 850327

Aberdour: St Fillan's (H) (Website: www.stfillans.presbytery.org)

Peter S. Gerbrandy-Baird MA BD MSc FRSA FRGS	2004	St Fillan's Manse, 36 Bellhouse Road, Aberdour, Fife KY3 0TL	01383 861522

Beath and Cowdenbeath: North (H)

David W. Redmayne BSc BD	2001	10 Stuart Place, Cowdenbeath KY4 9BN [E-mail: david@redmayne.freeserve.co.uk]	01383 511033

Cairneyhill (H) (01383 882352) linked with Limekilns (H) (01383 873337)

Norman M. Grant BD	1990	The Manse, 10 Church Street, Limekilns, Dunfermline KY11 3HT [E-mail: norman.grant@which.net]	01383 872341

Carnock and Oakley (H)

Elizabeth S.S. Kenny BD RGN SCM	1989	The Manse, Carnock, Dunfermline KY12 9JG [E-mail: esskenny@ecosse.net]	01383 850327

Cowdenbeath: Trinity (H)

David G. Adams BD	1991	66 Barclay Street, Cowdenbeath KY4 9LD [E-mail: trinity@fsmail.net]	01383 515089
John Wyllie (Pastoral Assistant)	1999	51 Seafar Street, Kelty KY4 0JX	01383 839200

Culross and Torryburn (H)

Thomas Moffat BSc BD	1976	Culross, Dunfermline KY12 8JD [E-mail: tom@gallus.org.uk]	01383 880231

Dalgety (H) (01383 824092) (E-mail: office@dalgety-church.co.uk) (Website: www.dalgety-church.co.uk)

Donald G.B. McCorkindale BD DipMin	1992	9 St Colme Drive, Dalgety Bay, Dunfermline KY11 9LQ [E-mail: donald@dalgety-church.co.uk]	01383 822316 (Tel/Fax)

Dunfermline: Abbey (H) (Website: www.dunfabbey.freeserve.co.uk)

Alistair L. Jessamine MA BD	1979 1991	12 Garvock Hill, Dunfermline KY12 7UU [E-mail: alistairjessamine@dunfermlineabbey.wanadoo.co.uk]	01383 721022

Dunfermline: Gillespie Memorial (H) (01383 621253) (E-mail: gillespie.church@btopenworld.com)
A. Gordon Reid BSc BD   1982   1988   4 Killin Court, Dunfermline KY12 7XF   01383 723329
                                                    [E-mail: reid501@fsmail.net]

Dunfermline: North
Vacant   13 Barbour Grove, Dunfermline KY12 9YB   01383 851078
Andrew E. Paterson (Aux)   6 The Willows, Kelty KY4 0FQ   01383 830998

Dunfermline: St Andrew's Erskine (01383 841660)
Ann Allison BSc PhD BD   2000   71A Townhill Road, Dunfermline KY12 0BN   01383 734657
                                                    [E-mail: ann.allison@homecall.co.uk]

Dunfermline: St Leonard's (01383 620106) (E-mail: stleonards_dunf@lineone.net) (Website: www.stleonardsparishchurch.org.uk)
Andrew J. Philip BSc BD   1996   2004   12 Torvean Place, Dunfermline KY11 4YY   01383 721054 (Tel)
                                                    [E-mail: andrewphilip@minister.com]   0871 242 5222 (Fax)

Dunfermline: St Margaret's
Iain M. Greenshields   1985   2007   38 Garvock Hill, Dunfermline KY12 7UU   01383 723955
BD DipRS ACMA MSc MTh   [E-mail: rev_imaclg@hotmail.com]

Dunfermline: St Ninian's
Elizabeth A. Fisk (Mrs) BD   1996   51 St John's Drive, Dunfermline KY12 7TL   01383 722256
Jacqueline Thomson (Mrs) DCS   2004   1 Barron Terrace, Leven KY8 4DL   01333 301115

Dunfermline: St Paul's East (New Charge Development)
Alan Childs BA BD MBA   2000   2003   9 Dover Drive, Dunfermline KY11 8HQ   01383 620704
                                                    [E-mail: alan@kingdomkirk.org.uk]

Dunfermline: Townhill and Kingseat (H)
David M. Almond BD   1996   2007   161 Main Street, Townhill, Dunfermline KY12 0EZ   01383 727275
                                                    [E-mail: rev.almond@btinternet.com]

Inverkeithing linked with North Queensferry (T)
Christopher D. Park BSc BD   1977   2005   1 Dover Way, Dunfermline KY11 8HR   01383 432158
                                                    [E-mail: chrispark8649@hotmail.com]
          (Inverkeithing is the name for the united charge of Inverkeithing: St John's and Inverkeithing: St Peter's)

Kelty (Website: www.keltykirk.org.uk)
Vacant   15 Arlick Road, Kelty KY4 0BH   01383 830291

Limekilns See Cairneyhill

Lochgelly and Benarty: St Serf's

Elisabeth M. Stenhouse (Ms) BD	2006	82 Main Street, Lochgelly KY5 9AA [E-mail: elisabeth@stenhouse.freeserve.co.uk]	01592 780435
Patricia Munro (Miss) BSc DCS	1986 2007		

North Queensferry See Inverkeithing

Rosyth

Violet C.C. McKay (Mrs) BD	1988 2002	42 Woodside Avenue, Rosyth KY11 2LA [E-mail: v.mckay@btinternet.com]	01383 412776
Morag Crawford (Miss) MSc DCS		118 Wester Drylaw Place, Edinburgh EH4 2TG [E-mail: morag.crawford@virgin.net]	0131-332 2253

Saline and Blairingone

Robert P. Boyle LTh	1990 2003	8 The Glebe, Saline, Dunfermline KY12 9UT [E-mail: boab.boyle@btinternet.com]	01383 853062

Tulliallan and Kincardine

Jock Stein MA BD	1973 2002	62 Toll Road, Kincardine, Alloa FK10 4QZ [E-mail: handsel@dial.pipex.com]	01259 730538
Margaret E. Stein (Mrs) DA BD DipRE	1984 2002	62 Toll Road, Kincardine, Alloa FK10 4QZ [E-mail: handsel@dial.pipex.com]	01259 730538

Name			Charge	Address	Phone
Brown, Peter MA BD FRAScot	1953	1987	(Holm)	24 Inchmickery Avenue, Dalgety Bay, Dunfermline KY11 5NF	(Home) 01383 822456 / (Office) 0131-343 3089
Evans, Mark DCS	2006		Chaplain: Queen Margaret Hospital, Dunfermline	13 Easter Drylaw Drive, Edinburgh EH4 2QA	01383 674136
Farquhar, William E. BA BD	1987	2006	(Dunfermline: Townhill and Kingseat)	29 Queens Drive, Middlewich, Cheshire CW10 0DG	01606 835097
Jenkins, Gordon F.C. MA BD PhD	1968	2006	(Dunfermline: North)	59 Porterfield, Comrie, Dunfermline KY12 9XQ	01383 851078
Macpheran, Stewart M. MA	1953	1990	(Dunfermline: Abbey)	176 Halbeath Road, Dunfermline KY11 4LB	01383 722851
Orr, J. McMichael MA BD PhD	1949	1986	(Aberfoyle with Port of Menteith)	9 Overhaven, Limekilns, Dunfermline KY11 3JH	01383 872245
Pogue, Victor C. BA BD	1945	1980	(Baird Research Fellow)	5/2 Plewlands Court, Edinburgh EH10 5JY	0131-445 1628
Reid, David MSc LTh FSAScot	1961	1992	(St Monans with Largoward)	North Lethans, Saline, Dunfermline KY12 9TE	01383 733144
Scott, John LTh	1969	1996	(Aberdour: St Fillan's)	32 White's Quay, St David's Harbour, Dalgety Bay, Dunfermline	01383 82089
Shewan, Frederick D.F. MA BD	1970	2005	(Edinburgh: Muirhouse St Andrew's)	38 Tremayne Place, Dunfermline KY12 9YH	01383 734354
Stuart, Anne (Miss) DCS			(Deaconess)	19 St Colme Crescent, Aberdour, Burntisland KY3 0ST	01383 860049
Taylor, David J. MA BD	1982	2007	(Irongray, Lochrutton and Terregles)	32 Croft an Righ, Inverkeithing KY11 1PF	01383 413227
Whyte, Isabel H. (Mrs) BD	1993		(Chaplain: Queen Margaret Hospital, Dunfermline)	14 Carlingnose Point, North Queensferry, Inverkeithing KY11 1ER [E-mail: iainisabel@whytes28.fsnet.co.uk]	01383 410732

(25) KIRKCALDY

Meets at Kirkcaldy, in St Brycedale Hall, on the first Tuesday of February, March, April, May, November and December, on the second Tuesday of September, and on the fourth Tuesday of June.

Clerk:	REV. ROSEMARY FREW (Mrs) MA BD	83 Milton Road, Kirkcaldy KY1 1TP [E-mail: kirkcaldy@cofscotland.org.uk]	**01592 260315**
Depute Clerk:	MR DOUGLAS G. HAMILL BEM	41 Abbots Mill, Kirkcaldy KY2 5PE [E-mail: hamilldg@tiscali.co.uk]	**01592 267500**

Auchterderran: St Fothad's linked with Kinglassie
Vacant

Auchtertool linked with Kirkcaldy: Linktown (H) (01592 641080)

Catriona M. Morrison (Mrs) MA BD	1995 2000	7 Woodend Road, Cardenden, Lochgelly KY5 0NE	01592 720213
		16 Raith Crescent, Kirkcaldy KY2 5NN	01592 265536

Buckhaven (01592 715577)

Wilma Cairns (Miss) BD	1999 2004	181 Wellesley Road, Buckhaven, Leven KY8 1JA	01592 712870

Burntisland (H)

Alan Sharp BSc BD	1980 2001	21 Ramsay Crescent, Burntisland KY3 9JL [E-mail: alansharp03@aol.com]	01592 874303

Dysart (H)

Tilly Wilson (Miss) MTh	1990 1998	1 School Brae, Dysart, Kirkcaldy KY1 2XB	01592 655887

Glenrothes: Christ's Kirk (H)

Peter A.D. Berrill MA BD	1983 2005	12 The Limekilns, Glenrothes KY6 3QJ [E-mail: peterberrill@hotmail.com]	01592 620536

Glenrothes: St Columba's (01592 752539)

Diane L. Hobson (Mrs) BA BD	2002 2005	40 Liberton Drive, Glenrothes KY6 3PB [E-mail: diane.hobson@btclick.com]	01592 741215
Sarah McDowall (Mrs) DCS		116 Scott Road, Glenrothes KY6 1AE	01592 562386

Glenrothes: St Margaret's (H) (01592 610310)

John P. McLean BSc BPhil BD	1994	8 Alburne Park, Glenrothes KY7 5RB [E-mail: john@stmargaretschurch.org.uk]	01592 752241

Glenrothes: St Ninian's (H) (01592 610560) (E-mail: st-ninians@tiscali.co.uk)

Allistair Roy BD DipSW PGDip	2007	1 Cawdor Drive, Glenrothes KY6 2HN [E-mail: alli@stninians.co.uk]	01592 611963

Innerleven: East (H)
James L. Templeton BSc BD | 1975 | 77 McDonald Street, Methil, Leven KY8 3AJ | 01333 426310

Kennoway, Windygates and Balgonie: St Kenneth's (01333 351372) (E-mail: administration@st-kenneths.freeserve.co.uk)
Richard Baxter MA BD | 1997 | 2 Fernhill Gardens, Windygates, Leven KY8 5DZ [E-mail: richard-baxter@msn.com] | 01333 352329

Maureen Paterson (Mrs) BSc (Aux) | 1992 1994 | 91 Dalmahoy Crescent, Kirkcaldy KY2 6TA | 01592 262300

Kinghorn
James Reid BD | 1985 1997 | 17 Myre Crescent, Kinghorn, Burntisland KY3 9UB [E-mail: jim17reid@aol.com] | 01592 890269

Kinglassie See Auchterderran: St Fothad's

Kirkcaldy: Abbotshall (H)
Rosemary Frew (Mrs) MA BD | 1988 2005 | 83 Milton Road, Kirkcaldy KY1 1TP [E-mail: rosiefrew@blueyonder.co.uk] | 01592 260315

Kirkcaldy: Linktown (01592 641080) See Auchtertool

Kirkcaldy: Pathhead (H) (Tel/Fax: 01592 204635) (E-mail: pathhead@btinternet.com) (Website: www.pathheadparishchurch.co.uk)
Andrew C. Donald BD DPS | 1992 2005 | 73 Loughborough Road, Kirkcaldy KY1 3DD [E-mail: andrewdonald@blueyonder.co.uk] | 01592 652215

Kirkcaldy: St Andrew's (H)
Donald M. Thomson BD | 1975 2000 | 15 Harcourt Road, Kirkcaldy KY2 5HQ [E-mail: dmaclthomson@aol.com] | 01592 260816

Kirkcaldy: St Bryce Kirk (H) (01592 640016) (E-mail: office@stbee.freeserve.co.uk)
Ken Froude MA BD | 1979 | 6 East Fergus Place, Kirkcaldy KY1 1XT [E-mail: kenfroude@blueyonder.co.uk] | 01592 264480

Kirkcaldy: St John's
Nicola Frail BLE MBA MDiv | 2000 2004 | 25 Bennochy Avenue, Kirkcaldy KY2 5QE | 01592 263821

Kirkcaldy: Templehall (H)
Anthony J.R. Fowler BSc BD | 1982 2004 | 35 Appin Crescent, Kirkcaldy KY2 6EJ | 01592 260156

Kirkcaldy: Torbain
Ian Elston BD MTh | 1999 | 91 Sauchenbush Road, Kirkcaldy KY2 5RN | 01592 263015

Kirkcaldy: Viewforth (H) linked with Thornton
Anne J. Job | 2000 | 66 Viewforth Street, Kirkcaldy KY1 3DJ | 01592 652502

Leslie: Trinity
Melvyn J. Griffiths BTh DipTheol — 1978 — 2006 — 4 Valley Drive, Leslie, Glenrothes KY6 3BQ
[E-mail: mel@thehavyn.wanadoo.co.uk] — 01592 741008

Leven
Gilbert C. Nisbet CA BD — 1993 — 2007 — 5 Forman Road, Leven KY8 4HH — 01333 303339

Markinch
Alexander R. Forsyth TD BA MTh — 1973 — 2002 — 7 Guthrie Crescent, Markinch, Glenrothes KY7 6AY — 01592 758264

Methil (H)
Vacant — Alma House, 2 School Brae, Methilhill, Leven KY8 2BT — 01592 713708

Methilhill and Denbeath
Elisabeth F. Cranfield (Miss) MA BD — 1988 — 9 Chemiss Road, Methilhill, Leven KY8 2BS
[E-mail: ecranfield@btinternet.com] — 01592 713142
(Charge formed by the union of Methilhill and Denbeath)

Thornton See Kirkcaldy: Viewforth

Wemyss
Kenneth W. Donald BA BD — 1982 — 1999 — 33 Main Road, East Wemyss, Kirkcaldy KY1 4RE
[E-mail: kenneth@kdonald.freeserve.co.uk] — 01592 713260

Name			Charge / Role	Address	Tel
Campbell, J. Ewen R. MA BD	1967	2005	(Auchterderran: St Fothad's with Kinglassie)	93 The Moorings, Dalgety Bay, Dunfermline KY11 9GP	01383 820765
Collins, Mitchell BD CPS	1996	2005	(Creich, Flisk and Kilmany with Monimail)	6 Netherby Park, Glenrothes KY6 3PL	
Connolly, Daniel BD DipTheol DipMin	1983		Army Chaplain	2 CS Reg, RLC, BFPO 47	
Cooper, M.W. MA	1944	1979	(Kirkcaldy: Abbotshall)	Applegarth, Sunny Park, Kinross KY13 7BX	01577 263204
Dick, James S. MA BTh	1988	1997	(Glasgow: Ruchazie)	1 Hawkmuir, Kirkcaldy KY1 2AN	01592 260289
Duncan, John C. BD MPhil	1987	2001	Army Chaplain	4 Bn The Royal Regiment of Scotland (The Highlanders), St Barbara's Barracks, BFPO 38	
Elston, Peter K.	1963	2000	(Dalgety)	6 Cairngorm Crescent, Kirkcaldy KY2 5RF	01592 205622
Ferguson, David J.	1966	2001	(Bellie with Speymouth)	4 Russell Gardens, Ladybank, Cupar KY15 7LT	01337 831406
Forrester, Ian L. MA	1964	1996	(Friockheim, Kinnell with Inverkeilor and Lunan)		
Gatt, David W.	1981	1995	(Thornton)	8 Bennochy Avenue, Kirkcaldy KY2 5QE	01592 260251
Gibson, Ivor MA	1957	1993	(Abercorn with Dalmeny)	15 Beech Avenue, Thornton, Kirkcaldy KY1 4AT	01592 774328
Gordon, Ian D. LTh	1972	2001	(Markinch)	15 McInnes Road, Glenrothes KY7 6BA	01592 759982
			(Deaconess)	2 Somerville Way, Glenrothes KY7 5GE	01592 742487
Howden, Margaret (Miss) DCS	1988	1997	Adviser in Mission and Evangelism	38 Munro Street, Kirkcaldy KY1 1PY	01592 205913
McAlpine, Robin J. BDS BD				10 Seton Place, Kirkcaldy KY2 6UX [E-mail: robin.mcalpine@virgin.net]	01592 643518
McDonald, Ian J.M. MA BD	1984	1996	Chaplain, Kirkcaldy Acute Hospitals	11 James Grove, Kirkcaldy KY1 1TN	01592 203775

McLeod, Alistair G.	1988 2005	(Glenrothes: St Columba's)	13 Greenmantle Way, Glenrothes KY6 3QG [E-mail: alistair@mcleod3246.freeserve.co.uk]	01592 744558
MacLeod, Norman	1960 1988	(Orwell with Portmoak)	324 Muirfield Drive, Glenrothes KY6 2PZ	01592 610281
McNaught, Samuel M. MA BD MTh	1968 2002	(Kirkcaldy: St John's)	6 Munro Court, Glenrothes KY7 5GD	01592 742352
Munro, Andrew MA BD PhD	1972 2000	(Glencaple with Lowther)	7 Dunvegan Avenue, Kirkcaldy KY2 5SG	01592 566129
Simpson, Gordon M. MA BD	1959 1996	(Leslie: Trinity)	37 Spottiswoode Gardens, St Andrews KY16 8SA	01334 473406
Sutherland, William	1964 1993	(Bo'ness Old)	88 Dunrobin Road, Kirkcaldy KY2 5YT	01592 205510
Thomson, Gilbert L. BA	1965 1996	(Glenrothes: Christ's Kirk)	3 Fortharfield, Freuchie, Cupar KY15 7JJ	01337 857431
Thomson, John D. BD	1985 2005	(Kirkcaldy: Pathhead)	3 Tottenham Court, Hill Street, Dysart, Kirkcaldy KY1 2XY	01592 655313
Tomlinson, Bryan L. TD	1969 2003	(Kirkcaldy: Abbotshall)	2 Duddingston Drive, Kirkcaldy KY2 6JP [E-mail: abbkirk@blueyonder.co.uk]	01592 564843
Webster, Elspeth H. (Miss) DCS		(Deaconess)	82 Broomhill Avenue, Burntisland KY3 0BP	01592 873616

KIRKCALDY ADDRESSES

Abbotshall	Abbotshall Road
Linktown	Nicol Street x High Street
Pathhead	Harriet Street x Church Street
St Andrew's	Victoria Road x Victoria Gdns
St Bryce Kirk	St Brycedale Avenue x Kirk Wynd
St John's	Elgin Street
Templehall	Beauty Place
Torbain	Lindores Drive
Viewforth	Viewforth Street x Viewforth Terrace

(26) ST ANDREWS

Meets at Cupar, in St John's Church Hall, on the second Wednesday of February, March, April, May, September, October, November and December; and on the last Wednesday of June.

Clerk: DR RAYMOND K. MACKIE

Depute Clerk: REV. DAVID I. SINCLAIR BSc BD PhD DipSW   c/o The Scottish Churches Parliamentary Office, The Scottish Storytelling Centre, 43–45 High Street, Edinburgh EH1 1SR   **0131-558 1638**
[E-mail: standrews@cofscotland.org.uk]

The Presbytery Office is manned Monday to Thursday inclusive from 1:30 until 3:30pm.

Abdie and Dunbog (H) linked with Newburgh (H)
Lynn Brady (Miss) BD DipMin   1996   2002   2 Guthrie Court, Cupar Road, Newburgh, Cupar KY14 6HA   01337 842228
[E-mail: lynn@revbrady.freeserve.co.uk]

Anstruther
Vacant   The James Melville Manse, Anstruther KY10 3EX   01333 311808

Auchtermuchty (H) Ann G. Fraser (Mrs) BD CertMin	1990	2 Burnside, Auchtermuchty, Cupar KY14 7AJ [E-mail: anngilfraser@btinternet.com]	01337 828519
Balmerino (H) linked with Wormit (H) James Connolly Dip'Th CertMin	1982 2004	5 Westwater Place, Newport-on-Tay DD6 8NS [E-mail: jim@connollyuk.wanadoo.co.uk]	01382 542626
Boarhills and Dunino linked with St Andrews: Martyrs' Vacant		49 Irvine Crescent, St Andrews KY16 8LG	01334 472948
Cameron linked with St Andrews: St Leonard's (01334 478702) Alan D. McDonald LLB BD MTh	1979 1998	1 Cairnhill Gardens, St Andrews KY16 8QY [E-mail: alan.d.mcdonald@talk21.com]	01334 472793
Carnbee linked with Pittenweem Margaret E.S. Rose BD	2007	29 Milton Road, Pittenweem, Anstruther KY10 2LN [E-mail: mgt.r@btopenworld.com]	01333 312838
Cellardyke (H) linked with Kilrenny David J.H. Laing BD DPS	1976 1999	Toll Road, Cellardyke, Anstruther KY10 3BH [E-mail: davith@v21mail.co.uk]	01333 310810
Ceres, Kemback and Springfield Eric G. McKimmon BA BD MTh	1983 2005	The Manse, St Andrews Road, Ceres, Cupar KY15 5NQ [E-mail: McKimmonCeres@aol.com]	01334 829466
Crail linked with Kingsbarns (H) Michael J. Erskine MA BD	1985 2002	Church Manse, St Andrews Road, Crail, Anstruther KY10 3UH	01333 450358
Creich, Flisk and Kilmany linked with Monimail Neil McLay BA BD	2006	Creich Manse, Brunton, Cupar KY15 4PA [E-mail: neilmclay@gmail.com]	01337 870332
Cupar: Old (H) and St Michael of Tarvit Kenneth S. Jeffrey BA BD PhD	2002	76 Hogarth Drive, Cupar KY15 5YH [E-mail: ksjeffrey@btopenworld.com]	01334 653196
Cupar: St John's linked with Dairsie A. Sheila Blount (Mrs) BD BA	1978 2002	23 Hogarth Drive, Cupar KY15 5YH [E-mail: asblount@fish.co.uk]	01334 656408
Dairsie See Cupar: St John's			

Edenshead and Strathmiglo
James G. Redpath BD DipPTh — 1988 — 2006 — The Manse, Kirk Wynd, Strathmiglo, Cupar KY14 7QS [E-mail: james.redpath2@btinternet.com] — 01337 860256

Elie (H) linked with Kilconquhar and Colinsburgh (H)
Brian McDowell BA BD — 1999 — 2007 — 30 Bank Street, Elie, Leven KY9 1BW — 01333 330685

Falkland (01337 858442) linked with Freuchie (H)
George G. Nicol BD DPhil — 1982 — 2006 — 1 Newton Road, Falkland, Cupar KY15 7AQ [E-mail: ggnicol@totalise.co.uk] — 01337 858557

Freuchie (H) See Falkland

Howe of Fife
Marion J. Paton (Miss) BMus BD — 1991 — 1994 — 83 Church Street, Ladybank, Cupar KY15 7ND [E-mail: marion@marionpaton.f9.co.uk] — 01337 830513
Cameron Harrison (Aux) — 2006 — Woodfield House, Prior Muir, St Andrews KY16 8LP — 01334 478067

Kilconquhar and Colinsburgh See Elie
Kilrenny See Cellardyke
Kingsbarns See Crail

Largo and Newburn (H) linked with Largo: St David's
John A.H. Murdoch BA BD DPSS — 1979 — 2006 — The Manse, Church Place, Upper Largo, Leven KY8 6EH [E-mail: jm.largo@btinternet.com] — 01333 360286

Largo: St David's See Largo and Newburn

Largoward (H) linked with St Monans (H)
Donald G. MacEwan MA BD PhD — 2001 — The Manse, St Monans, Anstruther KY10 2DD [E-mail: maiadona@fish.co.uk] — 01333 730258

Leuchars: St Athernase
Caroline Taylor (Mrs) MA BD — 1995 — 2003 — 7 David Wilson Park, Balmullo, St Andrews KY16 0NP [E-mail: caro234@btinternet.com] — 01334 870038

Monimail See Creich, Flisk and Kilmany
Newburgh See Abdie and Dunbog

Newport-on-Tay (H)
W. Kenneth Pryde DA BD — 1994 — 57 Cupar Road, Newport-on-Tay DD6 8DF [E-mail: wkpryde@hotmail.com] — 01382 543165 (Tel/Fax)

Pittenweem See Carnbee

St Andrews: Holy Trinity
| Rory MacLeod BA MBA BD | 1994 | 2004 | 19 Priory Gardens, St Andrews KY16 8XX
[E-mail: anniecrory@hotmail.com] | 01334 461098 |

St Andrews: Hope Park (H) linked with Strathkinness
| A. David K. Arnott MA BD | 1971 | 1996 | 20 Priory Gardens, St Andrews KY16 8XX
[E-mail: adka@arnotts.wanadoo.co.uk] | 01334 472912 (Tel/Fax) |

St Andrews: Martyrs' (H) See Boarhills and Dunino
St Andrews: St Leonard's (H) See Cameron
St Monans See Largoward
Strathkinness See St Andrews: Hope Park

Tayport
| Colin J. Dempster BD CertMin | 1990 | 27 Bell Street, Tayport DD6 9AP
[E-mail: demps@tayportc.fsnet.co.uk] | 01382 552861 |

Wormit See Balmerino

Alexander, James S. MA BD BA PhD	1966	1973	University of St Andrews	5 Strathkinness High Road, St Andrews KY16 9RP	01334 472680
Bennett, G. Alestair A. TD MA	1938	1976	(Strathkinness)	7 Bonfield Park, Strathkinness, St Andrews KY16 9SY	01334 850249
Bews, James MA	1942	1981	(Dundee: Craigiebank)	21 Balrymonth Court, St Andrews KY16 8XT	01334 476087
Blount, Graham K. LLB BD PhD	1976	1998	Parliamentary Officer	23 Hogarth Drive, Cupar KY15 5YH	01334 656408
Bradley, Ian MA BD DPhil	1990	1990	University of St Andrews	4 Donaldson Gardens, St Andrews KY16 9DN	01334 475389
Brown, Lawson R. MA	1960	1997	(Cameron with St Andrew's: St Leonard's)	10 Park Street, St Andrews KY16 8AQ	01334 473413
Cameron, James K. MA BD PhD FRHistS	1953	1989	(University of St Andrews)	Priorscroft, 71 Hepburn Gardens, St Andrews KY16 9LS	01334 473996
Casebow, Brian C. MA BD	1959	1993	(Edinburgh: Salisbury)	'The Rowans', 67 St Michael's Drive, Cupar KY15 5BP	01334 656385
Douglas, Peter C. JP	1966	1993	(Boarhills linked with Dunino)	The Old Schoolhouse, Flisk, Newburgh, Cupar KY14 6HN	01337 870218
Earnshaw, Philip BA BSc BD	1986	1996	(Glasgow: Pollokshields)	22 Castle Street, St Monans, Anstruther KY10 2AP	01333 730640
Edington, George L.	1952	1989	(Tayport)	64B Burghmuir Road, Perth PH1 1LH	
Fairlie, George BD BVMS MRCVS	1971	2002	(Crail with Kingsbarns)	41 Warrack Street, St Andrews KY16 8DR	01334 475868
Galloway, Robert W.C. LTh	1970	1998	(Cromarty)	22 Haughgate, Leven KY8 4SG	01333 426223
Gibson, Henry M. MA BD PhD	1960	1999	(Dundee: The High Kirk)	4 Comerton Place, Drumoig, Leuchars, St Andrews KY16 0NQ	01382 542199
Gordon, Peter M. MA BD	1958	1995	(Airdrie: West)	3 Cupar Road, Cuparmuir, Cupar KY15 5RH [E-mail: machrie@madasafish.com]	01334 652341
Hegarty, John D. LTh ABSC	1988	2004	(Buckie: South and West with Enzie)	26 Montgomery Way, Kinross KY13 8FD [E-mail: john.hegarty@tesco.net]	01577 863829
Henney, William MA DD	1957	1996	(St Andrews: Hope Park)	30 Doocot Road, St Andrews KY16 9LP	01334 472560
Hill, Roy MA	1962	1997	(Lisbon)	Forgan Cottage, Kinnessburn Road, St Andrews KY16 8AD	01334 472121
Jarvie, John W. BD CertMin MTh	1990	2005	(Falkland with Freuchie)	62 Glebe Park, Kirkcaldy KY1 1BL [E-mail: john@jarvie.info]	(Mbl) 07740 256120
Learmonth, Walter LTh	1968	1997	(Ceres with Springfield)	14 Marionfield Place, Cupar KY15 5JN	01334 656290
Lithgow, Thomas MA	1945	1982	(Banchory Devenick with Maryculter)	c/o Milne, Bairds (Lawyers), 7 St Catherine Street, Cupar KY15 4LS	

Name / Qualifications	(Charge / Role)			Address	Telephone
McCartney, Alexander C. BTh	(Caputh and Clunie with Kinclaven)	1973	1995	10 The Glebe, Crail, Anstruther KY10 3UT	01333 451194
McGregor, Duncan J. MIFM	(Channelkirk with Lauder: Old)	1982	1996	14 Mount Melville, St Andrews KY16 8NG	01334 478314
Macintyre, William J. MA BD DD	(Crail with Kingsbarns)	1951	1989	Tigh a' Ghobhainn, Lochton, Crail, Anstruther KY10 3XE	01333 450327
Mackenzie, A. Cameron MA	(Biggar)	1955	1995	Hedgerow, 5 Shiels Avenue, Freuchie, Cupar KY15 7JD	01337 857763
MacNab, Hamish S.D. MA	(Kilrenny)	1948	1987	Fairhill, Northmuir, Kirriemuir DD8 4PF	01575 572564
Meager, Peter MA BD CertMgmt(Open)	(Elie with Kilconquhar and Colinsburgh)	1971	1998	7 Lorraine Drive, Cupar KY15 5DY	01334 656991
Ord, J.K.	(Falkirk: Condorrat)	1963	1968	24 Forth Street, St Monance, Anstruther KY10 2AX	01333 730461
Paton, Iain F. BD FCIS	(Elie with Kilconquhar and Colinsburgh)	1980	2006	Lindisfarne, 19 Links Road, Lundin Links, Leven KY8 6AS	01333 320765
Portchmouth, Roland John NDD ATD	(Bendochy)	1980	1989	1 West Braes, Pittenweem, Anstruther KY10 2PS	01333 311448
Porteous, James K. DD	(Cupar: St John's)	1944	1997	16 Market Street, St Andrews KY16 9NS	
Reid, Alan A.S. MA BD STM	(Bridge of Allan: Chalmers)	1962	1995	Wayside Cottage, Bridgend, Ceres, Cupar KY15 5LS	01334 828509
Robb, Nigel J. FCP MA BD ThM MTh	Associate Secretary: Worship and Doctrine: Mission and Discipleship Council	1981	1998	c/o 121 George Street, Edinburgh EH2 4YN [E-mail: nrobb@cofscotland.org.uk]	0131-225 5722
Robertson, Norma P. (Miss) BD DMin MTh	(Kincardine O'Neil with Lumphanan)	1993	2002	82 Hogarth Drive, Cupar KY15 5YU [E-mail: normapr@fish.co.uk]	01334 650595
Roy, Alan J. BSc BD	(Aberuthven with Dunning)	1960	1999	14 Comerton Place, Drumoig, Leuchars, St Andrews KY16 0NQ [E-mail: roma.roy@btopenworld.com]	01382 542225
Salters, Robert B. MA BD PhD	(University of St Andrews)	1966	1971	Vine Cottage, 119 South Street, St Andrews KY16 9UH	01334 473198
Scot, J. Miller MA BD FSAScot DD	(Jerusalem)	1949	1988	St Martins, 6 Trinity Place, St Andrews KY16 8SG	01334 479518
Sinclair, David I. BSc BD PhD DipSW	Secretary: Church and Society Council	1990	1998	42 South Road, Cupar KY15 5JF	01334 656957
Stevenson, A.L. LLB MLitt DPA FPEA	(Balmerino linked with Wormit)	1984	1993	41 Main Street, Dairsie, Cupar KY15 4SR	01334 870582
Stoddart, David L.	(Laggan with Newtonmore)	1961	1987	3 Castle Street, Anstruther KY10 3DD	01333 310668
Strong, Clifford LTh	(Creich, Flisk and Kilmany with Monimail)	1983	1995		
Taylor, Ian BSc MA LTh DipEd	(Abdie and Dunbog with Newburgh)	1983	1997	60 Maryknowe, Gauldry, Newport-on-Tay DD6 8SL	01382 330445
Thomson, P.G. MA BD MTh ThD	(Irvine: Fullarton)	1947	1989	Lundie Cottage, Arncroach, Anstruther KY10 2RN	01333 720222
Thrower, Charles G. BSc	(Carnbee with Pittenweem)	1965	2002	Fullarton, 2 Beech Walk, Crail, Anstruther KY10 3UN	01333 450423
				Grange House, Wester Grangemuir, Pittenweem, Anstruther KY10 2RB [E-mail: c-thrower@pittenweem2.freeserve.co.uk]	01333 312631
Torrance, Alan J. MA BD DrTheol	University of St Andrews	1984	1999	Kincaple House, Kincaple, St Andrews KY16 9SH	(Home) 01334 850755 (Office) 01334 462843
Turnbull, James J. MA	(Arbirlot with Colliston)	1940	1981	Woodlands, Beech Avenue, Ladybank, Cupar KY15 7NG	(Tel) 01337 830279
Walker, James B. MA BD DPhil	Chaplain: University of St Andrews	1975	1993	1 Gillespie Terrace, The Scores, St Andrews KY16 9AT [E-mail: james.walker@st-andrews.ac.uk]	(Fax) 01334 462866 01334 462868
Wilson, Robert McL. MA BD PhD DD FBA	(University of St Andrews)	1946	1983	10 Murrayfield Road, St Andrews KY16 9NB	01334 474331
Wotherspoon, Ian G. BA LTh	(Coatbridge: St Andrew's)	1967	2004	11 Bowiehill, Auchtermuchty, Cupar KY14 7AQ [E-mail: wotherspoonrg@aol.com]	01337 827561
Wright, Lynda (Miss) BEd DCS	Deacon: Retreat Leader, Key House			6 Key Cottage, High Street, Falkland, Cupar KY15 7BD	01337 857705
Young, Evelyn M. (Mrs) BSc BD	(Kilmun (St Munn's) with Strone and Ardentinny)	1984	2003	2 Priestden Place, St Andrews KY16 8DP	01334 479662

(27) DUNKELD AND MEIGLE

Meets at Pitlochry on the first Tuesday of September and December, on the third Tuesday of February, April and October, and at the Moderator's church on the third Tuesday of June.

Clerk:	REV. JOHN RUSSELL MA		Kilblaan, Gladstone Terrace, Birnam, Dunkeld PH8 0DP [E-mail: dunkeldmeigle@cofscotland.org.uk]	01350 728896
Aberfeldy (H) linked with Amulree (H) and Strathbraan linked with Dull and Weem (H)				
Mark Drane BD	2007		The Manse, Taybridge Terrace, Aberfeldy PH15 2BS [E-mail: mark_drane@hotmail.co.uk]	01887 820656
Alyth (H)				
Sheila M. Kirk BA LLB BD	2007		The Manse, Cambridge Street, Alyth, Blairgowrie PH11 8AW [E-mail: sheilamkirk@tiscali.co.uk]	01828 632104
Amulree and Strathbraan See Aberfeldy				
Ardler, Kettins and Meigle				
Linda Stewart (Mrs) BD	2001		The Manse, Dundee Road, Meigle, Blairgowrie PH12 8SB [E-mail: lindacstewart@tiscali.co.uk]	01828 640278
Bendochy linked with Coupar Angus: Abbey				
Bruce Dempsey BD	1997		Caddam Road, Coupar Angus, Blairgowrie PH13 9EF [E-mail: revbruce.dempsey@btopenworld.com]	01828 627331
Blair Atholl and Struan linked with Tenandry				
Brian Ian Murray BD	2002		Blair Atholl, Pitlochry PH18 5SX [E-mail: athollkirks@yahoo.co.uk]	01796 481213
Blairgowrie				
Donald Macleod BD LRAM DRSAM	1987	2002	The Manse, Upper David Street, Blairgowrie PH10 6HB [E-mail: donmac@fish.co.uk]	01250 872146
Braes of Rannoch linked with Foss and Rannoch (H)				
Christine A.Y. Ritchie (Mrs) BD DipMin	2002	2005	The Manse, Kinloch Rannoch, Pitlochry PH16 5QA [E-mail: critchie@fish.co.uk]	01882 632381
Caputh and Clunie (H) linked with Kinclaven (H)				
William Ewart BSc BD	1972	2004	Caputh Manse, Caputh, Perth PH1 4JH [E-mail: ewe@surefish.co.uk]	01738 710520
Coupar Angus: Abbey See Bendochy				
Dull and Weem See Aberfeldy				

Dunkeld (H)
R. Fraser Penny BA BD   1984 2001   Cathedral Manse, Dunkeld PH8 0AW   01350 727249
[E-mail: fraserpenn@aol.com]   01350 727102 (Fax)

Fortingall and Glenlyon linked with Kenmore and Lawers
Anne J. Brennan BSc BD MTh   1999   The Manse, Balnaskeag, Kenmore, Aberfeldy PH15 2HB   01887 830218
[E-mail: annebrennan@yahoo.co.uk]

Foss and Rannoch See Braes of Rannoch

Grantully, Logierait and Strathtay
Rosemary Legge (Mrs) BSc BD MTh   1992 2006   The Manse, Strathtay, Pitlochry PH9 0PG   01887 840251
[E-mail: GLScofs@aol.com]

Kenmore and Lawers (H) See Fortingall and Glenlyon
Kinclaven See Caputh and Clunie

Kirkmichael, Straloch and Glenshee linked with Rattray (H)
Malcolm H. MacRae MA PhD   1971 2005   The Manse, Alyth Road, Rattray, Blairgowrie PH10 7HF   01250 872462
[E-mail: malcolm.macrae1@btopenworld.com]

Pitlochry (H) (01796 472160)
Malcolm Ramsay BA LLB DipMin   1986 1998   Manse Road, Moulin, Pitlochry PH16 5EP   01796 472774
[E-mail: amramsay@aol.com]

Rattray See Kirkmichael, Straloch and Glenshee
Tenandry See Blair Atholl and Struan

Cassells, Alexander K. MA BD	1961	1997	(Leuchars: St Athernase and Guardbridge)	Balloch Cottage, Keltneyburn, Aberfeldy PH15 2LS	01887 830758
Creegan, Christine M. (Mrs) MTh	1993	2005	(Grantully, Logierait and Strathtay)	Lonaig, 28 Lettoch Terrace, Pitlochry PH16 5BA [E-mail: christine@creegans.co.uk]	01796 472422
Dick, Tom MA	1951	1990	(Dunkeld)	Mo Dhachaidh, Callybrae, Dunkeld PH8 0EP	01350 727338
Duncan, James BTh FSAScot	1980	1995	(Blair Atholl and Struan)	25 Knockard Avenue, Pitlochry PH16 5JE	01796 474096
Forsyth, David Stuart MA	1948	1992	(Belhelvie)	39 Homemount House, Gogoside Road, Largs KA30 9LS	
Fulton, Frederick H. MA	1942	1983	(Clunie, Lethendy and Kinloch)	Grampian Cottage, Chapel Brae, Braemar, Ballater AB35 5YT	01339 741277
Gisbey, John E. MA BD MSc DipEd	1964	2002	(Thornhill)	Cherry House, Perth Road, Rosemount, Blairgowrie PH10 6QB	01250 872573
Hamilton, David G. MA BD	1971	2004	(Braes of Rannoch with Foss and Rannoch)	79 Finlay Rise, Milngavie, Glasgow G62 6QL [E-mail: davidhamilton@onetel.com]	0141-956 4202
Henderson, John D. MA BD	1953	1992	(Cluny with Monymusk)	Aldersyde, George Street, Blairgowrie PH10 6HP	01250 875181
Knox, John W. MTheol	1992	1997	(Lochgelly: Macainsh)	Heatherlea, Main Street, Ardler, Blairgowrie PH12 8SR	01828 640731
McAlister, D.J.B. MA BD PhD	1951	1989	(North Berwick: Blackadder)	2 Duff Avenue, Moulin, Pitlochry PH16 5EN	01796 473591
MacVicar, Kenneth MBE DFC TD MA	1950	1990	(Kenmore with Lawers with Fortingall and Glenlyon)	Illeray, Kenmore, Aberfeldy PH15 2HE	01887 830514

Ormiston, Hugh C. BSc BD MPhil PhD	1969	2004	(Kirkmichael, Straloch and Glenshee with Rattray)	Cedar Lea, Main Road, Woodside, Blairgowrie PH13 9NP	01828 670539
Robertson, Iain M. MA	1967	1992	(Carriden)	St Colme's, Perth Road, Birnam, Dunkeld PH8 0BH	01350 727455
Robertson, Matthew LTh	1968	2002	(Cawdor with Croy and Dalcross)	Inver, Strathtay, Pitlochry PH9 0PG	01887 840780
Russell, John MA	1959	2000	(Tillicoultry)	Kilblaan, Gladstone Terrace, Birnam, Dunkeld PH8 0DP	01350 728896
Shannon, W.G. MA BD	1955	1998	(Pitlochry)	19 Knockard Road, Pitlochry PH16 5HJ	01796 473533
Tait, Thomas W. BD	1972	1997	(Rattray)	20 Cedar Avenue, Blairgowrie PH10 6TT	01250 874833
White, Brock A. LTh	1971	2001	(Kirkcaldy: Templehall)	1 Littlewood Gardens, Blairgowrie PH10 6XZ	01250 870399
Whyte, William B. BD	1973	2003	(Nairn: St Ninian's)	The Old Inn, Park Hill Road, Rattray, Blairgowrie PH10 7DS	01250 874401
Wilson, John M. MA BD	1965	2004	(Altnaharra and Farr)	Berbice, The Terrace, Blair Atholl, Pitlochry PH18 5SZ	01796 481619
Wilson, Mary D. (Mrs) RGN SCM DTM	1990	2004	(Auxiliary Minister)	Berbice, The Terrace, Blair Atholl, Pitlochry PH18 5SZ	01796 481619
Young, G. Stuart	1961	1996	(Blairgowrie: St Andrew's)	7 James Place, Stanley, Perth PH1 4PD	01738 828473

(28) PERTH

Meets at Scone: Old, at 7:00pm, in the Elizabeth Ashton Hall, on the second Tuesday of February, March, June, September, November and December in each year.

Clerk:	REV. DOUGLAS M. MAIN BD		
Presbytery Office:		209 High Street, Perth PH1 5PB	01738 451177
		[E-mail: perth@cofscotland.org.uk]	
		[E-mail: perth@uk.uumail.com]	

Abernethy and Dron and Arngask

Vacant			3 Manse Road, Abernethy, Perth PH2 9JP	01738 850607

(Charge formed by the union of the charge of Abernethy and Dron with the charge of Arngask)

Almondbank Tibbermore

Vacant			The Manse, Pitcairngreen, Perth PH1 3EA	01738 583217

Ardoch (H) linked with Blackford (H)

Stuart D.B. Picken MA BD PhD	1966	2005	3 Millhill Crescent, Greenloaning, Dunblane FK15 0LH	01786 880217
			[E-mail: picken@eikoku.demon.co.uk]	

Auchterarder (H)

Michael R.R. Shewan MA BD CPS	1985	1998	24 High Street, Auchterarder, Perth PH3 1DF	01764 662210
			[E-mail: michaelshewan@onetel.net]	

Auchtergaven and Moneydie

Iain McFadzean MA BD	1989	2005	Bankfoot, Perth PH1 4BS	01738 787235
			[E-mail: iainmcfadzean@hotmail.com]	

Blackford See Ardoch

Cargill Burrelton linked with Collace
Jose R. Carvalho BD   2002   Manse Road, Woodside, Blairgowrie PH13 9NQ   01828 670352
[E-mail: joecarvalho@btinternet.com]

Cleish (H) linked with Fossoway: St Serf's and Devonside
Joanne G. Finlay (Mrs)   1996 2005   The Manse, Cleish, Kinross KY13 7LR   01577 850231
DipTMus BD AdvDipCouns   [E-mail: joanne.finlay196@btinternet.com]

Collace See Cargill and Burrelton

Comrie (H) linked with Dundurn (H)
Graham McWilliams BSc BD   2005   The Manse, Strowan Road, Comrie, Crieff PH6 2ES   01764 671045 (Tel/Fax)
[E-mail: Themansefamily@aol.com]

Crieff (H)
James W. MacDonald BD   1976 2002   8 Strathearn Terrace, Crieff PH7 3AQ   01764 653907
[E-mail: revup@tesco.net]

Dunbarney (H) and Forgandenny
Vacant   Dunbarney Manse, Bridge of Earn, Perth PH2 9DY   01738 812463

Dundurn See Comrie

Errol (H) linked with Kilspindie and Rait
Douglas M. Main BD   1986 2005   South Bank, Errol, Perth PH2 7PZ   01821 642279
[E-mail: revdmain@aol.com]

Fossoway: St Serf's and Devonside See Cleish

Fowlis Wester, Madderty and Monzie
Vacant   Beechview, Abercairney, Crieff PH7 3NF   01764 652116
(Charge formed by the union of Madderty, Fowlis Wester and Monzie)

Gask (H) linked with Methven and Logiealmond (H)
Brian Bain LTh   1980 1986   Sauchob Road, Methven, Perth PH1 3QD   01738 840274 (Tel/Fax)
[E-mail: brian.bain4@btinternet.com]

Kilspindie and Rait See Errol

Kinross (H) John P.L. Munro MA BD PhD	1977 1998	15 Station Road, Kinross KY13 8TG [E-mail: john@lochleven.freeserve.co.uk]	01577 862952
Methven and Logiealmond See Gask			
Muthill (H) linked with Trinity Gask and Kinkell John Oswald BSc PhD BD	1997 2002	Muthill, Crieff PH5 2AR [E-mail: revdocoz@bigfoot.com]	01764 681205
Orwell (H) and Portmoak (H) Robert G.D.W. Pickles BD MPhil	2003	3 Perth Road, Milnathort, Kinross KY13 9XU [E-mail: robert.pickles1@btopenworld.com]	01577 863461
Perth: Craigie (H) Vacant		46 Abbot Street, Perth PH2 0EE	01738 623748
Perth: Kinnoull (H) David I. Souter BD	1996 2001	1 Mount Tabor Avenue, Perth PH2 7BT [E-mail: d.souter@blueyonder.co.uk]	01738 626046
Perth: Letham St Mark's (H) James C. Stewart BD DipMin	1997	35 Rose Crescent, Perth PH1 1NT [E-mail: jimstewartrev@lineone.net]	01738 624167
Kenneth McKay DCS		11F Balgowan Road, Perth PH1 2JG [E-mail: kennydandcs@hotmail.com]	01738 621169
Perth: Moncreiffe (T) Isobel Birrell (Mrs) BD	1994 1999	Hiddlehame, 5 Hewat Place, Perth PH1 2UD [E-mail: isobel.birrell@peacenik.co.uk]	01738 625694
Perth: North (01738 622298) David W. Denniston BD DipMin	1981 1996	127 Glasgow Road, Perth PH2 0LU [E-mail: david.denniston@blueyonder.co.uk]	01738 625728
Perth: Riverside (New Charge Development) Grant MacLaughlan BA BD	1998 2007	44 Hay Street, Perth PH1 5HS [E-mail: revgrm2@aol.com]	01738 621305
Christine Palmer (Miss) DCS	2003 2005	39 Fortingall Place, Perth PH1 2NF [E-mail: chrisjpalmer@blueyonder.co.uk]	01738 587488
Perth: St John the Baptist's (H) (01738 626159) Vacant		15 Comely Bank, Perth PH2 7HU	
Elizabeth Brown (Mrs)	1996	25 Highfield Road, Scone, Perth PH2 6RN [E-mail: liz.brown@blueyonder.co.uk]	01738 621755 01738 552391 (Tel/Fax)

Perth: St Leonard's-in-the-Fields and Trinity (H) (01738 632238)
Vacant — 5 Strathearn Terrace, Perth PH2 0LS — 01738 621709

Perth: St Matthew's (Office: 01738 636757; Vestry: 01738 630725)
Scott Burton BD DipMin — 1999 2007 — 23 Kincarrathie Crescent, Perth PH2 7HH [E-mail: sburton@supanet.com] — 01738 626828

Redgorton and Stanley
Derek G. Lawson LLB BD — 1998 — 22 King Street, Stanley, Perth PH1 4ND [E-mail: dglawson@talktalk.net] — 01738 828247

St Madoes and Kinfauns
Marc F. Bircham BD MTh — 2000 — Glencarse, Perth PH2 7NF [E-mail: mark.bircham@btinternet.com] — 01738 860837

St Martin's linked with Scone: New (H) (01738 553900)
James Gemmell BD MTh — 1999 2007 — 24 Victoria Road, Scone, Perth PH2 6JW [E-mail: jasgemmell@aol.com] — 01738 551467

Scone: New See St Martin's

Scone: Old (H)
J. Bruce Thomson JP MA BD — 1972 1983 — Burnside, Scone, Perth PH2 6LP [E-mail: jock.tamson@talk21.com] — 01738 552030

The Stewartry of Strathearn (H) (01738 621674) (E-mail: office@stewartryofstrathearn.org.uk)
Colin R. Williamson LLB BD — 1972 2000 — Manse of Aberdalgie, Aberdalgie, Perth PH2 0QD [E-mail: stewartry@beeb.net] — 01738 625854

Trinity Gask and Kinkell See Muthill

Name			Charge	Address	Phone
Barr, George K. ARIBA BD PhD	1967	1993	(Uddingston: Viewpark)	7 Tay Avenue, Comrie, Crieff PH6 2PE [E-mail: gbarr2@compuserve.com]	01764 670454
Barr, T. Leslie LTh	1969	1997	(Kinross)	8 Fairfield Road, Kelty KY4 0BY	01383 839330
Bartholomew, Julia (Mrs) BSc BD	2002		Auchterarder: Associate	Kippenhill, Dunning, Perth PH2 0RA [E-mail: Julia@auchpc.fsnet.co.uk]	01764 684929
Bertram, Thomas A.	1972	1995	(Patna: Waterside)	3 Scrimgeours Corner, 29 West High Street, Crieff PH7 4AP	01764 652066
Birrell, John M. MA LLB BD	1974	1996	Hospital Chaplain: Perth Royal Infirmary	Hiddlehame, 5 Hewat Place, Perth PH1 2JD [E-mail: john.birrell@nhs.net]	01738 625694
Buchan, William DipTheol BD	1987	2001	(Kilwinning: Abbey)	34 Bridgewater Avenue, Auchterarder PH3 1DQ [E-mail: wbuchan3@aol.com]	01764 660306

Name			Charge / Appointment	Address	Tel.
Cairns, Evelyn BD	2004		Chaplain: Rachel House	15 Tala Park, Kinross KY13 8AB [E-mail: revelyn@chas.org.uk]	01577 863990
Campbell, Andrew B. BD DPS MTh	1979	2006	Mission and Discipleship Council	The Haven, 21 Skye Crescent, Crieff PH7 3FB [E-mail: acampbell@cofscotland.org.uk]	01764 654226
Carr, W. Stanley MA	1951	1991	(Largs: St Columba's)	16 Gannochy Walk, Perth PH2 7LW	01738 627422
Coleman, Sidney H. BA BD MTh	1961	2001	(Glasgow: Merrylea)	'Blaven', 11 Clyde Place, Perth PH2 0EZ [E-mail: sidney.coleman@blueyonder.co.uk]	01738 565072
Craig, Joan H. (Miss) MTheol	1986	2005	(Orkney: East Mainland)	7 Jedburgh Place, Perth PH1 1SJ [E-mail: joanhcraig@bigfoot.com]	01738 580180
Denniston, Jane MA BD	2002		Ministries Council	127 Glasgow Road, Perth PH2 0LU [E-mail: jdenniston@cofscotland.org.uk]	01738 565379
Donaldson, Robert B. BSocSc	1953	1997	(Kilchoman with Portnahaven)	11 Strathearn Court, Crieff PH7 3DS	01764 654976
Drummond, Alfred G. BD DMin	1991	2006	Scottish General Secretary: Evangelical Alliance	10 Errochty Court, Perth PH1 2SU	
Fleming, Hamish K. MA	1966	2001	(Banchory Ternan: East)	36 Earnmuir Road, Comrie, Crieff PH6 2EY	01764 679178
Galbraith, W. James L. BSc BD MICE	1973	1996	(Kilchrenan and Dalavich with Muckairn)	19 Mayfield Gardens, Kinross KY13 9GD	01577 863887
Gaston, A. Ray C. MA BD	1969	2002	(Leuchars: St Athernase)	'Hamewith', 13 Manse Road, Dollar FK14 7AL	01259 743202
Gregory, J.C. LTh	1968	1986	(Blantyre: St Andrew's)	2 Southlands Road, Auchterarder PH3 1BA	01764 664594
Grimson, John A. MA	1950	1986	(Glasgow: Wellington: Associate)	29 Highland Road, Turret Park, Crieff PH7 4LE	01764 653063
Gunn, Alexander M. MA BD	1967	2006	(Aberfeldy with Amulree and Strathbraan with Dull and Weem)	Navarone, 12 Cornhill Road, Perth PH1 1LR [E-mail: sandygunn@btinternet.com]	01738 443216
Halliday, Archibald R. BD MTh	1964	1999	(Duffus, Spynie and Hopeman)	2 Pittenzie Place, Crieff PH7 3JL	01764 656464
Henry, Malcolm N. MA BD	1951	1987	(Perth: Craigie)	Kelton, Castle Douglas DG7 1RU	01556 504144
Houston, Alexander McR.	1939	1977	(Tibbermore)	120 Glasgow Road, Perth PH2 0LU	01738 628056
Hughes, Clifford E. MA BD	1993	2001	(Haddington: St Mary's)	Pavilion Cottage, Briglands, Rumbling Bridge, Kinross KY13 0PS	01577 840506
Kelly, T. Clifford	1973	1995	(Ferintosh)	7 Bankfoot Park, Scotlandwell, Kinross KY13 7JP	01592 840387
Lacey, Eric R. BD	1971	1992	(Creich with Rosehall)	The Bungalow, Forteviot, Perth PH2 9BT [E-mail: revela.cey@homecall.co.uk]	01764 684041
Lawson, James B. MA BD	1961	2002	(South Uist)	4 Cowden Way, Comrie, Crieff PH6 2NW [E-mail: james.lawson7@btopenworld.com]	01764 679180
Lawson, Ronald G. MA BD	1964	1999	(Greenock: Wellpark Mid Kirk)	6 East Brougham Street, Stanley, Perth PH1 4NJ	01738 828871
Low, J.E. Stewart MA	1957	1997	(Tarbat)	15 Stormont Place, Scone, Perth PH2 6SR	01738 552023
McCormick, Alastair F.	1962	1998	(Creich with Rosehall)	14 Balmanno Park, Bridge of Earn, Perth PH2 9RJ	01738 813588
McGregor, William F. LTh	1987	2003	(Auchtergaven and Moneydie)	Ard Choille, 7 Taypark Road, Luncarty, Perth PH1 3FE [E-mail: bill.mcgregor@ukonline.co.uk]	01738 827866
MacKenzie, Donald W. MA	1941	1983	(Auchterarder: The Barony)	81 Kingswell Terrace, Perth PH1 2DA	01738 633716
MacLean, Nigel R. MA BD	1940	1986	(Perth: St Paul's)	9 Hay Street, Perth PH1 5HS	01738 626728
MacMillan, Riada M. (Mrs) BD	1991	1998	(Perth: Craigend Moncreiffe with Rhynd)	73 Muirend Gardens, Perth PH1 1JR	01738 628867
McNaughton, David J.H. BA CA	1976	1995	(Killin and Ardeonaig)	30 Hollybush Road, Crieff PH7 3HB	01764 653028
McPhee, Duncan P.	1951	1980	(Braemar with Crathie: Associate)	c/o Valley House, Torlundy, Fort William PH33 6SN	
McQuilken, John E. MA BD	1969	1992	(Glenaray and Inveraray)	18 Clark Terrace, Crieff PH7 3QE	01764 655764
Millar, Alexander M. MA BD MBA	1980	2001	Associate Secretary: Mission and Discipleship Council	c/o 121 George Street, Edinburgh EH2 4YN [E-mail: amillar@cofscotland.org.uk]	0131-225 5722
Millar, Archibald E. DipTh	1965	1991	(Perth: St Stephen's)	7 Maple Place, Perth PH1 1RT	01738 621813
Millar, Jennifer M. (Mrs) BD DipMin	1986	1995	Teacher: Religious and Moral Education	17 Mapledene Road, Scone, Perth PH2 6NX	01738 550270

Name	Dates	Charge / Position	Address	Telephone
Munro, Gillian (Miss) BSc BD	1989 2003	Head of Department of Spiritual Care, NHS Tayside		
Pattison, Kenneth J. MA BD STM	1967 2004	(Kilmuir and Logie Easter)	Royal Dundee Liff Hospital, Liff, Dundee DD2 5ND	01382 423116
Reid, David T. BA BD	1954 1993	(Cleish with Fossoway: St Serf's and Devonside)	2 Castle Way, St Madoes, Glencarse, Perth PH2 7NY	01738 860340
Robertson, Thomas G.M. LTh	1971 2004	(Edenshead and Strathmiglo)	Benarty, Wester Balgedie, Kinross KY13 9HE	01592 840214
Shirra, James MA	1945 1987	(St Martin's with Scone: New)	23 Muirend Avenue, Perth PH1 1JL	01738 624432
Simpson, James A. BSc BD STM DD	1960 2000	(Dornoch Cathedral)	'Dornoch', Perth Road, Bankfoot, Perth PH1 4ED [E-mail: dr.j.simpson@btinternet.com]	01738 812610 01738 787710
Sloan, Robert P. MA BD	1968 2007	(Braemar and Crathie)	1 Broomhill Avenue, Perth PH1 1EN [E-mail: sloans1@btinternet.com]	01738 443904
Stenhouse, W. Duncan MA BD	1989 2006	(Dunbarney and Forgandenny)	32 Sandport Gait, Kinross KY13 8FB [E-mail: duncan.stenhouse@btinternet.com]	01577 866992
Stewart, Anne E. (Mrs) BD CertMin	1998	Prison Chaplain	35 Rose Crescent, Perth PH1 1NT [E-mail: jahare06@tiscali.co.uk]	01738 624167
Stewart, Gordon G. MA	1961 2000	(Perth: St Leonard's-in-the-Fields and Trinity)	'Balnoe', South Street, Rattray, Blairgowrie PH10 7BZ	01250 870626
Stewart, Robin J. MA BD STM	1959 1995	(Orwell with Portmoak)	Oakbrae, Perth Road, Murthly, Perth PH1 4HF	01738 710220
Tait, Henry A.G. MA BD	1966 1997	(Crieff: South and Monzievaird)	14 Shieling Hill Place, Crieff PH7 4ER	01764 652325
Taylor, A.H.S. MA BA BD	1957 1992	(Brydekirk with Hoddam)	41 Anderson Drive, Perth PH1 1LF	01738 626579
Thomson, Peter D. MA BD	1968 2004	(Comrie with Dundurn)	34 Queen Street, Perth PH2 0EJ [E-mail: revpdt@the-manse.freeserve.co.uk]	01738 622418

PERTH ADDRESSES

Craigie	Abbot Street	
Kinnoull	Dundee Rd near Queen's Bridge	
Letham St Mark's	Rannoch Road	
Moncreiffe	Glenbruar Crescent	
North	Mill Street near Kinnoull Street	
Riverside	Bute Drive	
St John's	St John's Street	
St Leonard's-in-the-Fields and Trinity	Marshall Place	
St Matthew's	Tay Street	

(29) DUNDEE

Meets at Dundee, Meadowside St Paul's Church Halls, Nethergate, on the second Wednesday of February, March, May, September, October, November and December; and on the fourth Wednesday of June.

Clerk:	REV. JAMES L. WILSON BD CPS	[E-mail: dundee@cofscotland.org.uk] [E-mail: r3vjw@aol.com]	01382 459249 (Home) 07885 618659 (Mobile) 01382 503012
Presbytery Office:	Whitfield Parish Church, Haddington Crescent, Dundee DD4 0NA	

Abernyte linked with Inchture and Kinnaird linked with Longforgan (H)

Ian McIlroy BSS BD | 1996 2006 | The Manse, Longforgan, Dundee DD2 5EU | 01382 360238
[E-mail: ian.mcilroy@dundeepresbytery.org.uk]

Auchterhouse (H) linked with Murroes and Tealing (T)
David A. Collins BSc BD   1993 2006   New Kirk Manse, 25 Ballinard Gardens, Broughty Ferry, Dundee DD5 1BZ   01382 778874
[E-mail: david.collins@dundeepresbytery.org.uk]

Dundee: Balgay (H)
George K. Robson LTh DPS BA   1983 1987   150 City Road, Dundee DD2 2PW   01382 668806
[E-mail: george.robson@dundeepresbytery.org.uk]

Dundee: Barnhill St Margaret's (H)
Fraser M.C. Stewart BSc BD   1980 2000   The Manse, Invermark Terrace, Broughty Ferry, Dundee DD5 2QU   01382 779278

Dundee: Broughty Ferry New Kirk (H)
Catherine E.E. Collins (Mrs) MA BD   1993 2006   New Kirk Manse, 25 Ballinard Gardens, Broughty Ferry, Dundee DD5 1BZ   01382 778874
[E-mail: catherine.collins@dundeepresbytery.org.uk]

Dundee: Broughty Ferry St James' (H)
Alberto A. de Paula BD MTh   1991 2005   2 Ferry Road, Monifieth, Dundee DD5 4NT   01382 534468
[E-mail: alberto.depaula@dundeepresbytery.org.uk]

Dundee: Broughty Ferry St Luke's and Queen Street
C. Graham Taylor BSc BD FIAB   2001   22 Albert Road, Broughty Ferry, Dundee DD5 1AZ   01382 779212
[E-mail: graham.taylor@dundeepresbytery.org.uk]

Dundee: Broughty Ferry St Stephen's and West (H)
John U. Cameron BA BSc PhD BD ThD   1974   33 Camperdown Street, Broughty Ferry, Dundee DD5 3AA   01382 477403

Dundee: Camperdown (H) (01382 623958)
Vacant   Camperdown Manse, Myrekirk Road, Dundee DD2 4SF   01382 621383

Dundee: Chalmers Ardler (H)
Kenneth D. Stott MA BD   1989 1997   The Manse, Turnberry Avenue, Dundee DD2 3TP   01382 827439
[E-mail: arkstotts@aol.com]
Jane Martin (Miss) DCS   16 Wentworth Road, Ardler, Dundee DD2 8SD   01382 813786

Dundee: Clepington and Fairmuir
Vacant   9 Abercorn Street, Dundee DD4 7HY   01382 458314

Dundee: Craigiebank (H) (01382 731173) linked with Dundee: Douglas and Mid Craigie
Vacant   244 Arbroath Road, Dundee DD4 7SB   01382 452337
Edith F. McMillan (Mrs) MA BD (Assoc)   1981 1999   19 Americanmuir Road, Dundee DD3 9AA   01382 812423
Jeannie Allan (Mrs) DCS   2005   12C Hindmarsh Avenue, Dundee DD3 7LW   01382 827299

Dundee: Douglas and Mid Craigie See Dundee: Craigiebank

Dundee: Downfield South (H) (01382 810624)			
Lezley J. Kennedy BD ThM MTh	2000	15 Elgin Street, Dundee DD3 8NL [E-mail: lezley.kennedy@dundeepresbytery.org.uk]	01382 889498
Dundee: Dundee (St Mary's) (H) (01382 226271)			
Keith F. Hall MA BD	1980 1994	33 Strathern Road, West Ferry, Dundee DD5 1PP	01382 778808
Dundee: Lochee (H)			
Hazel Wilson (Ms) MA BD DipEd DMS	1991 2006	32 Clayhills Drive, Dundee DD2 1SX [E-mail: hazel.wilson@dundeepresbytery.org.uk]	01382 561989
(New charge formed by the union of Dundee: Lochee Old and St Luke's with Dundee: Lochee West)			
Dundee: Logie and St John's Cross (H)			
David S. Scott MA BD	1987 1999	7 Hyndford Street, Dundee DD2 1HQ [E-mail: david.scott@dundeepresbytery.org.uk]	01382 641572
Dundee: Mains (H) (01382 812166)			
John M. Pickering BSc BD DipEd	1997 2004	9 Elgin Street, Dundee DD3 8NL	01382 827207
Dundee: Mains of Fintry (01382 508191)			
Colin M. Brough BSc BD	1998 2002	4 Clive Street, Dundee DD4 7AW [E-mail: colin.brough@dundeepresbytery.org.uk]	01382 458629
Dundee: Meadowside St Paul's (H) (01382 225420)			
Maudeen I. MacDougall (Miss) BA BD	1978 1984	36 Blackness Avenue, Dundee DD2 1HH	01382 668828
Dundee: Menzieshill			
Harry J. Brown LTh	1991 1996	The Manse, Charleston Drive, Dundee DD2 4ED [E-mail: harrybrown@aol.com]	01382 667446
David Sutherland (Aux)		6 Cromarty Drive, Dundee DD2 2UQ [E-mail: dave.sutherland@dundeepresbytery.org.uk]	01382 621473
Dundee: St Andrew's (H) (01382 224860)			
Ian D. Petrie MA BD	1970 1986	77 Blackness Avenue, Dundee DD2 1JN	01382 641695
Dundee: St David's High Kirk (H)			
Vacant		6 Adelaide Place, Dundee DD3 6LF	01382 322955
Dundee: Steeple (H) (01382 223880)			
David M. Clark MA BD	1989 2000	128 Arbroath Road, Dundee DD4 7HR	01382 455411
Dundee: Stobswell (H)			
Vacant		23 Shamrock Street, Dundee DD4 7AH	01382 459119

Dundee: Strathmartine (H) (01382 825817)				
Stewart McMillan BD	1983	1990	19 Americanmuir Road, Dundee DD3 9AA	01382 812423
Dundee: Trinity (H) (01382 459997)				
Vacant			5 Castlewood Avenue, Emmock Woods, The Barns of Claverhouse, Dundee DD4 9FP	01382 501334
Dundee: West				
Andrew T. Greaves BD	1985	2000	Manse of Dundee West Church, Wards of Keithock, by Brechin DD9 7PZ [E-mail: andrew.greaves@dundeepresbytery.org.uk]	01356 624479
Dundee: Whitfield (E) (H) (01382 503012) (New Charge Development)				
James L. Wilson BD CPS	1986	2001	53 Old Craigie Road, Dundee DD4 7JD [E-mail: r3vjw@aol.com]	01382 459249
Fowlis and Liff linked with Lundie and Muirhead of Liff (H)				
Donna M. Hays (Mrs) MTheol DipEd DipTMHA		2004	149 Coupar Angus Road, Muirhead of Liff, Dundee DD2 5QN [E-mail: dmhays32@aol.com]	01382 580210
Inchture and Kinnaird See Abernyte				
Invergowrie (H)				
Robert J. Ramsay LLB NP BD	1986	1997	2 Boniface Place, Invergowrie, Dundee DD2 5DW [E-mail: robert.ramsay@dundeepresbytery.org.uk]	01382 561118
Longforgan See Abernyte				
Lundie and Muirhead of Liff See Fowlis and Liff				
Monifieth: Panmure (H)				
David B. Jamieson MA BD STM	1974		8A Albert Street, Monifieth, Dundee DD5 4JS	01382 532772
Monifieth: St Rule's (H)				
Vacant			Church Street, Monifieth, Dundee DD5 4JP	01382 532607
Monifieth: South				
Donald W. Fraser MA	1958	1959	Queen Street, Monifieth, Dundee DD5 4HG	01382 532646
Monikie and Newbigging				
Vacant			59B Broomwell Gardens, Monikie, Dundee DD5 3QP	01382 370200
Murroes and Tealing See Auchterhouse				

Name	Ordained	Inducted	Position/Charge	Address	Tel
Barrett, Leslie M. BD FRICS	1991	2001	Chaplain: University of Abertay, Dundee	Dunelm Cottage, Logie, Cupar KY15 4SJ [E-mail: l.barrett@abertay.ac.uk]	01334 870396
Campbell, Gordon MA BD CDipAF DipHSM MCMI MIHM AFRIN FRSGS FRGS FSAScot				2 Falkland Place, Kingoodie, Invergowrie, Dundee DD2 5DY [E-mail: gordon.campbell@dundeepresbytery.org.uk]	01382 561383
Clarkson, Robert G.	1950	1989	Auxiliary Minister: Chaplain: University of Dundee (Dundee: Strathmartine)	320 Strathmartine Road, Dundee DD3 8QG [E-mail: rob.gov@virgin.net]	01382 825380
Craik, Sheila (Mrs) BD	1989	2001	(Dundee: Camperdown)	35 Haldane Terrace, Dundee DD3 0HT	01382 802078
Cramb, Erik M. LTh	1973	1989	(Industrial Mission Organiser)	Flat 35, Braehead, Methven Walk, Dundee DD2 3FJ [E-mail: erikcramb@aol.com]	01382 526196
Donald, Robert M. LTh BA	1969	2005	(Kilmodan and Colintraive)	2 Blacklaw Drive, Birkhill, Dundee DD2 5RJ [E-mail: robandmoiradonald@yahoo.com]	01382 581337
Douglas, Fiona C. (Miss) MA BD PhD	1989	1997	Chaplain: University of Dundee	10 Springfield, Dundee DD1 4JE	01382 344157
Ferguson, John F. MA BD	1987	2001	(Perth: Kinnoull)	10 Glamis Crescent, Inchture, Perth PH14 9QU	0828 687881
Gammack, George BD	1985	1999	(Dundee: Whitfield)	13A Hill Street, Broughty Ferry, Dundee DD5 2JP	01382 778636
Hawdon, John E. BA MTh AICS	1961	1995	(Dundee: Clepington)	53 Hillside Road, Dundee DD2 1QT [E-mail: john.hawdon@dundeepresbytery.org.uk]	01382 646212
Hudson, J. Harrison DipTh MA BD	1961	1999	(Dundee: St Peter's McCheyne)	22 Hamilton Avenue, Tayport DD6 9BW	01382 552052
Ingram, J.R.	1954	1978	(Chaplain: RAF)	48 Marlee Road, Broughty Ferry, Dundee DD5 3EX	01382 736400
Kay, Elizabeth (Miss) DipYCS	1993	2007	(Auxiliary Minister)	1 Kintail Walk, Inchture, Perth PH14 9RY [E-mail: lizkay@clara.co.uk]	0828 686029
Laidlaw, John J. MA	1964	1973	(Adviser in Religious Education)	14 Dalhousie Road, Barnhill, Dundee DD5 2SQ	01382 477458
McLeod, David C. BSc MEng BD	1969	2001	(Dundee: Fairmuir)	6 Carseview Gardens, Dundee DD2 1NE [E-mail: david@mcleod6098.freeserve.co.uk]	01382 641371
McMillan, Charles D. LTh	1979	2004	(Elgin: High)	11 Troon Terrace, The Orchard, Ardler, Dundee DD2 3FX	01382 831358
Mair, Michael V.A. MA BD	1967	2007	(Craigiebank with Dundee: Douglas and Mid Craigie)	6 Emmockwoods Drive, Dundee DD4 9FD	01382 502114
Malvenan, Dorothy DCS	1964	1990	The Deaf Association, Dundee	Flat 19, 6 Craigie Street, Dundee DD4 6PF	01382 462495
Miller, Charles W. MA	1953	1994	(Fowlis and Liff)	'Palm Springs', Parkside, Auchterhouse, Dundee DD3 0RF	01382 320407
Milroy, Tom	1960	1992	(Monifieth: St Rule's)	9 Long Row, Westhaven, Carnoustie DD7 6BE	01241 856654
Mitchell, Jack MA BD CTh	1987	1996	(Dundee: Menzieshill)	10 Invergowrie Drive, Dundee DD2 1RF	01382 642301
Mowat, Gilbert M. MA	1948	1986	(Dundee: Albany-Butterburn)	7 Dunmore Gardens, Dundee DD2 1PP	01382 566013
Powrie, James E. LTh	1969	1995	(Dundee: Chalmers Ardler)	3 Kirktonhill Road, Kirriemuir DD8 4HU	01575 572503
Quigley, Barbara D. (Mrs) MTheol ThM DPS	1979		Religious Education Teacher	7 Albany Terrace, Dundee DD3 6HQ	01382 223059
Rae, Robert LTh	1968	1983	Chaplain: Dundee Acute Hospitals	14 Neddertoun View, Liff, Dundee DD3 5RU	01382 581790
Robertson, Thomas P.	1963	2001	(Dundee: Broughty Ferry St James')	4 Blair Gardens, Balgillo Park, Broughty Ferry DD5 3BQ [E-mail: tom.robertson@dundeepresbytery.org.uk]	01382 778229
Rogers, James M. BA DB DCult	1955	1996	(Gibraltar)	24 Mansion Drive, Dalclaverhouse, Dundee DD4 9DD	01382 506162
Roy, James A. MA BD	1965	2006	(Dundee: Lochee West)	'Beechwood', 7 Northview Terrace, Wormit, Newport-on-Tay DD6 8PP [E-mail: j.roy@btinternet.com]	01382 543578
Scroggie, John C.	1951	1985	(Mains)	23 Cliffburn Gardens, Broughty Ferry, Dundee DD5 3NB	01382 739354
Scoular, Stanley	1963	2000	(Rosyth)	31 Duns Crescent, Dundee DD4 0RY	01382 501653
Simpson, James H. BSc	1996	2005	(Auxiliary Minister)	11 Claypotts Place, Broughty Ferry, Dundee DD5 1LG	01382 776520
Smith, Lilian MA DCS			(Deaconess)	6 Fintry Mains, Dundee DD4 9HF	01382 500052
Strickland, Alexander LTh	1971	2005	(Dairsie with Kemback with Strathkinness)	12 Ballumbie Braes, Dundee DD5 0UN	01382 505551

DUNDEE ADDRESSES

Balgay	200 Lochee Road	
Barnhill St Margaret's	10 Invermark Terrace	
Broughty Ferry		
New Kirk	5 Fort Street	
St James'	5 West Queen Street	
St Luke's and Queen Street	96 Dundee Road	
St Stephen's and West	22 Brownhill Road	
Camperdown	Turnberry Avenue	
Chalmers Ardler		

Clepington and Fairmuir	Isla Street x Main Street/ 329 Clepington Road
Craigiebank	Craigie Avenue at Greendykes Road
Douglas and Mid Craigie	Balbeggie Place/ Longtown Terrace
Downfield South	Haldane Street off Strathmartine Road
Dundee (St Mary's)	Nethergate
Lochee	191 High Street, Lochee
Logie and St John's (Cross)	Shaftesbury Rd x Blackness Ave
Mains	Foot of Old Glamis Road

Mains of Fintry	Fintry Road x Fintry Drive
Meadowside St Paul's	114 Nethergate
Menzieshill	Charleston Drive, Lochee
St Andrew's	2 King Street
St David's High Kirk	119A Kinghorne Road and 273 Strathmore Avenue
Steeple	Nethergate
Stobswell	Top of Albert Street
Strathmartine	513 Strathmartine Road
Trinity	73 Crescent Street
West	130 Perth Road
Whitfield	Haddington Crescent

(30) ANGUS

Meets at Forfar in St Margaret's Church Hall, on the first Tuesday of each month, except June when it meets on the last Tuesday, and January, July and August when there is no meeting.

Clerk: **REV. MATTHEW S. BICKET BD**
Depute Clerk: **MRS HELEN McLEOD MA**
Presbytery Office: **St Margaret's Church, West High Street, Forfar DD8 1BJ   01307 464224**
[E-mail: angus@cofscotland.org.uk]

Aberlemno (H) linked with Guthrie and Rescobie
Brian Ramsay BD DPS MLitt   1980   The Manse, Guthrie, Forfar DD8 2TP   01241 828243

Arbirlot linked with Carmyllie
Ian O. Coltart CA BD   1988   2004   The Manse, Arbirlot, Arbroath DD11 2NX   01241 434479

Arbroath: Knox's (H) linked with Arbroath: St Vigeans (H)
Ian G. Gough MA BD MTh DMin   1974   1990   The Manse, St Vigeans, Arbroath DD11 4RD   01241 873206
[E-mail: ianggough@btinternet.com]

Arbroath: Old and Abbey (H) (Church office: 01241 877068)
Valerie L. Allen (Ms) BMus MDiv   1990   1996   51 Cliffburn Road, Arbroath DD11 5BA   01241 872196 (Tel/Fax)
[E-mail: VL2allen@aol.com]

Arbroath: St Andrew's (H) (E-mail: st_andrews_arbroath@lineone.net)
W. Martin Fair BA BD DMin   1992   92 Grampian Gardens, Arbroath DD11 4AQ   01241 873238 (Tel/Fax)
[E-mail: martinfair@aol.com]

Arbroath: St Vigeans See Arbroath: Knox's

Arbroath: West Kirk (H)
Alasdair G. Graham BD DipMin   1981   1986   1 Charles Avenue, Arbroath DD11 2EY   01241 872244
[E-mail: alasdair.graham@lineone.net]

Barry linked with Carnoustie
Michael S. Goss BD DPS   1991   2003   44 Terrace Road, Carnoustie DD7 7AR   01241 410194 (Tel/Fax)
[E-mail: michaelgoss@blueyonder.co.uk]   07787 141567 (Mbl)

Brechin: Cathedral (H) (Cathedral office: 01356 629360) (Website: www.brechincathedral.org.uk)
Scott Rennie MA BD STM   1999   Chanonry Wynd, Brechin DD9 6JS   01356 622783
[E-mail: scottrennie@tiscali.co.uk]

Brechin: Gardner Memorial (H)
Moira Herkes (Mrs) BD   1985   1999   15 Caldhame Gardens, Brechin DD9 1JJ   01356 622789
[E-mail: mossherkes@aol.com]

Carmyllie See Arbirlot
Carnoustie See Barry

Carnoustie: Panbride (H)
Matthew S. Bicket BD   1989   8 Arbroath Road, Carnoustie DD7 6BL   01241 854478 (Tel)
[E-mail: matthew@bicket.freeserve.co.uk]   01241 855088 (Fax)

Colliston linked with Friockheim Kinnell linked with Inverkeilor and Lunan (H)
Peter A. Phillips BA   1995   2004   18 Middlegate, Friockheim, Arbroath DD11 4TS   01241 828781
[E-mail: peter-rona@revphillips.freeserve.co.uk]

Dun and Hillside
Linda J. Broadley (Mrs) LTh DipEd   1996   2004   4 Manse Road, Hillside, Montrose DD10 9FB   01674 830288

Dunnichen, Letham and Kirkden
Allan F. Webster MA BD   1978   1990   7 Brachead Road, Letham, Forfar DD8 2PG   01307 818916
[E-mail: allanfwebster@aol.com]

Eassie and Nevay linked with Newtyle
Carleen Robertson (Miss) BD   1992   2 Kirkton Road, Newtyle, Blairgowrie PH12 8TS   01828 650461
[E-mail: carleen.robertson@tesco.net]

Edzell Lethnot Glenesk (H) linked with Fern Careston Menmuir
Alan G.N. Watt MTh DipCommEd CQSW   1996   2003   Glenesk Cottage, Dunlappie Road, Edzell, Edzell, Brechin   DD9 7UB   01356 648455
[E-mail: alangnwatt@aol.com]
(Edzell Lethnot and Glenesk have united)

Farnell
Vacant   01674 672060

Fern Careston Menmuir See Edzell Lethnot Glenesk

Forfar: East and Old (H)
Vacant   The Manse, Lour Road, Forfar DD8 2BB   01307 464303

Forfar: Lowson Memorial (H)
Karen Fenwick PhD MPhil BSc BD   2006   1 Jamieson Street, Forfar DD8 2HY   01307 468585
[E-mail: kmfenwick@talktalk.net]

Forfar: St Margaret's (H) (Church office: 01307 464224)
Vacant   15 Potters Park Crescent, Forfar DD8 1HH   01307 466390

Friockheim Kinnell See Colliston

Glamis (H), Inverarity and Kinnettles
John F. Davidson BSc DipEdTech   1970   2005   12 Turfbeg Road, Forfar DD8 3LT   01307 466038
[E-mail: jfraserdavid@tiscali.co.uk]

Guthrie and Rescobie See Aberlemno

Inchbrayock linked with Montrose: Melville South
David S. Dixon MA BD   1976   1994   The Manse, Ferryden, Montrose DD10 9SD   01674 672108
[E-mail: david@inchbrayock.wanadoo.co.uk]

Inverkeilor and Lunan See Colliston

Kirriemuir: St Andrew's (H) linked with Oathlaw Tannadice
David J. Taverner MCIBS ACIS BD   1996   2002   26 Quarry Park, Kirriemuir DD8 4DR   01575 575561
[E-mail: rahereuk@hotmail.com]

Montrose: Melville South See Inchbrayock

Montrose: Old and St Andrew's
Vacant   2 Rosehill Road, Montrose DD10 8ST   01674 672447

238 Presbytery of ANGUS (30)

Newtyle See Eassie and Nevay
Oathlaw Tannadice See Kirriemuir: St Andrew's

The Glens and Kirriemuir: Old (H) (Church office: 01575 572819) (Website: www.gkopc.co.uk)

Malcolm I.G. Rooney DPE BEd BD	1993	1999	20 Strathmore Avenue, Kirriemuir DD8 4DJ [E-mail: malcolm@gkopc.co.uk]	01575 573724 / 07909 993233 (Mbl)
Linda Stevens (Mrs) BSc BD (Team Minister)		2006	17 North Latch Road, Brechin DD9 6LE [E-mail: Linda@gkopc.co.uk]	01356 623415 / 07701 052552 (Mbl)

The Isla Parishes

Ben Pieterse BA BTh LTh	2001	Balduff House, Kilry, Blairgowrie PH11 8HS [E-mail: benhp1@gmail.com]	01575 560260

Name			(Former charge)	Address	Phone
Anderson, James W. BSc MTh	1986	1997	(Kincardine O'Neil with Lumphanan)	47 Glebe Road, Arbroath DD11 4HJ	01674 672029
Anderson, John F. MA BD FSAScot	1966	2006	(Aberdeen: Mannofield)	8 Eider Close, Montrose DD10 9NE [E-mail: jfa941@aol.com]	
Brodie, James BEM MA BD STM	1955	1974	(Hurlford)	25A Keptie Road, Arbroath DD11 3ED	01241 873298
Butters, David	1964	1998	(Turriff: St Ninian's and Forglen)	68A Millgate, Friockheim, Arbroath DD11 4TN	01241 828030
Douglas, Iain M. MA BD MPhil DipEd	1960	2002	(Farnell with Montrose: St Andrew's)	Old School House, Kinnell, Friockheim, Arbroath DD11 4UL	01241 828717
Drysdale James P.R.	1967	1999	(Brechin: Gardner Memorial)	51 Airlie Street, Brechin DD9 6JX	01356 625201
Duncan, Robert F. MTheol	1986	2001	(Lochgelly: St Andrew's)	25 Rowan Avenue, Kirriemuir DD8 4TB	01575 573973
Finlay, Quintin BA BD	1975	1996	(North Bute)	Ivy Cottage, Greenlees Farm, Kelso TD5 8BT	
Hodge, William N.T.	1966	1995	(Longside)	'Tullochgorum', 61 South Street, Forfar DD8 2BS	01307 461944
Jones, William	1952	1987	(Kirriemuir: St Andrew's)	14 Muir Street, Forfar DD8 3JY	01307 463193
Milton, Eric G. RD	1963	1994	(Blairdaff)	16 Bruce Court, Links Parade, Carnoustie DD7 7JE	01241 854928
Norrie, Graham MA BD	1967	2007	(Forfar: East and Old)	'Novar', 14A Wyllie Street, Forfar DD8 3DN	01307 818741
Perry, Joseph B.	1955	1989	(Farnell)	19 Guthrie Street, Letham, Forfar DD8 2PS	01307 818416
Reid, Albert B. BD BSc	1996	2001	(Ardler, Kettins and Meigle)	1 Dundee Street, Letham, Forfar DD8 2PQ	
Robertson, George R. LTh	1985	2004	(Udny and Pitmedden)	3 Slateford Gardens, Edzell, Brechin DD9 7SX [E-mail: george.robertson@tesco.net]	01356 647322
Searle, David C. MA DipTh	1965	2003	(Warden: Rutherford House)	12 Cairnie Road, Arbroath DD11 3DY	01241 872794
Smith, Hamish G.	1965	1993	(Auchterless with Rothienorman)	11A Guthrie Street, Letham, Forfar DD8 2PS	01307 818973
Thomas, Martyn R.H. CEng MIStructE	1987	2002	(Fowlis and Liff with Lundie and Muirhead of Liff)	14 Kirkgait, Letham, Forfar DD8 2XQ	01307 818084
Thomas, Shirley (Mrs) (Aux)	2000	2006	(Auxiliary Minister)	14 Kirkgait, Letham, Forfar DD8 2XQ	01307 818084
Tyre, Robert	1960	1998	(Aberdeen: St Ninian's with Stockethill)	8 Borrowfield Crescent, Montrose DD10 9BR	01674 676961
Warnock, Denis MA	1952	1990	(Kirkcaldy: Torbain)	19 Keptie Road, Arbroath DD11 3ED	01241 872740
Williamson, Tom MA BD	1941	1982	(Dyke with Edinkillie)	Storyville Residential Home, Beechwood Place, Kirriemuir DD8 5DZ	
Youngson, Peter	1961	1996	(Kirriemuir: St Andrew's)	Coreen, Woodside, Northmuir, Kirriemuir DD8 4PG	01575 572832

ANGUS ADDRESSES

Arbroath
Knox's — Howard Street
Old and Abbey — West Abbey Street
St Andrew's — Hamilton Green
West Kirk — Keptie Street

Brechin
Cathedral — Bishops Close
Gardner Memorial — South Esk Street

Carnoustie
Panbride — Dundee Street
  Arbroath Road

Forfar
East and Old — East High Street
Lowson Memorial — Jamieson Street
St Margaret's — West High Street

Kirriemuir
Old — High Street
St Andrew's — Glamis Road

Montrose
Melville South — Castle Street
Old and St Andrew's — High Street

(31) ABERDEEN

Meets at Queen's Cross Church, Albyn Place, Aberdeen AB10 1UN, on the first Tuesday of February, March, April, May, September, October, November and December; and on the fourth Tuesday of June.

Clerk:	REV. IAN A. McLEAN BSc BD DMin	
Presbytery Office:	Mastrick Church, Greenfern Road, Aberdeen AB16 6TR [E-mail: aberdeen@cofscotland.org.uk]	**01224 690494**
Hon. Treasurer:	MR A. SHARP	
	27 Hutchison Terrace, Aberdeen AB10 7NN	**01224 315702**

Aberdeen: Bridge of Don Oldmachar (01224 709299) (Website: www.oldmacharchurch.org)

Jim Ritchie BD MTh	2000	2004	60 Newburgh Circle, Aberdeen AB22 8QZ [E-mail: jim.ritchie@btopenworld.com]	01224 708137

Aberdeen: Cove (E)

David Swan BVMS BD	2005		4 Charleston Way, Cove, Aberdeen AB12 3FA [E-mail: david@covechurch.org.uk]	01224 899933
Mark Johnston BSc BD DipMin (Assoc)	1998	2003	5 Bruce Walk, Redmoss, Aberdeen AB12 3LX [E-mail: mark@covechurch.org.uk]	01224 874269

Aberdeen: Craigiebuckler (H) (01224 315649)

Kenneth L. Petrie MA BD	1984	1999	185 Springfield Road, Aberdeen AB15 8AA [E-mail: patandkenneth@aol.com]	01224 315125

Aberdeen: Ferryhill (H) (01224 213093)

John H.A. Dick MA MSc BD	1982		54 Polmuir Road, Aberdeen AB11 7RT [E-mail: jhadick01@talktalk.net]	01224 586933

Aberdeen: Garthdee (H)
Vacant — 27 Ramsay Gardens, Aberdeen AB10 7AE — 01224 317452

Aberdeen: Gilcomston South (H) (01224 647144)
D. Dominic Smart BSc BD MTh — 1988 — 37 Richmondhill Road, Aberdeen AB15 5EQ [E-mail: smartdd@btconnect.com] — 01224 314326

Aberdeen: High Hilton (H) (01224 494717)
A. Peter Dickson BSc BD — 1996 — 24 Rosehill Drive, Aberdeen AB24 4JJ [E-mail: peter@highhilton.com] — 01224 484155

Aberdeen: Holburn West (H) (01224 571120)
Duncan C. Eddie MA BD — 1992 1999 — 31 Cranford Road, Aberdeen AB10 7NJ [E-mail: nacnud@ceddie.freeserve.co.uk] — 01224 325873

Aberdeen: Mannofield (H) (01224 310087) (E-mail: mannofieldchurch@xalt.co.uk)
Keith T. Blackwood BD DipMin — 1997 2007 — 21 Forest Avenue, Aberdeen AB15 4TU [E-mail: k2blackwood@btinternet.com] — 01224 315748

Aberdeen: Mastrick (H) (01224 694121)
Lesley P. Risby (Mrs) BD — 1994 2005 — 8 Corse Wynd, Kingswells, Aberdeen AB15 8TP [E-mail: mrsrisby@hotmail.com] — 01224 749346
Benjamin D.W. Byun BA MDiv MTh PhD (Parish Assistant) — 2 Eastside Gardens, Bucksburn, Aberdeen AB21 9SN [E-mail: benjamin@byun1.fsnet.co.uk] — 01224 710274

Aberdeen: Middlefield (H)
This charge is to be served by two ministers, each of whom will serve on the basis of a 50 per cent time commitment. One appointment has been made; a second is awaited.
Elspeth Harley BA MTh — 1991 2007 — 8 Donmouth Road, Aberdeen AB23 8DT [E-mail: eharley@hotmail.co.uk] — 01224 703017
Vacant
Michael Phillippo MTh BSc BVetMed MRCVS (Aux) — 25 Deeside Crescent, Aberdeen AB15 7PT — 01224 318317

Aberdeen: Midstocket
Marian Cowie MA BD MTh — 1990 2006 — 54 Woodstock Road, Aberdeen AB15 5JF [E-mail: mcowieou@aol.com] — 01224 208001

Aberdeen: New Stockethill (New Charge Development)
Ian M. Aitken MA BD — 1999 — 52 Ashgrove Road West, Aberdeen AB16 5EE [E-mail: ncdstockethill@uk.uumail.com] — 01224 686929

Congregation	Minister	Ord.	Ind.	Address	Tel
Aberdeen: Northfield	Scott C. Guy BD	1989	1999	28 Byron Crescent, Aberdeen AB16 7EX [E-mail: scott.guy@surefish.co.uk]	01224 692332
Aberdeen: Queen Street	Vacant			51 Osborne Place, Aberdeen AB25 2BX	01224 646429
Aberdeen: Queen's Cross (H) (01224 644742)	Robert F. Brown MA BD ThM	1971	1984	1 St Swithin Street, Aberdeen AB10 6XH [E-mail: minister@queenscrosschurch.org.uk]	01224 322549
Aberdeen: Rubislaw (H) (01224 645477)	Andrew G.N. Wilson MA BD DMin	1977	1987	45 Rubislaw Den South, Aberdeen AB15 4BD [E-mail: agn.wilson@virgin.net]	01224 314878
Aberdeen: Ruthrieston West (H)	Sean Swindells BD DipMin	1996		451 Great Western Road, Aberdeen AB10 6NL [E-mail: seanswinl@aol.com]	01224 313075
Aberdeen: St Columba's Bridge of Don (H) (01224 825653)	Louis Kinsey BD DipMin	1991		151 Jesmond Avenue, Aberdeen AB22 8UG [E-mail: louis@stcolumbaschurch.org.uk]	01224 705337
Aberdeen: St George's Tillydrone (H) (01224 482204)	James Weir BD	1991	2003	127 Clifton Road, Aberdeen AB24 4RH [E-mail: rjimw@sky.com]	01224 483976
	Ann V. Lundie (Miss) DCS			20 Langdykes Drive, Cove, Aberdeen AB12 3HW	01224 898416
Aberdeen: St John's Church for Deaf People (H) (01224 494566)	John R. Osbeck BD	1979	1991	15 Deeside Crescent, Aberdeen AB15 7PT [E-mail: info@aneds.org.uk]	(Voice/Text) 01224 315595
Aberdeen: St Machar's Cathedral (H) (01224 485988)	Alan D. Falconer MA BD DLitt			18 The Chanonry, Old Aberdeen AB24 1RQ [E-mail: minister@stmachar.com]	01224 483688
Aberdeen: St Mark's (H) (01224 640672)	John M. Watson LTh	1989		65 Mile-end Avenue, Aberdeen AB15 5PU [E-mail: drjohn@johnmutchwatson.wanadoo.co.uk]	01224 622470
Aberdeen: St Mary's (H) (01224 487227)	Elsie J. Fortune (Mrs) BSc BD	2003		456 King Street, Aberdeen AB24 3DE	01224 633778
Aberdeen: St Nicholas Kincorth, South of	Edward C. McKenna BD DPS	1989	2002	The Manse, Kincorth Circle, Aberdeen AB12 5NX	01224 872820

Aberdeen: St Nicholas Uniting, Kirk of (H) (01224 643494)
B. Stephen C. Taylor BA BBS MA MDiv   1984   2005
12 Louisville Avenue, Aberdeen AB15 4TX
[E-mail: minister@kirk-of-st-nicholas.org.uk]
01224 314318
01224 649242 (Fax)

Aberdeen: St Stephen's (H) (01224 624443)
James M. Davies BSc BD   1982   1989
6 Belvidere Street, Aberdeen AB25 2QS
[E-mail: daviesjim@btinternet.com]
01224 635694

Aberdeen: South Holburn (H) (01224 211730)
George S. Cowie BSc BD   1991   2006
54 Woodstock Road, Aberdeen AB15 5JF
[E-mail: gscowie@aol.com]
01224 315042

Aberdeen: Summerhill (H) (Website: www.summerhillchurch.org.uk)
Ian A. McLean BSc BD DMin   1981
36 Stronsay Drive, Aberdeen AB15 6JL
[E-mail: iamclean@lineone.net]
01224 324669

Aberdeen: Torry St Fittick's (H) (01224 899183)
Iain C. Barclay   1976   1999
MBE TD MA BD MTh MPhil PhD
11 Devanha Gardens East, Aberdeen AB11 7UH
[E-mail: i.c.barclay@virgin.net]
01224 588245
07968 131930 (Mbl)
07625 383830 (Pager)

Aberdeen: Woodside (H) (01224 277249)
Markus Auffermann DipTheol   1999   2006
322 Clifton Road, Aberdeen AB24 4HQ
[E-mail: mauffermann@yahoo.com]
01224 484562
Ann V. Lundie DCS
20 Langdykes Drive, Cove, Aberdeen AB12 3HW
01224 898416

Bucksburn Stoneywood (H) (01224 712411)
Nigel Parker BD MTh DMin   1994
25 Gilbert Road, Bucksburn, Aberdeen AB21 9AN
[E-mail: nigel@revparker.fsnet.co.uk]
01224 712635

Cults (H)
Ewen J. Gilchrist BD DipMin DipComm   1982   2005
1 Cairnlee Terrace, Bieldside, Aberdeen AB15 9AE
[E-mail: hobgoblins@kincarrathie.fsnet.co.uk]
01224 861692

Dyce (H) (01224 771295)
Russel Moffat BD MTh PhD   1986   1998
144 Victoria Street, Dyce, Aberdeen AB21 7BE
01224 722380

Kingswells
Dolly Purnell BD   2003   2004
Kingswells Manse, Lang Stracht, Aberdeen AB15 8PL
[E-mail: neilanddolly.purnell@btinternet.com]
01224 740229

Newhills (H) (Tel/Fax: 01224 716161)

Hugh M. Wallace MA BD	1980	2007	Newhills Manse, Bucksburn, Aberdeen AB21 9SS [E-mail: revhugh@hotmail.com]	01224 712655

Peterculter (H) (01224 735845)

John A. Ferguson BD DipMin DMin	1988	1999	7 Howie Lane, Peterculter AB14 0LJ [E-mail: jc.ferguson@virgin.net]	01224 735041

Name			Charge/Ministry	Address	Tel.
Aitchison, James W. BD	1993		Chaplain: Army	2 Bn Prince of Wales Royal Regiment, Clive Barracks, Tern Hill, Shropshire TF9 3QE	
Alexander, William M. BD	1971	1998	(Berriedale and Dunbeath with Latheron)	110 Fairview Circle, Danestone, Aberdeen AB22 8YR	01224 703752
Beattie, Walter G. MA BD	1956	1995	(Arbroath: Old and Abbey)	126 Seafield Road, Aberdeen AB15 7YQ	01224 329259
Black, W. Graham MA BD	1983	1999	Urban Prayer Ministry	72 Linksview, Linksfield Road, Aberdeen AB24 5RG [E-mail: graham.black@virgin.net]	01224 492491
Bryden, Agnes Y. (Mrs) DCS	1970	2003	(Deaconess)	Angusfield House, 226 Queen's Road, Aberdeen AB15 8DN	07761 235815
Campbell, W.M.M. BD CPS	1973	1989	(Hospital Chaplain)	43 Murray Terrace, Aberdeen AB11 7SA	01779 841320
Coutts, Fred MA BD	1966	2002	Hospital Chaplain	Ladebank, 1 Manse Place, Hatton, Peterhead AB42 0QU	01224 208341
Crawford, Michael S.M. LTh	1950	1987	(Aberdeen: St Mary's)	9 Craigton Avenue, Aberdeen AB15 7RP	01330 826236
Dickson, John C. MA	1957	1995	(Aberdeen: St Fittick's)	36 Queen Victoria Park, Inchmarlo, Banchory AB31 4AL	01224 311932
Douglas, Andrew M. MA	1982	1991	(High Hilton)	219 Countesswells Road, Aberdeen AB15 7RD	01224 744621
Falconer, James B. BD	1953	1995	Hospital Chaplain	3 Brimmond Walk, Westhill AB32 6XH	01224 321147
Finlayson, Ena (Miss) DCS	1960	1995	(Deaconess)	16E Denwood, Aberdeen AB15 6JF	01224 322503
Goldie, George D. ALCM	1971	2005	(Greyfriars)	27 Broomhill Avenue, Aberdeen AB10 6JL	01224 782703
Gordon, Laurie Y.	1975	2004	(John Knox)	1 Alder Drive, Portlethen, Aberdeen AB12 4WA	01224 648041
Graham, A. David M. BA BD			(Aberdeen: Rosemount)	Elmhill House, 27 Shaw Crescent, Aberdeen AB25 3BT	01224 739824
Grainger, Harvey L. LTh			(Kingswells)	13 St Ronan's Crescent, Peterculter, Aberdeen AB14 0RL [E-mail: harveygrainger@tiscali.co.uk]	07768 333216 (Mbl)
Haddow, Angus BSc	1963	1999	(Methlick)	25 Lerwick Road, Aberdeen AB16 6RF	01224 696362
Hamilton, Helen (Miss) BD	1991	2003	(Glasgow: St James' Pollok)	The Cottage, West Tilbouries, Maryculter, Aberdeen AB12 5GD	01224 739632
Hutchison, A. Scott MA BD DD	1957	1991	(Hospital Chaplain)	Ashfield, Drumoak, Banchory AB31 5AG	01330 811309
Hutchison, Alison M. (Mrs) BD DipMin	1988	1988	Hospital Chaplain	Ashfield, Drumoak, Banchory AB31 5AG [E-mail: amhutch62@aol.com]	01330 811309
Hutchison, David S. BSc BD ThM	1991	1999	(Aberdeen: Torry St Fittick's)	51 Don Street, Aberdeen AB24 1UH	01224 276122
Jack, David LTh	1984	1999	(West Mearns)	7 Cromwell Road, Aberdeen AB15 4UH [E-mail: david@cromwell7.fsnet.co.uk]	01224 325355
Johnstone, William MA BD	1963	2001	(University of Aberdeen)	9/5 Mount Alvernia, Edinburgh EH16 6AW	0131-664 3140
Jolly, Andrew J. BD CertMin	1983	2006	Chaplain to the Oil Industry	Chaplain's Office, Total E and P (UK) PLC, Crawpeel Road, Altens, Aberdeen AB12 3FG	01224 297532/3
Kerr, Hugh F. MA BD	1968	2006	(Aberdeen: Ruthrieston South)	134C Great Western Road, Aberdeen AB10 6QE	01224 580091
McCallum, Moyra (Miss) MA BD DCS			(Deaconess)	176 Hilton Drive, Aberdeen AB24 4LT [E-mail: moymac@aol.com]	01224 486240
Maciver, Norman MA BD DMin	1976	2006	(Newhills)	4 Mundi Crescent, Newmachar, Aberdeen AB21 0LY [E-mail: norirene@aol.com]	01651 869442

Main, Alan TD MA BD STM PhD DD	1963	2001	(University of Aberdeen)	Kirkfield, Barthol Chapel, Inverurie AB51 8TD [E-mail: amain@talktalk.net]	01651 806773
Mirrilees, J.B. MA BD	1937	1977	(High Hilton)	22 King's Gate, Aberdeen AB15 4EJ	01224 638351
Montgomerie, Jean B. (Miss) MA BD	1973	2005	(Forfar: St Margaret's)	12 St Ronan's Place, Peterculter, Aberdeen AB14 0QX [E-mail: revjeanb@tiscali.co.uk]	01224 732350
Richardson, Thomas C. LTh ThB	1971	2004	(Cults: West)	19 Kinkell Road, Aberdeen AB15 8HR [E-mail: thomas.richardson7@btinternet.com]	01224 315328
Rodgers, D. Mark BA BD MTh	1987	2003	Hospital Chaplain	152D Gray Street, Aberdeen AB10 6JW	01224 210810
Sefton, Henry R. MA BD STM PhD	1957	1992	(University of Aberdeen)	25 Albury Place, Aberdeen AB11 6TQ	01224 572305
Skakle, George S. MA	1945	1987	(Aberdeen: Powis)	30 Whitehall Terrace, Aberdeen AB25 2RY	01224 646478
Smith, Angus MA LTh	1965	2006	(Industrial Chaplain)	3/7 West Powburn, West Savile Gait, Edinburgh EH9 3EW	0131-667 1761
Stewart, James C. MA BD STM	1960	2000	(Aberdeen: Kirk of St Nicholas)	54 Murray Terrace, Aberdeen AB11 7SB	01224 587071
Strachan, Ian M. MA BD	1959	1994	(Ashkirk with Selkirk)	'Cardenwell', Glen Drive, Dyce, Aberdeen AB21 7EN	01224 772028
Swinton, John BD PhD	1999		University of Aberdeen	51 Newburgh Circle, Bridge of Don, Aberdeen AB22 8XA [E-mail: j.swinton@abdn.ac.uk]	01224 825637
Torrance, Iain R. TD DPhil DD DTheol LHD CorrFRSE	1982	2005	President: Princeton Theological Seminary	64 Mercer Street, PO Box 552, Princeton, NJ 08542-0803, USA	001 609 497 7800
Watt, William G.	1970	1977	(Aberdeen: South of St Nicholas Kincorth)	Alastrean House, Tarland, Aboyne AB34 4TA	01224 321915
Wilkie, William E. LTh	1978	2001	(Aberdeen: St Nicholas Kincorth, South of)	32 Broomfield Park, Portlethen, Aberdeen AB12 4XT	01224 782052
Wilson, Thomas F. BD	1984	1996	Education	55 Allison Close, Cove, Aberdeen AB12 3WG	01224 873501
Wood, James L.K.	1967	1995	(Ruthrieston West)	1 Glen Drive, Dyce, Aberdeen AB21 7EN	01224 722543

ABERDEEN ADDRESSES

Place	Address	Place	Address	Place	Address
Bridge of Don Oldmachar	Ashwood Park	Kingswells	Old Skene Road, Kingswells	St Machar's	The Chanonry
Cove	Loirston Primary School, Loirston Avenue	Mannofield	Great Western Road x Craigton Road	St Mark's	Rosemount Viaduct
Craigiebuckler	Springfield Road	Mastrick	Greenfern Road	St Mary's	King Street
Cults	Quarry Road, Cults	Middlefield	Manor Avenue	St Nicholas Kincorth, South of	Kincorth Circle
Dyce	Victoria Street, Dyce	Midstocket	Mid Stocket Road	St Nicholas Uniting, South of	Union Street
Ferryhill	Fonthill Road x Polmuir Road	New Stockethill		Kirk of	Powis Place
Garthdee	Ramsay Gardens	Northfield	Byron Crescent	St Stephen's	Holburn Street
Gilcomston South	Union Street x Summer Street	Peterculter	Craigton Crescent	South Holburn	Stronsay Drive
High Hilton	Hilton Drive	Queen Street	Queen Street	Summerhill	Walker Road
Holburn West	Great Western Road	Queen's Cross	Albyn Place	Torry St Fittick's	Church Street, Woodside
		Rubislaw	Queen's Gardens	Woodside	
		Ruthrieston West	Broomhill Road		
		St Columba's	Braehead Way, Bridge of Don		
		St George's	Hayton Road, Tillydrone		
		St John's for the Deaf	Smithfield Road		

(32) KINCARDINE AND DEESIDE

Meets in Birse and Feughside Church, Finzean, Banchory on the first Tuesday of September, October, November, December, March and May, and on the last Tuesday of June at 7pm.

Clerk:	REV. JACK HOLT BSc BD		The Manse, Finzean, Banchory AB31 6PB [E-mail: kincardinedeeside@cofscotland.org.uk]	01330 850339

Aberluthnott linked with Laurencekirk (H)

Ronald Gall BSc BD	1985	2001	Aberdeen Road, Laurencekirk AB30 1AJ [E-mail: ronniegall@aol.com]	01561 378838

Aboyne and Dinnet (H) (01339 886989) linked with Cromar (E-mail: aboynedinnet.cos@virgin.net)

Douglas I. Campbell BD DPS		2004	49 Charlton Crescent, Aboyne AB34 5GN [E-mail: douglas.campbell@btinternet.com]	01339 886447

Arbuthnott and Bervie

Georgina M. Baxendale (Mrs) BD	1981	2006	10 Kirkburn, Inverbervie, Montrose DD10 0RT [E-mail: georgiebaxendale6@tiscali.co.uk]	01561 362633

Banchory-Devenick and Maryculter/Cookney

Bruce K. Gardner MA BD PhD	1988	2002	The Manse, Kirkton of Maryculter, Aberdeen AB12 5FS [E-mail: ministerofbdmc@aol.com]	01224 735776

Banchory-Ternan: East (H) (Tel: 01330 820380) (E-mail: eastchurch@banchory.fsbusiness.co.uk)

Mary M. Haddow (Mrs) BD		2001	East Manse, Station Road, Banchory AB31 5YP [E-mail: mary_haddow@ntlworld.com]	01330 822481
Anthony Stephen MA BD (Assistant Minister and Youth Leader)		2001	72 Grant Road, Banchory AB31 5UU [E-mail: tonys@edgerock.org]	01330 825038

Banchory-Ternan: West (H)

Donald K. Walker BD	1979	1995	2 Wilson Road, Banchory AB31 5UY [E-mail: btw@uk2.net]	01330 822811
Anthony Stephen MA BD (Assistant Minister and Youth Leader)		2001	72 Grant Road, Banchory AB31 5UU [E-mail: tonys@edgerock.org]	01330 825038

Birse and Feughside

Jack Holt BSc BD	1985	1994	The Manse, Finzean, Banchory AB31 6PB [E-mail: jholt@finzeanmanse.wanadoo.co.uk]	01330 850237

Braemar and Crathie
Kenneth I. Mackenzie BD CPS — 1990 — 2005 — Manse, Crathie, Ballater AB35 5UL [E-mail: crathiemanse@tiscali.co.uk] — 01339 742208

Cromar See Aboyne and Dinnet

Drumoak (H) and Durris (H)
James Scott MA BD — 1973 — 1992 — Manse, Durris, Banchory AB31 6BU [E-mail: jimscott73@yahoo.co.uk] — 01330 844557

Glenmuick (Ballater) (H)
Anthony Watts BD DipTechEd JP — 1999 — The Manse, Craigendarroch Walk, Ballater AB35 5ZB [E-mail: tony.watts6@btinternet.com] — 01339 754014

Kinneff linked with Stonehaven: South (H)
David J. Stewart BD MTh DipMin — 2000 — South Church Manse, Cameron Street, Stonehaven AB39 2HE [E-mail: brigodon@clara.co.uk] — 01569 762576

Laurencekirk See Aberluthnott

Mearns Coastal
George I. Hastie MA BD — 1971 — 1998 — The Manse, Kirkton, St Cyrus, Montrose DD10 0BW — 01674 850880 (Tel/Fax)

Mid Deeside
Norman Nicoll BD — 2003 — The Manse, Torphins, Banchory AB31 4GQ — 01339 882276

Newtonhill
Hugh Conkey BSc BD — 1987 — 2001 — 39 St Ternans Road, Newtonhill, Stonehaven AB39 3PF [E-mail: hugh@conkey.plus.com] — 01569 730143

Portlethen (H) (01224 782883)
Flora J. Munro (Mrs) BD DMin — 1993 — 2004 — 18 Rowanbank Road, Portlethen, Aberdeen AB12 4QY [E-mail: floramunro@aol.co.uk] — 01224 780211

Stonehaven: Dunnottar (H)
Vacant — Dunnottar Manse, Stonehaven AB39 3XL — 01569 762874

Stonehaven: Fetteresso (H) (Tel: 01569 767689) (E-mail: office@fetteressokirk.org.uk)
John R. Notman BSc BD — 1990 — 2001 — 11 South Lodge Drive, Stonehaven AB39 2PN [E-mail: notman@clara.co.uk] — 01569 762876

Stonehaven: South See Kinneff

West Mearns

Catherine A. Hepburn (Miss) BA BD	1982	2000	West Mearns Parish Church Manse, Fettercairn, Laurencekirk AB30 1UE [E-mail: chepburn@fish.co.uk]	01561 340203

Brown, J.W.S. BTh	1960	1995	(Cromar)	10 Forestside Road, Banchory AB31 5ZH	01330 824353
Christie, Andrew C. LTh	1975	2000	(Banchory-Devenick and Maryculter/Cookney)	17 Broadstraik Close, Elrick, Aberdeen AB32 6JP	01224 746888
Forbes, John W.A. BD	1973	1999	(Edzell Lethnot with Fern, Careston and Menmuir with Glenesk)		
Gray, Robert MA BD	1942	1982	(Stonehaven: Fetteresso)	Mid Clune, Finzean, Banchory AB31 6PL	01330 850283
Kinmiburgh, Elizabeth B.F. (Miss) MA BD	1970	1986	(Birse with Finzean with Strachan)	4 Park Drive, Stonehaven AB39 2NW 7 Huntly Cottages, Aboyne AB31 5HD	01569 767027 01339 886757
Lamb, A. Douglas MA	1964	2002	(Dalry: St Margaret's)	130 Denstrath Road, Edzell Woods, Brechin DD9 7XF [E-mail: lamb.edzell@talk21.com]	01356 648139
Massie, Robert W. LTh	1989	2007	(Monifieth: St Rule's)	73 Boswell Road, Portlethen, Aberdeen AB12 4BA [E-mail: revrwm@lineone.net]	
Nicholson, William	1949	1986	(Banchory-Ternan: East with Durris)	10 Pantoch Gardens, Banchory AB31 5ZD	01330 823875
Rennie, Donald B. MA	1956	1996	(Industrial Chaplain)	Mernis Howe, Inverurie Street, Auchenblae, Laurencekirk AB30 1XS	01561 320622
Smith, Albert E. BD	1983	2006	(Methlick)	42 Haulkerton Crescent, Laurencekirk AB30 1FB [E-mail: aesmethlick@aol.com]	01561 376111
Taylor, Peter R. JP BD	1977	2001	(Torphins)	42 Beltie Road, Torphins, Banchory AB31 4JT	01339 882780
Tierney, John P. MA	1945	1985	(Peterhead West Associate)	3 Queenshill Drive, Aboyne AB34 5DG	01339 886741
Watt, William D. LTh	1978	1996	(Aboyne – Dinnet)	2 West Toll Crescent, Aboyne AB34 5GB	01339 886943

(33) GORDON

Meets at various locations on the first Tuesday of February, March, April, May, September, October, November and December, and on the fourth Tuesday of June.

Clerk:	REV. G. EUAN D. GLEN BSc BD		The Manse, 26 St Ninian's, Monymusk, Inverurie AB51 7HF [E-mail: gordon@cofscotland.org.uk]	01467 651941

Barthol Chapel linked with Tarves

Isabel C. Buchan (Mrs) BSc BD RE(PgCE)	1975	2006	8 Murray Avenue, Tarves, Ellon AB41 7LZ [E-mail: revicbuchan@tiscali.co.uk]	01651 851250

Belhelvie (H)

Paul McKeown BSc PhD BD	2000	2005	Belhelvie Manse, Balmedie, Aberdeen AB23 8YR [E-mail: prmckeown@tiscali.co.uk]	01358 742227

Blairdaff and Chapel of Garioch
Vacant

John C. Mack JP (Aux)   1985 2004   The Manse, Chapel of Garioch, Inverurie AB51 5HE   01467 681619
                                           The Willows, Auchleven, Insch AB52 6QB   01464 820387
                                           (Charge formed by the union of Blairdaff and Chapel of Garioch)

Cluny (H) linked with Monymusk (H)
G. Euan D. Glen BSc BD   1992   The Manse, 26 St Ninian's, Monymusk, Inverurie AB51 7HF   01467 651470
                                           [E-mail: euanglen@aol.com]

Culsalmond and Rayne linked with Daviot (H)
Mary M. Cranfield (Miss) MA BD DMin   1989   The Manse, Daviot, Inverurie AB51 0HY   01467 671241
                                               [E-mail: marymc@ukgateway.net]

Cushnie and Tough (T) (H)
Margaret J. Garden (Miss) BD   1993 2000   The Manse, Muir of Fowlis, Alford AB33 8JU   01975 581239
                                                [E-mail: m.garden@virgin.net]

Daviot See Culsalmond and Rayne

Drumblade linked with Huntly Strathbogie
Neil I.M. MacGregor BD   1995   Deveron Road, Huntly AB54 8DU   01466 792702

Echt linked with Midmar (T)
Alan Murray BSc BD PhD   2003   The Manse, Echt, Westhill AB32 7AB   01330 860004
                                          [E-mail: ladecottage@btinternet.com]

Ellon
Stephen Emery BD DPS   2006   The Manse, 12 Union Street, Ellon AB41 9BA   01358 720476
                                          [E-mail: stephen.emery2@btinternet.com]
Sheila Craggs (Mrs) (Aux) 2001   7 Morar Court, Ellon AB41 9GG   01358 723055

Fintray Kinellar Keithhall
Ellen Larson Davidson BA MDiv   2007   20 Kinmhor Rise, Blackburn, Aberdeen AB21 0LJ   01224 790701

Foveran
Neil Gow BSc MEd BD   1996 2001   The Manse, Foveran, Ellon AB41 6AP   01358 789288
                                          [E-mail: ngow@beeb.net]

Howe Trinity
John A. Cook MA BD   1986 2000   The Manse, 110 Main Street, Alford AB33 8AD   01975 562282
                                          [E-mail: j-a-cook@howe-trinity.freeserve.co.uk]

Huntly Cairnie Glass Thomas R. Calder LLB BD WS	1994	The Manse, Queen Street, Huntly AB54 8EB [E-mail: cairniechurch@aol.com]	01466 792630
Huntly Strathbogie See Drumblade			
Insch-Leslie-Premnay-Oyne (H) Jane C. Taylor (Miss) BD DipMin	1990 2001	22 Western Road, Insch AB52 6JR	01464 820914
Inverurie: St Andrew's T. Graeme Longmuir KGSJ MA BEd	1976 2001	St Andrew's Manse, 1 Ury Dale, Inverurie AB51 3XW [E-mail: standrew@ukonline.co.uk]	01467 620468
Inverurie: West Ian B. Groves BD CPS	1989	West Manse, 1 Westburn Place, Inverurie AB51 5QS [E-mail: i.groves@inveruriewestchurch.org]	01467 620285
Kemnay John P. Renton BA LTh	1976 1990	Kemnay, Inverurie AB51 9ND [E-mail: johnrenton@btinternet.com]	01467 642219 (Tel/Fax)
Kintore (H) Alan Greig BSc BD	1977 1992	28 Oakhill Road, Kintore, Inverurie AB51 0FH [E-mail: greig@kincarr.free-online.co.uk]	01467 632219 (Tel/Fax)
Meldrum and Bourtie Hugh O'Brien CSS MTheol	2001	The Manse, Urquhart Road, Oldmeldrum, Inverurie AB51 0EX [E-mail: minister@meldrum-bourtiechurch.org]	01651 872250
Methlick Matthew Christopher Canlis BA MDiv MLitt	2007	The Manse, Manse Road, Methlick. Ellon AB41 7DG	01651 806215
Midmar See Echt **Monymusk** See Cluny			
New Machar Manson C. Merchant BD CPS	1992 2001	The Manse, Disblair Road, Newmachar, Aberdeen AB21 0RD [E-mail: mcmerchant@btopenworld.com]	01651 862278
Noth Vacant		Manse of Noth, Kennethmont, Huntly AB54 4NP	01464 831244
Skene (H) Iain U. Thomson MA BD Marion G. Stewart (Miss) DCS	1970 1972	The Manse, Kirkton of Skene, Skene AB32 6LX Kirk Cottage, Kirkton of Skene, Skene AB32 6XE	01224 743277 01224 743407

Tarves See Barthol Chapel

Udny and Pitmedden
Regine U. Cheyne (Mrs) MA BSc BD | 1988 | 2005 | Manse Road, Udny Green, Udny, Ellon AB41 7RS | 01651 842052

Upper Donside (H)
Brian Dingwall BTh CQSW | 1999 | 2006 | The Manse, Lumsden, Huntly AB54 4GQ | 01464 861757
[E-mail: briandingwall@tiscali.co.uk]

Name			Charge	Address	Tel
Andrew, John MA BD DipRE DipEd	1961	1995	(Teacher: Religious Education)	Cartar's Croft, Midmar, Inverurie AB51 7NJ	01330 833208
Bowie, Alfred LTh	1974	1998	(Alford with Keig with Tullynessle Forbes)	17 Stewart Road, Alford AB33 8UA	01975 563824
Buchan, Alexander MA BD PGCE	1975	1992	(North Ronaldsay with Sanday)	8 Murray Avenue, Tarves, Ellon AB41 7LZ [E-mail: revabuchan@bluebucket.org]	01651 851250
Collie, Joyce P. (Miss) MA PhD	1966	1994	(Corgarff Strathdon and Glenbuchat Towie)	35 Foudland Court, Insch AB52 6LG	01464 820945
Dryden, Ian MA DipEd	1988	2001	(New Machar)	16 Glenhome Gardens, Dyce, Aberdeen AB21 7FG	01224 722820
Hawthorn, Daniel MA BD DMin	1965	2004	(Belhelvie)	7 Crimond Drive, Ellon AB41 8BT [E-mail: donhawthorn@compuserve.com]	01358 723981
Jones, Robert A. LTh CA	1966	1997	(Marnoch)	13 Gordon Terrace, Inverurie AB51 4GT	01467 622691
Lister, Douglas	1945	1986	(Largo and Newburn)	Gowanbank, Port Elphinstone, Inverurie AB51 3UN [E-mail: pastillister@surf.scotland.uk]	01467 621262
Macalister, Eleanor	1994	2006	(Ellon)	2 Crimond Drive, Ellon AB41 8BT [E-mail: macal1ster@aol.com]	01358 722711
Macallan, Gerald B.	1954	1992	(Kintore)	38 Thorngrove House, 500 Great Western Road, Aberdeen AB10 6PF	01224 316125
McLean, John MA BD	1967	2003	(Bathgate: Boghall)	16 Eastside Drive, Westhill AB32 6QN	01224 747701
McLeish, Robert S.	1970	2000	(Insch-Leslie-Premnay-Oyne)	19 Western Road, Insch AB52 6JR	01464 820749
Rodger, Matthew A. BD	1978	1999	(Ellon)	15 Meadowlands Drive, Westhill AB32 6EJ	01224 743184
Scott, Allan D. BD	1977	1989	(Culsalmond with Daviot with Rayne)	20 Barclay Road, Inverurie AB51 3QP	01467 625161
Stewart, George C. MA	1952	1995	(Drumblade with Huntly Strathbogie)	104 Scott Drive, Huntly AB54 8PF	01466 792503
Stoddart, A. Grainger	1975	2001	(Meldrum and Bourtie)	6 Mayfield Gardens, Insch AB52 6XL	01464 821124
Wallace, R.J. Stuart MA	1947	1986	(Foveran)	Manse View, Manse Road, Methlick, Ellon AB41 7DW	01651 806843

(34) BUCHAN

Meets at St Kane's Centre, New Deer, Turriff on the first Tuesday of February, March, May, September, October, November and December; and on the third Tuesday of June.

Clerk: | MR GEORGE W. BERSTAN | Faithlie, Victoria Terrace, Turriff AB53 4EE | 01888 562392
[E-mail: buchan@cofscotland.org.uk]

Aberdour linked with Pitsligo linked with Sandhaven
Vacant | The Manse, 49 Pitsligo Street, Rosehearty, Fraserburgh AB43 7JL | 01346 571237

Auchaber United linked with Auchterless
Alison Jaffrey (Mrs) MA BD

1990   1999   The Manse, Auchterless, Turriff AB53 8BA   01888   511217
[E-mail: alison.jaffrey@bigfoot.com]

Auchterless See Auchaber United

Banff linked with King Edward (E-mail: banffkirk@bigfoot.com)
Alan Macgregor BA BD

1992   1998   7 Colleonard Road, Banff AB45 1DZ   01261   812107

Crimond linked with Lonmay linked with St Fergus
Vacant
The Manse, Crimond, Fraserburgh AB43 8QJ   01346   532431

Cruden
Rodger Neilson JP BSc BD

1972   1974   Hatton, Peterhead AB42 0QQ   01779   841229
[E-mail: rodger.neilson@virgin.net]

Deer (H)
James Wishart JP BD

1986   The Manse, Old Deer, Peterhead AB42 5JB   01771   623582
[E-mail: jWishart06@aol.com]

Fordyce
Iain A. Sutherland BSc BD

1996   2000   Seafield Terrace, Portsoy, Banff AB45 2QB   01261   842272
[E-mail: RevISutherland@aol.com]

Fraserburgh: Old
Vacant
The Old Parish Church Manse, 4 Robbies Road, Fraserburgh   01346   518536
AB43 7AF

Fraserburgh: South (H) linked with Inverallochy and Rathen: East
Ronald F. Yule

1982   15 Victoria Street, Fraserburgh AB43 9PJ   01346   518244 (Tel)
0870 055 4665 (Fax)

Fraserburgh: West (H) linked with Rathen: West
B. Andrew Lyon LTh

1971   1978   23 Strichen Road, Fraserburgh AB43 9SA   01346   513303 (Tel)

Fyvie linked with Rothienorman
Robert J. Thorburn BD

1978   2004   The Manse, Fyvie, Turriff AB53 8RD   01651   891230
[E-mail: rjthorburn@aol.com]

Gardenstown
Donald N. Martin BD

1996   The Manse, Fernie Brae, Gardenstown, Banff AB45 3YL   01261   851256
[E-mail: ferniebrae@googlemail.com]

Inverallochy and Rathen: East See Fraserburgh: South
King Edward See Banff

Longside
Robert A. Fowlie BD — 2007 — 9 Anderson Drive, Longside, Peterhead AB42 4XG
[E-mail: bobfowlie@tiscali.co.uk] — 01779 821224

Lonmay See Crimond

Macduff
David J. Randall MA BD ThM — 1971 — The Manse, Macduff AB45 3QL
[E-mail: djrandall479@btinternet.com] — 01261 832316

Marnoch
Paul van Sittert BA BD — 1997 2007 — Marnoch Manse, 53 South Street, Aberchirder, Huntly AB54 7TS
[E-mail: vansittert@btinternet.com] — 01466 781143

Maud and Savoch linked with New Deer: St Kane's
Alistair P. Donald MA PhD BD — 1999 — The Manse, New Deer, Turriff AB53 6TD
[E-mail: ap.donald@googlemail.com] — 01771 644216

Monquhitter and New Byth linked with Turriff: St Andrew's
James Cook MA MDiv — 1999 2002 — Balmellie Road, Turriff AB53 4SP
[E-mail: jmscook9@aol.com] — 01888 560304

New Deer: St Kane's See Maud and Savoch

New Pitsligo linked with Strichen and Tyrie
Iain Macnee LTh BD MA PhD — 1975 2004 — Kingsville, Strichen, Fraserburgh AB43 6SQ
[E-mail: strichen_tyrie@talktalk.net] — 01771 637365

Ordiquhill and Cornhill (H) linked with Whitehills
Brian Hendrie BD — 1992 2005 — 6 Craigneen Place, Whitehills, Banff AB45 2NE
[E-mail: brianandyvonne@98duncansby.freeserve.co.uk] — 01261 861671

Peterhead: Old
Pauline Thomson MA BD — 2006 — 1 Hawthorn Road, Peterhead AB42 2DW — 01779 472618

Peterhead: St Andrew's (H)
David G. Pitkeathly LLB BD — 1996 — 1 Landale Road, Peterhead AB42 1QN
[E-mail: david-gp@fish.co.uk] — 01779 472141

Peterhead: Trinity
L. Paul McClenaghan BA — 1973 1996 — 18 Landale Road, Peterhead AB42 1QP
[E-mail: paul.mcclenaghan@gmail.com] — 01779 472405

Pitsligo See Aberdour

Rathen: West See Fraserburgh: West
Rothienorman See Fyvie
St Fergus See Crimond
Sandhaven See Aberdour
Strichen and Tyrie See New Pitsligo
Turriff: St Andrew's See Monquhitter and New Byth

Turriff: St Ninian's and Forglen
Murdo C. Macdonald MA BD   2002   4 Deveronside Drive, Turriff AB53 4SP   01888 563850

Whitehills See Ordiquhill and Cornhill

Birnie, Charles J. MA	1969	1995	(Aberdour and Tyrie)		
Blaikie, James BD	1972	1997	(Berwick-on-Tweed: St Andrew's Wallace Green and Lowick)	'The Dookit', 23 Water Street, Strichen, Fraserburgh AB43 6ST	01771 637775
Douglas, Ian P. LTh	1974	1998	(Aberdeen: Craigiebuckler)	57 Glenugie View, Peterhead AB42 2BW	01779 490625
				'Stonecroft', 1 Tortorston Drive, Tortorston, Blackhills, Peterhead AB42 3LY	01779 474728
Dunlop, M. William B. LLB BD	1981	1995	(Peterhead: St Andrew's)	18 Iona Avenue, Peterhead AB42 1NZ	01779 479189
Fawkes, G.M. Allan BA BSc JP	1979	2000	(Lonmay with Rathen: West)	3 Northfield Gardens, Hatton, Peterhead AB42 0SW	01779 841814
Hendrie, Yvonne (Mrs)	1995		Hospital Chaplain	6 Craigneen Place, Whitehills, Banff AB45 2NE	01261 861671
McKay, Margaret (Mrs) MA BD MTh	1991	2003	(Auchaber United with Auchterless)	The Smithy, Knowes of Elrick, Aberchirder, Huntly AB54 7PP	(Tel) 01466 780208
				[E-mail: mg_mckay@yahoo.com.uk]	(Fax) 01466 780015
Mackenzie, Seoras L. BD	1996	1998	Chaplain: Army	1 Logistic Support Regiment, BFPO 47	
McMillan, William J. CA LTh BD	1969	2004	(Sandsting and Aithsting with Walls and Sandness)	7 Ardinn Drive, Turriff AB53 4PR [E-mail: revbillymcmillan@aol.com]	01888 560727
Noble, George S. DipTh	1972	2000	(Carfin with Newarthill)	Craigowan, 3 Main Street, Inverallochy, Fraserburgh AB43 8XX	01346 582749
Ross, David S. MSc PhD BD	1978	2003	Prison Chaplain Service	3–5 Abbey Street, Old Deer, Peterhead AB42 5LN [E-mail: padsross@btinternet.com]	01771 623994
Steenbergen, Pauline (Ms) MA BD	1996			1 Landale Road, Peterhead AB42 1QN	01779 472141
Taylor, William MA MEd	1984	1996	(Buckie: North)	23 York Street, Peterhead AB42 1SN [E-mail: william.taylor@globalnet.co.uk]	01779 481798

(35) MORAY

Meets at St Andrew's-Lhanbryd and Urquhart on the first Tuesday of February, March, May, September, October, November and December; and at the Moderator's church on the fourth Tuesday of June.

Clerk:	REV. HUGH M.C. SMITH LTh	Mortlach Manse, Dufftown, Keith AB55 4AR [E-mail: moray@cofscotland.org.uk] [E-mail: clerk@moraypresbytery.plus.com]	01340 820538
Depute Clerk:	REV. GRAHAM W. CRAWFORD BSc BD STM	The Manse, Prospect Terrace, Lossiemouth IV31 6JS	01343 810676

Aberlour (H)

Elizabeth M. Curran (Miss) BD	1995	1998	Mary Avenue, Aberlour AB38 9QN [E-mail: ecurran8@aol.com]	01340 871027

Alves and Burghead linked with Kinloss and Findhorn

Duncan Shaw LTh CPS	1984	2006	The Manse, 4 Manse Road, Kinloss, Forres IV36 3GH	01309 690931

Bellie linked with Speymouth

Alison C. Mehigan BD DPS	2003	11 The Square, Fochabers IV32 7DG [E-mail: alisonc@mehigan-ug.fsnet.co.uk]	01343 820256
Margaret King MA DCS	2007	56 Murrayfield, Fochabers IV32 7EZ	01343 820937

Birnie and Pluscarden linked with Elgin High

Julie M. Woods (Mrs) BTh	2005	Daisy Bank, 5 Forteath Avenue, Elgin IV30 1TQ [E-mail: missjulie@btinternet.com]	01343 542449
Anne Attenburrow BSc MBChB (Aux)	2006	4 Jock Inksons Brae, Elgin IV30 1QE	01343 552330

Buckie: North (H)

J. Gordon Mathew MA BD	1973	2006	14 St Peter's Road, Buckie AB56 1DL [E-mail: jgmathew@lineone.net]	01542 831328

Buckie: South and West (H) linked with Enzie

Vacant	41 East Church Street, Buckie AB56 1ES	01542 832103

Cullen and Deskford

Wilma A. Johnston MTheol MTh	2006	3 Seafield Place, Cullen, Buckie AB56 4UU [E-mail: revwilmaj@btinternet.com]	01542 841851

Dallas linked with Forres: St Leonard's (H) linked with Rafford

Paul Amed LTh DPS	1992	2000	St Leonard's Manse, Nelson Road, Forres IV36 1DR [E-mail: paulamed@stleonardsmanse.freeserve.co.uk]	01309 672380

Duffus, Spynie and Hopeman (H)

Bruce B. Lawrie BD	1974	2001	The Manse, Duffus, Elgin IV30 5QP [E-mail: blawrie@zetnet.co.uk]	01343 830276

Dyke linked with Edinkillie

Gordon R. Mackenzie BScAgr BD	1977	2003	Manse of Dyke, Brodie, Forres IV36 2TD [E-mail: rev.g.mackenzie@btopenworld.com]	01309 641239

Edinkillie See Dyke
Elgin: High See Birnie and Pluscarden

Elgin: St Giles' (H) and St Columba's South (01343 551501)   (Office and Church Halls: Greyfriars Street, Elgin IV30 1LF)
George B. Rollo BD   1974   1986   18 Reidhaven Street, Elgin IV30 1QH   [E-mail: gbrstgiles@hotmail.com]   01343 547208

James M. Cowie BD (Associate)   1977   2007   2 Hay Place, Elgin IV30 1LZ   [E-mail: jim911@btinternet.com]   01343 544957

Enzie See Buckie South and West

Findochty linked with Portknockie linked with Rathven
Graham Austin BD   1997   20 Netherton Terrace, Findochty, Buckie AB56 4QD   [E-mail: grahamaustin1@btopenworld.com]   01542 833484

Forres: St Laurence (H)
Barry J. Boyd LTh DPS   1993   12 Mackenzie Drive, Forres IV36 2JP   [E-mail: barryj.boydstlaurence@btinternet.com]   01309 672260 / 07778 731018 (Mbl)

Forres: St Leonard's See Dallas

Keith: North, Newmill, Boharm and Rothiemay (H) (01542 886390)
T. Douglas McRoberts BD CPS FRSA   1975   2002   North Manse, Church Road, Keith AB55 5BR   [E-mail: doug.mcroberts@btinternet.com]   01542 882559

Ian Cunningham DCS   The Manse, Rothiemay, Huntly AB54 7NE   [E-mail: icunninghamdcs@btinternet.com]   01466 711334

Keith: St Rufus, Botriphnie and Grange (H)
Ranald S.R. Gauld MA LLB BD   1991   1995   Church Road, Keith AB55 5BR   01542 882799

Kay Gauld (Mrs) BD STM PhD (Assoc)   1999   Church Road, Keith AB55 5BR   [E-mail: kay_gauld@strufus.fsnet.co.uk]   01542 882799

Kinloss and Findhorn See Alves and Burghead

Knockando, Elchies and Archiestown (H) linked with Rothes
Robert J.M. Anderson BD   1993   2000   Manse Brae, Rothes, Aberlour AB38 7AF   [E-mail: robert@carmanse.freeserve.co.uk]   01340 831381 (Tel/Fax)

Lossiemouth: St Gerardine's High (H)
Thomas M. Bryson BD   1997   2002   The Manse, St Gerardine's Road, Lossiemouth IV31 6RA   [E-mail: thomas@bryson547.fsworld.co.uk]   01343 813146

Lossiemouth: St James'
Graham W. Crawford BSc BD STM   1991   2003   The Manse, Prospect Terrace, Lossiemouth IV31 6JS   [E-mail: pictishreiver@aol.com]   01343 810676

Mortlach and Cabrach (H)
Hugh M.C. Smith LTh   1973   1982   Mortlach Manse, Dufftown, Keith AB55 4AR   01340 820380
[E-mail: clerk@moraypresbytery.plus.com]

Pluscarden See Birnie
Portknockie See Findochty
Rafford See Dallas
Rathven See Findochty
Rothes See Knockando, Elchies and Archiestown

St Andrew's-Lhanbryd (H) and Urquhart
Rolf H. Billes BD   1996   2001   39 St Andrews Road, Lhanbryde, Elgin IV30 8PU   01343 843995
[E-mail: rolf.billes@lineone.net]

Speymouth See Bellie

Davidson, A.A.B. MA BD	1960	1997	(Grange with Rothiemay)	11 Sutors Rise, Nairn IV12 5BU	
Douglas, Christina A. (Mrs)	1987	1993	(Inveraven and Glenlivet)	White Cottage, St Fillans, Crieff PH6 2ND	
Evans, John W. MA BD	1945	1984	(Elgin High)	15 Weaver Place, Elgin IV30 1HB	01343 543607
Henig, Gordon BSc BD	1997	2003	(Bellie with Speymouth)	59 Woodside Drive, Forres IV36 2UF	01309 672558
King, Margaret R. (Miss) MA DCS	2002			56 Murrayfield, Fochabers IV32 7EZ [E-mail: margaretrking@aol.com]	01343 820937
Macaulay, Alick Hugh MA	1943	1981	(Bellie with Speymouth)	5 Duke Street, Fochabers IV32 7DN	
Miller, William B.	1950	1987	(Cawdor with Croy and Dalcross)	10 Kirkhill Drive, Lhanbryde, Elgin IV30 8QA	01343 820726
Morton, Alasdair J. MA BD DipEd FEIS	1960	2000	(Bowden with Newtown)	16 St Leonard's Road, Forres IV36 1DW [E-mail: alasgilmor@compuserve.com]	01343 842368 / 01309 671719
Morton, Gillian M. (Mrs) MA BD PGCE	1983	1996	(Hospital Chaplain)	16 St Leonard's Road, Forres IV36 1DW [E-mail: alasgilmor@compuserve.com]	01309 671719
Munro, Sheila BD	1995	2003	Chaplain: RAF	RAF Lossiemouth, Lossiemouth IV31 6SD	
Poole, Ann McColl (Mrs) DipEd ACE LTh	1983	2003	(Dyke with Edinkillie)	Kirkside Cottage, Dyke, Forres IV36 2TF	01309 641046
Scotland, Ronald J. BD	1993	2003	(Birnie with Pluscarden)	7A Rose Avenue, Elgin IV30 1NX	01343 543086
Spence, Alexander	1944	1989	(Elgin: St Giles': Associate)	16 Inglis Court, Edzell, Brechin DD9 7SR	01356 648502
Wright, David L. MA BD	1957	1998	(Stornoway: St Columba)	84 Wyvis Drive, Nairn IV12 4TP	01667 451613
Thomson, James M. BA	1952	2000	(Elgin: St Giles' and St Columba's South: Associate)	48 Mayne Road, Elgin IV30 1PD	01343 547664

(36) ABERNETHY

Meets at Boat of Garten on the first Tuesday of February, March, April, June, September, October, November and December.

Clerk:	REV. JAMES A.I. MACEWAN MA BD		The Manse, Nethy Bridge PH25 3DG [E-mail: abernethy@cofscotland.org.uk]	01479 821280
Abernethy (H) linked with Cromdale (H) and Advie James A.I. MacEwan MA BD	1973		The Manse, Nethy Bridge PH25 3DG [E-mail: manse@nethybridge.freeserve.co.uk]	01479 821280
Alvie and Insh (T) (H) Vacant			Kincraig, Kingussie PH21 1NA	
Boat of Garten (H) and Kincardine linked with Duthil (H) David W. Whyte LTh	1993	1999	Deshar Road, Boat of Garten PH24 3BN [E-mail: djwhyte@fish.co.uk]	01479 831252
Cromdale and Advie See Abernethy				
Dulnain Bridge (H) linked with Grantown-on-Spey (H) Morris Smith BD	1988		The Manse, Golf Course Road, Grantown-on-Spey PH26 3HY [E-mail: mosmith.themanse@virgin.net]	01479 872084
Duthil See Boat of Garten and Kincardine **Grantown-on-Spey** See Dulnain Bridge				
Kingussie (H) Helen Cook (Mrs) BD	1974	2003	The Manse, 18 Hillside Avenue, Kingussie PH21 1PA [E-mail: bhja@cookville.fsnet.co.uk]	01540 661311
Laggan linked with Newtonmore (H) Douglas F. Stevenson BD DipMin	1991	2001	The Manse, Fort William Road, Newtonmore PH20 1DG [E-mail: dfstevenson@aol.com]	01540 673238
Newtonmore See Laggan				
Rothiemurchus and Aviemore (H) Ron C. Whyte BD CPS	1990		The Manse, 8 Dalfaber Park, Aviemore PH22 1QF [E-mail: ron4xst@aol.com]	01479 810280
Tomintoul (H), Glenlivet and Inveraven Sven S. Bjarnason CandTheol	1975	1992	The Manse, Tomintoul, Ballindalloch AB37 9HA [E-mail: sven@bjarnason.org.uk]	01807 580254

(37) INVERNESS

Meets at Inverness, in the Dr Black Memorial Hall, on the first Tuesday of February, March, April, May, September, October, November and December, and at the Moderator's church on the fourth Tuesday of June.

Clerk:	REV. ALASTAIR S. YOUNGER BScEcon ASCC			3 Elm Park, Inverness IV2 4WN [E-mail: inverness@cofscotland.org.uk]	01463 232462 (Tel/Fax)

Ardersier (H) linked with Petty
Alexander Whiteford LTh	1996		Ardersier, Inverness IV2 7SX [E-mail: a.whiteford@ukonline.co.uk]	01667 462224

Auldearn and Dalmore linked with Nairn: St Ninian's
Richard Reid BSc BD MTh	1991	2005	The Manse, Auldearn, Nairn IV12 5SX	01667 451675

Cawdor (H) linked with Croy and Dalcross (H)
Janet S. Mathieson MA BD	2003		The Manse, Croy, Inverness IV2 5PH [E-mail: jan@mathieson99.fsnet.co.uk]	01667 493217

Croy and Dalcross See Cawdor

Culloden: The Barn (H)
James H. Robertson BSc BD	1975	1994	45 Oakdene Court, Culloden IV2 7XL [E-mail: revjimrobertson@netscape.net]	01463 790504

Daviot and Dunlichity linked with Moy, Dalarossie and Tomatin
Reginald F. Campbell BD DipChEd	1979	2003	The Manse, Daviot, Inverness IV2 5XL	01463 772242

Dores and Boleskine
Vacant			The Manse, Foyers, Inverness IV2 6XU	01456 486206

Inverness: Crown (H) (01463 238929)
Peter H. Donald MA PhD BD	1991	1998	39 Southside Road, Inverness IV2 4XA [E-mail: pdonald7@aol.com]	01463 230537

Inverness: Dalneigh and Bona (GD) (H)
Fergus A. Robertson MA BD	1971	1999	9 St Mungo Road, Inverness IV3 5AS	01463 232339

Inverness: East (H)
Aonghas I. MacDonald MA BD	1967	1981	2 Victoria Drive, Inverness IV2 3QD [E-mail: aonghas@ukonline.co.uk]	01463 231269

Inverness: Hilton
Duncan MacPherson LLB BD
1994
66 Culduthel Mains Crescent, Inverness IV2 6RG
[E-mail: duncan@hiltonchurch.freeserve.uk]
01463 231417

Inverness: Inshes (H)
Alistair Malcolm BD DPS
1976 1992
48 Redwood Crescent, Milton of Leys, Inverness IV2 6HB
[E-mail: alimalcolm@7inverness.freeserve.co.uk]
01463 772402

Inverness: Kinmylies (E) (H)
Peter M. Humphris BSc BD
1976 2001
2 Balnafettack Place, Inverness IV3 8TQ
[E-mail: peter@humphris.co.uk]
01463 709893

Inverness: Ness Bank (T) (H)
S. John Chambers OBE BSc
1972 1998
15 Ballifeary Road, Inverness IV3 5PJ
[E-mail: chambers@ballifeary.freeserve.co.uk]
01463 234653

Inverness: Old High St Stephen's
Peter W. Nimmo BD ThM
1996 2004
24 Damfield Road, Inverness IV2 3HU
[E-mail: peternimmo@minister.com]
01463 250802

Inverness: St Columba High (H)
Alastair S. Younger BScEcon ASCC
1969 1976
3 Elm Park, Inverness IV2 4WN
[E-mail: asyounger@aol.com]
01463 232462   (Tel/Fax)

Inverness: Trinity (H)
Alistair Murray BD
1984 2004
60 Kenneth Street, Inverness IV3 5PZ
[E-mail: a.murray111@btinternet.com]
01463 234756

Kilmorack and Erchless
Edgar J. Ogston BSc BD
1976 2007
'Roselynn', Croyard Road, Beauly IV4 7DJ
[E-mail: edgar.ogston@macfish.com]
01463 782260

Kiltarlity linked with Kirkhill
Vacant
Wardlaw Manse, Wardlaw Road, Kirkhill, Inverness IV5 7NZ
01463 831662

Kirkhill See Kiltarlity
Moy, Dalarossie and Tomatin See Daviot and Dunlichity

Nairn: Old (H)
Ian W.F. Hamilton BD LTh ALCM AVCM
1978 1986
3 Manse Road, Nairn IV12 4RN
[E-mail: reviwfh@btinternet.com]
01667 452203

Nairn: St Ninian's (H) See Auldearn and Dalmore
Petty See Ardersier

Urquhart and Glenmoriston (H)
Hugh F. Watt BD DPS   1986 1996 Blairbeg, Drumnadrochit, Inverness IV3 6UG   01456 450231
[E-mail: hw@tinyworld.co.uk]

Name			Charge	Address	Phone
Black, Archibald T. BSc	1964	1997	(Inverness: Ness Bank)	16 Elm Park, Inverness IV2 4WN	01463 230588
Brown, Derek G. BD DipMin DMin	1989	1994	Chaplain: NHS Highland	Cathedral Manse, Cnoc-an-Lobht, Dornoch IV25 3HN [E-mail: revsbrown@aol.com]	01862 810296
Buell, F. Bart BA MDiv	1980	1995	(Urquhart and Glenmoriston)	6 Towerhill Place, Cradlehall, Inverness IV2 5FN [E-mail: bart@tower22.freeserve.co.uk]	01463 794634
Charlton, George W.	1952	1992	(Fort Augustus with Glengarry)	61 Drumfield Road, Inverness IV2 4XL	01463 242802
Chisholm, Archibald F. MA	1957	1997	(Braes of Rannoch with Foss and Rannoch)	32 Seabank Road, Nairn IV12 4EU	01667 452001
Christie, James LTh	1993	2003	(Dores and Boleskine)	20 Wester Inshes Crescent, Inverness IV2 5HL	01463 710534
Clyne, Douglas R. BD	1973	2004	(Fraserburgh: Old)	27 River Park, Nairn IV12 5SP [E-mail: manse1@supanet.com]	01667 456372
Donn, Thomas M. MA	1932	1969	(Duthil)	Clachnaharry Residential Home, Inverness	
Frizzell, R. Stewart BD	1961	2000	(Wick: Old)	98 Boswell Road, Inverness IV2 3EW	01463 231907
Jeffrey, Stewart D. BSc BD	1962	1997	(Banff with King Edward)	10 Grigor Drive, Inverness IV2 4LP	
Livesley, Anthony LTh	1979	1997	(Kiltearn)	87 Beech Avenue, Nairn IV12 5SX [E-mail: a.livesley@tesco.net]	01667 455126
Logan, Robert J.V. MA BD	1962	2001	(Abdie and Dunbog with Newburgh)	Lindores, 1 Murray Place, Smithton, Inverness IV2 7PX [E-mail: rjvlogan@btinternet.com]	01463 790226
Macritchie, Iain A.M. BSc BD STM PhD	1987	1998	Chaplain: Inverness Hospitals	7 Merlin Crescent, Inverness IV2 3TE	01463 235204
Morrison, Hector BSc BD MTh	1981	1994	Lecturer: Highland Theological College	24 Oak Avenue, Inverness IV2 4NX	01463 238561
Rettie, James A. BTh	1981	1999	(Melness and Eriboll with Tongue)	2 Trantham Drive, Westhill, Inverness IV2 5QT	01463 798896
Robb, Rodney P.T.	1995	2004	(Stirling: St Mark's)	2A Mayfield Road, Inverness IV2 4AE	
Stirling, G. Alan S. MA	1960	1999	(Leochel Cushnie and Lynturk linked with Tough)		
Turner, Fraser K. LTh	1994	2007	(Kiltarlity with Kirkhill)	97 Lochlann Road, Culloden, Inverness IV2 7HJ [E-mail: fraseratq@yahoo.co.uk]	01463 798313
Waugh, John L. LTh	1973	2002		58 Wyvis Drive, Nairn IV12 4TP [E-mail: jswaugh@care4free.net]	(Tel/Fax) 01667 456397
Wilson, Ian M.	1988	1993	(Cawdor with Croy and Dalcross)	17 Spires Crescent, Nairn IV12 5PZ	01667 452977

INVERNESS ADDRESSES

Inverness

Crown	Kingsmills Road x Midmills Road	
Dalneigh and Bona	St Mary's Avenue	
East	Academy Street x Margaret Street	
Hilton	Druid Road x Tomatin Road	
Inshes	Inshes Retail Park	
Kinmylies	Kinmylies Way	
Ness Bank	Ness Bank x Castle Road	
St Columba High	Bank Street x Fraser Street	
St Stephen's	Old Edinburgh Road x Southside Road	
The Old High	Church Street x Church Lane	
Trinity	Huntly Place x Upper Kessock Street	

Nairn

Old	Academy Street x Seabank Road
St Ninian's	High Street x Queen Street

(38) LOCHABER

Meets at Caol, Fort William, in Kilmallie Church Hall at 6pm, on the first Tuesday of September and December, on the last Tuesday of October and on the fourth Tuesday of March. The June meeting is held at 6pm on the first Tuesday in the church of the incoming Moderator.

Clerk: REV. DAVID M. ANDERSON MSc FCOptom
'Mirlos', 1 Dumfries Place, Fort William PH33 6UQ
[E-mail: lochaber@cofscotland.org.uk]
[E-mail: lochaber@uk.uumail.com]   01397 703203

Acharacle (H) linked with Ardnamurchan
Vacant   The Manse, Acharacle, Argyll PH36 4JU   01967 431561

Ardgour linked with Strontian
Vacant   The Manse, Ardgour, Fort William PH33 7AH   01855 841230

Ardnamurchan See Acharacle

Arisaig and the Small Isles linked with Mallaig: St Columba and Knoydart
John C. Christie BSc BD   1968   2007   10 Cumberland Avenue, Helensburgh G84 8QG   01436 674078
[E-mail: rev.jcc@btinternet.com]

Janet Anderson (Miss) DCS   4 Clanranald Place, Arisaig PH39 4NN   01687 450398
[E-mail: Janet.A_@tiscali.co.uk]

Duror (H) linked with Glencoe: St Munda's (H) (T)
Alison H. Burnside (Mrs) MA BD   1991   2002   The Manse, Ballachulish PH49 4JG   01855 811998
[E-mail: alisonskyona@aol.com]

David M. Anderson MSc FCOptom (Aux)   1984   2001   'Mirlos', 1 Dumfries Place, Fort William PH33 6UQ   01397 703203
[E-mail: lochaber@uk.uumail.com]

Fort Augustus linked with Glengarry
Adrian P.J. Varwell BA BD PhD   1983   2001   The Manse, Fort Augustus PH32 4BH   01320 366210
[E-mail: a-varwell@ecosse.net]

Fort William: Duncansburgh MacIntosh (H) linked with Kilmonivaig

Donald A. MacQuarrie BSc BD	1979	1990	The Manse of Duncansburgh, The Parade, Fort William PH33 6BA [E-mail: pdmacq@ukgateway.net]	01397 702297

(Charge formed by the union of Fort William: Duncansburgh and Fort William: MacIntosh Memorial)

Glencoe: St Munda's See Duror
Glengarry See Fort Augustus

Kilmallie

Richard T. Corbett BSc MSc PhD BD	1992	2005	Kilmallie Manse, Corpach, Fort William PH33 7JS [E-mail: revcorbett@pgen.net]	01397 772736

Kilmonivaig See Fort William: Duncansburgh

Kinlochleven (H) linked with Nether Lochaber (H)

Vacant			Lochaber Road, Kinlochleven, Argyll PA40 4QW	01855 831227
David M. Anderson MSc FCOptom (Aux)	1984	2001	'Mirlos', 1 Dumfries Place, Fort William PH33 6UQ [E-mail: lochaber@uk.uumail.com]	01397 703203

Mallaig: St Columba and Knoydart See Arisaig and the Small Isles

Morvern

Vacant	The Manse, Lochaline, Morvern, Oban PA34 5UU 01967 421267

Nether Lochaber See Kinlochleven
Strontian See Ardgour

Beaton, Jamesina (Miss) DCS			(Deaconess)	Farhills, Fort Augustus PH32 4DS	01320 366252
Burnside, William A.M. MA BD PGCE	1990		Teacher: Religious Education	The Manse, Ballachulish PH49 4JG	01855 811998
Carmichael, James A. LTh	1976	2006	(Ardgour with Strontian)	Linnhe View, 5 Clovulin, Ardgour, Fort William PH33 7AB	01855 841351
Cobain, Alan R. BD	2000		Teacher: Religious Education	1 Parkan Dubh, Inverlochy, Fort William PH33 6NH	01397 700105
Lamb, Alan H.W. BA MTh	1959	2005	(Associate Minister)	Smiddy House, Arisaig PH39 4NH [E-mail: handalamb@talktalk.net]	01687 450227
Millar, John L. MA BD	1981	1990	(Fort William: Duncansburgh with Kilmonivaig)	17 Whittingehame Court, 1350 Great Western Road, Glasgow G12 0BH	0141-339 4098
Olsen, Heather C. (Miss) BD	1978	2003	(Creich with Rosehall)	4 Riverside Park, Lochyside, Coull, Fort William PH33 7RA	01397 700023
Rae, Peter C. BSc BD	1968	2000	(Beath and Cowdenbeath North)	Rodane, Badabrie, Banavie, Fort William PH33 7LX	01397 772603
Winning, A. Ann MA DipEd BD	1984	2006	(Morvern)	'Westering', 13C Carnoch, Glencoe, Ballachulish PH49 4HQ [E-mail: annw@morvern13.fslife.co.uk]	01855 811929

LOCHABER   Communion Sundays

Acharacle	1st Mar, Jun, Sep, Dec	Fort William Duncansburgh	1st Apr, Jun, Oct
Ardgour	1st Jun, Sep, Dec, Easter	MacIntosh	
Ardnamurchan	1st Apr, Aug, Dec	Glencoe	1st Apr, Oct
Arisaig and Moidart	1st May, Nov	Glengarry	1st Jan, Apr, Jul, Oct
Duror	2nd Jun, 3rd Nov	Kilmallie	3rd Mar, May, Sep, 1st Dec
Fort Augustus	1st Jan, Apr, Jul, Oct	Kilmonivaig	1st May, Nov

Kinlochleven	1st Feb, Apr, Jun, Oct, Dec
Mallaig	4th May, 3rd Nov
Morvern	Easter, 1st Jul, 4th Sep, 1st Dec
Nether Lochaber	1st Apr, Oct
Strontian	1st Jun, Sep, Dec

(39) ROSS

Meets in Dingwall on the first Tuesday of each month, except January, May, July and August.

Clerk:	REV. THOMAS M. McWILLIAM MA BD		Guidhadden, 7 Woodholme Crescent, Culbokie, Dingwall IV7 8JH [E-mail: ross@cofscotland.org.uk]	01349 877014

Alness Ronald Morrison BD	1996		27 Darroch Brae, Alness IV17 0SD [E-mail: ranald@morrison89.freeserve.co.uk]	01349 882238
Avoch linked with Fortrose and Rosemarkie Alison J. Grainger BD	1995	2006	5 Nessway, Fortrose IV10 8SS [E-mail: revajgrainger@btinternet.com]	01381 620068
Contin Gordon McLean LTh	1972	2005	The Manse, Contin, Strathpeffer IV14 9ES [E-mail: gmaclean@hotmail.co.uk]	01997 421380
Cromarty John Tallach MA MLitt	1970	1999	Denny Road, Cromarty IV11 8YT [E-mail: john.t@ecosse.net]	01381 600802
Dingwall: Castle Street (H) Bruce Ritchie BSc BD	1977	2006	16 Achany Road, Dingwall IV15 9JB	01349 863167
Dingwall: St Clement's (H) Russel Smith BD	1994		8 Castlehill Road, Dingwall IV15 9PB [E-mail: russel@stclementschurch.fsnet.co.uk]	01349 861011

Fearn Abbey and Nigg linked with Tarbat David V. Scott BTh	1994	2006	Church of Scotland Manse, Fearn, Tain IV20 1TN	01862 832626 (Tel/Fax)
Ferintosh Andrew F. Graham BTh DPS	2001	2006	Ferintosh Manse, Leanaig Road, Conon Bridge, Dingwall IV7 8BE [E-mail: andy@afg1960.wanadoo.co.uk]	01349 861275
Fodderty and Strathpeffer Ivan C. Warwick MA BD TD	1980	1999	The Manse, Strathpeffer IV14 9DL [E-mail: L70rev@btinternet.com]	01997 421398 07775 530709 (Mbl)
Fortrose and Rosemarkie See Avoch				
Invergordon Kenneth Donald Macleod BD CPS	1989	2000	The Manse, Cromlet Drive, Invergordon IV18 0BA [E-mail: kd-macleod@tiscali.co.uk]	01349 852273
Killearnan linked with Knockbain Iain Ramsden BTh	1999		The Church of Scotland Manse, Coldwell Road, Artafallie, North Kessock, Inverness IV1 3ZE [E-mail: s4rev@cqm.co.uk]	01463 731333
Kilmuir and Logie Easter Thomas J.R. Mackinnon LTh DipMin	1996	2005	Delny, Invergordon IV18 0NW [E-mail: tmackinnon@aol.com]	01862 842280
Kiltearn (H) Donald A. MacSween BD	1991	1998	The Manse, Swordale Road, Evanton, Dingwall IV16 9UZ [E-mail: donaldmacsween@hotmail.com]	01349 830472
Knockbain See Killearnan				
Lochbroom and Ullapool (GD) Vacant			The Manse, Garve Road, Ullapool IV26 2SX	01854 612050
Resolis and Urquhart (T) C.J. Grant Bell	1983	2002	The Manse, Culbokie, Dingwall IV7 8JN	01349 877452

Rosskeen
Robert Jones BSc BD — 1990 — Rosskeen Manse, Perrins Road, Alness IV17 0SX
[E-mail: rob-jones@freeuk.com] — 01349 882265

Tain
Douglas A. Horne BD — 1977 — 14 Kingsway Avenue, Tain IV19 1NJ
[E-mail: douglas.horne@virgin.net] — 01862 894140

Tarbat (T) See Fearn Abbey and Nigg

Urray and Kilchrist
J. Alastair Gordon BSc BD — 2000 — The Manse, Corrie Road, Muir of Ord IV6 7TL
[E-mail: jagordon_muir@tiscali.co.uk] — 01463 870259

Buchan, John BD MTh	1968	1993	(Fodderty and Strathpeffer)	'Faithlie', 45 Swanston Avenue, Inverness IV3 6QW	01463 713114
Dupar, Kenneth W. BA BD PhD	1965	1993	(Christ's College, Aberdeen)	The Old Manse, The Causeway, Cromarty IV11 8XJ	01381 600428
Forsyth, James LTh	1970	2000	(Fearn Abbey with Nigg Chapelhill)	Rhives Lodge, Golspie, Sutherland KW10 6DD	
Glass, Alexander OBE MA	1998		Auxiliary Minister: Attached to Presbytery Clerk	Craigton, Tulloch Avenue, Dingwall IV15 9TU	01349 863258
Holroyd, Gordon BTh FPhS FSAScot	1959	1993	(Dingwall: St Clement's)	22 Stuarthill Drive, Maryburgh, Dingwall IV15 9HU	01349 863379
Liddell, Margaret (Miss) BD DipTh	1987	1997	(Contin)	20 Wyvis Crescent, Conon Bridge, Dingwall IV7 8BZ [E-mail: margaretliddell@talktalk.net]	01349 865997
McGowan, Prof. Andrew T.B. BD STM PhD	1979	1994	Highland Theological College	4 Kintail Place, Dingwall IV15 9RL [E-mail: andrew.mcgowan@htc.uhi.ac.uk]	(Home) 01349 867639 (Work) 01349 780208 (Fax) 01349 780001
Macgregor, John BD	2001	2006	Chaplain: Army	2 Bn The Royal Regiment of Scotland (Highland Fusiliers), Glencorse Barracks, Penicuik EH26	
Mackinnon, R.M. LTh	1968	1995	(Kilmuir and Logie Easter)	27 Riverford Crescent, Conon Bridge, Dingwall IV7 8HL	01349 866293
MacLennan, Alasdair J. BD DCE	1978	2001	(Resolis and Urquhart)	Airdale, Seaforth Road, Muir of Ord IV6 7TA	01463 870704
Macleod, John MA	1959	1993	(Resolis and Urquhart)	'Benview', 19 Balvaird, Muir of Ord IV6 7RG [E-mail: sheilaandjohn@yahoo.co.uk]	01463 871286
McWilliam, Thomas M. MA BD	1964	2003	(Contin)	Guidhadden, 7 Woodholme Crescent, Culbokie, Dingwall IV7 8JH	01349 877014
Niven, William W. BTh	1982	1995	(Alness)	4 Obsdale Park, Alness IV17 0TP	01349 882427
Rutherford, Ellen B. (Miss) MBE DCS			(Deaconess)	41 Duncanston, Conon Bridge, Dingwall IV7 8JB	01349 877439

(40) SUTHERLAND

Meets at Lairg on the first Tuesday of March, May, September, November and December, and on the first Tuesday of June at the Moderator's church.

Clerk: REV. J.L. GOSKIRK LTh — The Manse, Lairg, Sutherland IV27 4EH — 01549 402373
[E-mail: sutherland@cofscotland.org.uk]

Altnaharra and Farr Continued Vacancy			The Manse, Bettyhill, Thurso KW14 7SZ	01641 521208
Assynt and Stoer Vacant			Canisp Road, Lochinver, Lairg IV27 4LH	01571 844342
Clyne (H) linked with Kildonan and Loth Helmsdale (H) Ian W. McCree BD	1971	1987	Golf Road, Brora KW9 6QS [E-mail: ian@mccree.f9.co.uk]	01408 621239
Creich linked with Rosehall Vacant			Church of Scotland Manse, Dornoch Road, Bonar Bridge, Ardgay IV24 3EB	01863 766256
Dornoch Cathedral (H) Susan M. Brown (Mrs) BD DipMin	1985	1998	Cnoc-an-Lobht, Dornoch IV25 3HN [E-mail: revsbrown@aol.com]	01862 810296
Durness and Kinlochbervie John T. Mann BSc BD	1990	1998	Manse Road, Kinlochbervie, Lairg IV27 4RG [E-mail: jtmklb@aol.com]	01971 521287
Eddrachillis John MacPherson BSc BD	1993		Church of Scotland Manse, Scourie, Lairg IV27 4TQ	01971 502431
Golspie John B. Sterrett BA BD PhD	2007		The Manse, Fountain Road, Golspie KW10 6TH [E-mail: johnbsterrett@yahoo.co.uk]	01408 633295 (Tel/Fax)
Kildonan and Loth Helmsdale (H) See Clyne				
Kincardine Croick and Edderton Graeme W.M. Muckart MTh MSc FSAScot	1983	2004	The Manse, Ardgay IV24 3BG [E-mail: avqt18@dsl.pipex.com]	01863 766285
Lairg (H) linked with Rogart (H) J.L. Goskirk LTh	1968		The Manse, Lairg IV27 4EH	01549 402373
Melness and Tongue (H) John F. Mackie BD	1979	2000	New Manse, Glebelands, Tongue, Lairg IV27 4XL [E-mail: john.mackie1@virgin.net]	01847 611230

Rogart See Lairg
Rosehall See Creich

Macdonald, Michael	2004	Auxiliary Minister	73 Firhill, Alness IV17 0RT [E-mail: michaeljmac2@btinternet.com]	01349 884268

(41) CAITHNESS

Meets alternately at Wick and Thurso on the first Tuesday of February, March, May, September, November and December, and the third Tuesday of June.

Clerk: MR JAMES R.H. HOUSTON MBA MA		Lyndene House, Weydale, Thurso KW14 8YN [E-mail: caithness@cofscotland.org.uk]	01847 893955

Bower linked with Watten

Alastair H. Gray MA BD	1978	2005	Station Road, Watten, Wick KW1 5YN [E-mail: alastair.h.gray@btinternet.com]	01955 621220

Canisbay linked with Dunnet linked with Keiss

Vacant	The Manse, Canisbay, Wick KW1 4YH	01955 611309

Dunnet See Canisbay

Halkirk and Westerdale

Kenneth Warner BD DA DipTD	1981		Abbey Manse, Halkirk KW12 6UU [E-mail: wrnrkenn@aol.com]	01847 831227

Keiss See Canisbay

Olrig linked with Thurso: St Peter's and St Andrew's (H)
Vacant

The North Coast Parish

Paul R. Read BSc MA	2000	2006	Church of Scotland Manse, Reay, Thurso KW14 7RE [E-mail: PRead747@aol.com]

The Parish of Latheron

Vacant	Central Manse, Lybster KW3 6BN	01593 721231
John Craw DCS	Craiglockhart, Latheronwheel, Latheron KW5 6DW	01593 741779

Thurso: St Peter's and St Andrew's See Olrig

Thurso: West (H)
Ronald Johnstone BD   1977   1984   Thorkel Road, Thurso KW14 7LW   01847 892663
[E-mail: ronaldjohnstone@tiscali.co.uk]

Watten See Bower

Wick: Bridge Street linked with Wick: Old (H) (L)
Vacant   Mansefield, Miller Avenue, Wick KW1 4DF   01955 602822

Wick: Old See Wick: Bridge Street

Wick: Pulteneytown (H) and Thrumster
William F. Wallace BDS BD   1968   1974   The Manse, Coronation Street, Wick KW1 5LS   01955 603166
[E-mail: williamwallace39@btopenworld.com]

Mappin, Michael G. BA   1961 1998   (Bower with Watten)   Mundays, Banks Road, Watten, Wick KW1 5YL   01955 621720
Roy, Alistair A. MA BD   1955 2007   (Wick: Bridge Street)   1 Broaddykes Close, Kingswells, Aberdeen AB15 8UF   01224 743310

CAITHNESS Communion Sundays

Bower	1st Jul, Dec	North Coast	Mar, Easter, Jun, Sep, Dec	Watten	1st Jul, Dec
Canisbay	1st Jun, Nov	Olrig	last May, Nov	Wick	1st Apr, Oct
Dunnet	last May, Nov	Thurso		Bridge Street	4th Apr, Sep
Halkirk and Westerdale	Apr, Jul, Oct	St Peter's and		Old	
Keiss	1st May, 3rd Nov	St Andrew's	Mar, Jun, Sep, Dec	Pulteneytown and	
Latheron	Apr, Jul, Sep, Nov	West	4th Mar, Jun, Nov	Thrumster	1st Mar, Jun, Sep, Dec

(42) LOCHCARRON – SKYE

Meets in Kyle on the first Tuesday of each month, except January, May, July and August.

Clerk: REV. ALLAN J. MACARTHUR BD   High Barn, Croft Road, Lochcarron, Strathcarron IV54 8YA   01520 722278 (Tel)
[E-mail: lochcarronskye@cofscotland.org.uk]   01520 722674 (Fax)
[E-mail: a.macarthur@btinternet.com]

Applecross, Lochcarron and Torridon (GD)
Vacant

Bracadale and Duirinish (GD)
Vacant

Gairloch and Dundonnell			
Derek Morrison	1995	2000	Church of Scotland Manse, The Glebe, Gairloch IV21 2BT [E-mail: derekmorrison1@aol.com]	01445 712053 (Tel/Fax)

Glenelg and Kintail			
Roderick N. MacRae BTh	2001	2004	Church of Scotland Manse, Inverinate, Kyle IV40 8HE [E-mail: barvalous@msn.com]	01599 511245

Kilmuir and Stenscholl (GD)			
Ivor MacDonald BSc MSc BD	1993	2000	Staffin, Portree, Isle of Skye IV51 9JX [E-mail: ivormacdonald@btinternet.com]	01470 562759 (Tel/Fax)

Lochalsh			
John M. Macdonald	2002		The Church of Scotland Manse, Main Street, Kyle IV40 8DA [E-mail: john.macdonald53@btinternet.com]	01599 534294

Portree (GD)			
Sandor Fazakas BD MTh	1976	2007	Viewfield Road, Portree, Isle of Skye IV51 9ES [E-mail: fazakass52@yahoo.com]	01478 611868

Snizort (H) (GD)
Vacant
The Manse, Kensaleyre, Snizort, Portree, Isle of Skye IV51 9XE — 01470 532260

Strath and Sleat (GD)			
Ben Johnstone MA BD DMin	1973	2003	The Manse, 6 Upper Breakish, Isle of Skye IV42 8PY [E-mail: benonskye@onetel.com]	01471 820063
John D. Urquhart BA BD	1998	2003	The Manse, The Glebe, Kilmore, Teangue, Isle of Skye IV44 8RG [E-mail: ministear@hotmail.co.uk]	01471 844469

Note: The following addresses/numbers appear alongside the Vacant charges —
The Manse, Colonel's Road, Lochcarron, Strathcarron IV54 8YG — 01520 722829
Kinloch Manse, Dunvegan, Isle of Skye IV55 8WQ — 01470 521457

Beaton, Donald MA BD MTh	1961	2002	(Glenelg and Kintail)	Kilmaluag Croft, North Duntulm, Isle of Skye IV51 9UF	01470 552296
Ferguson, John LTh BD DD	1973	2002	(Portree)	9 Braeview Park, Beauly, Inverness IV4 7ED	01463 783900
Kellas, David J. MA BD	1966	2004	(Kilfinan with Kyles)	Babhunn, Glenelg, Kyle IV40 8LA [E-mail: davidkellas@beeb.net]	01599 522257
Macarthur, Allan J. BD	1973	1998	(Applecross, Lochcarron and Torridon)	High Barn, Croft Road, Lochcarron, Strathcarron IV54 8YA [E-mail: a.macarthur@btinternet.com]	(Tel) 01520 722278 (Fax) 01520 722674
McCulloch, Alen J.R. MA BD	1990	1995	Chaplain: Royal Navy	The Chaplaincy, HMS Drake, HMNB Devonport, Plymouth PL2 2BG	

MacDonald, Kenneth	1965 1992	(Associate: Applecross l/w Lochcarron)	Tigharry, Main Street, Lochcarron, Strathcarron IV54 8YB	01520 722433
Macleod, Donald LTh	1988 2000	(Snizort)	20 Caulfield Avenue, Cradlehall, Inverness IV1 2GA	01463 798093
Martin, George M. MA BD	1987 2005	(Applecross, Lochcarron and Torridon)	8(1) Buckingham Terrace, Edinburgh EH4 3AA	0131-343 3937
Matheson, James G. MA BD DD	1936 1979	(Portree)	The Elms, 148 Whitehouse Loan, Edinburgh EH9 2EZ	0131-446 6211
Murray, John W.	2003	Auxiliary Minister	Totescore, Kilmuir, Portree, Isle of Skye IV51 9YN	01470 542297

LOCHCARRON – SKYE   Communion Sundays

Applecross	4th Jun		Kilmuir	1st Mar, Sep
Arnisort	1st Sep		Kintail	3rd Apr, Jul
Bracadale	3rd Mar, Sep		Kyleakin	Easter, 4th Sep
Duirinish	3rd Jan, Easter, 3rd Sep		Lochalsh and	4th Jan, Jun, Sep, Christmas,
Dundonnell	4th Jun		Stromeferry	Easter
Elgol	1st Aug		Lochcarron	
Gairloch	3rd Jun, Nov		and Shieldaig	Easter, 3rd Jun, 1st Oct
Glenelg	2nd Jun, Nov		Plockton and Kyle	2nd May, 1st Oct
Glenshiel	1st Jul			

Portree	Easter, Pentecost, Christmas, 2nd Mar, Aug, 1st Nov
Sleat	4th Nov
Snizort	1st Jan, 4th Mar
Stenscholl	1st Jun, Dec
Strath	4th Jan
Torridon and Kinlochewe	2nd May

(43) UIST

Meets on the first Tuesday of February, March, September and November in Berneray, and on the third Tuesday of June in Leverburgh.

Clerk: REV. MURDO SMITH MA BD   Scarista, Isle of Harris HS3 3HX   **01859 550200**
[E-mail: uist@cofscotland.org.uk]

Barra (GD)
Eleanor D. Muir (Miss) MTheol DipP'Theol   1986   2005   Cuithir, Castlebay, Isle of Barra HS9 5XD   01871 810230
[E-mail: cuithir.manse@tesco.net]

Benbecula (GD) (H)
Andrew A. Downie BD BSc DipEd DipMin ThB   1994   2006   Church of Scotland Manse, Griminish, Isle of Benbecula HS7 5QA   01870 602180
[E-mail: andownie@yahoo.co.uk]

Berneray and Lochmaddy (GD) (H)
Donald Campbell MA BD DipTh   1997   2004   Church of Scotland Manse, Lochmaddy, Isle of North Uist HS6 5AA 01876 500414
[E-mail: donald13712@aol.com]

Carinish (GD) (H)
Iain Maciver BD
2007
Church of Scotland Manse, Clachan, Locheport, Lochmaddy,
Isle of North Uist HS6 5HD
[E-mail: iain.erica@btinternet.com]
01876 580219

Kilmuir and Paible (GE)
Iain M. Campbell BD
2004
Paible, Isle of North Uist HS6 5ED
[E-mail: ianmstudy@aol.com]
01876 510310

Manish-Scarista (GD) (H)
Murdo Smith MA BD
1988
Scarista, Isle of Harris HS3 3HX
[E-mail: uist@cofscotland.org.uk]
01859 550200

South Uist (GD)
Jackie G. Petrie
1989 2004
Daliburgh, Isle of South Uist HS8 5SS
[E-mail: jackiegpetrie@yahoo.com]
01878 700265

Tarbert (GE) (H)
Norman MacIver BD
1976 1988
The Manse, Manse Road, Tarbert, Isle of Harris HS3 3DF
[E-mail: norman@n-cmaciver.freeserve.co.uk]
01859 502231

Name	Years	Charge	Address	Phone
MacDonald, Angus J. BSc BD	1995 2001	(Lochmaddy and Trumisgarry)	7 Memorial Avenue, Stornoway, Isle of Lewis HS1 2QR	01851 706634
MacInnes, David MA BD	1966 1999	(Kilmuir and Paible)	9 Golf View Road, Kinmylies, Inverness IV3 8SZ	01463 717377
Macpherson, Kenneth J. BD	1988 2002	(Benbecula)	70 Baile na Cille, Balivanich, Isle of Benbecula HS7 5ND	01870 602751
Morrison, Donald John	2001	Auxiliary Minister	Lagnam, Brisgean 22, Kyles, Isle of Harris HS3 3BS	01859 502341
Muir, Alexander MA BD	1982 1996	(Carinish)	14 West Mackenzie Park, Inverness IV2 3ST	01463 712096
Smith, John M.	1956 1992	(Lochmaddy)	Hamersay, Clachan, Isle of North Uist HS6 5HD	01876 580332

UIST Communion Sundays

Barra	2nd Mar, June, Sep, Easter, Advent
Benbecula	2nd Mar, Sep
Berneray and Lochmaddy	4th Jun, last Oct
Carinish	4th Mar, Aug
Kilmuir and Paible	1st Jun, 3rd Nov
Manish-Scarista	3rd Apr, 1st Oct
South Uist – Iochdar	1st Mar
Howmore	1st Jun
Daliburgh	1st Sep
Tarbert	2nd Mar, 3rd Sep

(44) LEWIS

Meets at Stornoway, in St Columba's Church Hall, on the first Tuesday of February, March, June, September and November. It also meets if required in April and December on dates to be decided.

Clerk: REV. THOMAS S. SINCLAIR MA LTh BD

An Caladh, East Tarbert,
Tarbert, Isle of Harris HS3 3DB
[E-mail: lewis@cofscotland.org.uk]
[E-mail: thomas@sinclair0438.freeserve.co.uk]

01859 502849
07816 455820 (Mbl)

Barvas (GD) (H)
Vacant
Barvas, Isle of Lewis HS2 0QY
01851 840218

Carloway (GD) (H)
Vacant
Knock, Carloway, Isle of Lewis HS2 9AU
01851 643255

Cross Ness (GE) (H)
Ian Murdo M. Macdonald DPA BD   2001
Cross Manse, Swainbost, Ness, Isle of Lewis HS2 0TB
[E-mail: ianmurdo@crosschurch.fsnet.co.uk]
01851 810375

Kinloch (GE) (H)
Vacant
Laxay, Lochs, Isle of Lewis HS2 9LA
01851 830218

Knock (GE) (H)
Fergus J. MacBain BD DipMin   1999   2002
Knock Manse, Garrabost, Point, Isle of Lewis HS2 0PW
[E-mail: fergusjohn@macbain.freeserve.co.uk]
01851 870362

Lochs-Crossbost (GD) (H)
Andrew W.F. Coghill BD DPS   1993
Leurbost, Lochs, Isle of Lewis HS2 9NS
[E-mail: andcoghill@aol.com]
01851 860243 (Tel/Fax)
07776 480748 (Mbl)

Lochs-in-Bernera (GD) (H)
Vacant
Great Bernera, Isle of Lewis HS2 9LU

Stornoway: High (GD) (H)
William B. Black MA BD   1972   1998
1 Goathill Road, Stornoway, Isle of Lewis HS1 2NJ
[E-mail: willieblack@lineone.net]
01851 703106

Stornoway: Martin's Memorial (H) (Church office: 01851 700820)
Thomas MacNeil MA BD   2002   2006
Matheson Road, Stornoway, Isle of Lewis HS1 2LR
[E-mail: tommymacneil@hotmail.com]
01851 702206

Stornoway: St Columba (GD) (H) (Church office: 01851 701546)

| Angus Morrison MA BD PhD | 1979 | 2000 | Lewis Street, Stornoway, Isle of Lewis HS1 2JF | 01851 703350 |

[E-mail: morrisonangus@btconnect.com]

Uig (GE) (H)

| Vacant | | | Miavaig, Uig, Isle of Lewis HS2 9HW | 01851 672216 |

| Macdonald, Alexander | 1957 1991 | (Cross Ness) | 5 Urquhart Gardens, Stornoway, Isle of Lewis HS1 2TX | 01851 702825 |

[E-mail: almar@fivegardens.fsnet.co.uk]

| Macdonald, James LTh CPS | 1984 2001 | (Knock) | Elim, 8A Lower Bayble, Point, Isle of Lewis HS2 0QA | 01851 870173 |

[E-mail: elim8a@hotmail.co.uk]

| Maclean, Donald A. DCS | 1975 2006 | (Deacon) | 8 Upper Barvas, Isle of Lewis HS2 0QX | 01851 840454 |
| MacLennan, Donald Angus | | (Kinloch) | 4 Kestrel Place, Inverness IV2 3YH | 01463 243750 |

[E-mail: maclennankinloch@btinternet.com]   (Mbl) 07799 668270

Macleod, William	1957 2006	(Uig)	54 Lower Barvas, Isle of Lewis HS2 0QY	01851 840217
MacSween, Norman	1952 1986	(Kinloch)	7 Balmerino Drive, Stornoway, Isle of Lewis HS1 2TD	01851 703369
Sinclair, Thomas Suter MA LTh BD	1966 2004	(Stornoway: Martin's Memorial)	An Caladh, East Tarbert, Tarbert, Isle of Harris HS3 3DB	01859 502849

[E-mail: lewis@cofscotland.org.uk]   (Mbl) 07816 455820
[E-mail: thomas@sinclair0438.freeserve.co.uk]

LEWIS Communion Sundays

Barvas	3rd Mar, Sep
Carloway	1st Mar, last Sep
Cross Ness	2nd Mar, Oct
Kinloch	3rd Mar, 2nd Jun, 2nd Sep
Knock	3rd Apr, 1st Nov
Lochs-Crossbost	4th Mar, Sep
Lochs-in-Bernera	1st Apr, 2nd Sep
Stornoway	
High	3rd Feb, last Aug
Martin's Memorial	3rd Feb, last Aug
Stornoway	3rd Feb, last Aug
St Columba	3rd Jun, 1st Sep
Uig	1st Dec, Easter

(45) ORKNEY

Normally meets at Kirkwall, in the East Church King Street Halls, on the second Tuesday of September, February and May, and on the last Tuesday of November.

| Clerk: | REV. TREVOR G. HUNT BA BD | The Manse, Finstown, Orkney KW17 2EG | 01856 761328 (Tel/Fax) |
| | | | 07753 423333 (Mbl) |

[E-mail: orkney@cofscotland.org.uk]
[E-mail (personal): trevorghunt@yahoo.co.uk]

Birsay, Harray and Sandwick

| Andrea E. Price (Mrs) | 1997 | 2001 | The Manse, North Biggings Road, Dounby, Orkney KW17 2HZ | 01856 771803 |

[E-mail: andreaneil@andreaneil.plus.com]

East Mainland
Vacant
West Manse, Holm, Orkney KW17 2SB
01856 781422 (Tel/Fax)

Eday linked with Stronsay: Moncur Memorial (H)
Jennifer D. George (Ms) BA MDiv PhD   2000
Manse, Stronsay, Orkney KW17 2AF
[E-mail: jennifergeorge@btinternet.com]
01857 616311

Evie (H) linked with Firth (H) linked with Rendall
Trevor G. Hunt BA BD   1986
Manse, Finstown, Orkney KW17 2EG
[E-mail: trevorghunt@yahoo.co.uk]
01856 761328 (Tel/Fax)
07753 423333 (Mbl)

Firth (H) (01856 761117) See Evie

Flotta linked with Hoy and Walls
Vacant
South Isles Manse, Longhope, Stromness, Orkney KW16 3PG
01856 701325

Hoy and Walls See Flotta

Kirkwall: East (H)
Allan McCafferty BSc BD   1993
East Church Manse, Thoms Street, Kirkwall, Orkney KW15 1PF
[E-mail: amccafferty@beeb.net]
01856 875469

Kirkwall: St Magnus Cathedral (H)
G. Fraser H. Macnaughton MA BD   1982
Berstane Road, Kirkwall, Orkney KW15 1NA
[E-mail: fmacnaug@fish.co.uk]
01856 873312

North Ronaldsay linked with Sanday (H)
John L. McNab MA BD   1997
The Manse, Sanday, Orkney KW17 2BW
01857 600429

Orphir (H) linked with Stenness (H)
Thomas L. Clark BD   1985
Stenness Manse, Stenness, Stromness, Orkney KW16 3HH
[E-mail: toml.clark@btopenworld.com]
01856 761331

Papa Westray linked with Westray
Iain D. MacDonald BD   1993
The Manse, Hilldavale, Westray, Orkney KW17 2DW
[E-mail: idmacdonald@btinternet.com]
01857 677357 (Tel/Fax)
07710 443780 (Mbl)

Rendall See Evie

Rousay (Church centre: 01856 821271)
Continuing Vacancy

Sanday See North Ronaldsay

Shapinsay (50 per cent part-time)
Vacant

South Ronaldsay and Burray
Graham D.S. Deans MA BD MTh DMin   1978   2002   St Margaret's Manse, Church Road, St Margaret's Hope, Orkney KW17 2SR   01856 831288
[E-mail: graham.deans@btopenworld.com]

Stenness See Orphir

Stromness (H)
Fiona L. Lillie (Mrs) BA BD MLitt   1995   1999   5 Manse Lane, Stromness, Orkney KW16 3AP   01856 850203
[E-mail: fionalillie@btinternet.com]

Stronsay: Moncur Memorial See Eday
Westray See Papa Westray

Brown, R. Graeme BA BD   1961 1998   (Birsay with Rousay)   Bring Deeps, Orphir, Orkney KW17 2LX   (Tel/Fax) 01856 811707
[E-mail: graeme_sibyl@btinternet.com]

(46) SHETLAND

Meets at Lerwick on the first Tuesday of March, April, June, September, October, November and December.

Clerk: REV. CHARLES H.M. GREIG MA BD   The Manse, Sandwick, Shetland ZE2 9HW   01950 431244
[E-mail: shetland@cofscotland.org.uk]

Burra Isle linked with Tingwall
Vacant   Park Neuk, Meadowfield Place, Scalloway, Shetland ZE1 0UE   01595 880865

Delting linked with Northmavine
Vacant   The Manse, Grindwell, Brae, Shetland ZE2 9QJ   01806 522219
Robert M. MacGregor (Aux)   2004   Olna Cottage, Brae, Shetland ZE2 9QS   01806 522773
CMIOSH DipOSH RSP   [E-mail: shetlandsafety@aol.com]

Dunrossness and St Ninian's inc. Fair Isle linked with Sandwick, Cunningsburgh and Quarff
Charles H.M. Greig MA BD   1976   1997   The Manse, Sandwick, Shetland ZE2 9HW   01950 431244
[E-mail: chm.greig@btopenworld.com]

Fetlar linked with Unst linked with Yell
Vacant

Lerwick and Bressay

| Gordon Oliver BD | 1979 | 2002 | The Manse, 82 St Olaf Street, Lerwick, Shetland ZE1 0ES | 01595 692125 |

[E-mail: stolaf@tiscali.co.uk]

Nesting and Lunnasting linked with Whalsay and Skerries

| Irene A. Charlton (Mrs) BTh | 1994 | 1997 | The Manse, Marrister, Symbister, Whalsay, Shetland ZE2 9AE | 01806 566767 |

[E-mail: irene.charlton@virgin.net]

| Richard M. Charlton (Aux) | 2001 | | The Manse, Marrister, Symbister, Whalsay, Shetland ZE2 9AE | 01806 566767 |

[E-mail: richardm.charlton@virgin.net]

Northmavine See Delting

Sandsting and Aithsting linked with Walls and Sandness

| Thomas Macintyre MA BD | 1972 | 2006 | The Rock, Whiteness, Shetland ZE2 9LJ | 01595 830344 |

[E-mail: the2macs.macintyre@btinternet.com]

Sandwick, Cunningsburgh and Quarff See Dunrossness and St Ninian's
Tingwall See Burra Isle
Unst See Fetlar
Walls and Sandness See Sandsting and Aithsting
Whalsay and Skerries See Nesting and Lunnasting
Yell See Fetlar

Blair, James N.	1962	1986	(Sandsting and Aithsting with Walls)	2 Swinister, Sandwick, Shetland ZE2 9HH	01950 431472
Douglas, Marilyn (Miss) DCS	1988	2004	Presbytery Assistant	Heimdal, Quarff, Shetland ZE2 9EZ	01950 477584
Kirkpatrick, Alice H. (Miss) MA BD FSAScot	1987	2000	(Northmavine)	4 Stendaal, Skellister, South Nesting, Shetland ZE2 9XA	
Knox, R. Alan MA LTh AlnstAM	1965	2005	(Fetlar with Unst with Yell)	27 Killyvalley Road, Garvagh, Co. Londonderry, Northern Ireland BT51 5LX	02829 558925
Smith, Catherine (Mrs) DCS	1964	2003	(Presbytery Assistant)	21 Lingaro, Bixter, Shetland ZE2 9NN	01595 810207
Williamson, Magnus J.C.	1982	1999	(Fetlar with Yell)	Creekhaven, Houll Road, Scalloway, Shetland ZE1 0XA	01595 880023
Wilson, W. Stewart DA	1980	1997	(Kirkcudbright)	Aesterhoull, Fair Isle, Shetland ZE2 9JU	01595 760273

(47) ENGLAND

Meets at London, in Crown Court Church, on the second Tuesday of March and December, and at St Columba's, Pont Street, on the second Tuesday of June and October.

Clerk:	REV. SCOTT J. BROWN BD RN		35 Stag Way, Funtley, Fareham, Hants PO15 6TW	01329 236895 (Home)
			[E-mail: england@cofscotland.org.uk]	02392 625552 (Work)
			[E-mail: clerk@presbyteryofengland.org.uk]	07769 847876 (Mbl)

Corby: St Andrew's (H)

| Vacant | | | 6 Honiton Gardens, Corby, Northants NN18 8BW | 01536 203175 |

Corby: St Ninian's (H) (01536 265245)

Vacant				
Marjory Burns (Mrs) DCS	2003	1998	46 Glyndebourne Gardens, Corby, Northants NN18 0PZ	01536 747378
			25 Barnsley Square, Corby, Northants NN18 0PQ	01536 264819
			[E-mail: mburns8069@aol.com]	

Guernsey: St Andrew's in the Grange (H)

| Graeme W. Beebee BD | 1993 | 2003 | The Manse, Le Villocq, Castel, Guernsey GY5 7SB | 01481 257345 |
| | | | [E-mail: beehive@cwgsy.net] | |

Jersey: St Columba's (H)

| Randolph Scott MA BD | 1991 | 2006 | 18 Claremont Avenue, St Saviour, Jersey JE2 7SF | 01534 730659 |
| | | | [E-mail: rev.rs@tinyworld.co.uk] | |

Liverpool: St Andrew's

| Continued Vacancy | | | | |
| Session Clerk: Mr Robert Cottle | | | | 0151-524 1915 |

London: Crown Court (H) (020 7836 5643)

Vacant				
Timothy Fletcher BA FCMA (Aux)		1998	53 Sidmouth Street, London WC1H 8JX	020 7278 5022
			37 Harestone Valley Road, Caterham, Surrey CR3 6HN	01883 340826

London: St Columba's (H) (020 7836 5643) linked with Newcastle: St Andrew's (H)

Barry W. Dunsmore MA BD	1982	2000	29 Hollywood Road, Chelsea, London SW10 9HT	020 7376 5230
			[E-mail: office@stcolumbas.org.uk]	
Dorothy Lunn (Aux)	2001	2002	14 Bellerby Drive, Ouston, Co. Durham DH2 1TW	0191-492 0647
			[E-mail: dorothylunn@hotmail.com]	

Newcastle: St Andrews See London: St Columba's

Name			Designation	Address	Telephone
Bowie, A. Glen CBE BA BSc MA BD	1954	1984	(Principal Chaplain: RAF)	16 Weir Road, Hemingford Grey, Huntingdon PE18 9EH	01480 381425
Britchfield, Alison E.P. (Mrs)	1987	1992	Chaplain: RN	Director RN, Armed Forces Chaplaincy Centre, Amport House, Amport, Andover, Hants	
Brown, Scott J. BD RN	1993		Principal Chaplain: Royal Navy	Principal Church of Scotland and Free Churches Chaplain (Naval), and Director Naval Chaplaincy Service (Capability), Directorate General Naval Chaplaincy Service, MP 1.2, Leach Building, Whale Island, Portsmouth PO2 8BY [E-mail: clerk@presbyteryofengland.org.uk]	02392 625552 (Mbl) 07769 847876
Cairns, W. Alexander BD	1978	2006	(Corby: St Andrew's)	Kirkton House, Kirkton of Craig, Montrose DD10 9TB [E-mail: sandy.cairns@btinternet.com]	(Mbl) 07808 588045
Cameron, R. Neil	1975	1981	Chaplain: Community	The Church Centre, Rhine Area Support Unit, BFPO 40	0049 2161 472770
Coulter, David G. BA BD MDA PhD CF	1989	1994	Chaplain: Army	8 Ashdown Terrace, Tidworth, Wilts SP9 7SQ [E-mail: padredgcoulter@aol.com]	01980 842175
Craig, Gordon T. BD	1988	1988	Chaplain: RAF	40 Aiden Road, Quarrington, Sleaford, Lincs NG34 8UU	01529 300264
Dalton, Mark BD DipMin	2002	2002	Chaplain: RN	Fleet Pool Chaplain, Room 112, Defiance Building, HMNB Devonport, Plymouth, Devon PL2 2BG [E-mail: mark.dalton242@mod.uk]	01752 555921
Devenney, David J. BD	1997	2003	Chaplain: RN	8 Hunton Close, Lympstone, Exmouth, Devon EX8 5JG [E-mail: davidjdevenney@freeuk.com]	01395 266570
Dowswell, James A.M.	1991	2001	(Lerwick and Bressay)	Mill House, High Street, Staplehurst, Tonbridge, Kent TN12 0AV	01580 891271
Drummond, J.S. MA	1949	1978	(Corby: St Ninian's)	77 Low Road, Hellesdon, Norwich NR6 5AG	01603 417736
Duncan, Denis M. BD PhD	1944	1986	(Editor: *The British Weekly*)	80A Woodland Rise, London N10 3UJ	(Tel) 020 8883 1831 (Fax) 020 8374 4708
Fields, James MA BD STM	1988	1997	School Chaplain	The Bungalow, The Ridgeway, Mill Hill, London NW7 1QX	020 8201 1397
Hood, Adam J.J. MA BD DPhil	1989		Lecturer	67A Farquhar Road, Edgbaston, Birmingham B15 2QP [E-mail: adamhood1@hotmail.com]	0121-452 2606
Hughes, O. Tudor MBE BA	1934	1976	(Guernsey: St Andrew's in the Grange)	4 Belcher Court, Dorchester on Thames, Oxon	01865 340779
Kingston, David V.F. BD DipPTH	1993	1993	Chaplain: Army	CSFC Chaplain, RAF Akrotiri, Cyprus, BFPO 57	
Lugton, George L. MA BD	1955	1997	(Guernsey: St Andrew's in the Grange)	6 Clos de Beauvoir, Rue Cohu, Guernsey GY5 7TE	(Tel/Fax) 01481 254285
Macfarlane, Peter T. BA LTh	1970	1994	(Chaplain: Army)	4 rue de Rives, 37160 Abilly, France	
McIndoe, John H. MA BD STM DD	1966	2000	(London: St Columba's with Newcastle: St Andrew's	5 Dunlin, Westerlands Park, Glasgow G12 0FE	0141-579 1366
MacLeod, C. Angus BD	1996		Chaplain: Army	1 Mechanised Brigade, Delhi Barracks, Tidworth, Wilts SP9 7DX [E-mail: padreangusmac@hotmail.com]	(Work) 01980 602326 (Home) 01980 842380
MacLeod, R.N. MA BD	1986	1992	Chaplain: Army	25 Redford Gardens, Edinburgh EH13 0AP	0131-441 6522
Majcher, Philip L. BD	1982	1987	Chaplain: Army	Assistant Chaplain General, 2 Div, HQ 2nd Division, Craigiehall, South Queensferry EH30 9TN	
Martin, Anthony M. BA BD	1989	1989	Chaplain: Army	3 Lea Wood Road, Fleet, Hants GU51 5AL	01189 763409
Milloy, A. Miller DPE LTh DipTrMan	1979	1998	General Secretary: United Bible Societies		01252 628455
Mills, Peter W. BD CPS	1984		Chaplain-in-Chief, Royal Air Force		
Norwood, David W. BA	1948	1980	(Lisbon)	6 Kempton Close, Thundersley, Benfleet, Essex SS7 3SG	01268 747219

Prentice, Donald K. BSc BD	1989 1992	Chaplain: Army	SEME Bordon, Hampshire GU35 0JE	
Rennie, Alistair M. MA BD	1939 1986	(Kincardine Croick and Edderton)	Noble's Yard, St Mary's Gate, Wirksworth, Derbyshire DE4 4DQ	01629 820289
			[E-mail: alistairrennie@lineone.net]	
Stewart, Charles E. BSc BD PhD	1976 2000	School Chaplain	The Royal Hospital School, Holbrook, Ipswich IP9 2RX	01473 326200
Thomson, Steven	2001 2004	Chaplain: Royal Navy	Royal Navy SME, HMS Sultan, Military Road, Gosport PO12 3BY	
Trevorrow, James A. LTh	1971 2003	(Glasgow: Cranhill)	12 Test Green, Corby, Northants NN17 2HA	01536 264018
			[E-mail: jimtrevorrow@compuserve.com]	
Walker, R. Forbes BSc BD ThM	1987 2000	School Chaplain	2 Holmleigh, Priory Road, Ascot, Berks SL5 8EA	01344 883272
Wallace, Donald S.	1950 1980	(Chaplain: RAF)	7 Dellfield Close, Watford, Herts WD1 3BL	01923 223289
Ward, Michael J. BSc BD PhD MA	1983 2004	Chaplain: College	19 Devonshire Avenue, Grimsby, Lincs DN32 0BW	01472 877079
			[E-mail: revmw@btopenworld.com]	
Whitton, John P.	1977 1999	(Deputy Chaplain General)	Trenchard Lines, Upavon, Wilts SN9 6BE	01980 615802

ENGLAND – Church Addresses

Corby	Occupation Road	Liverpool	The Western Rooms, Anglican Cathedral	
St Andrew's				
St Ninian's	Beanfield Avenue	Newcastle	Sandyford Road	
		London		
		Crown Court	Crown Court WC2	
		St Columba's	Pont Street SW1	

(48) EUROPE

Clerk:	**REV. JOHN A. COWIE BSc BD**	**Jan Willem Brouwersstraat 9, NL-1071 LH Amsterdam**	**Tel: 0031 20 672 2288**
		[E-mail: europe@cofscotland.org.uk]	**Fax: 0031 842 221513**
		[E-mail: j.cowie@chello.nl]	

Amsterdam

John A. Cowie BSc BD	1983 1989	Jan Willem Brouwersstraat 9, NL-1071 LH Amsterdam, The Netherlands	0031 20 672 2288
			Fax: 0031 842 221513
		[E-mail: j.cowie@chello.nl]	

Brussels (E-mail: secretary@churchofscotland.be)

Andrew Gardner BSc BD PhD	1997 2004	23 Square des Nations, B-1000 Brussels, Belgium	0032 2 672 40 56
		[E-mail: minister@churchofscotland.be]	

Budapest (Church telephone: +36 13730725)

Aaron Stevens	2006	H-1145 Budapest, Uzsoki u. 34b, Hungary	+36 (1) 2516896
		[E-mail: revastevens@yahoo.co.uk]	(Mbl) +36 (30) 203179592
Otto Pecsuk (Assoc)	2006	1119 Budapest, Allende Park 9. III/11, Hungary	+36 (7) 2947635
		[E-mail: opecsuk@yahoo.com]	

Costa del Sol John Shedden CBE BD DipPSS	1971	2005	Lux Mundi Centro Ecumenico, Calle Nueva 3, Fuengirola, E-29460 Malaga, Spain	0034 951 260 982
Geneva Ian A. Manson BA BD	1989	2001	20 Ancienne Route, 1218 Grand Saconnex, Geneva, Switzerland (Office) [E-mail: cofsg@pingnet.ch]	0041 22 798 29 09 0041 22 788 08 31
Gibraltar Stewart J. Lamont BSc BD	1972	2003	St Andrew's Manse, 29 Scud Hill, Gibraltar [E-mail: lamont@gibraltar.gi]	00350 77040
Lausanne G. Melvyn Wood MA BD	1982	2004	26 Avenue de Rumine, CH-1005 Lausanne, Switzerland (Tel/Fax) [E-mail: scotskirklausanne@bluewin.ch]	0041 21 323 98 28
Lisbon William B. Ross LTh CPS	1988	2006	Av. Eng. Adelino Amaro da Costa, 2086, 2750 Cascais, Portugal	00351 21 483 7885
Malta David Morris	2002		La Romagnola, 13 Triq is-Seiqia, Mosra Kola, Attard (Tel/Fax) BZN 05, Malta [E-mail: djlmorris@onvol.net] Church address: 210 Old Baker Street, Valletta, Malta	00356 214 15465
Paris Alan Miller BA MA BD	2000	2006	10 Rue Thimmonier, F-75009 Paris, France [E-mail: scotskirk@wanadoo.fr] [E-mail: afmiller@orange.fr]	0033 1 48 78 47 94
Regensburg (University) Rhona Dunphy (Mrs)	2005		Hirtensteig 1, 93155 Hemau-Laufenthal, Germany [E-mail: rhona@dunphy.de]	0049 (949) 1903666
Rome: St Andrew's William B. McCulloch BD	1997	2002	Via XX Settembre 7, 00187 Rome, Italy (Tel) [E-mail: revwbmcculloch@hotmail.com] (Fax)	0039 06 482 7627 0039 06 487 4370
Rotterdam Robert A. Calvert BSc BD DMin	1983	1995	Meeuwenstraat 4A, NL-3071 PE Rotterdam, The Netherlands [E-mail: scotsintchurch@cs.com]	0031 10 220 4199
Joanne Evans-Boiten BD (Community Minister)	2004		Oude Veerdam 2, NL-3212 MA Simonshaven, The Netherlands	0031 181 454229

Turin
Vacant

Via Sant Anselmo 6, 10125 Turin, Italy — 0039 011 650 9467

Conference of European Churches
Matthew Z. Ross LLB BD MTh FSAScot   1998   2003

Church and Society Commission, Ecumenical Centre, Rue Joseph II 174, B-1000 Brussels, Belgium
[E-mail: mzr@cec-kek.be]
(Tel) 0032 2 230 1732
(Fax) 0032 2 231 1413
(Mbl) 0044 7711 706950

James M. Brown MA BD   1982
Neustrasse 15, D-4630 Bochum, Germany
[E-mail: j.brown@web.de]
0049 234 133 65

Professor A.I.C. Heron BD DTheol   1975   1987
University of Erlangen, Kochstrasse 6, D-91054 Erlangen, Germany
[E-mail: arheron@theologie.uni-erlangen.de]
0049 9131 852202

James Sharp (Aux)   2005
102 Rue des Eaux-Vives, CH-1207 Geneva, Switzerland
[E-mail: jsharp@scout.org]
0041 22 786 4847

Bertalan Tamas
St Columba's Scottish Mission, Vorosmarty utca 51, H-1064 Budapest, Hungary
[E-mail: rch@mail.elender.hu]
0036 1 343 8479

Derek Yarwood   1962   (2001)
Chaplain's Department, Garrison HQ, Princess Royal Barracks, BFPO 47, Germany
0044 5241 77924

(Rome) David F. Huie MA BD   1962
15 Rosebank Gardens, Largs KA30 8TD
[E-mail: david.huie@btopenworld.com]
01475 670733

(Brussels) Charles C. McNeill OBE BD   1962   (1991)
17 All Saints Way, Beachamwell, Swaffham, Norfolk PE37 8BU

(Gibraltar) D. Stuart Philip MA   1952   (1990)
6 St Bernard's Crescent, Edinburgh EH4 1NP
0131-332 7499

(Brussels) Thomas C. Pitkeathly MA CA BD   1984   2004
1 Lammermuir Court, Gullane EH31 2HU
01620 843373

(Rotterdam) Joost Pot BSc (Aux)   1992   2004
[E-mail: j.pot@wanadoo.nl]

(49) JERUSALEM

Jerusalem: St Andrew's
Jane L. Barron (Mrs) BA DipEd BD   1999   2006
PO Box 8619, Jerusalem 91086, Israel
[E-mail: stachjer@netvision.net.il]
(Tel) 00972 2 673 2401
(Fax) 00972 2 673 1711

Tiberias: St Andrew's
Jennifer C. Zielinski (Mrs) (Reader)
PO Box 104, Tiberias 14100, Israel
[E-mail: scottie2@netvision.net.il]
(Tel) 00972 4 671 0710
(Fax) 00972 4 671 0711

SECTION 6

Additional Lists
of Personnel

		Page
A	Auxiliary Ministers	284
B	Chaplains to HM Forces	285
C	Chaplains, Hospital	287
D	Chaplains, Full-time Industrial	295
E	Chaplains, Prison	295
F	Chaplains, University	296
G	The Diaconate	297
H	Ministers having Resigned Membership of Presbytery	301
I	Ministers holding Practising Certificates	303
J	Presbytery Advisers and Facilitator	306
K	Overseas Locations	306
L	Overseas Resigned and Retired Mission Partners	310
M	Parish Assistants and Project Workers	314
N	Readers	314
O	Representatives on Council Education Committees	326
P	Retired Lay Agents	328
Q	Ministers Ordained for Sixty Years and Upwards	328
R	Deceased Ministers	331

LIST A – AUXILIARY MINISTERS

NAME	ORD	ADDRESS	TEL	PR
Anderson, David M. MSc FCOptom	1984	1 Dumfries Place, Fort William PH33 6UQ	01397 703203	38
Attenburrow, Anne BSc MBChB	2006	4 Jock Inksons Brae, Elgin IV30 1QE	01343 552330	35
Binks, Mike	2007	Holly Bank, Corsbie Road, Newton Stewart DG8 6JD	01671 402201	9
Birch, Jim PGDip FRSA FIOC (Retired)	2001	1 Kirkhill Grove, Cambuslang, Glasgow G72 8EH	0141-583 1722	16
Brown, Elizabeth (Mrs) JP RGN	1996	25 Highfield Road, Scone, Perth PH2 6RN	01738 552391	28
Burroughs, Kirsty-Ann (Mrs) BA BD CertTheol DRM PhD	2007	Lorne and Lowland Manse, Castlehill, Campbeltown PA28 6AN	01586 552468	19
Cameron, Ann	2005	30 Wilson Road, Banchory AB31 5UY	01330 825953	32
Campbell, Gordon MA BD CDipAF DipHSM MCMI MIHM AFRIN FRSGS FRGS FSAScot	2001	2 Falkland Place, Kingoodie, Invergowrie, Dundee DD2 5DY	01382 561383	29
Charlton, Richard	2001	The Manse, Symbister, Whalsay, Shetland ZE2 9AE	01806 566767	46
Cloggie, June (Mrs) (Retired)	1997	11A Tulipan Crescent, Callander FK17 8AR	01877 331021	23
Craggs, Sheila (Mrs)	2001	7 Morar Court, Ellon AB41 9GG	01358 723055	33
Cruikshank, Alistair A.B. MA (Retired)	1991	Thistle Cottage, 2A Chapel Place, Dollar FK14 7DW	01259 742549	23
Don, Andrew	2006	5 Eskdale Court, Penicuik EH26 8HT	01968 675766	3
Durno, Richard C. DSW CQSW (Community Minister)	1989	Durnada House, 31 Springfield Road, Bishopbriggs, Glasgow G64 1PJ	0141-772 1052	16
Ferguson, Archibald M. MSc PhD CEng FRINA	1989	The Whins, 2 Barrowfield, Station Road, Cardross, Dumbarton G82 5NL	01389 841517	18
Fletcher, Timothy E.G. BA FCMA	1998	37 Hareston Valley Road, Caterham, Surrey CR3 6HN	01883 340826	47
Forrest, Kenneth P. CBE BSc PhD	2006	5 Carruth Road, Bridge of Weir PA11 3HQ	01505 615033	14
Glass, Alexander OBE MA	1998	Craigton, Tulloch Avenue, Dingwall IV15 9TU	01349 863258	39
Griffiths, Ruth (Mrs)	2004	Kirkwood, Mathieson Lane, Innellan, Dunoon PA23 7TA	01369 830145	19
Harrison, Cameron	2006	Woodfield House, Priormuir, St Andrews KY16 8LP	01334 478067	26
Hood, Catriona A.	2006	2 Bellmhor Court, Campbeltown PA28 6AN	01586 552065	19
Howie, Marion L.K. (Mrs) MA ARCS	1992	51 High Road, Stevenston KA20 3DY	01294 466571	12
Jenkinson, John J. JP LTCL ALCM DipEd DipSen (Retired)	1991	8 Rosehall Terrace, Falkirk FK1 1PY	01324 625498	22
Kay, Elizabeth (Miss) Dip YCS	1993	1 Kintail Walk, Inchture, Perth PH14 9RY	01828 686029	29
Kemp, Tina MA	2005	12 Oaktree Gardens, Dumbarton G82 1EV	01389 730477	18
Landale, William	2005	Green Hope Guest House, Green Hope, Duns TD11 3SG	01361 890242	5
Lunn, Dorothy	2002	14 Bellerby Drive, Ouston, Co. Durham DH2 1TN	0191-492 0647	47
McAlpine, John BSc (Retired)	1988	Braeside, 201 Bonkle Road, Newmains, Wishaw ML2 9AA	01698 384610	17
MacDonald, Kenneth MA BA (Retired)	2001	5 Henderland Road, Bearsden, Glasgow G61 1AH	0141-943 1103	16
Macdonald, Michael	2004	73 Firhill, Alness IV17 0RT	01349 884268	40
MacDougall, Lorna A. MA	2003	34 Miller Place, Greenmount Park, Falkirk FK2 9QB	01324 552739	22
MacGregor, Robert M. MIOSH DipOSH RSP	2004	Olna Cottage, Brae, Shetland ZE2 9QS	01806 522604	46
Mack, Elizabeth (Miss) Dip PEd	1994	24 Roberts Crescent, Dumfries DG2 7RS	01387 264847	8

NAME	ORD	ADDRESS	TEL	No.
Mack, John C. JP	1985	The Willows, Auchleven, Insch AB52 6QD	01464 820387	33
Mailer, Colin (Retired)	2000	Innis Chonain, Back Row, Polmont, Falkirk FK2 0RD	01324 712401	22
Manson, Eileen (Mrs) DCE	1994	1 Cambridge Avenue, Gourock PA19 1XT	01475 632401	14
Mills, Iain	2006	4 Farden Place, Prestwick KA9 2HS	01292 475212	10
Moore, Douglas T.	2003	9 Midton Avenue, Prestwick KA9 1PU	01292 671352	10
Morrison, Donald John	2001	22 Kyles, Tarbert, Isle of Harris HS3 3BS	01859 502341	43
Munro, Mary (Mrs) BA (Retired)	1993	14 Auchneel Crescent, Stranraer DG9 0JH	01776 870250	9
Murray, John W.	2003	1 Totescore, Kilmuir, Portree, Isle of Skye IV51 9YN	01470 542297	42
Paterson, Andrew E. JP	1994	6 The Willows, Kelty KY4 0FQ	01383 830998	24
Paterson, Maureen (Mrs) BSc	1992	91 Dalmahoy Crescent, Kirkcaldy KY2 6TA	01592 262300	25
Phillippo, Michael MTh BSc BVetMed MRCVS	2003	25 Deeside Crescent, Aberdeen AB15 7PT	01224 318317	31
Pot, Joost BSc (Retired)	1992	Rijksstraatweg 12, NL-2988 BJ Ridderkerk, The Netherlands	0031 18 042 0894	48
Ramage, Alistair E. MA BA ADB CertEd	1996	16 Claremont Gardens, Milngavie, Glasgow G62 6PG	0141-956 2897	18
Riddell, Thomas S. BSc CEng FIChemE	1993	4 The Maltings, Linlithgow EH49 6DS	01506 843251	2
Robson, Brenda (Dr)	2005	Old School House, 2 Baird Road, Ratho, Newbridge EH28 8RA	0131-333 2746	1
Sharp, James	2005	102 Rue des Eaux-Vivres, CH-1207 Geneva, Switzerland	0041 22 786 4847	48
Shaw, Catherine A.M. MA (Retired)	1998	40 Merrygreen Place, Stewarton, Kilmarnock KA3 5EP	01560 483352	11
Simpson, James H. BSc (Retired)	1996	11 Claypotts Place, Broughty Ferry, Dundee DD5 1LG	01382 776520	29
Sutherland, David	2001	6 Cronarty Drive, Dundee DD2 2UQ	01382 621473	29
Thomas, Shirley A. (Mrs) DipSocSci AMIA (Retired)	1988	14 Kirkgait, Letham, Forfar DD8 2XQ	01307 818084	30
Vivers, Katherine (Mrs)	2004	Blacket House, Eaglesfield, Lockerbie DG11 3AA	01461 500412	7
Wandrum, David	1993	5 Cawder View, Carrickstone Meadows, Cumbernauld, Glasgow G68 0BN	01236 723288	22
Watson, Jean S. (Miss) MA (Retired)	1993	29 Strachan Crescent, Dollar FK14 9HL	01259 742872	23
Wilson, Mary D. (Mrs) RGN SCM DTM (Retired)	1990	'Berbice', The Terrace, Bridge of Tilt, Blair Atholl, Pitlochry PH18 5SZ	01796 481619	27
Zambonini, James LLADip	1997	100 Old Manse Road, Netherton, Wishaw ML2 0EP	01698 350889	17

LIST B – CHAPLAINS TO HM FORCES

NAME	ORD	COM	BCH	ADDRESS
Abeledo, Benjamin J.A. BTh DipTh PTh	1991	1999	A	2 Bn Infantry Training Centre, Vimy Barracks, Catterick Garrison, North Yorks DL9 3PS
Aitchison, James W. BD	1993	1993	A	2 Bn The Parachute Regiment, Clive Barracks, Tern Hill, Shropshire TF9 3QE
Anderson, David P. BSc BD	2002	2007	A	3 Bn The Royal Regiment of Scotland (Black Watch), BFPO 806
Britchfield, Alison E.P. (Mrs) MA BD	1987	1992	RN	Director Royal Navy, Armed Forces Chaplaincy Centre, Amport House, Amport, Andover SP11 8BG
Brown, Scott J. BD	1993	1993	RN	Staff Chaplain to the Chaplain of the Fleet, Directorate Royal Naval Chaplaincy Service, MP 1.2, Leach Building, Whale Island, Portsmouth, Hants PO2 8BY
Connolly, Daniel BD DipTheol DipMin	1983		A	1 Bn Infantry Training Centre, Vimy Barracks, Catterick Garrison, North Yorks DL9 3PS
Coulter, David G. BA BD PhD	1989	1994	A	Headquarters 3 (UK) Division, Bulford Camp, Salisbury SP4 9NY

Craig, Gordon T. BD DipMin	1988	1988	RAF	Deputy Director Chaplaincy Operations and Training, HQ Strike Command, RAF High Wycombe, Bucks HP14 4UE
Dailly, J.R. BD DipPS	1979	1979	A	Warminster Training Centre, Warminster, Wiltshire BA12 0DJ
Dalton, Mark BD DipMin	2002	2002	RN	c/o The Chaplaincy, Fleet Pool, Devonport, Water Front Office, Room 132 Defence Building, HMNB Devonport, Plymouth PL2 2BG
Devenney, David BD	1997	2002	RN	The Chaplaincy Centre, Command Training Centre, Royal Marines, Lympstone, Exmouth, Devon EX8 5AR
Duncan, John C. BD MPhil	1987	2001	A	4 Bn The Royal Regiment of Scotland (The Highlanders), BFPO 38
Kennon, Stan MA BD	1992	2000	RN	c/o The Chaplaincy, HMS Raleigh, Tor Point, Cornwall PL2 2PD
Kingston, David V.F. BD DipPTH	1993	1993	A	Senior Chaplain, 101 Brigade, Buller Barracks, Aldershot, Hants GU11 2BX
McCulloch, Alen J.R. MA BD	1990	1995	RN	c/o The Chaplaincy, HMS Drake, HMNB Devonport, Plymouth PL2 2BG
Macgregor, John BD	2001	2006	A	2 Bn The Royal Regiment of Scotland (Highland Fusiliers), Glencorse Barracks, Penicuik EH26
Mackenzie, Seoras L. BD	1996	1998	A	1 Logistic Support Regiment, BFPO 47
MacLeod, C. Angus MA BD	1996	1996	A	Senior Chaplain, 1 (Mechanised) Brigade, Delhi Barracks, Tidworth SP9 7DX
MacLeod, Rory N. MA BD	1986	1992	A	2 Bn The Light Infantry, Redford Barracks, Edinburgh EH13 0PP
MacPherson Duncan J. BSc BD	1993	2002	A	Household Cavalry Regiment, Combermere Barracks, Windsor, Berkshire SL4 3DN
Majcher, Philip L. BD	1982	1987	A	Assistant Chaplain General, 2 Div, HQ 2nd Division, Craigiehall, South Queensferry EH30 9TN
Mills, Peter W. BD CPS	1984	1984	RAF	Chaplain-in-Chief and Principal Chaplain (Church of Scotland and Free Churches), HQ Strike Command, RAF High Wycombe, Bucks HP14 4UE
Munro, Sheila BD	1995	2003	RAF	Chaplaincy Centre, RAF Lossiemouth IV31 6SD
Prentice, Donald K. BSc BD	1987	1992	A	Senior Chaplain, SEME Bordon, Hampshire GU35 0JE
Shackleton, Scott J.S. BA BD	1993	1993	RN	The Chaplaincy Centre, HMS Neptune, HM Naval Base Clyde, Faslane, Helensburgh G84 8HL
Thomson, Steven BSc BD	2001	2004	RN	The Chaplaincy, HMS Sultan, Military Road, Gosport, Hants PO12 3BY

CHAPLAINS TO HM FORCES (Territorial Army)
CHAPLAINS TO HM FORCES (Army Cadet Force)
CHAPLAINS TO HM FORCES (Royal Naval Reserve)

In recent years, the *Year Book* has included details of those serving as Chaplains with the Territorial Army and with the Army Cadet Force. These lists have not always been as complete as those concerned with full-time Chaplains to the Forces. Fresh consideration is being given to the preparation and updating of these lists so that they can be included in future editions of the *Year Book* in accurate and appropriate forms. It is also intended that these lists will include the new category of Chaplains to the Royal Naval Reserve. The Rev. Marjory A. MacLean LLB BD PhD has been commissioned as Chaplain Royal Naval Reserve at HMS *Scotia*. The Rev. Ross McDonald has joined the RNR and will undertake new entry Chaplains' training this year, and has responsibility at HMS *Dalriada*.

LIST C – HOSPITAL CHAPLAINS ('Full-time' Chaplains are listed first in each area)

LOTHIAN

EDINBURGH – LOTHIAN UNIVERSITY HOSPITALS

ROYAL INFIRMARY
- Rev. Alexander Young — 32 Alnwickhill Park, Edinburgh EH16 6UH — 0131-242 1991
- Rev. Iain Telfer — 27A Craigour Avenue, Edinburgh EH17 7NH — 0131-242 1996
- Anne Mulligan

WESTERN GENERAL HOSPITAL [0131-537 1000]
- Rev. Alistair K. Ridland — 13 Stewart Place, Kirkliston EH29 2BQ — 0131-537 1400

LOTHIAN PRIMARY CARE

ROYAL EDINBURGH HOSPITAL [0131-537 6734]
- Rev. John McMahon
- Rev. Lynne MacMurchie
- Rev. Patricia Allen — 1 Westgate, Dunbar EH42 1JL

ROYAL HOSPITAL FOR SICK CHILDREN [0131-536 0000]
- Rev. Caroline Upton — 10 (3FL) Montagu Terrace, Edinburgh EH3 5QX — 0131-536 0144

EDINBURGH COMMUNITY MENTAL HEALTH
- Rev. Lynne MacMurchie — 41 George IV Bridge, Edinburgh EH1 1EL — 0131-220 5150

LIVINGSTON – ST JOHN'S HOSPITAL [01506 419666]
- Rev. Dr Georgina Nelson — Chaplain's Office, St John's Hospital, Livingston

HOSPICES

MARIE CURIE CENTRE	Rev. Tom Gordon	Frogston Road West, Edinburgh EH10 7DR	(Tel) 0131-445 2141 / (Fax) 0131-445 5845
ST COLUMBA'S HOSPICE	Rev. Ewan Kelly	15 Boswall Road, Edinburgh EH5 3RW	0131-551 1381

HOSPITALS

CORSTORPHINE	Rev. J. William Hill	33/9 Murrayfield Road, Edinburgh EH12 6EP	0131-554 1842
EASTERN GENERAL	Rev. John Tait	52 Pilrig Street, Edinburgh EH6 5AS	01506 419666
LINLITHGOW ST MICHAEL'S	Rev. Dr Georgina Nelson	Chaplain's Office, St John's Hospital, Livingston	01368 863098
BELHAVEN	Rev. Laurence H. Twaddle	The Manse, Belhaven Road, Dunbar EH42 1NH	01875 614442
EDENHALL	Rev. Anne M. Jones	7 North Elphinstone Farm, Tranent EH33 2ND	01875 614442
HERDMANFLAT	Rev. Anne M. Jones	7 North Elphinstone Farm, Tranent EH33 2ND	0131-667 2995
LOANHEAD	Mrs Susan Duncan	35 Kilmaurs Road, Edinburgh EH16 5DB	
ROODLANDS	Rev. Kenneth D.F. Walker	The Manse, Athelstaneford, North Berwick EH39 5BE	01620 880378

Hospital	Chaplain	Address	Telephone
ROSSLYNLEE	Rev. John W. Fraser	North Manse, Penicuik EH26 8AG	01968 672213
BORDERS			
MELROSE – BORDERS GENERAL HOSPITAL [01896 754333]	Rev. J. Ronald Dick	Chaplaincy Centre, Borders General Hospital, Melrose TD6 9BS	
DINGLETON	Rev. John Riddell	Orchid Cottage, Gingham Row, Earlston TD4 6ET	
HAY LODGE, PEEBLES	Rev. James H. Wallace	Innerleithen Road, Peebles EH45 8BD	01721 721749
KNOLL	Rev. Andrew Morrice	The Manse, Castle Street, Duns TD11 3DG	01361 883755
INCH	Rev. Robin McHaffie	Kirk Yetholm, Kelso TD5 8RD	01573 420308
DUMFRIES AND GALLOWAY			
DUMFRIES AND GALLOWAY ROYAL INFIRMARY [01387 241625]	Rev. Alexander E. Strachan		
THOMAS HOPE, LANGHOLM	Rev. Robert B. Milne	The Manse, Langholm DG13 0BL	01896 668577
LOCHMABEN	Rev. Alexander C. Stoddart	The Manse, Hightae, Lockerbie DG11 1JL	01387 811499
MOFFAT	Rev. David M. McKay	The Manse, Moffat DG10 9LR	01683 220128
NEW ANNAN	Rev. Mairi C. Byers	Meadowbank, Plumdon Road, Annan DG12 6SJ	01461 206512
CASTLE DOUGLAS	Rev. Robert Malloch	1 Castle View, Castle Douglas DG7 1BG	01556 502171
DUMFRIES AND GALLOWAY ROYAL INFIRMARY			
KIRKCUDBRIGHT	Rev. Douglas R. Irving	6 Bourtree Avenue, Kirkcudbright DG6 4AU	01557 330489
THORNHILL	Rev. Donald Keith	The Manse, Mansepark, Thornhill D63 5ER	01848 331191
NEWTON STEWART			
AYRSHIRE AND ARRAN			
AYRSHIRE AND ARRAN PRIMARY CARE [01292 513023]			
AILSA HOSPITAL, AYR	Rev. Sheila Mitchell		
AYR HOSPITAL	Rev. Paul Russell	Chaplaincy Centre, Dalmellington Road, Ayr KA6 6AB	
AYRSHIRE AND ARRAN ACUTE HOSPITALS [01563 521133]			
CROSSHOUSE HOSPITAL KILMARNOCK	Rev. Alex Welsh	8 Greenside Avenue, Prestwick KA9 2HB	01292 475341
	Rev. Judith Huggett	4 Westmoor Crescent, Kilmarnock KA1 1TX	
AYR/BIGGART HOSPITALS [01292 610555]			
AYR	Rev. Roderick H. McNidder	6 Hollow Park, Alloway, Ayr KA7 4SR	01292 442554
	Rev. Kenneth Elliott	68 St Quivox Road, Prestwick KA9 1JF	01292 478788
EAST AYRSHIRE COMMUNITY	Rev. John Paterson	33 Barrhill Road, Cumnock KA18 1PJ	01290 420769

Institution	Chaplain	Address	Telephone
WAR MEMORIAL, ARRAN	Rev. Elizabeth Watson	The Manse, Whiting Bay, Isle of Arran KA27 8RE	01770 700289
LADY MARGARET, MILLPORT	Rev. Marjory H. Mackay	The Manse, Millport, Isle of Cumbrae KA28 0ED	01475 530416

LANARKSHIRE

Institution	Chaplain	Address	Telephone
LOCKHART	Rev. Alison Meikle	2 Kaimhill Court, Lanark ML11 9HU	01555 662600
CLELAND			
KELLO	Rev. James Francis	61 High Street, Biggar ML12 6DA	01899 220227
LADY HOME			
ROADMEETINGS	Rev. Geoff McKee	Kirkstyle Manse, Church Street, Carluke ML8 4BA	
WISHAW GENERAL	Rev. James S.G. Hastie	Chalmers Manse, Quarry Road, Larkhall ML9 1HH	01698 882238
	Rev. J. Allardyce	6 Kelso Crescent, Wishaw ML2 7HD	01698 372657
	Rev. Sharon Colvin	48 Dunrobin Road, Airdrie ML6 8LR	01236 763154
	Rev. Mhorag MacDonald	350 Kirk Road, Wishaw ML2 8LH	01698 381305
STRATHCLYDE	Rev. David W. Doyle	19 Orchard Street, Motherwell ML1 3JE	01698 263472
HAIRMYRES	Rev. John Brewster	21 Turnberry Place, East Kilbride, Glasgow G75 8TB	01355 242564
	Rev. Dr John McPake	30 Eden Grove, East Kilbride, Glasgow G75 8XY	01355 234196
	Rev. James S.G. Hastie	Chalmers Manse, Quarry Road, Larkhall ML9 1HH	01698 882238
KIRKLANDS	Rev. James P. Fraser	26 Hamilton Road, Strathaven ML10 6JA	01357 522758
STONEHOUSE	Rev. J. Stanley Cook	137A Old Manse Road, Netherton, Wishaw ML2 0EW	01698 299600
UDSTON	Rev. James Munton	2 Moorcroft Drive, Airdrie ML6 8ES	01236 754848
COATHILL	Rev. James Grier	47 Blair Road, Coatbridge ML5 1JQ	01236 432427
MONKLANDS GENERAL	Rev. James Munton	2 Moorcroft Drive, Airdrie ML6 8ES	01263 754848
WESTER MOFFAT	Rev. Derek Pope	35 Birrens Road, Motherwell ML1 3NS	01698 266716
HARTWOODHILL	Rev. Colin Cuthbert	Yieldshields Farm, Carluke ML8 4QB	01555 771157
HATTONLEA	Rev. Agnes Moore	16 Croftpark Street, Bellshill ML4 1EY	01698 842877
MOTHERWELL PSYCHIATRIC	Rev. John Handley	12 Airbles Crescent, Motherwell ML1 3AR	01698 262733
COMMUNITY MENTAL HEALTH CARE	Rev. J. Stanley Cook	137A Old Manse Road, Netherton, Wishaw ML2 0EW	01698 299600
	Rev. Sharon Colvin	48 Dunrobin Road, Airdrie ML6 8LR	01236 763154

GREATER GLASGOW AND CLYDE

NORTH GLASGOW UNIVERSITY HOSPITALS
GLASGOW ROYAL INFIRMARY
[0141-211 4000/4661]

Institution	Chaplain	Address	Telephone
GLASGOW ROYAL INFIRMARY	Rev. Anne J.M. Harper	122 Greenock Road, Bishopton PA7 5AS	
WESTERN INFIRMARY [0141-211 2000]	Rev. Keith Saunders	1 Beckfield Drive, Robroyston, Glasgow G33 1SR	0141-211 2000/2812
GARTNAVEL GENERAL [0141-211 3000]	Rev. Keith Saunders	1 Beckfield Drive, Robroyston, Glasgow G33 1SR	0141-211 3000/3026
GLASGOW HOMŒOPATHIC [0141-211 1600]	Rev. Keith Saunders	1 Beckfield Drive, Robroyston, Glasgow G33 1SR	0141-211 1600

GREATER GLASGOW PRIMARY CARE	Rev. Cameron H. Langlands: Co-ordinator		
GARTNAVEL ROYAL HOSPITAL [0141-211 3686]	Rev. Gordon B. Armstrong: North/East Sector	Chaplain's Office, Old College of Nursing, Stobhill Hospital, 133 Balornock Road, Glasgow G21 3UW	0141-232 0609
	Ms Anne MacDonald: South Sector	Chaplain's Office, Leverndale Hospital, 510 Crookston Road, Glasgow G53 7TU	0141-211 6695
SOUTH GLASGOW UNIVERSITY HOSPITALS			
SOUTHERN GENERAL HOSPITAL [0141-201 2156]	Rev. Ann Purdie		
	Rev. Blair Robertson: Co-ordinator		
VICTORIA INFIRMARY	Rev. Iain Reid	Chaplain's Office, Langside Road, Glasgow G42 9TT	0141-201 5164
YORKHILL NHS TRUST [0141-201 0595]	Rev. Alistair Bull	Royal Hospital for Sick Children, Glasgow G3 8SG	
GREATER GLASGOW PRIMARY CARE	Rev. David Torrance	19 Redhills View, Lennoxtown, Glasgow G65 7BL	01360 312527
	Rev. Alastair MacDonald	42 Roman Way, Dunblane FK15 9DJ	
ROYAL INFIRMARY	Mrs Sandra Bell	62 Loganswell Road, Thornliebank, Glasgow G46 8AX	0141-883 5618
STOBHILL	Rev. John Beaton	33 North Birbiston Road, Lennoxtown, Glasgow G65 7LZ	0141-632 1514
LEVERNDALE	Miss Anne MacDonald	62 Berwick Drive, Glasgow G52 3JA	0141-959 7158
VICTORIA INFIRMARY/MEARNSKIRK	Rev. Alan Raeburn	110 Mount Annan Drive, Glasgow G44 4RZ	0141-569 8547
KNIGHTSWOOD/DRUMCHAPEL	Rev. Andrew McMillan	1 Swallow Gardens, Glasgow G13 4QD	0141-647 6178
RUTHERGLEN TAKARE	Rev. J.W. Drummond	12 Albert Drive, Rutherglen, Glasgow G73 3RT	0141-429 5599
	Rev. Alexander Thomson	31 Highburgh Drive, Rutherglen, Glasgow G73 3RR	0141-762 1844
PRINCE AND PRINCESS OF WALES HOSPICE	Rev. Stuart Webster	71 Carlton Place, Glasgow G5 9TD	0141-531 1346
FOURHILLS NURSING HOME	Rev. W.G. Ramsay	3 Tofthill Avenue, Bishopbriggs, Glasgow G64 3PN	
HUNTERS HILL MARIE CURIE CENTRE	Miss Dawn Allan	1 Belmont Drive, Glasgow G21 3AY	
INVERCLYDE ROYAL HOSPITAL (Whole-time) GREENOCK [01475 633777]	Rev. Fergus McLachlan	Chaplain's Office, Inverclyde Royal Hospital, Larkfield Road, Greenock PA16 0XN	
DYKEBAR (Part-time)	Mrs Joyce Nicol	93 Brisbane Street, Greenock PA16 8NY	01475 723235
	Rev. Alistair Morrison	92 St Leonard's Road, Ayr KA7 2PU	01292 266121
	Rev. George Mackay	109 Ormonde Avenue, Glasgow G44 3SN	0141-637 4976
MERCHISTON HOUSE	Rev. Thomas Cant	18 Oldhall Road, Paisley PA1 3HL	0141-882 2277
JOHNSTONE	Rev. Thomas Cant	18 Oldhall Road, Paisley PA1 3HL	0141-882 2277
ROYAL ALEXANDRA	Rev. Arthur Sherratt	West Manse, Kilbarchan, Johnstone PA10 2JR	01805 702669
	Rev. Douglas Ralph	24 Kinpurnie Road, Paisley PA1 3HH	0141-883 3505
	Rev. Esther J. Ninian	28 Fulbar Crescent, Paisley PA2 9AS	01505 812304
	Rev. Ritchie Gillon	31 Southfield Avenue, Paisley PA2 8BX	0141-884 6215
	Rev. David Kay	6 Southfield Avenue, Paisley PA2 8BY	0141-884 3600
	Rev. E. Lorna Hood (Mrs)	North Manse, 1 Alexandra Drive, Renfrew PA4 8UB	0141-886 2074
	Rev. Owain Jones	East Manse, Kilbarchan PA10 2JQ	01505 702621
RAVENSCRAIG	Rev. David Mill	105 Newark Street, Greenock PA16 7TW	01475 639602
	Rev. Douglas Cranston	6 Churchill Road, Kilmacolm PA13 4LH	01505 873271

DUMBARTON JOINT	Rev. Daniel Cheyne	217 Glasgow Road, Dumbarton G82 1EE	01389 763075
VALE OF LEVEN GENERAL	Rev. Ian Miller	1 Glebe Gardens, Bonhill, Alexandria G83 9HB	01389 753039
VALE OF LEVEN GERIATRIC	Rev. Ian Wilkie	38 Main Street, Renton, Dumbarton G82 4PU	01389 752017

FORTH VALLEY

PRIMARY CARE	Rev. Robert MacLeod	13 Cannons Way, Falkirk FK2 7QG	01324 631008
BO'NESS	Mr Frank Hartley	49 Argyll Place, Kilsyth, Glasgow G65 0PY	01236 824135
FALKIRK ROYAL INFIRMARY	Rev. Helen Christie	5 Watson Place, Dennyloanhead, Bonnybridge FK4 2BG	01324 813786
	Rev. Margery Collin	2 Saughtonhall Crescent, Edinburgh EH12 5RF	0131-337 7153
BANNOCKBURN	Rev. James Landels	Allan Manse, Bogend Road, Bannockburn, Stirling FK7 8NP	01786 814692
CLACKMANNAN COUNTY	Rev. Eleanor Forgan	18 Alexandra Drive, Alloa FK10 2DQ	01259 212836
KILDEAN	Rev. Eleanor Forgan	18 Alexandra Drive, Alloa FK10 2DQ	01259 212836
SAUCHIE	Rev. Eleanor Forgan	18 Alexandra Drive, Alloa FK10 2DQ	01259 212836
STIRLING ROYAL INFIRMARY	Rev. Gary McIntyre	7 Randolph Road, Stirling FK8 2AJ	01786 474421
	Rev. Kenneth Russell	5 Clifford Road, Stirling FK8 2QU	01786 475802

FIFE

QUEEN MARGARET HOSPITAL, DUNFERMLINE [01383 674136]	Mr Mark Evans DCS	Queen Margaret Hospital, Whitefield Road, Dunfermline KY12 0SU	01383 674136
VICTORIA HOSPITAL, KIRKCALDY [01592 643355]	Rev. Ian J.M. McDonald	11 James Grove, Kirkcaldy KY1 1TN	01592 203775
LYNEBANK	Rev. Elizabeth Fisk	51 St John's Drive, Dunfermline KY12 7TL	01383 720256
CAMERON	Rev. James L. Templeton	Innerleven Manse, McDonald Street, Methil, Leven KY8 3AJ	01333 426310
	Rev. Kenneth Donald	33 Main Road, East Wemyss, Kirkcaldy KY1 4RE	01592 713260
GLENROTHES	Rev. Ian D. Gordon	2 Somerville Way, Forester's Grove, Glenrothes KY7 5GE	01592 742487
RANDOLPH WEMYSS	Rev. Elizabeth Cranfield	9 Chemiss Road, Methilhill, Leven KY8 2BS	01592 713142
ADAMSON, CUPAR	Rev. Lynn Brady	2 Guthrie Court, Cupar Road, Newburgh, Cupar KY14 6HA	01337 842228
NETHERLEA, NEWPORT	Rev. James Connolly	5 Westwater Place, Newport-on-Tay DD6 8NS	01382 542626
STRATHEDEN, CUPAR	Rev. John Jarvie	62 Glebe Park, Kirkcaldy KY1 1BL	07740 256120
ST ANDREWS MEMORIAL	Rev. David Arnott	20 Priory Gardens, St Andrews KY16 8XX	01334 472912

TAYSIDE

Institution	Name	Address	Telephone
Head of Spiritual Care	Rev. Gillian Munro	Royal Dundee Liff Hospital, Dundee DD2 5NF	01382 423116
DUNDEE NINEWELLS HOSPITAL [01382 660111]	Rev. David J. Gordon		

Hospital	Chaplain	Address	Phone
PERTH ROYAL INFIRMARY [01738 473896]	Rev. John M. Birrell		
ABERFELDY			
BLAIRGOWRIE RATTRAY	Rev. Ian Knox	Heatherlea, Main Street, Ardler, Blairgowrie PH12 8SR	01828 640731
IRVINE MEMORIAL	Rev. Ian Murray	The Manse, Blair Atholl, Pitlochry PH18 5SX	01796 481213
CRIEFF COTTAGE	Rev. James W. MacDonald	8 Strathearn Terrace, Crieff PH7 3AQ	01764 653907
MACMILLAN HOSPICE	Rev. John M. Birrell	2 Rhynd Lane, Perth PH2 8TP	01738 625694
MURRAY ROYAL	Rev. Peter Meager	7 Lorraine Drive, Cupar KY15 5DY	01334 656991
ST MARGARET'S COTTAGE	Rev. Randal MacAlister	St Kessog's Rectory, High Street, Auchterarder PH3 1AD	01764 662525
ROYAL VICTORIA	Rev. Janet Foggie	39 Tullidelph Road, Dundee DD2 2JD	01382 660152
	Rev. Roy Massie	St Rule's Manse, 8 Church Street, Monifieth DD5 4JP	01382 532607
ASHLUDIE	Rev. David Jamieson	Panmure Manse, 8A Albert Street, Monifieth DD5 4JS	01382 532772
DUNDEE, ROYAL LIFF	Rev. Janet Foggie	39 Tullidelph Road, Dundee DD2 2JD	01382 660152
NINEWELLS			
STRATHMARTINE	Rev. Janet Foggie	39 Tullidelph Road, Dundee DD2 2JD	01382 660152
ARBROATH INFIRMARY	Rev. Alasdair G. Graham	1 Charles Avenue, Arbroath DD11 2EZ	01241 872244
BRECHIN INFIRMARY	Mr Gordon Anderson	33 Grampian View, Montrose DD10 9SU	01674 674915
FORFAR INFIRMARY			
LITTLE CAIRNIE	Rev. Ian G. Gough	St Vigeans Manse, Arbroath DD11 4RD	01241 873206
MONTROSE ROYAL	Rev. Iain Coltart	The Manse, Arbirlot, Arbroath DD11 2NX	01241 434479
STRACATHRO	Mr Gordon Anderson	33 Grampian View, Montrose DD10 9SU	01674 674915
SUNNYSIDE ROYAL	Mr Gordon Anderson	33 Grampian View, Montrose DD10 9SU	01674 674915

GRAMPIAN

Head of Spiritual Care:
Rev. Fred Coutts, Chaplains' Office, Aberdeen Royal Infirmary, Foresterhill, Aberdeen AB25 2ZN

1. ACUTE SECTOR
ABERDEEN ROYAL INFIRMARY, ABERDEEN MATERNITY HOSPITAL
Chaplains' Office, Aberdeen Royal Infirmary, Foresterhill, Aberdeen AB25 2ZN
Rev. Fred Coutts   01224 553166
Rev. Sylvia Spencer (Chaplain's Assistant)   01224 553316
Ms Monica Stewart (Chaplain's Assistant)

ROYAL ABERDEEN CHILDREN'S HOSPITAL
Chaplain's Office, Royal Aberdeen Children's Hospital, Westburn Drive, Aberdeen AB25 2ZG
Rev. James Falconer   01224 554905

ROXBURGHE HOUSE
Chaplains' Office, Roxburghe House, Ashgrove Road, Aberdeen AB25 2ZH
Rev. Alison Hutchison   01224 557077
Ms Monica Stewart

WOODEND HOSPITAL
Chaplain's Office, Woodend Hospital, Eday Road, Aberdeen AB15 6XS
Rev. Mark Rodgers — 01224 556788

DR GRAY'S HOSPITAL, ELGIN
Rev. George Rollo, 18 Reidhaven Street, Elgin IV30 1QH — 01343 547208
Rev. Andrew Willis, Deanshaugh Croft, Mulben, Keith AB55 6YJ — 01542 860240

THE OAKS, ELGIN
Rev. Stuart Macdonald, 55 Forsyth Street, Hopeman, Elgin IV30 2SY — 01343 831175

2. MENTAL HEALTH
ROYAL CORNHILL HOSPITAL, WOODLANDS
Chaplain's Office, Royal Cornhill Hospital, Cornhill Road, Aberdeen AB25 2ZH. — 01224 557293
Rev. Muriel Knox
Miss Pamela Adam (Chaplain's Assistant)
Mr Donald Meston (Chaplain's Assistant)

3. COMMUNITY HOSPITALS

ABOYNE	Rev. Douglas Campbell	49 Charlton Crescent, Aboyne AB24 5GN	01339 886447
GLEN O'DEE, BANCHORY	Rev. Donald Walker	2 Wilson Road, Banchory AB31 3UY	01330 822811
CAMPBELL, PORTSOY	Rev. Iain Sutherland	The Manse, Portsoy, Banff AB45 2QB	01261 842272
CHALMERS, BANFF	Rev. Alan Macgregor	7 Colleonard Road, Banff AB45 1DZ	01261 812107
FLEMING, ABERLOUR	Rev. Andrew Willis	Deanshaugh Croft, Mulben, Keith AB55 6YJ	01542 860240
FRASERBURGH	Rev. Andrew Lyon	23 Strichen Road, Fraserburgh AB43 9SA	01346 513303
INVERURIE	Rev. Ian B. Groves	1 Westburn Place, Inverurie AB51 5QS	01467 620285
INSCH	Rev. Thomas Calder	The Manse, Queen Street, Huntly AB54 5EB	01466 792630
JUBILEE, HUNTLY	Rev. David Stewart	South Manse, Cameron Street, Stonehaven AB39 2HE	01569 762576
KINCARDINE COMMUNITY, STONEHAVEN	Rev. Douglas Lamb	130 Denstrath Road, Edzell Woods, Brechin DD9 7XF	01356 648139
LEANCHOIL, FORRES	Rev. David Young	15 Mannachie Rise, Forres IV36 2US	01309 672284
MAUD	Rev. Alastair Donald	New Deer Manse, Turriff AB53 6TG	01771 644216
MUIRTON	Rev. Andrew Willis		
PETERHEAD COMMUNITY	Rev. David S. Ross	3–5 Abbey Street, Deer, Peterhead AB42 5LN	01771 623994
SEAFIELD, BUCKIE	Rev. Andrew Willis	Deanshaugh Croft, Mulben, Keith AB55 6YJ	01542 860240
STEPHEN, DUFFTOWN	Rev. Hugh M.C. Smith	The Manse, Church Street, Dufftown, Keith AB55 4AR	01340 820380
TURNER, KEITH	Rev. Kay Gauld	The Manse, Church Road, Keith AB55 5BR	01542 882799
TURRIFF	Rev. Yvonne Hendrie	6 Craigneen Place, Whitehills, Banff AB45 2NE	01261 861671
UGIE, PETERHEAD	Mrs Sena Allen	Berea Cottage, Kirk Street, Peterhead AB42 1RY	01779 477327

HIGHLAND

THE RAIGMORE HOSPITAL [01463 704000]
Rev. Iain MacRitchie — 7 Merlin Crescent, Inverness IV2 3TE
Rev. Derek Brown — Cathedral Manse, Dornoch IV25 3HV

IAN CHARLES	Rev. Morris Smith	Golf Course Road, Grantown-on-Spey PH26 3HY	01479 872084
ST VINCENT	Rev. Helen Cook	The Manse, West Terrace, Kingussie PH21 1HA	01340 661311
NEW CRAIGS	Rev. Michael Hickford	Chaplain's Office, New Craigs Hospital, Leachkin Road, Inverness IV3 8NP	01463 704000
NAIRN TOWN AND COUNTY	Rev. Ian Hamilton	3 Manse Road, Nairn IV12 4RN	01667 452203
BELFORD AND BELHAVEN	Rev. Donald A. MacQuarrie	Manse of Duncansburgh, Fort William PH33 6BA	01397 702297
GLENCOE	Rev. Alison Burnside	The Manse, Ballachulish PH49 4JG	01855 811998
ROSS MEMORIAL, DINGWALL	Rev. Russel Smith	8 Castlehill Road, Dingwall IV15 9PB	01349 861011
INVERGORDON COUNTY	Rev. Kenneth D. Macleod	The Manse, Cromlet Drive, Invergordon IV18 0BA	01349 852273
LAWSON MEMORIAL	Rev. Eric Paterson	Free Church Manse, Golspie KW10 6TT	01408 633529
MIGDALE	Rev. Kenneth Hunter	Free Church Manse, Gower Street, Brora KW9 6PU	01408 621271
CAITHNESS GENERAL	Mr John Craw	'Craiglockhart', Latheronwheel, Latheron KW5 6DW	01593 741779
DUNBAR	Rev. Alastair H. Gray	The Manse, Station Road, Watten, Wick KW1 5YN	01955 621220
BROADFORD MACKINNON MEMORIAL	Rev. Dr Ben Johnstone	The Shiants, 5 Upper Breakish, Breakish, Isle of Skye IV42 8PY	01471 822538
PORTREE	Rev. Iain Greenshields	The Manse, Kensaleyre, Snizort, Portree, Isle of Skye IV51 9XE	01470 532260
CAMPBELTOWN	Mrs Janice Forrest	The Manse, Southend, Campbeltown PA28 6RQ	01586 830274
LOCHGILPHEAD	Mrs Margaret Sinclair	2 Quarry Park, Furnace, Inveraray PA32 8XW	01499 500633
ISLAY	Rev. Stephen Fulcher	The Manse, Main Street, Port Charlotte, Isle of Islay PA48 7TW	01496 850241
DUNOON	Rev. Austin Erskine	99 Sandhaven, Sandbank, Dunoon PA23 8QW	01369 701295
DUNOON ARGYLL UNIT	Rev. Austin Erskine	99 Sandhaven, Sandbank, Dunoon PA23 8QW	01369 701295
ROTHESAY	Mr Raymond Deans	60 Ardmory Road, Rothesay PA20 0PG	01700 504893
LORN AND THE ISLANDS DISTRICT GENERAL	Rev. Elizabeth Gibson	Rudha-na-Cloiche, The Esplanade, Oban PA34 5AQ	01631 562759

WESTERN ISLES HEALTH BOARD

UIST AND BARRA HOSPITAL WESTERN ISLES, STORNOWAY	Rev. James MacDonald	8A Lower Bayble, Point, Lewis HS2 0QA	01851 870173

ORKNEY HEALTH BOARD

BALFOUR AND EASTBANK	Mrs Marion Dicken	6 Claymore Brae, Kirkwall KW15 1UQ	01856 879509

LIST D – FULL-TIME INDUSTRIAL CHAPLAINS

EDINBURGH (Edinburgh City Mission Appointment)	Mr John Hopper	26 Mulberry Drive, Dunfermline KY11 5BZ	01383 737189
EDINBURGH (Methodist Appointment)	Rev. Linda Bandelier	5 Dudley Terrace, Edinburgh EH6 4QQ	0131-554 1636
EDINBURGH (part-time)	Mrs Dorothy Robertson	45 Kirklands Park Crescent, Kirkliston EH29 9EP	0131-333 5414
GREATER GLASGOW AND LANARKSHIRE	Rev. Elisabeth Spence	45 Selvieland Road, Glasgow G52 4ES	0141-883 8973
WEST OF SCOTLAND	Rev. Alister Goss	79 Weymouth Crescent, Gourock PA19 1HR	01475 638944
OFFSHORE OIL INDUSTRY	Rev. Andrew Jolly	Total E and P UK PLC, Crawpeel Road, Aberdeen AB12 3FG	(Office) 01224 297532
ABERDEEN CITY CENTRE (part-time)	Mrs Cate Adams	15 Rousay Place, Aberdeen AB15 6HG	01224 643494/647470
NORTH OF SCOTLAND and NATIONAL CO-ORDINATOR	Mr Lewis Rose DCS	16 Gean Drive, Blackburn, Aberdeen AB21 0YN	01224 790145
TAYSIDE	Rev. John A. Jackson	65 Clepington Road, Dundee DD4 7BQ	01382 458764

LIST E – PRISON CHAPLAINS

ADVISER TO SCOTTISH PRISON SERVICE (NATIONAL)	Rev. William Taylor	HM Prison, Edinburgh EH11 3LN	0131-444 3082
ABERDEEN CRAIGINCHES	Rev. Dr David Ross	HM Prison, Aberdeen AB1 2NE	01224 238300
	Rev. Louis Kinsey	HM Prison, Aberdeen AB1 2NE	01224 238300
	Rev. Iain Barclay	HM Prison, Aberdeen AB1 2NE	01224 238300
CASTLE HUNTLY	Rev. Anne Stewart	HM Prison, Castle Huntly, Longforgan, Dundee DD2 5HL	01382 319333
CORNTON VALE	Rev. Kay Gilchrist	HM Prison, Cornton Vale, Stirling FK9 5NU	01786 832591
DUMFRIES	Rev. Neil Campbell	HM Prison, Dumfries DG2 9AX	01387 261218

EDINBURGH: SAUGHTON	Rev. Colin Reed	Chaplaincy Centre, HMP Edinburgh EH11 3LN	0131-444 3115
	Rev. William Taylor	HM Prison, Edinburgh EH11 3LN	0131-444 3082
	Rev. Robert Akroyd	HM Prison, Edinburgh EH11 3LN	0131-444 3115
GLASGOW: BARLINNIE	Rev. Edward V. Simpson	5 Langtree Avenue, Glasgow G46 7LN	0141-638 8767
	Rev. Ian McInnes	46 Earlbank Avenue, Glasgow G14 9HL	0141-954 0328
	Rev. Douglas Clark	41 Kirkintilloch Road, Lenzie, Glasgow G66 4LB	0141-770 2184
	Rev. Alexander Wilson	HM Prison, Barlinnie, Glasgow G33 2QX	0141-770 2059
	Rev. Dr William D. Moore	Chaplaincy Centre, HM Prison, Barlinnie, Glasgow G33 2QX	0141-770 2059
GLENOCHIL	Rev. Alan F.M. Downie	37A Claremont, Alloa FK10 2DG	01259 213872
GREENOCK	Rev. James Munro	80 Bardrainney Avenue, Port Glasgow PA14 6UD	01475 701213
INVERNESS	Rev. James Robertson	45 Oakdene Court, Culloden, Inverness IV2 7XZ	01463 790504
	Rev. Alexander Shaw	HM Prison, Inverness IV2 3HN	01463 229000
	Rev. Christopher Smart	HM Prison, Inverness IV2 3HN	01463 229000
KILMARNOCK	Rev. Andrew Black	HMP Bowhouse, Mauchline Road, Kilmarnock KA1 5AA	01563 548928
	Rev. Morag Dawson	206 Bank Street, Irvine KA12 0YB	01294 211403
NORANSIDE	Rev. Anne Stewart	HM Prison, Noranside DD8 3QY	01382 319333
PERTH INCLUDING FRIARTON	Rev. Graham Matthews	Chaplaincy Centre, HMP Perth PH2 8AT	01738 622293
	Mrs Deirdre Yellowlees	Ringmill House, Gannochy Farm, Perth PH2 7JH	01738 633773
PETERHEAD	Rev. Dr David Ross	HM Prison, Peterhead AB42 6YY	01779 479101
POLMONT	Rev. Donald H. Scott	Chaplaincy Centre, HMYOI Polmont, Falkirk FK2 0AB	01324 711558
	Rev. Daniel L. Mathers	10 Ercall Road, Brightons, Falkirk FK2 0RS	01324 872253
SHOTTS	Rev. Allan Brown	Chaplaincy Centre, HMP Shotts ML7 4LE	01501 824071

LIST F – UNIVERSITY CHAPLAINS

ABERDEEN	Easter Smart MDiv	01224 484271
ABERTAY, DUNDEE	Leslie M. Barrett BD FRICS	01382 308447
CALEDONIAN	Ewen MacLean BA BD (Honorary)	0141-558 7451
CAMBRIDGE	Keith Riglin (U.R.C. and C. of S.)	01223 503726

DUNDEE	Fiona C. Douglas BD PhD	01382 344157
EDINBURGH	Diane Williams	0131-650 2595
GLASGOW	Stuart D. MacQuarrie JP BD BSc	0141-330 5419
HERIOT-WATT	Howard G. Taylor BSc BD	0131-449 5111 (ext 4508)
NAPIER	Marion Chatterley	0131-455 4694
OXFORD	Susan Durber (U.R.C. and C. of S.)	01865 554358
PAISLEY	Morris M. Dutch BD BA	0141-571 4059
ROBERT GORDON	Daniel French	01224 262000 (ext 3506)
ST ANDREWS	James B. Walker MA BD DPhil	01334 462866
STIRLING	Gillian Weighton BD STM (Honorary)	01786 832753
STRATHCLYDE	Marjory Macaskill LLB BD	0141-553 4144

LIST G – THE DIACONATE

NAME	COM	APP	ADDRESS	TEL	PRES
Allan, Jean (Mrs) DCS	1989	2005	12C Hindmarsh Avenue, Dundee DD3 7LW	01382 827299	29
Anderson, Janet (Miss) DCS	1979	2006	4 Clanranald Place, Arisaig PH39 4NN [E-mail: jaskye@tiscali.co.uk]	01687 450398	38
Beaton, Margaret (Miss) DCS	1989	1988	64 Gardenside Grove, Carmyle, Glasgow G32 8EZ	0141-646 2297	16
Bell, Sandra (Mrs)	2001	2004	62 Loganswell Road, Thornliebank, Glasgow G46 8AX	0141-638 5884	16
Black, Linda (Miss) BSc DCS	1993	2004	148 Rowan Road, Abronhill, Cumbernauld, Glasgow G67 3DA [E-mail: lnan@blueyonder.co.uk]	01236 786265	22
Buchanan, John (Mr) DCS	1988	2004	19 Gillespie Crescent, Edinburgh EH10 4HJ	0131-229 0794	3
Buchanan, Marion (Mrs) MA DCS	1983	2006	2 Lenzie Road, Stepps, Glasgow G33 6DX	0141-779 5746	16
Burns, Marjorie (Mrs) DCS	1997	1998	25 Barnsley Square, Corby, Northants NN18 0PQ [E-mail: mburns8069@aol.com]	01536 264819 07989 148464 (Mbl)	47
Carson, Christine (Miss) MA DCS	2006		36 Upper Wellhead, Limekilns, Dunfermline KY11 3JQ	01383 873131 07919 137294 (Mbl)	24
Cathcart, John Paul (Mr) DCS	2000		59 Glen Isla, St Leonards, East Kilbride, Glasgow G74 3TG [E-mail: paulcathcart@msn.com]	01355 521906 07708 396074 (Mbl)	17
Clark, Jean (Ms) DCS	2006		Flat 1/1, 15 Colston Grove, Bishopbriggs, Glasgow G64 1BF	07729 316321 (Mbl)	16
Corrie, Margaret (Miss) DCS	1989	1998	44 Sunnyside Street, Camelon, Falkirk FK1 4BH	01324 670656	22
Craw, John (Mr) DCS	1998	2002	'Craiglockhart', Latheronwheel, Latheron KW5 6DW	01593 741779	41
Crawford, Morag (Miss) MSc DCS	1977	1998	118 Wester Drylaw Place, Edinburgh EH4 2TG [E-mail: morag.crawford@virgin.net]	0131-332 2253 (Tel/Fax) 07970 982563 (Mbl)	24
Crocker, Elizabeth (Mrs) DipComEd	1985	2003	77C Craigcrook Road, Edinburgh EH4 3PH [E-mail: crock@crook77c.freeserve.co.uk]	0131-332 0227	1
Cunningham, Ian (Mr) DCS	1994	2002	The Manse, Rothiemay, Huntly AB54 7NE	01466 711334	35

Name			Address	Phone	No.
Cuthbertson, Valerie Dip'TMus DCS	2003		105 Bellshill Road, Motherwell ML1 3SJ [E-mail: vcuthbertson@tiscali.co.uk]	01698 259001	22
Deans, Raymond (Mr) DCS	1994	2003	60 Ardmory Road, Rothesay, Isle of Bute PA20 0PG [E-mail: deans@fish.co.uk]	01700 504893	19
Douglas, Marilyn (Miss) DCS	1988	2004	Heimdal, Quarff, Shetland ZE2 9JA	01950 447584	46
Dunnett, Linda (Mrs)	1976	2000	3 Branklyn Crescent, Glasgow G13 1GJ	0141-959 3732	[16]
Evans, Mark (Mr) BSc RGN DCS	1988	2006	13 Easter Drylaw Drive, Edinburgh EH4 2QA [E-mail: mevansdcs@aol.com] (Office)	0131-343 3089 / 01383 674136	24
Gargrave, Mary (Mrs) DCS	1989	2002	229/2 Calder Road, Edinburgh EH11 4RG (Office)	0131-476 3493 / 0131-443 9452	1
Getliffe, Dorothy (Mrs)	2006		3 Woodview Terrace, Hamilton ML3 9DP [E-mail: DGetliffe@aol.com]	01698 423504	17
Gordon, Margaret (Mrs) DCS	1998	2001	92 Lanark Road West, Currie EH14 5LA	0131-449 2554	1
Gray, Greta (Miss) DCS	1992	1998	67 Crags Avenue, Paisley PA2 6SG	0141-884 6178	14
Hamilton, James (Mr) DCS	1997	2002	6 Beckfield Gate, Glasgow G33 1SW [E-mail: j.hamilton111@btinternet.com]	0141-558 3195	16
Hamilton, Karen (Mrs) DCS	1995	2004	6 Beckfield Gate, Glasgow G33 1SW [E-mail: k.hamilton6@btinternet.com]	0141-558 3195	16
Hughes, Helen (Miss) DCS	1977	2002	2/2, 43 Burnbank Terrace, Glasgow G20 6UQ [E-mail: helenhughes@fish.co.uk]	0141-333 9459	16
King, Chris (Mrs) DCS	2002	2005	28 Kilnford, Dundonald, Kilmarnock KA2 9ET [E-mail: chrisking99@tiscali.co.uk]	01563 851197	10
King, Margaret (Miss) DCS	2002		56 Murrayfield, Fochabers IV32 7EZ	01343 820937	35
Love, Joanna (Ms) BSc DCS	2006		92 Everard Drive, Glasgow G21 1XQ	0141-563 5859	16
Lundie, Ann V. (Miss) DCS	1972	2002	20 Langdykes Drive, Cove, Aberdeen AB12 3HW	01224 898416	31
Lyall, Ann (Miss) DCS	1980	2003	117 Barlia Drive, Glasgow G45 0AY [E-mail: annlyall@btinternet.com]	0141-631 3643	16
MacDonald, Anne (Miss) BA	1980	2002	502 Castle Gait, Paisley PA1 2PA	0141-840 1875	16
McDowall, Sarah (Mrs) DCS	1991	2003	116 Scott Road, Glenrothes KY6 1AE	01592 562386	25
McKay, Kenneth (Mr) DCS	1996	1998	11F Balgowan Road, Letham, Perth PH1 2JG [E-mail: kennydandcs@hotmail.com] (Mbl)	01738 621169 / 07952 076331	28
MacKinnon, Ronald (Mr) DCS	1996	2004	71 Cromarty Road, Cairnhill, Airdrie ML6 9RL	01236 762024	22
McLellan, Margaret (Mrs)	1986	2000	18 Broom Road East, Newton Mearns, Glasgow G77 5SD	0141-639 6853	16
McNaughton, Janette (Miss) DCS	1982	1997	4 Dunellan Avenue, Moodiesburn, Glasgow G69 0GB	01236 870180	22
McPheat, Elspeth (Miss)	1985	2001	11/5 New Orchardfield, Edinburgh EH6 5ET	0131-554 4143	1
Martin, Jane (Miss) DCS	1979	1979	16 Wentworth Road, Dundee DD2 3SD [E-mail: janimar@aol.com]	01382 813786	29
Mitchell, Joyce (Mrs) DCS	1994	1993	16/4 Murrayburn Place, Edinburgh EH14 2RR [E-mail: joyce@mitchell71.freeserve.co.uk]	0131-453 6548	1
Mulligan, Anne MA DCS	1974	1986	27A Craigour Avenue, Edinburgh EH17 7NH [E-mail: mulliganne@aol.com]	0131-664 3426	1
Munro, Patricia (Miss) BSc DCS	1986	2002	11 Hurlingham Square, Peterborough Road, London SW6 3DZ [E-mail: patmunro@tiscali.co.uk] (Office)	0131-242 1996 / 020 7610 6994	47

NAME	COM		ADDRESS	TEL	PRES
Nicholson, David (Mr) DCS	1994	1993	2D Doonside, Kildrum, Cumbernauld, Glasgow G67 2HX	01236 732260 / (Mbl) 07703 332270	22
Nicol, Joyce (Mrs) BA DCS	1974	1998	93 Brisbane Street, Greenock PA16 8NY	01475 723235 / (Mbl) 07957 642709	14
Ogilvie, Colin (Mr) DCS	1998	2003	32 Upper Bourtree Court, Glasgow G67 2HX	0141-442 1965	16
Palmer, Christine (Ms) DCS	2003	2005	39 Fortingall Place, Perth PH1 2NF	01738 587488	28
Rennie, Agnes M. (Miss) DCS	1974	1979	3/1 Craigmillar Court, Edinburgh EH16 4AD	0131-661 8475	1
Rose, Lewis (Mr) DCS	1993	2005	16 Gean Drive, Blackburn, Aberdeen AB21 0YN [E-mail: scimnorth@uk.uumail.com]	01224 790145 / (Mbl) 07899 790466	31
Ross, Duncan (Mr) DCS	1996	2006	4 Glasgow Road, Cambuslang, Glasgow G72 7BW [E-mail: ssornacnud@hotmail.com]	0141-641 1699	16
Rycroft-Sadi, Pauline (Mrs) DCS	2003	2006	6 Ashville Terrace, Edinburgh EH6 8DD	0131-554 6564 / (Mbl) 07759 436303	1
Steele, Marilynn J. (Mrs) BD DCS	1999	1999	2 Northfield Gardens, Prestonpans EH32 9LQ	01875 811497	1
Steven, Gordon BD DCS	1997	2004	51 Nantwich Drive, Edinburgh EH7 6RB	0131-669 2054 / (Mbl) 07904 385256	3
Stewart, Marion (Miss) DCS	1991	1994	Kirk Cottage, Kirkton of Skene, Westhill, Skene AB32 6XE	01224 743407	33
Thomson, Jacqueline (Mrs) MTh DCS	2004	2004	1 Barron Terrace, Leven KY8 4DL [E-mail: jacquelinethomson@blueyonder.co.uk]	01333 301115	24
Thomson, Phyllis (Miss) DCS	2003	2003	63 Caroline Park, Mid Calder, Livingston EH53 0SJ	01506 883207	2
Urquhart, Barbara (Mrs) DCS	1986	2006	9 Standalane, Kilmaurs, Kilmarnock KA3 2NB	01563 538289	11
Wilson, Glenda (Mrs) DCS	1990	2006	Charity Cottage, Blairmore, Dunoon PA23 8TP	01369 810397	19
Wilson, Muriel (Miss) MA BD DCS	1997	2001	28 Bellevue Crescent, Ayr KA7 2DR [E-mail: muriel.wilson4@btinternet.com]	01292 264939	10
Wishart, William (Mr) DCS	1994	2004	10 Stanley Drive, Paisley PA2 6HE	0141-884 4177 / (Mbl) 07971 422201	14
Wright, Lynda (Miss) BEd DCS	1979	1992	Key Cottage, High Street, Falkland, Cupar KY15 7BU	01337 857705	26

THE DIACONATE (Retired List)

NAME	COM	ADDRESS	TEL	PRES
Anderson, Catherine B. (Mrs) DCS	1975	13 Mosshill Road, Bellshill, Motherwell ML4 1NQ	01698 745907	17
Anderson, Mary (Miss) DCS	1955	33 Ryehill Terrace, Edinburgh EH6 8EN	0131-553 2818	1
Bayes, Muriel C. (Mrs) DCS	1963	Flat 6, Carleton Court, 10 Fenwick Road, Glasgow G46 4AN	0141-633 0865	16
Beaton, Jamesina (Miss) DCS	1953	Fairhills, Fort Augustus PH32 4DS	01320 366252	38
Cameron, Margaret (Miss) DCS	1961	2 Rowans Gate, Paisley PA2 6RD	0141-840 2479	14
Copland, Agnes M. (Mrs) MBE DCS	1950	3 Craigmuschat Road, Gourock PA19 1SE	01475 635870	14

Name	Year	Address	Telephone	No.
Cunningham, Alison W. (Miss) DCS	1961	23 Strathblane Road, Milngavie, Glasgow G62 8DL	0141-563 9232	18
Drummond, Rhoda (Miss) DCS	1960	23 Grange Loan, Edinburgh EH9 2ER	0131-668 3631	1
Erskine, Morag (Miss) DCS	1979	111 Mains Drive, Park Mains, Erskine PA8 7JJ	0141-812 6096	14
Finlayson, Ellena B. (Miss) DCS	1963	16E Denwood, Summerhill, Aberdeen AB15 6JF	01224 321147	31
Flockhart, Andrew (Mr) DCS	1988	Flat 0/1, 8 Hardie Avenue, Rutherglen, Glasgow G73 3AS	0141-569 0716	16
Gillespie, Ann M. (Miss) DCS	1969	Barlochan House, Palnackie, Castle Douglas DG7 1PF	01556 600378	8
Gillon, Phyllis (Miss) DCS	1957	The Hermitage Home, 15 Hermitage Drive, Edinburgh EH10 6BX	0131-447 0664	1
Gordon, Fiona S. (Mrs) MA DCS	1958	Machrie, 3 Cupar Road, Cuparmuir, Cupar KY15 5RH [E-mail: machrie@madasafish.com]	01334 652341	26
Gray, Catherine (Miss) DCS	1969	10C Eastern View, Gourock PA19 1RJ	01475 637479	14
Gray, Christine (Mrs) DCS	1969	11 Woodside Avenue, Thornliebank, Glasgow G46 7HR	0141-571 1008	16
Howden, Margaret (Miss) DCS	1954	38 Munro Street, Kirkcaldy KY1 1PY	01592 205913	25
Hutchison, Alan E.W. (Mr) DCS	1988	132 Lochbridge Road, North Berwick EH39 4DR	01620 894077	3
Hutchison, Maureen (Mrs) DCS	1961	23 Drylaw Crescent, Edinburgh EH4 2AU	0131-332 8020	1
Johnston, Mary (Miss) DCS	1988	19 Lounsdale Drive, Paisley PA2 9ED	0141-849 1615	14
McBain, Margaret (Miss) DCS	1974	33 Quarry Road, Paisley PA2 7RD	0141-884 2920	14
McCallum, Moyra (Miss) MA BD DCS	1965	176 Hilton Drive, Aberdeen AB24 4LT [E-mail: moymac@aol.com]	01224 486240	31
McCully, M. Isobel (Miss) DCS	1974	10 Broadstone Avenue, Port Glasgow PA14 5BB	01475 742240	14
MacLean, Donald A. (Mr) DCS	1988	8 Upper Barvas, Isle of Lewis HS2 0QX	01851 840454	44
MacPherson, James B. (Mr) DCS	1988	104 Cartside Street, Glasgow G42 9TQ	0141-616 6468	16
MacQuien, Duncan (Mr) DCS	1988	35 Criffel Road, Mount Vernon, Glasgow G32 9JE	0141-575 1137	14
Malvenan, Dorothy (Miss) DCS	1937	Flat 19, 6 Craigie Street, Dundee DD4 6PF	01382 462495	29
Martin, Neil (Mr) DCS	1988	3 Strathmiglo Place, Stenhousemuir, Larbert FK5 4UQ	01324 551362	22
Merrilees, Ann (Miss) DCS	1994	23 Cuthill Brae, Willow Wood Residential Park, West Calder EH55 8QE [E-mail: ann@merrilees.freeserve.co.uk]		45
Miller, Elsie M. (Miss) DCS	1974	30 Swinton Avenue, Rowanbank, Baillieston, Glasgow G69 6JR	0141-771 0857	22
Morrison, Jean (Dr) DCS	1964	45 Corslet Road, Currie EH14 5LZ [E-mail: jean.morrison@blueyonder.co.uk]	0131-449 6859	1
Mortimer, Aileen (Miss) BSc DCS	1976	38 Sinclair Way, Knightsridge, Livingston EH54 8HW	01506 430504	2
Moyes, Sheila (Miss) DCS	1957	158 Pilton Avenue, Edinburgh EH5 2JZ	0131-551 1731	1
Nicol, Senga (Miss) DCS	1993	Forthbank Nursing Home, Drip Road, Raploch, Stirling FK8 1RR		16
Potts, Jean M. (Miss) DCS	1973	28B East Claremont Street, Edinburgh EH7 4JP	0131-557 2144	1
Ramsay, Katherine (Miss) MA DCS	1958	25 Homeroyal House, 2 Chalmers Crescent, Edinburgh EH9 1TP	0131-667 4791	1
Ronald, Norma A. (Miss) MBE DCS	1961	2B Saughton Road North, Edinburgh EH12 7HG	0131-334 8736	1
Rutherford, Ellen B. (Miss) MBE DCS	1962	41 Duncanston, Conon Bridge, Dingwall IV7 8JB	01349 877439	39
Smith, Catherine (Mrs) DCS	1964	21 Lingaro, Bixter, Shetland ZE2 9NN	01595 810207	46
Smith, Lillian (Miss) MA DCS	1977	6 Fintry Mains, Dundee DD4 9HF	01382 500052	29
Stuart, Anne (Miss) DCS	1966	19 St Colme Crescent, Aberdour, Burntisland KY3 0ST	01383 860049	24

	ORD		TEL	PRES
Tait, Agnes (Mrs) DCS	1995	10 Carnoustie Crescent, Greenhills, East Kilbride, Glasgow G75 8TE		
Teague, Yvonne (Mrs) DCS	1965	46 Craigcrook Avenue, Edinburgh EH4 3PX	0131-336 3113	1
Thom, Helen (Miss) BA DipEd MA DCS	1959	84 Great King Street, Edinburgh EH3 6QU	0131-556 5687	1
Trimble, Robert DCS	1988	5 Templar Rise, Livingston EH54 6PJ	01506 412504	2
Webster, Elspeth H. (Miss) DCS	1950	82 Broomhill Avenue, Burntisland KY3 0BP	01592 873616	25
Weir, Minnie Mullo (Miss) MA DCS	1934	37 Strathearn Court, Strathearn Terrace, Crieff PH7 3DS	01764 654189	28
White, Elizabeth (Miss) DCS	1950	Rodger Park Nursing Home, Rutherglen, Glasgow G73 3QZ		16

THE DIACONATE (Supplementary List)

	ORD		TEL
Forrest, Janice (Mrs)	1990	The Manse, Southend, Campbeltown PA28 6RQ	01586 830274
Gilroy, Lorraine (Mrs)	1988	5 Bluebell Drive, Cheverel Court, Bedward CV12 0GE	02476 366031
Guthrie, Jennifer M. (Miss) DCS		14 Eskview Terrace, Ferryden, Montrose DD10 9RD	01674 660345
Harris, Judith (Mrs)	1993	243 Western Avenue, Sandfields, Port Talbot, West Glamorgan SA12 7NF	01639 884855
Hood, Katrina (Mrs)	1988	67C Farquhar Road, Edgbaston, Birmingham B18 2QP	
Hudson, Sandra (Mrs)	1982	10 Albany Green, Rutherglen, Glasgow G73 3QN	
McIntosh, Kay (Mrs) DCS	1990	4 Jacklin Green, Livingston EH54 8PZ	01506 495472
Muir, Alison M. (Mrs)	1969	77 Arthur Street, Dunfermline KY12 0JJ	
Ramsden, Christine (Miss)	1978	2 Wykeham Close, Bassett, Southampton SO16 7LZ	
Walker, Wikje (Mrs)	1970	24 Brodie's Yard, Queen Street, Coupar Angus PH13 9RA	01828 628251
Wallace, Catherine (Mrs)		4 Thornwood Court, Setauket, NY 11733, USA	

LIST H – MINISTERS HAVING RESIGNED MEMBERSHIP OF PRESBYTERY
(in Terms of Act III 1992)

(Resignation of Presbytery membership does not imply the lack of a practising certificate.)

NAME	ORD	ADDRESS	TEL	PRES
Anderson, Kenneth G. MA BD	1967	8 School Road, Arbroath DD11 2LT	01241 874825	30
Bailey, W. Grahame MA BD	1939	148 Craiglea Drive, Edinburgh EH10 5PU	0131-447 1663	1
Barbour, Robin A.S. KCVO MC BD STM DD	1954	Old Fincastle, Pitlochry PH16 5RJ	01796 473209	27
Beck, John C. BD	1975	43A Balvenie Street, Dufftown, Keith AB55 4AS		35

Name	Year	Address	Tel	No.
Bonar, Sandy LTh	1988	7 Westbank Port, Westbank Terrace, Macmerry, Tranent EH33 1QS [E-mail: sandy.bonar@btinternet.com]	01875 615165	3
Brown, Alastair BD	1986	52 Henderson Drive, Kintore, Inverurie AB51 0FB	01467 632787	32
Caie, Albert LTh	1983	34 Ringwell Gardens, Stonehouse, Larkhall ML9 3QW	01698 792187	32
Cooper, George MA BD	1943	8 Leighton Square, Alyth, Blairgowrie PH11 8AQ	01828 633746	27
Craig, Eric MA BD BA	1959	5 West Relugas Road, Edinburgh EH9 2PW	0131-667 8210	1
Craig, Gordon W. MBE MA BD	1972	1 Beley Bridge, Dunino, St Andrews KY16 8LT	01334 880285	26
Craig, John W. MA BD	1951	83 Milton Road East, Edinburgh EH15 2NL	0131-657 2309	1
Crawford, S.G. Victor	1980	Crofton, 65 Main Road, East Wemyss, Kirkcaldy KY1 4RL	01592 712325	25
Cumming, David P.L. MA	1957	Shillong, Tarbat Ness Road, Portmahomack, Tain IV20 1YA	01862 871794	19
Donaldson, Colin V.	1982	3A Playfair Terrace, St Andrews KY16 9HX	01334 472889	3
Drummond, R. Hugh	1953	19 Winton Park, Edinburgh EH10 7EX [E-mail: hughdrummond1@activemail.co.uk]	0131-445 3634	1
Ferguson, Ronald MA BD ThM	1972	Vinbreck, Orphir, Orkney KW17 2RE [E-mail: ronbluebrazil@aol.com]	01856 811378	45
Finlayson, Duncan MA	1943	Flat 3, Nicholson Court, Kinnettas Road, Strathpeffer IV14 9BG	01997 420014	39
Gordon, Alasdair B. BD LLB EdD	1970	31 Binghill Park, Milltimber, Aberdeen AB13 0EE [E-mail: alasdairbgordon@hotmail.com]	01224 732464	31
Greig, James C.G. MA BD STM	1955	Block 2, Flat 2, Station Lofts, Strathblane, Glasgow G63 9BD [E-mail: jgreig@netcomuk.co.uk]	01360 771915	16
Grubb, George D.W. BA BD BPhil DMin	1962	10 Wellhead Close, South Queensferry EH30 9WA	0131-331 2072	1
Hamilton, David S.M. MA BD STM	1958	Hilbre, Baycrofts, Strachur, Cairndow, Argyll PA27 8BY	01369 860634	47
Hosie, James MA BD MTh	1959	26 Morgan Road, Aberdeen AB16 5JY	01224 483669	19
Howie, William MA BD STM	1964	Flat 6, 21 Bulldale Place, Glasgow G14 0NE	0141-959 2604	31
Hurst, Frederick R. MA	1965	1 Mercat Loan, Biggar ML12 6DG	01899 221352	40
Lambie, Andrew E. BD	1957	2 Gillsland Road, Edinburgh EH10 5BW	0131-228 3118	13
Levison, Mary I. (Mrs) BA BD DD	1978	3 Drummond Place, Calderwood, East Kilbride, Glasgow G74 3AD	01355 234169	1
Lindsay, W. Douglas BD CPS	1978	Simbister, Sanday, Orkney KW17	01857 600289	16
Lynn, Joyce (Mrs) MIPM BD	1995	7 Blacket Place, Edinburgh EH9 1RN	0131-667 2100	1
McDonald, William J.G. DD	1953	Flat 12, Homeburn House, 177 Fenwick Road, Giffnock, Glasgow G46 6JD	0141-620 3235	1
Macfarlane, Alwyn J.C. MA	1957	8 Muirfield Gardens, Inverness IV2 4HF	01463 231977	37
Macfarlane, Donald MA	1940	8 Bonnington Road, Peebles EH45 9HF	01721 723609	4
Macfarlane, Kenneth	1963	West Lodge, Inverness Road, Nairn IV12 4SD	01667 452827	26
Mackenzie, J.A.R. MA	1947	4 Dunellan Avenue, Moodiesburn, Glasgow G69 0GB	01236 870180	16
McKenzie, Mary O. (Miss)	1976	38 Grange Loan, Edinburgh EH9 2NR	0131-667 9532	1
Mackie, Steven G. MA BD	1956	21 Kenilworth Avenue, Helensburgh G84 7JR	01436 671744	18
Mair, John BSc	1965	25 St Mary's Street, St Andrews KY16 8AZ	01334 476136	26
Marshall, James S. MA PhD	1939	5 Braeside Park, Aberfeldy PH15 2DT	01887 829396	27
Miller, Irene B. (Mrs) MA BD	1984			1
Monro, George D. TD MA	1935			
Morton, Andrew Q. MA BSc BD FRSE	1949	Sunnyside, 4A Manse Street, Aberdour, Burntisland KY3 0TY		18

NAME	ORD	ADDRESS	TEL	PRES
Nelson, John MA BD	1941	7 Manse Road, Roslin EH25 9LF	0131-440 3321	3
Ogston, David D. MA BD	1970	13 Alder Grove, Scone, Perth		28
Ramsay, Alan MA	1967	12 Riverside Grove, Lochyside, Fort William PH33 7NY		38
Reid, William M. MA BD	1966	10 Rue Rossini, F-75009 Paris, France		48
Shaw of Chapelverna, Duncan Bundesverdienstkreuz Drhc PhD ThDr JP	1951	4 Sydney Terrace, Edinburgh EH7 6SL	0131-337 2130	19
Shaw, D.W.D. BA BD LLB WS DD	1960	4/13 Succoth Court, Edinburgh EH12 6BZ	01330 823032	26
Skinner, Silvester MA	1960	29 Silverbank Gardens, Banchory AB31 5YZ	01339 882780	32
Smith, J.A. Wemyss MA	1947	Rapplaroan, 42 Beltie Road, Torphins, Banchory AB31 4JT	0131-663 1234	32
Smith, Ralph C.P. MA STM	1960	2A Waverley Road, Eskbank, Dalkeith EH22 3DJ [E-mail: rcpsmith@waitrose.com]		3
Speed, David K. LTh	1969	153 West Princes Street, Helensburgh G84 8EZ	01436 674493	16
Spowart, Mary G. (Mrs) BD	1978	Aldersyde, St Abbs Road, Coldingham, Eyemouth TD14 5NR	01890 771697	26
Swan, Andrew MA	1941	11 The Terrace, Ardbeg, Rothesay, Isle of Bute PA20 0NP	01700 502138	14
Taylor, Alexander T.H. MA BD	1938	4 The Pleasance, Strathkinness, St Andrews KY16 9SD	01334 850585	26
Todd, James F. BD CPS	1984	21 Harrow Terrace, Wick KW1 5AX	01955 605320	41
Urie, D.M.L. MA BD PhD	1940	7 Glebe Park, Kincardine O'Neil, Aboyne AB34 5ED	01339 884204	32
Weatherhead, James L. CBE MA LLB DD	1960	59 Brechin Road, Kirriemuir DD8 4DE	01575 572237	30
Webster, John G. BSc	1964	Plane Tree, King's Cross, Brodick, Isle of Arran KA27 8RG	01770 700747	16
Westmarland, Colin A.	1971	PO Box 5, Cospicua, CSPOI, Malta	00356 216 923552	48
Wilkie, George D. OBE BL	1948	2/37 Barnton Avenue West, Edinburgh EH4 6EB	0131-339 3973	1
Wylie, W. Andrew	1953	Well Rose Cottage, Peat Inn, Cupar KY15 5LH	01334 840600	26

LIST I – MINISTERS HOLDING PRACTISING CERTIFICATES (under Act II, as amended by Act VIII 2000)

Not all Presbyteries have stated whether or not some of those listed have taken a seat in Presbytery. There is still some variation in practice.

NAME	ORD	ADDRESS	TEL	PRES
Alexander, Helen J.R.	1981	112B Maling Road, Canterbury, Victoria 3126, Australia	0061 3983 01476	1
Alexander, Ian W. BA BD STM	1990	5 Comiston Gardens, Edinburgh EH10 5QH	0131-447 4519	1
Anderson, David MA BD	1975	Rowan Cottage, Aberlour Gardens, Aberlour AB38 9LD	01340 871906	35
Anderson, Kenneth G. MA BD	1967	8 School Road, Arbroath DD11 2LT	01241 874825	30
Arbuthnott, Joan (Mrs) MA BD	1993	139/1 New Street, Musselburgh EH21 6DH	0131-665 6736	3
Archer, Nicholas D.C. BA BD	1971	Hillview, Edderton, Tain IV19 4AJ	01862 821494	47
Barbour, Robin A.S. KCVO MC BD STM DD	1954	Old Fincastle, Pitlochry PH16 5RJ	01796 473209	27

Name	Year	Address	Telephone	No.
Bardgett, Frank D. MA BD PhD	1987	Tigh an Iasgair, Street of Kincardine, Boat of Garten PH24 3BY [E-mail: tigh@bardgett.plus.com]	01479 831751	36
Beattie, Warren BSc BD	1991	33A Chancery Lane, Singapore 908554	0065 256 3208	1
Black, James S. BD DPS	1976	7 Breck Terrace, Penicuik EH26 0RJ [E-mail: jsb.black@btopenworld.com]	01968 677559	3
Blane, Quintin A. BSc BD MSc	1979	18D Kirkhill Road, Penicuik EH26 8HZ [E-mail: quintin@qab.org.uk]	01968 670017	3
Bonar, Sandy LTh	1988	7 Westbank Port, Westbank Terrace, Macmerry, Tranent EH33 1QS [E-mail: sandy.bonar@btinternet.com]	01875 615165	3
Bowman, Norman M. MA BD	1940	Abbotsford Nursing Home, 98 Eglinton Road, Ardrossan KA22 8NN		12
Boyd, Ian R. MA BD PhD	1989	33 Castleton Drive, Newton Mearns, Glasgow G77 3LE		32
Caie, Albert LTh	1983	34 Ringwell Gardens, Stonehouse, Larkhall ML9 3QW	01698 792187	14
Campbell, Thomas R. MA BD	1986	Craigleith, Bowfield Road, Howwood, Johnstone PA9 1BS	01505 702461	2
Currie, Gordon C.M. MA BD	1975	43 Deanburn Park, Linlithgow EH49 6HA	01506 842759	33
Davidson, Mark R. MA BD STM	2005	20 Kinmhor Rise, Blackburn, Aberdeen AB21 0LJ	01224 790701	24
Davies, Gareth W. BA BD	1979	Pitadro House, Fordell Gardens, Dunfermline KY11 7EY	01383 417634	1
Dickson, Graham T. MA BD	1985	19/4 Stead's Place, Edinburgh EH6 5DY [E-mail: grd22@blueyonder.co.uk]	0131-476 0187	3
Donaldson, Colin V.	1982	3A Playfair Terrace, St Andrews KY16 9HX	01334 472889	42
Drummond, Norman W. MA BD	1976	c/o Columba 1400 Ltd, Staffin, Isle of Skye IV51 9JY	01478 611400	16
Ellis, David W. GIMechE GIProdE	1962	4 Wester Tarsappie, Rhynd Road, Perth PH2 8PT	01738 449618	45
Ferguson, Ronald MA BD ThM	1972	Vinbreck, Orphir, Orkney KW17 2RE [E-mail: ronbluebrazil@aol.com]	01856 811378	22
Fleming, Thomas G.	1961	Longwood, Humbie EH36 5PN	01875 833208	3
Flockhart, D. Ross OBE BA BD DUniv	1955	[E-mail: rossflock@ednet.co.uk]		
Fowler, Richard C.A. BSc MSc BD	1978	4 Gardentown, Whalsay, Shetland ZE2 9AB	01806 566538	46
Fraser, Ian M. MA BD PhD	1946	Ferndale, Gargunnock, Stirling FK8 3BW	01786 860612	23
Frew, John M. MA BD	1946	17 The Furrows, Walton-on-Thames KT12 3JQ		16
Gillies, Jan E. (Mrs) BD	1998	18 McIntyre Lane, Macmerry, Tranent EH33 1QL [E-mail: jgillies@fish.co.uk]	01875 614774	3
Gilmour, Robert M. MA BD	1942	'Bellevue', Station Road, Watten, Wick KW1 5YN	01955 621317	37
Grubb, George D.W. BA BD BPhil DMin	1962	10 Wellhead Close, South Queensferry EH30 9WA	0131-331 2072	1
Hamilton, David S.M. MA BD STM	1958	4 Cemydd Terrace, Senghenydd, Caerphilly, Mid Glamorgan CF83 4HL	02920 831653	1
Hibbert, Frederick W. BD	1986	150 Broughty Ferry Road, Dundee DD4 6JJ	01382 461288	29
Higgins, G.K.	1957	Hilbre, Baycrofts, Strachur, Cairndow PA27 8BY	01369 860634	19
Hosie, James MA BD MTh	1959	48 Jubilee Court, St Margaret's Street, Dunfermline KY12 7PE	01383 732223	24
Ireland, Andrew BA BTh DipRD	1963	Glenallan, Doune Road, Dunblane FK15 9AT	01786 823241	23
Jack, Alison M. (Mrs) MA BD PhD	1998			
Jamieson, Esther M.M. (Mrs) BD	1984	1 Redburn, Bayview, Stornoway HS1 2UV [E-mail: ejamieson@freeuk.com]	01851 704789	44

Name and Qualifications	Year	Address	Tel	Pr.
Jenkinson, John J. JP LTCL ALCM DipEd DipSen	1991	8 Rosehall Terrace, Falkirk FK1 1PY	01324 625498	22
Johnstone, Donald B.	1969	22 Glenhove Road, Cumbernauld, Glasgow G67 2JZ	01236 612479	22
Johnstone, Robert MTheol	1973	59 Cliffburn Road, Arbroath DD11 5BA	01241 439292	32
Lawrie, Robert M. BD MSc DipMin LLCM(TD)	1994	West Benview, Main Road, Langbank, Port Glasgow PA14 6XP	01475 540240	14
Liddiard, F.G.B. MA	1957	34 Trinity Fields Crescent, Brechin DD9 6YF	01356 622966	30
Logan, Thomas M. LTh	1971	3 Duncan Court, Kilmarnock KA3 7TF	01563 524398	11
Lyall, David BSc BD STM PhD	1965	16 Brian Crescent, Tunbridge Wells, Kent TN4 0AP	01892 670323	1
Macaskill, Donald MA BD PhD	1994	44 Forfar Avenue, Glasgow G52 3JQ	0141-883 5956	16
McDonald, Ross J. BA BD ThM	1998	HMS Dalriada, Navy Buildings, Eldon Street, Greenock PA16 7SL	(Mbl) 07952 558767	16
Macfarlane, Kenneth	1963	9 Bonnington Road, Peebles EH45 9HF	01721 723609	4
McKean, Martin J. BD DipMin	1984	56 Kingsknowe Drive, Edinburgh EH14 2JX	0131-466 1157	1
Mackie, Steven G. MA BD	1956	38 Grange Loan, Edinburgh EH9 2NR	0131-667 9532	1
MacPherson, Gordon C.	1963	203 Capelrig Road, Patterton, Newton Mearns, Glasgow G77 6ND	0141-616 2107	16
McPherson, William BD DipEd	1993	83 Laburnum Avenue, Port Seton, Prestonpans EH32 0UD	01875 812252	3
Mailer, Colin (Aux)	1996	Innis Chonain, Back Row, Polmont, Falkirk FK2 0RD	01324 712401	22
Main, Arthur W.A. BD	1954	13/3 Eildon Terrace, Edinburgh EH3 5NL	0131-556 1344	1
Marr, Ian MA BD	1984	116 Jeanfield Road, Perth PH1 1LP	01738 632530	28
Masson, John D. MA BD PhD BSc	1984	2 Beechgrove, Craw Hall, Brampton CA8 1TS [E-mail: john@masson.demon.co.uk]	ex-directory	7
Matheson, Iain G. BD BMus	1985	16 New Street, Musselburgh EH21 6JP [E-mail: igmatheson@tiscali.co.uk]	0131-665 2128	3
Millar, Peter W. MA BD PhD	1971	35/6 Mid Steil, Edinburgh EH10 5XB [E-mail: ionacottage@hotmail.com]	0131-447 6186	1
Miller, Irene B. (Mrs) MA BD	1984	5 Braeside Park, Aberfeldy PH15 2DT	01887 829396	27
Mills, Archibald MA PhD	1953	32 High Street, South Queensferry EH30 9PP	0131-331 3906	1
Moodie, Alastair R. MA BD	1978	5 Buckingham Terrace, Glasgow G12 8EB		16
Morton, Andrew Q. MA BSc BD FRSE	1949	Sunnyside, 4A Manse Street, Aberdour, Burntisland KY3 0TY		18
Mowbray, Harry (Aux)	2003	Viewlands, Beechwood Place, Kirriemuir DD8 5DZ	01575 574937	30
Munro, Alexander W. MA BD	1978	Columba House, 12 Alexandra Road, Southport PR9 0NB [E-mail: awmunro@tiscali.co.uk]	01704 543044	47
Newell, Alison M. (Mrs) BD	1986	1A Inverleith Terrace, Edinburgh EH3 5NS [E-mail: alinewell@aol.com]	0131-556 3505	1
Newell, J. Philip MA BD PhD	1982	1A Inverleith Terrace, Edinburgh EH3 5NS	0131-556 3505	1
Ogston, David D. MA BD	1970	13 Alder Grove, Scone, Perth		28
Ostler, John H. MA LTh	1975	5 Osborne Terrace, Port Seton, Prestonpans EH32 0BZ [E-mail: anna.rodwell@googlemail.com]	01875 814358	
Owen, Catherine W. MTh	1984	10 Waverley Park, Kirkintilloch, Glasgow G66 2BP	0141-776 0407	16
Provan, Iain W. MA BA PhD	1991	Regent College, 5800 University Boulevard, Vancouver BC V6T 2E4, Canada	001 604 224 3245	
Reamonn, Paraic BA BD	1982			
Rodwell, Anna J. (Mrs) BD DipMin	1998	Bargrennan, Mainhouse, Kelso TD5 8AA [E-mail: anna.rodwell@googlemail.com]	01573 440761	6

Name	Year	Address	Phone	
Sawers, Hugh BA	1968	2 Rosemount Meadows, Castlepark, Bothwell, Glasgow G71 8EL	01698 853960	17
Scouller, Hugh BSc BD	1985	The Mercat Hotel, High Street, Haddington EH41 3EP [E-mail: hughscouller@hotmail.com]		3
Shaw, D.W.D. BA BD LLB WS DD	1960	4/13 Succoth Court, Edinburgh EH12 6BZ	0131-337 2130	26
Stewart, Margaret L. (Mrs) BSc MB ChB BD	1985	28 Inch Crescent, Bathgate EH48 1EU	01506 653428	2
Storrar, William F. MA BD PhD	1984	Director, Centre of Theological Enquiry, 50 Stockton Street, Princeton, NJ 08540, USA		1
Strachan, David G. BD DPS	1978	1 Deeside Park, Aberdeen AB15 7PQ	01224 324101	31
Strachan, Gordon MA BD PhD	1963	59 Merchiston Crescent, Edinburgh EH10 5AH	0131-229 3654	1
Tollick, Frank BSc DipEd	1958	3 Bellhouse Road, Aberdour, Burntisland KY3 0TL	01383 860559	24
Turnbull, Julian S. BSc BD MSc CEng MBCS	1980	25 Hamilton Road, Gullane EH31 2HP [E-mail: jules-turnbull@zetnet.co.uk]	01620 842958	3
Weatherhead, James L. CBE MA LLB DD	1960	59 Brechin Road, Kirriemuir DD8 4DE	01575 572237	30
Weir, Mary K. (Mrs) BD PhD	1968	1249 Millar Road RR1, SITEH-46, BC V0N 1G0, Canada	001 604 947 0636	1
Winn, Fiona M.M. MA BD RGN	1994	35 Ashwood Avenue, Melbourne 3190, Australia	0061 3 9555 2038	1
Wood, Peter J. MA BD	1993	97 Broad Street, Cambourne, Cambridgeshire CB3 6DH	01954 205216	47

LIST J – PRESBYTERY ADVISERS AND FACILITATOR

GLASGOW PRESBYTERY CONGREGATIONAL FACILITATOR	Rev. John K. Collard MA BD 1 Nelson Terrace, East Kilbride, Glasgow G74 2EY	01355 520093

Appointments and job titles within these categories have been under review.

LIST K – OVERSEAS LOCATIONS

EUROPE

AMSTERDAM	Rev. John A. Cowie (1990) and Mrs Gillian Cowie Jan Willem Brouwersstraat 9, NL–1071 LH Amsterdam, The Netherlands [E-mail: j.cowie2@chello.nl; Website: www.ercadam.nl] The English Reformed Church, The Begijnhof (off the Spui). Service each Sunday at 10:30am.	(Tel) 0031 20 672 2288 (Fax) 0031 20 676 4895

BRUSSELS

Rev. Dr Andrew Gardner (2004) and Mrs Julie Gardner   (Tel/Fax) 0032 2 672 40 56
23 Square des Nations, B-1000 Brussels, Belgium
[E-mail: andrewgar@pro.tiscali.be; Website: www.welcome.to/st-andrews]
St Andrew's Church, Chaussée de Vleurgat 181 (off Ave. Louise). Service each Sunday at 11:00am.
[E-mail: st-andrews@welcome.to]

BUDAPEST

St Columba's Scottish Mission, Vorosmarty utca 51, H-1064 Budapest, Hungary   (Church Tel) 0036 1 343 8479
Service in English and Sunday School each Sunday at 11:00am.
The General Synod of the Reformed Church in Hungary, 1440 Budapest, PF5, Hungary
[E-mail: zsinat.kulugy@zsinatiroda.hu]   (Tel/Fax) 0036 1 460 0708

COSTA DEL SOL

Rev. John Shedden and Mrs Jeannie Shedden (2005)
Services at Lux Mundi Ecumenical Centre, Calle Nueva 7, Fuengirola. Service each Sunday at 10:30am.

GENEVA

Rev. Ian A. Manson (2001) and Mrs Roberta Manson   (Tel/Fax) 0041 22 798 29 09
[E-mail: cofsg@pingnet.ch; Website: www.churchofscotlandgeneva.com]
20 Ancienne Route, CH-1218 Grand Saconnex, Geneva, Switzerland
The Calvin Auditoire, Place de la Taconnerie (beside Cathedral of St Pierre). Service each Sunday at 11:00am.

GIBRALTAR

Rev. Stewart J. Lamont (2003) and Mrs Lara Lamont   (Tel) 00335 63670377
St Andrew's Manse, 29 Scud Hill, Gibraltar   (Fax) 00350 40852
St Andrew's Church, Governor's Parade. Service each Sunday at 10:30am.
[E-mail: lamont@gibraltar.gi]

LAUSANNE

Rev. Melvyn Wood (2004) and Mrs Doreen Wood   (Tel/Fax) 0041 21 323 98 28
26 Avenue de Rumine, CH-1005 Lausanne, Switzerland
[E-mail: scotskirklausanne@bluewin.ch]
Service each Sunday at 10:30am.

LISBON

Rev. William B. Ross and Mrs Maureen Ross (2006)
St Andrew's Church, Rua da Arriaga 13–15, Lisbon, Portugal. Service each Sunday at 11:00am.

MALTA

Rev. David Morris (2003) and Mrs Jacky Morris (not Church of Scotland)   (Tel/Fax) 00356 222 643
[E-mail: davidmorris486@hotmail.com]
La Romagnola, 13 Triq is-Sieqjamisrah Eola, Attard BZN 05, Malta
St Andrew's Church, 210 Old Bakery Street, Valletta. Service each Sunday at 10:30am.

PARIS

Rev. Alan Miller (2006)   (Tel/Fax) 0033 1 48 78 47 94
10 Rue Thimmonier, F-75009 Paris, France
[E-mail: scotskirk@wanadoo.fr; Website: www.scotskirkparis.com]
The Scots Kirk, 17 Rue Bayard, F-75008 Paris (Metro: Roosevelt)
Service each Sunday at 10:30am.

ROME   Rev. William B. McCulloch (2001) and Mrs Jean McCulloch
[E-mail: revwbmcculloch@hotmail.com]
Via XX Settembre 7, 00187 Rome, Italy. Service each Sunday at 11:00am.
(Tel) 0039 06 482 7627
(Fax) 0039 06 487 4370

ROTTERDAM   Rev. Robert A. Calvert (1995) and Mrs Lesley-Ann Calvert
Meeuwenstraat 4A, 3071 PE Rotterdam, The Netherlands
[E-mail: scotsintchurch@cs.com; Website: www.scotsintchurch.com]
The Scots Kirk, Schiedamsevest 121, Rotterdam. Service each Sunday at 10:30am. Informal service at 9:15am.
(Tel/Fax) 0031 10 220 4199
(Tel) 0031 10 412 4779

AFRICA

MALAWI   **Church of Central Africa Presbyterian**
Synod of Blantyre

Synod of Livingstonia
Dr Andrew and Mrs Felicity Gaston (1997)
Miss Helen Scott (2000, held previous appointment)
LISAP, PO Box 279, Ekwendeni, Malawi
CCAP Girls' Secondary School, PO Box 2, Ekwendeni, Malawi

ZAMBIA   **United Church of Zambia**
Rev. Colin D. Johnston (1994) (Ecum)
PO Box 21225, Kitwe, Zambia
[E-mail: revcdj@zamnet.zm]
United Church of Zambia Synod Office, Lusaka, Zambia
[E-mail: uczsynod@zamnet.zm]
(Tel) 00260 1 250 641
(Fax) 00260 1 252 198

THE CARIBBEAN, CENTRAL AND SOUTH AMERICA

BAHAMAS   Vacant
St Andrew's Manse, PO Box N1099, Nassau
(Tel) 001 242 322 5475
(Fax) 001 242 323 1960

Rev. Scott R.McL. Kirkland (2006)
Lucaya Presbyterian Kirk, PO Box F-40777, Freeport, Bahamas
(Tel) 001 242 373 2568
(Fax) 001 242 373 4961

BERMUDA   Rev. T. Alan W. Garrity (1999) and Mrs Elizabeth Garrity
The Manse, PO Box PG88, Paget PGBX, Bermuda
[E-mail: revtawg@logic.bm and christchurch@logic.bm] and
[Church website: www.christchurch.bm]
(Tel) 001 441 236 0400
(Tel) 001 441 236 1882
(Fax) 001 441 232 0552

TRINIDAD   Rev. Garwell Bacchas
Church of Scotland Greyfriars St Ann's,
50 Frederick Street, Port of Spain, Trinidad
[E-mail: greyfriars@tstt.net.tt]
(Tel) 001 868 627 9312

ASIA

BANGLADESH

Church of Bangladesh
Mr James Pender (2004) (Ecum)

c/o St Thomas' Church, 54 Johnston Road, Dhaka 1100,   (Tel: 0121-472 4744)
Bangladesh
[E-mail: ohenepender@yahoo.co.uk]

Mr David Hall and Mrs Sarah Hall (2005) (Ecum)

c/o St Thomas' Church, 54 Johnston Road, Dhaka 1100,
Bangladesh

Dr Helen Brannam (2006) (Ecum)

c/o St Thomas' Church, 54 Johnston Road, Dhaka 1100,
Bangladesh

Ecumenical Appointments

CHINA

Together with Scottish Churches China Group
Ian Groves
Anne and Mick Kavanagh (1997)

York University: returning to China in autumn 2008 as a Long Term Amity Teacher
Hezuo Teachers' College for Minority Nationalities, Hezuo, Gansu Province, 747000,
P. R. of China

Kate Jarman (2006)
Angela Evans (2006)
Christine Green (2006)

Hechi Teachers' College, Yizhou, Guangxi Province, 546300, P. R. of China
Dingxi Teachers' College, Dingxi, Gansu Province, 743000, P. R. of China
Wuwei Occupational College, 21 Xian Jian Road, Wuwei, Gansu Province, 743000,
P. R. of China

David Clements (2006)

Northwest Normal University, 803 East Anning Road, Lanzhou, Gansu Province,
730070, P. R. of China

Placements are not yet confirmed for Kath Saltwell and Gordon Paterson (2007).

SRI LANKA

Presbytery of Lanka
Rev. John P.S. Purves BSc BD (2003)

St Andrew's Scots Kirk, Colombo
St Andrew's Church Manse, 73 Galle Road, Colombo 3,   (Tel) 0094 1386 774
Sri Lanka
[E-mail: reverend@sltnet.lk]

MIDDLE EAST AND NORTH AFRICA

ISRAEL

[Note: Church Services are held in St Andrew's Scots Memorial Church, Jerusalem, each Sunday at 10am, and at St Andrew's, Galilee (contact minister for worship time)]

Jerusalem
Rev. Jane Barron

St Andrew's, Jerusalem, PO Box 8619, Jerusalem 91086, Israel
(Tel: 00972 2 6732401; Fax: 00972 2 673 1711)
[E-mail: janebarron23@hotmail.com]
[Websites: www.janeinisraelpalestine.bigspot.com; www.scothotels.co.il]

Tiberias
Rev. Jane Barron

St Andrew's, Galilee, PO Box 104, Tiberias, Israel
(Tel: 00972 6 6721165; Fax: 00972 6 6790145)
[Website: www.scothotels.co.il]

Jaffa

Tabeetha School, PO Box 8170, 21 Yefet Street, Jaffa, Israel
(Tel: 00972 3 6821581; Fax: 00972 3 6819357)
[E-mail: costab@zahav.net.il;
Website: www.tabeetha.htmlplant.com]
Tabeetha School

LIST L – OVERSEAS RESIGNED AND RETIRED MISSION PARTNERS (ten or more years' service)

NAME	APP	RET	AREA	ADDRESS
Aitken, Faith (Mrs)	1957	1968	Nigeria	High West, Urlar Road, Aberfeldy PH15 2ET
Anderson, Karen (Mrs)	1987	1990	Zambia	23 Allanpark Street, Largs KA30 9AG
Anderson, Kathleen (Mrs)	1992	2006	Israel	1A Elms Avenue, Great Shelford, Cambridge CB2 5LN
Archibald, Mary L. (Miss)	1955	1968	Pakistan	490 Low Main Street, Wishaw ML2 7PL
Barbour, Edith R. (Miss)	1964	1982	Nigeria/Ghana	13/11 Pratik Nagar, Yerwada, Pune 411006, Maharashta, India
Baxter, Rev. Richard and Mrs Ray	1952	1983	North India	
Berkeley, Dr John	1954	1969	Malawi	138 Braid Road, Edinburgh EH10 6JB
and Dr Muriel	1967	1977	Bhutan	Drumbeg, Coylumbridge, Aviemore PH22 1QU
Boyle, Lexa (Miss)	1995	1998	Yemen	7 Maxwell Grove, Glasgow G41 5JP
Bone, Mr David and Mrs Isobel	1959	1992	Aden/Yemen/Sudan	315 Blackness Road, Dundee DD2 1SH
Bone, Elizabeth (Mrs)	1977	1988	Malawi	2A Elm Street, Dundee DD2 2AY
	1950	1964	Malawi	
Brodie, Rev. Jim	1980	1984	North India	25A Keptie Road, Arbroath DD11 3ED
	1955	1974	Nepal	
Brown, Janet H. (Miss)	1996	1998	Pakistan	6 Baxter Park Terrace, Dundee DD4 6NL
Burnett, Dr Fiona	1967	1980	Zambia	The Glenholm Centre, Broughton, Biggar ML12 6JF
Burnett, Dr Robin	1988	1998	Nigeria	79 Bank Street, Irvine KA12 0LL
and Mrs Storm	1964	1967	South Africa	
Burt, M.R.C. (Miss)	1968	1977	Kenya	22 The Loaning, Chirnside, Duns TD11 3YE
Byers, Rev. Alan and Rev. Mairi	1940	1975	Ghana	Meadowbank, Plumdon Road, Annan DG12 6SJ
	1960	1971		

Name	Country	From	To	Address
Campbell, George H.	Livingstonia	1957	1971	20 Woodlands Grove, Kilmarnock KA3 1TZ
Coltart, Rev. Ian O.	North India	1967	1985	The Manse, Arbirlot, Arbroath DD11 2NX
Conacher, Marion (Miss)	India	1963	1993	41 Magdalene Drive, Edinburgh EH15 3BG
Cooper, Rev. George	Kenya	1966	1986	8 Leighton Square, Alyth, Blairgowrie PH11 8AQ
Crosbie, Ann R. (Miss)	Nigeria	1955	1967	21 Fieldhead Square, Glasgow G43 1HL
Dawson, Miss Anne	Malawi	1976	2000	5 Cattle Market, Clackmannan FK10 4EH
Dick, Dr James and Mrs Anne	North India	1954	1957	1 Tummel Place, Comrie, Crieff PH6 2PG
	Nepal	1957	1968	
Dodman, Rev. Roy and Mrs Jane	Jamaica	1983	2006	PO Box 64, Stony Hill, Kingston 9, Jamaica
Dougall, Ian C.	Kenya	1960	1990	60B Craigmillar Park, Edinburgh EH16 5PU
Drever, Dr Bryan	Aden/Yemen/Pakistan	1962	1982	188 Addison Road, King's Head, Birmingham
Duncan, Mr David and Mrs Allison	Nigeria	1952	1969	7 Newhailes Avenue, Musselburgh EH21 6DW
Duncan, Rev. Graham and Mrs Sandra	South Africa	1977	1987	56 Daphne Road, Maroelana, 0081 Pretoria, South Africa
Dunlop, Mr Walter T. and Mrs Jennifer	Malawi/Israel	1998	2006	50 Oxgangs Road, Edinburgh EH13 9DR
Fauchelle, Rev. Don and Mrs Margaret	Zambia, Malawi, Zimbabwe	1979	1994	Flat 3, 22 North Avenue, Devonport, Auckland 1309, New Zealand
Ferguson, Mr. John K.P.	Pakistan	1971	1979	15 Ashgrove, Craigshill, Livingston EH54 5JQ
Finlay, Carol (Ms)	Malawi	1991	1999	96 Broomfield Crescent, Edinburgh EH12 7LX
Fischbacher, Dr Colin M. and Mrs Sally	Malawi	1977	1989	11 Barclay Square, Gosforth, Newcastle-upon-Tyne NE3 2JB
Foster, Joyce (Miss) BSc	Kenya	1990	2001	99 Sixth Street, Newtongrange EH22 4LA
Fowler, Rev. Margaret	Malawi	1986	1998	PO Box 3097, Negril, Westmorland, Jamaica
	Kenya	1968	1972	
	Malawi	1972	1981	
Fucella, Rev. Mike	Jamaica	1988	2007	95/5 Sathorn SOI 9, Pikul, Sathorn Road, Yannawa, Sathorn, Bangkok 10120, Thailand
	Thailand	1990	2006	
Gall, E.G. (Miss)	Blantyre	1940	1962	151 Raeburn Heights, Glenrothes KY16 1BW
Hutchison, C.M. (Mr)	Calabar	1951	1972	75 Grampian Road, Torry, Aberdeen AB11 8ED
Irvine, Mr Clive and Mrs Su	Nepal	1984	1999	McGregor Flat, 92 Blackford Avenue, Edinburgh EH9 3ES
Irvine, Elsabe (Mrs)	Malawi	1951	1987	60 Thirlestane Road, Edinburgh EH9 1AR
Irvine, Dr Geoffrey C. and Mrs Dorothy	Kenya	1952	1989	Lakeside, PO Box 1356 Naivasha, Kenya
Karam, Ishbel (Mrs)	Pakistan	1968	1985	Hillsgarth, Baltasound, Unst, Shetland ZE2 9DY
King, Mrs Betty	North India	1955	1971	23 Main Street, Newstead, Melrose TD6 9DX
Knowles, Dr John K. and Mrs Heather	Malawi	1976	1992	Trollopes Hill, Monton Combe, Bath BA2 7HX
Laidlay, Dr Rorie and Mrs Una	Yemen	1961	1968	Isles View, 5 Bell's Road, Lerwick, Shetland ZE1 0QB
	Pakistan	1968	1971	
	Yemen	1971	1978	
Liddell, Margaret (Miss)	Zambia	1964	1980	20 Wyvis Crescent, Conon Bridge, Dingwall IV7 8BZ
Logie, Robina (Mrs)	North India	1950	1960	23 Stonefield Drive, Inverurie AB5 9DZ

Lyon, Rev. D.H.S.	1952	1972	Nagpur	30 Mansfield Road, Balerno EH14 7JZ
McArthur, G. (Mr)	1956	1972	South Africa	3 Craigcrook Road, Edinburgh EH4 3NQ
McCulloch, Lesley (Mrs)	1982	1992	Malawi/Pakistan	316 North Jones Street, Port Angeles, WA 98362-4218, USA
McCutcheon, Agnes W.F. (Miss)	1957	1989	India	10A Hugh Murray Grove, Cambuslang, Glasgow G72 7NG
MacDonald, Dr Alistair and Mrs Freda	1949	1962	Nigeria	10 Millside, Morpeth, Northumberland NE61 1PN
McDougall, Rev. John N.	1935	1960	West Pakistan	Everill Orr Home, Allendale Road, Mount Albert, Auckland 3, New Zealand
McGoff, A.W. (Miss)	1954	1974	Kolhapur	6 Mossvale Walk, Craigend, Glasgow G33 5PF
MacGregor, Rev. Margaret	1959	1994	India	Gordon Flat, 16 Learmonth Court, Edinburgh EH4 1PB
McKenzie, Rev. Robert P.	1936	1951	India	23 Foulis Crescent, Edinburgh EH14 5BN
McKenzie, Rev. W.M.	1958	1974	Zambia	Troqueer Road, Dumfries DG2 7DF
MacKinnon, E.L. (Miss)	1952	1972	Nigeria	
McMahon, Rev. Robert and Mrs Jessie	1959	1976	North India	7 Ridgepark Drive, Lanark ML11 7PG
McMillan, Helen (Miss)	1981	2003	Pakistan	17/1 New Orchardfield, Edinburgh EH6 5ET
Macrae, Rev. Norman	1943	1960	Nigeria	49 Lixmount Avenue, Edinburgh EH5 3EW
Malley, Beryl Stevenson (Miss)	1982	1992	Malawi	272/2 Craigcrook Road, Edinburgh EH4 7TF
Marshall, Rev. Fred J.	1946	1992	Bermuda	Flat 3, 31 Oswald Road, Edinburgh EH9 2HT
Millar, Rev. Margaret R.M.	1967	1996	Malawi/Zambia	The Manse, Taynuilt, Argyll PA35 1HW
Millar, Rev. Peter	1976	1989	South India	
Moir, Rev. Ian and Mrs Elsie	1962	1973	South Africa	28/6 Comely Bank Avenue, Edinburgh EH4 1EL
Moore, Rev. J. Wilfred and Mrs Lillian	1943	1957	Ghana	31 Lennox Gardens, Linlithgow EH49 7PZ
Morrice, Rev. Dr Charles and Mrs Margaret	1971	1998	Buenos Aires/Kenya	104 Baron's Hill Avenue, Linlithgow EH49 7JG
Morton, Rev. Alasdair J.	1960	1973	Zambia	St Leonard's, 16 St Leonard's Road, Forres IV36 1DW
Morton, Rev. Colin	1988	1998	Israel	313 Lanark Road West, Currie EH14 5RS
Munro, Harriet (Miss)	1959	1969	Malawi	26 The Forge, Braidpark Drive, Glasgow G46 6LB
Murison, Rev. W.G.	1951	1971	Santalia	21 Hailes Gardens, Edinburgh EH13 0JL
Murray, Rev. Douglas and Mrs Sheila	1994	2004	Switzerland	Flat 9, 4 Bonnington Gait, Edinburgh EH6 5NZ
Murray, Mr Ian and Mrs Isabel	1962	2000	Pakistan	17 Piershill Terrace, Edinburgh EH8 7EY
Musgrave, Rev. Clarence W. and Mrs Joan	1966	1980	Zambia	4 Ravelston Heights, Edinburgh EH4 3LX
Musgrave, Rev. Clarence W. and Mrs Joan	2000	2006	Jerusalem	
Musk, Mrs Lily	1959	1959	Malawi	1 Tulloch Place, St Andrews KY16 8XJ
Musk, Mrs Lily	1959	1974	Zambia	
Nelson, Rev. John and Mrs Anne	1947	1952	Pakistan	7 Manse Road, Roslin EH25 9LF
Nelson, Rev. John and Mrs Anne	1952	1959	North India	
Nelson, Rev. John and Mrs Anne	1970	1973	North India	
Nicholson, Rev. Thomas S.	1981	1995	Taiwan	Todholes, Greenlaw, Duns TD10 6XD
Nicol, Catherine (Miss)	1960	2000	Pakistan	St Columba Christian Girls' RTC, Barah Patthar, Sialkot 2, Pakistan
Nutter, Margaret (Miss)	1966	1979	Pakistan	Kilmorich, 14 Balloch Road, Balloch, Alexandria G83 8SR

Name			Location	Address
Pacitti, Rev. Stephen A.	1977	1996	Taiwan	157 Nithsdale Road, Pollokshields, Glasgow G41 5RD
Pattison, Rev. Kenneth and Mrs Susan	1966	1977		2 Castle Way, St Madoes, Glencarse, Perth PH2 7NY
Philip, Rev. David Stuart	1978	1991	Malawi	6 St Bernard's Crescent, Edinburgh EH4 1NP
Philip, Mrs Margaret	1951	1968	Gibraltar	Penlan, Holm Farm Road, Catrine, Mauchline KA5 6TA
Philp, Rev. Robert	1937	1961	Nigeria	Bybrook Nursing Home, Middlehill, Box, Wilts SN13 8QP
Philpot, Rev. David	1981	1995	Kenya	2/27 Pentland Drive, Edinburgh EH10 6PX
Reid, Dr Ann	1988	1996	WCC Geneva	19 Cloughwood Crescent, Shevington, Lancs WN6 8EP
Reid, Margaret I. (Miss)	1964	1982	Ghana	26A Angle Park Terrace, Edinburgh EH11 2JT
Rennie, Rev. Alistair M.	1939	1976	Malawi	Noble's Yard, St Mary's Gate, Wirksworth, Derbyshire DE4 4DQ
Ritchie, Isbhel M. (Miss)	1955	1996	Malawi	8 Ross Street, Dunfermline KY12 0AN
Ritchie, Rev. J.M.	1974	1977	Eastern Himalaya	46 St James' Gardens, Penicuik EH26 9DU
Ritchie, Margaret (Miss)	1968	1978	Yemen	1 Afton Bridgend, New Cumnock KA18 4AX
Ritchie, Mary Scott (Miss)	1968	1991	Zambia	Afton Villa, 1 Afton Bridgend, New Cumnock KA18 4AX
Ross, Rev. Prof. Kenneth and Mrs Hester	1988	1998	Malawi/Zambia/Israel	35 Madeira Street, Edinburgh EH6 4AJ
Rough, Mary E. (Miss)	1966	1987	Malawi	6 Glebe Street, Dumfries DG1 2LF
Roy, Rev. Alan J.	1960	1972	Blantyre	14 Comerton Place, Drumoig, St Andrews KY16 0NQ
Russell, M.M. (Miss)		1969	Zambia	14 Hozier Street, Carluke ML8 5DW
Samuel, Lynda (Mrs)	1974	1990	Nigeria	28 Braehead, Methven Walk, Dundee DD2 3FJ [E-mail: rasam42@onetel.com]
Shepherd, Dr Clyne	1956	1968	Madras	10 Kingsknowe Road South, Edinburgh EH14 2JE
Smith, Mr Harry and Mrs Margaret	1959	1967	Nigeria	31 Woodville Crescent, Sunderland SR4 8RE
Smith, M.L. (Miss)	1968	1970	Nigeria	6 Fintry Mains, Dundee DD4 9HF
Smith, Rev. W. Ewing	1956	1973	Malawi	8 Hardy Gardens, Bathgate EH48 1NH
Sneddon, Mr Sandy and Mrs Marie	1962	1978	Madras	84 Greenend Gardens, Edinburgh EH17 7QH
Steedman, Martha (Mrs) (née Hamilton)	1986	2003	Delhi	Muir of Blebo, Blebo Craigs, Cupar KY15 5TZ
Stewart, Marion G. (Miss)	1955	1966	Pakistan	Kirk Cottage, Kirkton of Skene, Westhill, Skene AB32 6XX
Stiven, Rev. Iain	1976	1989	North India	7 Gloucester Place, Edinburgh EH3 6EE
Stone, W. Vernon MA BD	1959	1969	Malawi/Israel	36 Woodrow Court, Port Glasgow Road, Kilmacolm PA13 4QA
Taylor, Rev. A.T.H.	1949	1966	Pakistan	4 The Pleasance, Strathkinness, St Andrews KY16 9SD
Tennant, Frances (Miss)	1938	1972	Zambia	101 St John's Road, Edinburgh EH12 6NN
Wallace, A. Dorothy (Miss)	1965	1977	Nigeria/Jamaica	7 Bynack Place, Nethy Bridge PH25 3DU
Walker, Rev. Donald and Mrs Judith	1953	1991	Pakistan	2 Wilson Road, Banchory AB31 3UY
Westmarland, Rev. Colin	1981	1994	North India	PO Box 5, Cospicua, CSPO1, Malta
Wilkie, Rev. James L.	1975	2001	Zambia	7 Comely Bank Avenue, Edinburgh EH4 1EW
Wilkinson, Dr Alison	1959	1976	Malta	5 Birch Avenue, Stirling FK8 2PL
Wilkinson, Rev. John	1992	2007	Zambia	70 Craigleith Hill Gardens, Edinburgh EH4 2JH
Wilson, Irene (Ms)	1946	1975	Kenya	7 Lady's Well, Moat Road, Annan DG12 5AD
Wilson, M.H. (Miss)	1993	2004	Kenya	37 Kings Avenue, Longniddry EH32 0QN
Wilson, Rev. Mark	1946	1977	Israel	

LIST M – PARISH ASSISTANTS AND PROJECT WORKERS

NAME	APP	ADDRESS	APPOINTMENT	TEL	PRES
Bauer, Alex (Mrs)	2001	Linwood Parish Church, Clippens Road, Linwood, Paisley PA3 3PY	Linwood	(Mbl) 07900 531196	14
Black, Colm	2001	54 Provost Smith Crescent, Inverness IV2 3TG	Inverness: Hilton	01463 717208	37
Brown, Sarah (Miss)	2003	2/1, 3 Bathgate Street, Glasgow G31 1DZ	Govan Old, Linthouse St Kenneth's and New Govan	0141-556 2959	16
Campbell, Alasdair	2000	3 Gellatly Road, Dunfermline KY11 4BH	Dunfermline: Dalgety	01383 726238	24
Close, David	2001	12–14 Wallace Street, Paisley PA3 2BU	The Star Project: Paisley North	0141-889 5850	14
Conlin, Melodie	2000	Bridgeton Business Centre, Suite 313, 285 Abercromby Street, Glasgow G40 2DD	Glasgow East End	0141-554 0997	16
Cowie, Marjorie	2002	35 Balbirnie Avenue, Markinch, Glenrothes KY7 6BS	Glenrothes: St Margaret's	01592 758402	25
Finch, John	2002	71 Maxwell Avenue, Westerton Garden Suburb, Glasgow G61 8NZ	Glasgow: St Francis in the East	0141-587 7390	16
Haringman, Paul MSc	2003	19 Dewartown, Gorebridge EH23 4NX	Newbattle	01875 320687	3
Hutchison, John BA	2001	30/4 West Pilton Gardens, Edinburgh EH4 4EA	Edinburgh: The Old Kirk	0131-538 1622	1
Johnston, Mark (Rev.)	2003	5 Bruce Walk, Redmoss, Nigg, Aberdeen AB12 3LX	Cove New Charge Development	01224 874269	31
Philip, Elizabeth MA BA	2001	12 Torvean Place, Dunfermline KY11 4YY [E-mail: elizabethphilip@cheerful.com]	Dunfermline: St Paul's East	01383 721054	16
Reford, Susan	2001	32 Jedburgh Street, Blantyre, Glasgow G72 0SU	East Kilbride: Moncreiff	01698 820122	17
Smith, David	2003	66 Hendry Road, Kirkcaldy KY2 5DB	Benarty and Lochgelly		24
Wyllie, John	2007	51 Seafar Drive, Kelty KY4 0JX	Cowdenbeath: Trinity	01383 839200	24
Young, Neil James	2001	Holmlea, Main Street, Banton, Kilsyth, Glasgow G65 0QY	Glasgow: St Paul's	01236 825883	16

LIST N – READERS

1. EDINBURGH

Christie, Gillian L. (Mrs)	45 Allan Park Drive, Edinburgh EH16 1LW	0131-443 4472
Davies, Ruth (Mrs) (attached to Liberton)	4 Hawkhead Grove, Edinburgh EH16 6LS	0131-664 3608
Farrant, Yvonne (Mrs)	Flat 7, 14 Duddingston Mills, Edinburgh EH8 7NF [E-mail: yfarrant@charis.org.uk]	0131-661 0672

Farrell, William J. — 50 Ulster Crescent, Edinburgh EH8 7JS [E-mail: will.farrell@freeuk.com] — 0131-661 1026

Farrow, Edmund — 14 Brunswick Terrace, Edinburgh EH7 5PG [E-mail: efsc18422@blueyonder.co.uk] — 0131-558 8210

Kerrigan, Herbert A. MA LLB QC — Airdene, 20 Edinburgh Road, Dalkeith EH22 1JY [E-mail: kerriganqc@btconnect.com] — 0131-660 3007

Kinnear, Dr Malcolm — 25 Thorburn Road, Edinburgh EH13 0BH [E-mail: andrewk@kinnear25.fsnet.co.uk] — 0131-441 3150

McPherson, Alistair — 77 Bonaly Wester, Edinburgh EH13 0RQ [E-mail: anjihmcpherson@blueyonder.co.uk] — 0131-478 5384

Morrison, Peter K. — 14 Eildon Terrace, Edinburgh EH3 5LU [E-mail: pmorriso@fish.co.uk] — 0131-556 1962

Pearce, Martin — 4 Corbiehill Avenue, Edinburgh EH4 5DR [E-mail: martin.j.pearce@blueyonder.co.uk] — 0131-336 4864

Wyllie, Anne (Miss) — 46 Jordan Lane, Edinburgh EH10 4QX — 0131-447 9035

2. WEST LOTHIAN

Blackwood, Michael — Inshaig Cottage, Hatton, Kirknewton EH27 8DZ — 0131-333 1448

Coyle, Charlotte (Mrs) — 28 The Avenue, Whitburn EH47 0DA — 01501 740687

Elliot, Sarah (Miss) — 105 Seafield, Bathgate EH47 7AW — 01506 654950

Galloway, Brenda (Miss) — Lochend, St Ninian's Road, Linlithgow EH49 7BN — 01506 842028

Notman, Jean G.S. (Miss) — 31 South Loch Park, Bathgate EH48 2QZ — 01506 633820

Scoular, Iain W. — 'The Wee Hoose', Ecclesmachan Road, Uphall, Broxburn EH52 6JP [E-mail: iain@iwsconsultants.com] — 01506 855794

Wilkie, David — 53 Goschen Place, Broxburn EH52 5JH — 01506 854777

3. LOTHIAN

Cannon, S. Christopher MA — Briarwood, Winterfield Place, Belhaven, Dunbar EH42 1QQ — 01368 864991

Evans, W. John IEng MIIE(Elec) — Edenwood, 29 Smileyknowes Court, North Berwick EH39 4RG [E-mail: jevans7is@hotmail.com] — 01620 894309

Gibson, C.B. Stewart — 27 King's Avenue, Longniddry EH32 0QN [E-mail: stewartgibson27@tiscali.co.uk] — 01875 853464

Herkes, Chistine W.S. (Mrs) — Viewfield, 224 Galashiels Road, Stow, Galashiels TD1 2RA — 01578 730413

Hogg, David MA — 82 Eskhill, Penicuik EH26 8DQ — 01968 676350

Johnston, June E. (Ms) BSc MEd BD — 49 Braeside Road South, Gorebridge EH23 4DL — 01875 823086

Lyall, George JP — Mossgiel, 13 Park Road, Bonnyrigg EH19 2AW [E-mail: george.lyall@bigfoot.com] — 0131-663 9343

Millan, Mary (Mrs) — 33 Polton Vale, Loanhead EH20 9DF [E-mail: marymillan@fsmail.net] — 0131-440 1624

Trevor, A. Hugh MA MTh — 29A Fidra Road, North Berwick EH39 4NE [E-mail: htrevor@talktalk.net] — 01620 894924

Yeoman, Edward T.N. FSAScot — 75 Newhailes Crescent, Musselburgh EH21 6EF — 0131-653 2291

4. MELROSE AND PEEBLES

Butcher, John W.	'Sandal', 13 Ormiston Grove, Melrose TD6 9SR	01896 822339
Cashman, Margaret D. (Mrs)	38 Abbotsford Road, Galashiels TD1 3HR	01896 752711
Selkirk, Frances (Mrs)	2 The Glebe, Ashkirk, Selkirk TD7 4PJ	01750 32204

5. DUNS

Deans, M. (Mrs) BA	The Lodge, Edrington House, Mordington, Berwick-on-Tweed TD15 1UF	01289 386222
Elphinston, Enid (Mrs)	Edrington House, Berwick-on-Tweed TD15 1UF	01289 386359
Landale, Alison (Mrs)	Green Hope, Duns TD11 3SG	01361 890242

6. JEDBURGH

Findlay, Elizabeth (Mrs)	10 Inch Park, Kelso TD5 7EQ [E-mail: elizabeth@findlay8124.fsworld.co.uk]	01573 226641
Knox, Dagmar (Mrs)	3 Stichill Road, Ednam, Kelso TD5 7QQ [E-mail: dagmar@knox-riding.wanadoo.co.uk]	01573 224883
Thomson, Robert R.	34/36 Fisher Avenue, Hawick TD9 9NB	01450 373851

7. ANNANDALE AND ESKDALE

Boncey, David	Redbrae, Beattock, Moffat DG10 9RF [E-mail: bonceyofredbrae@yahoo.co.uk]	01683 300613
Brown, Martin J.	Lochhouse Farm, Beattock, Moffat DG10 9SG [E-mail: martin@lochhousefarm.com]	01683 300451
Brown, S. Jeffrey BA	Skara Brae, 8 Ballplay Road, Moffat DG10 9AR	01683 220475
Chisholm, Dennis A.G. MA BSc	Moss-side, Hightae, Lockerbie DG11 1JR	01387 811803
Dodds, Alan	Trinco, Battlehill, Annan DG12 6SN [E-mail: alandodds46@btinternet.com]	01461 201235
Jackson, Susan (Mrs)	48 Springbells Road, Annan DG12 6LQ [E-mail: shjackson@supanet.com]	01461 204159
Morton, Andrew A. BSc	19 Sherwood Park, Lockerbie DG11 2DX [E-mail: andrew_a_morton@btinternet.com]	01576 203164
Saville, Hilda A. (Mrs)	32 Crosslaw Burn, Moffat DG10 9LP	01683 222854

8. DUMFRIES AND KIRKCUDBRIGHT

Carroll, J. Scott	17 Downs Place, Heathhall, Dumfries DG1 3RF	01387 265350
Greer, Kathleen (Mrs) MEd	10 Watling Street, Dumfries DG1 1HF	01387 256113
Ogilvie, D.W. MA FSAScot	Lingerwood, 2 Nelson Street, Dumfries DG2 9AY	01387 264267
Paterson, Ronald M. (Dr)	Mirkwood, Ringford, Castle Douglas DG7 2AL	01557 820202
Piggins, Janette (Mrs)	Cleugh Wood, Dalbeattie DG5 4PF	01387 780655
Wallace, Mhairi (Mrs)	The Manse, Twynholm, Kirkcudbright DG6 4NY	01557 860381

9. WIGTOWN AND STRANRAER

Clough, Alan	Dowiesbank, Whauphill, Newton Stewart DG8 9PN	01988 700824
Connery, Graham	Skellies Knowe, West Ervie, Stranraer DG9	01776 854277

Harvey, Joyce (Mrs) — 4A Allanfield Place, Newton Stewart DG8 6BS — 01671 403693
McQuistan, Robert — Old School House, Carsluith, Newton Stewart DG8 7DT — 01671 820327
Williams, Roy — 120 Belmont Road, Stranraer DG9 7BG

10. AYR

Anderson, James (Dr)
  BVMS PhD DVM FRCPath FIBiol MRCVS — 67 Henrietta Street, Girvan KA26 9AN — 01465 710059
Jamieson, Iain — 2 Whinfield Avenue, Prestwick KA9 2BH — 01242 476898
Morrison, James — 27 Monkton Road, Prestwick KA9 1AP — 01292 479313
Murphy, Ian — 56 Lamont Crescent, Cumnock KA18 3DU — 01290 423675
Riome, Elizabeth (Mrs) — Monkwood Mains, Minishant, Maybole KA19 8EY — 01292 443440

11. IRVINE AND KILMARNOCK

Bircham, James — 8 Holmlea Place, Kilmarnock KA1 1UU — 01563 532287
Cuthbert, Helen (Miss) MA MSc — 63 Haining Avenue, Kilmarnock KA1 3QN — 01563 550403
Crosbie, Shona (Mrs) — 4 Campbell Street, Darvel KA17 0PA — 01560 322229
Findlay, Elizabeth (Mrs) — 19 Keith Place, Kilmarnock KA3 7NS — 01563 528084
Hamilton, Margaret A. (Mrs) — 59 South Hamilton Street, Kilmarnock KA1 2DT — 01563 534431
Jamieson, John BSc(Hons) DEP AFBPSS — 22 Moorfield Avenue, Kilmarnock KA1 1TS — 01563 534065
Lightbody, Hunter B. — 36 Rannoch Place, Irvine KA12 9NQ — 01294 273955
McAllister, Anne C. (Mrs) — 39 Bowes Rigg, Stewarton KA3 5EN — 01560 483191
McLean, Donald — 1 Four Acres Drive, Kilmaurs, Kilmarnock KA3 2ND — 01563 381475
MacTaggart, Elspeth (Miss) — 21 Scargie Road, Kilmarnock KA3 1QR — 01563 527713
Mills, Catherine (Mrs) — 59 Crossdene Road, Crosshouse, Kilmarnock KA2 0JU — 01563 535305
Raleigh, Gavin — 21 Landsborough Drive, Kilmarnock KA3 1RY — 01563 520836
Scott, William BA DipEd — 6 Elgin Avenue, Stewarton, Kilmarnock KA3 3HJ — 01560 484273
Storm, Iain — 17 Kilwinning Road, Irvine KA12 8RR — 01294 277647
Wilson, Robert L.S. MA BD — 57 West Woodstock Street, Kilmarnock KA1 2JH — 01563 526658

12. ARDROSSAN

Barclay, Elizabeth (Mrs) — 2 Jacks Road, Saltcoats KA21 5NT — 01294 471855
Currie, Archie — 55 Central Avenue, Kilbirnie KA25 6JP — 01505 681474
Hunter, Jean C.Q. (Mrs) BD — The Manse, Lamlash, Brodick, Isle of Arran KA27 8LE — 01770 860380
McCool, Robert — 17 McGregor Avenue, Stevenston KA20 4BA — 01294 466548
Mackay, Brenda H. (Mrs) — 19 Eglinton Square, Ardrossan KA22 8LN — 01294 464491
Nimmo, M. (Mrs) — 12 Muirfield Place, Kilwinning KA13 6NL — 01294 553718
Ross, Magnus — 39 Beachway, Largs KA30 8QH — 01475 689572
Smith, N. (Mrs) — 5 Kames Street, Millport, Isle of Cumbrae KA28 0BN — 01475 530747
Spencer, P. (Mrs) — 43 Gateside Street, Largs KA30 9LH — 01475 686293

13. LANARK

Allan, Robert — 59 Jennie Lee Drive, Overtown, Wishaw ML2 0EE — 01698 376738
Grant, Alan — 25 Moss-side Avenue, Carluke ML8 5UG — 01555 771419
Kerr, Sheilah I. (Mrs) — Dunvegan, 29 Wilsontown Road, Forth, Lanark ML11 8ER — 01555 812214
Love, William — 30 Barmore Avenue, Carluke ML8 4PE — 01555 751243

14. GREENOCK AND PAISLEY

Name	Address / E-mail	Telephone
Banks, Russell	18 Aboyne Drive, Paisley PA2 7SJ [E-mail: cbanks25@aol.com]	0141-884 6925
Campbell, Tom BA DipCPC	100 Craigielea Road, Renfrew PA4 8NJ [E-mail: thomas.campbell1180@ntlworld.co.uk]	0141-886 2503
Davey, Charles L.	16 Divert Road, Gourock PA19 1DT [E-mail: charles.davey@talktalk.net]	01475 631544
Glenny, John C.	49 Cloch Road, Gourock PA19 1AT [E-mail: jacklizg@aol.com]	01475 636415
Hood, Eleanor (Mrs)	12 Clochoderick Avenue, Kilbarchan, Johnstone PA10 2ES [E-mail: eleanor.hood.kilbarchan@ntlworld.com]	01505 704208
Jamieson, J.A.	148 Finnart Street, Greenock PA16 8HY	01475 729531
McFarlan, Elizabeth (Miss)	20 Fauldswood Crescent, Paisley PA2 9PA [E-mail: elizabeth.mcfarlan@ntlworld.com]	01505 358411
McHugh, Jack	'Earlshaugh', Earl Place, Bridge of Weir PA11 3HA [E-mail: jrmchugh@btinternet.com]	01505 612789
Marshall, Leon M.	Glenisla, Gryffe Road, Kilmacolm PA13 4BA [E-mail: lm@stevenson-kyles.co.uk]	01505 872417
Maxwell, Margaret (Mrs) BD	2 Grants Avenue, Paisley PA2 6AZ [E-mail: sandra1.maxwell@virgin.net]	0141-884 3710
Noonan, Pam (Mrs)	18 Woodburn Place, Houston, Johnstone PA6 7NA	01505 326254
Orry, Geoff	'Rhu Ellan', 4 Seaforth Crescent, Barrhead, Glasgow G78 1PL	0141-881 9748
Robertson, William	69 Colinbar Circle, Barrhead, Glasgow G78 2BG	0141-571 4338
Shaw, Ian	The Grove, 8 Commercial Road, Barrhead, Glasgow G78 1AJ	0141-881 2038

16. GLASGOW

Name	Address / E-mail	Telephone
Adams, Mary	44 Springcroft Crescent, Glasgow G69 6SB	0141-771 1957
Birchall, Edwin R.	11 Sunnybank Grove, Clarkston, Glasgow G76 7SU	0141-638 4332
Callander, Thomas M.S.	31 Dalkeith Avenue, Bishopbriggs, Glasgow G64 2HQ	0141-563 6955
Campbell, Jack T. BD BEd	40 Kenmure Avenue, Bishopbriggs, Glasgow G64 2DE	0141-563 5837
Dickson, Hector	'Gwito', 61 Whitton Drive, Giffnock, Glasgow G46 6EF	0141-637 0080
Fullarton, Andrew	225 Aros Drive, Glasgow G52 1TJ	0141-883 9518
Galbraith, Iain B.	Beechwood, Overton Road, Alexandria G83 0LJ	01389 753563
Gibson, James N.	153 Peveril Avenue, Glasgow G41 3SF	0141-632 4162
Hunt, Roland BSc PhD CertEd	4 Flora Gardens, Bishopbriggs, Glasgow G64 1DS	0141-548 3658 (Daytime – Mon–Fri) 0141-563 3257 (Evenings and weekends)
McFarlane, Robert	25 Avenel Road, Glasgow G13 2PB	0141-954 5540
McLaughlin, Cathy (Mrs)	8 Lamlash Place, Glasgow G33 3XH	0141-774 2483
MacLeod, John	2 Shuna Place, Newton Mearns, Glasgow G77 6TN	0141-639 6862
Phillips, John B.	2/3, 30 Handel Place, Glasgow G5 0TP [E-mail: johnphillips@fish.co.uk]	0141-429 7716
Robertson, Adam	423 Amulree Street, Glasgow G32 7SS	0141-573 6662
Stuart, Alex	107 Baldorran Crescent, Cumbernauld, Glasgow G68 9EX	01236 727710

Name	Address	Telephone
Tindall, Margaret (Mrs)	23 Ashcroft Avenue, Lennoxtown, Glasgow G65 7EN [E-mail: margarettindall@aol.com]	01360 310911
Wilson, George A.	46 Maxwell Drive, Garrowhill, Baillieston, Glasgow G69 6LS	0141-771 3862

17. HAMILTON

Anderson, Malcolm	5 Anford Place, Blantyre, Glasgow G72 0NR [E-mail: andersoncalvin1@aol.com]	01698 820510
Beattie, Richard	4 Bent Road, Hamilton ML3 6QB	01698 420806
Bell, Sheena	2 Langdale, East Kilbride, Glasgow G74 4RP	01355 248217
Clemenson, Anne	25 Dempsey Road, Lochview, Bellshill ML4 2UF [E-mail: aclemenson@msn.com]	01698 291019
Cruickshanks, William	63 Progress Drive, Caldercruix, Airdrie ML6 7PU	01236 843352
Haggarty, Frank	46 Glen Road, Caldercruix, Airdrie ML6 7PZ	01236 842182
Hawthorne, William G. MBE	172 Main Street, Plains, Airdrie ML6 7JH	01236 842230
Hewitt, Samuel	3 Corrie Court, Earnock, Hamilton ML3 9XE	01698 457403
Hislop, Eric	1 Castlegait, Strathaven ML10 6FF	01357 520003
Keir, Dickson	46 Brackenhill Drive, Hamilton ML3 8AY	01698 457351
Leckie, Elizabeth	41 Church Street, Larkhall ML9 1EZ	01698 308933
McCleary, Isaac	719 Coatbridge Road, Bargeddie, Glasgow G69 7PH	0141-236 0158
MacMillan, Georgina	1 Darngaber Gardens, Quarter, Hamilton ML3 7XX	01698 424040
Queen, Leslie	60 Loch Assynt, East Kilbride, Glasgow G74 2DW	01355 233932
Robertson, Rowan	68 Townhead Road, Coatbridge ML5 2HU	01236 425703
Smith, Alexander (Reader Emeritus)	6 Coronation Street, Wishaw ML2 8LF	01698 385797
Stevenson, Thomas	34 Castle Wynd, Quarter, Hamilton ML3 7XD	01698 282263
White, Ian	21 Muirhead, Stonehouse, Larkhall ML9 3HG	01698 792772
Wilson, William (Reader Emeritus)	115 Chatelherault Crescent, Low Waters Estate, Hamilton ML3 9PL	01698 421856

18. DUMBARTON

Name	Address	Telephone
Foster, Peter	The Forge, Colgrain Steading, Colgrain, Cardross, Dumbarton G82 5JL	01389 849200
Giles, Donald (Dr)	Levern House, Stuckenduff, Shandon, Helensburgh G84 8NW	01436 820565
Harold, Sandy	The Laurels, Risk Street, Clydebank G81 3LW	0141-952 3673
Hart, R.J.M. BSc	7 Kidston Drive, Helensburgh G84 8QA	01436 672039
Nutter, Margaret (Miss)	14 Balloch Road, Balloch, Alexandria G83 8SR	01436 754505
Rettie, Sara (Mrs)	86 Dennistoun Crescent, Helensburgh G84 7JF	01436 677984
Robertson, Ishbell (Miss)	81 Bonhill Road, Dumbarton G82 2DU	01389 763436

19. ARGYLL

Binner, Aileen (Mrs)	'Ailand', Connel, Oban PA37 1QX	01631 710264
Challis, John O.	Bay Villa, Strachur, Cairndow PA27 8DE	01369 860436
Elwis, Michael	Erray Farm, Tobermory, Mull PA75 6PS	01688 302331
Goodison, Michael	Dalriada Cottage, Bridge of Awe, Taynuilt PA35 1HT [E-mail: dalriada@btinternet.com]	01866 822479
Holden, Robert	Orsay, West Bank Road, Ardrishaig, Lochgilphead PA30 8HG	01546 603211
Logue, David	3 Braeface, Tayvallich, Lochgilphead PA31 8PN	01546 870647

Name	Address	Telephone
McLellan, James A.	West Drimvore, Lochgilphead PA31 8SU [E-mail: james.mclellan@argyll-bute.gov.uk]	01546 606403
Mitchell, James S.	4 Main Street, Port Charlotte, Isle of Islay PA48 7TX	01496 850650
Morrison, John L.	Tigh na Barnashaig, Tayvallich, Lochgilphead PA31 8PN	01546 870637
Ramsay, Matthew M.	Portnastorm, Carradale, Campbeltown PA28 6SB [E-mail: portnastorm@tiscali.co.uk]	01583 431381
Roberts, John V.	20 Toberonochy, Isle of Luing, Oban PA34 4UE	01852 314301
Sinclair, Margaret (Mrs)	2 Quarry Place, Furnace, Inveraray PA32 8XW [E-mail: margaret_sinclair@btinternet.com]	01499 500633 (Prefix 18001 Text, prefix 18002 Voice)
Stather, Angela (Mrs)	9 Gartness Cottages, Ballygrant, Isle of Islay PA45 7QN	01496 840527
Stewart, Agnes (Mrs)	Creagdhu Mansions, New Quay Street, Campbeltown PA28 6BB	01586 552805

22. FALKIRK

Name	Address	Telephone
Duncan, Lorna (Mrs) BA	Richmond, 28 Solway Drive, Head of Muir, Denny FK5 5NS	01324 813020
Mathers, S. (Mrs)	10 Ercall Road, Brightons, Falkirk FK2 0RS	01324 872253
O'Rourke, Edith (Mrs)	16 Achray Road, Cumbernauld, Glasgow G67 4JH	01236 732813
Sarle, Andrew BSc BD	114 High Station Road, Falkirk FK1 5LN	01324 621648
Stewart, Arthur MA	51 Bonnymuir Crescent, Bonnybridge FK4 1GD	01324 812667
Struthers, I.	7 McVean Place, Bonnybridge FK4 1QZ [E-mail: ivar.struthers@btinternet.com]	01324 841145

23. STIRLING

Name	Address	Telephone
Brown, Kathryn (Mrs)	1 Callendar Park Walk, Callendar Grange, Falkirk FK1 1TA	01324 617352
Durie, Alastair	25 Forth Place, Stirling FK8 1UD	01786 451029
Grier, Hunter	17 Station Road, Bannockburn, Stirling FK7 8LG	01786 815192
Kimmitt, Alan	111 Glasgow Road, Stirling FK7 0PF	01786 817014
Lamont, John BD	62 Parkdyke, Stirling FK7 9LS	01786 474515
Mack, Lynne (Mrs)	36 Middleton, Menstrie FK11 7HD	01259 761465
Ross, Alastair	7 Elm Court, Doune FK16 6JG	01786 841648
Tilly, Patricia	4 Innerdownie Place, Dollar FK14 7BY	01259 742094
Weir, Andrew (Dr)	16 The Oaks, Killearn, Glasgow G63 9SF	01360 550779

24. DUNFERMLINE

Name	Address	Telephone
Adams, William	24 Foulford Street, Cowdenbeath KY4 0EQ	01383 510540
Arnott, Robert G.K.	25 Sealstrand, Dalgety Bay, Dunfermline KY11 5GH	01383 822293
Conway, Bernard	4 Centre Street, Kelty KY4 0DU	01383 830442
Grant, Allan	6 Normandy Place, Rosyth KY11 2HJ	01383 428760
McCaffery, Joyce (Mrs)	79 Union Street, Cowdenbeath KY4 9SA	01383 515775
McDonald, Elizabeth (Mrs)	Parleyhill, Culross, Dunfermline KY12 8JD	01383 880231
Meiklejohn, Barry	40 Lilac Grove, Dunfermline KY11 8AP	01383 731550
Mitchell, Ian G. QC	17 Carlingnose Point, North Queensferry, Inverkeithing KY11 1ER	01383 416240

25. KIRKCALDY

Name	Address	Telephone
Biernat, Ian	2 Formonthills Road, Glenrothes KY6 3BX	01592 741487
Weatherston, Catriona M.A. (Miss) BSc	'Cruachan', Church Road, Leven KY8 4JB	01333 424636

26. ST ANDREWS

Name	Address	Telephone
Elder, Morag (Mrs)	5 Provost Road, Tayport DD6 9JE	01382 552218
King, C.M. (Mrs)	8 Bankwell Road, Anstruther KY10 3DA	01333 310017
Kinnis, W.K.B. (Dr) (Reader Emeritus)	4 Dempster Court, St Andrews KY16 9EU	01334 476959
Sherriffs, Irene (Mrs)	Cragganmhor, 79 Tay Street, Newport-on-Tay DD1 8AQ	01382 542193
Smith, Elspeth (Mrs)	Whinstead, Dalgairn, Cupar KY15 4PH	01334 653269

27. DUNKELD AND MEIGLE

Name	Address	Telephone
Carr, Graham	St Helens, Meigle Road, Alyth PH11 8EU	01828 632474
Ewart, Ellen (Mrs)	Caputh Manse, Caputh, Perth PH1 4JH	01738 710520
Howat, David	Lilybank Cottage, Newton Street, Blairgowrie PH10 6MZ	01250 874715
Macmartin, Duncan M.	Teallach, Old Crieff Road, Aberfeldy PH15 2DG	01887 820693
Peacock, Graham	7 Glensla View, Alyth, Blairgowrie PH11 8LW	01828 633341
Saunders, Grace (Ms)	40 Perth Street, Blairgowrie PH10 6DQ	01250 873981
Templeton, Elizabeth (Mrs)	Milton of Pitgur Farmhouse, Dalcapon, Pitlochry PH9 0ND	01796 482232

28. PERTH

Name	Address	Telephone
Begg, James	8 Park Village, Turretba Road, Crieff PH7 4JN [E-mail: Bjimmy37@aol.com]	01764 655907
Brown, Stanley	14 Buchan Drive, Perth PH1 1NQ	01738 628818
Chappell, E. (Mrs)	Fiscal's House, Flat B, 1 South Street, Perth PH2 8NJ [E-mail: chappell@fish.co.uk]	01738 587808
Coulter, Hamish	95 Cedar Drive, Perth PH1 1RW [E-mail: hamishcoulter@btinternet.com]	01738 636761
Hastings, W.P.	5 Craigroyston Road, Scone, Perth PH2 6NB	01738 560498
Laing, John	10 Graybank Road, Perth PH2 0GZ [E-mail: laing_middlechurch@hotmail.com]	01738 623888
Livingstone, Alan	Meadowside, Lawmuir, Methven, Perth PH1 3SZ	01738 840682
Michie, Margaret (Mrs)	3 Loch Leven Court, Wester Balgedie, Kinross KY13 9NE [E-mail: margaretmichie@balgedie.freeserve.co.uk]	01592 840602
Ogilvie, Brian	67 Whitecraigs, Kinnesswood, Kinross KY13 9JN [E-mail: brianj.ogilvie1@btopenworld.com]	01592 840823
Packer, Joan (Miss)	11 Moredun Terrace, Perth PH2 0DA	
Thorburn, Susan (Mrs) MTh	3 Daleally Cottages, St Madoes Road, Errol, Perth PH2 7TJ [E-mail: s_thor2@yahoo.com]	01738 623873
Wilkie, Robert	24 Huntingtower Road, Perth PH1 2JS	01738 628301
Yellowlees, Deirdre (Mrs)	Ringmill House, Gannochy Farm, Perth PH2 7JH [E-mail: d.yellowlees@btinternet.com]	01738 633773

29. DUNDEE

Bell, Stephen (Dr)	10 Victoria Street, Newport-on-Tay DD6 8DJ	01382 542315
	[E-mail: stephen.bell@dundeepresbytery.org.uk]	
Brown, Isobel (Mrs)	10 School Wynd, Muirhead, Dundee DD2 5LW	01382 580545
Brown, Janet (Miss)	G2, 6 Baxter Park Terrace, Dundee DD4 6NL	01382 453066
Doig, Andrew	6 Lyndhurst Terrace, Dundee DD2 3HP	01382 610596
Owler, Harry G. (Emeritus)	43 Brownhill Road, Dundee DD2 4LH	01382 622902
Ramsay, T.	6 Inchcape Road, Broughty Ferry, Dundee DD5 2LP	01382 778915
Rodgers, Mary (Mrs)	12 Balmerino Road, Dundee DD4 8RN	01382 500291
Shepherd, Ewan	34 Dalmahoy Drive, Dundee DD2 3UT	01382 815825
Simpson, Webster	51 Wemyss Crescent, Monifieth, Dundee DD5 4RA	01382 535218
Webster, Charles A.	16 Bath Street, Broughty Ferry, Dundee DD5 2BY	01382 739520
	[E-mail: charles.webster@dundeepresbytery.org.uk]	
Woodley, Alan G. (Dr)	67 Marlee Road, Broughty Ferry, Dundee DD5 3UT	01382 739820
	[E-mail: alan.woodley@dundeepresbytery.org.uk]	
Xenophontos-Hellen, Tim	23 Ancrum Drive, Dundee DD2 2JG	01382 660355
	[E-mail: tim.xenophontos-hellen@dundeepresbytery.org.uk]	

30. ANGUS

Anderson, Gordon	33 Grampian View, Ferryden, Montrose DD10 9SU	01674 674915
Beedie, A.W.	62 Newton Crescent, Arbroath DD11 3JZ	01241 875001
Davidson, P.I.	95 Bridge Street, Montrose DD10 8AF	01674 674098
Edwards, Dougal	25 Mackenzie Street, Carnoustie DD7 6HD	01241 852666
Gray, Ian	'The Mallards', 15 Rossie Island Road, Montrose DD10 9NH	01674 677126
Gray, Linda (Mrs)	8 Inchgarth Street, Forfar DD8 3LY	01307 464039
Ironside, Colin (Emeritus)	21 Taillyour Crescent, Montrose DD10 9BL	01674 673959
Leslie Melville, Ruth (Hon. Mrs)	Little Deuchar, Fern, Forfar DD8 3RA	01356 650279
Nicol, Douglas C.	Edenbank, 16 New Road, Forfar DD8 2AE	01307 463264
Stevens, Peter J. BSc BA	7 Union Street, Montrose DD10 8PZ	01674 673710
Thompson, Anne	22 Braehead Drive, Carnoustie DD7 7SX	01241 852084
Wheat, M.	16A South Esk Street, Montrose DD10 8BJ	01674 676083

31. ABERDEEN

Anderson, William	1 Farepark Circle, Westhill, Skene AB32 6WJ	01224 740017
(attached to the congregations of Cove and St Nicholas Kincorth)		
Gray, Peter PhD	165 Countesswells Road, Aberdeen AB15 7RA	01224 318172
Morgan, Richard	73A Bon-Accord Street, Aberdeen AB11 6ED	01224 210270
Sinton, George P. (Emeritus) FIMLS	12 North Donside Road, Bridge of Don, Aberdeen AB23 8PA	01224 702273

32. KINCARDINE AND DEESIDE

Atkins, Sally (Mrs)	9 Feugh View, Strachan, Banchory AB31 6NF	01330 850434
Broere, Teresa (Mrs)	3 Balnastraid Cottages, Dinnet, Aboyne AB34 5NE	01339 880058

Coles, Stephen	43 Mearns Walk, Laurencekirk AB30 1FA	01561 378400
Harris, Michael	The Gables, Netherley Park, Netherley, Stonehaven AB39 3QM	01569 731091
McCafferty, W. John	Lynwood, Cammachmore, Stonehaven AB39 3NR	01569 730281
	[E-mail: john.mccafferty@opuscompany.com]	
McLuckie, John	7 Monaltrie Close, Ballater AB35 5PT	01339 755489
	[E-mail: j-r-mcluckie@supanet.com]	
Middleton, Robbie (Capt.)	7 St Ternan's Road, Newtonhill, Stonehaven AB39 2PF	01569 730852
Platt, David	2 St Michael's Road, Newtonhill, Stonehaven AB39 3RW	01569 730465
Simpson, Elizabeth (Mrs)	33 Golf Road, Ballater AB35 5QX	01339 755597
	[E-mail: connemara33@yahoo.com]	

33. GORDON

Doak, Alan B.	17 Chievres Place, Ellon AB41 9WH	01358 721819
Findlay, Patricia (Mrs)	Douglas View, Tullynessle, Alford AB33 8QR	01975 562379
Hart, Elsie (Mrs)	The Knoll, Craigearn, Kemnay AB51 9LN	01467 642105
Mitchell, Jean (Mrs)	6 Cowgate, Oldmeldrum, Inverurie AB51 0EN	01651 872745
Rennie, Lyall	Dunisla, Oyne, Insch AB52 6QU	01464 851587
Robb, Margaret (Mrs)	Chrislouan, Keithhall, Inverurie AB51 0LN	01651 882310
Robertson, James Y.	1 Nicol Road, Kintore, Inverurie AB51 0QA	01467 633001
Sutherland, Susan (Mrs)	53 Westhill Grange, Westhill, Skene AB32 6QJ	01224 741889

34. BUCHAN

Allen, Sena (Mrs)	88 Kirk Street, Peterhead AB42 1RY	01779 477327
	[E-mail: sama@allen159.fsnet.co.uk]	
Armitage, Rosaline (Mrs)	Whitecairn, Blackhills, Peterhead AB42 3LR	01779 477267
Brown, Lillian (Mrs)	Bank House, 45 Main Street, Aberchirder, Huntly AB54 7ST	01466 780330
Davidson, James	19 Great Stuart Street, Peterhead AB42 1JX	01779 470242
Forsyth, Alicia (Mrs)	Rothie Inn Farm, Rothienorman, Inverurie AB51 8YH	01651 821359
Givan, James	Zimra, Longmanhill, Banff AB45 3RP	01261 833318
	[E-mail: jim.givan@btopenworld.com]	
Higgins, Scott	St Ninian's, Manse Terrace, Turriff AB53 4BA	01888 569103
	[E-mail: mhairiandscott@binternet.com]	
Lumsden, Vera (Mrs)	8 Queen's Crescent, Portsoy, Banff AB45 2PX	01261 842712
	[E-mail: ivsd@lumsden77.freeserve.co.uk]	
McColl, John	East Cairnchina, Lonmay, Fraserburgh AB43 8RH	01346 532558
Macnee, Anthea (Mrs)	Kingsville, Strichen, Fraserburgh AB43 6SQ	01771 637941
Mair, Dorothy (Miss)	53 Dennyduff Road, Fraserburgh AB43 9LY	01346 513879
	[E-mail: dorothymair1@aol.com]	
Michie, William	34 Seafield Street, Whitehills, Banff AB45 2NR	01261 861439
Noble, John	44 Henderson Park, Peterhead AB42 2WR	01779 472522
	[E-mail: john.noble@onetel.net]	
Ogston, Norman	Rowandale, 6 Rectory Road, Turriff AB53 4SU	01888 560342
	[E-mail: norman.ogston@virgin.net]	

Simpson, Andrew C. — 10 Wood Street, Banff AB45 1JX [E-mail: andy.louise1@btinternet.com] — 01261 812538

Smith, Ian M.G. MA — Chomriach, 2 Hill Street, Cruden Bay, Peterhead AB42 0HF — 01779 812698
Smith, Jenny (Mrs) — 5 Seatown Place, Cairnbulg, Fraserburgh AB43 8WP [E-mail: jennyfsmith@hotmail.com] — 01346 582980

Sneddon, Richard — 8 School Road, Peterhead AB42 2BE [E-mail: CARICHCARICH@aol.com] — 01779 480803

Stewart, William — Denend. Strichen AB43 6RN — 01771 637256
Williams, Paul — 20 Soy Burn Gardens, Portsoy AB45 2QG — 01261 842338
Yule, Joseph — 5 Staffa Street, Peterhead AB42 1NF — 01779 476400

35. MORAY
Benson, F. Stewart — 8 Springfield Court, Forres IV36 3WY — 01309 671525
Carson, John — 2 Woodside Drive, Forres IV36 2UF — 01309 674541
Finnie, Les — 83 Robertson Road, Lhanbryde, Elgin IV30 8IQ — 01343 842789
Forbes, Jean (Mrs) — Greenmoss, Drybridge, Buckie AB56 5JB — 01542 831646
MacKenzie, Stuart G. MA — Woodend Cottage, Blackburn, Fochabers IV32 7LN — 01343 843248
Middleton, Alex — Coral Cottage, Pilmuir Road West, Forres IV36 2HL — 01309 676912

36. ABERNETHY
Bardgett, Alison (Mrs) — Tigh an Iasgair, Street of Kincardine, Boat of Garten PH24 3BY [E-mail: alison@bardgett.plus.com] — 01479 831751

Duncanson, Mary (Mrs) — Falas-an-Duin, Catlodge, Laggan, Newtonmore PH20 1BS [E-mail: maryb@mduncanson.freeserve.co.uk] — 01528 544399

37. INVERNESS
Archer, Morven (Mrs) — 42 Firth View Drive, Inverness IV3 8QE — 01463 237840
Barry, Dennis — 50 Holm Park, Inverness IV2 4XU — 01463 225883
Cazaly, Leonard — 9 Moray Park, Culloden, Inverness IV2 4SX — 01463 794469
Cook, Arnett D. — 128 Laurel Avenue, Inverness IV3 5RS — 01463 242586
Davidson, Margaret (Mrs) — 11 Souters Rise, Nairn IV12 5BU — 01667 859938
Robertson, Hendry — 'Park House', 51 Glenurquhart Road, Inverness IV3 5PB — 01463 231858
Robertson, Stewart J.H. — 27 Towerhill Drive, Inverness IV2 5FD — 01463 793144
Roden, Vivien — 15 Oldmill Road, Tomatin, Inverness IV13 7YW — 01808 511355

38. LOCHABER
Chalkley, Andrew BSc — 2 Telford Place, Claggan, Fort William PH33 6QG [E-mail: andrew.chalkley@btinternet.com] — 01397 700271

Dick, Robert MA — 8 Lanark Place, Fort William PH33 6UD — 01397 704833
Fraser, John A. BA — 26 Clunes Avenue, Caol, Fort William PH33 7BJ [E-mail: john.afraser@btopenworld.com] — 01397 703467

Maitland, John	St Monance, Ardgour, Fort William PH33 7AA	01855 841267
Thomas, Geoff	Drumcannach, Station Road, Arisaig PH39 4NJ [E-mail: geoffthomas@tiscali.co.uk]	01687 450230
Walker, Eric	Tigh a Chlann, Inverroy, Roy Bridge PH31 4AQ [E-mail: line15@btinternet.com]	01397 712028
Walker, Pat (Mrs)	Tigh a Chlann, Inverroy, Roy Bridge PH31 4AQ [E-mail: pw-15@tiscali.co.uk]	01397 712028

39. ROSS

Finlayson, Michael R.	Amberlea, Evanton, Dingwall IV16 9UY	01349 830598
Gilbertson, Ian	Firth View, Craigrory, North Kessock, Inverness IV1 1XH	01463 731538
Jamieson, Patricia A. (Mrs)	7 Craig Avenue, Tain IV19 1JP	01862 893154
McCreadie, Frederick	Highfield, Highfield Park, Conon Bridge, Dingwall IV7 8AP	01349 862171
Riddell, Keith	2 Station Cottages, Fearn, Tain IV20 1RR [E-mail: shirleyriddell@yahoo.co.uk]	01862 832867

40. SUTHERLAND

Bruce, Dorothy (Mrs)	Eastwood, Altass, Rosehall, by Lairg IV27 4EU	01549 441285
Henderson, Angela (Mrs)	Kildale, Clashmore, Dornoch IV25 3RG	01862 881286
Innes, Derek	Hill Cottage, Lairg Muir, Lairg IV27 4ED	01549 402215
Reid, Rosie (Dr)	The Old Manse, Creich, Bonar Bridge, Ardgay IV24 3AB	01863 766257
Stobo, Mary (Mrs)	Druim-an-Sgairnich, Lower Gledfield, Ardgay IV24 3BG	01863 766868
Weidner, Karl	St Vincent Road, Tain IV19 1JR	01862 894202

41. CAITHNESS

Duncan, Esme (Miss)	Avalon, Upper Warse, Canisbay, Wick KW1 4YD [E-mail: esmeduncan@btinternet.com]	01955 611455
Stewart, Heather (Mrs)	Burnthill, Thrumster, Wick KW1 5AX [E-mail: heatherburnthill@btopenworld.com]	01955 651717

42. LOCHCARRON – SKYE

Mackenzie, Hector	53 Strath, Gairloch IV21 2DB	01445 712433
Macrae, D.E.	Nethania, 52 Strath, Gairloch IV21 2DB	01445 712235
Ross, R. Ian	St Conal's, Inverinate, Kyle IV40 8HB	01599 511371

43. UIST

Browning, Margaret	1 Middlequarter, Sollar, Lochmaddy, Isle of North Uist HS6	01876 560392
Lines, Charles	Flat 1/02, 8 Queen Margaret Road, Glasgow G20 6DP	0141-946 2142
MacAulay, John	Flodabay, Isle of Harris HS3 3HA	01859 530340
MacNab, Ann (Mrs)	Druim Skilivat, Scolpaig, Lochmaddy, Isle of North Uist HS6 5DH	01876 510701
MacSween, John	5 Scott Road, Tarbert, Isle of Harris HS3 3DL	01859 502338
Taylor, Hamish	Tigh na Tobair, Flodabay, Isle of Harris HS3 3HA	01859 530310

44. LEWIS

Name	Address	Tel
Forsyth, William	1 Berisay Place, Stornoway, Isle of Lewis HS1 2TF	01851 702332
McAlpin, Robert J.G. MA FEIS	42A Upper Coll, Back, Isle of Lewis HS2 0LS	01851 820288
Murray, Angus	4 Ceann Chilleagraidh, Stornoway, Isle of Lewis HS1 2UJ	01851 703550

45. ORKNEY

Name	Address	Tel
Robertson, Johan (Mrs)	Old Manse, Eday, Orkney KW17 2AA	01857 622251
Steer, John	Beckington, Hillside Road, Stromness, Orkney KW16 3AH	01856 850815

46. SHETLAND

Name	Address	Tel
Christie, William C.	11 Fullaburn, Bressay, Shetland ZE2 9ET	01595 820244
Greig, Diane (Mrs) MA	The Manse, Sandwick, Shetland ZE2 9HW	01950 431244
Harrison, Christine (Mrs) BA	Gerdavatn, Baltasound, Unst, Shetland ZE2 9DY	01957 711578
Jamieson, Ian MA	Linksview, Ringesta, Quendale, Shetland ZE2 9JD	01950 460477
Laidlay, Una (Mrs)	5 Bells Road, Lerwick, Shetland ZE1 0QB	01595 695147
Smith, M. Beryl (Mrs) DCE MSc	Vakterlee, Cumliewick, Sandwick, Shetland ZE2 9HH	01950 431280

47. ENGLAND

Dick, R.G.	Duneagle, Church Road, Sparkford, Somerset	01963 40475
Green, Peter (Dr)	Samburu Cottage, Russells Green Road. Ninfield, East Sussex	01424 892033
Mackay, Donald (Reader Emeritus)	90 Hallgarth Street, Elvet, Durham DH1 3AS	0191-383 2110
Menzies, Rena (Mrs)	49 Elizabeth Avenue, St Brelade's, Jersey JE3 8GR	01534 741095

48. EUROPE

Name	Address	Tel
Ross, David	URB EL Campanario, EDF Granada, Esc 14, Baja B, Ctra Cadiz N-340, Km 168, 29680 Estepona, Malaga, Spain [E-mail: rosselcampanario@yahoo.co.uk]	(Tel/Fax) 0034 952 88 26 34

49. JERUSALEM

Name	Address	Tel
Zielinski, Jennifer C. (Mrs)	PO Box 104, Tiberias 14100, Israel [E-mail: scottie2@netvision.net.il]	(Tel) 00972 4 671 0710 (Fax) 00972 4 671 0711

LIST O – REPRESENTATIVES ON COUNCIL EDUCATION COMMITTEES

COUNCIL	NAME	ADDRESS	TEL
ABERDEEN CITY	Mr David Yacamini	29 Rubislaw Park Crescent, Aberdeen AB15 8BT [E-mail: jeananddave.yacamini@googlemail.com]	01224 316128

ABERDEENSHIRE	Mr Alexander Corner	4 Bain Road, Mintlaw, Peterhead AB42 5EW [E-mail: sandycorner@hotmail.com]	01771 622562
ANGUS	Mr David Adams	Glebe House, Farnell, by Brechin DD9 6UH	01674 820227
ARGYLL and BUTE	Miss Fiona Fisher	2 Nursery Cottages, Kilmun, Dunoon PA23 8SE [E-mail: fionae@tiscali.co.uk]	01369 840766
BORDERS	Mr Graeme Donald	1 Upper Loan Park, Lauder TD2 6TR [E-mail: graeme.donald@btopenworld.com]	01578 722422
CLACKMANNAN	Rev. Mairi Lovett	The Manse, 7 Long Row, Menstrie FK11 7BA [E-mail: mairi@kanyo.co.uk]	01259 761461
DUMFRIES and GALLOWAY	Mr Robert McQuistan	Kirkdale Schoolhouse, Carsluith, Newton Stewart DG8 7DT [E-mail: mcquistan@quista.net]	01387 722165
DUNDEE	Rev. James L. Wilson	53 Old Craigie Road, Dundee DD4 7JD [E-mail: R3VJW@aol.com]	01382 459249
EAST AYRSHIRE	Mr William McGregor	25 Blackburn Drive, Ayr KA7 2XW [E-mail: Bill.McGregor@east-ayrshire.gov.uk]	01292 293918
EAST DUNBARTONSHIRE	Mrs Barbara Jarvie	18 Cannerton Crescent, Milton of Campsie, Glasgow G66 8DR [E-mail: bj@bjarvie.fsnet.co.uk]	01360 319729
EAST LOTHIAN	Mrs Marjorie K. Goldsmith	20 St Lawrence, Haddington EH41 3RL	01620 823349
EAST RENFREWSHIRE	Rev. Maureen Leitch	14 Maxton Avenue, Barrhead, Glasgow G78 1DY [E-mail: maureen.leitch@ntlworld.com]	0141-881 1462
EDINBURGH CITY	Mr A. Craig Duncan	2 East Barnton Gardens, Edinburgh EH4 6AR [E-mail: acraigduncan@aol.com]	0131-336 4432
EDINBURGH SCRUTINY PANEL	Dr J. Mitchell Manson	17 Huntingdon Place, Edinburgh EH7 4AX [E-mail: MitchellManson@aol.com]	0131-557 1933
FALKIRK	Mrs Margaret Coutts	34 Pirleyhill Gardens, Falkirk FK1 5NB [E-mail: margaret.coutts1@tiscali.co.uk]	01324 628732
FIFE	Rev. Alistair McLeod	13 Greenmantle Way, Glenrothes KY6 2QG [E-mail: alistair@mcleod3246.freeserve.co.uk]	01592 744558
GLASGOW CITY	Rev. Graham Cartledge	5 Briar Grove, Newlands, Glasgow G43 2TG [E-mail: g.cartledge@ntlworld.com]	0141-637 3228
HIGHLAND	Rev. Alexander Glass	Craigton, Tulloch Avenue, Dingwall IV15 9LH	01349 863258
INVERCLYDE	Rev. William Douglas Hamilton	67 Forsyth Street, Greenock PA16 8SX [E-mail: revwdhamilton@hotmail.com]	01475 724003
MIDLOTHIAN	Mr Paul Hayes	Kingsway Management Services Ltd, 127 Deanburn, Penicuik EH26 0JA [E-mail: paul.hayes@basilicon.com]	
MORAY	Mrs Alexandra Rose MacLennan	The Old Steading, Wester Golford, Auldearn, Nairn IV12 5QQ [E-mail: ian.maclennan3@btinternet.com]	01309 641342
NORTH AYRSHIRE	Mr John S. Scott	2 West Lynn, Dalry KA24 4LJ [E-mail: scott.lynn1@btopenworld.com]	
NORTH LANARKSHIRE	Mr Alistair MacLeod	21 Cairnhill Avenue, Airdrie ML6 9HQ [E-mail: alistairmacleod@blueyonder.co.uk]	01236 754760
ORKNEY	Mrs Carole Macnaughton	The Cathedral Manse, Berstane Road, Kirkwall, Orkney KW15 1NA [E-mail: fmacnaug@fish.co.uk]	01856 873312

PERTH and KINROSS	Mrs Hilary Spencer Bridge	House of Cardean, Meigle, Blairgowrie PH12 8RB [E-mail: hilary.bridge@btinternet.com]	01828 640452
RENFREWSHIRE	Mr George Hamilton	33 St Ninian's Road, Paisley PA2 6TP	0141-840 2233
SHETLAND	Rev. Tom Macintyre	The Rock, Whiteness, Shetland ZE2 9LJ [E-mail: the2macs.macintyre@btinternet.com]	
SOUTH AYRSHIRE	Rev. Dr John Lochrie	The Manse, Colmonell, Girvan KA26 0SA	01465 881224
SOUTH LANARKSHIRE	Mrs Marion Dickie	2 Murchison Drive, East Kilbride, Glasgow G75 8HF [E-mail: marion.ekmc.wpc@ukgateway.net]	
STIRLING	Mrs Joan Kerr	36 Strathallan Court, Bridge of Allan, Stirling FK9 4BW	01786 834939
WEST DUNBARTONSHIRE	Miss Sheila Rennie	128 Dumbuie Avenue, Dumbarton G82 2JW [E-mail: sheila_rennie@tiscali.co.uk]	01389 763246
WEST LOTHIAN	Rev. Dr Robert A. Anderson	The Manse, 5 MacDonald Gardens, Blackburn, Bathgate EH47 7RE [E-mail: robertaland@supanet.com]	01506 652825
WESTERN ISLES	Rev. Andrew W.F. Coghill	Leurbost, Lochs, Isle of Lewis HS2 9NS [E-mail: andcoghill@aol.com]	01851 860243

LIST P – RETIRED LAY AGENTS

Forrester, Arthur A.	158 Lee Crescent North, Bridge of Don, Aberdeen AB22 8FR
Scott, John W.	15 Manor Court, Forfar DD8 1BR
Shepherd, Dennis	Mission House, Norby, Sandness, Shetland ZE2 9PL

LIST Q – MINISTERS ORDAINED FOR SIXTY YEARS AND UPWARDS

Until 1992, the *Year Book* contained each year a list of those ministers who had been ordained 'for fifty years and upwards'. For a number of reasons, that list was thereafter discontinued. The current Editor was encouraged to reinstate such a list, and the edition for 2002 included the names of those ordained for sixty years and upwards. With ministers, no less than the rest of society, living longer, it was felt reasonable to proceed on that basis. Correspondence made it clear that this list was welcomed, and it has been included in an appropriately revised form each year since then. Again this year, an updated version is offered following the best enquiries that could be made. The date of ordination is given in full where it is known.

1932	14 August	Thomas Mackenzie Donn (Duthil)
1933	20 October	The Very Rev. William Roy Sanderson (Stenton with Whittingehame)

1934	3 November	Owain Tudor Hughes (Guernsey: St Andrew's in the Grange)
1935	10 April	George Douglas Monro (Yester)
1936	September	The Very Rev. James Gunn Matheson (Portree)
1937	31 March	James Brown Mirrilees (Aberdeen: High Hilton)
	15 October	Robert Anderson Philp (Stepps: St Andrew's)
1938	26 February	John Macgregor MacKechnie (Kilchrenan and Dalavich)
	29 June	George Alestair Alison Bennett (Strathkinness)
	1 July	Alexander Thomas Hain Taylor (Dunoon: Old and St Cuthbert's)
	13 October	Robert Hamilton (Kelso: Old)
1939	2 June	David Noel Fisher (Glasgow: Sherbrooke St Gilbert's)
	27 October	James Scott Marshall (Associate Minister: Leith South)
	12 November	Alexander McRae Houston (Tibbermore)
	18 November	David Sloan Walker (Makerstoun with Smailholm with Stichill, Hume and Nethorn)
	10 December	Wellesley Grahame Bailey (Ladykirk with Whitsome)
	22 December	Alastair McRae Rennie (Kincardine Croick and Edderton)
1940	24 February	James Johnstone Turnbull (Arbirlot with Colliston)
	20 March	The Very Rev. Thomas Forsyth Torrance (Professor of Christian Dogmatics: Edinburgh University)
	22 March	Donald MacKellar Leitch Urie (Kincardine O'Neil)
	29 May	Norman McGathan Bowman (Edinburgh: St Mary's)
	14 July	Nigel Ross MacLean (Perth: St Paul's)
	21 August	Donald MacFarlane (Inverness: East)
	3 September	Arthur Thomas Hill (Ormiston with Prestonpans: Grange)
1941	29 May	Harry Galbraith Miller (Iona and Ross of Mull)
	6 June	Thomas Williamson (Dyke with Edinkillie)
	3 July	Donald William MacKenzie (Auchterarder: The Barony)
	21 September	Silvester Skinner (Lumphanan)
	21 September	Andrew Swan (Greenock: St Margaret's)
	9 December	John Nelson (Crawford and Elvanfoot with Leadhills and Wanlockhead)
1942	2 January	James Gilbert Morrison (Rotterdam)
	4 February	Robert Macbean Gilmour (Kiltarlity)
	15 April	Frank Haughton (Kirkintilloch: St Mary's)
	5 July	Norman Christopher Macrae (Loanhead)
	26 August	Arthur William Bruce (Fortingall and Glenlyon)
	3 September	James Robert Moffett (Paisley: St Matthew's)
	22 November	Robert Gray (Stonehaven: Fetteresso)
	23 November	Frederick Haslehurst Fulton (Clunie, Lethendy and Kinloch)
	24 December	James Bews (Dundee: Craigiebank)

1943	4 March	Matthew Liddell (Glasgow: St Paul's (Outer High) and St David's (Ramshorn))
	11 May	Leon David Levison (Ormiston with Pencaitland)
	2 June	Duncan Finlayson (Morvern)
	22 June	William Cadzow McCormick (Glasgow: Maryhill Old)
	24 June	James Murray Hutcheson (Glasgow: Possilpark)
	3 September	George Cooper (Delting with Nesting and Lunnasting)
	1 October	Alick Hugh McAulay (Bellie with Speymouth)
	7 October	Hugh Talman (Polmont: Old)
	28 November	David Hutchison Whiteford (Gullane)
1944	3 January	Magnus William Cooper (Kirkcaldy: Abbotshall)
	21 June	Denis Macdonald Duncan (Editor: *The British Weekly*)
	12 July	James Kirk Porteous (Cupar: St John's)
	10 November	Alexander Spence (Elgin: St Giles': Associate)
1945	4 January	Victor Charles Pogue (Baird Research Fellow)
	24 January	Thomas Morton (Rutherglen: Stonelaw)
	4 February	James Shirra (St Martin's with Scone New)
	20 April	Thomas Lithgow (Banchory-Devenick with Maryculter)
	5 May	Robert Stockbridge Whiteford (Shapinsay)
	27 June	Ian Arthur Girdwood Easton (University of Strathclyde)
	4 July	Douglas Lister (Largo and Newburn)
	1 August	John Walter Evans (Elgin: High)
	5 August	Richard Anderson Baigrie (Kirkurd with Newlands)
	4 September	John Paul Tierney (Peterhead West: Associate)
	5 September	Allan MacInnes Macleod (Gordon: St Michael's with Legerwood with Westruther)
	7 October	George Scott Skakle (Aberdeen: Powis)
1946	11 April	James Martin (Glasgow: High Carntyne)
	19 May	John McClymont Frew (Glasgow: Dennistoun)
	3 June	John Geddes Sim (Kirkcaldy: Old)
	6 June	Robert McLachlan Wilson (University of St Andrews)
	23 June	Ian Masson Fraser (Selly Oak Colleges)
	18 September	John Wilkinson (Kikuyu)
	25 September	Frederick John Marshall (Bermuda)
	3 October	John Henry Whyte (Gourock: Ashton)
	13 November	Ian Bruce Doyle (Department of National Mission)
	18 December	Ronald Neil Grant Murray (Pardovan and Kingscavil with Winchburgh)
1947	23 January	Peter George Thomson (Irvine: Fullarton)
	30 April	Neil Douglas Craig (Dalbeattie: Craignair with Urr)
	22 June	James Alexander Robertson Mackenzie (Largo: St David's)
	24 July	James Alexander Wemyss Smith (Garvock St Cyrus)

27 November William Duncan Crombie (Glasgow: Calton New with Glasgow: St Andrew's)
10 December Robert James Stuart Wallace (Foveran)

LIST R – DECEASED MINISTERS

The Editor has been made aware of the following ministers who have died since the publication of the previous volume of the *Year Book*.

Bruce, William Craik (Motherwell: Dalziel)
Campbell, John (Urquhart)
Cant, Harry William McPhail (Kirkwall: St Magnus Cathedral)
Craig, Iain Robeson (Invergowrie)
Donaldson, Moses (Fort Augustus with Glengarry)
Edwards, William Geraint (Amsterdam)
Harries, David Arthur (British Sailors Society)
Jackson, John (Bonnybridge)
Jamieson, George Thomas (Stirling: Viewfield)
Kenrick, Bruce (Calcutta)
Lawson, Ruth Elaine Auxiliary Minister: Presbytery of Lochaber
McCallum, John Noth
McCann, George McDonald (Auxiliary Minister: Presbytery of Melrose and Peebles)
McConnell, Robert (Hawick: St Margaret's and Wilton South with Roberton)
Mackay, Donald (Ardrossan: St John's)
Mackenzie, Donald Macfarlane (Auchtertool with Burntisland)
Mackenzie, Iain (Tarbat)
Mackenzie, Ian Murdo (BBC)
MacLeod, Ian Ingram Scott (Arbroath: St Andrew's)
MacLeod, William John (Kirkintilloch: St David's Memorial)
McPhail, Peter (Creich, Flisk and Kilmany)
Mellis, Robert James (Shapinsay)
Montgomery, David (North Knapdale)
Paterson, Ian Manson (Eccles with Greenlaw)
Paterson, John Wallace (St Andrews: Martyrs')
Paul, Alison (Rhu and Shandon)
Rae, David Lionel (Kolhapur)
Reid, Martin Robertson Betsworth Coutts (Falkirk: West)
Robertson, Daniel McCallum (Auchinleck)
Smith, John Rankine (Glasgow: Barmulloch)
Squires, James Finlay Robertson (Principal Lecturer: Aberdeen College of Education)
Stewart, Walter Thomas Andrew (Barry)
Walker, Robert Bernard William (Lesmahagow: Abbeygreen)
Wardlaw, Elliot Gray Stirrat (Bathgate: St David's)

SECTION 7

Scottish Charity Numbers for Individual Congregations

1. Presbytery of Edinburgh

Balerno	SC018012
Currie	SC001554
Dalmeny	SC010971
Edinburgh: Albany Deaf Church	SC018321
Edinburgh: Barclay	SC014757
Edinburgh: Blackhall St Columba	SC008756
Edinburgh: Bristo Memorial, Craigmillar	SC011625
Edinburgh: Broughton St Mary's	SC012642
Edinburgh: Canongate	SC015251
Edinburgh: Carrick Knowe	SC004783
Edinburgh: Colinton	SC010313
Edinburgh: Colinton Mains	SC015982
Edinburgh: Corstorphine Craigsbank	SC014719
Edinburgh: Corstorphine Old	SC016009
Edinburgh: Corstorphine St Anne's	SC006300
Edinburgh: Corstorphine St Ninian's	SC016557
Edinburgh: Craigentinny St Christopher's	SC003466
Edinburgh: Craiglockhart	SC010545
Edinburgh: Craigmillar Park	SC017061
Edinburgh: Cramond	SC003430
Edinburgh: Davidson's Mains	SC009470
Edinburgh: Dean	SC001692
Edinburgh: Drylaw	SC005744
Edinburgh: Duddingston	SC016610
Edinburgh: Fairmilehead	SC015967
Edinburgh: Gilmerton (New Charge Dev)	SC011155
Edinburgh: Gorgie	SC009146
Edinburgh: Granton	SC011985
Edinburgh: Greenbank	SC011325
Edinburgh: Greenside	SC009749
Edinburgh: Greyfriars Tolbooth and Highland Kirk	SC003761
Edinburgh: High (St Giles')	SC003565
Edinburgh: Holy Trinity	SC012562
Edinburgh: Holyrood Abbey	SC000052
Edinburgh: Inverleith	SC015442
Edinburgh: Juniper Green	SC005197
Edinburgh: Kaimes Lockhart Memorial	SC004950
Edinburgh: Kirk o' Field	SC014430
Edinburgh: Leith North	SC004932
Edinburgh: Leith South	SC004695
Edinburgh: Leith St Andrew's	SC012680
Edinburgh: Leith St Serf's	SC008572
Edinburgh: Leith St Thomas' Junction Road	SC010072
Edinburgh: Leith Wardie	SC008710
Edinburgh: Liberton	SC011602
Edinburgh: Liberton Northfield	SC008891
Edinburgh: London Road	SC000896
Edinburgh: Marchmont St Giles'	SC009338
Edinburgh: Mayfield Salisbury	SC000785
Edinburgh: Morningside	SC034396
Edinburgh: Morningside United	SC015552
Edinburgh: Muirhouse St Andrew's	SC000871
Edinburgh: Murrayfield	SC005198
Edinburgh: New Restalrig	SC000963
Edinburgh: Newhaven	SC019117
Edinburgh: Old Kirk	SC006457
Edinburgh: Palmerston Place	SC004291

Edinburgh: Pilrig St Paul's	SC007277
Edinburgh: Polwarth	SC004183
Edinburgh: Portobello Old	SC002328
Edinburgh: Portobello St James'	SC007372
Edinburgh: Portobello St Philip's Joppa	SC011728
Edinburgh: Priestfield	SC014499
Edinburgh: Reid Memorial	SC014027
Edinburgh: Richmond Craigmillar	SC009035
Edinburgh: Slateford Longstone	SC030896
Edinburgh: St Andrew's and St George's	SC003470
Edinburgh: St Andrew's Clermiston	SC002748
Edinburgh: St Catherine's Argyle	SC009379
Edinburgh: St Colm's	SC013227
Edinburgh: St Cuthbert's	SC010592
Edinburgh: St David's Broomhouse	SC004746
Edinburgh: St George's West	SC008990
Edinburgh: St John's Oxgangs	SC030819
Edinburgh: St Margaret's	SC004779
Edinburgh: St Martin's	SC013918
Edinburgh: St Michael's	SC009038
Edinburgh: St Nicholas' Sighthill	SC007068
Edinburgh: St Stephen's Comely Bank	SC004487
Edinburgh: Stenhouse St Aidan's	SC010004
Edinburgh: Stockbridge	SC002499
Edinburgh: Tron Moredun	SC009274
Edinburgh: Viewforth	SC015373
Kirkliston	SC013924
Queensferry	SC002329
Ratho	SC001169

2. Presbytery of West Lothian

Abercorn	SC013100
Armadale	SC000791
Avonbridge	SC007454
Bathgate: Boghall	SC001881
Bathgate: High	SC007418
Bathgate: St David's	SC015799
Bathgate: St John's	SC016755
Blackburn and Seafield	SC024154
Blackridge	SC006811
Breich Valley	SC000800
Broxburn	SC017180
Fauldhouse: St Andrew's	SC016313
Harthill: St Andrew's	SC007601
Kirk of Calder	SC013461
Kirknewton and East Calder	SC006973
Linlithgow: St Michael's	SC016185
Linlithgow: St Ninian's Craigmailen	SC011348
Livingston Ecumenical	SC012054
Livingston: Old	SC011826
Pardovan, Kingscavil and Winchburgh	SC026230
Polbeth Harwood	SC017373
Strathbrock	SC006336
Torphichen	SC021516
Uphall: South	SC024255
West Kirk of Calder	SC004703
Whitburn: Brucefield	SC003362
Whitburn: South	SC001053

3. Presbytery of Lothian

Aberlady	SC004580
Athelstaneford	SC009401

Belhaven	SC007231
Bilston	SC032180
Bolton and Saltoun	SC003230
Bonnyrigg	SC003482
Borthwick	SC015775
Cockenzie and Port Seton: Chalmers	
Memorial	SC004630
Cockenzie and Port Seton: Old	SC007052
Cockpen and Carrington	SC013139
Cranstoun, Crichton and Ford	SC006926
Dalkeith: St John's and King's Park	SC008958
Dalkeith: St Nicholas Buccleuch	SC014158
Dirleton	SC004533
Dunbar	SC000455
Dunglass	SC014299
Fala and Soutra	SC007860
Garvald and Morham	SC014972
Gladsmuir	SC005996
Glencorse	SC030433
Gorebridge	SC004673
Gullane	SC005237
Haddington: St Mary's	SC010614
Haddington: West	SC022183
Howgate	SC014364
Humbie	SC016765
Lasswade	SC015878
Loanhead	SC014420
Longniddry	SC016556
Musselburgh: Northesk	SC004722
Musselburgh: St Andrew's High	SC000129
Musselburgh: St Clement's and	
St Ninian's	SC001726
Musselburgh: St Michael's Inveresk	SC013559
Newbattle	SC035087
Newton	SC030879
North Berwick: Abbey	SC004761
North Berwick: St Andrew Blackadder	SC006421
Ormiston	SC014810
Pencaitland	SC004871
Penicuik: North	SC010902
Penicuik: South	SC011871
Penicuik: St Mungo's	SC005838
Prestonpans: Prestongrange	SC031191
Rosewell	SC004927
Roslin	SC005457
Spott	SC008667
Tranent	SC017423
Traprain	SC012277
Whitekirk and Tyninghame	SC000494
Yester	SC015414

4. Presbytery of Melrose and Peebles

Ashkirk	SC010768
Bowden	SC008083
Bowden and Melrose	SC006480
Broughton, Glenholm and Kilbucho	SC030062
Caddonfoot	SC016990
Carlops	SC004340
Channelkirk	SC003176
Channelkirk and Lauder	SC009892
Earlston	SC003895
Eddleston	SC010081

Ettrick and Yarrow	SC034662
Galashiels: Old and St Paul's	SC010389
Galashiels: St Aidan's	SC016768
Galashiels: St John's	SC000281
Galashiels: St Ninian's	SC001386
Galashiels: Trinity	SC001386
Innerleithen, Traquair and Walkerburn	SC001100
Kirkurd and Newlands	SC018087
Lauder: Old	SC009892
Lyne and Manor	SC021456
Maxton and Mertoun	SC013481
Melrose	SC006480
Newtown	SC000575
Peebles: Old	SC013316
Peebles: St Andrew's Leckie	SC009159
Selkirk	SC014883
Skirling	SC004728
St Boswells	SC010210
Stobo and Drumelzier	SC001866
Stow: St Mary of Wedale and Heriot	SC000228
Tweedsmuir	SC013564
West Linton: St Andrew's	SC003938

5. Presbytery of Duns

Ayton and Burnmouth	SC001208
Berwick-upon-Tweed: St Andrew's	
Wallace Green and Lowick	SC000867
Bonkyl and Preston	SC000246
Chirnside	SC006722
Coldingham and St Abb's	SC009185
Coldstream	SC001456
Duns	SC005161
Eccles	SC000031
Edrom: Allanton	SC007567
Eyemouth	SC006499
Fogo and Swinton	SC002789
Foulden and Mordington	SC024535
Gordon: St Michael's	SC022349
Grantshouse and Houndwood and	
Reston	SC016400
Greenlaw	SC013136
Hutton and Fishwick and Paxton	SC002216
Kirk of Lammermuir and Langton and	
Polwarth	SC010680
Kirk of Lammermuir	SC024026
Ladykirk	SC009995
Langton and Polwarth	SC010680
Legerwood	SC004582
Leitholm	SC005115
Westruther	SC004903
Whitsome	SC001611

6. Presbytery of Jedburgh

Ale and Teviot United	SC016457
Cavers and Kirkton	SC004550
Hawick: Burnfoot	SC004517
Hawick: St Mary's and Old	SC005574
Hawick: Teviot and Roberton	SC005191
Hawick: Trinity	SC013892
Hawick: Wilton	SC017381
Hobkirk and Southdean	SC012830
Jedburgh: Old and Edgerston	SC004530

Jedburgh: Old and Trinity	SC004530
Jedburgh: Trinity	SC002728
Kelso Country Churches	SC000958
Kelso: North and Ednam	SC014039
Kelso: Old and Sprouston	SC015229
Linton, Morebattle, Hownam and Yetholm	SC003023
Oxnam	SC010593
Ruberslaw	SC034629
Teviothead	SC006917

7. Presbytery of Annandale and Eskdale

Annan: Old	SC010555
Annan: St Andrews'	SC010891
Applegarth, Sibbaldbie and Johnstone	SC013947
Brydekirk	SC012516
Canonbie United	SC000717
Dalton	SC006344
Dornock	SC004542
Eskdalemuir	SC001974
Gretna: Old, Gretna: St Andrew's and Half Morton and Kirkpatrick Fleming	SC016747
Hightae	SC022170
Hoddam	SC013467
Hutton and Corrie	SC015197
Kirkpatrick Juxta	SC005701
Kirtle-Eaglesfield	SC012479
Langholm, Ewes and Westerkirk	SC011946
Liddesdale	SC006519
Lochmaben	SC004644
Lockerbie: Dryfesdale	SC007116
Middlebie	SC000722
Moffat: St Andrew's	SC012236
St Mungo	SC001060
The Border Kirk	SC0eng00
Tundergarth	SC013190
Wamphray	SC007536
Waterbeck	SC013922

8. Presbytery of Dumfries and Kirkcudbright

Auchencairn and Rerrick	SC016850
Balmaclellan and Kells	SC016053
Balmaghie	SC000498
Borgue	SC004450
Buittle and Kelton	SC003844
Caerlaverock	SC008648
Carsphairn	SC015242
Castle Douglas	SC011037
Closeburn	SC005624
Colvend, Southwick and Kirkbean	SC009384
Corsock and Kirkpatrick Durham	SC007152
Crossmichael and Parton	SC014901
Cummertrees	SC013341
Dalbeattie	SC002443
Dalry	SC013121
Dumfries: Lincluden and Holywood	SC009615
Dumfries: Lochside	SC019944
Dumfries: Maxwelltown West	SC015925
Dumfries: St George's	SC006404
Dumfries: St Mary's-Greyfriars	SC009432
Dumfries: St Michael's and South	SC016201

Dumfries: Troqueer	SC000973
Dunscore	SC016060
Durisdeer	SC014783
Gatehouse of Fleet	SC000961
Glencairn and Moniaive	SC014663
Irongray, Lochrutton and Terregles	SC033058
Kirkconnel	SC014150
Kirkcudbright	SC005883
Kirkgunzeon	SC002286
Kirkmahoe	SC010508
Kirkmichael, Tinwald and Torthorwald	SC030785
Lochend	SC007990
Lochend and New Abbey	SC014590
Mouswald	SC001144
New Abbey	SC014590
Penpont, Keir and Tynron	SC015087
Ruthwell	SC015399
Sanquhar: St Bride's	SC000845
Tarff and Twynholm	SC004475
Thornhill	SC012722
Urr	SC014465

9. Presbytery of Wigtown and Stranraer

Ervie Kirkcolm	SC003122
Glasserton and Isle of Whithorn	SC001705
Inch	SC007375
Kirkcowan	SC007136
Kirkinner	SC001946
Kirkmabreck	SC010150
Kirkmaiden	SC007708
Leswalt	SC009412
Mochrum	SC003300
Monigaff	SC006014
New Luce	SC006316
Old Luce	SC005302
Penninghame	SC031847
Portpatrick	SC015452
Sorbie	SC010621
Stoneykirk	SC007346
Stranraer: High Kirk	SC017312
Stranraer: St Ninian's	SC002247
Stranraer: Town Kirk	SC001693
Whithorn: St Ninian's Priory	SC016881
Wigtown	SC014552

10. Presbytery of Ayr

Alloway	SC012456
Annbank	SC013225
Arnsheen Barrhill	SC006710
Auchinleck	SC006707
Ayr: Auld Kirk of Ayr	SC016648
Ayr: Castlehill	SC001792
Ayr: Newton on Ayr	SC001994
Ayr: St Andrew's	SC001757
Ayr: St Columba	SC014338
Ayr: St James'	SC009336
Ayr: St Leonard's	SC016860
Ayr: St Quivox	SC004906
Ayr: Wallacetown	SC018489
Ballantrae	SC008536
Barr	SC015366
Catrine	SC013689

Colmonell	SC014381	Kilmaurs: St Maur's Glencairn	SC009036
Coylton	SC005283	Newmilns: Loudoun	SC013880
Craigie	SC002633	Stewarton: John Knox	SC015890
Crosshill	SC017520	Stewarton: St Columba's	SC013595
Dailly	SC012591		
Dalmellington	SC031474	**12. Presbytery of Ardrossan**	
Dalrymple	SC013503	Ardrossan: Barony St John's	SC002350
Drongan: The Schaw Kirk	SC030714	Ardrossan: Park	SC004736
Dundonald	SC008482	Beith: High	SC004660
Fisherton	SC008226	Beith: Trinity	SC005680
Girvan: North (Old and St Andrew's)	SC007347	Brodick	SC012017
Girvan: South	SC010381	Corrie	SC005030
Kirkmichael	SC031952	Cumbrae	SC004919
Kirkoswald	SC000213	Dalry: St Margaret's	SC013170
Lugar	SC014055	Dalry: Trinity	SC006882
Mauchline	SC007714	Fairlie	SC017304
Maybole	SC003164	Fergushill	SC012902
Monkton and Prestwick: North	SC004271	Kilbirnie: Auld Kirk	SC016024
Muirkirk	SC010606	Kilbirnie: St Columba's	SC013750
New Cumnock	SC014794	Kilmory	SC023602
Ochiltree	SC000130	Kilwinning: Abbey	SC001856
Old Cumnock: Old	SC006025	Kilwinning: Erskine	SC009891
Old Cumnock: Trinity	SC034504	Kilwinning: Mansefield Trinity	SC016499
Patna: Waterside	SC008562	Kilwinning: Old	SC001856
Prestwick: Kingcase	SC001940	Lamlash	SC015072
Prestwick: South	SC007403	Largs: Clark Memorial	SC002782
Prestwick: St Nicholas'	SC011750	Largs: St Columba's	SC002294
Sorn	SC015899	Largs: St John's	SC009048
Stair	SC035601	Lochranza and Pirnmill	SC009377
Straiton: St Cuthbert's	SC013366	Saltcoats: New Trinity	SC023003
Symington	SC002144	Saltcoats: North	SC003299
Tarbolton	SC014767	Saltcoats: St Cuthbert's	SC002905
Troon: Old	SC007246	Shiskine	SC005323
Troon: Portland	SC003477	Stevenston: Ardeer	SC015397
Troon: St Meddan's	SC015019	Stevenston: High	SC009848
		Stevenston: Livingstone	SC000452
11. Presbytery of Irvine and Kilmarnock		West Kilbride: Overton	SC004565
Ayrshire Mission to the Deaf		West Kilbride: St Andrew's	SC013464
Crosshouse	SC011414	Whiting Bay and Kildonan	SC014005
Darvel	SC012014		
Dreghorn and Springside	SC008684	**13. Presbytery of Lanark**	
Dunlop	SC000447	Biggar	SC000333
Fenwick	SC010062	Black Mount	SC000603
Galston	SC010370	Cairngryffe	SC017001
Hurlford	SC001084	Carluke: Kirkton	SC026539
Irvine: Fullarton	SC008725	Carluke: St Andrew's	SC013968
Irvine: Girdle Toll	SC005491	Carluke: St John's	SC004066
Irvine: Mure	SC002299	Carnwath	SC016360
Irvine: Old	SC008345	Carstairs	SC002994
Irvine: Relief Bourtreehill	SC002469	Carstairs and Carstairs Junction,	
Irvine: St Andrew's	SC010167	The United Church of	SC028124
Kilmarnock: Grange	SC006920	Carstairs Junction	SC028124
Kilmarnock: Henderson	SC008154	Coalburn	SC016493
Kilmarnock: Howard St Andrew's	SC001059	Crossford	SC014659
Kilmarnock: Laigh West High	SC031334	Culter	SC018252
Kilmarnock: Old High Kirk	SC008405	Forth: St Paul's	SC003080
Kilmarnock: Riccarton	SC006040	Glencaple	SC017506
Kilmarnock: Shortlees	SC029057	Kirkfieldbank	SC011211
Kilmarnock: St John's Onthank	SC001580	Kirkmuirhill	SC014451
Kilmarnock: St Kentigern's	SC001324	Lanark: Greyfriars	SC016504
Kilmarnock: St Marnock's	SC006345	Lanark: St Nicholas'	SC011368
Kilmarnock: St Ninian's Bellfield	SC012430	Law	SC013217

Lesmahagow: Abbeygreen	SC006516	Port Glasgow: St Martin's	SC002410
Lesmahagow: Old	SC017014	Renfrew: North	SC006605
Libberton and Quothquan	SC016304	Renfrew: Old	SC004411
Lowther	SC034654	Renfrew: Trinity	SC003785
Symington	SC009095	Skelmorlie and Wemyss Bay	SC003309
The Douglas Valley Church	SC001718		

14. Presbytery of Greenock and Paisley

16. Presbytery of Glasgow

		Banton	SC017638
Barrhead: Arthurlie	SC015730	Bishopbriggs: Kenmure	SC012329
Barrhead: Bourock	SC016467	Bishopbriggs: Springfield	SC005642
Barrhead: South and Levern	SC007776	Broom	SC003290
Bishopton	SC006109	Burnside Blairbeth	SC006633
Bridge of Weir: Freeland	SC002293	Busby	SC016612
Bridge of Weir: St Machar's Ranfurly	SC003766	Cadder	SC015193
Caldwell	SC008214	Cambuslang: Flemington Hallside	SC006638
Elderslie Kirk	SC015701	Cambuslang: Old	SC000061
Erskine	SC017177	Cambuslang: St Andrew's	SC023596
Gourock: Old Gourock and Ashton	SC007324	Cambuslang: Trinity St Paul's	SC011456
Gourock: St John's	SC006412	Campsie	SC000835
Greenock: Ardgowan	SC010818	Chryston	SC006752
Greenock: East End	SC037023	Eaglesham	SC006377
Greenock: Finnart St Paul's	SC014076	Fernhill and Cathkin	SC001077
Greenock: Mount Kirk	SC008357	Gartcosh	SC007541
Greenock: Old West Kirk	SC004855	Giffnock: Orchardhill	SC009774
Greenock: St George's North	SC015301	Giffnock: South	SC007807
Greenock: St Luke's	SC005106	Giffnock: The Park	SC002965
Greenock: St Margaret's	SC016711	Glasgow: Anderston Kelvingrove	SC014631
Greenock: St Ninian's	SC008059	Glasgow: Baillieston Mure Memorial	SC002220
Greenock: Wellpark Mid Kirk	SC001043	Glasgow: Baillieston St Andrew's	SC005625
Greenock: Westburn	SC005106	Glasgow: Balshagray Victoria Park	SC000885
Houston and Killellan	SC012822	Glasgow: Barlanark Greyfriars	SC025730
Howwood	SC003487	Glasgow: Battlefield East	SC008946
Inchinnan	SC011778	Glasgow: Blawarthill	SC006410
Inverkip	SC001079	Glasgow: Bridgeton St Francis in the	
Johnstone: High	SC009588	East	SC012535
Johnstone: St Andrew's Trinity	SC011696	Glasgow: Broomhill	SC007820
Johnstone: St Paul's	SC011747	Glasgow: Calton Parkhead	SC006958
Kilbarchan: East	SC012123	Glasgow: Cardonald	SC010265
Kilbarchan: West	SC017140	Glasgow: Carmunnock	SC011224
Kilmacolm: Old	SC009291	Glasgow: Carmyle	SC000532
Kilmacolm: St Columba	SC007992	Glasgow: Carntyne Old	SC009154
Langbank	SC015085	Glasgow: Carnwadric	SC030150
Linwood	SC020972	Glasgow: Castlemilk East	SC015309
Lochwinnoch	SC014518	Glasgow: Castlemilk West	SC009813
Neilston	SC035155	Glasgow: Cathcart Old	SC002727
Paisley: Abbey	SC007633	Glasgow: Cathcart Trinity	SC033802
Paisley: Castlehead	SC003906	Glasgow: Cathedral (High or	
Paisley: Glenburn	SC006718	St Mungo's)	SC013966
Paisley: Laigh Kirk	SC006437	Glasgow: Colston Milton	SC012939
Paisley: Lylesland	SC012648	Glasgow: Colston Wellpark	SC005709
Paisley: Martyrs'	SC011798	Glasgow: Cranhill	SC009874
Paisley: Oakshaw Trinity	SC005362	Glasgow: Croftfoot	SC009761
Paisley: Sandyford (Thread Street)	SC003497	Glasgow: Dennistoun Blackfriars	SC001093
Paisley: Sherwood Greenlaw	SC007484	Glasgow: Dennistoun Central	SC008824
Paisley: St Columba Foxbar	SC005770	Glasgow: Dennistoun New	SC008824
Paisley: St James'	SC000949	Glasgow: Drumchapel Drumry St Mary's	SC026241
Paisley: St Luke's	SC000558	Glasgow: Drumchapel St Andrew's	SC022128
Paisley: St Mark's Oldhall	SC011210	Glasgow: Drumchapel St Mark's	SC008954
Paisley: St Ninian's Ferguslie	SC004753	Glasgow: Eastbank	SC004642
Paisley: Wallneuk North	SC012650	Glasgow: Easterhouse St George's and	
Port Glasgow: Hamilton Bardrainney	SC005421	St Peter's	SC003021
Port Glasgow: St Andrew's	SC009018	Glasgow: Eastwood	SC000277

Glasgow: Gairbraid	SC030168	Glasgow: St John's Renfield	SC012920
Glasgow: Gardner Street	SC009218	Glasgow: St Luke's and St Andrew's	SC032738
Glasgow: Garthamlock and Craigend		Glasgow: St Margaret's Tollcross Park	SC005764
East	SC016862	Glasgow: St Nicholas' Cardonald	SC011527
Glasgow: Gorbals	SC002214	Glasgow: St Paul's	SC016306
Glasgow: Govan Old	SC013596	Glasgow: St Rollox	SC015459
Glasgow: Govanhill Trinity	SC012752	Glasgow: St Thomas' Gallowgate	SC006549
Glasgow: High Carntyne	SC006729	Glasgow: Temple Anniesland	SC015579
Glasgow: Hillington Park	SC002614	Glasgow: Toryglen	SC009399
Glasgow: Househillwood		Glasgow: Trinity Possil and Henry	
St Christopher's	SC007798	Drummond	SC009578
Glasgow: Hyndland	SC002398	Glasgow: Tron St Mary's	SC017015
Glasgow: Ibrox	SC009841	Glasgow: Victoria Tollcross	SC004821
Glasgow: John Ross Memorial (for		Glasgow: Wallacewell	SC008840
Deaf People)	SC027651	Glasgow: Wellington	SC000289
Glasgow: Jordanhill	SC015683	Glasgow: Whiteinch (New Charge Dev)	SC030362
Glasgow: Kelvin Stevenson Memorial	SC014414	Glasgow: Yoker	SC017408
Glasgow: Kelvinside Hillhead	SC006629	Glenboig	SC002834
Glasgow: Kenmuir Mount Vernon	SC008980	Greenbank	SC011453
Glasgow: King's Park	SC017040	Kilsyth: Anderson	SC009866
Glasgow: Kinning Park	SC014895	Kilsyth: Burns and Old	SC009912
Glasgow: Knightswood St Margaret's	SC007757	Kirkintilloch: Hillhead	SC002424
Glasgow: Langside	SC007055	Kirkintilloch: St Columba's	SC008735
Glasgow: Lansdowne	SC015778	Kirkintilloch: St David's Memorial Park	SC007427
Glasgow: Linthouse St Kenneth's	SC005923	Kirkintilloch: St Mary's	SC007260
Glasgow: Lochwood	SC002161	Lenzie: Old	SC008935
Glasgow: Martyrs', The	SC009428	Lenzie: Union	SC015287
Glasgow: Maryhill	SC002102	Maxwell Mearns Castle	SC017317
Glasgow: Merrylea	SC004016	Mearns	SC007125
Glasgow: Mosspark	SC013281	Milton of Campsie	SC014735
Glasgow: Mount Florida	SC010138	Netherlee	SC015303
Glasgow: New Govan	SC004153	Newton Mearns	SC004219
Glasgow: Newlands South	SC000042	Rutherglen: Old	SC006856
Glasgow: North Kelvinside	SC003264	Rutherglen: Stonelaw	SC013558
Glasgow: Partick South	SC008315	Rutherglen: Wardlawhill	SC001080
Glasgow: Partick Trinity	SC007632	Rutherglen: West	SC007585
Glasgow: Penilee St Andrew's	SC022874	Rutherglen: West and Wardlawhill	SC007585
Glasgow: Pollokshaws	SC006683	Stamperland	SC003155
Glasgow: Pollokshields	SC013690	Stepps	SC014212
Glasgow: Possilpark	SC003241	Thornliebank	SC008426
Glasgow: Priesthill and Nitshill	SC015858	Torrance	SC016058
Glasgow: Queen's Park	SC001575	Twechar	SC011672
Glasgow: Renfield St Stephen's	SC011423	Williamwood	SC009939
Glasgow: Robroyston	SC032401		
Glasgow: Ruchazie	SC003149	**17. Presbytery of Hamilton**	
Glasgow: Ruchill	SC014538	Airdrie: Broomknoll	SC016464
Glasgow: Sandyford Henderson		Airdrie: Clarkston	SC011239
Memorial	SC002155	Airdrie: Flowerhill	SC014555
Glasgow: Sandyhills	SC009460	Airdrie: High	SC024357
Glasgow: Scotstoun	SC030418	Airdrie: Jackson	SC004083
Glasgow: Shawlands	SC012969	Airdrie: New Monkland	SC011674
Glasgow: Sherbrooke St Gilbert's	SC015155	Airdrie: St Columba's	SC002900
Glasgow: Shettleston Old	SC001070	Airdrie: The New Wellwynd	SC012944
Glasgow: South Carntyne	SC010899	Bargeddie	SC004209
Glasgow: South Shawlands	SC005196	Bellshill: Macdonald Memorial	SC012556
Glasgow: Springburn	SC004397	Bellshill: Orbiston	SC006007
Glasgow: St Andrew's East	SC009600	Bellshill: West	SC008340
Glasgow: St Columba	SC006342	Blantyre: Livingstone Memorial	SC004084
Glasgow: St David's Knightswood	SC017297	Blantyre: Old	SC018492
Glasgow: St Enoch's Hogganfield	SC004918	Blantyre: St Andrew's	SC005955
Glasgow: St George's Tron	SC004931	Bothwell	SC009819
Glasgow: St James' (Pollok)	SC013313	Calderbank	SC015831

Caldercruix and Longriggend	SC030492
Carfin	SC036085
Chapelhall	SC008486
Chapelton	SC011817
Cleland	SC017084
Coatbridge: Blairhill Dundyvan	SC009704
Coatbridge: Calder	SC006854
Coatbridge: Clifton	SC003105
Coatbridge: Middle	SC016362
Coatbridge: Old Monkland	SC010236
Coatbridge: St Andrew's	SC013521
Coatbridge: Townhead	SC008809
Dalserf	SC016156
East Kilbride: Claremont	SC007396
East Kilbride: Greenhills	SC030300
East Kilbride: Moncreiff	SC016751
East Kilbride: Mossneuk	SC012692
East Kilbride: Old	SC000609
East Kilbride: South	SC008332
East Kilbride: Stewartfield	SC034242
East Kilbride: West	SC000250
East Kilbride: Westwood	SC001857
Glasford	SC014716
Greengairs	SC018154
Hamilton: Burnbank	SC015042
Hamilton: Cadzow	SC006611
Hamilton: Gilmour and Whitehill	SC011571
Hamilton: Hillhouse	SC005376
Hamilton: North	SC014508
Hamilton: Old	SC010855
Hamilton: South	SC022166
Hamilton: St Andrew's	SC007145
Hamilton: St John's	SC008779
Hamilton: Trinity	SC007051
Hamilton: West	SC008451
Holytown	SC012888
Kirk o' Shotts	SC013269
Larkhall: Chalmers	SC013309
Larkhall: St Machan's	SC002870
Larkhall: Trinity	SC008611
Motherwell: Crosshill	SC008810
Motherwell: Dalziel St Andrew's	SC015503
Motherwell: Manse Road	SC008601
Motherwell: North	SC016821
Motherwell: South	SC002209
Motherwell: South Dalziel	SC016967
Motherwell: St Margaret's	SC010924
Motherwell: St Mary's	SC012233
New Stevenston: Wrangholm Kirk	SC004688
Newarthill	SC005427
Newmains: Bonkle	SC006540
Newmains: Coltness Memorial	SC001381
Overtown	SC007360
Quarter	SC009689
Shotts: Calderhead Erskine	SC006538
Stonehouse: St Ninian's	SC003239
Strathaven: Avendale Old and Drumclog	SC001956
Strathaven: East	SC015591
Strathaven: Rankin	SC001020
Strathaven: West	SC016435
Uddingston: Burnhead	SC010039
Uddingston: Old	SC016893

Uddingston: Park	SC000928
Uddingston: Viewpark	SC009991
Wishaw: Cambusnethan North	SC013037
Wishaw: Cambusnethan Old and Morningside	SC011532
Wishaw: Craigneuk and Belhaven	SC013841
Wishaw: Old	SC011253
Wishaw: South Wishaw	SC010775
Wishaw: St Mark's	SC012529

18. Presbytery of Dumbarton

Alexandria	SC001268
Arrochar	SC008929
Baldernock	SC006355
Bearsden: Baljaffray	SC037739
Bearsden: Cross	SC009082
Bearsden: Killermont	SC009748
Bearsden: New Kilpatrick	SC012997
Bearsden: North	SC005429
Bearsden: South	SC009082
Bearsden: Westerton Fairlie Memorial	SC004489
Bonhill	SC000886
Cardross	SC003494
Clydebank: Abbotsford	SC004596
Clydebank: Faifley	SC005108
Clydebank: Kilbowie St Andrew's	SC015005
Clydebank: Radnor Park	SC013242
Clydebank: St Cuthbert's	SC003077
Craigrownie	SC001725
Dalmuir: Barclay	SC013599
Dumbarton: Riverside	SC002937
Dumbarton: St Andrew's	SC006235
Dumbarton: West Kirk	SC010474
Duntocher	SC008854
Garelochhead	SC016699
Helensburgh: Park	SC007801
Helensburgh: St Columba	SC014837
Helensburgh: The West Kirk	SC012053
Jamestown	SC012346
Kilmaronock Gartocharn	SC002145
Luss	SC017192
Milngavie: Cairns	SC009913
Milngavie: St Luke's	SC003870
Milngavie: St Paul's	SC002737
Old Kilpatrick Bowling	SC011630
Renton: Trinity	SC014833
Rhu and Shandon	SC010086
Rosneath: St Modan's	SC001510

19. Presbytery of Argyll

Appin	SC015795
Ardchattan	SC000680
Ardrishaig	SC010713
Campbeltown: Highland	SC002493
Campbeltown: Lorne and Lowland	SC011686
Coll	SC035582
Colonsay and Oronsay	SC031271
Connel	SC006738
Craignish	SC003718
Cumlodden, Lochfyneside and Lochgair	SC016097
Dunoon: St John's	SC003216
Dunoon: The High Kirk	SC017524

Gigha and Cara	SC002567	Cumbernauld: St Mungo's	SC036366
Glassary, Kilmartin and Ford	SC002121	Denny: Dunipace	SC002943
Glenaray and Inveraray	SC016665	Denny: Old	SC016255
Glenorchy and Innishael	SC003179	Denny: Westpark	SC007072
Innellan	SC013247	Falkirk: Bainsford	SC004142
Iona	SC036399	Falkirk: Camelon	SC014816
Jura	SC002925	Falkirk: Erskine	SC007546
Kilarrow	SC009853	Falkirk: Grahamston United	SC016991
Kilberry	SC006941	Falkirk: Laurieston	SC007383
Kilbrandon and Kilchattan	SC017005	Falkirk: Old and St Modan's	SC000652
Kilcalmonell	SC006948	Falkirk: St Andrew's West	SC005066
Kilchoman	SC013203	Falkirk: St James'	SC007665
Kilchrenan and Dalavich	SC009417	Grangemouth: Abbotsgrange	SC000775
Kildalton and Oa	SC006032	Grangemouth: Dundas	SC002631
Kilfinan	SC003483	Grangemouth: Kerse	SC000775
Kilfinichen and Kilvickeon and the		Grangemouth: Kirk of the Holy Rood	SC001603
Ross of Mull	SC013473	Grangemouth: Zetland	SC013114
Killean and Kilchenzie	SC016020	Haggs	SC014536
Kilmeny	SC015317	Larbert: East	SC006456
Kilmodan and Colintraive	SC021449	Larbert: Old	SC000445
Kilmore and Oban	SC011171	Larbert: West	SC012251
Kilmun (St Munn's)	SC001694	Muiravonside	SC007571
Kilninver and Kilmelford	SC002458	Polmont: Old	SC003421
Kirn	SC001976	Redding and Westquarter	SC008787
Kyles	SC014928	Slamannan	SC013602
Lismore	SC030972	Stenhouse and Carron	SC002263
Lochgilphead	SC016311		
Lochgoilhead and Kilmorich	SC006458	**23. Presbytery of Stirling**	
Muckairn	SC013377	Aberfoyle	SC001308
Mull, Isle of, Kilninian and Kilmore	SC025506	Alloa: North	SC002898
North Knapdale	SC001002	Alloa: St Mungo's	SC007821
Portnahaven	SC004086	Alloa: West	SC007605
Rothesay: Trinity	SC006420	Alva	SC000006
Saddell and Carradale	SC002609	Balfron	SC005335
Salen and Ulva	SC026099	Balquhidder	SC012316
Sandbank	SC006657	Bannockburn: Allan	SC002953
Skipness	SC004280	Bannockburn: Ladywell	SC011345
South Knapdale	SC010782	Bridge of Allan	SC015171
Southend	SC005484	Buchanan	SC012927
Strachur and Strachlachlan	SC001767	Buchlyvie	SC000833
Strathfillan	SC004088	Callander	SC000396
Strone and Ardentinny	SC003410	Cambusbarron: The Bruce Memorial	SC001913
Tarbert	SC002622	Clackmannan	SC002324
The United Church of Bute	SC030563	Cowie	SC022328
Tiree	SC000878	Cowie and Plean	SC016296
Tobermory	SC002878	Dollar	SC009713
Torosay and Kinlochspelvie	SC003909	Drymen	SC004824
Toward	SC015531	Dunblane: Cathedral	SC004454
		Dunblane: St Blane's	SC005185
22. Presbytery of Falkirk		Fallin	SC028465
Airth	SC011038	Fintry	SC012537
Blackbraes and Shieldhill	SC002512	Gargunnock	SC012154
Bo'ness: Old	SC008191	Gartmore	SC009788
Bo'ness: St Andrew's	SC011448	Glendevon	SC003028
Bonnybridge: St Helen's	SC015225	Killearn	SC012140
Bothkennar and Carronshore	SC009754	Killin and Ardeonaig	SC010198
Brightons	SC001385	Kilmadock	SC012031
Carriden	SC007811	Kincardine-in-Menteith	SC000802
Cumbernauld: Abronhill	SC029326	Kippen	SC004286
Cumbernauld: Condorrat	SC011839	Lecropt	SC014031
Cumbernauld: Kildrum	SC004564	Logie	SC001298
Cumbernauld: Old	SC000877	Menstrie	SC004778

Muckhart	SC009418	Kirkcaldy: Linktown	SC012039
Norrieston	SC028719	Kirkcaldy: Pathhead	SC002858
Plean	SC016296	Kirkcaldy: St Andrew's	SC011722
Port of Menteith	SC001864	Kirkcaldy: St Bryce Kirk	SC031064
Sauchie and Coalsnaughton	SC018155	Kirkcaldy: St John's	SC005628
Stirling: Allan Park South	SC001414	Kirkcaldy: Templehall	SC012756
Stirling: Church of the Holy Rude	SC011473	Kirkcaldy: Torbain	SC015807
Stirling: North	SC011795	Kirkcaldy: Viewforth	SC004264
Stirling: St Columba's	SC013444	Leslie: Trinity	SC014025
Stirling: St Mark's	SC005432	Leven	SC031969
Stirling: St Ninian's Old	SC016320	Markinch	SC005820
Stirling: Viewfield	SC007533	Methil	SC009581
Strathblane	SC007261	Methilhill	SC007949
Tillicoultry	SC016570	Methilhill and Denbeath	SC007949
Tullibody: St Serf's	SC005918	Thornton	SC003417
		Wemyss	SC006847

24. Presbytery of Dunfermline

Aberdour: St Fillan's	SC005851	**26. Presbytery of St Andrews**	
Beath and Cowdenbeath: North	SC031695	Abdie and Dunbog	SC004848
Cairneyhill	SC012892	Anstruther	SC012986
Carnock and Oakley	SC010676	Auchtermuchty	SC005402
Cowdenbeath: Trinity	SC003799	Balmerino	SC002542
Culross and Torryburn	SC015149	Boarhills and Dunino	SC001108
Dalgety	SC020926	Cameron	SC005565
Dunfermline: Abbey	SC016883	Carnbee	SC016744
Dunfermline: Gillespie Memorial	SC011659	Cellardyke	SC000181
Dunfermline: North	SC013226	Ceres and Springfield	SC017442
Dunfermline: St Andrew's Erskine	SC007302	Ceres, Kemback and Springfield	SC017442
Dunfermline: St Leonard's	SC007799	Crail	SC001601
Dunfermline: St Margaret's	SC007080	Creich, Flisk and Kilmany	SC001907
Dunfermline: St Ninian's	SC007453	Cupar: Old and St Michael of Tarvit	SC013123
Dunfermline: St Paul's East (New		Cupar: St John's	SC031896
Charge Dev)	SC035690	Dairsie	SC015721
Dunfermline: Townhill and Kingseat	SC008085	Edenshead and Strathmiglo	SC015226
Inverkeithing	SC000968	Elie	SC003163
Inverkeithing: St John's	SC000968	Falkland	SC012247
Inverkeithing: St Peter's	SC016219	Freuchie	SC016622
Kelty	SC011004	Howe of Fife	SC005381
Limekilns	SC002435	Kemback	SC004755
Lochgelly and Benarty: St Serf's	SC032353	Kilconquhar and Colinsburgh	SC012750
North Queensferry	SC007414	Kilrenny	SC002653
Rosyth	SC013620	Kingsbarns	SC012192
Saline and Blairingone	SC013688	Largo and Newburn	SC003465
Tulliallan and Kincardine	SC002951	Largo: St David's	SC013705
		Largoward	SC009474
25. Presbytery of Kirkcaldy		Leuchars: St Athernase	SC015677
Auchterderran: St Fothad's	SC031143	Monimail	SC015182
Auchtertool	SC025310	Newburgh	SC004607
Buckhaven	SC009495	Newport-on-Tay	SC006758
Burntisland	SC016418	Pittenweem	SC015271
Denbeath	SC001703	St Andrews: Holy Trinity	SC017173
Dysart	SC008991	St Andrews: Hope Park	SC014934
Glenrothes: Christ's Kirk	SC007397	St Andrews: Martyrs'	SC014986
Glenrothes: St Columba's	SC016386	St Andrews: St Leonard's	SC013586
Glenrothes: St Margaret's	SC009845	St Monans	SC005556
Glenrothes: St Ninian's	SC002472	Strathkinness	SC014710
Innerleven: East	SC009342	Tayport	SC008659
Kennoway, Windygates and Balgonie:		Wormit	SC006447
St Kenneth's	SC016733		
Kinghorn	SC007848	**27. Presbytery of Dunkeld and Meigle**	
Kinglassie	SC012030	Aberfeldy	SC007899
Kirkcaldy: Abbotshall	SC002586	Alyth	SC000540

Amulree and Strathbraan	SC028023	Redgorton	SC012736
Ardler, Kettins and Meigle	SC000098	Redgorton and Stanley	SC010629
Bendochy	SC004358	Scone: New	SC007094
Blair Atholl and Struan	SC013516	Scone: Old	SC002844
Blairgowrie	SC033757	St Madoes and Kinfauns	SC014964
Braes of Rannoch	SC011351	St Martin's	SC002000
Caputh and Clunie	SC001957	Stanley	SC010629
Coupar Angus: Abbey	SC014438	The Stewartry of Strathearn	SC030799
Dull and Weem	SC001465	Trinity Gask and Kinkell	SC000004
Dunkeld	SC009867		
Fortingall and Glenlyon	SC003310	**29. Presbytery of Dundee**	
Foss and Rannoch	SC006570	Abernyte	SC007847
Grantully, Logierait and Strathtay	SC004275	Auchterhouse	SC016717
Kenmore and Lawers	SC006260	Dundee: Balgay	SC017449
Kinclaven	SC009251	Dundee: Barnhill St Margaret's	SC011017
Kirkmichael, Straloch and Glenshee	SC008021	Dundee: Broughty Ferry East	SC007031
Pitlochry	SC008361	Dundee: Broughty Ferry New Kirk	SC007031
Rattray	SC000323	Dundee: Broughty Ferry St Aidan's	SC016420
Tenandry	SC001984	Dundee: Broughty Ferry St James'	SC005210
		Dundee: Broughty Ferry St Luke's and	
28. Presbytery of Perth		Queen Street	SC000088
Abernethy and Dron and Arngask	SC000586	Dundee: Broughty Ferry St Stephen's	
Abernethy and Dron	SC000586	and West	SC003714
Almondbank Tibbermore	SC005203	Dundee: Camperdown	SC003677
Ardoch	SC000139	Dundee: Chalmers Ardler	SC021763
Arngask	SC007308	Dundee: Clepington and Fairmuir	SC012089
Auchterarder	SC001688	Dundee: Craigiebank	SC016701
Auchtergaven and Moneydie	SC010247	Dundee: Douglas and Mid Craigie	SC010030
Blackford	SC005594	Dundee: Douglas and Angus	SC010030
Cargill Burrelton	SC007283	Dundee: Downfield South	SC005707
Cleish	SC003168	Dundee: Dundee (St Mary's)	SC002198
Collace	SC009031	Dundee: Lochee	SC033313
Comrie	SC001878	Dundee: Lochee Old and St Luke's	SC006637
Crieff	SC010776	Dundee: Lochee West	SC033313
Dunbarney	SC009638	Dundee: Logie and St John's Cross	SC009115
Dunbarney and Forgandenny	SC009638	Dundee: Mains	SC013884
Dundurn	SC010311	Dundee: Mains of Fintry	SC020742
Errol	SC015895	Dundee: Meadowside St Paul's	SC013162
Forgandenny	SC004599	Dundee: Menzieshill	SC004496
Fossoway: St Serf's and Devonside	SC013157	Dundee: Mid Craigie	SC022116
Fowlis Wester	SC010819	Dundee: St Andrew's	SC011775
Fowlis Wester, Madderty and Monzie	SC002209	Dundee: St David's High Kirk	SC000723
Gask	SC009632	Dundee: Steeple	SC014314
Kilspindie and Rait	SC010838	Dundee: Stobswell	SC000384
Kinross	SC012555	Dundee: Strathmartine	SC018015
Madderty	SC002209	Dundee: Trinity	SC011021
Methven and Logiealmond	SC010807	Dundee: West	SC017136
Monzie	SC002807	Dundee: Whitfield	SC000316
Muthill	SC004984	Fowlis and Liff	SC002792
Orwell	SC015523	Inchture and Kinnaird	SC009839
Orwell and Portmoak	SC015523	Invergowrie	SC009454
Perth: Craigie	SC001330	Longforgan	SC012230
Perth: Kinnoull	SC007509	Lundie and Muirhead of Liff	SC001085
Perth: Letham St Mark's	SC002467	Monifieth: Panmure	SC013282
Perth: Moncreiffe	SC006021	Monifieth: South	SC015950
Perth: North	SC013014	Monifieth: St Rule's	SC008965
Perth: Riverside	SC011113	Monikie and Newbigging	SC014775
Perth: St John the Baptist's	SC017132	Murroes and Tealing	SC012137
Perth: St Leonard's-in-the-Fields and			
Trinity	SC002919	**30. Presbytery of Angus**	
Perth: St Matthew's	SC016829	Aberlemno	SC018944
Portmoak	SC008008	Airlie Ruthven and Kingoldrum	SC031461

Arbirlot	SC017413
Arbroath: Knox's	SC011361
Arbroath: Old and Abbey	SC013052
Arbroath: St Andrew's	SC005478
Arbroath: St Vigeans	SC003049
Arbroath: West Kirk	SC006482
Barry	SC002545
Brechin: Cathedral	SC010332
Brechin: Gardner Memorial	SC008630
Carmyllie	SC017424
Carnoustie	SC015146
Carnoustie: Panbride	SC004594
Colliston	SC001293
Dun and Hillside	SC000572
Dunnichen, Letham and Kirkden	SC003833
Eassie and Nevay	SC016937
Edzell Lethnot	SC013105
Edzell Lethnot Glenesk	SC013105
Farnell	SC007997
Fern Careston Menmuir	SC003236
Forfar: East and Old	SC004921
Forfar: Lowson Memorial	SC002417
Forfar: St Margaret's	SC001506
Friockheim Kinnell	SC005085
Glamis, Inverarity and Kinnettles	SC011205
Glenesk	SC014587
Glenisla, Kilry and Lintrathen	SC031548
Guthrie and Rescobie	SC017327
Inchbrayock	SC009017
Inverkeilor and Lunan	SC017785
Kirriemuir: St Andrew's	SC004395
Montrose: Melville South	SC009016
Montrose: Old and St Andrew's	SC009934
Newtyle	SC013352
Oathlaw Tannadice	SC006317
The Glens and Kirriemuir: Old	SC015123
The Isla Parishes	SC031461

31. Presbytery of Aberdeen

Aberdeen: Beechgrove	SC010643
Aberdeen: Bridge of Don Oldmachar	SC025324
Aberdeen: Cove	SC032413
Aberdeen: Craigiebuckler	SC017158
Aberdeen: Denburn	SC001962
Aberdeen: Ferryhill	SC010756
Aberdeen: Garthdee	SC022497
Aberdeen: Gilcomston South	SC013916
Aberdeen: High Hilton	SC003789
Aberdeen: Holburn Central	SC004461
Aberdeen: Holburn West	SC013318
Aberdeen: Mannofield	SC001680
Aberdeen: Mastrick	SC013459
Aberdeen: Middlefield	SC031459
Aberdeen: Midstocket	SC010643
Aberdeen: New Stockethill (New Charge Dev)	SC030587
Aberdeen: Northfield	SC034441
Aberdeen: Queen Street	SC014117
Aberdeen: Queen's Cross	SC002019
Aberdeen: Rosemount	SC008188
Aberdeen: Rubislaw	SC015841
Aberdeen: Ruthrieston South	SC003976

Aberdeen: Ruthrieston West	SC013020
Aberdeen: South Holburn	SC017516
Aberdeen: St Columba's Bridge of Don	SC027440
Aberdeen: St George's Tillydrone	SC024795
Aberdeen: St John's Church for Deaf People	SC021283
Aberdeen: St Machar's Cathedral	SC008157
Aberdeen: St Mark's	SC015451
Aberdeen: St Mary's	SC018173
Aberdeen: St Nicholas Kincorth, South of	SC016043
Aberdeen: St Nicholas Uniting, Kirk of	SC008689
Aberdeen: St Ninian's	SC013146
Aberdeen: St Stephen's	SC014120
Aberdeen: Summerhill	SC007076
Aberdeen: Torry St Fittick's	SC009020
Aberdeen: Woodside	SC001966
Bucksburn Stoneywood	SC017404
Cults	SC017517
Cults: East	SC014009
Cults: West	SC017517
Dyce	SC016950
Kingswells	SC006865
Newhills	SC011204
Peterculter	SC001452

32. Presbytery of Kincardine and Deeside

Aberluthnott	SC016449
Aboyne and Dinnet	SC014112
Arbuthnott	SC001312
Arbuthnott and Bervie	SC009239
Banchory-Devenick and Maryculter/ Cookney	SC013648
Banchory-Ternan: East	SC011251
Banchory-Ternan: West	SC003306
Bervie	SC009239
Birse and Feughside	SC018517
Braemar and Crathie	SC012075
Cromar	SC015856
Drumoak and Durris	SC033779
Glenmuick (Ballater)	SC005522
Kinneff	SC007436
Laurencekirk	SC014830
Mearns Coastal	SC011997
Mid Deeside	SC012967
Newtonhill	SC005679
Portlethen	SC007420
Stonehaven: Dunnottar	SC013165
Stonehaven: Fetteresso	SC011191
Stonehaven: South	SC016565
West Mearns	SC016193

33. Presbytery of Gordon

Barthol Chapel	SC010960
Belhelvie	SC016387
Blairdaff	SC003116
Blairdaff and Chapel of Garioch	SC004050
Chapel of Garioch	SC004050
Cluny	SC003429
Culsalmond and Rayne	SC010911
Cushnie and Tough	SC030817

Daviot	SC003254	Turriff: St Ninian's and Forglen	SC007470
Drumblade	SC010765	Whitehills	SC002085
Echt	SC003215		
Ellon	SC008819	**35. Presbytery of Moray**	
Fintray and Kinellar	SC013066	Aberlour	SC001336
Fintray Kinellar Keithhall	SC003115	Alves and Burghead	SC010330
Foveran	SC011701	Bellie	SC005310
Howe Trinity	SC007979	Birnie and Pluscarden	SC016720
Huntly Cairnie Glass	SC001405	Buckie: North	SC001235
Huntly Strathbogie	SC000534	Buckie: South and West	SC005608
Insch-Leslie-Premnay-Oyne	SC000935	Cullen and Deskford	SC011231
Inverurie: St Andrew's	SC008791	Dallas	SC015881
Inverurie: West	SC016907	Duffus, Spynie and Hopeman	SC004853
Keithhall	SC003115	Dyke	SC000585
Kemnay	SC014790	Edinkillie	SC009986
Kintore	SC001406	Elgin: High	SC005240
Meldrum and Bourtie	SC015960	Elgin: St Giles' and St Columba's South	SC015164
Methlick	SC016542	Enzie	SC015093
Midmar	SC009556	Findochty	SC010045
Monymusk	SC004525	Forres: St Laurence	SC000711
New Machar	SC024017	Forres: St Leonard's	SC005094
Noth	SC007582	Keith: North, Newmill, Boharm and	
Skene	SC009462	Rothiemay	SC033804
Tarves	SC017161	Keith: St Rufus, Botriphnie and Grange	SC031791
Udny and Pitmedden	SC006056	Kinloss and Findhorn	SC014557
Upper Donside	SC014679	Knockando, Elchies and Archiestown	SC014428
		Lossiemouth: St Gerardine's High	SC009793
34. Presbytery of Buchan		Lossiemouth: St James'	SC000880
Aberdour	SC007197	Mortlach and Cabrach	SC010193
Auchaber United	SC017101	Portknockie	SC014485
Auchterless	SC009168	Rafford	SC022567
Banff	SC015501	Rathven	SC015906
Crimond	SC006889	Rothes	SC016116
Cruden	SC006408	Speymouth	SC007113
Deer	SC012985	St Andrews-Lhanbryd and Urquhart	SC008850
Fordyce	SC000522		
Fraserburgh: Old	SC013119	**36. Presbytery of Abernethy**	
Fraserburgh: South	SC005714	Abernethy	SC003652
Fraserburgh: West	SC016334	Alvie and Insh	SC000043
Fyvie	SC001475	Boat of Garten and Kincardine	SC008346
Gardenstown	SC012282	Cromdale and Advie	SC002884
Inverallochy and Rathen: East	SC000375	Dulnain Bridge	SC014015
King Edward	SC015077	Duthil	SC001064
Longside	SC008873	Grantown-on-Spey	SC010001
Lonmay	SC008813	Kingussie	SC021546
Macduff	SC015786	Laggan	SC008016
Marnoch	SC001107	Newtonmore	SC005490
Maud and Savoch	SC009773	Rothiemurchus and Aviemore	SC003282
Monquhitter and New Byth	SC010291	Tomintoul, Glenlivet and Inveravon	SC001802
New Deer: St Kane's	SC007917		
New Pitsligo	SC014620	**37. Presbytery of Inverness**	
Ordiquhill and Cornhill	SC001971	Ardclach	SC012321
Peterhead: Old	SC011147	Ardersier	SC015446
Peterhead: St Andrew's	SC010841	Auldearn and Dalmore	SC026653
Peterhead: Trinity	SC009990	Cawdor	SC001695
Pitsligo	SC005498	Croy and Dalcross	SC013601
Rathen: West	SC015604	Culloden: The Barn	SC000662
Rothienorman	SC032016	Daviot and Dunlichity	SC003301
Sandhaven	SC024874	Dores and Boleskine	SC013579
St Fergus	SC000710	Inverness: Crown	SC018159
Strichen and Tyrie	SC007273	Inverness: Dalneigh and Bona	SC011773
Turriff: St Andrew's	SC015620	Inverness: East	SC016866

Inverness: Hilton	SC016775
Inverness: Inshes	SC005553
Inverness: Kinmylies	SC020888
Inverness: Ness Bank	SC010870
Inverness: Old High St Stephen's	SC035073
Inverness: St Columba High	SC008109
Inverness: Trinity	SC015432
Kilmorack and Erchless	SC008121
Kiltarlity	SC014918
Kirkhill	SC003866
Moy, Dalarossie and Tomatin	SC015653
Nairn: Old	SC000947
Nairn: St Ninian's	SC015361
Petty	SC004952
Urquhart and Glenmoriston	SC016627

38. Presbytery of Lochaber

Acharacle	SC002916
Ardgour	SC008222
Ardnamurchan	SC030394
Arisaig and the Small Isles	SC021584
Duror	SC018259
Fort Augustus	SC022635
Fort William: Duncansburgh	SC013279
Fort William: MacIntosh Memorial	SC003723
Glencoe: St Munda's	SC005211
Glengarry	SC023413
Kilmallie	SC005687
Kilmonivaig	SC014745
Kinlochleven	SC030288
Mallaig: St Columba and Knoydart	SC009485
Morvern	SC015532
Nether Lochaber	SC006700
Strontian	SC008982

39. Presbytery of Ross

Alness	SC015227
Avoch	SC003921
Contin	SC011897
Cromarty	SC006666
Dingwall: Castle Street	SC001167
Dingwall: St Clement's	SC001056
Fearn Abbey and Nigg	SC009309
Ferintosh	SC012675
Fodderty and Strathpeffer	SC003499
Fortrose and Rosemarkie	SC004472
Invergordon	SC010964
Killearnan	SC010319
Kilmuir and Logie Easter	SC013375
Kiltearn	SC009180
Knockbain	SC014467
Lochbroom and Ullapool	SC015631
Resolis and Urquhart	SC013643
Rosskeen	SC010093
Tain	SC012425
Tarbat	SC021420
Urray and Kilchrist	SC009902

40. Presbytery of Sutherland

Altnaharra and Farr	SC016038
Assynt and Stoer	SC010171
Clyne	SC004973

Creich	SC003840
Dornoch Cathedral	SC000315
Durness and Kinlochbervie	SC005079
Eddrachillis	SC007326
Golspie	SC004560
Kildonan and Loth Helmsdale	SC004056
Kincardine Croick and Edderton	SC016877
Lairg	SC020871
Melness and Tongue	SC014066
Rogart	SC010035
Rosehall	SC017558

41. Presbytery of Caithness

Berriedale and Dunbeath	SC034424
Bower	SC001363
Canisbay	SC032164
Dunnet	SC030261
Halkirk and Westerdale	SC008544
Keiss	SC010874
Latheron	SC011166
Lybster and Bruan	SC006296
Olrig	SC010296
Reay	SC005947
Strathy and Halladale	SC001815
The North Coast Parish	SC001815
The Parish of Latheron	SC034424
Thurso: St Peter's and St Andrew's	SC016691
Thurso: West	SC007248
Watten	SC003365
Wick: Bridge Street	SC013840
Wick: Old	SC011338
Wick: Pulteneytown and Thrumster	SC001291

42. Presbytery of Lochcarron – Skye

Applecross, Lochcarron and Torridon	Sc032334
Bracadale and Duirinish	Sc022592
Gairloch and Dundonnell	Sc015448
Glenelg and Kintail	Sc017510
Kilmuir and Stenscholl	Sc014072
Lochalsh	Sc016505
Portree	Sc000416
Snizort	Sc030117
Strath and Sleat	Sc001285

43. Presbytery of Uist

Barra	SC003980
Benbecula	SC002191
Berneray and Lochmaddy	SC016358
Carinish	SC016461
Kilmuir and Paible	SC030955
Manish-Scarista	SC001770
South Uist	SC031790
Tarbert	SC004787

44. Presbytery of Lewis

Barvas	SC006563
Carloway	SC032250
Cross Ness	SC000991
Kinloch	SC008004
Knock	SC014492
Lochs-Crossbost	SC024236
Lochs-in-Bernera	SC008746

Stornoway: High	SC010164	Stenness	SC008306
Stornoway: Martin's Memorial	SC000753	Stromness	SC003099
Stornoway: St Columba	SC006777	Stronsay: Moncur Memorial	SC006572
Uig	SC007879	Westray	SC025053

45. Presbytery of Orkney

46. Presbytery of Shetland

Birsay, Harray and Sandwick	SC035048	Burra Isle	SC030483
East Mainland	SC019770	Delting	SC029873
Eday	SC005404	Dunrossness and St Ninian's inc.	
Evie	SC005062	Fair Isle	SC015253
Firth	SC013330	Fetlar	
Flotta	SC016203	Lerwick and Bressay	SC017535
Hoy and Walls	SC023194	Nesting and Lunnasting	SC031996
Kirkwall: East	SC018002	Northmavine	SC002341
Kirkwall: St Magnus Cathedral	SC005322	Sandsting and Aithsting	SC012345
North Ronaldsay	SC030098	Sandwick, Cunningsburgh and Quarff	SC014545
Orphir	SC016221	Tingwall	SC002674
Papa Westray	SC013661	Unst	SC007954
Rendall	SC016806	Walls and Sandness	SC030748
Rousay	SC001078	Whalsay and Skerries	SC000293
Sanday	SC000271	Yell	SC020628
Shapinsay	SC006097		
South Ronaldsay and Burray	SC003298		

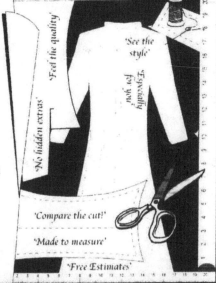

SECTION 8

Congregational
Statistics
2006

CHURCH OF SCOTLAND
Comparative Statistics: 1966–2006

	2006	1996	1986	1976	1966
Communicants	504,363	680,062	854,311	1,020,403	1,233,808
Elders	40,651	45,999	47,336	47,736	48,661

NOTES ON CONGREGATIONAL STATISTICS

Com Number of communicants at 31 December 2006.

Eld Number of elders at 31 December 2006.

G Membership of the Guild including Young Woman's Group and others as recorded on the 2006 annual return submitted to the Guild Office.

In 06 Ordinary General Income for 2006. Ordinary General Income consists of members' offerings, contributions from congregational organisations, regular fund-raising events, income from investments, deposits and so on. This figure does not include extraordinary or special income, or income from special collections and fund-raising for other charities.

M&M Final amount allocated to congregations after allowing for Presbytery-approved amendments up to 31 December 2006, but before deducting stipend endowments and normal allowances given for stipend purposes in a vacancy.

–18 This figure shows 'the number of children and young people aged 17 years and under who are involved in the life of the congregation'.

(NB Figures may not be available for new charges created or for congregations which have entered into readjustment late in 2006 or during 2007. Figures might also not be available for congregations which failed to submit the appropriate schedule.)

Congregation	Com	Eld	G	In 06	M&M	–18
1. Edinburgh						
Albany Deaf Church of Edinburgh	124	10	–	–	–	–
Balerno	800	65	45	110,848	57,559	60
Barclay	276	30	–	109,717	69,102	35
Blackhall St Columba	1,059	84	42	181,842	95,169	63
Bristo Memorial Craigmillar	126	6	22	–	14,928	30
Broughton St Mary's	268	31	–	58,613	40,069	73
Canongate	395	48	–	69,596	46,446	18
Carrick Knowe	508	51	84	61,046	42,853	175
Colinton	1,021	89	–	213,651	103,084	212
Colinton Mains	204	15	–	49,870	29,312	68
Corstorphine Craigsbank	624	32	–	95,537	64,611	104
Corstorphine Old	539	52	55	73,702	58,965	16
Corstorphine St Anne's	449	50	51	71,952	58,322	61
Corstorphine St Ninian's	975	80	50	147,456	92,625	65
Craigentinny St Christopher's	136	12	–	27,604	13,730	22
Craiglockhart	532	56	42	152,725	79,724	390
Craigmillar Park	283	21	30	91,224	57,492	26
Cramond	1,268	104	24	212,914	114,355	69
Currie	733	58	83	155,233	86,999	84
Dalmeny	115	8	–	12,746	11,950	–
Queensferry	769	53	69	85,363	36,665	120
Davidson's Mains	773	66	56	186,312	95,728	100
Dean	231	27	–	61,318	43,062	22
Drylaw	198	16	–	22,603	12,562	1
Duddingston	865	63	48	–	57,627	175
Fairmilehead	845	60	34	99,350	73,525	447
Gilmerton	–	–	–	–	–	–
Gorgie	301	34	–	75,271	54,637	87
Granton	327	25	–	–	26,221	14
Greenbank	923	96	55	245,943	112,318	137
Greenside	215	32	–	–	35,837	30
Greyfriars Tolbooth and Highland Kirk	398	53	19	98,632	71,640	24
High (St Giles')	584	38	–	253,854	102,516	8
Holyrood Abbey	265	32	20	136,143	93,146	77
Holy Trinity	195	23	–	81,853	43,783	20
Inverleith	347	43	–	94,625	59,984	10
Juniper Green	413	32	–	85,828	57,279	50
Kaimes Lockhart Memorial	85	6	10	–	10,720	4
Kirkliston	333	41	50	75,854	42,207	44
Kirk o' Field	188	28	–	34,734	33,403	5
Leith North	426	42	–	63,459	58,009	219
Leith St Andrew's	267	28	–	56171	38,164	140
Leith St Serf's	295	24	15	57,123	40,095	23
Leith St Thomas' Junction Road	257	23	–	51,901	30,796	5
Leith South	521	79	–	112,864	51,826	115
Leith Wardie	572	72	34	119,098	74,866	102

Congregation	Com	Eld	G	In 06	M&M	–18
Liberton	853	79	61	152,836	80,590	136
Liberton Northfield	274	10	36	52,276	26,002	30
London Road	338	29	39	53,598	37,076	55
Marchmont St Giles'	275	36	28	59,095	61,120	40
Mayfield Salisbury	686	69	27	231,895	112,311	60
Morningside	730	97	24	156,674	85,807	43
Morningside United	242	34	–	101,939	8,786	33
Muirhouse St Andrew's	113	7	–	11,102	246	72
Murrayfield	548	67	–	131,227	66,539	56
Newhaven	237	18	41	60,878	46,779	62
New Restalrig	270	16	20	101,581	64,964	45
Old Kirk	135	15	–	21,287	13,245	11
Palmerston Place	466	67	–	158,383	99,241	112
Pilrig St Paul's	308	28	–	47,432	31,460	37
Polwarth	311	26	18	89,190	54,727	50
Portobello Old	373	37	34	72,917	45,925	124
Portobello St James'	381	35	–	54,599	37,417	15
Portobello St Philip's Joppa	637	66	81	129,850	82,707	140
Priestfield	212	21	23	62,347	42,053	10
Ratho	236	19	18	43,647	24,678	42
Reid Memorial	377	26	–	–	63,085	25
Richmond Craigmillar	115	11	–	–	8,074	23
St Andrew's and St George's	339	39	–	184,383	91,375	24
St Andrew's Clermiston	303	19	–	–	29,510	14
St Catherine's Argyle	285	29	20	131,383	81,314	157
St Colm's	141	15	22	25,567	25,670	10
St Cuthbert's	471	58	–	172,492	103,515	2
St David's Broomhouse	184	15	–	41,877	31,130	25
St George's West	167	35	–	103,074	63,400	10
St John's Oxgangs	294	25	45	31,006	17,346	18
St Margaret's	421	36	20	44,765	38,675	82
St Martin's	114	13	–	21,656	4,038	80
St Michael's	430	39	–	53,539	40,373	24
St Nicholas' Sighthill	466	31	23	52,670	37,579	70
St Stephen's Comely Bank	408	25	53	101,335	62,036	10
Slateford Longstone	304	24	53	–	34,734	20
Stenhouse St Aidan's	199	13	–	30,671	19,369	35
Stockbridge	337	34	26	101,264	46,891	16
Tron Moredun	143	15	–	–	3,655	21
Viewforth	212	28	–	–	39,605	19

2. West Lothian

Abercorn	80	10	10	13,593	9,364	–
Pardovan, Kingscavil and Winchburgh	299	30	14	51,889	27,724	74
Armadale	615	46	28	67,628	38,925	214
Avonbridge	94	10	8	15,938	6,390	20
Torphichen	271	18	–	–	22,974	25
Bathgate: Boghall	286	35	20	62,905	37,216	84

Congregation	Com	Eld	G	In 06	M&M	–18
Bathgate: High.	545	43	34	78,478	48,609	80
Bathgate: St David's	271	11	16	43,642	30,793	–
Bathgate: St John's	358	25	35	51,949	37,250	108
Blackburn and Seafield	513	38	–	61,328	35,794	85
Blackridge	103	7	–	18,161	9,219	–
Harthill: St Andrew's.	246	17	34	58,711	34,911	87
Breich Valley	222	11	–	22,836	18,944	16
Broxburn	499	30	48	64,624	37,583	142
Fauldhouse: St Andrew's.	251	11	13	42,598	28,156	11
Kirknewton and East Calder	362	40	28	100,228	50,521	96
Kirk of Calder	649	45	25	74,958	43,947	80
Linlithgow: St Michael's	1,493	104	55	264,974	114,625	346
Linlithgow: St Ninian's Craigmailen	508	49	70	72,410	44,724	111
Livingston Ecumenical	786	51	–	–	27,288	270
Livingston: Old	452	36	25	74,542	45,580	61
Polbeth Harwood.	227	33	–	28,121	13,146	8
West Kirk of Calder	327	27	43	36,322	30,636	27
Strathbrock	361	43	20	100,875	64,516	25
Uphall: South.	216	22	–	–	26,016	65
Whitburn: Brucefield.	462	30	21	91,170	39,613	20
Whitburn: South	423	35	40	62,860	42,734	123

3. Lothian

Congregation	Com	Eld	G	In 06	M&M	–18
Aberlady	297	28	–	35,715	21,652	37
Gullane	461	40	47	60,147	34,260	38
Athelstaneford	215	20	–	20,720	14,002	20
Whitekirk and Tyninghame.	160	17	–	–	20,455	17
Belhaven	746	41	61	68,531	37,607	134
Spott.	103	7	–	13,881	7,319	10
Bilston	106	5	20	10,315	2,111	–
Glencorse.	342	11	–	25,228	16,792	12
Roslin.	283	9	–	28,347	16,603	–
Bolton and Saltoun	162	16	16	24,590	15,703	10
Humbie	87	9	12	14,217	10,108	15
Yester.	211	21	18	24,991	15,040	15
Bonnyrigg	824	72	51	96,245	60,661	52
Borthwick	73	8	–	19,101	6,989	15
Cranstoun, Crichton and Ford.	261	20	–	42,892	26,045	12
Fala and Soutra	71	6	14	9,373	8,284	3
Cockenzie and Port Seton: Chalmers Memorial.	278	31	38	62,370	39,136	40
Cockenzie and Port Seton: Old.	447	16	28	42,818	14,525	24
Cockpen and Carrington	333	24	46	21,263	18,651	36
Lasswade	309	20	–	24,009	17,222	2
Rosewell	137	9	–	10,692	7,746	–
Dalkeith: St John's and King's Park	547	43	23	82,092	45,445	40
Dalkeith: St Nicholas' Buccleuch	469	29	–	47,403	32,247	12
Dirleton	259	17	16	30,607	21,552	12
North Berwick: Abbey	328	32	49	70,629	38,709	59

Congregation	Com	Eld	G	In 06	M&M	–18
Dunbar	809	22	41	86,828	48,942	44
Dunglass	352	17	17	27,916	17,418	2
Garvald and Morham	53	9	–	16,001	8,784	32
Haddington: West	510	33	57	72,688	40,139	52
Gladsmuir	215	15	–	22,307	13,028	–
Longniddry	430	40	37	73,649	46,341	44
Gorebridge	469	17	–	74,753	36,303	24
Haddington: St Mary's	663	61	–	–	74,595	50
Howgate	45	5	7	14,706	7,917	10
Penicuik: South	191	12	–	81,658	60,389	40
Loanhead	385	29	40	53,107	27,786	57
Musselburgh: Northesk	410	37	39	61,856	39,251	105
Musselburgh: St Andrew's High	381	34	26	62,473	33,709	21
Musselburgh: St Clement's and St Ninian's	371	28	9	31,037	19,024	15
Musselburgh: St Michael's Inveresk	518	35	25	47,500	40,426	26
Newbattle	639	38	–	66,913	36,031	253
Newton	167	6	15	16,104	10,818	–
North Berwick: St Andrew Blackadder	702	45	32	99,242	63,043	144
Ormiston	178	8	23	31,217	16,260	–
Pencaitland	267	11	14	–	31,333	50
Penicuik: North	622	37	–	98,522	51,712	72
Penicuik: St Mungo's	458	22	31	64,219	38,097	12
Prestonpans: Prestongrange	374	51	27	40,425	33,087	20
Tranent	293	14	25	48,838	30,883	38
Traprain	506	32	–	58,053	44,125	6
4. Melrose and Peebles						
Ashkirk	65	7	9	9,447	5,439	4
Selkirk	579	23	33	56,294	42,453	18
Bowden	95	11	–	24,282	19,350	–
Newtown	182	11	–	12,797	10,338	–
Broughton, Glenholm and Kilbucho	170	14	27	16,922	8,715	8
Skirling	87	8	–	9,286	5,309	12
Stobo and Drumelzier	99	–	–	12,355	9,105	5
Tweedsmuir	42	6	–	6,472	4,189	13
Caddonfoot	229	16	–	14,065	7,437	11
Galashiels: Trinity	944	64	–	83,175	57,007	51
Carlops	69	14	–	13,829	6,704	–
Kirkurd and Newlands	113	7	14	17,466	10,542	–
West Linton: St Andrew's	244	17	–	32,313	20,061	–
Channelkirk and Lauder	440	28	–	42,362	26,649	34
Earlston	508	15	13	38,845	29,403	33
Eddleston	120	8	11	9,576	5,890	17
Peebles: Old	640	51	–	85,389	53,242	110
Ettrick and Yarrow	216	21	–	32,753	21,232	18
Galashiels: Old and St Paul's	352	24	26	62,866	44,437	47
Galashiels: St John's	258	17	–	42,167	21,266	75
Innerleithen, Traquair and Walkerburn	465	33	–	59,213	44,597	95

Congregation	Com	Eld	G	In 06	M&M	–18
Lyne and Manor	104	–	–	22,656	15,399	–
Maxton and Mertoun	148	10	–	17,392	14,725	8
St Boswells	288	24	28	33,943	21,762	11
Melrose	870	46	54	112,211	66,142	40
Peebles: St Andrew's Leckie	692	40	–	92,294	52,026	45
Stow: St Mary of Wedale and Heriot	197	14	–	30,527	20,947	38

5. Duns

Congregation	Com	Eld	G	In 06	M&M	–18
Ayton and Burnmouth	195	6	–	16,475	11,780	17
Grantshouse and Houndwood and Reston	120	8	–	11,468	9,569	–
Berwick-upon-Tweed: St Andrew's Wallace Green and Lowick	471	32	39	56,372	33,510	15
Bonkyl and Preston	87	8	–	9,167	4,742	–
Chirnside	329	21	–	24,767	15,998	15
Edrom: Allanton	80	9	–	9,049	4,485	–
Coldingham and St Abb's	92	6	–	30,478	16,128	11
Eyemouth	284	23	43	37,135	23,150	24
Coldstream	410	28	19	40,861	24,434	1
Eccles	99	10	18	7,555	6,776	3
Duns	549	28	40	51,675	29,774	40
Fogo and Swinton	133	5	–	13,924	7,514	2
Ladykirk	36	6	11	7,946	4,866	–
Leitholm	90	9	–	13,929	6,451	6
Whitsome	49	4	10	8,333	2,936	1
Foulden and Mordington	98	11	12	4,529	7,408	–
Hutton and Fishwick and Paxton	92	8	12	10,776	7,011	4
Gordon: St Michael's	71	7	–	6,417	7,661	8
Greenlaw	131	10	19	17,561	12,732	12
Legerwood	65	7	–	7,841	4,117	6
Westruther	46	6	9	7,197	4,313	9
Kirk of Lammermuir	82	10	–	10,015	11,422	6
Langton and Polwarth	107	7	27	12,510	10,848	–

6. Jedburgh

Congregation	Com	Eld	G	In 06	M&M	–18
Ale and Teviot United	489	39	–	40,401	32,850	15
Cavers and Kirkton	151	9	–	9,907	8,651	12
Hawick: Trinity	848	31	52	48,177	35,116	80
Hawick: Burnfoot	141	13	12	28,514	14,998	90
Hawick: St Mary's and Old	588	26	48	37,367	30,283	122
Hawick: Teviot and Roberton	363	10	6	55,117	35,205	47
Hawick: Wilton	416	30	28	39,924	25,676	28
Teviothead	79	6	9	5,201	3,217	4
Hobkirk and Southdean	183	18	14	11,140	13,029	14
Ruberslaw	320	25	–	29,652	21,255	26
Jedburgh: Old and Edgerston	608	19	21	42,730	30,388	9
Jedburgh: Trinity	221	11	–	35,905	25,966	–
Kelso Country Churches	224	17	–	25,761	22,565	–
Kelso: North and Ednam	1,310	73	53	112,877	67,421	33

Congregation	Com	Eld	G	In 06	M&M	–18
Kelso: Old and Sprouston	626	45	–	55,214	35,499	12
Linton, Morebattle, Hownam and Yetholm	490	28	–	49,882	33,871	25
Oxnam	109	7	–	8,993	3,593	1

7. Annandale and Eskdale

Annan: Old	426	37	52	67,408	41,118	55
Annan: St Andrew's	766	40	92	61,887	39,484	108
Brydekirk	57	5	–	7,087	4,788	12
Applegarth, Sibbaldbie and Johnstone	194	12	–	10,741	9,714	–
Lochmaben	557	25	41	51,763	24,362	25
Canonbie United	140	13	–	23,112	12,630	18
Liddesdale	154	10	–	38,203	22,765	30
Dalton	118	7	5	17,626	8,651	8
Hightae	90	8	15	9,839	7,288	45
St Mungo	140	10	14	15,973	9,314	8
Dornock	156	13	–	13,418	7,491	40
Eskdalemuir	31	–	–	3,815	2,961	–
Hutton and Corrie	76	6	–	6,861	9,325	–
Tundergarth	76	7	11	9,174	3,852	–
Gretna: Old, Gretna: St Andrew's and Half Morton and Kirkpatrick Fleming	403	29	28	–	23,020	60
Hoddam	149	8	–	8,975	7,469	–
Kirtle-Eaglesfield	93	10	17	13,474	8,627	–
Middlebie	101	9	14	–	5,885	3
Waterbeck	69	4	–	6,121	3,448	–
Kirkpatrick Juxta	154	10	–	12,886	7,186	–
Moffat: St Andrew's	513	46	36	79,725	39,322	35
Wamphray	59	6	–	6,463	4,263	–
Langholm, Ewes and Westerkirk	519	29	57	39,424	29,588	35
Lockerbie: Dryfesdale	829	44	45	52,865	31,123	31
The Border Kirk	382	48	–	59,833	29,425	17

8. Dumfries and Kirkcudbright

Auchencairn and Rerrick	119	11	–	9,822	7,500	8
Buittle and Kelton	216	20	16	26,717	16,140	12
Balmaclellan and Kells	142	10	15	16,192	11,806	8
Carsphairn	110	10	–	8,264	4,200	3
Dalry	193	15	25	12,032	5,756	17
Balmaghie	130	7	17	13,851	6,903	–
Tarff and Twynholm	194	18	27	26,677	19,060	12
Borgue	56	6	11	4,605	3,500	5
Gatehouse of Fleet	324	24	27	51,118	29,763	13
Caerlaverock	162	8	–	10,773	5,500	18
Dumfries: St Mary's-Greyfriars	847	63	–	68,460	44,153	14
Castle Douglas	533	36	48	55,661	39,189	25
Closeburn	247	14	–	19,739	15,023	20
Durisdeer	167	5	22	24,905	13,044	20
Colvend, Southwick and Kirkbean	365	26	21	69,784	38,771	25

Congregation	Com	Eld	G	In 06	M&M	–18
Corsock and Kirkpatrick Durham	135	15	24	18,051	14,648	30
Crossmichael and Parton	183	14	16	22,060	13,000	19
Cummertrees	49	4	–	5,434	3,244	–
Mouswald	80	5	15	6,371	7,000	–
Ruthwell	100	8	17	10,260	8,500	10
Dalbeattie	648	37	64	51,124	32,350	60
Urr	210	11	–	16,057	12,063	18
Dumfries: Lincluden and Holywood	291	19	–	24,997	20,030	30
Dumfries: Lochside	376	18	25	20,520	14,592	65
Dumfries: Maxwelltown West	679	49	48	74,714	36,000	127
Dumfries: St George's	566	48	42	85,289	42,650	67
Dumfries: St Michael's and South	936	50	35	80,918	42,650	115
Dumfries: Troqueer	401	28	20	90,052	50,874	43
Dunscore	255	21	11	31,688	18,677	36
Glencairn and Moniaive	214	11	–	28,731	15,783	18
Irongray, Lochrutton and Terregles	511	34	–	32,865	27,422	–
Kirkconnel	352	11	12	49,127	32,953	8
Kirkcudbright	704	36	–	64,256	48,169	40
Kirkgunzeon	58	9	–	6,863	3,000	–
Kirkmahoe	376	16	30	27,035	21,000	10
Kirkmichael, Tinwald and Torthorwald	560	44	–	60,215	44,008	35
Lochend and New Abbey	277	20	–	24,341	14,626	11
Penpont, Keir and Tynron	185	12	–	18,920	14,367	30
Thornhill	263	12	16	24,065	18,624	–
Sanquhar: St Bride's	500	29	24	44,044	28,580	36

9. Wigtown and Stranraer

Congregation	Com	Eld	G	In 06	M&M	–18
Ervie Kirkcolm	249	16	–	20,820	12,967	19
Leswalt	307	14	16	29,352	15,646	19
Glasserton and Isle of Whithorn	117	8	–	18,597	9,664	–
Whithorn: St Ninian's Priory	324	15	24	24,509	18,231	21
Inch	262	18	13	18,875	11,489	20
Stranraer: Town Kirk	696	46	–	69,880	53,802	99
Kirkcowan	148	9	–	32,758	16,186	9
Wigtown	230	12	15	29,972	22,703	32
Kirkinner	171	6	14	13,715	9,333	–
Sorbie	163	10	9	19,079	9,631	–
Kirkmabreck	173	9	29	19,468	14,388	10
Monigaff	412	25	–	29,708	22,751	25
Kirkmaiden	236	20	16	24,470	17,746	–
Stoneykirk	386	26	16	33,823	22,742	10
Mochrum	280	22	36	27,574	18,127	23
New Luce	107	10	–	10,462	7,859	10
Old Luce	170	24	34	36,512	24,202	38
Penninghame	560	38	–	60,887	49,357	8
Portpatrick	249	10	31	17,824	13,642	18
Stranraer: St Ninian's	439	23	25	42,265	27,114	18
Stranraer: High Kirk	628	36	33	65,540	36,164	83

Congregation	Com	Eld	G	In 06	M&M	–18
10. Ayr						
Alloway	1,277	96	33	209,001	108,819	280
Annbank	305	19	22	36,070	17,927	19
Tarbolton	531	33	27	44,632	27,299	14
Arnsheen Barrhill	73	5	–	–	3,993	–
Colmonell	208	14	–	18,895	10,340	–
Auchinleck	378	21	28	–	29,185	30
Catrine	110	16	24	20,707	11,712	–
Ayr: Auld Kirk of Ayr	636	82	40	75,386	60,000	28
Ayr: Castlehill	704	43	66	103,482	55,520	40
Ayr: Newton on Ayr	421	45	52	105,008	63,004	300
Ayr: St Andrew's	508	37	16	78,075	50,090	80
Ayr: St Columba	1,462	139	47	202,960	100,030	110
Ayr: St James'	457	32	54	64,061	40,587	271
Ayr: St Leonard's	608	55	38	75,654	48,756	41
Ayr: St Quivox	382	–	21	46,966	34,488	22
Ayr: Wallacetown	370	25	33	40,382	28,220	8
Ballantrae	276	23	41	34,792	27,300	15
Barr	73	5	–	6,600	2,795	10
Dailly	181	13	18	15,689	10,022	4
Girvan: South	334	26	36	33,827	20,954	31
Coylton	342	17	–	39,559	13,373	103
Drongan: The Schaw Kirk	253	23	23	28,817	11,001	90
Craigie	125	8	–	12,780	6,509	15
Symington	383	21	27	53,618	35,649	15
Crosshill	196	10	26	17,031	10,571	11
Dalrymple	268	15	–	23,891	17,942	–
Dalmellington	311	26	72	47,565	29,441	125
Patna: Waterside	159	15	–	25,921	11,082	64
Dundonald	532	50	55	–	45,876	100
Fisherton	145	9	10	10,389	8,164	–
Kirkoswald	256	14	16	32,999	23,486	12
Girvan: North (Old and St Andrew's)	966	66	–	73,407	49,282	150
Kirkmichael	225	–	22	18,946	11,689	14
Straiton: St Cuthbert's	167	13	16	14,062	8,647	20
Lugar	169	11	18	17,376	7,808	4
Old Cumnock: Old	409	19	46	60,862	29,197	63
Mauchline	591	24	65	67,230	44,674	125
Maybole	583	29	–	57,371	30,600	24
Monkton and Prestwick: North	516	42	46	100,629	57,660	87
Muirkirk	233	16	25	34,175	12,945	7
Sorn	169	12	21	20,508	16,519	6
New Cumnock	602	38	52	59,596	33,737	95
Ochiltree	270	24	19	22,225	17,230	36
Stair	226	14	12	22,857	17,424	47
Old Cumnock: Trinity	408	24	–	42,215	29,932	19
Prestwick: Kingcase	985	92	57	116,177	62,536	260
Prestwick: St Nicholas'	786	75	77	102,296	60,764	141

Congregation	Com	Eld	G	In 06	M&M	–18
Prestwick: South	354	35	44	75,156	48,467	100
Troon: Old	1,185	74	–	146,952	85,966	104
Troon: Portland	692	49	42	118,818	66,072	–
Troon: St Meddan's	1,083	111	68	160,105	93,599	80

11. Irvine and Kilmarnock

Congregation	Com	Eld	G	In 06	M&M	–18
Crosshouse	336	28	24	42,300	25,093	16
Darvel	590	36	55	41,521	27,000	19
Dreghorn and Springside	614	66	44	67,989	46,000	–
Dunlop	416	37	36	56,051	35,000	45
Fenwick	392	24	23	59,014	37,000	33
Galston	795	67	75	108,662	68,000	78
Hurlford	557	24	39	66,079	36,204	30
Irvine: Fullarton	458	36	51	99,781	60,899	149
Irvine: Girdle Toll	189	18	28	37,248	20,800	115
Irvine: Mure	441	30	32	75,998	50,000	67
Irvine: Old	515	30	26	86,944	60,000	–
Irvine: Relief Bourtreehill	363	28	30	51,199	27,000	12
Irvine: St Andrew's	335	19	32	40,689	33,000	20
Kilmarnock: Grange	414	35	57	66,013	41,400	29
Kilmarnock: Henderson	583	79	68	114,922	74,000	28
Kilmarnock: Howard St Andrew's	409	40	32	66,073	51,000	2
Kilmarnock: Laigh West High	897	71	–	136,454	91,000	215
Kilmarnock: Old High Kirk	280	18	20	55,146	26,500	21
Kilmarnock: Riccarton	344	32	32	62,863	43,000	98
Kilmarnock: St John's Onthank	293	28	26	43,140	27,900	82
Kilmarnock: St Kentigern's	289	26	–	48,820	31,000	167
Kilmarnock: St Marnock's	751	85	–	117,081	68,000	346
Kilmarnock: St Ninian's Bellfield	226	19	24	29,990	19,000	30
Kilmarnock: Shortlees	118	13	–	29,457	18,500	6
Kilmaurs: St Maur's Glencairn	341	23	24	49,134	34,000	25
Newmilns: Loudoun	362	10	–	82,154	48,449	47
Stewarton: John Knox	275	33	23	71,368	44,500	80
Stewarton: St Columba's	482	42	45	64,162	48,000	48

12. Ardrossan

Congregation	Com	Eld	G	In 06	M&M	–18
Ardrossan: Barony St John's	341	19	35	46,906	30,278	20
Ardrossan: Park	473	35	40	59,596	39,880	123
Beith: High	824	75	26	56,476	35,787	52
Beith: Trinity	252	31	37	47,483	26,190	37
Brodick	208	24	–	38,140	21,181	27
Corrie	77	7	–	16,447	6,321	3
Lochranza and Pirnmill	63	10	12	13,443	7,051	–
Shiskine	70	8	14	18,843	9,026	14
Cumbrae	295	26	59	41,642	28,680	58
Dalry: St Margaret's	850	54	36	90,443	56,477	148
Dalry: Trinity	254	23	41	77,132	48,166	58
Fairlie	275	33	55	66,237	35,366	22

Congregation	Com	Eld	G	In 06	M&M	–18
Fergushill	50	5	–	5,734	2,057	9
Kilbirnie: Auld Kirk	471	37	20	47,878	29,350	16
Kilbirnie: St Columba's	624	34	32	61,366	35,894	91
Kilmory	48	8	–	12,164	4,698	8
Kilwinning: Mansefield Trinity	253	15	45	41,478	12,438	–
Kilwinning: Old	739	52	–	98,062	48,939	71
Lamlash	139	13	27	32,724	14,288	17
Largs: Clark Memorial	966	91	54	116,744	66,970	43
Largs: St Columba's	511	50	56	102,157	56,462	36
Largs: St John's	937	52	79	147,334	79,514	101
Saltcoats: New Trinity	336	44	26	57,178	41,973	20
Saltcoats: North	359	26	38	54,921	30,646	90
Saltcoats: St Cuthbert's	515	54	39	89,874	58,755	85
Stevenston: Ardeer	331	28	30	37,994	19,574	75
Stevenston: Livingstone	367	44	39	45,859	23,049	15
Stevenston: High	275	28	53	74,900	42,359	35
West Kilbride: Overton	348	29	29	48,201	34,460	34
West Kilbride: St Andrew's	645	52	26	–	47,159	30
Whiting Bay and Kildonan	123	15	–	38,036	21,864	21

13. Lanark

Congregation	Com	Eld	G	In 06	M&M	–18
Biggar	662	37	62	75,705	47,315	38
Black Mount	107	7	16	11,824	8,000	9
Culter	89	11	–	10,449	6,125	5
Libberton and Quothquan	90	12	–	11,797	3,895	12
Cairngryffe	179	15	22	23,678	20,000	21
Symington	247	20	27	39,451	16,537	32
Carluke: Kirkton	835	50	25	100,674	59,000	300
Carluke: St Andrew's	361	18	16	45,913	29,900	32
Carluke: St John's	799	51	38	77,437	50,000	49
Carnwath	336	17	26	41,807	25,610	34
Carstairs and Carstairs Junction	317	23	–	43,267	24,759	22
Coalburn	164	8	20	18,278	8,500	7
Lesmahagow: Old	638	32	24	74,937	37,400	60
Crossford	197	9	–	27,860	18,040	20
Kirkfieldbank	125	8	18	17,636	9,250	55
Forth: St Paul's	404	30	52	45,677	28,800	33
Glencaple	219	13	14	25,764	22,120	15
Lowther	39	5	–	8,573	4,223	8
Kirkmuirhill	322	17	64	102,616	61,000	80
Lanark: Greyfriars	844	47	45	82,910	47,500	103
Lanark: St Nicholas'	656	51	38	85,417	51,000	130
Law	178	20	37	–	20,750	150
Lesmahagow: Abbeygreen	238	17	3	80,334	47,000	57
The Douglas Valley Church	419	33	–	52,770	24,100	20

Congregation	Com	Eld	G	In 06	M&M	–18
14. Greenock and Paisley						
Barrhead: Arthurlie	343	28	26	93,881	47,698	72
Barrhead: Bourock	513	53	57	77,313	49,715	252
Barrhead: South and Levern	445	32	26	69,062	49,356	181
Bishopton	829	58	–	95,248	54,044	127
Bridge of Weir: Freeland	424	54	–	109,340	68,811	112
Bridge of Weir: St Machar's Ranfurly	488	41	38	91,757	48,504	42
Caldwell	261	16	–	55,915	34,374	50
Elderslie Kirk	595	61	59	114,655	65,878	170
Erskine	388	33	58	95,211	62,817	289
Gourock: Old Gourock and Ashton	876	70	56	126,349	79,746	260
Gourock: St John's	665	69	24	103,798	60,447	345
Greenock: Ardgowan	465	43	32	81,532	52,543	149
Greenock: East End	–	–	–	–	888	–
Greenock: Finnart St Paul's	382	30	–	77,197	48,547	71
Greenock: Mount Kirk	346	43	20	56,191	44,957	170
Greenock: Old West Kirk	349	28	35	70,095	54,673	21
Greenock: St George's North	318	32	–	42,529	40,173	37
Greenock: St Luke's	709	83	53	114,449	77,819	197
Greenock: St Margaret's	188	16	25	26,933	16,847	15
Greenock: St Ninian's	258	20	–	–	15,120	92
Greenock: Wellpark Mid Kirk	617	37	31	82,261	52,387	125
Houston and Killellan	752	57	57	132,647	76,930	420
Howwood	220	13	21	53,159	29,486	24
Inchinnan	382	39	28	67,096	42,208	174
Inverkip	438	30	37	51,533	32,026	90
Johnstone: High	322	41	34	84,535	52,348	35
Johnstone: St Andrew's Trinity	262	31	36	46,977	28,285	134
Johnstone: St Paul's	558	75	31	77,988	47,189	38
Kilbarchan: East	400	44	26	75,595	41,333	50
Kilbarchan: West	470	48	37	97,239	67,660	53
Kilmacolm: Old	547	53	–	121,151	75,604	50
Kilmacolm: St Columba	575	33	23	107,340	65,534	55
Langbank	146	15	–	30,922	20,933	12
Linwood	485	45	28	57,852	40,463	36
Lochwinnoch	155	14	–	39,628	22,208	167
Neilston	664	47	47	–	58,036	40
Paisley: Abbey	788	54	–	151,602	72,481	115
Paisley: Castlehead	278	31	14	52,841	36,967	22
Paisley: Glenburn	271	21	–	42,862	28,088	36
Paisley: Laigh Kirk	480	70	69	119,670	49,723	50
Paisley: Lylesland	456	65	49	78,027	51,959	51
Paisley: Martyrs'	475	57	–	68,226	52,387	97
Paisley: Oakshaw Trinity	658	89	51	116,971	64,151	40
Paisley: St Columba Foxbar	226	29	29	38,950	26,596	142
Paisley: St James'	370	32	–	53,210	29,817	35
Paisley: St Luke's	284	32	–	–	33,470	8
Paisley: St Mark's Oldhall	611	60	105	113,162	67,343	254

Congregation	Com	Eld	G	In 06	M&M	–18
Paisley: St Ninian's Ferguslie	42	–	–	12,171	749	15
Paisley: Sandyford (Thread Street)	292	21	21	48,344	31,736	12
Paisley: Sherwood Greenlaw	751	97	48	119,452	72,977	54
Paisley: Wallneuk North	479	54	–	–	39,243	22
Port Glasgow: Hamilton Bardrainney	344	18	22	45,375	26,953	69
Port Glasgow: St Andrew's	660	59	46	75,237	51,313	284
Port Glasgow: St Martin's	173	16	–	21,441	11,565	16
Renfrew: North	677	65	38	104,924	61,324	150
Renfrew: Old	609	43	50	82,936	51,829	–
Renfrew: Trinity	383	32	60	76,432	49,819	25
Skelmorlie and Wemyss Bay	405	29	–	73,121	44,040	30

16. Glasgow

Congregation	Com	Eld	G	In 06	M&M	–18
Banton	83	12	–	17,888	7,311	25
Twechar	76	–	–	14,333	5,402	14
Bishopbriggs: Kenmure	340	28	49	80,562	48,830	150
Bishopbriggs: Springfield	922	51	82	103,100	64,515	194
Broom	817	66	41	136,900	82,750	75
Burnside Blairbeth	713	56	–	247,320	112,372	312
Busby	356	44	40	62,684	41,518	40
Cadder	891	86	74	150,050	94,622	222
Cambuslang: Flemington Hallside	211	13	13	43,797	19,956	90
Cambuslang: Old	384	47	40	71,395	53,413	20
Cambuslang: St Andrew's	403	37	–	81,598	52,689	80
Cambuslang: Trinity St Paul's	304	22	–	73,436	48,740	56
Campsie	207	19	21	–	33,144	100
Chryston	700	41	25	167,029	83,310	95
Eaglesham	677	55	67	117,919	69,197	180
Fernhill and Cathkin	312	25	48	42,655	27,071	111
Gartcosh	148	–	10	16,174	11,770	–
Glenboig	139	8	13	12,576	6,857	11
Giffnock: Orchardhill	519	52	28	177,504	106,537	392
Giffnock: South	956	96	59	192,060	114,251	108
Giffnock: The Park	308	28	–	56,427	32,479	103
Greenbank	1,071	82	51	213,805	120,674	300
Kilsyth: Anderson	412	20	60	88,100	53,053	132
Kilsyth: Burns and Old	485	38	45	86,168	46,451	100
Kirkintilloch: Hillhead	143	10	15	13,573	10,558	55
Kirkintilloch: St Columba's	553	51	49	89,593	56,425	100
Kirkintilloch: St David's Memorial Park	713	63	37	121,236	80,094	137
Kirkintilloch: St Mary's	794	65	74	135,400	74,805	250
Lenzie: Old	491	43	–	104,534	51,298	43
Lenzie: Union	778	72	87	168,521	97,810	242
Maxwell Mearns Castle	303	32	–	151,324	83,803	225
Mearns	901	50	–	160,105	92,862	73
Milton of Campsie	358	40	35	48,728	34,291	120
Netherlee	828	79	61	205,401	114,105	433
Newton Mearns	711	59	27	124,915	77,484	142

Congregation	Com	Eld	G	In 06	M&M	–18
Rutherglen: Old	379	27	–	55,771	35,202	70
Rutherglen: Stonelaw	423	44	44	123,885	74,012	28
Rutherglen: Wardlawhill	354	42	47	46,665	30,164	100
Rutherglen: West	487	30	27	68,083	39,340	91
Stamperland	429	31	31	74,710	52,694	252
Stepps	387	29	18	47,955	32,569	160
Thornliebank	234	18	51	56,666	31,764	58
Torrance	306	17	–	75,702	32,680	154
Williamwood	511	75	36	122,015	78,255	274
Glasgow: Anderston Kelvingrove	66	18	11	11,653	13,461	18
Glasgow: Baillieston Mure Memorial	527	35	101	83,770	54,352	305
Glasgow: Baillieston St Andrew's	389	26	39	62,863	41,006	119
Glasgow: Balshagray Victoria Park	284	39	34	86,901	53,004	64
Glasgow: Barlanark Greyfriars	158	21	20	34,329	18,422	170
Glasgow: Battlefield East	150	11	36	42,445	26,064	3
Glasgow: Blawarthill	191	22	43	29,801	17,466	83
Glasgow: Bridgeton St Francis in the East	98	16	9	–	19,151	56
Glasgow: Broomhill	607	63	58	144,250	84,497	120
Glasgow: Calton Parkhead	97	13	–	16,200	15,483	5
Glasgow: Cardonald	474	49	90	125,286	80,001	233
Glasgow: Carmunnock	349	31	32	58,121	38,336	50
Glasgow: Carmyle	119	5	25	22,551	12,369	42
Glasgow: Kenmuir Mount Vernon	154	10	31	49,621	26,813	90
Glasgow: Carntyne Old	149	24	–	39,642	26,442	57
Glasgow: Eastbank	159	16	29	39,013	20,131	42
Glasgow: Carnwadric	142	19	28	33,278	15,564	48
Glasgow: Castlemilk East	159	12	16	29,517	18,020	30
Glasgow: Castlemilk West	130	19	16	24,051	13,627	24
Glasgow: Cathcart Old	312	50	47	68,262	52,614	639
Glasgow: Cathcart Trinity	571	45	–	186,320	92,047	82
Glasgow: Cathedral (High or St Mungo's)	417	56	–	89,642	61,488	12
Glasgow: Colston Milton	105	17	–	25,809	15,309	80
Glasgow: Colston Wellpark	179	14	–	–	19,749	91
Glasgow: Cranhill	36	7	–	11,386	2,883	33
Glasgow: Croftfoot	330	49	39	80,939	49,910	61
Glasgow: Dennistoun Blackfriars	141	18	22	40,302	32,645	4
Glasgow: Dennistoun Central	229	23	25	42,841	30,103	135
Glasgow: Drumchapel Drumry St Mary's	107	11	–	8,260	1,737	15
Glasgow: Drumchapel St Andrew's	427	42	–	48,704	33,996	26
Glasgow: Drumchapel St Mark's	70	10	–	13,492	1,187	8
Glasgow: Easterhouse St George's and St Peter's	70	8	–	–	120	12
Glasgow: Eastwood	352	51	43	80,411	58,670	61
Glasgow: Gairbraid	229	20	16	33,786	25,245	16
Glasgow: Gardner Street	40	8	–	–	32,016	2
Glasgow: Garthamlock and Craigend East	83	15	–	–	2,111	70
Glasgow: Gorbals	95	11	–	24,100	16,035	9
Glasgow: Govan Old	155	29	22	51,227	28,156	38
Glasgow: Govanhill Trinity	124	17	25	25,247	20,973	5

Congregation	Com	Eld	G	In 06	M&M	–18
Glasgow: High Carntyne	410	33	77	77,696	52,178	132
Glasgow: Hillington Park	406	32	45	78,677	46,022	145
Glasgow: Househillwood St Christopher's	128	–	27	–	11,406	–
Glasgow: Hyndland	278	39	28	98,191	56,734	45
Glasgow: Ibrox	222	16	29	47,582	32,775	111
Glasgow: John Ross Memorial (for Deaf People)	68	8	–	–	–	–
Glasgow: Jordanhill	641	75	27	196,771	92,472	190
Glasgow: Kelvin Stevenson Memorial	168	30	18	37,667	27,452	103
Glasgow: Kelvinside Hillhead	174	24	–	67,416	44,304	85
Glasgow: King's Park	760	79	55	158,375	92,518	342
Glasgow: Kinning Park	153	16	21	35,701	24,190	15
Glasgow: Knightswood St Margaret's	651	31	37	55,891	35,433	130
Glasgow: Langside	249	42	21	60,650	32,093	148
Glasgow: Lansdowne	103	12	–	7,392	8,086	5
Glasgow: Linthouse St Kenneth's	98	15	12	17,560	16,762	46
Glasgow: Lochwood	74	4	10	–	4,547	80
Glasgow: Martyrs', The	124	8	–	24,758	15,321	60
Glasgow: Maryhill	195	16	–	–	25,635	150
Glasgow: Merrylea	457	78	46	90,408	55,820	155
Glasgow: Mosspark	196	37	50	61,764	39,867	68
Glasgow: Mount Florida	280	30	46	103,766	56,733	181
Glasgow: New Govan	108	17	25	50,139	35,276	58
Glasgow: Newlands South	614	74	32	177,429	104,993	35
Glasgow: North Kelvinside	62	5	23	38,169	22,244	15
Glasgow: Partick South	189	32	32	63,055	35,926	–
Glasgow: Partick Trinity	184	25	–	61,408	26,179	60
Glasgow: Penilee St Andrew's	158	26	–	34,458	24,270	82
Glasgow: Pollokshaws	170	23	31	42,964	26,354	57
Glasgow: Pollokshields	286	42	54	107,168	72,331	47
Glasgow: Possilpark	178	18	19	30,340	20,814	59
Glasgow: Priesthill and Nitshill	128	18	21	34,974	19,085	27
Glasgow: Queen's Park	249	31	–	80,646	56,522	83
Glasgow: Renfield St Stephen's	172	30	37	78,837	46,205	11
Glasgow: Robroyston	67	–	–	8,396	0	58
Glasgow: Ruchazie	68	6	–	13,919	7,454	75
Glasgow: Ruchill	93	21	–	43,971	31,850	15
Glasgow: St Andrew's East	119	21	25	36,140	22,668	52
Glasgow: St Columba	136	11	18	–	20,758	27
Glasgow: St David's Knightswood	464	28	46	92,816	59,102	56
Glasgow: St Enoch's Hogganfield	202	13	37	40,825	29,049	–
Glasgow: St George's Tron	417	30	–	242,209	120,039	50
Glasgow: St James' (Pollok)	181	29	22	56,419	31,406	62
Glasgow: St John's Renfield	428	51	–	161,222	85,694	140
Glasgow: St Luke's and St Andrew's	79	9	12	–	12,299	–
Glasgow: St Margaret's Tollcross Park	148	5	–	28,459	18,132	36
Glasgow: St Nicholas' Cardonald	336	31	10	53,673	40,725	322
Glasgow: St Paul's	57	7	–	–	3,057	9
Glasgow: St Rollox	120	11	–	27,611	14,407	11

Congregation	Com	Eld	G	In 06	M&M	–18
Glasgow: St Thomas' Gallowgate	34	6	–	–	3,778	9
Glasgow: Sandyford Henderson Memorial	196	22	21	132,302	66,808	44
Glasgow: Sandyhills	346	29	55	71,913	49,156	95
Glasgow: Scotstoun	263	14	–	72,325	44,188	65
Glasgow: Shawlands	431	26	–	106,310	67,778	32
Glasgow: Sherbrooke St Gilbert's	389	50	25	129,463	74,109	110
Glasgow: Shettleston Old	218	23	25	31,936	31,944	80
Glasgow: South Carntyne	78	9	–	26,394	15,697	50
Glasgow: South Shawlands	211	26	–	68,768	34,189	140
Glasgow: Springburn	281	41	27	69,731	46,911	130
Glasgow: Temple Anniesland	408	33	56	91,231	53,484	80
Glasgow: Toryglen	128	10	–	20,909	8,443	14
Glasgow: Trinity Possil and Henry Drummond	105	7	–	50,643	28,559	12
Glasgow: Tron St Mary's	147	21	–	34,885	22,282	120
Glasgow: Victoria Tollcross	140	16	21	26,149	17,918	32
Glasgow: Wallacewell	133	16	–	–	21,007	27
Glasgow: Wellington	255	34	–	77,682	56,826	23
Glasgow: Whiteinch	31	–	–	46,080	0	150
Glasgow: Yoker	92	–	–	24,676	15,650	–

17. Hamilton

Airdrie: Broomknoll	357	40	38	72,622	39,869	139
Calderbank	131	10	15	23,289	8,725	10
Airdrie: Clarkston	443	38	36	64,363	41,672	100
Airdrie: Flowerhill	721	66	25	111,124	63,656	204
Airdrie: High	405	28	–	43,856	34,437	86
Airdrie: Jackson	323	45	19	60,985	37,908	89
Airdrie: New Monkland	347	27	21	44,651	17,704	120
Greengairs	144	8	–	20,615	11,242	–
Airdrie: St Columba's	242	10	–	20,407	16,122	51
Airdrie: The New Wellwynd	725	82	14	109,514	56,613	76
Bargeddie	139	11	–	71,576	32,729	12
Bellshill: Macdonald Memorial	286	21	20	40,855	26,840	18
Bellshill: Orbiston	243	23	17	17,420	9,022	8
Bellshill: West	773	64	40	65,978	42,775	50
Blantyre: Livingstone Memorial	277	22	31	54,708	27,309	125
Blantyre: Old	347	16	20	43,909	42,987	15
Blantyre: St Andrew's	277	24	25	68,579	38,237	54
Bothwell	534	53	45	117,799	75,426	100
Caldercruix and Longriggend	224	12	19	54,917	33,176	18
Carfin	51	8	–	7,919	3,425	–
Newarthill	431	31	21	48,963	33,367	130
Chapelhall	291	24	40	39,850	27,615	72
Chapelton	200	15	27	25,693	15,315	48
Strathaven: Rankin	582	64	45	81,584	51,269	177
Cleland	225	18	–	27,609	16,173	19
Coatbridge: Blairhill Dundyvan	396	29	30	60,504	38,332	101
Coatbridge: Calder	454	27	43	58,590	33,574	105

Congregation	Com	Eld	G	In 06	M&M	–18
Coatbridge: Clifton	232	24	21	43,850	30,145	24
Coatbridge: Middle	389	35	37	46,525	30,755	161
Coatbridge: Old Monkland	325	22	31	47,571	27,388	65
Coatbridge: St Andrew's	681	62	42	90,682	59,286	235
Coatbridge: Townhead	335	23	33	–	29,951	130
Dalserf	255	20	22	–	38,755	57
East Kilbride: Claremont	754	87	40	108,756	57,889	214
East Kilbride: Greenhills	172	15	35	32,695	15,456	20
East Kilbride: Moncreiff	853	69	52	113,042	64,706	300
East Kilbride: Mossneuk	265	19	–	41,898	17,387	230
East Kilbride: Old	694	73	56	91,799	56,782	129
East Kilbride: South	386	44	48	84,402	60,677	25
East Kilbride: Stewartfield	–	–	–	10,770	–	–
East Kilbride: West	601	39	71	60,073	42,637	175
East Kilbride: Westwood	694	44	128	81,848	53,977	1
Glasford	187	10	25	18,828	10,964	–
Strathaven: East	295	32	34	50,235	28,633	40
Hamilton: Burnbank	116	13	–	31,676	15,247	7
Hamilton: North	153	31	28	34,129	22,451	18
Hamilton: Cadzow	732	64	75	103,508	67,579	159
Hamilton: Gilmour and Whitehill	182	27	–	31,220	25,209	70
Hamilton: Hillhouse	440	50	31	83,292	55,857	38
Hamilton: Old	579	69	39	113,751	82,509	98
Hamilton: St Andrew's	343	35	27	61,320	41,599	143
Hamilton: St John's	583	57	53	110,352	74,179	224
Hamilton: South	297	31	37	55,296	34,206	34
Quarter	98	12	17	23,155	8,956	19
Hamilton: Trinity	321	29	–	40,920	27,729	116
Hamilton: West	387	29	–	66,914	44,587	25
Holytown	319	20	34	42,664	31,547	99
Kirk o' Shotts	200	11	14	28,666	18,732	20
Larkhall: Chalmers	159	16	26	33,808	24,399	13
Larkhall: St Machan's	572	54	52	106,142	56,053	119
Larkhall: Trinity	324	19	37	53,994	32,427	142
Motherwell: Crosshill	483	56	62	72,181	49,527	110
Motherwell: Dalziel St Andrew's	583	75	60	108,965	66,724	150
Motherwell: Manse Road	236	33	26	45,147	27,462	130
Motherwell: North	209	29	43	46,163	28,680	250
Motherwell: St Margaret's	374	18	23	–	26,293	144
Motherwell: St Mary's	936	106	91	111,609	64,648	285
Motherwell: South Dalziel	375	60	16	86,775	58,601	90
Newmains: Bonkle	166	18	–	38,251	18,317	20
Newmains: Coltness Memorial	236	28	26	51,996	27,070	83
New Stevenston: Wrangholm Kirk	183	11	18	41,445	25,396	55
Overtown	295	27	49	44,794	27,854	210
Shotts: Calderhead Erskine	596	38	40	65,534	48,067	160
Stonehouse: St Ninian's	442	47	48	70,465	48,539	25
Strathaven: Avendale Old and Drumclog	741	63	40	–	73,862	105

Congregation	Com	Eld	G	In 06	M&M	–18
Strathaven: West	235	18	31	48,931	29,128	50
Uddingston: Burnhead	289	20	12	39,052	27,780	95
Uddingston: Old	699	63	72	106,071	69,279	152
Uddingston: Park	179	14	25	61,697	42,110	42
Uddingston: Viewpark	481	51	37	77,191	37,454	300
Wishaw: Cambusnethan North	534	44	–	75,939	51,642	150
Wishaw: Cambusnethan Old and Morningside	535	48	22	73,183	55,694	166
Wishaw: Craigneuk and Belhaven	221	24	27	47,387	33,214	22
Wishaw: Old	353	35	–	40,545	29,525	82
Wishaw: St Mark's	465	40	42	66,979	47,107	171
Wishaw: South Wishaw	599	38	–	98,849	64,709	26

18. Dumbarton

Congregation	Com	Eld	G	In 06	M&M	–18
Alexandria	432	40	27	64,018	41,494	40
Arrochar	58	–	12	18,909	6,228	54
Luss	93	9	29	37,366	11,592	39
Baldernock	232	18	–	47,269	27,443	21
Bearsden: Killermont	706	71	69	139,473	83,345	194
Bearsden: New Kilpatrick	1,702	130	113	285,183	149,729	170
Bearsden: North	596	81	73	86,050	70,046	20
Bearsden: South	791	82	41	169,745	95,370	62
Bearsden: Westerton Fairlie Memorial	470	49	48	77,301	56,582	60
Bonhill	909	59	–	83,664	52,530	140
Cardross	442	33	35	93,773	60,311	50
Clydebank: Abbotsford	330	26	–	49,212	36,040	27
Clydebank: Faifley	234	23	39	41,348	20,446	18
Clydebank: Kilbowie St Andrew's	309	23	33	44,465	31,629	140
Clydebank: Radnor Park	234	32	31	47,317	34,091	6
Clydebank: St Cuthbert's	132	18	23	–	12,851	5
Duntocher	325	–	25	63,611	29,038	–
Craigrownie	224	23	21	33,448	24,334	18
Rosneath: St Modan's	173	11	24	26,483	16,057	9
Dalmuir: Barclay	295	13	29	41,989	26,876	45
Dumbarton: Riverside	699	80	78	114,496	67,909	338
Dumbarton: St Andrew's	134	27	16	31,988	19,671	10
Dumbarton: West Kirk	334	45	20	–	35,375	45
Garelochhead	180	19	–	56,860	35,849	88
Helensburgh: Park	466	51	35	73,151	54,605	21
Helensburgh: St Columba	538	49	39	103,647	64,627	62
Helensburgh: The West Kirk	612	56	47	119,541	77,966	50
Jamestown	382	23	23	52,955	34,513	15
Kilmaronock Gartocharn	270	11	–	29,034	20,237	16
Milngavie: Cairns	676	46	–	122,173	69,954	60
Milngavie: St Luke's	408	41	30	68,621	43,563	37
Milngavie: St Paul's	1,118	97	101	213,168	102,949	110
Old Kilpatrick Bowling	312	29	32	50,560	29,769	155
Renton: Trinity	284	24	–	34,062	23,237	10
Rhu and Shandon	294	33	50	72,382	50,037	32

Congregation	Com	Eld	G	In 06	M&M	–18
19. Argyll						
Appin	85	14	19	14,790	9,959	12
Lismore	54	8	10	12,400	5,310	13
Ardchattan	140	11	8	19,654	9,932	14
Ardrishaig	176	26	30	36,816	26,295	43
South Knapdale	37	6	–	6,099	5,130	–
Campbeltown: Highland	478	36	29	50,081	33,213	10
Campbeltown: Lorne and Lowland	912	61	60	79,556	51,697	73
Coll	16	3	–	3,358	1,293	–
Connel	151	24	20	46,850	23,367	18
Colonsay and Oronsay	16	2	–	3,524	2,763	–
Craignish	41	–	–	13,367	4,928	–
Kilbrandon and Kilchattan	90	–	–	23,170	11,668	–
Kilninver and Kilmelford	60	6	–	9,599	6,299	2
Cumlodden, Lochfyneside and Lochgair	101	12	13	20,741	11,738	18
Dunoon: St John's	237	29	30	38,931	27,017	20
Sandbank	147	13	–	18,279	12,075	5
Dunoon: The High Kirk	410	41	39	–	33,627	19
Innellan	112	11	–	25,932	12,108	–
Toward	113	–	–	17,941	9,074	–
Gigha and Cara	38	7	–	10,334	6,231	–
Glassary, Kilmartin and Ford	119	11	–	23,096	16,394	10
North Knapdale	71	10	–	29,670	22,101	–
Glenaray and Inveraray	117	15	11	20,582	15,308	2
Glenorchy and Innishael	82	7	–	10,125	4,079	–
Strathfillan	47	4	–	11,038	3,712	–
Iona	23	–	–	5,212	4,529	–
Kilfinichen and Kilvickeon and the Ross of Mull	33	–	–	13,357	6,394	–
Jura	44	6	–	13,542	5,444	18
Kilarrow	94	17	14	26,838	16,905	10
Kilberry	12	–	–	5,437	998	–
Tarbert	167	18	28	33,099	20,712	17
Kilcalmonell	56	7	10	9,021	2,947	7
Kilchoman	88	10	–	16,844	17,668	17
Kilmeny	40	6	–	10,283	7,471	20
Portnahaven	19	5	16	5,350	2,865	4
Kilchrenan and Dalavich	35	4	8	9,702	8,555	–
Muckairn	132	15	13	22,857	11,473	25
Kildalton and Oa	122	15	16	31,951	18,992	26
Kilfinan	30	6	8	4,639	2,354	–
Kilmodan and Colintraive	139	13	–	19,405	15,460	20
Kyles	167	17	22	25,696	18,893	2
Killean and Kilchenzie	175	12	26	32,196	20,753	15
Kilmore and Oban	622	59	49	95,877	50,057	37
Kilmun (St Munn's)	116	11	27	16,374	9,211	7
Strone and Ardentinny	125	9	14	21,957	14,520	9
Kirn	357	31	–	77,796	43,793	12
Lochgilphead	217	–	17	–	20,348	–

Congregation	Com	Eld	G	In 06	M&M	–18
Lochgoilhead and Kilmorich	103	13	15	23,787	18,384	7
Mull, Isle of, Kilninian and Kilmore	33	4	–	11,314	5,213	–
Salen and Ulva	42	7	–	13,110	5,298	–
Tobermory	79	14	–	21,371	8,899	–
Torosay and Kinlochspelvie	25	5	–	5,817	4,177	2
Rothesay: Trinity	459	43	42	59,487	37,688	90
Saddell and Carradale	225	13	26	28,055	19,018	2
Skipness	30	3	–	7,169	4,438	7
Southend	250	14	18	33,763	20,381	22
Strachur and Strachlachlan	138	21	20	30,775	21,970	11
The United Church of Bute	652	45	–	67,343	49,535	25
Tiree	106	–	22	19,324	13,105	–

22. Falkirk

Congregation	Com	Eld	G	In 06	M&M	–18
Airth	157	8	19	–	27,109	35
Blackbraes and Shieldhill	185	14	17	23,242	15,661	13
Bo'ness: Old	463	39	30	63,348	39,952	96
Bo'ness: St Andrew's	557	32	–	67,553	43,294	85
Bonnybridge: St Helen's	360	17	32	47,582	34,051	123
Bothkennar and Carronshore	271	30	–	31,330	24,257	10
Brightons	736	42	55	123,017	58,523	244
Carriden	519	50	22	52,586	34,639	17
Cumbernauld: Abronhill	300	34	37	58,416	28,980	313
Cumbernauld: Condorrat	456	35	34	64,363	34,517	140
Cumbernauld: Kildrum	399	36	–	47,876	25,163	193
Cumbernauld: Old	492	40	–	60,458	41,755	103
Cumbernauld: St Mungo's	326	–	–	51,481	19,108	104
Denny: Dunipace	405	37	19	61,114	35,525	111
Denny: Old	456	61	26	66,561	41,874	100
Denny: Westpark	652	50	36	74,916	52,539	100
Falkirk: Bainsford	307	13	–	–	27,350	66
Falkirk: Camelon	394	31	–	79,895	52,757	24
Falkirk: Erskine	526	46	42	76,031	49,659	20
Falkirk: Grahamston United	444	46	37	68,679	45,398	72
Falkirk: Laurieston	252	19	30	39,115	24,759	12
Redding and Westquarter	189	13	36	29,146	13,953	30
Falkirk: Old and St Modan's	728	50	32	113,088	68,589	117
Falkirk: St Andrew's West	568	39	–	–	64,119	59
Falkirk: St James'	264	27	15	33,005	26,591	–
Grangemouth: Abbotsgrange	708	67	–	72,515	60,897	133
Grangemouth: Kirk of the Holy Rood	660	40	–	59,584	35,408	88
Grangemouth: Zetland	884	80	75	110,115	65,938	153
Haggs	301	33	14	46,402	29,544	77
Larbert: East	672	46	36	92,582	52,743	201
Larbert: Old	640	37	19	95,435	60,707	210
Larbert: West	523	42	41	71,293	47,276	214
Muiravonside	220	18	12	30,524	23,919	–
Polmont: Old	438	29	75	77,779	47,155	23

Congregation	Com	Eld	G	In 06	M&M	–18
Slamannan	252	8	–	–	21,175	12
Stenhouse and Carron	451	44	23	73,459	47,151	19

23. Stirling

Congregation	Com	Eld	G	In 06	M&M	–18
Aberfoyle	134	12	19	20,800	12,436	40
Port of Menteith	67	8	–	12,692	4,113	25
Alloa: North	280	17	21	47,054	29,306	26
Alloa: St Mungo's	627	43	50	59,598	46,284	15
Alloa: West	225	14	40	39,653	28,666	4
Alva	595	55	32	71,157	43,349	152
Balfron	162	18	17	77,051	37,440	15
Fintry	149	10	16	13,091	12,041	–
Balquhidder	98	5	–	19,669	14,656	6
Killin and Ardeonaig	156	9	19	25,043	16,334	10
Bannockburn: Allan	466	39	–	63,967	37,355	65
Bannockburn: Ladywell	483	32	22	–	25,240	13
Bridge of Allan	804	51	–	116,859	81,586	65
Buchanan	105	7	–	23,187	13,209	20
Drymen	306	18	24	60,282	30,658	25
Buchlyvie	237	13	16	30,673	17,522	15
Gartmore	80	13	–	15,336	11,960	6
Callander	679	52	43	116,111	69,793	102
Cambusbarron: The Bruce Memorial	381	27	–	40,703	26,493	31
Clackmannan	502	32	45	67,561	51,703	48
Cowie and Plean	327	17	–	34,295	17,924	–
Fallin	264	8	–	36,599	25,199	110
Dollar	651	46	54	100,604	54,997	65
Glendevon	51	3	–	6,851	2,298	–
Muckhart	131	8	–	16,930	10,748	15
Dunblane: Cathedral	998	88	68	205,143	105,747	288
Dunblane: St Blane's	405	42	31	90,914	57,201	25
Gargunnock	192	14	–	22,602	17,087	15
Kilmadock	202	9	–	9,695	9,596	8
Kincardine-in-Menteith	98	8	–	11,353	6,403	20
Killearn	565	40	47	74,988	46,293	70
Kippen	305	22	21	30,697	22,603	2
Norrieston	139	13	13	15,185	12,704	5
Lecropt	254	15	26	43,212	30,697	–
Logie	578	44	47	95,010	59,729	33
Menstrie	397	29	26	60,876	41,970	32
Sauchie and Coalsnaughton	811	36	15	57,103	42,408	18
Stirling: Allan Park South	239	41	28	53,520	29,808	26
Stirling: Church of the Holy Rude	263	33	–	40,864	26,610	12
Stirling: North	527	39	26	66,836	38,068	35
Stirling: St Columba's	554	66	–	92,702	57,674	103
Stirling: St Mark's	267	9	–	32,350	26,100	–
Stirling: St Ninians Old	813	59	–	83,836	57,427	45
Stirling: Viewfield	409	22	35	50,408	44,083	25

Congregation	Com	Eld	G	In 06	M&M	–18
Strathblane	203	26	39	70,125	46,896	52
Tillicoultry	825	57	47	80,958	57,248	110
Tullibody: St Serf's	522	19	30	70,003	44,188	93

24. Dunfermline

Congregation	Com	Eld	G	In 06	M&M	–18
Aberdour: St Fillan's	393	27	–	68,111	42,100	43
Beath and Cowdenbeath: North	214	18	–	44,112	24,000	79
Cairneyhill	192	19	–	26,077	14,600	32
Limekilns	319	47	–	70,807	45,000	30
Carnock and Oakley	220	21	15	56,600	31,600	24
Cowdenbeath: Trinity	420	25	–	51,467	28,500	68
Culross and Torryburn	307	22	–	43,907	28,400	12
Dalgety	627	39	33	115,561	59,000	180
Dunfermline: Abbey	772	70	–	123,360	75,600	200
Dunfermline: Gillespie Memorial	354	64	23	113,036	65,200	80
Dunfermline: North	215	17	–	34,312	20,800	15
Dunfermline: St Andrew's Erskine	244	26	16	43,403	24,000	180
Dunfermline: St Leonard's	501	42	30	70,558	34,000	101
Dunfermline: St Margaret's	399	48	29	54,258	36,000	24
Dunfermline: St Ninian's	325	39	37	40,734	24,000	90
Dunfermline: St Paul's East	–	–	–	11,139	–	–
Dunfermline: Townhill and Kingseat	422	32	34	61,546	37,400	30
Inverkeithing: St John's	186	19	–	34,963	21,000	82
North Queensferry	89	7	–	18,033	10,000	29
Inverkeithing: St Peter's	310	7	–	17,970	18,000	20
Kelty	378	25	49	73,472	35,000	78
Lochgelly and Benarty: St Serf's	562	49	–	56,035	31,862	30
Rosyth	307	24	–	36,444	23,000	56
Saline and Blairingone	185	14	21	42,882	31,000	20
Tulliallan and Kincardine	564	49	60	62,403	30,300	12

25. Kirkcaldy

Congregation	Com	Eld	G	In 06	M&M	–18
Auchterderran: St Fothad's	408	24	–	33,210	27,178	17
Kinglassie	189	12	–	–	13,160	3
Auchtertool	79	7	–	8,190	3,126	8
Kirkcaldy: Linktown	400	41	30	50,870	36,225	24
Buckhaven	226	23	–	35,201	23,678	9
Burntisland	574	41	50	44,502	44,578	28
Denbeath	80	4		5,683	4,870	8
Methilhill	163	16		23,825	11,048	9
Dysart	373	31	25	50,975	31,379	37
Glenrothes: Christ's Kirk	304	24	43	–	18,428	21
Glenrothes: St Columba's	608	35	20	61,272	41,089	43
Glenrothes: St Margaret's	399	36	38	62,704	37,069	65
Glenrothes: St Ninian's	300	44	13	61,461	38,231	23
Innerleven: East	168	8	20	26,123	14,956	57
Kennoway, Windygates and Balgonie: St Kenneth's	742	50	78	82,145	36,765	31
Kinghorn	445	29	–	62,232	44,897	52

Congregation	Com	Eld	G	In 06	M&M	–18
Kirkcaldy: Abbotshall	671	62	–	69,924	51,863	81
Kirkcaldy: Pathhead	568	43	65	85,354	55,002	164
Kirkcaldy: St Andrew's	277	24	30	45,917	28,876	11
Kirkcaldy: St Bryce Kirk	683	47	–	82,291	58,582	49
Kirkcaldy: St John's	379	48	51	71,100	41,439	15
Kirkcaldy: Templehall	338	14	20	46,928	22,108	12
Kirkcaldy: Torbain	261	29	23	36,877	21,897	25
Kirkcaldy: Viewforth	334	12	–	33,312	19,707	5
Thornton	220	10	–	20,043	14,302	24
Leslie: Trinity	286	23	31	30,666	22,555	4
Leven	716	45	–	93,254	49,874	75
Markinch	607	40	45	59,130	39,531	28
Methil	368	18	33	31,797	24,715	8
Wemyss	146	11	27	20,648	23,442	14

26. St Andrews

Congregation	Com	Eld	G	In 06	M&M	–18
Abdie and Dunbog	174	19	–	15,695	11,470	–
Newburgh	269	16	–	23,819	14,251	–
Anstruther	343	27	–	45,548	28,143	27
Auchtermuchty	306	20	22	36,755	19,509	22
Balmerino	156	14	17	–	17,447	8
Wormit	296	18	35	29,272	18,057	20
Boarhills and Dunino	163	8	–	16,521	12,825	–
St Andrews: Martyrs'	335	–	31	37,633	32,524	–
Cameron	93	11	15	16,918	8,782	17
St Andrews: St Leonard's	621	48	28	105,420	67,902	30
Carnbee	111	16	22	16,853	8,746	10
Pittenweem	307	18	27	30,820	19,146	17
Cellardyke	305	23	47	40,196	21,796	12
Kilrenny	119	11	18	23,393	15,032	15
Ceres, Kemback and Springfield	466	46	–	108,757	62,373	34
Crail	425	32	47	48,274	34,710	15
Kingsbarns	100	9	–	–	8,286	–
Creich, Flisk and Kilmany	123	9	18	21,435	14,486	8
Monimail	113	11	–	17,239	14,636	20
Cupar: Old and St Michael of Tarvit	635	50	18	–	64,846	74
Cupar: St John's	818	43	45	68,316	42,506	56
Dairsie	130	9	17	16,976	8,628	6
Edenshead and Strathmiglo	232	13	19	29,614	16,197	7
Elie	392	32	63	61,073	45,351	10
Kilconquhar and Colinsburgh	215	17	–	31,262	21,002	12
Falkland	316	22	–	–	20,446	16
Freuchie	239	16	26	26,370	14,641	–
Howe of Fife	776	37	–	53,293	41,255	–
Largo and Newburn	280	7	–	40,154	25,396	15
Largo: St David's	185	17	51	27,316	17,771	4
Largoward	89	6	–	11,301	4,622	20
St Monans	302	15	47	–	32,528	60

Congregation	Com	Eld	G	In 06	M&M	–18
Leuchars: St Athernase	502	26	34	58,179	36,555	14
Newport-on-Tay	396	42	–	69,304	48,962	90
St Andrews: Holy Trinity	600	31	52	69,628	45,657	40
St Andrews: Hope Park	695	87	42	122,597	80,743	45
Strathkinness	125	12	12	18,726	12,759	–
Tayport	462	35	29	42,640	30,368	25

27. Dunkeld and Meigle

Aberfeldy	254	19	16	54,654	23,774	135
Amulree and Strathbraan	15	3	–	–	2,897	–
Dull and Weem	97	11	19	15,195	9,173	15
Alyth	818	45	40	81,562	44,433	31
Ardler, Kettins and Meigle	464	25	43	41,555	32,919	30
Bendochy	91	11	–	19,032	9,133	5
Coupar Angus: Abbey	372	33	17	48,981	31,480	84
Blair Atholl and Struan	148	20	13	19,974	17,500	12
Tenandry	68	7	–	22,080	9,409	3
Blairgowrie	969	56	–	83,538	55,000	24
Braes of Rannoch	35	9	–	14,415	7,500	–
Foss and Rannoch	122	17	23	28,710	16,000	11
Caputh and Clunie	188	24	15	26,423	18,216	20
Kinclaven	153	16	11	18,046	12,500	–
Dunkeld	437	29	24	88,863	62,849	37
Fortingall and Glenlyon	50	9	–	15,901	10,178	4
Kenmore and Lawers	90	8	22	28,835	18,000	–
Grantully, Logierait and Strathtay	163	16	13	34,232	23,281	26
Kirkmichael, Straloch and Glenshee	139	14	–	12,552	10,450	8
Rattray	482	39	32	37,333	21,886	16
Pitlochry	482	38	25	84,080	50,833	80

28. Perth

Abernethy and Dron	247	18	16	–	19,482	11
Arngask	141	13	23	13,361	12,204	35
Almondbank Tibbermore	330	25	46	34,093	23,873	45
Ardoch	172	17	35	34,945	16,900	20
Blackford	92	14	–	23,444	7,514	10
Auchterarder	702	44	58	84,641	52,445	33
Auchtergaven and Moneydie	513	21	30	41,181	29,484	49
Cargill Burrelton	342	17	37	43,264	27,141	20
Collace	127	9	20	16,679	11,254	10
Cleish	262	21	18	61,177	35,283	–
Fossoway: St Serf's and Devonside	220	21	–	37,994	24,218	–
Comrie	481	31	28	65,816	38,775	15
Dundurn	62	7	–	15,464	6,987	5
Crieff	943	55	48	102,287	49,398	40
Dunbarney and Forgandenny	630	37	43	59,555	38,783	39
Errol	299	21	21	31,017	24,682	22
Kilspindie and Rait	72	6	–	–	5,626	9

Congregation	Com	Eld	G	In 06	M&M	–18
Fowlis Wester	122	11	–	16,635	7,386	10
Madderty	102	14	13	16,580	7,387	17
Monzie	101	9	–	14,468	8,019	–
Gask	128	12	14	13,406	12,991	–
Methven and Logiealmond	346	25	18	25,806	17,205	–
Kinross	668	32	30	73,300	50,061	110
Muthill	298	22	13	32,459	24,322	31
Trinity Gask and Kinkell	61	4	–	8,369	2,896	–
Orwell and Portmoak	519	46	–	73,391	40,730	100
Perth: Craigie	676	31	40	56,891	34,252	26
Perth: Kinnoull	464	33	29	60,272	39,147	50
Perth: Letham St Mark's	596	8	31	76,287	47,882	50
Perth: Moncreiffe	245	13	–	8,785	10,674	361
Perth: North	1,287	101	26	203,700	109,154	41
Perth: Riverside	70	9	–	–	3,134	30
Perth: St John the Baptist's	741	41	–	91,589	58,902	–
Perth: St Leonard's-in-the-Fields and Trinity	596	73	–	100,161	64,312	10
Perth: St Matthew's	936	59	42	107,040	65,903	38
Redgorton and Stanley	412	34	–	37,111	25,314	35
St Madoes and Kinfauns	347	28	27	35,900	19,899	45
St Martin's	188	6	16	9,769	6,032	12
Scone: New	561	40	63	63,517	37,840	47
Scone: Old	667	39	39	59,967	41,578	–
The Stewartry of Strathearn	504	37	–	57,214	34,427	51

29. Dundee

Congregation	Com	Eld	G	In 06	M&M	–18
Abernyte	92	10	–	12,220	9,002	25
Inchture and Kinnaird	249	28	–	26,981	15,958	10
Longforgan	221	19	23	32,627	18,617	–
Auchterhouse	160	13	22	22,674	16,068	18
Murroes and Tealing	317	18	16	63,223	16,468	12
Dundee: Balgay	500	44	34	75,317	46,427	65
Dundee: Barnhill St Margaret's	829	68	50	111,522	75,857	37
Dundee: Broughty Ferry New Kirk	1,078	83	–	144,145	82,454	43
Dundee: Broughty Ferry St James'	242	13	32	52,668	29,648	47
Dundee: Broughty Ferry St Luke's and Queen Street	511	55	41	80,165	53,620	46
Dundee: Broughty Ferry St Stephen's and West	356	23	–	40,014	27,224	12
Dundee: Camperdown	187	20	16	27,930	17,872	10
Dundee: Chalmers Ardler	244	20	31	72,505	41,855	161
Dundee: Clepington and Fairmuir	469	34	–	49,803	30,604	100
Dundee: Craigiebank	284	12	–	51,865	33,025	98
Dundee: Douglas and Mid Craigie	208	25	–	34,555	17,478	76
Dundee: Downfield South	373	37	28	67,631	42,288	169
Dundee: Dundee (St Mary's)	660	62	30	73,373	64,887	24
Dundee: Lochee Old and St Luke's	240	22	–	27,543	26,296	6
Dundee: Lochee West	506	38	14	32,605	28,854	62
Dundee: Logie and St John's Cross	363	18	30	123,435	59,408	60
Dundee: Mains	152	11	–	16,982	13,640	7

Congregation	Com	Eld	G	In 06	M&M	–18
Dundee: Mains of Fintry	137	13	–	43,295	28,194	18
Dundee: Meadowside St Paul's	538	282	33	71,549	48,184	69
Dundee: Menzieshill	399	26	–	39,723	28,681	140
Dundee: St Andrew's	716	74	31	–	59,978	27
Dundee: St David's High Kirk	391	49	–	54,650	36,722	75
Dundee: Steeple	342	38	–	122,190	62,982	40
Dundee: Stobswell	553	43	–	70,116	47,322	18
Dundee: Strathmartine	431	36	38	–	39,187	8
Dundee: Trinity	664	55	33	52,822	33,125	930
Dundee: West	424	27	–	69,642	46,104	–
Dundee: Whitfield	–	–	–	14,127	0	–
Fowlis and Liff	156	14	13	19,748	21,004	17
Lundie and Muirhead of Liff	358	24	–	40,854	20,046	24
Invergowrie	449	45	63	71,703	36,966	121
Monifieth: Panmure	426	33	–	43,700	32,836	49
Monifieth: St Rule's	615	29	40	55,205	37,504	15
Monifieth: South	410	22	38	47,216	29,351	142
Monikie and Newbigging	250	18	–	–	20,524	8

30. Angus

Congregation	Com	Eld	G	In 06	M&M	–18
Aberlemno	199	11	–	16,531	12,226	14
Guthrie and Rescobie	232	9	14	21,710	13,483	16
Arbirlot	214	12	–	18,923	16,459	20
Carmyllie	133	6	12	15,331	14,316	8
Arbroath: Knox's	395	27	34	39,096	23,979	9
Arbroath: St Vigeans	649	49	29	60,270	40,705	30
Arbroath: Old and Abbey	664	45	45	87,566	53,547	65
Arbroath: St Andrew's	791	50	25	131,363	60,845	150
Arbroath: West Kirk	1,014	86	54	86,173	63,291	91
Barry	240	16	16	26,001	16,177	10
Carnoustie	468	40	35	70,169	45,113	53
Brechin: Cathedral	989	41	17	–	47,404	20
Brechin: Gardner Memorial	571	36	12	43,196	34,097	5
Carnoustie: Panbride	766	37	–	61,444	38,434	65
Colliston	200	9	12	17,727	11,022	15
Friockheim Kinnell	229	16	24	18,894	13,629	10
Inverkeilor and Lunan	205	10	18	21,614	14,922	4
Dun and Hillside	471	41	8	54,730	28,260	50
Dunnichen, Letham and Kirkden	363	20	30	42,227	25,384	24
Eassie and Nevay	60	8	–	8,564	8,301	–
Newtyle	299	16	21	26,051	20,334	20
Edzell Lethnot	407	26	34	37,872	27,103	10
Fern Careston Menmuir	130	10	–	14,488	11,773	4
Glenesk	59	2	–	4,474	5,039	–
Farnell	111	7	–	4,313	9,029	–
Forfar: East and Old	1,347	50	36	85,588	61,194	83
Forfar: Lowson Memorial	979	38	29	71,428	45,666	113
Forfar: St Margaret's	937	40	26	67,578	54,558	85

Congregation	Com	Eld	G	In 06	M&M	–18
Glamis, Inverarity and Kinnettles	421	33	–	43,320	31,189	36
Inchbrayock	212	11	–	42,254	23,282	–
Montrose: Melville South	349	19	–	33,524	21,634	–
Kirriemuir: St Andrew's	387	27	49	53,283	29,887	16
Oathlaw Tannadice	184	8	–	14,504	13,466	22
Montrose: Old and St Andrew's	961	53	–	123,776	63,319	150
The Glens and Kirriemuir: Old	1,188	96	–	159,247	85,021	50
The Isla Parishes	308	21	13	–	24,017	20

31. Aberdeen

Congregation	Com	Eld	G	In 06	M&M	–18
Aberdeen: Bridge of Don Oldmachar	299	6	–	–	24,840	200
Aberdeen: Cove	72	4	–	13,699	0	32
Aberdeen: Craigiebuckler	844	70	58	107,700	53,910	217
Aberdeen: Ferryhill	493	63	34	78,504	45,015	27
Aberdeen: Garthdee	273	17	29	–	17,735	12
Aberdeen: Gilcomston South	319	26	–	157,097	75,301	63
Aberdeen: High Hilton	575	52	50	138,314	65,436	55
Aberdeen: Holburn West	524	45	38	98,379	69,741	25
Aberdeen: Mannofield	1,593	125	65	181,469	112,380	180
Aberdeen: Mastrick	429	25	17	46,701	23,755	60
Aberdeen: Middlefield	169	9	–	13,311	1,014	25
Aberdeen: Midstocket	782	68	–	118,443	98,347	30
Aberdeen: New Stockethill	89	–	–	26,531	0	19
Aberdeen: Northfield	311	14	23	27,399	17,414	60
Aberdeen: Queen Street	909	68	–	72,565	63,605	42
Aberdeen: Queen's Cross	659	53	38	152,019	95,463	72
Aberdeen: Rubislaw	651	86	42	137,320	83,840	–
Aberdeen: Ruthrieston West	410	35	29	60,554	36,738	16
Aberdeen: St Columba's Bridge of Don	367	28	–	80,005	54,284	231
Aberdeen: St George's Tillydrone	161	10	19	19,694	8,077	12
Aberdeen: St John's Church for Deaf People	106	5	–	–	–	–
Aberdeen: St Machar's Cathedral	631	42	–	102,813	65,937	20
Aberdeen: St Mark's	528	48	28	86,979	53,076	71
Aberdeen: St Mary's	500	55	21	51,705	26,391	76
Aberdeen: St Nicholas Kincorth, South of	472	34	32	54,807	34,446	65
Aberdeen: St Nicholas Uniting, Kirk of	509	62	18	85,373	17,405	4
Aberdeen: St Stephen's	257	29	17	57,963	31,252	51
Aberdeen: South Holburn	937	61	–	115,573	82,690	45
Aberdeen: Summerhill	194	20	–	27,206	17,164	20
Aberdeen: Torry St Fittick's	538	31	29	49,404	30,922	3
Aberdeen: Woodside	348	33	27	47,548	27,321	87
Bucksburn Stoneywood	555	22	27	47,684	33,292	17
Cults	853	65	–	136,782	81,597	35
Dyce	1,313	76	36	–	52,776	271
Kingswells	442	44	24	48,210	29,361	32
Newhills	926	43	61	91,027	61,659	175
Peterculter	717	52	–	86,901	53,730	202

Congregation	Com	Eld	G	In 06	M&M	–18
32. Kincardine and Deeside						
Aberluthnott	225	9	19	17,656	11,896	5
Laurencekirk	511	13	35	28,247	18,949	18
Aboyne and Dinnet	451	12	32	64,311	37,779	25
Cromar	265	11	–	–	16,585	8
Arbuthnott and Bervie	581	35	–	57,239	33,030	40
Banchory-Devenick and Maryculter/						
Cookney	377	19	–	45,712	26,767	52
Banchory-Ternan: East	645	50	36	98,310	47,080	108
Banchory-Ternan: West	670	39	37	111,885	51,216	50
Birse and Feughside	276	31	20	34,739	31,355	15
Braemar and Crathie	280	32	–	64,391	32,521	21
Drumoak and Durris	466	23	–	65,986	31,741	74
Glenmuick (Ballater)	358	24	30	49,901	28,536	10
Kinneff	155	5	5	7,623	6,621	–
Stonehaven: South	298	26	12	44,238	25,520	16
Mearns Coastal	334	18	–	26,845	24,113	6
Mid Deeside	814	50	24	55,489	42,390	–
Newtonhill	395	16	20	31,814	23,644	155
Portlethen	518	20	–	53,621	38,103	177
Stonehaven: Dunnottar	862	33	23	63,150	46,241	21
Stonehaven: Fetteresso	936	49	35	172,859	67,795	278
West Mearns	562	–	52	40,921	33,134	–
33. Gordon						
Barthol Chapel	98	10	10	7,468	6,134	20
Tarves	496	31	37	–	28,690	15
Belhelvie	396	38	24	67,843	32,756	61
Blairdaff	98	8	–	7,203	7,377	–
Chapel of Garioch	325	29	19	37,001	22,551	66
Cluny	202	12	10	20,184	15,507	12
Monymusk	122	4	–	17,456	10,198	28
Culsalmond and Rayne	231	7	–	8,725	7,705	20
Daviot	156	8	–	15,558	13,060	10
Cushnie and Tough	289	18	–	29,418	20,608	20
Drumblade	122	7	11	–	4,816	4
Huntly Strathbogie	787	43	28	61,423	37,310	103
Echt	281	14	14	22,200	16,685	17
Midmar	164	7	–	13,774	10,962	3
Ellon	1,745	94	–	123,592	69,489	45
Fintray Kinellar Keithhall	233	21	–	–	24,971	25
Foveran	366	20	–	–	24,466	40
Howe Trinity	672	31	48	46,630	36,946	32
Huntly Cairnie Glass	801	24	35	38,222	33,289	10
Insch-Leslie-Premnay-Oyne	554	43	38	–	34,101	8
Inverurie: St Andrew's	1,237	39	45	106,134	57,476	10
Inverurie: West	780	56	35	88,231	45,514	73
Kemnay	622	41	–	46,977	38,063	137

Congregation	Com	Eld	G	In 06	M&M	–18
Kintore	881	50	30	84,832	57,929	122
Meldrum and Bourtie	547	33	47	65,801	36,928	41
Methlick	356	23	26	43,893	30,368	15
New Machar	489	25	36	48,897	31,697	43
Noth	356	12	–	24,639	15,941	13
Skene	1,568	97	52	132,825	64,267	191
Udny and Pitmedden	488	–	13	62,827	35,125	–
Upper Donside	449	19	–	37,179	24,436	38

34. Buchan

Aberdour	144	10	10	9,859	8,907	12
Pitsligo	135	11	–	19,689	15,409	25
Sandhaven	81	7	–	10,067	7,174	21
Auchaber United	172	13	13	12,637	12,798	10
Auchterless	207	19	13	19,841	13,031	15
Banff	811	31	28	72,472	60,809	185
King Edward	167	27	10	18,218	11,014	16
Crimond	267	12	–	18,067	11,989	21
Lonmay	172	13	12	9,686	8,388	–
St Fergus	207	11	9	9,427	6,925	14
Cruden	489	30	31	53,359	33,466	36
Deer	843	32	20	49,809	29,255	18
Fordyce	514	27	32	53,153	38,400	19
Fraserburgh: Old	817	60	80	117,649	83,852	256
Fraserburgh: South	330	24	–	37,740	30,838	36
Inverallochy and Rathen: East	95	11	–	18,553	3,623	12
Fraserburgh: West	657	41	–	47,509	34,141	70
Rathen: West	113	8	–	11,465	6,237	8
Fyvie	391	25	40	42,695	28,498	–
Rothienorman	154	12	16	13,556	7,205	–
Gardenstown	72	11	34	49,943	29,544	55
Longside	567	26	–	45,731	35,501	132
Macduff	867	43	67	88,488	52,365	140
Marnoch	379	18	11	31,045	25,253	–
Maud and Savoch	250	17	22	25,912	13,950	9
New Deer: St Kane's	466	22	19	41,656	23,728	128
Monquhitter and New Byth	384	21	11	24,311	15,426	17
Turriff: St Andrew's	562	31	19	38,966	25,874	49
New Pitsligo	350	9	–	19,871	14,257	24
Strichen and Tyrie	635	22	–	50,441	24,576	28
Ordiquhill and Cornhill	160	9	10	10,763	8,930	20
Whitehills	302	20	38	33,216	19,847	13
Peterhead: Old	474	34	37	60,925	36,470	50
Peterhead: St Andrew's	576	37	30	55,144	32,889	40
Peterhead: Trinity	360	24	31	113,245	59,649	18
Turriff: St Ninian's and Forglen	967	42	44	69,941	43,952	100

Congregation	Com	Eld	G	In 06	M&M	–18
35. Moray						
Aberlour	345	–	24	37,571	29,631	–
Alves and Burghead	161	18	39	23,108	14,457	9
Kinloss and Findhorn	93	27	10	15,308	11,803	6
Bellie	315	16	37	44,991	32,378	40
Speymouth	222	10	22	20,475	12,354	13
Birnie and Pluscarden	314	26	–	33,517	24,017	10
Elgin: High	711	47	–	72,564	44,785	61
Buckie: North	499	42	57	57,137	34,913	40
Buckie: South and West	318	30	33	–	22,904	221
Enzie	97	7	12	13,924	9,603	5
Cullen and Deskford	387	33	41	39,256	31,493	12
Dallas	60	7	–	8,862	8,223	10
Forres: St Leonard's	274	17	42	62,922	35,963	105
Rafford	78	4	–	16,019	7,270	4
Duffus, Spynie and Hopeman	358	38	28	46,801	30,708	17
Dyke	158	12	17	20,425	14,179	22
Edinkillie	89	13	–	13,936	14,446	5
Elgin: St Giles' and St Columba's South	1,260	101	–	129,890	75,113	159
Findochty	54	10	11	25,726	11,934	30
Portknockie	90	11	28	24,237	10,695	55
Rathven	112	14	21	17,738	10,348	7
Forres: St Laurence	609	40	43	72,088	43,536	12
Keith: North, Newmill, Boharm and Rothiemay	679	62	–	84,640	50,170	132
Keith: St Rufus, Botriphnie and Grange	1,049	63	–	76,274	36,328	130
Knockando, Elchies and Archiestown	274	17	14	19,020	18,038	2
Rothes	329	18	24	28,911	18,430	34
Lossiemouth: St Gerardine's High	389	22	38	–	34,027	22
Lossiemouth: St James'	347	21	42	47,223	30,050	25
Mortlach and Cabrach	406	19	16	22,715	19,854	5
St Andrew's-Lhanbryd and Urquhart	498	28	31	53,910	40,475	45
36. Abernethy						
Abernethy	158	18	–	40,281	22,967	62
Cromdale and Advie	95	2	–	13,358	9,402	5
Alvie and Insh	72	8	–	23,936	16,120	13
Boat of Garten and Kincardine	91	9	20	22,198	13,499	12
Duthil	72	8	17	15,504	5,094	15
Dulnain Bridge	36	5	–	10,848	8,488	2
Grantown-on-Spey	257	18	21	38,280	25,331	12
Kingussie	124	16	–	21,149	7,912	19
Laggan	35	5	–	12,876	7,045	10
Newtonmore	87	14	–	26,073	13,196	8
Rothiemurchus and Aviemore	91	5	–	18,788	13,443	6
Tomintoul, Glenlivet and Inveraven	172	13	–	–	15,569	20

Congregation	Com	Eld	G	In 06	M&M	–18
37. Inverness						
Ardersier	65	14	10	15,384	10,622	17
Petty	75	12	9	19,061	10,206	14
Auldearn and Dalmore	82	6	15	12,148	9,953	5
Nairn: St Ninian's	260	17	32	38,728	25,454	30
Cawdor	183	18	–	29,062	17,495	15
Croy and Dalcross	58	–	10	11,525	8,159	–
Culloden: The Barn	345	28	26	81,802	42,589	140
Daviot and Dunlichity	61	7	–	15,926	10,527	13
Moy, Dalarossie and Tomatin	33	5	9	9,004	7,394	36
Dores and Boleskine	84	7	–	11,650	13,019	10
Inverness: Crown	680	87	64	140,060	73,275	–
Inverness: Dalneigh and Bona	288	19	29	84,687	51,535	47
Inverness: East	337	46	–	139,505	77,329	144
Inverness: Hilton	276	10	25	91,667	32,160	112
Inverness: Inshes	207	15	–	108,959	52,514	45
Inverness: Kinmylies	129	12	–	56,410	15,112	30
Inverness: Ness Bank	619	–	39	114,853	59,467	–
Inverness: Old High St Stephen's	538	60	–	102,782	67,997	72
Inverness: St Columba High	232	–	21	44,601	33,518	–
Inverness: Trinity	346	30	20	76,697	47,525	68
Kilmorack and Erchless	138	17	25	43,260	19,568	30
Kiltarlity	42	6	–	13,284	11,633	–
Kirkhill	75	4	13	14,561	8,802	–
Nairn: Old	878	63	37	106,715	63,430	56
Urquhart and Glenmoriston	130	7	4	52,950	32,389	32
38. Lochaber						
Acharacle	38	2	–	19,576	8,049	12
Ardnamurchan	20	4	–	6,292	4,523	7
Ardgour	56	7	10	12,070	8,185	11
Strontian	27	4	10	9,623	4,042	12
Arisaig and the Small Isles	65	8	17	12,561	6,274	10
Mallaig: St Columba and Knoydart	54	5	–	21,766	16,341	16
Duror	44	7	14	20,663	3,890	10
Glencoe: St Munda's	65	8	23	16,839	9,346	12
Fort Augustus	76	7	15	22,353	11,012	7
Glengarry	33	5	12	13,493	6,811	10
Fort William: Duncansburgh	289	25	21	60,543	37,185	84
Kilmonivaig	83	6	15	17,582	14,142	10
Fort William: MacIntosh Memorial	203	26	17	43,162	28,815	13
Kilmallie	166	18	26	–	29,126	15
Kinlochleven	67	9	19	19,301	10,481	15
Nether Lochaber	52	10	–	–	8,691	7
Morvern	46	6	11	–	7,393	–

Congregation	Com	Eld	G	In 06	M&M	–18
39. Ross						
Alness	97	14	–	35,323	20,940	22
Avoch	32	5	15	15,241	8,360	19
Fortrose and Rosemarkie	116	17	–	36,170	24,855	7
Contin	61	11	–	24,982	13,834	16
Cromarty	53	6	17	20,996	12,563	36
Dingwall: Castle Street	131	16	19	44,450	27,333	4
Dingwall: St Clement's	253	29	26	56,263	35,089	48
Fearn Abbey and Nigg	116	16	–	29,014	18,508	–
Tarbat	70	10	–	16,904	10,178	–
Ferintosh	199	23	31	49,574	29,436	25
Fodderty and Strathpeffer	141	19	22	34,474	18,196	24
Invergordon	167	13	–	52,114	28,883	29
Killearnan	134	19	–	33,203	20,156	19
Knockbain	64	12	–	19,434	11,102	2
Kilmuir and Logie Easter	78	10	27	–	19,339	14
Kiltearn	88	7	–	26,241	16,714	38
Lochbroom and Ullapool	56	5	10	41,663	19,331	20
Resolis and Urquhart	88	7	–	24,638	17,483	14
Rosskeen	135	10	21	45,331	26,674	55
Tain	156	12	21	62,757	31,787	25
Urray and Kilchrist	118	15	17	43,865	24,448	58
40. Sutherland						
Altnaharra and Farr	34	2	–	12,311	7,585	3
Assynt and Stoer	28	1	–	13,723	7,971	14
Clyne	73	9	–	19,770	13,423	8
Kildonan and Loth Helmsdale	39	6	–	11,452	6,312	15
Creich	30	4	16	14,806	11,496	–
Rosehall	23	3	–	7,010	5,130	8
Dornoch Cathedral	390	34	44	101,375	58,797	70
Durness and Kinlochbervie	35	3	10	21,590	13,427	14
Eddrachillis	18	2	–	14,023	7,800	4
Golspie	90	18	14	–	19,115	11
Kincardine Croick and Edderton	77	11	16	26,872	18,274	18
Lairg	51	6	21	23,988	10,130	12
Rogart	24	4	10	14,481	6,485	4
Melness and Tongue	49	7	–	13,744	11,190	7
41. Caithness						
Bower	38	6	11	12,871	6,387	12
Watten	45	4	–	13,454	7,666	28
Canisbay	43	3	19	–	8,866	15
Keiss	29	2	9	10,903	5,228	4
Dunnet	19	3	9	–	5,016	–
Olrig	56	4	11	9,417	5,112	15
Halkirk and Westerdale	49	6	18	18,391	9,260	15
The North Coast Parish	47	14	–	18,322	14,569	11

Congregation	Com	Eld	G	In 06	M&M	–18
The Parish of Latheron	73	12	–	22,974	17,835	35
Thurso: St Peter's and St Andrew's	230	17	44	52,260	41,347	30
Thurso: West	274	25	35	48,421	34,548	38
Wick: Bridge Street	169	12	–	29,285	24,503	–
Wick: Old	213	40	35	50,669	38,659	17
Wick: Pulteneytown and Thrumster	237	14	25	52,104	32,295	280

42. Lochcarron – Skye

Congregation	Com	Eld	G	In 06	M&M	–18
Applecross, Lochcarron and Torridon	84	5	–	34,344	21,243	22
Bracadale and Duirinish	73	9	–	29,059	19,288	55
Gairloch and Dundonnell	103	5	–	67,126	41,057	30
Glenelg and Kintail	55	11	–	29,043	17,348	29
Kilmuir and Stenscholl	74	9	–	39,363	22,261	45
Lochalsh	79	9	29	40,347	23,114	25
Portree	124	8	–	47,744	35,198	33
Snizort	71	8	–	41,297	29,423	41
Strath and Sleat	195	15	18	93,572	44,765	80

43. Uist

Congregation	Com	Eld	G	In 06	M&M	–18
Barra	38	2	–	19,626	5,719	59
Benbecula	74	11	10	39,271	17,509	32
Berneray and Lochmaddy	58	5	–	35,323	16,309	6
Carinish	81	9	18	41,847	27,500	20
Kilmuir and Paible	31	4	–	38,012	19,513	43
Manish-Scarista	41	3	–	30,070	20,543	20
South Uist	60	10	8	21,469	13,687	19
Tarbert	147	13	–	79,817	49,789	60

44. Lewis

Congregation	Com	Eld	G	In 06	M&M	–18
Barvas	91	9	–	65,967	33,823	33
Carloway	45	3	–	29,720	15,390	22
Cross Ness	65	8	–	61,308	21,004	30
Kinloch	42	7	–	29,309	16,375	32
Knock	58	2	–	47,740	26,451	12
Lochs-Crossbost	22	4	–	23,203	9,215	12
Lochs-in-Bernera	30	3	–	22,770	8,967	27
Stornoway: High	248	19	–	124,989	70,826	–
Stornoway: Martin's Memorial	133	10	14	70,668	31,999	80
Stornoway: St Columba	143	16	44	74,791	45,532	132
Uig	36	6	–	22,207	13,820	5

45. Orkney

Congregation	Com	Eld	G	In 06	M&M	–18
Birsay, Harray and Sandwick	376	31	15	35,687	26,937	35
East Mainland	282	23	–	23,547	22,901	8
Eday	6	3	–	2,963	1,092	–
Stronsay: Moncur Memorial	80	12	15	12,294	7,916	18
Evie	38	3	–	6,432	6,805	–
Firth	121	10	17	26,222	13,395	24

Congregation	Com	Eld	G	In 06	M&M	–18
Rendall	53	2	14	8,198	5,716	15
Flotta	26	8	–	3,936	1,769	–
Hoy and Walls	64	13	13	–	2,686	6
Kirkwall: East	460	48	32	58,199	37,634	50
Kirkwall: St Magnus Cathedral	677	51	31	71,638	48,184	–
North Ronaldsay	15	3	–	–	968	–
Sanday	81	10	13	8,732	7,966	10
Orphir	127	11	15	18,653	11,572	10
Stenness	88	9	–	11,985	8,870	2
Papa Westray	11	3	–	5,127	1,766	6
Westray	70	16	22	17,600	11,312	25
Rousay	26	4	8	3,643	2,758	–
Shapinsay	61	8	–	4,573	3,423	6
South Ronaldsay and Burray	173	12	15	17,586	11,949	20
Stromness	376	25	26	50,275	38,750	10

46. Shetland

Burra Isle	42	6	25	8,193	5,139	17
Tingwall	163	19	11	24,150	20,243	36
Delting	97	8	–	19,928	10,275	14
Northmavine	82	9	–	10,017	5,857	8
Dunrossness and St Ninian's inc. Fair Isle	70	18	–	16,725	9,183	55
Sandwick, Cunningsburgh and Quarff	132	11	23	25,125	14,849	43
Fetlar	20	5	–	–	1,323	–
Unst	130	10	17	18,259	9,054	–
Yell	121	13	14	11,414	8,118	–
Lerwick and Bressay	493	36	10	74,291	42,343	87
Nesting and Lunnasting	40	5	18	7,007	6,793	–
Whalsay and Skerries	234	18	20	30,251	13,731	25
Sandsting and Aithsting	48	7	–	8,502	5,619	35
Walls and Sandness	42	9	5	6,930	5,038	12

47. England

Corby: St Andrew's	304	21	31	48,885	30,489	19
Corby: St Ninian's	297	20	11	40,862	29,088	5
Guernsey: St Andrew's in the Grange	234	20	–	49,512	33,022	24
Jersey: St Columba's	130	18	–	58,447	34,933	32
Liverpool: St Andrew's	38	6	7	19,673	8,891	8
London: Crown Court	243	40	6	86,349	55,608	28
London: St Columba's	1,107	46	–	227,376	119,132	108
Newcastle: St Andrew's	113	20	–	–	4,038	12

INDEX OF MINISTERS

NOTE: Ministers who are members of a Presbytery are designated 'A' if holding a parochial appointment in that Presbytery, or 'B' if otherwise qualifying for membership.

'A-1, A-2' etc. indicate the numerical order of congregations in the Presbyteries of Edinburgh, Glasgow and Hamilton.

Also included are:

(1) Ministers who have resigned their seat in Presbytery (List 6-H)

(2) Ministers who hold a Practising Certificate (List 6-I)

(3) Ministers serving overseas (List 6-K)

(4) Auxiliary Ministers (List 6-A)

(5) Ministers ordained for sixty years and upwards (List 6-Q)

(6) Ministers who have died since the publication of the last *Year Book* (List 6-R)

NB *For a list of the Diaconate, see List 6-G.*

Abeledo, B.J.	Greenock/Paisley 14B	Andrew, R.J.M.	Ayr 10B
Acklam, C.R.	West Lothian 2A	Andrews, J.E.	Lothian 3B
Adams, D.G.	Dunfermline 24A	Annand, J.M.	Annandale/Eskdale 7B
Adamson, A.	Ardrossan 12A	Arbuthnott, Mrs J.	List 6-I
Adamson, H.	Irvine/Kilmarnock 11A	Archer, N.D.C.	List 6-I
Aiken, P.W.I.	Wigtown/Stranraer 9A	Armitage, W.L.	Edinburgh 1B
Aitchison, J.W.	Aberdeen 31B	Armstrong, W.R.	G'ock/Paisley 14A
Aitken, A.J.	Glasgow 16B	Arnott, A.D.K.	St Andrews 26A
Aitken, A.R.	Edinburgh 1B	Atkins, Mrs Y.E.S.	Lothian 3A
Aitken, E.D.	Stirling 23B	Atkinson, G.T.	Glasgow 16A-130
Aitken, E.R.	Edinburgh 1B	Attenburrow, A.	Moray 35A
Aitken, F.R.	Ayr 10A	Auffermann, M.	Aberdeen 31A
Aitken, I.M.	Aberdeen 31A	Auld, A.G.	Edinburgh 1B
Aitken, J.D.	Edinburgh 1A-79	Austin, G.	Moray 35A
Albon, D.W.	West Lothian 2A		
Alexander, D.N.	G'ock/Paisley 14B	Baigrie, R.A.	Edinburgh 1B
Alexander, E.J.	Glasgow 16B	Bailey, W.G.	List 6-H
Alexander, H.J.R.	List 6-I	Baillie, D.	Dum'/Kirkcudbright 8B
Alexander, I.W.	List 6-I	Bain, B.	Perth 28A
Alexander, J.S.	St Andrews 26B	Baird, K.S.	Edinburgh 1A-40
Alexander, W.M.	Aberdeen 31B	Baker, Mrs C.	Ayr 10A
Allan, A.G.	Glasgow 16B	Ballentine, Miss A.M.	W' Lothian 2A
Allan, R.T.	Falkirk 22A	Banks, J.	Ayr 10B
Allen, M.A.W.	Glasgow 16A-103	Barber, P.I.	Edinburgh 1A-27
Allen, Ms V.L.	Angus 30A	Barbour, R.A.S.	Lists 6H and 6I
Allison, A.	Dunfermline 24A	Barclay, I.C.	Aberdeen 31A
Allison, Ms M.M.	Glasgow 16A-81	Barclay, N.W.	Falkirk 22B
Allison, R.N.	G'ock/Paisley 14A	Barclay, S.G.	Irvine/Kilmarnock 11A
Almond, D.	Dunfermline 24A	Bardgett, F.D.	List 6-I
Alston, W.G.	Glasgow 16A-103	Barge, N.L.	Glasgow 16A-41
Amed, P.	Moray 35A	Barr, A.C.	Glasgow 16B
Anderson, A.F.	Edinburgh 1A-30	Barr, G.K.	Perth 28B
Anderson, C.M.	Glasgow 16B	Barr, G.R.	Edinburgh 1A-18
Anderson, D.	List 6-I	Barr, J.	Glasgow 16B
Anderson, D.M.	Lochaber 38A	Barr, T.L.	Perth 28B
Anderson, D.P.	Argyll 19B	Barrett, L.	Dundee 29B
Anderson, D.U.	Edinburgh 1A-69	Barrie, A.	Falkirk 22A
Anderson, J.F.	Angus 30B	Barrie, A.P.	Hamilton 17A-43
Anderson, J.W.	Angus 30B	Barrington, C.W.H.	Edinburgh 1B
Anderson, K.G.	Lists 6H and 6I	Barron, Mrs J.L.	Jerusalem 49A
Anderson, R.A.	West Lothian 2A	Bartholomew, D.S.	Dum'/K'cud' 8A
Anderson, R.J.M.	Moray 35A	Baxendale, Mrs G.M.	Kincardine/Deeside 32A
Anderson, R.S.	Edinburgh 1B	Baxter, R.	Kirkcaldy 25A
Anderson, Mrs S.M.	Irv'/K'nock 11A	Baxter, R.F.	Edinburgh 1B
Andrew, J.	Gordon 33B		

Bayne, A.L.	Lothian 3B
Beaton, D.	Lochcarron/Skye 42B
Beattie, J.A.	Glasgow 16B
Beattie, W.	List 6-I
Beattie, W.G.	Hamilton 17B
Beattie, W.G.	Aberdeen 31B
Beautyman, P.H.	Edinburgh 1A-26
Beck, J.C.	List 6-H
Beckett, D.M.	Edinburgh 1B
Beebee, G.W.	England 47A
Bell, C.J.G.	Ross 39A
Bell, D.W.	Argyll 19B
Bell, G.K.	Glasgow 16A-57
Bell, I.W.	Greenock/Paisley 14A
Bell, J.L.	Glasgow 16B
Bell, Mrs M.	Greenock/Paisley 14A
Bell, R.P.	Ayr 10B
Bennett, A.	St Andrews 26B
Bennett, A.G.	Melrose/Peebles 4A
Bennett, D.K.P.	Dum'/K'cudbright 8B
Benson, J.W.	Stirling 23B
Benzie, I.W.	Ardrossan 12A
Berrill, P.A.D.	Kirkcaldy 25A
Bertram, T.A.	Perth 28B
Beveridge, S.E.P.	Annan'/Eskdale 7B
Bews, J.	St Andrews 26B
Bezuidenhout, L.C.	Dum'/K'cudbright 8A
Bezuidenhout, W.J.	Stirling 23A
Bicket, M.S.	Angus 30A
Billes, R.H.	Moray 35A
Binks, M.	Wigtown/Stranraer 9A
Birch, J.	Glasgow 16B
Bircham, M.F.	Perth 28A
Birnie, C.J.	Buchan 34B
Birrell, Mrs I.	Perth 28A
Birrell, J.M.	Perth 28B
Birse, G.S.	Ayr 10A
Birss, A.D.	Greenock/Paisley 14A
Bjarnason, S.	Abernethy 36A
Black, A.G.	Lothian 3B
Black, A.R.	Irv'/Kilmarnock 11A
Black, A.T.	Inverness 37B
Black, D.R.	Glasgow 16A-108
Black, D.W.	West Lothian 2A

Black, G.W.G.   Hamilton 17A-58
Black, I.W.   Falkirk 22A
Black, J.M.   Hamilton 17B
Black, Mrs J.M.K.   G'ock/Paisley 14B
Black, J.S.   List 6-I
Black, Mrs S.   Glasgow 16A-140
Black, W.B.   Lewis 44A
Black, W.G.   Aberdeen 31B
Blackley, Mrs J.R.M.   Stirling 23B
Blackwood, K.T.   Aberdeen 31A
Blaikie, J.   Buchan 34B
Blair, D.B.   Falkirk 22B
Blair, J.N.   Shetland 46B
Blakey, R.S.   Edinburgh 1B
Blakey, S.A.   Glasgow 16A-132
Blane, Q.A.   List 6-I
Blount, Mrs A.S.   St Andrews 26A
Blount, G.K.   St Andrews 26B
Blyth, J.G.S.   Ayr 10B
Blythe, S.C.   Edinburgh 1A-85
Boag, J.A.S.   Glasgow 16A-4
Bogle, A.O.   Falkirk 22A
Bogle, T.C.   Ayr 10B
Bonar, S.   Lists 6H and 6I
Bond, M.S.   Dum'/Kirkcudbright 8A
Booth, F.M.   Dumbarton 18B
Booth, Mrs J.   Edinburgh 1B
Borthwick, K.S.   Edinburgh 1A-34
Boswell G.   Falkirk 22A
Bowie, A.   Gordon 33B
Bowie, A.G.   England 47B
Bowie, A.McC.   Melrose/Peebles 4B
Bowman, N.M.   List 6-I
Boyd, B.   Moray 35A
Boyd, I.R.   List 6-I
Boyd, K.M.   Edinburgh 1B
Boyd, R.M.H.   Ayr 10A
Boyle, E.   Wigtown/Stranraer 9A
Boyle, R.P.   Dunfermline 24A
Bradley, A.W.   Glasgow 16B
Bradley, I.   St Andrews 26B
Brady, I.D.   Edinburgh 1B
Brady, Miss L.   St Andrews 26A
Brain, E.J.   Glasgow 16B
Brain, Mrs I.J.   Glasgow 16B
Brennan, Ms A.J.   D'keld/Meigle 27A
Brewster, J.   Hamilton 17A-32
Brice, D.G.   Glasgow 16B
Bristow, Mrs I.A.   Ardrossan 12B
Bristow, W.H.G.   Argyll 19B
Britchfield, Mrs A.E.P.   England 47B
Broadley, Mrs L.J.   Angus 30A
Brockie, C.G.F.   Irv'/K'marnock 11A
Brodie, J.   Angus 30B
Brook, S.A.   Stirling 23A
Brough, C.H.   Dundee 29A
Brough, R.   Glasgow 16B
Brown, A.   List 6-H
Brown, A.B.   Hamilton 17B

Brown, D.G.   Inverness 37B
Brown, Mrs E.   Perth 28A
Brown, H.J.   Dundee 29A
Brown, H.T.   Irvine/Kilmarnock 11A
Brown, J.   Falkirk 22B
Brown, J.   Jedburgh 6B
Brown, J.H.   Stirling 23B
Brown, J.M.   Annan'/Eskdale 7A
Brown, J.M.   Europe 48
Brown, J.W.S.   Kincard'/Deeside 32B
Brown, L.R.   St Andrews 26B
Brown, Mrs M.D.   Jedburgh 6A
Brown, P.   Dunfermline 24B
Brown, R.   Melrose/Peebles 4B
Brown, R.F.   Aberdeen 31A
Brown, R.G.   Orkney 45B
Brown, R.H.   Lothian 3B
Brown, S.J.   England 47B
Brown, Mrs S.M.   Sutherland 40A
Brown, T.J.   Stirling 23B
Brown, W.   Lothian 3B
Brown, W.D.   Edinburgh 1B
Brown, W.D.   Edinburgh 1A-54
Browning, D.   Edinburgh 1A-51
Bruce, A.W.   G'ock/Paisley 14B
Bruce, Miss L.M.   Edinburgh 1B
Bruce, W.C.   List 6-R
Bryden, W.A.   Glasgow 16B
Bryson, T.M.   Moray 35A
Buchan, A.   Gordon 33B
Buchan, C.   Melrose/Peebles 4A
Buchan, Mrs I.C.   Gordon 33A
Buchan, J.   Ross 39B
Buchan, W.   Perth 28B
Buchanan, F.C.   Dumbarton 18A
Buchanan, N.   Glasgow 16A-39
Buckley, R.G.   Glasgow 16A-141
Buell, F.B.   Inverness 37B
Bull, A.W.   Glasgow 16B
Burns, J.H.   Wigtown/Stranraer 9A
Burnside, Mrs A.H.   Lochaber 38A
Burnside, W.A.M.   Lochaber 38B
Burroughs, Mrs K.-A.   Argyll 19A
Burroughs, P.   Argyll 19A
Burt, D.W.G.   Hamilton 17A-45
Burt, T.W.   Melrose/Peebles 4A
Burton, S.   Perth 28A
Butters, D.   Angus 30B
Buwert, K.O.F.   Hamilton 17A-84
Byers, A.J.   Annan'/Eskdale 7B
Byers, Mrs M.   Annan'/Eskdale 7B
Byun, B.D.W.   Aberdeen 31A

Caie, A.   Lists 6-H and 6-I
Cairns, A.B.   Wigtown/Stranraer 9B
Cairns, E.   Perth 28B
Cairns, J.B.   Lothian 3A
Cairns, Miss W.   Kirkcaldy 25A
Cairns, W.A.   England 47B

Calder, B.   Glasgow 16A-26
Calder, T.R.   Gordon 33A
Calvert, R.A.   Europe 48A
Cameron, A.F.   G'ock/Paisley 14A
Cameron, C.M.   Irv'/Kilmarnock 11A
Cameron, D.C.   Glasgow 16A-30
Cameron, D.J.R.   Argyll 19A
Cameron, D.S.   Irv'/Kilmarnock 11A
Cameron, G.G.   Edinburgh 1B
Cameron, I.   West Lothian 2B
Cameron, J.K.   St Andrews 26B
Cameron, J.U.   Dundee 29A
Cameron, J.W.M.   Edinburgh 1B
Cameron, R.   Glasgow 16A-131
Cameron, R.N.   England 47B
Cameron, S.   Ardrossan 12B
Campbell, A.B.   Perth 28B
Campbell, A.I.   Glasgow 16B
Campbell, A.M.   Hamilton 17A-61
Campbell, D.   Uist 43A
Campbell, D.   Dum'/K'cudbright 8A
Campbell, D.   Greenock/Paisley 14A
Campbell, D.I.   Kincard'/Deeside 32A
Campbell, Mrs E.C.   Ayr 10B
Campbell, F.   Jedburgh 6A
Campbell, G.   Dundee 29B
Campbell, G.H.   Irv'/Kilmarnock 11B
Campbell, I.M.   Uist 43A
Campbell, J.   Greenock/Paisley 14A
Campbell, J.   List 6-R
Campbell, J.A.   Irv'/Kilmarnock 11B
Campbell, J.E.R.   Kirkcaldy 25B
Campbell, J.W.   Melrose/Peebles 4A
Campbell, M.M.   Falkirk 22A
Campbell, N.G.   Dum'/K'cudbright 8A
Campbell, R.   Stirling 23A
Campbell, R.D.M.   Edinburgh 1A-69
Campbell, R.F.   Inverness 37A
Campbell, T.R.   List 6-I
Campbell, W.M.M.   Aberdeen 31B
Campbell-Jack, W.C.   Gl'w 16A-109
Canlis, M.C.   Gordon 33A
Cant, H.W.M.   List 6-R
Cant, T.M.   Irv'/Kilmarnock 11B
Carmichael, D.J.M.   Glasgow 16A-29
Carmichael, D.S.   Lanark 13A
Carmichael, J.A.   Lochaber 38B
Carr, W.S.   Perth 28B
Carrie, J.G.   Edinburgh 1A-20
Carruth, Mrs P.A.   Hamilton 17A-23
Carruthers, D.   Argyll 19A
Cartlidge, G.   Glasgow 16B
Cartwright, A.C.D.   Duns 5A
Carvalho, J.R.   Perth 28A
Casebow, B.C.   St Andrews 26B
Cashman, P.H.   Melrose/Peebles 4B
Caskie, J.C.   Dumbarton 18A
Cassells, A.K.   Dunkeld/Meigle 27B
Cathcart, I.A.   Lothian 3A

Chalmers, G.A. — Falkirk 22B
Chalmers, J.P. — Edinburgh 1B
Chalmers, M. — Edinburgh 1B
Chalmers, W.R. — Lothian 3B
Chambers, S.J. — Inverness 37A
Charlton, G.W. — Inverness 37B
Charlton, Mrs I.A. — Shetland 46A
Charlton, R. — Shetland 46A
Cherry, A.J. — Glasgow 16A-106
Chester, S.J. — Glasgow 16B
Chestnut, A. — Greenock/Paisley 14B
Cheyne, Mrs R.U. — Gordon 33A
Childs, A. — Dunfermline 24A
Chisholm, A.F. — Inverness 37B
Christie, A.A. — Ayr 10A
Christie, A.C. — Kincard'/Deeside 32B
Christie, Mrs H.F. — Falkirk 22A
Christie, J. — Inverness 37B
Christie, J.C. — Lochaber 38A
Christie, R.S. — Irv'/Kilmarnock 11B
Clancy, Mrs P.J. — G'ock/Paisley 14A
Clark, Mrs C.M. — Edinburgh 1A-9
Clark, D.M. — Dundee 29A
Clark, D.W. — Glasgow 16A-28
Clark, D.W. — Dumbarton 18A
Clark, T.L. — Orkney 45A
Clarkson, R.G. — Dundee 29B
Clegg, O.M.H. — Edinburgh 1A-34
Clelland, Mrs E. — Stirling 23A
Clinkenbeard, W.W. — Edinburgh 1B
Clipston, S.F. — Ayr 10A
Cloggie, Mrs J. — Stirling 23B
Clyne, D.R. — Inverness 37B
Cobain, A.R. — Lochaber 38B
Cochrane, J. — Stirling 23A
Coghill, A.W.F. — Lewis 44A
Coleman, S.H. — Perth 28B
Coley, R. — Glasgow 16B
Collard, J.K. — Glasgow 16B
Collie, Miss J.P. — Gordon 33B
Collins, Mrs C.E.E. — Dundee 29A
Collins, D.A. — Dundee 29A
Collins, M. — Kirkcaldy 25B
Coltart, I.O. — Angus 30A
Colvin, Mrs S.E.F. — Hamilton 17A-5
Combe, N.R. — Jedburgh 6A
Conkey, H. — Kin'/Deeside 32A
Connolly, D. — Kirkcaldy 25B
Connolly, J. — St Andrews 26A
Coogan, J.M. — Ardrossan 12B
Cook, Mrs H. — Abernethy 36A
Cook, J. — Edinburgh 1B
Cook, J.A. — Gordon 33A
Cook, J.M. — Buchan 34A
Cook, J.S. — Hamilton 17B
Cook, J.W. — Edinburgh 1B
Cooper, G. — List 6-H
Cooper, M.W. — Kirkcaldy 25B
Corbett, R.T. — Lochaber 38A
Coull, M.C. — Glasgow 16B
Coulter, D. — England 47B
Court, D.L. — Edinburgh 1A-56
Coutts, F. — Aberdeen 31B
Coutts, J.A. — Glasgow 16A-44
Cowan, J.S.A. — G'ock/Paisley 14A
Cowell, Miss S.G. — Lanark 13B
Cowie, G.S. — Aberdeen 31A
Cowie, J.A. — Europe 48A
Cowie, J.M. — Moray 35A
Cowie, Mrs M. — Aberdeen 31A
Cowieson, R.J. — Lanark 13A

Craggs, Mrs S. — Gordon 33A
Craig, A.J.D. — Glasgow 16A-97
Craig, E. — List 6-H
Craig, G.T. — England 47B
Craig, G.W. — List 6-H
Craig, I.R. — List 6-R
Craig, Miss J.H. — Perth 28B
Craig, J.W. — List 6-H
Craig, M.D. — Stirling 23B
Craig, N.D. — Dum'/K'cudbright 8B
Craig, R.A.S. — Glasgow 16A-134
Craig, W. — Lanark 13B
Craik, Mrs S. — Dundee 29B
Cramb, E.M. — Dundee 29B
Cranfield, Miss E.F. — Kirkcaldy 25A
Cranfield, Miss M.M. — Gordon 33A
Cranston, G. — Ayr 10B
Cranston, R.D. — G'ock/Paisley 14A
Crawford, G.W. — Moray 35A
Crawford, J.F. — Wigtown/Stranraer 9B
Crawford, M.S.M. — Aberdeen 31B
Crawford, S.G.V. — List 6-H
Creegan, Mrs C.M. — D'keld/Meigle 27B
Crichton, J. — Ayr 10A
Crichton, T. — Edinburgh 1B
Cringles, G.G. — Argyll 19A
Crombie, W.D. — Dumbarton 18B
Cross, B.F. — Edinburgh 1B
Crosthwaite, M.D. — Falkirk 22A
Cruickshank, A.A.B. — Stirling 23B
Cruickshank, N. — Ardrossan 12B
Crumlish, Mrs E.A. — G'ock/Paisley 14A
Cubie, J.P. — Greenock/Paisley 14B
Cullen, W.T. — Hamilton 17B
Cumming, D.P.L. — List 6-H
Cunningham, A. — Glasgow 16B
Cunningham, I.D. — Lanark 13A
Cunningham, J.S.A. — Glasgow 16B
Curran, Miss E.M. — Moray 35A
Currie, A.I. — Wigtown/Stranraer 9A
Currie, D.E.P. — Hamilton 17B
Currie, G.C.M. — List 6-I
Currie, I.S. — Argyll 19A
Currie, Ms M.F. — Hamilton 17A-7
Currie, R. — Glasgow 16B
Currie, R.D. — Hamilton 17B
Cuthbertson, M. — Glasgow 16A-71
Cuthell, T.C. — Edinburgh 1B
Cutler, J.S.H. — Lanark 13A

Dailly, J.R. — Ardrossan 12B
Dalton, M.F. — England 47B
Darroch, R.J.G. — West Lothian 2A
Davidge, Mrs A. — Ardrossan 12A
Davidge, P.R. — Glasgow 16A-128
Davidson, Mrs A. — Hamilton 17A-24
Davidson, A.A.B. — Moray 35B
Davidson, D.H. — Edinburgh 1A-35
Davidson, E.L. — Gordon 33A
Davidson, I.M.P. — Edinburgh 1B
Davidson, J. — Irvine/Kilmarnock 11B
Davidson, J.F. — Angus 30A
Davidson, M.R. — List 6-I
Davidson, R. — Dumbarton 18B
Davies, G.W. — List 6-I
Davies, J.M. — Aberdeen 31A
Dawson, M.A. — Melrose/Peebles 4A
Dawson, M.S. — Edinburgh 1B
de Groot, J. — Edinburgh 1A-81
de Paula, A.A. — Dundee 29A
Dean, R.A.F. — Wigtown/Stranraer 9B

Deans, G.D.S. — Orkney 45A
Dempsey, B. — Dunkeld/Meigle 27A
Dempster, C.J. — St Andrews 26A
Denniston, D.W. — Perth 28A
Denniston, J. — Perth 28B
Devenney, D.J. — England 47B
Devenny, R.P. — Melrose/Peebles 4B
Dewar, J.S. — Edinburgh 1A-36
Dick, A.B. — Lothian 3A
Dick, J.H.A. — Aberdeen 31A
Dick, J.R. — Melrose/Peebles 4B
Dick, J.S. — Kirkcaldy 25B
Dick, T. — Dunkeld/Meigle 27B
Dickie, M.M. — Ayr 10B
Dickson, A.P. — Aberdeen 31A
Dickson, G.T. — List 6-I
Dickson, J.C. — Aberdeen 31B
Dilbey, Miss M.D. — Edinburgh 1B
Dillon, A. — Glasgow 16A-91
Dingwall, B. — Gordon 33A
Dixon, D.S. — Angus 30A
Dobie, Mrs R.J.W. — Mel'/Peebles 4A
Dodd, Miss M.E. — Jedburgh 6A
Doherty, A.J. — Stirling 23B
Don, A. — Lothian 3A
Donaghy, L.G. — Dumbarton 18B
Donald, A.C. — Kirkcaldy 25A
Donald, A.P. — Buchan 34A
Donald, K.W. — Kirkcaldy 25A
Donald, P.H. — Inverness 37A
Donald, R.M. — Dundee 29B
Donald, T.W. — Melrose/Peebles 4B
Donaldson, C.V. — Lists 6H and 6I
Donaldson, D. — Dumbarton 18A
Donaldson, G.M. — Hamilton 17A-18
Donaldson, M. — List 6-R
Donaldson, R.B. — Perth 28B
Donn, T.M. — Inverness 37B
Dougall, Mrs E. — Edinburgh 1B
Dougall, N.J. — Lothian 3A
Douglas, A.B. — Edinburgh 1A-4
Douglas, A.M. — Aberdeen 31B
Douglas, Mrs C.A. — Moray 35B
Douglas, C.R. — Edinburgh 1B
Douglas, Miss F.C. — Dundee 29B
Douglas, I.M. — Angus 30B
Douglas, I.P. — Buchan 34B
Douglas, P.C. — St Andrews 26B
Downie, A.A. — Uist 43A
Downie, A.F.M. — Stirling 23A
Downie, A.S. — Ardrossan 12B
Dowswell, J.A.M. — England 47B
Doyle, D.W. — Hamilton 17A-62
Doyle, I.B. — Edinburgh 1B
Drake, Mrs W.F. — Lothian 3A
Drane, M. — Dunkeld/Meigle 27A
Drummond, A.G. — Perth 28B
Drummond, J.S. — England 47B
Drummond, J.W. — Glasgow 16A-37
Drummond, N.W. — List 6-H
Drummond, R.H. — List 6-H
Dryden, I. — Gordon 33B
Drysdale, J.H. — Ardrossan 12B
Drysdale, J.P.R. — Angus 30B
Duff, S.M. — Glasgow 16A-95
Duff, T.M.F. — Glasgow 16A-111
Duff, Miss V.J. — Glasgow 16A-75
Duffin, G.L. — Lothian 3A
Dunbar, Ms L.J. — Edinburgh 1A-60
Duncan, A.S. — Dumbarton 18A
Duncan, C.A. — Melrose/Peebles 4B

Duncan, D.M.	England 47B	Ferguson, D.J.	Kirkcaldy 25B	Fraser, Miss S.A.	Edinburgh 1B
Duncan, J.	Dunkeld/Meigle 27B	Ferguson, J.	Lochcarron/Skye 42B	Frater, A.	Dumbarton 18A
Duncan, J.C.	Kirkcaldy 25B	Ferguson, J.A.	Aberdeen 31A	Frazer, R.E.	Edinburgh 1A-31
Duncan, Mrs L.	Edinburgh 1A-44	Ferguson, J.B.	Glasgow 16B	Frew, J.M.	List 6-I
Duncan, Mrs M.M.	Irv'/K'nock 11A	Ferguson, J.F.	Dundee 29B	Frew, M.W.	Edinburgh 1A-82
Duncan, R.F.	Angus 30B	Ferguson, R.	Lists 6H and 6I	Frew, Mrs R.	Kirkcaldy 25A
Dundas, T.B.S.	West Lothian 2B	Ferguson, W.B.	Glasgow 16A-52	Frizzell, R.S.	Inverness 37B
Dunleavy, Miss S.	G'ock/Paisley 14A	Fergusson, D.A.S.	Edinburgh 1B	Froude, K.	Kirkcaldy 25A
Dunlop, A.J.	Argyll 19B	Fiddes, G.R.	Ayr 10A	Fulcher, S.	Argyll 19A
Dunlop, M.W.B.	Buchan 34B	Fields, J.T.	England 47B	Fulton, F.H.	Dunkeld/Meigle 27B
Dunn, W.I.C.	Edinburgh 1B	Finch, G.S.	Glasgow 16A-7	Fulton, R.S.M.	Stirling 23A
Dunn, W.S.	Hamilton 17B	Findlay, H.J.W.	Lanark 13B	Fulton, Mrs S.F.	Stirling 23A
Dunnett, A.L.	Glasgow 16A-104	Finlay, Mrs J.G.	Perth 28A	Fyall, R.S.	Edinburgh 1B
Dunphy, Mrs R.	Europe 48A	Finlay, Q.	Angus 30B		
Dunsmore, B.W.	England 47A	Finlay, W.P.	Glasgow 16B	Gaddes, D.R.	Duns 5B
Dupar, K.W.	Ross 39B	Finlayson, D.	List 6-H	Galbraith, D.	Edinburgh 1B
Durno, R.C.	Glasgow 16A-84	Finnie, C.J.	Jedburgh 6A	Galbraith, N.W.	Glasgow 16A-60
Dutch, M.M.	Greenock/Paisley 14A	Fisher, D.N.	Annandale/Eskdale 7B	Galbraith, W.J.L.	Perth 28B
Dutton, D.W.	Wigtown/Stranraer 9A	Fisher, M.L.	Glasgow 16B	Gale, R.A.A.	Duns 5B
		Fisk, Mrs E.A.	Dunfermline 24A	Gall, R.	Kincardine/Deeside 32A
Earl, J.	Jedburgh 6A	Fleming, A.F.	Stirling 23B	Gallacher, Miss J.W.	Falkirk 22A
Earnshaw, P.	St Andrews 26B	Fleming, H.K.	Perth 28B	Galloway, I.F.	Glasgow 16A-76
Easton, D.J.C.	Lanark 13B	Fleming, T.G.	List 6-I	Galloway, Mrs K.	Glasgow 16B
Easton, I.A.G.	Dumbarton 18B	Fletcher, G.G.	Glasgow 16A-55	Galloway, R.W.C.	St Andrews 26B
Easton, Mrs L.C.	Hamilton 17B	Fletcher, Mrs S.G.	Stirling 23A	Gammack, G.	Dundee 29B
Eddie, D.C.	Aberdeen 31A	Fletcher, T.	England 47A	Garden, Miss M.J.	Gordon 33A
Edington, G.L.	St Andrews 26B	Flockhart, D.R.	List 6-I	Gardner, A.	Europe 48A
Edwards, W.G.	List 6-R	Foggitt, E.W.	Lothian 3A	Gardner, B.K.	Kin'/Deeside 32A
Elder, A.B.	Dum'/Kirkcudbright 8B	Forbes, I.M.	Lothian 3B	Gardner, Mrs F.	Glasgow 16A-137
Elliott, G.J.	Edinburgh 1B	Forbes, J.W.A.	Kincard'/Deeside 32B	Gardner, F.J.	Greenock/Paisley 14B
Elliott, K.C.	Ayr 10A	Ford, A.A.	Glasgow 16A-138	Gardner, J.V.	Edinburgh 1B
Ellis, D.W.	List 6-I	Ford, C.H.M.	Edinburgh 1A-77	Gardner, N.N.	Edinburgh 1A-7
Elston, I.	Kirkcaldy 25A	Forrest, A.B.	Argyll 19B	Gardner, P.M.	Glasgow 16A-112
Elston, P.K.	Kirkcaldy 25B	Forrest, K.P.	Greenock/Paisley 14B	Garrity, T.A.W.	Ayr 10B and List 6-K
Embleton, B.M.	Edinburgh 1A-67	Forrest, M.R.	Argyll 19A	Gaston, A.R.C.	Perth 28B
Embleton, Mrs S.R.	Edinburgh 1A-42	Forrester, D.B.	Edinburgh 1B	Gatherer, J.F.	Dum'/K'cudbright 8A
Emery, S.	Gordon 33A	Forrester, I.L.	Kirkcaldy 25B	Gatt, D.W.	Kirkcaldy 25B
Erskine, A.U.	Argyll 19B	Forrester, Mrs M.R.	Edinburgh 1B	Gauld, B.G.D.D.	Lanark 13A
Erskine, M.J.	St Andrews 26A	Forsyth, A.R.	Kirkcaldy 25A	Gauld, Mrs K.	Moray 35A
Evans, J.W.	Moray 35B	Forsyth, D.S.	Dunkeld/Meigle 27B	Gauld, R.S.R.	Moray 35A
Evans-Boiten, J.	Europe 48A	Forsyth, J.	Ross 39B	Geddes, A.J.	Dum'/K'cudbright 8A
Eve, J.C.	Glasgow 16A-6	Fortune, Mrs E.J.	Aberdeen 31A	Gehrke, R.	West Lothian 2A
Ewart, W.	Dunkeld/Meigle 27A	Foster, M.	Edinburgh 1A-22	Gemmell, D.R.	Ayr 10A
		Fowler, A.J.R.	Kirkcaldy 25A	Gemmell, J.	Perth 28A
Fair, W.M.	Angus 30A	Fowler, R.C.A.	List 6-I	George, Ms J.D.	Orkney 45A
Fairful, J.	Hamilton 17A-9	Fowlie, R.A.	Buchan 34A	Gerbrandy-Baird, P.S.	
Fairlie, G.	St Andrews 26B	Fox, G.D.A.	Jedburgh 6B		Dunfermline 24A
Falconer, A.D.	Aberdeen 31A	Fox, G.H.	Lanark 13B	Gibb, J.D.M.	Annandale/Eskdale 7B
Falconer, J.B.	Aberdeen 31B	Frail, N.	Kirkcaldy 25A	Gibson, A.W.	Hamilton 17A-72
Faris, Mrs J.M.	Melrose/Peebles 4A	Francis, J.	Lanark 13A	Gibson, E.	Argyll 19A
Farquhar, W.E.	Dunfermline 24B	Frank, D.	Glasgow 16A-17	Gibson, F.S.	Argyll 19B
Farquharson, G.	Edinburgh 1B	Fraser, Mrs A.G.	St Andrews 26A	Gibson, H.M.	Glasgow 16B
Farrington, A.	Glasgow 16A-1	Fraser, A.M.	Glasgow 16A-16	Gibson, H.M.	St Andrews 26B
Faulds, N.L.	Edinburgh 1B	Fraser, D.W.	Dundee 29A	Gibson, I.	Kirkcaldy 25B
Fawkes, G.M.A.	Buchan 34B	Fraser, I.C.	Glasgow 16A-123	Gibson, J.C.L.	Edinburgh 1B
Fazakas, S.	Lochcarron/Skye 42A	Fraser, I.M.	List 6-I	Gibson, J.M.	Hamilton 17A-16
Fenemore, J.C.	Argyll 19B	Fraser, J.P.	Hamilton 17B	Gibson, M.	Glasgow 16B
Fenwick, K.	Angus 30A	Fraser, J.W.	Lothian 3A	Gilchrist, E.J.	Aberdeen 31A
Ferguson, A.M.	Dumbarton 18B	Fraser, J.W.	Lothian 3B	Gilchrist, Miss K.	Hamilton 17B

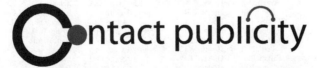

Gilfillan, J.	Lothian 3B	Haddow, A.H.	Aberdeen 31B	Hill, A.T.	Lothian 3B
Gillan, D.S.	West Lothian 2A	Haddow, Mrs M.M.	Kin'/Deeside 32A	Hill, J.W.	Edinburgh 1B
Gillespie, Mrs I.C.	Stirling 23B	Hair, P.R.	Edinburgh 1A-33	Hill, R.	Lothian 3A
Gillies, Mrs J.E.	List 6-I	Haley, D.	Glasgow 16B	Hill, R.	St Andrews 26B
Gillon, C.B.	Irv'/Kilmarnock 11B	Hall, K.F.	Dundee 29A	Hill, S.	Falkirk 22B
Gillon, D.R.M.	G'ock/Paisley 14A	Hall, W.M.	Irvine/Kilmarnock 11A	Hilsley, B.C.	Edinburgh 1A-45
Gilmour, I.Y.	Edinburgh 1A-44	Halliday, A.R.	Perth 28B	Hobson, Mrs D.	Kirkcaldy 25A
Gilmour, R.M.	List 6-I	Hamill, R.	Dum'/K'cudbright 8B	Hodge, W.N.T.	Angus 30B
Gilmour, W.M.	Stirling 23A	Hamilton, A.J.	Dumbarton 18A	Hogg, T.	Lothian 3A
Gisbey, J.E.	Dunkeld/Meigle 27B	Hamilton, D.G.	Dunkeld/Meigle 27B	Hogg, W.T.	Dum'/K'cudbright 8A
Glass, A.	Ross 39B	Hamilton, D.S.M.	Lists 6-H and 6-I	Holland, J.C.	Falkirk 22B
Glen, G.E.D.	Gordon 33A	Hamilton, Miss H.	Aberdeen 31B	Holland, W.	Dum'/K'cudbright 8A
Glencross, W.M.	Ayr 10B	Hamilton, I.W.F.	Inverness 37A	Holroyd, G.	Ross 39B
Glover, N.	Glasgow 16A-8	Hamilton, R.	Jedburgh 6B	Holt, J.	Kincardine/Deeside 32A
Glover, R.L.	Lothian 3A	Hamilton, R.A.	Hamilton 17A-8	Hood, A.J.J.	England 47B
Goldie, Miss C.	Glasgow 16A-64	Hamilton, R.G.	Dumbarton 18A	Hood, C.A.	Argyll 19B
Goldie, G.D.	Aberdeen 31B	Hamilton, W.D.	G'ock/Paisley 14A	Hood, D.P.	Glasgow 16A-98
Goodman, R.A.	Falkirk 22B	Hammond, R.J.	Dum'/K'bright 8B	Hood, Mrs E.L.	G'ock/Paisley 14A
Gordon, A.B.	List 6-H	Handley, J.	Hamilton 17B	Hood, H.S.C.	Argyll 19B
Gordon, D.C.	Ardrossan 12B	Hannah, W.	Ayr 10B	Hood, Miss J.C.	Edinburgh 1A-6
Gordon, Miss E.J.	Falkirk 22A	Harbison, D.J.H.	Ardrossan 12B	Hope, Miss E.P.	Glasgow 16B
Gordon, I.D.	Kirkcaldy 25B	Harbison, Mrs K.E.	Hamilton 17A-51	Hope, Mrs G.H.	Duns 5B
Gordon, J.A.	Ross 39A	Hardie, H.W.	Melrose/Peebles 4B	Horne, A.M.	Falkirk 22A
Gordon, L.Y.	Aberdeen 31B	Hardie, R.K.	Falkirk 22B	Horne, D.A.	Ross 39A
Gordon, P.M.	St Andrews 26B	Hare, M.M.W.	Irv'/Kilmarnock 11B	Horsburgh, A.G.	Lothian 3A
Gordon, T.	Edinburgh 1B	Harkes, G.	Wigtown/Stranraer 9B	Horsburgh, G.E.	Irv'/K'marnock 11A
Goring, I.M.	Hamilton 17A-53	Harkness, J.	Edinburgh 1B	Hosain, S.	Irvine/K'marnock 11B
Goskirk, J.L.	Sutherland 40A	Harley, E.	Aberdeen 31A	Hosie, J.	Lists 6H and 6I
Goss, A.J.	Glasgow 16B	Harper, Miss A.J.M.	Glasgow 16B	Houghton, Mrs C.	West Lothian 2A
Goss, M.S.	Angus 30A	Harper, D.L.	Ayr 10A	Houston, A.M.	Perth 28B
Gough, I.G.	Angus 30A	Harries, D.A.	List 6-R	Houston, Miss E.W.	Dumbarton 18A
Gow, N.	Gordon 33A	Harris, J.W.F.	Dumbarton 18A	Houston, G.R.	Lanark 13A
Graham, A.D.M.	Aberdeen 31B	Harris, S.McC.	Argyll 19A	Houston, P.M.	Dumbarton 18B
Graham, A.F.	Ross 39A	Harrison, C.	St Andrews 26A	Houston, T.C.	Glasgow 16B
Graham, A.G.	Angus 30A	Harvey, W.J.	Glasgow 16B	Houston, W.R.	West Lothian 2A
Graham, D.J.	Lothian 3A	Haslett, H.J.	Lothian 3A	Howie, Mrs M.L.K.	Ardrossan 12A
Graham, S.S.	Argyll 19A	Hastie, G.I.	Kincardine/Deeside 32A	Howie, W.	List 6-H
Graham, W.P.	Edinburgh 1B	Hastie, J.S.G.	Hamilton 17A-55	Howitt, Miss J.M.	Mel'/Peebles 4A
Grahame, R.P.	Ardrossan 12B	Haston, C.B.	Annandale/Eskdale 7A	Hudson, E.V.	Dumbarton 18B
Grainger, A.J.	Ross 39A	Haughton, F.	Glasgow 16B	Hudson, H.R.	Glasgow 16A-51
Grainger, H.L.	Aberdeen 31B	Hawdon, J.E.	Dundee 29B	Hudson, J.H.	Dundee 29B
Grainger, I.G.	Argyll 19B	Hawthorn, D.	Gordon 33B	Huggett, Miss J.A.	Irv'/K'nock 11B
Grant, D.I.M.	Glasgow 16B	Hay, B.J.L.	Duns 5B	Hughes, C.E.	Perth 28B
Grant, J.G.	Ayr 10B	Hay, J.W.	Edinburgh 1A-2	Hughes, D.W.	Hamilton 17A-59
Grant, N.M.	Dunfermline 24A	Hay, W.J.R.	Irvine/Kilmarnock 11B	Hughes, O.T.	England 47B
Grant, P.G.R.	Hamilton 17A-71	Hays D.	Dundee 29A	Huie, D.F.	Europe 48B
Gray, A.H.	Caithness 41A	Hebenton, D.J.	Ardrossan 12B	Humphris, P.M.	Inverness 37A
Gray, K.N.	Greenock/Paisley 14A	Hegarty, J.D.	St Andrews 26B	Hunt, T.G.	Orkney 45A
Gray, R.	Kincardine/Deeside 32B	Helon, G.G.	Ayr 10B	Hunter, A.G.	Glasgow 16B
Gray, W.	Argyll 19B	Henderson, C.M.	Argyll 19B	Hunter, J.E.	Hamilton 17B
Greaves, A.T.	Dundee 29A	Henderson, Miss E.M.	Edinb' 1A-68	Hunter, W.F.	Glasgow 16A-114
Green, A.H.	Stirling 23A	Henderson, F.M.	Lothian 3A	Hurst, F.R.	List 6-H
Greenshields, I.M.	Dunfermline 24A	Henderson, G.M.	Argyll 19A	Hutcheson, J.M.	Glasgow 16B
Greer, A.D.C.	Dum'/K'cudbright 8B	Henderson, J.D.	Dunkeld/Meigle 27B	Hutcheson, N.M.	Dum'/K'cud' 8A
Gregory, J.C.	Perth 28B	Henderson, Miss J.M.	Stirling 23A	Hutchison, Mrs A.M.	Aberdeen 31B
Gregson, Mrs E.M.	Glasgow 16B	Henderson, R.J.M.	Glasgow 16A-93	Hutchison, A.S.	Aberdeen 31B
Greig, A.	Gordon 33A	Hendrie, B.R.	Buchan 34A	Hutchison, D.S.	Aberdeen 31B
Greig, C.H.M.	Shetland 46A	Hendrie, Mrs Y.	Buchan 34A	Hutchison, H.	Glasgow 16B
Greig, J.C.G.	List 6-H	Hendry K.E.	Glasgow 16A-147		
Greig, R.G.	West Lothian 2A	Henig, G.	Moray 35B	Inglis, Mrs A.	Duns 5A
Grier, J.	Hamilton 17B	Henney, W.	St Andrews 26B	Inglis, D.B.C.	Argyll 19B
Griffiths, M.J.	Kirkcaldy 25A	Henry, M.N.	Perth 28B	Ingram, J.R.	Dundee 29B
Griffiths, R.I.	Argyll 19A	Hepburn, Miss C.A.	Kinc'/Dee' 32A	Ireland, A.	List 6-I
Grimson, J.A.	Perth 28B	Heriot, C.R.	Falkirk 22B	Irvine, Mrs E.H.C.	Glasgow 16B
Grimstone, A.F.	Glasgow 16B	Herkes, Mrs M.	Angus 30A	Irving, D.R.	Dum'/K'cudbright 8A
Groves, I.B.	Gordon 33A	(Heron, A.I.C.	Europe 48)	Irving, W.D.	Edinburgh 1B
Grubb, G.D.W.	Lists 6-H and 6-I	Hetherington, R.M.	G'ock/Paisley 14B	Izett, W.A.F.	Stirling 23B
Gunn, A.M.	Perth 28B	Hewitt, W.C.	Greenock/Paisley 14A		
Gunn, F.D.	Falkirk 22B	Hibbert, F.W.	List 6-I	Jack, Mrs A.M.	List 6-I
Guthrie, J.A.	Ayr 10B	Higgins, G.K.	List 6-I	Jack, C.	Stirling 23A
Guy, S.C.	Aberdeen 31A	Higham, R.D.	Duns 5B	Jack, D.	Aberdeen 31B

Jack, J.A.P.	Edinburgh 1A-24	Kelly, E.R.	Edinburgh 1B	Leask, Mrs R.M.	Ardrossan 12B
Jack, R.	Dumbarton 18B	Kelly, Miss I.J.M.	G'ock/Paisley 14A	Ledgard, J.C.	Duns 5B
Jackson, J.	List 6-R	Kelly, T.A.D.	Irvine/Kilmarnock 11B	Lees, A.P.	Dumbarton 18A
Jackson, J.A.	Hamilton 17A-22	Kelly, T.C.	Perth 28B	Legge, Mrs R.	Dunkeld/Meigle 27A
Jackson, W.	Falkirk 22A	Kelly, W.	Dum'/Kirkcudbright 8A	Leishman, J.S.	Dum'/K'cudbright 8B
Jaffrey, Mrs A.	Buchan 34A	Kemp, T.	Dumbarton 18B	Leitch, D.G.	Lothian 3A
Jamieson, A.	Glasgow 16A-70	Kennedy, G.	Wigtown/Stranraer 9A	Leitch, Mrs M.	G'ock/Paisley 14A
Jamieson, D.B.	Dundee 29A	Kennedy, L.J.	Dundee 29A	Lennox, L.I.	Ayr 10B
Jamieson, Mrs E.M.M.	List 6-I	Kennon, S.	Melrose/Peebles 4B	Levison, C.L.	Glasgow 16B
Jamieson, G.D.	Edinburgh 1B	Kenny, E.S.S.	Dunfermline 24A	Levison, L.D.	Lothian 3B
Jamieson, G.T.	List 6-R	Kenrick, B.	List 6-R	Levison, Mrs M.I.	List 6-H
Jamieson, Mrs H.E.	Lanark 13A	Kent, A.F.S.	Ayr 10B	Lewis, E.M.H.	Glasgow 18B
Jarvie, J.W.	St Andrews 26B	Kent, R.M.	Hamilton 17A-49	Liddell, M.	Glasgow 16B
Jarvie, T.W.	Irvine/Kilmarnock 11B	Kerr, A.	Duns 5B	Liddell, Miss M.	Ross 39B
Jeffrey, E.W.S.	Edinburgh 1B	Kerr, A.	Glasgow 16A-34	Liddiard, F.G.B.	List 6-I
Jeffrey, K.	St Andrews 26A	Kerr, B.	Lanark 13A	Lillie, Mrs F.L.	Orkney 45A
Jeffrey, S.D.	Inverness 37B	Kerr, H.F.	Aberdeen 31B	Lincoln, J.	Stirling 23A
Jenkins, G.F.C.	Dunfermline 24B	Kesting, S.M.	Falkirk 22B	Lind, G.K.	Annandale/Eskdale 7A
Jenkinson, J.J.	List 6-I	Keyes, Mrs J.A.	Falkirk 22A	Lind, M.J.	Argyll 19A
Jessamine, A.L.	Dunfermline 24A	King, C.S.	Hamilton 17B	Lindsay, D.G.	Duns 5B
Job, A.J.	Kirkcaldy 25A	Kingston, D.V.F.	England 47B	Lindsay, W.D.	List 6-H
Johnson, C.I.W.	G'ock/Paisley 14A	Kinniburgh, Miss E.B.	Kinc'/Dee' 32B	Lister, D.	Gordon 33B
Johnston, C.D.	List 6-K	Kinsey, L.	Aberdeen 31A	Lithgow, Mrs A.R.	Lothian 3A
Johnston, J.P.N.	Hamilton 17A-15	Kirk, S.M.	Dunkeld/Meigle 27A	Lithgow, T.	St Andrews 26B
Johnston, K.L.	Ayr 10B	Kirk, W.L.	Dum'/K'cudbright 8B	Livesley, A.	Inverness 37B
Johnston, M.	Aberdeen 31A	Kirkland, S.R.McL.		Lloyd, J.M.	Glasgow 16A-66
Johnston, M.H.	Glasgow 16A-90		Falkirk 22B and List 6-K	Lochrie, J.S.	Ayr 10A
Johnston, R.W.M.	Glasgow 16B	Kirkpatrick, Miss A.H.	Shetland 46B	Locke, D.	Glasgow 16A-48
Johnston, T.N.	Edinburgh 1A-64	Kirkwood, G.	Glasgow 16A-86	Lodge, B.P.	Glasgow 16B
Johnston, W.A.	Moray 35A	Knox, J.W.	Dunkeld/Meigle 27B	Logan, Mrs A.T.	Edinburgh 1A-84
Johnston, W.R.	Ardrossan 12A	Knox, R.A.	Shetland 46B	Logan, R.J.V.	Inverness 37B
Johnstone, B.	Lochcarron/Skye 42A			Logan, T.M.	List 6-I
Johnstone, D.B.	List 6-I	Lacey, E.R.	Perth 28B	Longmuir, T.G.	Gordon 33A
Johnstone, H.M.J.	Glasgow 16B	Lacy, D.W.	Irv'/Kilmarnock 11A	Longmuir, W.M.	Jedburgh 6B
Johnstone, M.E.	Glasgow 16A-27	Lafferty, J.M.M.	Ardrossan 12A	Lovett, M.F.	Stirling 23A
Johnstone, R.	List 6-I	Laidlaw, J.J.	Dundee 29B	Low, J.E.S.	Perth 28B
Johnstone, R.	Caithness 41A	Laidlaw, V.W.N.	Edinburgh 1A-71	Low, Mrs N.	Hamilton 17A-68
Johnstone, W.	Aberdeen 31B	Laing, D.J.H.	St Andrews 26A	Lowe, E.	Greenock/Paisley 14B
Jolly, A.J.	Aberdeen 31B	Laing, I.A.	Glasgow 16A-2	Lugton, G.L.	England 47B
Jones, A.	Jedburgh 6A	Laing, W.F.	Melrose/Peebles 4B	Lunan, D.W.	Glasgow 16B
Jones, Mrs A.M.	Lothian 3B	Lamb, A.D.	Kincard'/Deeside 32B	Lunn, D.	England 47A
Jones, J.O.	Greenock/Paisley 14A	Lamb, A.H.W.	Lochaber 38B	Lusk, A.S.	Hamilton 17A-33
Jones, P.H.	Lanark 13A	Lambie, A.E.	List 6-H	Lyall, D.	List 6-I
Jones, R.	Ross 39A	Lamont, A.	Argyll 19B	Lyall, M.G.	Hamilton 17A-78
Jones, R.A.	Gordon 33A	Lamont, S.J.	Europe 48A	Lynn, Mrs J.	List 6-H
Jones, W.	Angus 30B	Lancaster, C.	Glasgow 16A-82	Lynn, R.	Ayr 10A
Jones, W.G.	Ayr 10A	Landale, W.S.	Duns 5B	Lyon, B.A.	Buchan 34A
		Landels, J.	Stirling 23A	Lyon, D.H.S.	Edinburgh 1B
Kant, E.W.	Edinburgh 1B	Lang, Miss I.P.	Glasgow 16B	Lyons, E.D.	Wigtown/Stranraer 9A
Kavanagh, J.A.	Glasgow 16A-31	Langlands, C.H.	Glasgow 16B		
Kay, D.	Greenock/Paisley 14A	Lawrie, B.B.	Moray 35A	McAdam, D.J.	Glasgow 16A-13
Kay, Miss E.	Dundee 29B	Lawrie, R.M.	List 6-I	McAlister, D.J.B.	D'keld/Meigle 27B
Keating, Mrs G.J.	Edinburgh 1A-38	Lawson, A.H.	Dumbarton 18B	Macalister, E.	Gordon 33B
Keddie, D.A.	Glasgow 16B	Lawson, D.G.	Perth 28A	Macallan, G.B.	Gordon 33B
Keil, A.H.	Edinburgh 1A-70	Lawson, J.B.	Perth 28B	McAlpine, J.	Hamilton 17B
Keith, D.	Dum'/Kirkcudbright 8A	Lawson, K.C.	Edinburgh 1B	McAlpine, R.H.M.	Irv'/K'nock 11B
Kellas, D.J.	Lochcarron/Skye 42B	Lawson, R.E.	List 6-R	McAlpine, R.J.	Kirkcaldy 25B
Kellet, J.M.	Melrose/Peebles 4B	Lawson, R.G.	Perth 28B	McAreavey, W.	Glasgow 16B
Kelly, A.F.	Edinburgh 1A-1	Learmonth, W.	St Andrews 26B	Macarthur, A.J.	Lochcarron/Skye 42B

McArthur, M. Glasgow 16A-15
Macaskill, D. List 6-I
Macaskill, Mrs M. Glasgow 16B
Macaulay, A.H. Moray 35B
Macaulay, G.D. Falkirk 22A
MacBain, F.J. Lewis 44A
MacBain, I. Glasgow 16B
McCabe, G. Hamilton 17B
McCafferty, A. Orkney 45A
McCallum, A.D. Ardrossan 12B
McCallum, J. Falkirk 22B
McCallum, J. List 6-R
McCance, A.M. Ardrossan 12B
McCann, G.McD. List 6-R
McCarthy, D.J. G'ock/Paisley 14A
McCartney, A.C. St Andrews 26B
McCaskill, G.I.L. Edinburgh 1B
McChlery, L.M. Glasgow 16A-14
McClenaghan, L.P. Buchan 34A
MacColl, J. G'ock/Paisley 14B
MacColl, J.C. G'ock/Paisley 14B
McConnell, R. List 6-R
McCool, Mrs A.C. G'ock/Paisley 14A
McCorkindale, D.G.B. Dunf'line 24A
McCormick, A.F. Perth 28B
McCormick, J.A. Argyll 19A
MacCormick, M.G. Stirling 23B
McCormick, W.C. Lanark 13B
McCracken, G.A. Glasgow 16A-67
McCreadie, D.W. Stirling 23B
McCree, I.W. Sutherland 40A
McCrorie, W. Ayr 10B
McCrum, R. Ayr 10A
McCulloch, A.J.R. L'carron/Skye 42B
McCulloch, J.D. Irv'/K'marnock 11A
McCulloch, W.B. Europe 48A
McDonald, A. G'ock/Paisley 14B
Macdonald, A. G'ock/Paisley 14B
Macdonald, A. Lewis 44B
McDonald, A.D. St Andrews 26A
MacDonald, A.I. Inverness 37A
MacDonald, A.J. Uist 43B
McDonald, A.P. Lothian 3A
Macdonald, C.D. Glasgow 16A-19
Macdonald, F.A.J. Edinburgh 1B
MacDonald, G. Hamilton 17A-50
MacDonald, I. Edinburgh 1A-34
MacDonald, I. Lochcarron/Skye 42A
MacDonald, I.D. Orkney 45A
McDonald, I.J.M. Kirkcaldy 25B
Macdonald, I.M.M. Lewis 44A
McDonald, I.R.W. Hamilton 17A-4
Macdonald, I.U. Ayr 10B
Macdonald, J. Lewis 44B
McDonald, J.A. Hamilton 17B
MacDonald, J.M. Irv'/K'nock 11B
Macdonald J.M. Lochcarron/Skye 42A
MacDonald, J.W. Perth 28A
Macdonald, K. Glasgow 16B
MacDonald, K. Lochcarron/Skye 42B
Macdonald, Ms M. Hamilton 17A-79
McDonald, M. Edinburgh 1A-12
Macdonald, M. Sutherland 40B
Macdonald, M.C. Buchan 34A
Macdonald, P.J. Edinburgh 1A-75
MacDonald, R.I.T. Ardrossan 12A
McDonald, R.J. List 6-I
McDonald, T. Jedburgh 6A
McDonald, W.G. Falkirk 22B
Macdonald, W.J. Edinburgh 1B
McDonald, W.J.G. List 6-H

Macdonell, A.W. Lothian 3B
McDougall, H. Glasgow 16A-113
MacDougall, Miss L.A. Falkirk 22A
MacDougall, Miss M.I. Dundee 29A
Macdougall, M.M. Mel'/Peebles 4A
McDowall, R.J. Falkirk 22B
McDowell, B. St Andrews 26A
McEnhill, P. G'ock/Paisley 14A
MacEwan D.G. St Andrews 26A
MacEwan, J.A.I. Abernethy 36A
MacFadyen, Mrs A.M. Glasgow 16B
McFadyen, G. Dumbarton 18A
McFadzean, I. Perth 28A
Macfarlane, A.J.C. List 6-H
Macfarlane, D. List 6-H
MacFarlane, D.C. Mel'/Peebles 4B
Macfarlane, J. Argyll 19A
Macfarlane, K. Lists 6-H and 6-I
Macfarlane, P.T. England 47B
McFarlane, R.G. G'ock/Paisley 14A
Macfarlane, T.G. G'ock/Paisley 14B
McGill, Ms S. Glasgow 16A-125
McGill, T.W. Wigtown/Stranraer 9B
McGillivray, A.G. Edinburgh 1B
McGlynn, Mrs M. Glasgow 16A-72
McGowan, A.T.B. Ross 39B
Macgregor, A. Buchan 34A
McGregor, A.G.C. Edinburgh 1B
McGregor, D.J. St Andrews 26B
Macgregor, J. Ross 39B
MacGregor, J.B. Glasgow 16A-80
MacGregor, Miss M.S. Edinburgh 1B
MacGregor, N.I.M. Gordon 33A
MacGregor, R. Shetland 46A
McGregor, T.S. Edinburgh 1B
McGregor, W. Perth 28B
McGurk, A.F. Ardrossan 12A
McHaffie, R.D. Jedburgh 6A
McIlroy, I. Dundee 29A
McIndoe, J.H. England 47B
MacInnes, D. Uist 43B
MacInnes, D.M. Glasgow 16A-117
McInnes, I.M.S. Glasgow 16A-50
McIntosh, C.G. Stirling 23A
McIntosh, H.N.M. Stirling 23B
McIntyre, A.G. G'ock/Paisley 14A
McIntyre, G. Dumbarton 18A
McIntyre, G.J. Stirling 23A
McIntyre, J.A. Dumbarton 18B
Macintyre, T. Shetland 46A
Macintyre, W.J. St Andrews 26B
Maciver, I. Uist 43A
Maciver, N. Aberdeen 31B
MacIver, N. Uist 43A
McIvor, Miss A. Lanark 13A
Mack, Miss E.A. Dum'/K'bright 8A
Mack, J.C. Gordon 33A
Mack, K.L. Lothian 3A
McKaig, W.G. G'ock/Paisley 14A
MacKay, A.H. Glasgow 16A-38
Mackay, D. List 6-R
McKay, D.M. Annan'/Eskdale 7A
MacKay, G.C. Glasgow 16A-8
McKay, J.R. Ardrossan 12B
Mackay, K.J. West Lothian 2B
McKay, Mrs M. Buchan 34B
Mackay, Mrs M.H. Ardrossan 12A
Mackay, Mrs V.C.C. Dunfermline 24A
McKean, A.T. Stirling 23A
McKean, M.J. List 6-I
MacKechnie, J.M. Argyll 19B

McKee, N.B. Hamilton 17A-77
McKenna, E.C. Aberdeen 31A
McKenna, S.S. Edinburgh 1A-50
McKenzie, A. Hamilton 17A-10
Mackenzie, A.C. St Andrews 26B
Mackenzie, C. Lothian 3A
Mackenzie, D.M. List 6-R
MacKenzie, D.W. Perth 28B
Mackenzie, G.R. Moray 35A
Mackenzie, I. List 6-R
MacKenzie, I.C. Glasgow 16A-144
Mackenzie, I.M. List 6-R
Mackenzie, J.A.R. List 6-H
Mackenzie, J.G. Hamilton 17B
Mackenzie, K. Hamilton 17A-39
Mackenzie, K.I. Kin'/Deeside 32A
McKenzie, Miss M.O. List 6-H
Mackenzie, R.A. Edinburgh 1A-74
McKenzie, R.D. Hamilton 17A-42
Mackenzie, R.K. Argyll 19A
Mackenzie, S.L. Buchan 34B
McKenzie, W.M. Dum'/K'cud' 8B
McKeown, P. Gordon 33A
MacKichan, A.J. Dum'/K'cud' 8A
Mackie, J.F. Sutherland 40A
Mackie, S.G. Lists 6-H and 6-I
McKillop, A. Hamilton 17A-56
McKimmon, E.G. St Andrews 26A
Mackinnon, C. Glasgow 16A-47
MacKinnon, C.M. Glasgow 16A-22
McKinnon, E.W. Ardrossan 12A
McKinnon, Mrs L.F. Glasgow 16A-78
MacKinnon, N. Falkirk 22A
Mackinnon, R.M. Ross 39B
Mackinnon, T.J.R. Ross 39A
McLachlan, D.N. Glasgow 16A-92
McLachlan, E. Glasgow 16B
McLachlan, F.C. G'ock/Paisley 14B
McLachlan, I.K. Ayr 10A
McLachlan, T.A. Argyll 19A
MacLaine, Mrs M. G'ock/Paisley 14A
McLaren, D.M. Glasgow 16B
McLarty, R.R. Edinburgh 1A-53
McLauchlan, Mrs M.C. Ayr 10A
MacLaughlan, G. Perth 28A
McLay, A.D. Glasgow 16B
McLay, N. St Andrews 26A
Maclean, Mrs A.G. Edinburgh 1B
MacLean, A.T. G'ock/Paisley 14A
MacLean, E. Glasgow 16A-96
McLean, G. Ross 39A
Maclean, Mrs G.P. Edinburgh 1A-76
McLean, I.A. Aberdeen 31A
McLean, J. Gordon 33B
McLean, J.P. Kirkcaldy 25A
Maclean, M. Glasgow 16A-56
MacLean, Miss M.A. Edinburgh 1B
MacLean, N.R. Perth 28B
McLean-Foreman, T. Edinburgh 1A-57
McLeish, R.S. Gordon 33B
McLellan, A.R.C. Edinburgh 1B
MacLennan, A.J. Ross 39B
MacLennan, D.A. Lewis 44B
McLeod, A.G. Kirkcaldy 25B
Macleod, A.M. Duns 5B
MacLeod, C.A. England 47B
Macleod, D. Dunkeld/Meigle 27A
MacLeod, D. Lochcarron/Skye 42B
McLeod, D.C. Dundee 29B
MacLeod, I. Ardrossan 12B
MacLeod, I.I.S. List 6-R

Macleod, J.	Irvine/Kilmarnock 11A	
Macleod, J.	Ross 39B	
Macleod, K.D.	Ross 39A	
MacLeod, M.	Glasgow 16A-54	
MacLeod, N.	Hamilton 17A-48	
MacLeod, N.	Kirkcaldy 25B	
McLeod, R.	Edinburgh 1B	
MacLeod, R.	Argyll 19A	
MacLeod, R.A.R.	St Andrews 26A	
MacLeod, R.N.	England 47B	
Macleod, W.	Lewis 44B	
MacLeod, W.J.	List 6-R	
MacLeod-Mair, A.T.	Glasgow 16A-46	
McMahon, Miss E.J.	G'ock/Pais' 14A	
McMahon, J.K.S.	Edinburgh 1B	
MacMahon, Mrs J.P.H.	D'barton 18A	
McMahon, R.J.	Lanark 13B	
McMillan, C.D.	Dundee 29B	
McMillan, Mrs E.F.	Dundee 29A	
Macmillan, G.	Edinburgh 1A-32	
MacMillan, Mrs R.M.	Perth 28B	
McMillan, S.	Dundee 29A	
McMillan, W.J.	Buchan 34B	
MacMillan, W.M.	Annan'/Eskdale 7B	
McMullin, J.A.	Falkirk 22B	
MacMurchie, F.L.	Edinburgh 1B	
McNab, D.G.	Ayr 10A	
MacNab, H.S.D.	St Andrews 26B	
McNab, J.L.	Orkney 45A	
McNaught, N.A.	Ayr 10A	
McNaught, S.M.	Kirkcaldy 25B	
McNaughtan, J.	Irv/K'marnock 11A	
McNaughton, D.J.H.	Perth 28B	
Macnaughton, G.F.H.	Orkney 45A	
Macnaughton, J.A.	Glasgow 16B	
Macnee, I.	Buchan 34A	
McNeil, J.N.R.	Stirling 23A	
MacNeil, T.	Lewis 44A	
McNeill, C.C.	Europe 48B	
McNicol, B.	Jedburgh 6B	
McNidder, R.H.	Ayr 10B	
McPake, J.L.	Hamilton 17A-34	
McPake, J.M.	Edinburgh 1A-47	
McPhail, A.M.	Ayr 10B	
McPhail, P.	List 6-R	
McPhee, D.C.	Edinburgh 1B	
MacPhee, D.P.	Perth 28B	
MacPherson, A.J.	Stirling 23A	
Macpherson, A.S.	Edinburgh 1B	
Macpherson, C.C.R.	Edinburgh 1B	
MacPherson, D.	Inverness 37A	
McPherson, D.C.	Hamilton 17A-30	
Macpherson, D.J.	Annan'/Esk' 7B	
MacPherson, G.C.	List 6-I	
MacPherson, J.	Sutherland 40A	
Macpherson, K.J.	Uist 43B	
McPherson, S.M.	Edinburgh 1A-11	
Macpherson, S.M.	Dunfermline 24B	
McPherson, W.	List 6-I	
MacQuarrie, D.A.	Lochaber 38A	
McQuarrie, I.A.	Edinburgh 1A-10	
MacQuarrie, S.	Glasgow 16B	
McQuilken, J.E.	Perth 28B	
MacRae, Mrs E.H.	Stirling 23A	
MacRae, G.	Stirling 23A	
Macrae, Mrs J.	Glasgow 16A-87	
MacRae, M.H.	Dunkeld/Meigle 27A	
Macrae, N.C.	Lothian 3B	
MacRae, N.I.	West Lothian 2B	
MacRae, R.N.	Lochcarron/Skye 42A	
Macritchie, I.A.M.	Inverness 37B	
McRoberts, T.D.	Moray 35A	
MacSween, D.A.	Ross 39A	
MacSween, N.	Lewis 44B	
MacVicar, K.	Dunkeld/Meigle 27B	
McWhirter, T.M.	Wigtown/Stran' 9A	
McWilliam, A.	Glasgow 16A-146	
McWilliam, T.M.	Ross 39B	
McWilliams, G.	Perth 28A	
Mailer, C.	List 6-I	
Main, A.	Aberdeen 31B	
Main, A.W.A.	List 6-I	
Main, D.M.	Perth 28A	
Mair, J.	List 6-H	
Mair, M.V.A.	Dundee 29B	
Majcher, P.L.	England 47B	
Malcolm, A.	Inverness 37A	
Malcolm, M.	Lothian 3A	
Malloch, P.R.M.	Stirling 23A	
Malloch, R.J.	Dum'/K'cudbright 8A	
Mann, J.	Glasgow 16A-121	
Mann, J.T.	Sutherland 40A	
Manners, S.	Edinburgh 1B	
Manson, Mrs E.	G'ock/Paisley 14A	
Manson, I.A.	Europe 48A	
Manson, J.A.	Lothian 3B	
Manson, R.L.	West Lothian 2B	
Mappin, M.G.	Caithness 41B	
Marr, I.	List 6-I	
Marsh, S.	Dum'/K'cudbright 8A	
Marshall, A.S.	West Lothian 2A	
Marshall, Mrs F.	Argyll 19B	
Marshall, F.J.	Greenock/Paisley 14B	
Marshall, J.S.	List 6-H	
Marshall, T.E.	Irv'/Kilmarnock 11A	
Marten, S.	Edinburgh 1A-48	
Martin, A.M.	England 47B	
Martin, D.N.	Buchan 34A	
Martin, G.M.	Lochcarron/Skye 42B	
Martin, J.	Hamilton 17B	
Martindale, J.P.F.	Glasgow 16B	
Massie, R.W.	Kin'/Deeside 32B	
Masson, J.D.	List 6-I	
Mathers, D.L.	Falkirk 22B	
Matheson, I.G.	List 6-I	
Matheson, J.G.	Lochcarron/Skye 42B	
Mathew, J.G.	Moray 35A	
Mathieson, A.R.	Edinburgh 1B	
Mathieson, Mrs F.M.	Edinburgh 1A-8	
Mathieson, J.S.	Inverness 37A	
Matthews, J.C.	Glasgow 16A-115	
Matthews, S.C.	Glasgow 16A-97	
Maxton, R.M.	Falkirk 22B	
Maxwell, F.E.	Dumbarton 18A	
Maxwell, I.D.	Edinburgh 1A-39	
May, A.	Glasgow 16A-36	
Mayes, R.	Ayr 10A	
Mayne, K.A.L.	G'ock/Paisley 14A	
Mead, J.M.	Wigtown/Stranraer 9A	
Meager, P.	St Andrews 26B	
Mealyea, H.B.	Ayr 10A	
Mehigan, A.	Moray 35A	
Meikle, Mrs A.A.	Lanark 13A	
Mellis, R.J.	List 6-R	
Melrose, J.H.L.	Hamilton 17B	
Melville, D.D.	Dum'/K'cudbright 8A	
Merchant, M.C.	Gordon 33A	
Messeder, L.	Glasgow 16A-9	
Middleton, J.R.H.	Edinburgh 1B	
Middleton, P.	Edinburgh 1B	
Mill, D.	Greenock/Paisley 14A	
Millar, A.E.	Perth 28B	
Millar, A.M.	Perth 28B	
Millar, J.L.	Lochaber 38B	
Millar, Mrs J.M.	Perth 28B	
Millar, Miss M.R.M.	Argyll 19A	
Millar, P.W.	List 6-I	
Miller, A.	Europe 48A	
Miller, C.W.	Dundee 29B	
Miller, H.G.	Argyll 19B	
Miller, Mrs I.B.	Lists 6-H and 6-I	
Miller, I.H.	Dumbarton 18A	
Miller, J.D.	Glasgow 16B	
Miller, J.G.	Dum'/Kirkcudbright 8B	
Miller, J.R.	Dum'/Kirkcudbright 8B	
Miller, W.B.	Moray 35B	
Milliken, J.	Dum'/Kirkcudbright 8A	
Milloy, A.M.	England 47B	
Mills, A.	List 6-I	
Mills, I.A.M.	Ayr 10B	
Mills, P.W.	England 47B	
Milne, R.B.	Annandale/Eskdale	
Milroy, T.	Dundee 29B	
Milton, E.G.	Angus 30B	
Mirrilees, J.B.	Aberdeen 31B	
Mitchell, A.B.	Stirling 23A	
Mitchell, D.	Argyll 19A	
Mitchell, D.R.	Ardrossan 12B	
Mitchell, J.	Lothian 3A	
Mitchell, J.	Dundee 29B	
Mitchell, Miss S.M.	Ayr 10B	
Moffat, R.	Aberdeen 31A	
Moffat, T.	Dunfermline 24A	
Moffet, J.R.	Greenock/Paisley 14B	
Moir, I.A.	Edinburgh 1B	
Monro, G.D.	List 6-H	
Monteith, W.G.	Edinburgh 1B	

Montgomerie, Miss J.B.   Ab'deen 31B
Montgomery, D.   List 6-R
Montgomery, R.A.   G'ock/Paisley 14B
Moodie, A.R.   List 6-I
Moore, Miss A.A.   Hamilton 17A-12
Moore, D.T.   Ayr 10A
Moore, J.W.   West Lothian 2B
Moore, Ms N.   Dumbarton 18A
Moore, W.B.   Glasgow 16B
Moore, W.H.   Melrose/Peebles 4B
Morrice, A.A.   Duns 5A
Morrice, A.M.   List 6-I
Morrice, C.S.   West Lothian 2B
Morrice, W.G.   Edinburgh 1B
Morris, D.   Europe 48A
Morris, W.J.   Glasgow 16A-64
Morrison, A.   Lewis 44A
Morrison, A.H.   Irv'/K'marnock 11B
Morrison, A.W.   Argyll 19B
Morrison, Mrs C.M.   Kirkcaldy 25A
Morrison, D.   Lochcarron/Skye 42A
Morrison, D.J.   Uist 43B
Morrison, H.   Inverness 37B
Morrison, I.   Glasgow 16A-61
Morrison, I.C.   West Lothian 2B
Morrison, J.G.   Dum'/K'cudbright 8B
Morrison, Mrs M.B.   Edinburgh 1B
Morrison, R.   Glasgow 16A-74
Morrison, R.   Ross 39A
Morton, A.J.   Moray 35B
Morton, A.Q.   Lists 6-H and 6-I
Morton, A.R.   Edinburgh 1B
Morton, Mrs G.M.   Moray 35B
Morton, R.C.M.   Edinburgh 1B
Morton, T.   Glasgow 16B
Mowat, G.M.   Dundee 29B
Mowbray, H.   List 6-I
Muckart, G.W.M.   Sutherland 40A
Muir, A.   Uist 43B
Muir, Miss E.D.   Uist 43A
Muir, F.C.   Glasgow 16B
Muir, Miss M.A.   Lanark 13A
Munro, A.   Kirkcaldy 25B
Munro, A.W.   List 6-I
Munro, D.P.   Dumbarton 18B
Munro, Mrs F.J.   Kincardine/Deeside 32A
Munro, Miss G.   Perth 28B
Munro, G.A.M.   Edinburgh 1B
Munro, J.A.   Greenock/Paisley 14A
Munro, J.P.L.   Perth 28A
Munro, J.R.   Edinburgh 1A-25
Munro, Mrs M.   Wigtown/Stranraer 9B
Munro, S.   Moray 35B
Munroe, H.   Falkirk 22B
Munson, Ms W.   Melrose/Peebles 4B
Munton, J.G.   Hamilton 17B
Murdoch, C.   Greenock/Paisley 14A
Murdoch, I.C.   Hamilton 17A-80
Murdoch, J.A.H.   St Andrews 26A
Murdoch, W.M.   Dumbarton 18B
Murison, W.G.   Edinburgh 1B
Murning, J.   Falkirk 22A
Murphy, F.E.   Greenock/Paisley 14A
Murray, A.   Gordon 33A
Murray, A.   Inverness 37A
Murray, B.I.   Dunkeld/Meigle 27A
Murray, D.E.   Duns 5A
Murray, D.R.   Stirling 23B
Murray, G.M.   Glasgow 16A-124
Murray, J.W.   Lochcarron/Skye 42B

Murray, R.N.G.   West Lothian 2B
Murrie, J.   Edinburgh 1B
Musgrave, C.W.   Edinburgh 1B
Myers, F.   Glasgow 16B
Nash, G.   Greenock/Paisley 14A
Neill, B.F.   Melrose/Peebles 4B
Neilson, P.   Edinburgh 1B
Neilson, R.   Buchan 34A
Nelson, Mrs G.   West Lothian 2B
Nelson, J.   List 6-H
Nelson, R.C.   Argyll 19A
Nelson, T.   Glasgow 16A-33
Ness, D.T.   Ayr 10A
Newell, Mrs A.M.   List 6-I
Newell, J.P.   List 6-I
Newlands, G.M.   Glasgow 16B
Nicholas, M.S.   Lothian 3A
Nicholson, T.S.   Duns 5A
Nicholson, W.   Kincard'/Deeside 32B
Nicol, D.A.O.   Edinburgh 1B
Nicol, D.M.   Glasgow 16A-110
Nicol, G.G.   St Andrews 26A
Nicol, J.C.   Stirling 23B
Nicol, R.M.   West Lothian 2B
Nicol, Mrs S.E.C.   Edinburgh 1A-17
Nicoll, N.   Kin'/Deeside 32A
Nicolson, F.   Hamilton 17A-28
Nimmo, P.W.   Inverness 37A
Ninian, Miss E.J.   G'ock/Paisley 14A
Nisbet, G.C.   Kirkcaldy 25A
Niven, W.W.   Ross 39B
Noble, A.B.   Ardrossan 12A
Noble, G.S.   Buchan 34B
Norman, Miss N.M.   Mel'/Peebles 4A
Norrie, G.   Angus 30B
Norwood, D.W.   England 47B
Notman, J.R.   Kincardine/Deeside 32A
O'Brien, H.   Gordon 33A
O'Brien, J.   Falkirk 22A
Ogilvie, Mrs C.   Falkirk 22A
Ogilvy, O.M.   Wigtown/Stranraer 9B
Ogston, D.D.   Lists 6H and 6I
Ogston, E.J.   Inverness 37A
O'Leary, T.   Irv'/Kilmarnock 11B
Oliver, G.   Shetland 46A
Olsen, Miss H.C.   Lochaber 38B
Ord, J.K.   St Andrews 26B
Ormiston, H.C.   Dunkeld/Meigle 27B
Orr, J.M.   Dunfermline 24B
Osbeck, J.R.   Aberdeen 31A
Ostler, J.H.   List 6-I
Oswald, J.   Perth 28A
Ott, Mrs V.J.   Dum'/Kirkcudbright 8A
Ovens, S.B.   Stirling 23B
Owen, C.W.   List 6-I
Owen, J.J.C.   Dum'/Kirkcudbright 8B
Oxburgh, B.H.   Ardrossan 12A
Pacitti, S.A.   Lanark 13B
Page, J.R.   Greenock/Paisley 14B
Page, R.   Edinburgh 1B
Palmer, G.R.   Hamilton 17A-31
Palmer, S.W.   Greenock/Paisley 14B
Park, C.D.   Dunfermline 24A
Park, P.B.   Ayr 10A
Parker, N.   Aberdeen 31A
Paterson, A.E.   Dunfermline 24A
Paterson, D.S.   Edinburgh 1A-72
Paterson, I.M.   List 6-R

Paterson, J.H.   Ardrossan 12B
Paterson, J.L.   Stirling 23B
Paterson, J.M.K.   Edinburgh 1B
Paterson, J.W.   Ayr 10A
Paterson, Mrs M.   Kirkcaldy 25A
Paterson, S.J.   Hamilton 17A-21
Paterson, W.   Duns 5B
Paton, A.S.   Argyll 19A
Paton, I.F.   St Andrews 26B
Paton, J.H.   Argyll 19B
Paton, Miss M.J.   St Andrews 26A
Patterson, A.R.M.   Edinburgh 1A-61
Patterson, J.   Edinburgh 1A-5
Patterson, J.M.   Edinburgh 1B
Patterson, J.W.   List 6-R
Pattison, K.J.   Perth 28B
Paul, Miss A.   List 6-R
Paul, I.   Falkirk 22B
Pearson, Ms M.B.   Glasgow 16A-65
Pearson, Mrs W.   Glasgow 16A-61
Pecsuk, O.   Europe 48A
Penman, I.D.   Edinburgh 1A-37
Penny, R.F.   Dunkeld/Meigle 27A
Perry, J.B.   Angus 30B
Petrie, I.D.   Dundee 29A
Petrie, J.G.   Uist 43A
Petrie, K.L.   Aberdeen 31A
Philip, A.J.   Dunfermline 24A
Philip, D.S.   Europe 48B
Philip, G.M.   Glasgow 16B
Philip, J.   Edinburgh 1B
Philip, M.R.   Falkirk 22A
Philip, W.J.U.   Glasgow 16A-120
Phillippo, M.   Aberdeen 31A
Phillips, P.A.   Angus 30A
Philp, Miss C.   Edinburgh 1B
Philp, R.A.   Glasgow 16B
Philpot, D.   List 6-L
Picken, S.D.B.   Perth 28A
Pickering, J.M.   Dundee 29A
Pickles, R.G.D.W.   Perth 28A
Pieterse, B.   Angus 30A
Pirie, D.   Lothian 3B
Pitkeathly, D.G.   Buchan 34B
Pitkeathly, T.C.   Europe 48B
Plate, Miss M.A.G.   Edinburgh 1B
Pogue, V.C.   Dunfermline 24B
Pollock, T.L.   Glasgow 16A-133
Pollock, W.   Argyll 19B
Poole, Mrs A.M.   Moray 35B
Pope, D.H.N.   Hamilton 17A-60
Portchmouth, R.J.   St Andrews 26B
Porteous, B.   St Andrews 26B
Porter, R.   Glasgow 16B
Pot, J.   Europe 48B
Povey, J.M.   West Lothian 2A
Powrie, J.E.   Dundee 29B
Prentice, D.K.   England 47B
Prentice, G.   Greenock/Paisley 14B
Preston, T.   West Lothian 2A
Price, Mrs A.E.   Orkney 45A
Price, P.O.   Hamilton 17B
Provan, I.W.   List 6-I
Pryce, S.F.A.   Stirling 23B
Pryde, W.K.   St Andrews 26A
Purnell, D.   Aberdeen 31A
Purves, J.P.S.   List 6-K
Purves, J.S.   Glasgow 16A-69
Pyper, J.S.   Greenock/Paisley 14B

Quigley, Mrs B.D.   Dundee 29B

Raby, S.   Hamilton 17A-27
Rae, A.W.   Melrose/Peebles 4B
Rae, D.L.   List 6-R
Rae, P.C.   Lochaber 38B
Rae, R.   Dundee 29B
Rae, S.M.   Irv'/Kilmarnock 11B
Raeburn, A.C.   Glasgow 16A-49
Raeburn, G.   Hamilton 17A-65
Ramage, A.E.   Dumbarton 18B
Ramsay, A.   List 6-H
Ramsay, B.   Angus 30A
Ramsay, M.   Dunkeld/Meigle 27A
Ramsay, R.J.   Dundee 29A
Ramsay, W.G.   Glasgow 16B
Ramsden I.   Ross 39A
Randall, D.J.   Buchan 34A
Randall, D.S.   Falkirk 22A
Rankin, Miss L.-J.   Jedburgh 6A
Read, P.R.   Caithness 41A
Reamonn, P.   List 6-I
Redman, Mrs M.R.W.   Lothian 3A
Redmayne, D.   Dunfermline 24A
Redmayne, G.   Irv'/Kilmarnock 11A
Redpath, J.G.   St Andrews 26A
Reid, A.A.S.   St Andrews 26B
Reid, A.B.   Angus 30B
Reid, A.D.   Annandale/Eskdale 7A
Reid, A.G.   Dunfermline 24A
Reid, D.   Dunfermline 24B
Reid, D.T.   Perth 28B
Reid, I.M.A.   Glasgow 16A-43
Reid, J.   Kirkcaldy 25A
Reid, Miss J.G.   Glasgow 16A-116
Reid, M.R.B.C.   List 6-R
Reid, R.   Inverness 37A
Reid, R.G.   Falkirk 22A
Reid, S.   Lanark 13A
Reid, W.M.   List 6-H
Reid, W.S.   Edinburgh 1B
Rennie, A.M.   England 47B
Rennie, C.A.J.   Falkirk 22A
Rennie, D.B.   Kincard'/Deeside 32B
Rennie, J.B.   Stirling 23B
Rennie, J.D.   Annan'/Eskdale 7B
Rennie, Mrs M.R.   Edinburgh 1A-13
Rennie, S.   Angus 30
Renton, I.P.   Edinburgh 1B
Renton, J.P.   Gordon 33A
Renwick, C.C.   Glasgow 16A-85
Rettie, J.A.   Inverness 37B
Richardson, T.C.   Aberdeen 31B
Riddell, J.A.   Melrose/Peebles 4B
Riddell, T.S.   West Lothian 2A
Ridland, A.K.   Edinburgh 1B
Risby, Mrs L.   Aberdeen 31A
Ritchie, A.   Edinburgh 1A-16
Ritchie, B.   Ross 39A
Ritchie, Mrs C.   Dunkeld/Meigle 27A
Ritchie, G.W.M.   Jedburgh 6B
Ritchie, J.   Aberdeen 31A
Ritchie, J.McL.   Lothian 3B
Ritchie, M.A.   Argyll 19B
Ritchie, W.M.   Argyll 19B
Robb, N.J.   St Andrews 26B
Robb, R.P.T.   Inverness 37B
Roberts, P.   Dumbarton 18A
Robertson, A.   Glasgow 16B
Robertson, A.   Stirling 23B
Robertson, B.   Glasgow 16B
Robertson, C.   Edinburgh 1B
Robertson, Miss C.   Angus 30A

Robertson, D.McC.   List 6-R
Robertson, Miss E.M.D. Stirling 23A
Robertson, F.A.   Inverness 37A
Robertson, G.R.   Angus 30B
Robertson, I.M.   Dunkeld/Meigle 27B
Robertson, I.W.   Dum'/K'cud' 8B
Robertson, J.   Lothian 3B
Robertson, J.H.   Inverness 37A
Robertson, M.   Dunkeld/Meigle 27B
Robertson, Miss N.   St Andrews 26B
Robertson, T.G.M.   Perth 28B
Robertson, T.P.   Dundee 29B
Robson, A.   Lanark 13A
Robson, B.   Edinburgh 1A-53
Robson, G.K.   Dundee 29A
Roddick, J.   Glasgow 16A-21
Rodger, M.A.   Gordon 33B
Rodgers, D.M.   Aberdeen 31B
Rodwell, Mrs A.S.   List 6-I
Rogers, J.M.   Dundee 29B
Rogerson, S.D.   Hamilton 17B
Rollo, G.B.   Moray 35A
Rooney, M.I.G.   Angus 30A
Rose, D.S.   West Lothian 2A
Rose, M.E.S.   St Andrews 26A
Ross, A.C.   Edinburgh 1B
Ross, A.C.   Annandale/Eskdale 7B
Ross, D.M.   Glasgow 16B
Ross, D.S.   Buchan 34B
Ross, E.J.   Falkirk 22B
Ross, Mrs E.M.   Glasgow 16A-11
Ross, Ms F.C.   Ardrossan 12A
Ross, J.   Glasgow 16B
Ross, Miss J.   Glasgow 16A-79
Ross, K.R.   Edinburgh 1B
Ross, K.W.   Hamilton 17B
Ross, M.Z.   Europe 48B
Ross, Mrs S.L.   Lanark 13A
Ross, W.B.   Europe 48A
Roy, A.   Kirkcaldy 25A
Roy, A.A.   Caithness 41B
Roy, A.J.   St Andrews 26B
Roy, I.M.   Ardrossan 12B
Roy, J.   Irvine/Kilmarnock 11B
Roy, J.A.   Dundee 29B
Russell, A.   West Lothian 2B
Russell, J.   Dunkeld/Meigle 27B
Russell, K.G.   Stirling 23A
Russell, P.R.   Ayr 10B

Salmond, J.S.   Hamilton 17B
Salomon, M.M.   Glasgow 16A-143
Salters, R.B.   St Andrews 26B
Sanderson, A.M.   Ayr 10B
Sanderson, W.R.   Lothian 3B
Sangster, E.G.   Stirling 23B
Saunders, C.M.   Ayr 10B
Saunders, K.   Glasgow 16B
Savage, G.M.A.   Dum'/K'cud' 8A
Sawers, H.   List 6-I
Schluter, Miss L.   Hamilton 17A-57
Schofield, M.F.   Edinburgh 1B
Scobie, A.J.   Dumbarton 18A
Scotland, R.J.   Moray 35B
Scott, A.D.   Gordon 33B
Scott, D.D.   Dumbarton 18A
Scott, D.H.   Falkirk 22B
Scott, D.S.   Dundee 29A
Scott, D.V.   Ross 39A
Scott, E.M.   Greenock/Paisley 14B
Scott, I.G.   Edinburgh 1B

Scott, J.   Dunfermline 24B
Scott, J.   Kincardine/Deeside 32A
Scott, J.E.   List 6-I
Scott, J.F.   Stirling 23B
Scott, J.M.   St Andrews 26B
Scott, J.W.   Dum'/Kirkcudbright 8A
Scott, M.   Edinburgh 1B
Scott, R.   England 47A
Scott, T.T.   Irvine/Kilmarnock 11B
Scoular, J.M.   Stirling 23A
Scoular, S.   Dundee 29B
Scouler, M.D.   Melrose/Peebles 4A
Scouller, H.   List 6-I
Scroggie, J.C.   Dundee 29B
Seaman, R.S.   Annandale/Eskdale 7B
Searle, J.C.   Angus 30B
Seath, T.J.G.   Lanark 13B
Sefton, H.R.   Aberdeen 31B
Selemani, E.   Hamilton 17A-29
Selfridge, J.   Ardrossan 12B
Sewell, P.M.N.   Duns 5A
Shackleton, S.J.S.   Dumbarton 18B
Shackleton, W.   Glasgow 16B
Shand, G.C.   Edinburgh 1A-43
Shanks, N.J.   Glasgow 16B
Shannon, W.G.   Dunkeld/Meigle 27B
Sharp, A.   Kirkcaldy 25A
Sharp, J.   Europe 48B
Sharp, J.C.   Hamilton 17A-36
Sharp, S.   Falkirk 22A
Shaw, A.N.   Greenock/Paisley 14A
Shaw, C.A.M.   Irvine/Kilmarnock 11B
Shaw, D.   West Lothian 2A
Shaw, D.   Moray 35A
Shaw, D.   List 6-H
Shaw, D.W.D.   Lists 6-H and 6-I
Shedden, J.   Europe 48A
Sheppard, M.J.   Wigtown/Stranraer 9A
Sheret, B.S.   Glasgow 16A-68
Sherrard, H.D.   Dumbarton 18A
Sherratt, A.   Greenock/Paisley 14A
Sherry, G.T.   Stirling 23B
Shewan, F.D.F.   Edinburgh 1B
Shewan, M.R.R.   Perth 28A
Shields, J.M.   Melrose/Peebles 4B
Shields, R.B.   Dumbarton 18A
Shirra, J.   Perth 28B
Shuttleworth, A.   Ayr 10A
Silcox, J.R.   Stirling 23B
Silver, R.M.   Glasgow 16A-40
Sim, J.G.   Edinburgh 1B
Sime, Mrs C.   Dum'/K'cudbright 8A
Simpson, E.V.   Glasgow 16A-18
Simpson, G.M.   Kirkcaldy 25B
Simpson, J.A.   Perth 28B
Simpson, J.H.   Greenock/Paisley 14B
Simpson, J.H.   Dundee 29B
Simpson, N.A.   Glasgow 16B
Simpson, R.R.   Lothian 3A
Sinclair, C.A.M.   Edinburgh 1A-58
Sinclair, D.I.   St Andrews 26B
Sinclair, J.H.   Stirling 23B
Sinclair, T.S.   Lewis 44B
Siroky, S.   Melrose/Peebles 4A
Skakle, G.S.   Aberdeen 31B
Skinner, D.M.   Edinburgh 1B
Skinner, S.   List 6-H
Sloan, R.   Glasgow 16A-23
Sloan, R.P.   Perth 28B
Slorach, A.   Edinburgh 1B
Smart, D.D.   Aberdeen 31A

Smart, G.H.	Falkirk 22A	
Smillie, A.M.	Greenock/Paisley 14B	
Smith, A.	Aberdeen 31B	
Smith, A.E.	Kincard'/Deeside 32B	
Smith, D.J.	Falkirk 22A	
Smith, Mrs E.	West Lothian 2A	
Smith, G.S.	Glasgow 16B	
Smith, G.W.	West Lothian 2A	
Smith, Miss H.C.	Argyll 19A	
Smith, H.G.	Angus 30B	
Smith, H.M.C.	Moray 35A	
Smith, Miss H.W.	Edinburgh 1A-32	
Smith, J.A.W.	List 6-H	
Smith, J.M.	Uist 43B	
(Smith, J.R.	Edinburgh 1A-52)	
Smith, J.R.	List 6-R	
Smith, J.S.A.	Glasgow 16B	
Smith, M.	Abernethy 36A	
Smith, M.	Uist 43A	
Smith, N.A.	Edinburgh 1A-28	
Smith, R.	Dum'/Kirkcudbright 8B	
Smith, R.	Lothian 3A	
Smith, R.	Ross 39A	
Smith, Ms R.A.	Hamilton 17A-14	
Smith, R.C.P.	List 6-H	
Smith, R.W.	Falkirk 22A	
Smith, S.J.	Glasgow 16A-105	
Smith, S.J.	Ardrossan 12A	
Smith, W.E.	West Lothian 2B	
Sorensen, A.K.	G'ock/Paisley 14A	
Souter, D.I.	Perth 28A	
Speed, D.K.	List 6-H	
Speirs, A.	Greenock/Paisley 14A	
Spence, A.	Moray 35B	
Spence, C.K.O.	Dumbarton 18B	
Spence, Miss E.G.B.	Glasgow 16B	
Spence, Mrs S.M.	Hamilton 17A-54	
Spencer, J.	Glasgow 16B	
Spiers, J.M.	Glasgow 16B	
Spowart, Mrs M.G.	List 6-H	
Squires, J.F.R.	List 6-R	
Steel, G.H.B.	Greenock/Paisley 14A	
Steele, H.D.	Annan'/Eskdale 7A	
Steele, L.M.	Melrose/Peebles 4A	
Steele, Miss M.	West Lothian 2A	
Steell, S.C.	G'ock/Paisley 14A	
Steenbergen, Ms P.	Buchan 34A	
Stein, J.	Dunfermline 24A	
Stein, Mrs M.E.	Dunfermline 24A	
Stenhouse, Ms E.M.	Dunfermline 24A	
Stenhouse, W.D.	Perth 28B	
Stephen, A.	Kin'/Deeside 32A	
Stephen, D.M.	Edinburgh 1B	
Sterrett, J.B.	Sutherland 40A	
Steven, H.A.M.	Dumbarton 18B	
Stevens, A.	Europe 48A	
Stevens, L.	Angus 30A	
Stevenson, A.L.	St Andrews 26B	
Stevenson, D.F.	Abernethy 36A	
Stevenson, J.	Edinburgh 1B	
Stevenson, J.	Glasgow 16B	
Stewart, Mrs A.E.	Perth 28B	
Stewart, A.T.	Edinburgh 1A-14	
Stewart, A.T.	Stirling 23B	
Stewart, C.E.	England 47B	
Stewart, D.	G'ock/Paisley 14A	
Stewart, Ms D.E.	Glasgow 16B	
Stewart, D.J.	Kin'/Deeside 32A	
Stewart, F.M.C.	Dundee 29A	
Stewart, G.C.	Gordon 33B	
Stewart, G.G.	Perth 28B	

Stewart, J.	Argyll 19A	
Stewart, J.C.	Perth 28A	
Stewart, J.C.	Aberdeen 31B	
Stewart, Mrs J.E.	Argyll 19B	
Stewart, J.M.	Lanark 13B	
Stewart, L.	Dunkeld/Meigle 27A	
Stewart, Mrs M.L.	List 6-I	
Stewart, Ms N.D.	Glasgow 16B	
Stewart, R.J.	Perth 28B	
Stewart, Ms U.B.	Hamilton 17A-75	
Stewart, W.T.	Hamilton 17A-40	
Stewart, W.T.A.	List 6-R	
Stirling, A.D.	Edinburgh 1B	
Stirling, G.A.S.	Inverness 37B	
Stirling, I.R.	Ayr 10B	
Stitt, R.J.M.	Hamilton 17A-44	
Stiven, I.K.	Edinburgh 1B	
Stoddart, A.C.	Annandale/Eskdale 7A	
Stoddart, A.G.	Gordon 33B	
Stoddart, D.L.	St Andrews 26B	
Stone, W.V.	Greenock/Paisley 14B	
Storrar, W.F.	List 6-I	
Stott, K.D.	Dundee 29A	
Strachan, A.E.	Dum'/K'cudbright 8B	
Strachan, D.G.	List 6-I	
Strachan, G.	List 6-I	
Strachan, I.M.	Aberdeen 31B	
Strickland, A.	Dundee 29B	
Strong, C.	St Andrews 26B	
Strong, C.A.	Irvine/Kilmarnock 11A	
Sutcliffe, Miss C.B.	Irv'/K'nock 11A	
Sutherland, C.A.	Hamilton 17A-13	
Sutherland, D.	Dundee 29A	
Sutherland, D.I.	Glasgow 16B	
Sutherland, Miss E.W.	Glasgow 16B	
Sutherland, I.A.	Buchan 34A	
Sutherland, W.	Kirkcaldy 25B	
Swan, A.	List 6-H	
Swan, A.F.	Lothian 3B	
Swan, D.	Aberdeen 31A	
Swinburne, N.	Annan'/Eskdale 7B	
Swindells, Mrs A.J.	Edinburgh 1A-29	
Swindells, S.	Aberdeen 31A	
Swinton, J.	Aberdeen 31B	
Symington, A.H.	Ayr 10A	
Tait, A.	Glasgow 16B	
Tait, H.A.G.	Perth 28B	
Tait, J.M.	Edinburgh 1A-59	
Tait, T.W.	Dunkeld/Meigle 27B	
Tallach, J.	Ross 39A	
Talman, H.	Falkirk 22B	
(Tamas, B.	Europe 48A)	
Taverner, D.J.	Angus 30A	
Taverner, G.R.	Melrose/Peebles 4B	
Taylor, A.H.S.	Perth 28B	
Taylor, A.S.	Ardrossan 12B	
Taylor, A.T.	Argyll 19B	
Taylor, A.T.H.	List 6-H	
Taylor, B.S.C.	Aberdeen 31A	
Taylor, Mrs C.	St Andrews 26A	
Taylor, C.G.	Dundee 29A	
Taylor, D.J.	Dunfermline 24B	
Taylor, G.J.A.	G'ock/Paisley 14A	
Taylor, H.G.	Edinburgh 1B	
Taylor, I.	Glasgow 16A-3	
Taylor, I.	St Andrews 26B	
Taylor, Miss J.C.	Gordon 33A	
Taylor, J.H.B.	Irv'/Kilmarnock 11A	
Taylor, P.R.	Kincardine/Deeside 32B	
Taylor, T.	West Lothian 2A	

Taylor, W.	Buchan 34B	
Taylor, W.R.	Edinburgh 1B	
Telfer, A.B.	Ayr 10A	
Telfer, I.J.M.	Edinburgh 1B	
Templeton, J.L.	Kirkcaldy 25A	
Thain, G.M.	Glasgow 16A-118	
Thom, D.J.	Greenock/Paisley 14A	
Thom, I.G.	Hamilton 17A-70	
Thomas, M.R.H.	Angus 30B	
Thomas, Mrs S.	Angus 30B	
Thompson, W.M.D.	Jedburgh 6B	
Thomson, A.	Glasgow 16A-35	
Thomson, A.	Hamilton 17B	
Thomson, D.M.	Kirkcaldy 25A	
Thomson, E.P.L.	Jedburgh 6A	
Thomson, G.F.M.	Melrose/Peebles 4B	
Thomson, G.L.	Kirkcaldy 25B	
Thomson, I.U.	Gordon 33A	
Thomson, J.B.	Perth 28A	
Thomson, J.D.	Kirkcaldy 25B	
Thomson, J.M.	Moray 35B	
Thomson, J.M.A.	Hamilton 17A-47	
Thomson, M.	Ardrossan 12A	
Thomson, Mrs M.	Ardrossan 12B	
Thomson, P.	Buchan 34A	
Thomson, P.D.	Perth 28B	
Thomson, P.G.	St Andrews 26B	
Thomson, R.	Falkirk 22A	
Thomson, S.	England 47B	
Thomson, W.	Falkirk 22A	
Thomson, W.H.	Lothian 3B	
Thorburn, R.J.	Buchan 34A	
Thorne, L.W.	Hamilton 17B	
Thornthwaite, A.P.	Edinburgh 1A-86	
Thrower, C.G.	St Andrews 26B	
Tierney, J.P.	Kincardine/Deeside 32B	
Todd, A.S.	Stirling 23B	
Todd, J.F.	List 6-H	
Tollick, F.	List 6-I	
Tomlinson, B.L.	Kirkcaldy 25B	
Torrance, A.	St Andrews 26B	
Torrance, D.J.	Glasgow 16A-12	
Torrance, D.W.	Lothian 3B	
Torrance, I.R.	Aberdeen 31B	
Torrance, T.F.	Edinburgh 1B	
Torrens, J.K.	Glasgow 16A-127	
Torrens, S.A.R.	Edinburgh 1A-3	
Travers, R.	Irvine/Kilmarnock 11A	
Trevorrow, J.A.	England 47B	
Troup, H.J.G.	Argyll 19B	
Turnbull, J.	Lanark 13B	
Turnbull, J.J.	St Andrews 26B	
Turnbull, J.S.	List 6-I	
Turner, A.	Glasgow 16B	
Turner, F.K.	Inverness 37B	
Tuton, R.M.	Glasgow 16B	
Twaddle, L.H.	Lothian 3A	
Tyre, R.	Angus 30B	
Underwood, Mrs F.A.	Lothian 3B	
Underwood, G.H.	Lothian 3B	
Urie, D.M.L.	List 6-H	
Urquhart, J.A.	Irv'/Kilmarnock 11A	
Urquhart, J.D.	Lochcarron/Skye 42A	
Urquhart, N.	Irv'/Kilmarnock 11A	
van Sittert, P.	Buchan 34A	
Varwell, A.P.J.	Lochaber 38A	
Vermeulen, C.	Glasgow 16A-17	
Vidits, G.	Dumbarton 18A	
Vincent, C.R.	Dum'/K'cudbright 8B	

Vint, A.S.   Glasgow 16A-45
Vischer, J.   Argyll 19A
Vivers, K.A.   Annandale/Eskdale 7B

Waddell, Mrs E.A.   Hamilton 17A-52
Walker, A.L.   Glasgow 16B
Walker, D.K.   Kincard'/Deeside 32A
Walker, D.S.   Ardrossan 12B
Walker, I.   West Lothian 2B
Walker, J.B.   St Andrews 26B
Walker, K.D.F.   Lothian 3A
Walker, R.B.W.   List 6-R
Walker, R.F.   England 47B
Wallace, C.   Dum'/Kirkcudbright 8A
Wallace, D.S.   England 47B
Wallace, D.W.   Hamilton 17A-37
Wallace, H.M.   Aberdeen 31A
Wallace, J.H.   Melrose/Peebles 4A
Wallace, R.J.S.   Gordon 33B
Wallace, W.F.   Caithness 41A
Walton, A.   Glasgow 16B
Wandrum, D.   Falkirk 22A
Ward, A.H.   Greenock/Paisley 14A
Ward, M.J.   England 47B
Wardlaw, E.G.S.   List 6-R
Wark, A.C.   Greenock/Paisley 14A
Warner, K.   Caithness 41A
Warnock, D.   Angus 30B
Warwick, I.C.   Ross 39A
Watson, Mrs E.R.L.   Ardrossan 12A
Watson, I.M.   Lanark 13A
Watson, J.   Argyll 19B
Watson, J.B.   Duns 5A
Watson, J.M.   Aberdeen 31A
Watson, Miss J.S.   Stirling 23B
Watson, Mrs K.K.   Edinburgh 1A-49
Watson, Mrs P.   Edinburgh 1A-23
Watson, T.D.   Ayr 10A
Watson, V.G.C.   Ardrossan 12A
Watt, A.G.N.   Angus 30A
Watt, H.F.   Inverness 37A
Watt, R.   Stirling 23B
Watt, R.J.   Dumbarton 18A
Watt, W.D.   Kincardine/Deeside 32B
Watt, W.G.   Aberdeen 31B
Watts, A.   Kincardine/Deeside 32A
Waugh, J.L.   Inverness 37B
Weatherhead, J.L.   Lists 6-H and 6-I
Weaver, S.G.   Edinburgh 1A-63
Webster, A.F.   Angus 30A

Webster, B.G.   Stirling 23A
Webster, J.G.   List 6-H
Webster, P.   Edinburgh 1A-62
Weighton, Mrs G.   Stirling 23A
Weir, J.   Aberdeen 31A
Weir, Mrs M.K.   List 6-I
Wells, I.J.   Edinburgh 1A-66
Wells, J.R.   Lothian 3A
Welsh, A.M.   Irv'/Kilmarnock 11B
West, R.B.   Argyll 19A
Westmarland, C.A.   List 6-H
White, B.A.   Dunkeld/Meigle 27B
White, C.P.   Glasgow 16A-129
White, D.M.   Glasgow 16A-25
Whitecross, Mrs J.   Dumbarton 18A
Whiteford, A.   Inverness 37A
Whiteford, D.H.   Lothian 3B
Whiteford, J.D.   Glasgow 16A-102
Whiteford, R.S.   Falkirk 22B
Whiteman, D.   Ayr 10A
Whitley, L.A.B.   Glasgow 16A-62
Whitson, W.S.   West Lothian 2B
Whitton, J.P.   England 47B
Whyte, D.W.   Abernethy 36A
Whyte, G.J.   Edinburgh 1A-9
Whyte, I.A.   Edinburgh 1B
Whyte, Mrs I.H.   Dunfermline 24B
Whyte, J.   Ardrossan 12A
Whyte, J.H.   Greenock/Paisley 14B
Whyte, Mrs M.   Glasgow 16A-107
Whyte, N.R.   Duns 5A
Whyte, R.C.   Abernethy 36A
Whyte, W.B.   Dunkeld/Meigle 27B
Wigglesworth, J.C.   Edinburgh 1B
Wilkie, G.D.   List 6-H
Wilkie, I.   Falkirk 22A
Wilkie, J.L.   Aberdeen 31A
Wilkie, J.R.   Dum'/Kirkcudbright 8B
Wilkie, W.E.   Aberdeen 31B
Wilkinson, A.D.   Ayr 10A
Wilkinson, J.   Edinburgh 1B
Wilkinson, W.B.   Argyll 19B
Williams, Miss J.M.   Edinburgh 1B
Williams, T.C.   Annan'/Eskdale 7B
Williamson, C.R.   Perth 28A
Williamson, J.   Dum'/K'cud' 8A
Williamson, M.J.C.   Shetland 46A
Williamson, T.   Angus 30B
Willoughby, Mrs M.   Lothian 3A
Wilson, A.G.N.   Aberdeen 31A

Wilson, G.R.   Irvine/Kilmarnock 11A
Wilson, Ms H.   Dundee 29A
Wilson, I.M.   Inverness 37B
Wilson, J.   Glasgow 16A-139
Wilson, J.H.   Hamilton 17B
Wilson, J.H.C.   Glasgow 16A-32
Wilson, J.L.   Dundee 29A
Wilson, J.M.   Dunkeld/Meigle 27B
Wilson, J.M.   Edinburgh 1B
Wilson M.   List 6-L
Wilson, Miss M.   Kirkcaldy 25A
Wilson, Mrs M.D.   Dunkeld/Meigle 27B
Wilson, Mrs P.M.   Falkirk 22B
Wilson, R.M.   St Andrews 26B
Wilson, T.F.   Aberdeen 31B
Wilson, W.S.   Shetland 46B
Wilson, W.T.S.   Glasgow 16A-5
Winn, Mrs F.M.M.   List 6-I
Winning, A.A.   Lochaber 38B
Wishart, J.   Buchan 34A
Wood, G.M.   Europe 48A
Wood, J.L.K.   Aberdeen 31B
Wood, P.J.   List 6-I
Woods, Mrs J.M.   Moray 35A
Wotherspoon, I.G.   St Andrews 26B
Wotherspoon, R.C.   Dum'/K'cud' 8B
Wright, D.L.   Moray 35B
Wright, J.P.   Stirling 23B
Wright, M.   Dumbarton 18B
Wyatt, F.   Argyll 19A
Wylie, W.A.   List 6-H
Wyllie, H.R.   Hamilton 17B

Yorke, K.B.   Ayr 10A
Young, A.W.   Edinburgh 1B
Young, D.A.   Lanark 13B
Young, Mrs E.M.   St Andrews 26B
Young, G.S.   Dunkeld/Meigle 27B
Young, J.   Dum'/Kirkcudbright 8B
Young, J.N.   Edinburgh 1A-46
Young, Mrs R.M.   Ayr 10A
Younger, Mrs A.   Glasgow 16B
Younger, A.S.   Inverness 37A
Youngson, E.J.B.   Edinburgh 1A-41
Youngson, P.   Angus 30B
Yule, Mrs M.J.B.   Dumbarton 18A
Yule, R.F.   Buchan 34A

Zambonini, J.   Hamilton 17B

INDEX OF PARISHES AND PLACES

NOTE: Numbers on the right of the column refer to the Presbytery in which the district lies. Names in brackets are given for ease of identification. They may refer to the name of the Parish, which may be different from that of the district, or they distinguish places with the same name, or they indicate the first named charge in a union.

Abdie and Dunbog	26	Ardrossan	12	Bearsden	18	Botriphnie (Keith)	35
Abercorn	2	Arisaig and the		Beath	24	Bourtie (Meldrum)	33
Aberdeen	31	Small Isles	38	Beattock		Bowden and Melrose	4
Aberdour (Buchan)	34	Armadale	2	(Kirkpatrick Juxta)	7	Bower	41
Aberdour (Fife)	24	Arnsheen Barrhill		Beauly (Kilmorack)	37	Bowling	
Aberfeldy	27	(St Colmon)	10	Beith	12	(Old Kilpatrick)	18
Aberfoyle	23	Arrochar	18	Belhaven	3	Bowmore (Kilarrow)	19
Aberlady	3	Ashkirk	4	Belhelvie	33	Bracadale and Duirinish	42
Aberlemno	30	Assynt and Stoer	40	Bellie	35	Braemar and Crathie	32
Aberlour	35	Athelstaneford	3	Bellshill	17	Braes of Rannoch	27
Aberluthnott	32	Auchaber	34	Benarty (Lochgelly)	24	Brechin	30
Abernethy and Dron		Auchencairn		Benbecula	43	Breich Valley	2
and Arngask	28	and Rerrick	8	Bendochy	27	Bressay (Lerwick)	46
Abernethy	36	Auchinleck	10	Berneray and		Bridge of Allan	23
Abernyte	29	Auchterarder	28	Lochmaddy	43	Bridge of Earn	
Aboyne and Dinnet	32	Auchterderran	25	Bervie	32	(Dunbarney)	28
Acharacle	38	Auchtergaven and		Berwick-upon-Tweed		Bridge of Weir	14
Advie (Cromdale)	36	Moneydie	28	and Lowick	5	Brightons	22
Airdrie	17	Auchterhouse	29	Biggar	13	Broadford (Strath)	42
Airth	22	Auchterless	34	Bilston	3	Brodick	12
Aithsting (Sandsting)	46	Auchtermuchty	26	Birnie and Pluscarden	35	Broom	16
Alexandria	18	Auchtertool	25	Birsay, Harray and		Broughton, Glenholm	
Allanton (Edrom)	5	Auldearn and Dalmore	37	Sandwick	45	and Kilbucho	4
Alloa	23	Aviemore		Birse and Feughside	32	Broughty Ferry	
Alloway	10	(Rothiemurchus)	36	Bishopbriggs	16	(Dundee)	29
Almondbank		Avoch	39	Bishopton	14	Broxburn	2
Tibbermore	28	Avonbridge	2	Blackbraes and		Brydekirk	7
Alness	39	Ayr	10	Shieldhill	22	Buchanan	23
Altnaharra and Farr	40	Ayton and Burnmouth	5	Blackburn and Seafield	2	Buchlyvie	23
Alva	23			Blackford	28	Buckhaven	25
Alves and Burghead	35	Baldernock	18	Black Mount	13	Buckie	35
Alvie and Insh	36	Balfron	23	Blackridge	2	Bucksburn Stoneywood	31
Alyth	27	Balgonie (Kennoway)	25	Blair Atholl and Struan	27	Buittle and Kelton	8
Amulree and		Baljaffray (Bearsden)	18	Blairbeth	16	Bunessan	
Strathbraan	27	Ballantrae	10	Blairdaff and Chapel		(Kilfinichen)	21
Annan	7	Balloch (Jamestown)	18	of Garioch	33	Burghead (Alves)	35
Annbank	10	Balmaclellan and Kells	8	Blairgowrie	27	Burnmouth (Ayton)	5
Anstruther	26	Balmaghie	8	Blairingone (Saline)	24	Burnside	16
Appin	19	Balmedie (Belhelvie)	33	Blantyre	17	Burntisland	25
Applecross, Lochcarron		Balmerino	26	Boarhills and Dunino	26	Burra Isle	46
and Torridon	42	Balquhidder	23	Boat of Garten and		Burray	
Applegarth, Sibbaldbie		Banchory-Devenick		Kincardine	36	(South Ronaldsay)	45
and Johnstone	7	and Maryculter/		Boharm (Keith)	35	Burrelton (Cargill)	28
Arbirlot	30	Cookney	32	Boleskine (Dores)	37	Busby	16
Arbroath	30	Banchory-Ternan	32	Bolton and Saltoun	3	Bute, The United Church of	19
Arbuthnott	32	Banff	34	Bona (Inverness)	37		
Archiestown		Bankfoot		Bonar Bridge (Creich)	40	Cabrach (Mortlach)	35
(Knockando)	35	(Auchtergaven)	28	Bo'ness	22	Cadder	16
Ardchattan	19	Bannockburn	23	Bonhill	18	Caddonfoot	4
Ardentinny (Strone)	19	Banton	16	Bonkle (Newmains)	17	Caerlaverock	8
Ardeonaig (Killin)	23	Bargeddie	17	Bonkyl and Preston	5	Cairneyhill	24
Ardersier	37	Barr	10	Bonnybridge	22	Cairngryffe	13
Ardgay (Kincardine)	40	Barra	43	Bonnyrigg	3	Cairnie-Glass (Huntly)	33
Ardgour	38	Barrhead	14	Border Kirk, The	7	Calder, Kirk of	2
Ardler, Kettins and		Barrhill (Arnsheen)	10	Borgue	8	Calderbank	17
Meigle	27	Barry	30	Borthwick	3	Caldercruix and	
Ardnamurchan	38	Barthol Chapel	33	Bothkennar and		Longriggend	17
Ardoch	28	Barvas	44	Carronshore	22	Caldwell	14
Ardrishaig	19	Bathgate	2	Bothwell	17	Callander	23

Cambusbarron 23
Cambuslang 16
Cambusnethan (Wishaw) 17
Cameron 26
Campbeltown 19
Campsie 16
Canisbay 41
Canonbie 7
Caputh and Clunie 27
Cara (Gigha) 19
Cardross 18
Careston (Fern) 30
Carfin 17
Cargill Burrelton 28
Carinish 43
Carlops 4
Carloway 44
Carluke 13
Carmunnock (Glasgow) 16
Carmyllie 30
Carnbee 26
Carnock and Oakley 24
Carnoustie 30
Carnwath 13
Carradale (Saddell) 19
Carriden 22
Carrington (Cockpen) 3
Carron (Stenhouse) 22
Carronshore
  (Bothkennar) 22
Carsphairn 8
Carstairs and
  Carstairs Junction 13
Castle Douglas 8
Castletown (Olrig) 41
Cathkin (Glasgow
  Fernhill) 16
Catrine 10
Cavers and Kirkton 6
Cawdor 37
Cellardyke 26
Ceres and Springfield 26
Channelkirk and Lauder 4
Chapel of Garioch
  (Blairdaff) 33
Chapelhall 17
Chapelton 17
Chirnside 5
Chryston 16
Clackmannan 23
Cleish 28
Cleland 17
Closeburn 8
Clunie (Caputh) 27
Cluny 33
Clydebank 18
Clyne 40
Coalburn 13
Coalsnaughton (Sauchie) 23
Coatbridge 17
Cockenzie and
  Port Seton 3
Cockpen and Carrington 3
Coldingham and St Abb's 5
Coldstream 5
Colinsburgh
  (Kilconquhar) 26
Colintraive (Kilmodan) 19
Coll 19
Collace 28
Colliston 30

Colmonell (St Colmon) 10
Colonsay and Oronsay 19
Colvend, Southwick
  and Kirkbean 8
Comrie 28
Condorrat
  (Cumbernauld) 22
Connel 19
Contin 39
Cookney
  (Banchory-Devenick) 32
Corby 47
Cornhill (Ordiquhill) 34
Corpach (Kilmallie) 38
Corrie (Arran) 12
Corrie (Hutton) 7
Corsock and
  Kirkpatrick Durham 8
Coupar Angus 27
Cove (Craigrownie) 18
Cowdenbeath 24
Cowie and Plean 23
Coylton 10
Craigie 10
Craignish 19
Craigrownie 18
Crail 26
Cranstoun, Crichton
  and Ford 3
Crathie (Braemar) 32
Creich 40
Creich, Flisk and
  Kilmany 26
Crichton (Cranstoun) 3
Crieff 28
Crimond 34
Croick (Kincardine) 40
Cromar 32
Cromarty 39
Cromdale and Advie 36
Cross, Ness 44
Crossbost (Lochs) 44
Crossford 13
Crosshill 10
Crosshouse 11
Crossmichael and
  Parton 8
Croy and Dalcross 37
Cruden 34
Cullen and Deskford 35
Culloden 37
Culross and Torryburn 24
Culsalmond and Rayne 33
Culter 13
Cults 31
Cumbernauld 22
Cumbrae 12
Cuminestown
  (Monquhitter) 34
Cumlodden
  Lochfyneside and
  Lochgair 19
Cummertrees 8
Cumnock 10
Cunningsburgh
  (Sandwick) 46
Cushnie and Tough 33
Cupar 26

Dailly 10
Dairsie 26

Dalarossie (Moy) 37
Dalavich (Kilchrenan) 19
Dalbeattie 8
Dalcross (Croy) 37
Dalgety 24
Dalkeith 3
Dallas 35
Dalmally (Glenorchy) 19
Dalmellington 10
Dalmeny 1
Dalmore (Auldearn) 37
Dalmuir 18
Dalry (Ayrshire) 12
Dalry (St John's Town) 8
Dalrymple 10
Dalserf 17
Dalton 7
Dalziel (Motherwell) 17
Darvel 11
Daviot 33
Daviot and Dunlichity 37
Deer 34
Delting 46
Denbeath (Methilhill) 25
Denny 22
Deskford (Cullen) 35
Devonside (Fossoway) 28
Dingwall 39
Dinnet (Aboyne) 32
Dirleton 3
Dollar 23
Dores and Boleskine 37
Dornoch 40
Dornock 7
Douglas Valley
  Church, The 13
Doune (Kilmadock) 23
Dreghorn and Springside 11
Dron (Abernethy) 28
Drongan 10
Drumblade 33
Drumclog (Strathaven) 17
Drumelzier (Stobo) 4
Drummore
  (Kirkmaiden) 9
Drumnadrochit
  (Urquhart) 37
Drumoak and Durris 32
Drymen 23
Dufftown (Mortlach) 35
Duffus, Spynie and
  Hopeman 35
Duirinish (Bracadale) 42
Dull and Weem 27
Dulnain Bridge 36
Dumbarton 18
Dumfries 8
Dun and Hillside 30
Dunbar 3
Dunbarney and
  Forgandenny 28
Dunblane 23
Dunbog (Abdie) 26
Dundee 29
Dundonald 10
Dundonnell (Gairloch) 42
Dundrennan (Rerrick) 8
Dundurn 28
Dunfermline 24
Dunglass 3
Dunino (Boarhills) 26

Dunipace (Denny) 22
Dunkeld 27
Dunlichity (Daviot) 37
Dunlop 11
Dunnet 41
Dunnichen, Letham
  and Kirkden 30
Dunnottar (Stonehaven) 32
Dunoon 19
Dunrossness 46
Duns 5
Dunscore 8
Duntocher 18
Dunure (Fisherton) 10
Dunvegan (Bracadale
  and Duirinish) 42
Durisdeer 8
Durness and
  Kinlochbervie 40
Duror 38
Durris (Drumoak) 32
Duthil 36
Dyce 31
Dyke 35
Dysart 25

Eaglesfield (Kirtle) 7
Eaglesham 16
Earlston 4
Eassie and Nevay 30
East Calder
  (Kirknewton) 2
East Kilbride 17
East Linton (Traprain) 3
East Mainland 45
Eccles 5
Echt 33
Eday 45
Edderton (Kincardine) 40
Eddleston 4
Eddrachillis 40
Edenshead and
  Strathmiglo 26
Edinburgh 1
Edinkillie 35
Ednam (Kelso North) 6
Edrom Allanton 5
Edzell Lethnot Glenesk 30
Elchies (Knockando) 35
Ederslie 14
Elgin 35
Elie 26
Ellon 33
Enzie 35
Erchless (Kilmorack) 37
Errol 28
Erskine 14
Ervie Kirkcolm 9
Eskdalemuir (Langholm) 7
Ettrick and Yarrow 4
Evanton (Kiltearn) 39
Evie 45
Ewes (Langholm) 7
Eyemouth 5

Fair Isle (Dunrossness) 46
Fairlie 12
Fala and Soutra 3
Falkirk 22
Falkland 26
Fallin 23

Farnell 30
Farr (Altnaharra) 40
Fauldhouse 2
Fearn Abbey and Nigg 39
Fenwick 11
Fergushill 12
Ferintosh 39
Fern Careston Menmuir 30
Fernhill and Cathkin 16
Fetlar 46
Fetteresso (Stonehaven) 32
Feughside (Birse) 32
Findhorn (Kinloss) 35
Findochty 35
Fintray Kinellar
 Keithhall 33
Fintry 23
Firth 45
Fisherton 10
Fishwick (Hutton) 5
Flisk (Creich) 26
Flotta 45
Fodderty and
 Strathpeffer 39
Fogo and Swinton 5
Ford (Cranstoun) 3
Ford (Glassary) 19
Fordyce 34
Forfar 30
Forgandenny
 (Dunbarney) 28
Forglen (Turriff) 34
Forres 35
Fort Augustus 38
Forth 13
Fortingall and
 Glenlyon 27
Fortrose and
 Rosemarkie 39
Fort William 38
Foss and Rannoch 27
Fossoway and
 Devonside 28
Foulden and
 Mordington 5
Foveran 33
Fowlis and Liff 29
Fowlis Wester,
 Madderty and Monzie 28
Fraserburgh 34
Freuchie 26
Friockheim Kinnell 30
Fyvie 34

Gairloch and
 Dundonnell 42
Galashiels 4
Galston 11
Gardenstown 34
Garelochhead 18
Gargunnock 23
Gartcosh 16
Gartmore 23
Gartocharn
 (Kilmaronock) 18
Garvald and Morham 3
Gask 28
Gatehouse of Fleet 8
Gateside (Edenshead) 26
Giffnock 16
Gifford (Yester) 3

Gigha and Cara 19
Gilmerton (Edinburgh) 1
Gilmerton (Monzie) 28
Girvan 10
Gladsmuir 3
Glamis Inverarity and
 Kinnettles 30
Glasford 17
Glasgow 16
Glass (Huntly) 33
Glassary, Kilmartin and
 Ford 19
Glasserton and
 Isle of Whithorn 9
Glenaray and Inveraray 19
Glenboig 16
Glencairn and Moniaive 8
Glencaple 13
Glencoe 38
Glencorse 3
Glendaruel (Kilmodan) 20
Glendevon 23
Glenelg and Kintail 42
Glenesk (Edzell) 30
Glengarry 38
Glenholm (Broughton) 4
Glenlivet (Tomintoul) 36
Glenlyon (Fortingall) 27
Glenmoriston
 (Urquhart) 37
Glenmuick 32
Glenorchy and
 Innishael 19
Glenrothes 25
Glens, The and
 Kirriemuir Old 30
Glenshee (Kirkmichael) 27
Golspie 40
Gordon 5
Gorebridge 3
Gourock 14
Grange (Keith) 35
Grangemouth 22
Grantown-on-Spey 36
Grantshouse and
 Houndwood and
 Reston 5
Grantully, Logierait
 and Strathtay 27
Greenbank (Edinburgh) 1
Greenbank (Glasgow) 16
Greengairs 17
Greenlaw 5
Greenock 14
Gretna, Half Morton and
 Kirkpatrick-Fleming 7
Guernsey 47
Gullane 3
Guthrie and Rescobie 30

Haddington 3
Haggs 22
Half Morton (Gretna) 7
Halkirk and Westerdale 41
Hamilton 17
Harray (Birsay) 45
Harthill 2
Harwood (Polbeth) 2
Hawick 6
Helensburgh 18
Helmsdale (Kildonan) 40

Heriot (Stow) 4
Hightae 7
Hillside (Dun) 30
Hobkirk and
 Southdean 6
Hoddam 7
Holytown 17
Holywood
 (Dumfries Lincluden) 8
Hopeman (Duffus) 35
Houndwood
 (Grantshouse) 5
Houston and Killellan 14
Howe of Fife 26
Howe Trinity 33
Howgate 3
Hownam (Morebattle) 6
Howwood 14
Hoy and Walls 45
Humbie 3
Huntly 33
Hurlford 11
Hutton and Corrie 7
Hutton and Fishwick
 and Paxton 5

Inch 9
Inchbrayock 30
Inchinnan 14
Inchture and Kinnaird 29
Innellan 19
Innerleithen, Traquair
 and Walkerburn 4
Innerleven 25
Innishael (Glenorchy) 19
Insch-Leslie-
 Premnay-Oyne 33
Insh (Alvie) 36
Inverallochy and
 Rathen East 34
Inveraray (Glenaray) 19
Inverarity (Glamis) 30
Inveraven (Tomintoul) 36
Inverbervie (Bervie) 32
Invergordon 39
Invergowrie 29
Inverkeilor and Lunan 30
Inverkeithing 24
Inverkip 14
Inverness 37
Inverurie 33
Iona 19
Irongray, Lochrutton and
 Terregles 8
Irvine 11
Isla Parishes, The 30
Isle of Whithorn
 (Glasserton) 9

Jamestown 18
Jedburgh 6
Jersey 47
Johnstone (Applegarth) 7
Johnstone (Paisley) 14
Jura 19

Keir (Penpont) 8
Keiss 41
Keith 35
Keithhall (Fintray) 33
Kells (Balmaclellan) 8

Kelso 6
Kelso Country Churches 6
Kelton (Buittle) 8
Kelty 24
Kemback 26
Kemnay 33
Kenmore and Lawers 27
Kennoway, Windygates
 and Balgonie 25
Kettins (Ardler) 27
Kilarrow 19
Kilbarchan 14
Kilberry 19
Kilbirnie 12
Kilbrandon and
 Kilchattan 19
Kilbucho (Broughton) 4
Kilcalmonell 19
Kilchattan
 (Kilbrandon) 19
Kilchenzie (Killean) 19
Kilchoman 19
Kilchrenan and
 Dalavich 19
Kilchrist (Urray) 39
Kilconquhar and
 Colinsburgh 26
Kilcreggan
 (Craigrownie) 18
Kildalton and Oa 19
Kildonan (Whiting Bay) 12
Kildonan and Loth,
 Helmsdale 40
Kilfinan 19
Kilfinichen, Kilvickeon
 and the Ross of Mull 19
Killean and Kilchenzie 19
Killearn 23
Killearnan 39
Killellan (Houston) 14
Killin and Ardeonaig 23
Kilmacolm 14
Kilmadock 23
Kilmallie 38
Kilmany (Creich) 26
Kilmarnock 11
Kilmaronock Gartocharn 18
Kilmartin (Glassary) 19
Kilmaurs 11
Kilmelford (Kilninver) 19
Kilmeny 19
Kilmodan and
 Colintraive 19
Kilmonivaig 38
Kilmorack and Erchless 37
Kilmore and Oban 19
Kilmore (Kilninian) 19
Kilmorich
 (Lochgoilhead) 19
Kilmory 12
Kilmuir and
 Logie Easter 39
Kilmuir and Stenscholl
 (Skye) 42
Kilmuir and Paible 43
Kilmun 19
Kilninian and Kilmore 19
Kilninver and
 Kilmelford 19
Kilrenny 26
Kilspindie and Rait 28

Kilsyth	16
Kiltarlity	37
Kiltearn	39
Kilvickeon (Kilfinichen)	19
Kilwinning	12
Kincardine (Tulliallan)	24
Kincardine (Boat of Garten)	36
Kincardine, Croick and Edderton	40
Kincardine in Menteith	23
Kinclaven	27
Kinellar (Fintray)	33
Kinfauns (St Madoes)	28
King Edward	34
Kinghorn	25
Kinglassie	25
Kingsbarns	26
Kingscavil (Pardovan)	2
Kingswells	31
Kingussie	36
Kinkell (Trinity Gask)	28
Kinloch	44
Kinlochbervie (Durness)	40
Kinlochleven	38
Kinlochspelvie (Torosay)	19
Kinloss and Findhorn	35
Kinnaird (Inchture)	29
Kinneff	32
Kinnell (Friockheim)	30
Kinnettles (Glamis)	30
Kinross	28
Kintail (Glenelg)	42
Kintore	33
Kippen	23
Kirkbean (Colvend)	8
Kirkcaldy	25
Kirkcolm (Ervie)	9
Kirkconnel	8
Kirkcowan	9
Kirkcudbright	8
Kirkden (Dunnichen)	30
Kirkfieldbank	13
Kirkgunzeon	8
Kirkhill	37
Kirkinner	9
Kirkintilloch	16
Kirkliston (Edinburgh)	1
Kirkmabreck	9
Kirkmahoe	8
Kirkmaiden	9
Kirkmichael (Ayr)	10
Kirkmichael, Tinwald and Torthorwald	8
Kirkmichael, Straloch and Glenshee	27
Kirkmichael and Tomintoul	36
Kirkmuirhill	13
Kirknewton and East Calder	2
Kirk of Calder	2
Kirk of Lammermuir and Langton and Polwarth	5
Kirk o' Shotts	17
Kirkoswald	10
Kirkpatrick Durham (Corsock)	8

Kirkpatrick Fleming (Gretna)	7
Kirkpatrick Juxta	7
Kirkton (Cavers)	6
Kirkurd and Newlands	4
Kirkwall	45
Kirn	19
Kirriemuir	30
Kirtle-Eaglesfield	7
Knock	44
Knockando, Elchies and Archiestown	35
Knockbain	39
Knoydart (Mallaig)	38
Kyle of Lochalsh (Lochalsh)	42
Kyles	19
Ladykirk	5
Laggan	36
Lairg	40
Lamlash	12
Lammermuir, Kirk of	5
Lanark	13
Langbank	14
Langholm, Eskdalemuir, Ewes and Westerkirk	7
Langton and Polwarth (Kirk of Lammermuir)	5
Larbert	22
Largo	26
Largoward	26
Largs	12
Larkhall	17
Lasswade	3
Latheron	41
Lauder (Channelkirk)	4
Laurencekirk	32
Law	13
Lawers (Kenmore)	27
Lecropt	23
Legerwood	5
Leith (Edinburgh)	1
Leithholm	5
Lennoxtown (Campsie)	16
Lenzie	16
Lerwick and Bressay	46
Leslie	25
Leslie (Insch)	33
Lesmahagow	13
Leswalt	9
Letham (Dunnichen)	30
Lethnot (Edzell)	30
Leuchars	26
Leven	25
Levern (Barrhead)	14
Lhanbryd (St Andrew's)	35
Libberton and Quothquan	13
Liddesdale	7
Liff (Fowlis)	29
Limekilns	24
Linlithgow	2
Linton, Morebattle, Hownam and Yetholm	6
Linwood	14
Lismore	19
Liverpool	47
Livingston	2
Loanhead	3

Lochalsh	42
Lochbroom and Ullapool	39
Lochcarron (Applecross)	42
Lochend and New Abbey	8
Lochfyneside (Cumlodden)	19
Lochgair (Cumlodden)	19
Lochgelly	24
Lochgilphead	19
Lochgoilhead and Kilmorich	19
Lochinver (Assynt)	40
Lochmaben	7
Lochmaddy (Berneray)	43
Lochranza and Pirnmill	12
Lochrutton (Irongray)	8
Lochs in Bernera	44
Lochs-Crossbost	44
Lochwinnoch	14
Lockerbie	7
Logie	23
Logiealmond (Methven)	28
Logie Easter (Kilmuir)	39
Logierait (Grantully)	27
London	47
Longforgan	29
Longniddry	3
Longriggend (Caldercruix)	17
Longside	34
Lonmay	34
Lossiemouth	35
Loth (Kildonan)	40
Loudoun (Newmilns)	11
Lowick (Berwick)	5
Lowther (Glencaple)	13
Lugar	10
Lunan (Inverkeilor)	30
Lundie and Muirhead of Liff	29
Lunnasting (Nesting)	46
Luss	18
Lyne and Manor	4
Macduff	34
Madderty (Fowlis Wester)	28
Mallaig and Knoydart	38
Manish Scarista	43
Manor (Lyne)	4
Markinch	25
Marnoch	34
Maryculter (Banchory-Devenick)	32
Mauchline	10
Maud and Savoch	34
Maxton and Mertoun	4
Maxwell Mearns Castle	16
Maybole	10
Mearns (Glasgow)	16
Mearns Coastal	32
Meigle (Ardler)	27
Meldrum and Bourtie	33
Melness and Tongue	40
Melrose (Bowden)	4
Menmuir (Fern)	30

Menstrie	23
Mertoun (Maxton)	4
Methil	25
Methilhill and Denbeath	25
Methlick	33
Methven and Logiealmond	28
Mid Calder (Kirk of Calder)	2
Middlebie	7
Midmar	33
Milngavie	18
Milton of Campsie	16
Mochrum	9
Moffat	7
Moneydie (Auchtergaven)	28
Moniaive (Glencairn)	8
Monifieth	29
Monigaff	9
Monikie and Newbigging	29
Monimail	26
Monkton and Prestwick	10
Monquhitter and New Byth	34
Montrose	30
Monymusk	33
Monzie (Fowlis Wester)	28
Mordington (Foulden)	5
Morebattle and Hownam (Linton)	6
Morham (Garvald)	3
Mortlach and Cabrach	35
Morvern	38
Motherwell	17
Mouswald	8
Moy, Dalarossie and Tomatin	37
Muckairn	19
Muckhart	23
Muiravonside	22
Muirhead of Liff (Lundie)	29
Muirkirk	10
Mull, Isle of	19
Murroes and Tealing	29
Musselburgh	3
Muthill	28
Nairn	37
Neilston	14
Ness (Cross)	44
Nesting and Lunnasting	46
Netherlee	16
Nether Lochaber	38
Nevay (Eassie)	30
New Abbey (Lochend)	8
Newarthill	17
Newbattle	3
Newbigging (Monikie)	29
Newburgh	26
Newburgh (Foveran)	33
Newburn (Largo)	26
New Byth (Monquhitter)	34
Newcastle	47
New Cumnock	10
New Deer	34
New Galloway (Kells)	8
Newhills	31

New Kilpatrick	
(Bearsden)	18
Newlands (Kirkurd)	4
New Luce	9
New Machar	33
Newmains	17
Newmill (Keith)	35
Newmilns	11
New Monkland (Airdrie)	17
New Pitsligo	34
Newport on Tay	26
New Stevenston	17
Newton	3
Newtonhill	32
Newton Mearns	16
Newtonmore	36
Newtown	4
Newtyle	30
Nigg (Fearn)	39
Norrieston	23
North Berwick	3
North Coast Parish, The	41
North Knapdale	19
Northmavine	46
North Queensferry	24
North Ronaldsay	45
Noth	33
Oa (Kildalton)	19
Oakley (Carnock)	24
Oathlaw Tannadice	30
Oban (Kilmore)	19
Ochiltree	10
Old Cumnock	10
Old Kilpatrick Bowling	18
Old Luce	9
Old Monkland	
(Coatbridge)	17
Olrig	41
Onich (Nether Lochaber)	38
Ordiquhill and Cornhill	34
Ormiston	3
Oronsay (Colonsay)	19
Orphir	45
Orwell and Portmoak	28
Overtown	17
Oxnam	6
Oxton (Channelkirk)	4
Oyne (Insch)	33
Paible (Kilmuir)	43
Paisley	14
Panbride (Carnoustie)	30
Papa Westray	45
Pardovan, Kingscavil	
and Winchburgh	
(Abercorn)	2
Parton (Crossmichael)	8
Pathhead (Cranstoun)	3
Patna Waterside	10
Paxton (Hutton)	5
Peebles	4
Pencaitland	3
Penicuik	3
Penninghame	9
Penpont, Keir and	
Tynron	8
Perth	28
Peterculter	31
Peterhead	34
Petty	37

Pirnmill (Lochranza)	12
Pitlochry	27
Pitmedden (Udny)	33
Pitsligo	34
Pittenweem	26
Plean (Cowie)	23
Pluscarden (Birnie)	35
Polbeth Harwood	2
Polmont	22
Polwarth (Langton)	5
Port Charlotte	
(Kilchoman)	19
Port Glasgow	14
Portknockie	35
Portlethen	32
Portmahomack (Tarbat)	39
Portmoak (Orwell)	28
Portnahaven	19
Port of Menteith	23
Portpatrick	9
Portree	42
Port Seton (Cockenzie)	3
Premnay (Insch)	33
Preston (Bonkyl)	5
Prestonpans	3
Prestwick	10
Quarff (Sandwick)	46
Quarter	17
Queensferry	
(Edinburgh)	1
Quothquan (Libberton)	13
Rafford	35
Rait (Kilspindie)	28
Rannoch (Foss)	27
Rathen	34
Ratho (Edinburgh)	1
Rathven	35
Rattray	27
Rayne (Culsalmond)	33
Redding and	
Westquarter	22
Redgorton and Stanley	28
Rendall	45
Renfrew	14
Renton	18
Rerrick (Auchencairn)	8
Rescobie (Guthrie)	30
Resolis and Urquhart	39
Reston (Grantshouse)	5
Rhu and Shandon	18
Riccarton	
(Kilmarnock)	11
Rigside (Douglas	
Water)	13
Roberton (Hawick	
Teviot)	6
Rogart	40
Rosehall	40
Rosemarkie (Fortrose)	39
Rosewell	3
Roslin	3
Rosneath	18
Rosskeen	39
Ross of Mull	
(Kilfinichen)	19
Rosyth	24
Rothes	35
Rothesay	19
Rothiemay (Keith)	35

Rothiemurchus and	
Aviemore	36
Rothienorman	34
Rousay	45
Ruberslaw	6
Rutherglen	16
Ruthwell	8
Saddell and Carradale	19
St Abb's (Coldingham)	5
St Andrews	26
St Andrew's Lhanbryd	
and Urquhart	35
St Boswells	4
St Colman	10
St Fergus	34
St Fillan's (Dundurn)	28
St Madoes	
and Kinfauns	28
St Martin's	28
St Monans	26
St Mungo	7
St Ninians	
(Dunrossness)	46
St Quivox (Ayr)	10
Salen and Ulva	19
Saline and Blairingone	24
Saltcoats	12
Saltoun (Bolton)	3
Sanday	45
Sandbank	19
Sandhaven	34
Sandness (Walls)	46
Sandsting and Aithsting	46
Sandwick (Birsay)	45
Sandwick, Cunningsburgh	
and Quarff	46
Sandyhills (Glasgow)	16
Sanquhar	8
Sauchie and	
Coalsnaughton	23
Savoch (Maud)	34
Scarista (Manish)	43
Scone	28
Seafield (Blackburn)	2
Selkirk (Ashkirk)	4
Shandon (Rhu)	18
Shapinsay	45
Shieldhill (Blackbraes)	22
Shiskine	12
Shotts	17
Sibbaldbie (Applegarth)	7
Skelmorlie and	
Wemyss Bay	14
Skene	33
Skerries (Whalsay)	46
Skipness	19
Skirling	4
Slamannan	22
Sleat (Strath)	42
Small Isles (Arisaig)	38
Snizort	42
Sorbie	9
Sorn	10
Southdean (Hobkirk)	6
Southend	19
South Knapdale	19
South Queensferry	
(Queensferry)	1
South Ronaldsay and	
Burray	45
South Uist	43

Southwick (Colvend)	8
Soutra (Fala)	3
Spean Bridge	
(Kilmonivaig)	38
Speymouth	35
Spott	3
Springfield (Ceres)	26
Springside (Dreghorn)	11
Sprouston (Kelso Old)	6
Spynie (Duffus)	35
Stair	10
Stamperland	16
Stanley (Redgorton)	28
Stenhouse and Carron	22
Stenness (Orphir)	45
Stenscholl (Kilmuir)	42
Stepps	16
Stevenston	12
Stewarton	11
Stewartry of	
Strathearn, The	28
Stirling	23
Stobo and Drumelzier	4
Stoer (Assynt)	40
Stonehaven	32
Stonehouse	17
Stoneykirk	9
Stoneywood	
(Bucksburn)	31
Stornoway	44
Stow	4
Strachur and	
Strathlachlan	19
Straiton	10
Straloch (Kirkmichael)	27
Stranraer	9
Strath and Sleat	42
Strathaven	17
Strathblane	23
Strathbraan (Amulree)	27
Strathbrock	2
Strathfillan	19
Strathkinness	26
Strathlachlan (Strachur)	19
Strathmiglo (Edenshead)	26
Strathpeffer (Fodderty)	39
Strathtay (Grantully)	27
Strichen and Tyrie	34
Stromness	45
Strone and Ardentinny	19
Stronsay	45
Strontian	38
Struan (Blair Atholl)	27
Swinton (Fogo)	5
Symington (Ayr)	10
Symington (Lanark)	13
Tain	39
Tannadice (Oathlaw)	30
Tarbat	39
Tarbert (South Argyll)	19
Tarbert (Uist)	43
Tarbolton	10
Tarff and Twynholm	8
Tarves	33
Taynuilt (Muckairn)	19
Tayport	26
Tealing (Murroes)	29
Tenandry	27
Terregles (Irongray)	8
Teviothead	6

The Border Kirk	7	Torrance	16	Unst	46	Westerkirk
The Douglas Valley		Torridon (Applecross)	42	Uphall	2	(Langholm)	7
Church	13	Torryburn (Culross)	24	Uplawmoor (Caldwell)	14	Westhill (Skene)	33
The Glens and		Torthorwald		Upper Donside	33	Westquarter (Redding)	22
Kirriemuir Old	30	(Kirkmichael)	8	Urquhart and		Westray	45
The Isla Parishes	30	Tough (Cushnie)	33	Glenmoriston		Westruther	5
The North Coast Parish	41	Toward	19	(Inverness)	37	Whalsay and Skerries	46
The Parish of Latheron	41	Tranent	3	Urquhart (Resolis)	39	Whitburn	2
The Stewartry of		Traprain	3	Urquhart (St Andrew's		Whitehills	34
Strathearn	28	Traquair (Innerleithen)	4	Lhanbryd)	35	Whitekirk and
The United Church of Bute	19	Trinity Gask and		Urr	8	Tyninghame	3
Thornhill (Dumfries)	8	Kinkell	28	Urray and Kilchrist	39	Whithorn	9
Thornhill (Norrieston)	23	Troon	10			Whiting Bay and
Thornliebank	16	Troqueer (Dumfries)	8	Walkerburn		Kildonan	12
Thornton	25	Tulliallan and		(Innerleithen)	4	Whitsome	5
Thrumster (Wick)	41	Kincardine	24	Walls (Hoy)	45	Wick	41
Thurso	41	Tullibody	23	Walls and Sandness		Wigtown	9
Tibbermore		Tundergarth	7	(Shetland)	46	Williamwood	16
(Almondbank)	28	Turriff	34	Wamphray	7	Wilton (Hawick)	6
Tillicoultry	23	Twechar	16	Waterbeck	7	Winchburgh
Tingwall	46	Tweedsmuir	4	Waterside (Patna)	10	(Pardovan)	2
Tinwald (Kirkmichael)	8	Twynholm (Tarff)	8	Watten	41	Windygates
Tiree	19	Tyninghame (Whitekirk)	3	Weem (Dull)	27	(Kennoway)	25
Tobermory	19	Tynron (Penpont)	8	Wemyss	25	Wishaw	17
Tomatin (Moy)	37	Tyrie (Strichen)	34	Wemyss Bay		Wormit	26
Tomintoul, Glenlivet and				(Skelmorlie)	14	
Inveraven	36	Uddingston	17	West Calder	2	Yarrow (Ettrick)	4
Tongue (Melness)	40	Udny and Pitmedden	33	West Kilbride	12	Yell	46
Torosay and		Uig	44	West Linton	4	Yester	3
Kinlochspelvie	19	Ullapool (Lochbroom)	39	West Mearns	32	Yetholm (Linton)	6
Torphichen	2	Ulva (Salen)	19	Westerdale (Halkirk)	41	

INDEX OF DISCONTINUED PARISH AND CONGREGATIONAL NAMES

The following index updates and corrects the 'Index of Former Parishes and Congregations' printed in the previous edition of the *Year Book*. As before, it lists the parishes of the Church of Scotland and the congregations of the United Presbyterian Church (and its constituent denominations), the Free Church (1843–1900) and the United Free Church (1900–29) whose names have completely disappeared, largely as a consequence of union.

The observant will notice that this index appears this year under a different title. The hope is that this will make even more clear what the index does and does not contain. The introductory paragraphs to the index have from the outset contained a statement to the effect that this is *not* intended to offer 'a comprehensive guide to readjustment in the Church of Scotland'; that would require a considerably larger number of pages. Experience has shown, however, that there have been those who have been sufficiently misled by the apparent all-inclusiveness of the previous title to draw to the editor's attention the omission of this or that congregation whose name had been slightly altered – but not out of all recognition – as a result of union.

As was stated in previous years, the purpose of this index is to assist those who are trying to identify the present-day successor of some former parish or congregation whose name is now wholly out of use and which can therefore no longer be easily traced. Where the former name has not disappeared completely, and the whereabouts of the former parish or congregation may therefore be easily established by reference to the name of some existing parish, the former name has not been included in this index. The following examples will illustrate some of the criteria used to determine whether a name should be included or not:

- Where all the former congregations in a town have been united into one, as in the case of Melrose or Selkirk, the names of these former congregations have not been included; but, in the case of towns with more than one congregation, such as Galashiels or Hawick, the names of the various constituent congregations are listed.
- The same principle applies in the case of discrete areas of cities. For example, as Dundee: Lochee and Glasgow: Dennistoun New are now the only congregations in Lochee and Dennistoun respectively, there is no need to list Dundee: Lochee St Ninian's, Glasgow: Dennistoun South and any other congregations which had Lochee or Dennistoun in their names.
- Where a prefix such as North, Old, Little, Mid or the like has been lost but the substantive part of the name has been retained, the former name has not been included: it is assumed that someone searching for Little Dalton or Mid Yell will have no difficulty in connecting these with Dalton or Yell.
- Where the present name of a united congregation includes the names of some or all of its constituent parts, these former names do not appear in the list: thus, neither Glasgow: Anderston nor Glasgow: Kelvingrove appears, since both names are easily traceable to Glasgow: Anderston Kelvingrove.

Two other criteria for inclusion or exclusion may also be mentioned:

- Some parishes and congregations have disappeared, and their names have been lost, as a consequence of suppression, dissolution or secession. The names of rural parishes in this category have been included, together with the names of their Presbyteries to assist with identification, but those in towns and cities have not been included, as there will clearly be no difficulty in establishing the general location of the parish or congregation in question.
- Since 1929, a small number of rural parishes have adopted a new name (for example, Whitehills, formerly Boyndie). The former names of these parishes have been included, but it would have been too unwieldy to include either the vast numbers of such changes of name in towns and cities, especially those which occurred at the time of the 1900 and 1929 unions, or the very many older names of pre-Reformation parishes which were abandoned in earlier centuries (however fascinating a list of such long-vanished names as Fothmuref, Kinbathock and Toskertoun might have been).

In this index, the following abbreviations have been used:

C of S	Church of Scotland
FC	Free Church
R	Relief Church
RP	Reformed Presbyterian Church
UF	United Free Church
UP	United Presbyterian Church
US	United Secession Church

Name no longer used	Present name of parish
Abbey St Bathan's	Kirk of Lammermuir and Langton and Polwarth
Abbotrule	charge suppressed: Presbytery of Jedburgh
Aberargie	charge dissolved: Presbytery of Perth
Aberchirder	Marnoch
Aberdalgie	The Stewartry of Strathearn
Aberdeen: Beechgrove	Aberdeen: Midstocket
Aberdeen: Belmont Street	Aberdeen: St Mark's
Aberdeen: Carden Place	Aberdeen: Queen's Cross
Aberdeen: Causewayend	Aberdeen: St Stephen's
Aberdeen: East	Aberdeen: St Mark's
Aberdeen: Gallowgate	Aberdeen: St Mary's
Aberdeen: Greyfriars	Aberdeen: Queen Street
Aberdeen: Hilton	Aberdeen: Woodside
Aberdeen: Holburn Central	Aberdeen: South Holburn
Aberdeen: John Knox Gerrard Street	Aberdeen: Queen Street
Aberdeen: John Knox's (Mounthooly)	Aberdeen: Queen Street
Aberdeen: King Street	Aberdeen: Queen Street
Aberdeen: Melville	Aberdeen: Queen's Cross
Aberdeen: Nelson Street	Aberdeen: Queen Street
Aberdeen: North	Aberdeen: Queen Street
Aberdeen: North of St Andrew	Aberdeen: Queen Street
Aberdeen: Pittodrie	Aberdeen: St Mary's
Aberdeen: Powis	Aberdeen: St Stephen's
Aberdeen: Ruthrieston (C of S)	Aberdeen: South Holburn
Aberdeen: Ruthrieston (FC)	Aberdeen: Ruthrieston West
Aberdeen: South (C of S)	Aberdeen: South of St Nicholas, Kincorth
Aberdeen: South (FC)	Aberdeen: St Mark's
Aberdeen: St Andrew's	Aberdeen: Queen Street
Aberdeen: St Columba's	Aberdeen: High Hilton
Aberdeen: St Mary's	Aberdeen: St Machar's Cathedral
Aberdeen: St Ninian's	Aberdeen: Midstocket
Aberdeen: Trinity (C of S)	Aberdeen: Kirk of St Nicholas Uniting
Aberdeen: Trinity (FC)	Aberdeen: St Mark's
Aberuthven	The Stewartry of Strathearn
Abington	Glencaple
Addiewell	Breich Valley
Afton	New Cumnock
Airdrie: West	Airdrie: New Wellwynd
Airlie	The Isla Parishes
Aldbar	Aberlemno
Aldcambus	Dunglass
Alford	Howe Trinity
Alloa: Chalmers	Alloa: North
Alloa: Melville	Alloa: North
Alloa: St Andrew's	Alloa: North
Altries	charge dissolved: Presbytery of Kincardine and Deeside
Altyre	Rafford
Alvah	Banff
Ancrum	Ale and Teviot United
Annan: Erskine	Annan: St Andrew's
Annan: Greenknowe	Annan: St Andrew's
Anwoth	Gatehouse of Fleet
Arbroath: East	Arbroath: St Andrew's
Arbroath: Erskine	Arbroath: West Kirk
Arbroath: High Street	Arbroath: St Andrew's
Arbroath: Hopemount	Arbroath: St Andrew's
Arbroath: Ladyloan	Arbroath: West Kirk
Arbroath: Princes Street	Arbroath: West Kirk

Name no longer used	Present name of parish
Arbroath: St Columba's	Arbroath: West Kirk
Arbroath: St Margaret's	Arbroath: West Kirk
Arbroath: St Ninian's	Arbroath: St Andrew's
Arbroath: St Paul's	Arbroath: St Andrew's
Ardallie	Deer
Ardclach	charge dissolved: Presbytery of Inverness
Ardwell	Stoneykirk
Ascog	The United Church of Bute
Auchindoir	Upper Donside
Auchmithie	Arbroath: St Vigean's
Auldcathie	Dalmeny
Aultbea	Gairloch and Dundonnell
Ayr: Cathcart	Ayr: St Columba
Ayr: Darlington New	Ayr: Auld Kirk of Ayr
Ayr: Darlington Place	Ayr: Auld Kirk of Ayr
Ayr: Lochside	Ayr: St Quivox
Ayr: Martyrs'	Ayr: Auld Kirk of Ayr
Ayr: Sandgate	Ayr: St Columba
Ayr: St John's	Ayr: Auld Kirk of Ayr
Ayr: Trinity	Ayr: St Columba
Ayr: Wallacetown South	Ayr: Auld Kirk of Ayr
Back	charge dissolved: Presbytery of Lewis
Badcall	Eddrachillis
Balbeggie	Collace
Balfour	charge dissolved: Presbytery of Dundee
Balgedie	Orwell and Portmoak
Baliasta	Unst
Ballachulish	Nether Lochaber
Ballater	Glenmuick
Ballingry	Lochgelly and Benarty: St Serf's
Balmacolm	Howe of Fife
Balmullo	charge dissolved: Presbytery of St Andrews
Balnacross	Tarff and Twynholm
Baltasound	Unst
Banchory-Ternan: North	Banchory-Ternan: West
Banchory-Ternan: South	Banchory-Ternan: West
Bandry	Luss
Bara	Garvald and Morham
Bargrennan	Penninghame
Barnweil	Tarbolton
Barrhead: Westbourne	Barrhead: Arthurlie
Barrock	Dunnet
Bearsden: North	Bearsden: Cross
Bearsden: South	Bearsden: Cross
Bedrule	Ruberslaw
Beith: Hamilfield	Beith: Trinity
Beith: Head Street	Beith: Trinity
Beith: Mitchell Street	Beith: Trinity
Belkirk	Liddesdale
Benholm	Mearns Coastal
Benvie	Fowlis and Liff
Berriedale	The Parish of Latheron
Binny	Linlithgow: St Michael's
Blackburn	Fintray Kinellar Keithhall
Blackhill	Longside
Blairlogie	congregation seceded: Presbytery of Stirling
Blanefield	Strathblane
Blantyre: Anderson	Blantyre: St Andrew's

Name no longer used	Present name of parish
Blantyre: Burleigh Memorial	Blantyre: St Andrew's
Blantyre: Stonefield	Blantyre: St Andrew's
Blyth Bridge	Kirkurd and Newlands
Boddam	Peterhead: Trinity
Bonhill: North	Alexandria
Bothwell: Park	Uddingston: Viewpark
Bourtreebush	Newtonhill
Bow of Fife	Monimail
Bowmore	Kilarrow
Boyndie	Whitehills
Brachollie	Petty
Braco	Ardoch
Braehead	Forth
Brechin: East	Brechin: Gardner Memorial
Brechin: Maison Dieu	Brechin: Cathedral
Brechin: St Columba's	Brechin: Gardner Memorial
Brechin: West	Brechin: Gardner Memorial
Breich	Breich Valley
Bridge of Teith	Kilmadock
Brora	Clyne
Bruan	The Parish of Latheron
Buccleuch	Ettrick and Yarrow
Burnhead	Penpont, Keir and Tynron
Cairnryan	charge dissolved: Presbytery of Wigtown and Stranraer
Cambuslang: Rosebank	Cambuslang: St Andrew's
Cambuslang: West	Cambuslang: St Andrew's
Cambusmichael	St Martin's
Campbeltown: Longrow	Campbeltown: Lorne and Lowland
Campsail	Rosneath: St Modan's
Canna	Mallaig: St Columba and Knoydart
Carbuddo	Guthrie and Rescobie
Cardenden	Auchterderran: St Fothad's
Carlisle	The Border Kirk
Carmichael	Cairngryffe
Carnoch	Contin
Carnousie	Turriff: St Ninian's and Forglen
Carnoustie: St Stephen's	Carnoustie
Carrbridge	Duthil
Carruthers	Middlebie
Castle Kennedy	Inch
Castleton	Liddesdale
Caterline	Kinneff
Chapelknowe	congregation seceded: Presbytery of Annandale and Eskdale
Clatt	Noth
Clayshant	Stoneykirk
Climpy	charge dissolved: Presbytery of Lanark
Clola	Deer
Clousta	Sandsting and Aithsting
Clova	The Glens and Kirriemuir: Old
Clydebank: Bank Street	Clydebank: St Cuthbert's
Clydebank: Boquhanran	Clydebank: Kilbowie St Andrew's
Clydebank: Hamilton Memorial	Clydebank: St Cuthbert's
Clydebank: Linnvale	Clydebank: St Cuthbert's
Clydebank: St James'	Clydebank: Abbotsford
Clydebank: Union	Clydebank: Kilbowie St Andrew's
Clydebank: West	Clydebank: Abbotsford
Coatbridge: Cliftonhill	Coatbridge: Clifton
Coatbridge: Coatdyke	Coatbridge: Clifton

Name no longer used	Present name of parish
Coatbridge: Coats	Coatbridge: Clifton
Coatbridge: Dunbeth	Coatbridge: St Andrew's
Coatbridge: Gartsherrie	Coatbridge: St Andrew's
Coatbridge: Garturk	Coatbridge: Calder
Coatbridge: Maxwell	Coatbridge: St Andrew's
Coatbridge: Trinity	Coatbridge: Clifton
Coatbridge: Whifflet	Coatbridge: Calder
Cobbinshaw	charge dissolved: Presbytery of West Lothian
Cockburnspath	Dunglass
Coigach	charge dissolved: Presbytery of Lochcarron-Skye
Coldstone	Cromar
Collessie	Howe of Fife
Corgarff	Upper Donside
Cortachy	The Glens and Kirriemuir: Old
Coull	Cromar
Covington	Cairngryffe
Cowdenbeath: Cairns	Cowdenbeath: Trinity
Cowdenbeath: Guthrie Memorial	Beath and Cowdenbeath: North
Cowdenbeath: West	Cowdenbeath: Trinity
Craggan	Tomintoul, Glenlivet and Inveraven
Craig	Inchbrayock
Craigdam	Tarves
Craigend	Perth: Moncreiffe
Crailing	Ale and Teviot United
Cranshaws	Kirk of Lammermuir and Langton and Polwarth
Crawford	Glencaple
Crawfordjohn	Glencaple
Cray	Kirkmichael, Straloch and Glenshee
Creetown	Kirkmabreck
Crofthead	Fauldhouse St Andrew's
Crombie	Culross and Torryburn
Crossgates	Cowdenbeath: Trinity
Cruggleton	Sorbie
Cuikston	Farnell
Culbin	Dyke
Cullicudden	Resolis and Urquhart
Cults	Howe of Fife
Cumbernauld: Baird	Cumbernauld: Old
Cumbernauld: Bridgend	Cumbernauld: Old
Cumbernauld: St Andrew's	Cumbernauld: Old
Dalgarno	Closeburn
Dalguise	Dunkeld
Daliburgh	South Uist
Dalkeith: Buccleuch Street	Dalkeith: St Nicholas Buccleuch
Dalkeith: West (C of S)	Dalkeith: St Nicholas Buccleuch
Dalkeith: West (UP)	Dalkeith: St John's and King's Park
Dalmeath	Huntly Cairnie Glass
Dalreoch	charge dissolved: Presbytery of Perth
Dalry: Courthill	Dalry: Trinity
Dalry: St Andrew's	Dalry: Trinity
Dalry: West	Dalry: Trinity
Deerness	East Mainland
Denholm	Ruberslaw
Denny: Broompark	Denny: Westpark
Denny: West	Denny: Westpark
Dennyloanhead	charge dissolved: Presbytery of Falkirk
Dolphinton	Black Mount
Douglas	The Douglas Valley Church

Name no longer used	Present name of parish
Douglas Water	The Douglas Valley Church
Dowally	Dunkeld
Drainie	Lossiemouth St Gerardine's High
Drumdelgie	Huntly Cairnie Glass
Dumbarrow	charge dissolved: Presbytery of Angus
Dumbarton: Bridgend	Dumbarton: West
Dumbarton: Dalreoch	Dumbarton: West
Dumbarton: High	Dumbarton: Riverside
Dumbarton: Knoxland	Dumbarton: Riverside
Dumbarton: North	Dumbarton: Riverside
Dumbarton: Old	Dumbarton: Riverside
Dumfries: Maxwelltown Laurieknowe	Dumfries: Troqueer
Dumfries: Townhead	Dumfries: St Michael's and South
Dunbeath	The Parish of Latheron
Dunblane: East	Dunblane: St Blane's
Dunblane: Leighton	Dunblane: St Blane's
Dundee: Albert Square	Dundee: Meadowside St Paul's
Dundee: Baxter Park	Dundee: Trinity
Dundee: Broughty Ferry East	Dundee: Broughty Ferry New Kirk
Dundee: Broughty Ferry St Aidan's	Dundee: Broughty Ferry New Kirk
Dundee: Broughty Ferry Union	Dundee: Broughty Ferry St Stephen's and West
Dundee: Chapelshade (FC)	Dundee: Meadowside St Paul's
Dundee: Douglas and Angus	Dundee: Douglas and Mid Craigie
Dundee: Downfield North	Dundee: Strathmartine
Dundee: Hawkhill	Dundee: Meadowside St Paul's
Dundee: Martyrs'	Dundee: Balgay
Dundee: Maryfield	Dundee: Stobswell
Dundee: McCheyne Memorial	Dundee: West
Dundee: Ogilvie	Dundee: Stobswell
Dundee: Park	Dundee: Stobswell
Dundee: Roseangle	Dundee: West
Dundee: Ryehill	Dundee: West
Dundee: St Andrew's (FC)	Dundee: Meadowside St Paul's
Dundee: St Clement's Steeple	Dundee: Steeple
Dundee: St David's (C of S)	Dundee: Steeple
Dundee: St Enoch's	Dundee: Steeple
Dundee: St George's	Dundee: Meadowside St Paul's
Dundee: St John's	Dundee: West
Dundee: St Mark's	Dundee: West
Dundee: St Matthew's	Dundee: Trinity
Dundee: St Paul's	Dundee: Steeple
Dundee: St Peter's	Dundee: West
Dundee: Tay Square	Dundee: Meadowside St Paul's
Dundee: Victoria Street	Dundee: Stobswell
Dundee: Wallacetown	Dundee: Trinity
Dundee: Wishart Memorial	Dundee: Steeple
Dundurcas	charge suppressed: Presbytery of Moray
Duneaton	Glencaple
Dunfermline: Chalmers Street	Dunfermline: St Andrew's Erskine
Dunfermline: Maygate	Dunfermline: Gillespie Memorial
Dunfermline: Queen Anne Street	Dunfermline: St Andrew's Erskine
Dungree	Kirkpatrick Juxta
Duninald	Inchbrayock
Dunlappie	Brechin: Cathedral
Dunning	The Stewartry of Strathearn
Dunoon: Gaelic	Dunoon: St John's
Dunoon: Old	Dunoon: The High Kirk
Dunoon: St Cuthbert's	Dunoon: The High Kirk

Name no longer used	Present name of parish
Dunrod	Kirkcudbright
Dunsyre	Black Mount
Dupplin	The Stewartry of Strathearn
Ecclefechan	Hoddam
Ecclesjohn	Dun and Hillside
Ecclesmachan	Strathbrock
Ecclesmoghriodan	Abernethy and Dron and Arngask
Eckford	Ale and Teviot United
Edgerston	Jedburgh: Old and Trinity
Edinburgh: Abbey	Edinburgh: Greenside
Edinburgh: Abbeyhill	Edinburgh: Holyrood Abbey
Edinburgh: Arthur Street	Edinburgh: Kirk o' Field
Edinburgh: Barony	Edinburgh: Greenside
Edinburgh: Belford	Edinburgh: Palmerston Place
Edinburgh: Braid	Edinburgh: Morningside
Edinburgh: Bruntsfield	Edinburgh: Barclay
Edinburgh: Buccleuch	Edinburgh: Kirk o' Field
Edinburgh: Cairns Memorial	Edinburgh: Gorgie
Edinburgh: Candlish	Edinburgh: Polwarth
Edinburgh: Canongate (FC, UP)	Edinburgh: Holy Trinity
Edinburgh: Chalmers	Edinburgh: Barclay
Edinburgh: Charteris Memorial	Edinburgh: Kirk o' Field
Edinburgh: Cluny	Edinburgh: Morningside
Edinburgh: College	Edinburgh: Muirhouse St Andrew's
Edinburgh: College Street	Edinburgh: Muirhouse St Andrew's
Edinburgh: Cowgate (FC)	Edinburgh: Muirhouse St Andrew's
Edinburgh: Cowgate (R)	Edinburgh: Barclay
Edinburgh: Cowgate (US)	Edinburgh: Mayfield Salisbury
Edinburgh: Dalry	Edinburgh: St Colm's
Edinburgh: Davidson	Edinburgh: Stockbridge
Edinburgh: Dean (FC)	Edinburgh: Palmerston Place
Edinburgh: Dean Street	Edinburgh: Stockbridge
Edinburgh: Fountainhall Road	Edinburgh: Mayfield Salisbury
Edinburgh: Grange (C of S)	Edinburgh: Marchmont St Giles
Edinburgh: Grange (FC)	Edinburgh: St Catherine's Argyle
Edinburgh: Guthrie Memorial	Edinburgh: Greenside
Edinburgh: Haymarket	Edinburgh: St Colm's
Edinburgh: Henderson (C of S)	Edinburgh: Craigmillar Park
Edinburgh: Henderson (UP)	Edinburgh: Richmond Craigmillar
Edinburgh: Hillside	Edinburgh: Greenside
Edinburgh: Holyrood	Edinburgh: Holyrood Abbey
Edinburgh: Hope Park	Edinburgh: Mayfield Salisbury
Edinburgh: Hopetoun	Edinburgh: Greenside
Edinburgh: John Ker Memorial	Edinburgh: Polwarth
Edinburgh: Knox's	Edinburgh: Holy Trinity
Edinburgh: Lady Glenorchy's North	Edinburgh: Greenside
Edinburgh: Lady Glenorchy's South	Edinburgh: Holy Trinity
Edinburgh: Lady Yester's	Edinburgh: Greyfriars Tolbooth and Highland
Edinburgh: Lauriston	Edinburgh: Barclay
Edinburgh: Lochend	Edinburgh: St Margaret's
Edinburgh: Lothian Road	Edinburgh: Palmerston Place
Edinburgh: Mayfield North	Edinburgh: Mayfield Salisbury
Edinburgh: Mayfield South	Edinburgh: Craigmillar Park
Edinburgh: McCrie	Edinburgh: Kirk o' Field
Edinburgh: McDonald Road	Edinburgh: Broughton St Mary's
Edinburgh: Moray	Edinburgh: Holy Trinity
Edinburgh: Morningside High	Edinburgh: Morningside
Edinburgh: New North (C of S)	Edinburgh: Marchmont St Giles

Name no longer used	Present name of parish
Edinburgh: New North (FC)	Edinburgh: Greyfriars Tolbooth and Highland
Edinburgh: Newington East	Edinburgh: Kirk o' Field
Edinburgh: Newington South	Edinburgh: Mayfield Salisbury
Edinburgh: Nicolson Street	Edinburgh: Kirk o' Field
Edinburgh: North Morningside	Edinburgh: Morningside United
Edinburgh: North Richmond Street	Edinburgh: Richmond Craigmillar
Edinburgh: Pleasance (FC)	Edinburgh: Muirhouse St Andrew's
Edinburgh: Pleasance (UF)	Edinburgh: Kirk o' Field
Edinburgh: Prestonfield	Edinburgh: Priestfield
Edinburgh: Queen Street (FC)	Edinburgh: St Andrew's and St George's
Edinburgh: Queen Street (UP)	Edinburgh: Stockbridge
Edinburgh: Restalrig (C of S)	Edinburgh: St Margaret's
Edinburgh: Restalrig (FC)	Edinburgh: New Restalrig
Edinburgh: Rosehall	Edinburgh: Priestfield
Edinburgh: Roxburgh	Edinburgh: Kirk o' Field
Edinburgh: Roxburgh Terrace	Edinburgh: Kirk o' Field
Edinburgh: South Morningside	Edinburgh: Morningside
Edinburgh: St Bernard's	Edinburgh: Stockbridge
Edinburgh: St Bride's	Edinburgh: St Colm's
Edinburgh: St Columba's	Edinburgh: Greyfriars Tolbooth and Highland
Edinburgh: St David's (C of S)	Edinburgh: Viewforth
Edinburgh: St David's (FC)	Edinburgh: St David's Broomhouse
Edinburgh: St James' (C of S)	Edinburgh: Greenside
Edinburgh: St James' (FC)	Edinburgh: Inverleith
Edinburgh: St James' Place	Edinburgh: Greenside
Edinburgh: St John's	Edinburgh: Greyfriars Tolbooth and Highland
Edinburgh: St Luke's	Edinburgh: St Andrew's and St George's
Edinburgh: St Matthew's	Edinburgh: Morningside
Edinburgh: St Oran's	Edinburgh: Greyfriars Tolbooth and Highland
Edinburgh: St Oswald's	Edinburgh: Viewforth
Edinburgh: St Paul's	Edinburgh: Kirk o' Field
Edinburgh: St Stephen's (C of S)	Edinburgh: Stockbridge
Edinburgh: St Stephen's (FC)	Edinburgh: St Stephen's Comely Bank
Edinburgh: Tolbooth (C of S)	Edinburgh: Greyfriars Tolbooth and Highland
Edinburgh: Tolbooth (FC)	Edinburgh: St Andrew's and St George's
Edinburgh: Trinity College	Edinburgh: Holy Trinity
Edinburgh: Tynecastle	Edinburgh: Gorgie
Edinburgh: Warrender	Edinburgh: Marchmont St Giles
Edinburgh: West St Giles	Edinburgh: Marchmont St Giles
Eigg	Arisaig and the Small Isles
Eilean Finain	Ardnamurchan
Elgin: Moss Street	Elgin: St Giles and St Columba's South
Elgin: South Street	Elgin: St Giles and St Columba's South
Ellem	Kirk of Lammermuir and Langton and Polwarth
Elsrickle	Black Mount
Eshaness	Northmavine
Essie	Noth
Essil	Speymouth
Ethie	Inverkeilor and Lunan
Ettiltoun	Liddesdale
Ewes Durris	Langholm, Eskdalemuir, Ewes and Westerkirk
Falkirk: Graham's Road	Falkirk: Grahamston United
Farnua	Kirkhill
Ferryden	Inchbrayock
Fetterangus	Deer
Fettercairn	West Mearns
Fetternear	Blairdaff and Chapel of Garioch
Finzean	Birse and Feughside

Name no longer used	Present name of parish
Fochabers	Bellie
Forbes	Howe Trinity
Fordoun	West Mearns
Forfar: South	Forfar: St Margaret's
Forfar: St James'	Forfar: St Margaret's
Forfar: West	Forfar: St Margaret's
Forgan	Newport-on-Tay
Forgue	Auchaber United
Forres: Castlehill	Forres: St Leonard's
Forres: High	Forres: St Leonard's
Forteviot	The Stewartry of Strathearn
Forvie	Ellon
Foula	Walls and Sandness
Galashiels: East	Galashiels: Trinity
Galashiels: Ladhope	Galashiels: Trinity
Galashiels: South	Galashiels: Trinity
Galashiels: St Aidan's	Galashiels: Trinity
Galashiels: St Andrew's	Galashiels: Trinity
Galashiels: St Columba's	Galashiels: Trinity
Galashiels: St Cuthbert's	Galashiels: Trinity
Galashiels: St Mark's	Galashiels: Trinity
Galashiels: St Ninian's	Galashiels: Trinity
Galtway	Kirkcudbright
Gamrie	charge dissolved: Presbytery of Buchan
Garmouth	Speymouth
Gartly	Noth
Garvell	Kirkmichael, Tinwald and Torthorwald
Garvock	Mearns Coastal
Gauldry	Balmerino
Gelston	Buittle and Kelton
Giffnock: Orchard Park	Giffnock: The Park
Girthon	Gatehouse of Fleet
Girvan: Chalmers	Girvan: North (Old and St Andrew's)
Girvan: Trinity	Girvan: North (Old and St Andrew's)
Glasgow: Abbotsford	Glasgow: Gorbals
Glasgow: Albert Drive	Glasgow: Pollokshields
Glasgow: Auldfield	Glasgow: Pollokshaws
Glasgow: Baillieston Old	Glasgow: Baillieston St Andrew's
Glasgow: Baillieston Rhinsdale	Glasgow: Baillieston St Andrew's
Glasgow: Balornock North	Glasgow: Wallacewell
Glasgow: Barmulloch	Glasgow: Wallacewell
Glasgow: Barrowfield (C of S)	Glasgow: Bridgeton St Francis in the East
Glasgow: Barrowfield (RP)	Glasgow: St Luke's and St Andrew's
Glasgow: Bath Street	Glasgow: Renfield St Stephen's
Glasgow: Battlefield West	Glasgow: Langside
Glasgow: Bellahouston	Glasgow: Ibrox
Glasgow: Bellgrove	Glasgow: Dennistoun New
Glasgow: Belmont	Glasgow: Kelvinside Hillhead
Glasgow: Berkeley Street	Glasgow: Renfield St Stephen's
Glasgow: Blackfriars	Glasgow: Dennistoun New
Glasgow: Bluevale	Glasgow: Dennistoun New
Glasgow: Blythswood	Glasgow: Renfield St Stephen's
Glasgow: Bridgeton East	Glasgow: Bridgeton St Francis in the East
Glasgow: Bridgeton West	Glasgow: St Luke's and St Andrew's
Glasgow: Buccleuch	Glasgow: Renfield St Stephen's
Glasgow: Burnbank	Glasgow: Lansdowne
Glasgow: Calton New	Glasgow: St Luke's and St Andrew's
Glasgow: Calton Old	Glasgow: Calton Parkhead

Name no longer used	Present name of parish
Glasgow: Calton Relief	Glasgow: St Luke's and St Andrew's
Glasgow: Cambridge Street	Bishopbriggs: Springfield Cambridge
Glasgow: Candlish Memorial	Glasgow: Govanhill Trinity
Glasgow: Carntyne Old	Glasgow: Shettleston New
Glasgow: Cathcart South	Glasgow: Cathcart Trinity
Glasgow: Central	Glasgow: St Luke's and St Andrew's
Glasgow: Cessnock	Glasgow: Kinning Park
Glasgow: Chalmers (C of S)	Glasgow: St Luke's and St Andrew's
Glasgow: Chalmers (FC)	Glasgow: Gorbals
Glasgow: Claremont	Glasgow: Anderston Kelvingrove
Glasgow: College	Glasgow: Anderston Kelvingrove
Glasgow: Cowcaddens	Glasgow: Renfield St Stephen's
Glasgow: Cowlairs	Glasgow: Springburn
Glasgow: Crosshill	Glasgow: Queen's Park
Glasgow: Dalmarnock (C of S)	Glasgow: Calton Parkhead
Glasgow: Dalmarnock (UF)	Rutherglen: Old
Glasgow: Dean Park	Glasgow: New Govan
Glasgow: Dowanhill	Glasgow: Partick Trinity
Glasgow: Dowanvale	Glasgow: Partick South
Glasgow: Drumchapel Old	Glasgow: Drumchapel St Andrew's
Glasgow: East Campbell Street	Glasgow: Dennistoun New
Glasgow: East Park	Glasgow: Kelvin Stevenson Memorial
Glasgow: Eastbank	Glasgow: Shettleston New
Glasgow: Edgar Memorial	Glasgow: St Luke's and St Andrew's
Glasgow: Eglinton Street	Glasgow: Govanhill Trinity
Glasgow: Elder Park	Glasgow: Govan Old
Glasgow: Elgin Street	Glasgow: Govanhill Trinity
Glasgow: Erskine	Glasgow: Langside
Glasgow: Fairbairn	Rutherglen: Old
Glasgow: Fairfield	Glasgow: New Govan
Glasgow: Finnieston	Glasgow: Anderston Kelvingrove
Glasgow: Garnethill	Glasgow: Renfield St Stephen's
Glasgow: Garscube Netherton	Glasgow: Knightswood St Margaret's
Glasgow: Gillespie	Glasgow: St Luke's and St Andrew's
Glasgow: Gordon Park	Glasgow: Whiteinch
Glasgow: Govan Copland Road	Glasgow: New Govan
Glasgow: Govan Trinity	Glasgow: New Govan
Glasgow: Grant Street	Glasgow: Renfield St Stephen's
Glasgow: Greenhead	Glasgow: St Luke's and St Andrew's
Glasgow: Hall Memorial	Rutherglen: Old
Glasgow: Hamilton Crescent	Glasgow: Partick South
Glasgow: Highlanders' Memorial	Glasgow: Knightswood St Margaret's
Glasgow: Hyndland (UF)	Glasgow: St John's Renfield
Glasgow: John Knox's	Glasgow: Gorbals
Glasgow: Johnston	Glasgow: Springburn
Glasgow: Jordanvale	Glasgow: Whiteinch
Glasgow: Kelvinhaugh	Glasgow: Anderston Kelvingrove
Glasgow: Kelvinside Botanic Gardens	Glasgow: Kelvinside Hillhead
Glasgow: Kelvinside Old	Glasgow: Kelvin Stevenson Memorial
Glasgow: Kingston	Glasgow: Carnwadric
Glasgow: Lancefield	Glasgow: Anderston Kelvingrove
Glasgow: Langside Avenue	Glasgow: Shawlands
Glasgow: Langside Hill	Glasgow: Battlefield East
Glasgow: Langside Old	Glasgow: Langside
Glasgow: Laurieston (C of S)	Glasgow: Gorbals
Glasgow: Laurieston (FC)	Glasgow: Carnwadric
Glasgow: London Road	Glasgow: Bridgeton St Francis in the East
Glasgow: Lyon Street	Glasgow: Renfield St Stephen's

Name no longer used	Present name of parish
Glasgow: Macgregor Memorial	Glasgow: Govan Old
Glasgow: Macmillan	Glasgow: St Luke's and St Andrew's
Glasgow: Milton	Glasgow: Renfield St Stephen's
Glasgow: Netherton St Matthew's	Glasgow: Knightswood St Margaret's
Glasgow: New Cathcart	Glasgow: Cathcart Trinity
Glasgow: Newhall	Glasgow: Bridgeton St Francis in the East
Glasgow: Newton Place	Glasgow: Partick South
Glasgow: Nithsdale	Glasgow: Queen's Park
Glasgow: Old Partick	Glasgow: Partick Trinity
Glasgow: Paisley Road	Glasgow: Kinning Park
Glasgow: Partick Anderson	Glasgow: Partick South
Glasgow: Partick East	Glasgow: Partick Trinity
Glasgow: Partick High	Glasgow: Partick South
Glasgow: Phoenix Park	Glasgow: Springburn
Glasgow: Plantation	Glasgow: Kinning Park
Glasgow: Pollok St Aidan's	Glasgow: St James' Pollok
Glasgow: Pollok Street	Glasgow: Kinning Park
Glasgow: Polmadie	Glasgow: Govanhill Trinity
Glasgow: Queen's Cross	Glasgow: Ruchill
Glasgow: Renfield (C of S)	Glasgow: Renfield St Stephen's
Glasgow: Renfield (FC)	Glasgow: St John's Renfield
Glasgow: Renfield Street	Glasgow: Renfield St Stephen's
Glasgow: Renwick	Glasgow: Gorbals
Glasgow: Robertson Memorial	Glasgow: The Martyrs'
Glasgow: Rockcliffe	Rutherglen: Old
Glasgow: Rockvilla	Glasgow: Possilpark
Glasgow: Rose Street	Glasgow: Langside
Glasgow: Rutherford	Glasgow: Dennistoun New
Glasgow: Shamrock Street	Glasgow: Renfield St Stephen's
Glasgow: Shawholm	Glasgow: Pollokshaws
Glasgow: Shawlands Cross	Glasgow: Shawlands
Glasgow: Shawlands Old	Glasgow: Shawlands
Glasgow: Sighthill	Glasgow: Springburn
Glasgow: Somerville	Glasgow: Springburn
Glasgow: Springbank	Glasgow: Lansdowne
Glasgow: St Clement's	Glasgow: Bridgeton St Francis in the East
Glasgow: St Columba Gaelic	Glasgow: New Govan
Glasgow: St Cuthbert's	Glasgow: Ruchill
Glasgow: St Enoch's (C of S)	Glasgow: St Enoch's Hogganfield
Glasgow: St Enoch's (FC)	Glasgow: Anderston Kelvingrove
Glasgow: St George's (C of S)	Glasgow: St George's Tron
Glasgow: St George's (FC)	Glasgow: Anderston Kelvingrove
Glasgow: St George's Road	Glasgow: Renfield St Stephen's
Glasgow: St James' (C of S)	Glasgow: St James' Pollok
Glasgow: St James' (FC)	Glasgow: St Luke's and St Andrew's
Glasgow: St John's (C of S)	Glasgow: St Luke's and St Andrew's
Glasgow: St John's (FC)	Glasgow: St John's Renfield
Glasgow: St Kiaran's	Glasgow: New Govan
Glasgow: St Mark's	Glasgow: Anderston Kelvingrove
Glasgow: St Mary's Govan	Glasgow: New Govan
Glasgow: St Mary's Partick	Glasgow: Partick South
Glasgow: St Matthew's (C of S)	Glasgow: Renfield St Stephen's
Glasgow: St Matthew's (FC)	Glasgow: Knightswood St Margaret's
Glasgow: St Ninian's	Glasgow: Gorbals
Glasgow: St Peter's	Glasgow: Anderston Kelvingrove
Glasgow: Steven Memorial	Glasgow: Ibrox
Glasgow: Strathbungo	Glasgow: Queen's Park
Glasgow: Summerfield	Rutherglen: Old

Name no longer used	Present name of parish
Glasgow: Summertown	Glasgow: New Govan
Glasgow: Sydney Place	Glasgow: Dennistoun New
Glasgow: The Park	Giffnock: The Park
Glasgow: Titwood	Glasgow: Pollokshields
Glasgow: Tradeston	Glasgow: Gorbals
Glasgow: Trinity	Glasgow: St Luke's and St Andrew's
Glasgow: Trinity Duke Street	Glasgow: Dennistoun New
Glasgow: Tron St Anne's	Glasgow: St George's Tron
Glasgow: Union	Glasgow: Carnwadric
Glasgow: Victoria	Glasgow: Queen's Park
Glasgow: Wellfield	Glasgow: Springburn
Glasgow: Wellpark	Glasgow: Dennistoun New
Glasgow: West Scotland Street	Glasgow: Kinning Park
Glasgow: White Memorial	Glasgow: Kinning Park
Glasgow: Whitehill	Glasgow: Dennistoun New
Glasgow: Whitevale (FC)	Glasgow: St Thomas' Gallowgate
Glasgow: Whitevale (UP)	Glasgow: Dennistoun New
Glasgow: Wilton	Glasgow: Kelvin Stevenson Memorial
Glasgow: Woodlands	Glasgow: Wellington
Glasgow: Woodside	Glasgow: Lansdowne
Glasgow: Wynd (C of S)	Glasgow: St Luke's and St Andrew's
Glasgow: Wynd (FC)	Glasgow: Gorbals
Glasgow: Young Street	Glasgow: Dennistoun New
Glen Convinth	Kiltarlity
Glen Ussie	Fodderty and Strathpeffer
Glenapp	Ballantrae
Glenbervie	West Mearns
Glenbuchat	Upper Donside
Glenbuck	Muirkirk
Glencaple	Caerlaverock
Glendoick	St Madoes and Kinfauns
Glenfarg	Abernethy and Dron and Arngask
Glengairn	Glenmuick
Glengarnock	Kilbirnie: Auld Kirk
Glenisla	The Isla Parishes
Glenluce	Old Luce
Glenmoriston	Fort Augustus
Glenprosen	The Glens and Kirriemuir: Old
Glenrinnes	Mortlach and Cabrach
Glenshiel	Glenelg and Kintail
Glentanar	Aboyne – Dinnet
Gogar	Edinburgh: Corstorphine Old
Gordon	Monquhitter and New Byth
Graemsay	Stromness
Grangemouth: Dundas	Grangemouth: Abbotsgrange
Grangemouth: Grange	Grangemouth: Zetland
Grangemouth: Kerse	Grangemouth: Abbotsgrange
Grangemouth: Old	Grangemouth: Zetland
Greenloaning	Ardoch
Greenock: Augustine	Greenock: East End
Greenock: Cartsburn	Greenock: East End
Greenock: Cartsdyke	Greenock: East End
Greenock: Crawfordsburn	Greenock: East End
Greenock: Gaelic	Greenock: Westburn
Greenock: Greenbank	Greenock: Westburn
Greenock: Martyrs'	Greenock: Westburn
Greenock: Middle	Greenock: Westburn
Greenock: Mount Park	Greenock: Mount Kirk

Name no longer used	Present name of parish
Greenock: Mount Pleasant	Greenock: Mount Kirk
Greenock: North (C of S)	Greenock: Old West Kirk
Greenock: North (FC)	Greenock: Westburn
Greenock: Sir Michael Street	Greenock: Ardgowan
Greenock: South	Greenock: Mount Kirk
Greenock: South Park	Greenock: Mount Kirk
Greenock: St Andrew's	Greenock: Ardgowan
Greenock: St Columba's Gaelic	Greenock: Old West Kirk
Greenock: St George's	Greenock: Westburn
Greenock: St Luke's	Greenock: Westburn
Greenock: St Mark's	Greenock: Westburn
Greenock: St Thomas'	Greenock: Westburn
Greenock: The Old Kirk	Greenock: Westburn
Greenock: The Union Church	Greenock: Ardgowan
Greenock: Trinity	Greenock: Ardgowan
Greenock: Union Street	Greenock: Ardgowan
Greenock: West	Greenock: Westburn
Gress	Stornoway: St Columba
Guardbridge	Leuchars: St Athernase
Haddington: St John's	Haddington: West
Hamilton: Auchingramont North	Hamilton: North
Hamilton: Avon Street	Hamilton: St Andrew's
Hamilton: Brandon	Hamilton: St Andrew's
Hamilton: Saffronhall Assoc. Anti-Burgher	Hamilton: North
Hardgate	Urr
Hassendean	Ruberslaw
Hawick: East Bank	Hawick: Trinity
Hawick: Orrock	Hawick: St Mary's and Old
Hawick: St Andrew's	Hawick: Trinity
Hawick: St George's	Hawick: Teviot
Hawick: St George's West	Hawick: Teviot
Hawick: St John's	Hawick: Trinity
Hawick: St Margaret's	Hawick: Teviot
Hawick: West Port	Hawick: Teviot
Hawick: Wilton South	Hawick: Teviot
Haywood	Forth
Helensburgh: Old	Helensburgh: The West Kirk
Helensburgh: St Andrew's	Helensburgh: The West Kirk
Helensburgh: St Bride's	Helensburgh: The West Kirk
Heylipol	Tiree
Hillside	Unst
Hillswick	Northmavine
Hilton	Whitsome
Holm	East Mainland
Holywell	The Border Kirk
Hope Kailzie	charge suppressed: Presbytery of Melrose and Peebles
Horndean	Ladykirk
Howford	charge dissolved: Presbytery of Inverness
Howmore	South Uist
Hume	Kelso Country Churches
Huntly: Princes Street	Huntly: Strathbogie
Inchkenneth	Kilfinichen and Kilvickeon and the Ross of Mull
Inchmartin	Errol
Innerwick	Dunglass
Inverallan	Grantown-on-Spey
Inverchaolain	Toward
Inverkeithny	Auchaber United
Inverness: Merkinch St Mark's	Inverness: Trinity

Name no longer used	Present name of parish
Inverness: Queen Street	Inverness: Trinity
Inverness: St Mary's	Inverness: Dalneigh and Bona
Inverness: West	Inverness: Inshes
Irving	Gretna, Half Morton and Kirkpatrick Fleming
Johnshaven	Mearns Coastal
Johnstone: East	Johnstone: St Paul's
Johnstone: West	Johnstone: St Paul's
Kames	Kyles
Kearn	Upper Donside
Keig	Howe Trinity
Keith Marischal	Humbie
Keith: South	Keith: North, Newmill, Boharm and Rothiemay
Kelso: East	Kelso: North and Ednam
Kelso: Edenside	Kelso: North and Ednam
Kelso: St John's	Kelso: North and Ednam
Kelso: Trinity	Kelso: North and Ednam
Kennethmont	Noth
Kettle	Howe of Fife
Kilbirnie: Barony	Kilbirnie: Auld Kirk
Kilbirnie: East	Kilbirnie: St Columba's
Kilbirnie: West	Kilbirnie: St Columba's
Kilblaan	Southend
Kilblane	Kirkmahoe
Kilbride (Cowal)	Kyles
Kilbride (Dumfries and Kirkcudbright)	Sanquhar
Kilbride (Lorn)	Kilmore and Oban
Kilbride (Stirling)	Dunblane: Cathedral
Kilchattan Bay	The United Church of Bute
Kilchousland	Campbeltown: Highland
Kilcolmkill (Kintyre)	Southend
Kilcolmkill (Lochaber)	Morvern
Kildrummy	Upper Donside
Kilkerran	Campbeltown: Highland
Kilkivan	Campbeltown: Highland
Killintag	Morvern
Kilmacolm: St James'	Kilmacolm: St Columba
Kilmahew	Cardross
Kilmahog	Callander
Kilmarnock: King Street	Kilmarnock: Howard St Andrew's
Kilmarnock: Portland Road	Kilmarnock: Howard St Andrew's
Kilmarrow	Killean and Kilchenzie
Kilmichael (Inverness)	Urquhart and Glenmoriston
Kilmichael (Kintyre)	Campbeltown: Highland
Kilmoir	Brechin: Cathedral
Kilmore	Urquhart and Glenmoriston
Kilmoveonaig	Blair Atholl and Struan
Kilmun: St Andrew's	Strone and Ardentinny
Kilpheder	South Uist
Kilry	The Isla Parishes
Kilwinning: Abbey	Kilwinning: Old
Kilwinning: Erskine	Kilwinning: Old
Kinairney	Midmar
Kincardine O'Neil	Mid Deeside
Kincraig	Alvie and Insh
Kinedar	Lossiemouth: St Gerardine's High
Kingarth	The United Church of Bute
Kingoldrum	The Isla Parishes
Kininmonth	charge dissolved: Presbytery of Buchan

Name no longer used	Present name of parish
Kinkell	Fintray Kinellar Keithhall
Kinloch	Caputh and Clunie
Kinlochewe	Applecross, Lochcarron and Torridon
Kinlochluichart	Contin
Kinlochrannoch	Foss and Rannoch
Kinneil	Bo'ness: Old
Kinnettas	Fodderty and Strathpeffer
Kinnoir	Huntly Cairnie Glass
Kinrossie	Collace
Kirkandrews	Borgue
Kirkapol	Tiree
Kirkcaldy: Abbotsrood	Kirkcaldy: St Andrew's
Kirkcaldy: Bethelfield	Kirkcaldy: Linktown
Kirkcaldy: Dunnikier	Kirkcaldy: St Andrew's
Kirkcaldy: Gallatown	Kirkcaldy: Viewforth
Kirkcaldy: Invertiel	Kirkcaldy: Linktown
Kirkcaldy: Old	Kirkcaldy: St Bryce Kirk
Kirkcaldy: Raith	Kirkcaldy: Abbotshall
Kirkcaldy: Sinclairtown	Kirkcaldy: Viewforth
Kirkcaldy: St Brycedale	Kirkcaldy: St Bryce Kirk
Kirkcaldy: Victoria Road	Kirkcaldy: St Andrew's
Kirkchrist	Tarff and Twynholm
Kirkconnel	Gretna, Half Morton and Kirkpatrick Fleming
Kirkcormick	Buittle and Kelton
Kirkdale	Kirkmabreck
Kirkforthar	Markinch
Kirkhope	Ettrick and Yarrow
Kirkintilloch: St Andrew's	Kirkintilloch: St Columba's
Kirkintilloch: St David's	Kirkintilloch: St Columba's
Kirkmadrine (Machars)	Sorbie
Kirkmadrine (Rhinns)	Stoneykirk
Kirkmaiden	Glasserton and Isle of Whithorn
Kirkmichael	Tomintoul, Glenlivet and Inveraven
Kirkpottie	Abernethy and Dron and Arngask
Kirkwall: King Street	Kirkwall: East
Kirkwall: Paterson	Kirkwall: East
Kirriemuir: Bank Street	The Glens and Kirriemuir: Old
Kirriemuir: Barony	The Glens and Kirriemuir: Old
Kirriemuir: Livingstone	Kirriemuir: St Andrew's
Kirriemuir: South	Kirriemuir: St Andrew's
Kirriemuir: St Ninian's	The Glens and Kirriemuir: Old
Kirriemuir: West	The Glens and Kirriemuir: Old
Ladybank	Howe of Fife
Lagganallochie	Dunkeld
Lamberton	Foulden and Mordington
Lamington	Glencaple
Lanark: Broomgate	Lanark: Greyfriars
Lanark: Cairns	Lanark: Greyfriars
Lanark: St Kentigern's	Lanark: Greyfriars
Lanark: St Leonard's	Lanark: St Nicholas'
Largieside	Killean and Kilchenzie
Lassodie	Dunfermline: Townhill and Kingseat
Lathones	Largoward
Laurieston	Balmaghie
Laxavoe	Delting
Leadhills	Lowther
Leith: Bonnington	Edinburgh: Leith North
Leith: Claremont	Edinburgh: Leith St Andrew's

Name no longer used	Present name of parish
Leith: Dalmeny Street	Edinburgh: Pilrig St Paul's
Leith: Elder Memorial	Edinburgh: St John's Oxgangs
Leith: Harper Memorial	Edinburgh: Leith North
Leith: Kirkgate	Edinburgh: Leith South
Leith: South (FC)	Edinburgh: Leith St Andrew's
Leith: St Andrew's Place	Edinburgh: Leith St Andrew's
Leith: St John's	Edinburgh: St John's Oxgangs
Leith: St Nicholas	Edinburgh: Leith North
Leith: St Ninian's	Edinburgh: Leith North
Lemlair	Kiltearn
Lempitlaw	Kelso: Old and Sprouston
Leny	Callander
Leochel	Cushnie and Tough
Lesmahagow: Cordiner	Lesmahagow: Abbey Green
Lethendy	Caputh and Clunie
Lilliesleaf	Ale and Teviot United
Lindowan	Craigrownie
Linlithgow: East	Linlithgow: St Ninian's Craigmailen
Linlithgow: Trinity	Linlithgow: St Ninian's Craigmailen
Lintrathen	The Isla Parishes
Livingston: Tulloch	Livingston: Old
Livingston: West	Livingston: Old
Lochaline	Morvern
Lochcraig	Lochgelly and Benarty: St Serf's
Lochdonhead	Torosay and Kinlochspelvie
Lochearnhead	Balquhidder
Lochlee	Edzell Lethnot Glenesk
Lochryan	Inch
Logie (Dundee)	Fowlis and Liff
Logie (St Andrews)	charge dissolved: Presbytery of St Andrews
Logie Buchan	Ellon
Logie Mar	Cromar
Logie Pert	charge dissolved: Presbytery of Angus
Logie Wester	Ferintosh
Logiebride	Auchtergaven and Moneydie
Longcastle	Kirkinner
Longformacus	Kirk of Lammermuir and Langton and Polwarth
Longnewton	Ale and Teviot United
Longridge	Breich Valley
Longtown	The Border Kirk
Luce	Hoddam
Lude	Blair Atholl and Struan
Lumphanan	Mid Deeside
Lumphinnans	Beath and Cowdenbeath: North
Lumsden	Upper Donside
Luncarty	Redgorton and Stanley
Lund	Unst
Lybster	The Parish of Latheron
Lynturk	Cushnie and Tough
Mailor	The Stewartry of Strathearn
Mainsriddle	Colvend, Southwick and Kirkbean
Makerstoun	Kelso Country Churches
Maryburgh	Ferintosh
Marykirk	Aberluthnott
Maryton	Inchbrayock
Meadowfield	Caldercruix and Longriggend
Meathie	Glamis, Inverarity and Kinnettles
Megget	Ettrick and Yarrow

Name no longer used	Present name of parish
Melville	charge suppressed: Presbytery of Lothian
Memus	The Glens and Kirriemuir: Old
Methil: East	Innerleven: East
Mid Calder: Bridgend	Kirk of Calder
Mid Calder: St John's	Kirk of Calder
Midholm	congregation seceded: Presbytery of Jedburgh
Migvie	Cromar
Millbrex	Fyvie
Millerston	charge dissolved: Presbytery of Glasgow
Millport	Cumbrae
Milnathort	Orwell and Portmoak
Minto	Ruberslaw
Monecht	charge dissolved: Presbytery of Gordon
Monifieth: North	Monikie and Newbigging
Montrose: Knox's	Montrose: Melville South
Montrose: St George's	Montrose: Old and St Andrew's
Montrose: St John's	Montrose: Old and St Andrew's
Montrose: St Luke's	Montrose: Old and St Andrew's
Montrose: St Paul's	Montrose: Melville South
Montrose: Trinity	Montrose: Old and St Andrew's
Monzievaird	Crieff
Moonzie	charge dissolved: Presbytery of St Andrews
Morton	Thornhill
Mossbank	Delting
Mossgreen	Cowdenbeath: Trinity
Motherwell: Brandon	Motherwell: Crosshill
Motherwell: Cairns	Motherwell: Crosshill
Motherwell: Manse Road	Motherwell: South
Motherwell: South Dalziel	Motherwell: South
Moulin	Pitlochry
Mount Kedar	Ruthwell
Mow	Linton, Morebattle, Hownam and Yetholm
Moy	Dyke
Moyness	charge dissolved: Presbytery of Moray
Muckersie	The Stewartry of Strathearn
Muirton	Aberluthnott
Murthly	Caputh and Clunie
Musselburgh: Bridge Street	Musselburgh: St Andrew's High
Musselburgh: Millhill	Musselburgh: St Andrew's High
Nairn: High	Nairn: St Ninian's
Nairn: Rosebank	Nairn: St Ninian's
Navar	Edzell Lethnot Glenesk
Nenthorn	Kelso Country Churches
New Leeds	charge dissolved: Presbytery of Buchan
New Liston	Edinburgh: Kirkliston
Newcastleton	Liddesdale
Newdosk	Edzell Lethnot Glenesk
Newmills	Culross and Torryburn
Newseat	Rothienorman
Newton Stewart	Penninghame
Newtongrange	Newbattle
Nigg	charge dissolved: Presbytery of Aberdeen
Nisbet	Ale and Teviot United
North Bute	The United Church of Bute
Norwick	Unst
Ogston	Lossiemouth: St Gerardine's High
Old Cumnock: Crichton Memorial	Old Cumnock: Trinity
Old Cumnock: St Ninian's	Old Cumnock: Trinity

Name no longer used	Present name of parish
Old Cumnock: West	Old Cumnock: Trinity
Old Kilpatrick: Barclay	Dalmuir: Barclay
Oldhamstocks	Dunglass
Ollaberry	Northmavine
Olnafirth	Delting
Ord	Ordiquhill and Cornhill
Paisley: Canal Street	Paisley: Castlehead
Paisley: George Street	Paisley: Glenburn
Paisley: High	Paisley: Oakshaw Trinity
Paisley: Merksworth	Paisley: Wallneuk North
Paisley: Middle	Paisley: Castlehead
Paisley: Mossvale	Paisley: Wallneuk North
Paisley: New Street	Paisley: Glenburn
Paisley: North	Paisley: Wallneuk North
Paisley: Oakshaw West	Paisley: St Luke's
Paisley: Orr Square	Paisley: Oakshaw Trinity
Paisley: South	Paisley: St Luke's
Paisley: St Andrew's	Paisley: Laigh
Paisley: St George's	Paisley: Laigh
Paisley: St John's	Paisley: Oakshaw Trinity
Papa Stour	Walls and Sandness
Park	Kinloch
Pathhead	Ormiston
Pathstruie	The Stewartry of Strathearn
Pearston	Dreghorn and Springside
Peebles: West	Peebles: St Andrew's Leckie
Pennersaughs	Middlebie
Pentland	Lasswade
Persie	Kirkmichael, Straloch and Glenshee
Perth: Bridgend	Perth: St Matthew's
Perth: East	Perth: St Leonard's-in-the-Fields and Trinity
Perth: Knox's	Perth: St Leonard's-in-the-Fields and Trinity
Perth: Middle	Perth: St Matthew's
Perth: St Andrew's	Perth: Riverside
Perth: St Columba's	Perth: North
Perth: St Leonard's	Perth: North
Perth: St Stephen's	Perth: Riverside
Perth: West	Perth: St Matthew's
Perth: Wilson	Perth: St Matthew's
Perth: York Place	Perth: St Leonard's-in-the-Fields and Trinity
Peterhead: Charlotte Street	Peterhead: Trinity
Peterhead: East	Peterhead: St Andrew's
Peterhead: South	Peterhead: St Andrew's
Peterhead: St Peter's	Peterhead: Trinity
Peterhead: West Associate	Peterhead: Trinity
Pettinain	Cairngryffe
Pitcairn (C of S)	Redgorton and Stanley
Pitcairn (UF)	Almondbank Tibbermore
Pitlessie	Howe of Fife
Pitroddie	St Madoes and Kinfauns
Plockton	Lochalsh
Polmont South	Brightons
Poolewe	Gairloch and Dundonnell
Port Bannatyne	The United Church of Bute
Port Ellen	Kildalton and Oa
Port Glasgow: Clune Park	Port Glasgow: St Andrew's
Port Glasgow: Newark	Port Glasgow: St Andrew's
Port Glasgow: Old	Port Glasgow: St Andrew's

Name no longer used	Present name of parish
Port Glasgow: Princes Street	Port Glasgow: St Andrew's
Port Glasgow: West	Port Glasgow: St Andrew's
Port Sonachan	Glenorchy and Inishail
Port William	Mochrum
Portobello: Regent Street	Edinburgh: Portobello Old
Portobello: Windsor Place	Edinburgh: Portobello Old
Portsoy	Fordyce
Prestonkirk	Traprain
Prinlaws	Leslie: Trinity
Quarrier's Mount Zion	Kilmacolm: St Columba
Raasay	Portree
Rathillet	Creich, Flisk and Kilmany
Rathmuriel	Noth
Reay	The North Coast Parish
Redcastle	Killearnan
Restenneth	Forfar: East and Old
Rhynd	Perth: Moncreiffe
Rhynie	Noth
Rickarton	charge dissolved: Presbytery of Kincardine and Deeside
Rigg	Gretna, Half Morton and Kirkpatrick Fleming
Rigside	The Douglas Valley Church
Rinpatrick	Gretna, Half Morton and Kirkpatrick Fleming
Roberton	Glencaple
Rosehearty	Pitsligo
Rossie	Inchture and Kinnaird
Rothesay: Bridgend	The United Church of Bute
Rothesay: Craigmore High	Rothesay: Trinity
Rothesay: Craigmore St Brendan's	The United Church of Bute
Rothesay: High	The United Church of Bute
Rothesay: New	The United Church of Bute
Rothesay: St James'	Rothesay: Trinity
Rothesay: St John's	The United Church of Bute
Rothesay: West	Rothesay: Trinity
Roxburgh	Kelso Country Churches
Rutherglen: East	Rutherglen: Old
Rutherglen: Greenhill	Rutherglen: Old
Rutherglen: Munro	Rutherglen: West and Wardlawhill
Ruthven (Angus)	The Isla Parishes
Ruthven (Gordon)	Huntly Cairnie Glass
Saltcoats: Erskine	Saltcoats: New Trinity
Saltcoats: Landsborough	Saltcoats: New Trinity
Saltcoats: Middle	Saltcoats: New Trinity
Saltcoats: South Beach	Saltcoats: St Cuthbert's
Saltcoats: Trinity	Saltcoats: New Trinity
Saltcoats: West	Saltcoats: New Trinity
Sandhead	Stoneykirk
Saughtree	Liddesdale
Saulseat	Inch
Scalloway	Tingwall
Scatsta	Delting
Sclattie	Blairdaff and Chapel of Garioch
Scone: Abbey	Scone: New
Scone: West	Scone: New
Scoonie	Leven
Scourie	Eddrachillis
Seafield	Portknockie
Sennick	Borgue
Seton	Tranent

Name no longer used	Present name of parish
Shawbost	Carloway
Shebster	The North Coast Parish
Sheuchan	Stranraer: High
Shieldaig	Applecross, Lochcarron and Torridon
Shiels	Belhelvie
Shottsburn	Kirk o' Shotts
Shurrery	The North Coast Parish
Simprin	Fogo and Swinton
Skerrols	Kilarrow
Skinnet	Halkirk and Westerdale
Slains	Ellon
Smailholm	Kelso Country Churches
South Ballachulish	charge dissolved: Presbytery of Lochaber
Spittal (Caithness)	Halkirk and Westerdale
Spittal (Duns)	charge dissolved: Presbytery of Duns
Springfield	Gretna, Half Morton and Kirkpatrick Fleming
St Andrew's (Orkney)	East Mainland
St Cyrus	Mearns Coastal
St Ola	Kirkwall: St Magnus Cathedral
Stenton	Traprain
Stewartfield	Deer
Stewarton: Cairns	Stewarton: St Columba's
Stewarton: Laigh	Stewarton: St Columba's
Stichill	Kelso Country Churches
Stirling: Craigs	Stirling: St Columba's
Stirling: North (FC)	Stirling: St Columba's
Stobhill	Gorebridge
Stockbridge	Dunglass
Stonehaven: North	Stonehaven: South
Stoneyburn	Breich Valley
Stornoway: James Street	Stornoway: Martin's Memorial
Stracathro	Brechin: Cathedral
Strachan	Birse and Feughside
Stranraer: Bellevilla	Stranraer: St Ninian's
Stranraer: Bridge Street	Stranraer: St Ninian's
Stranraer: Ivy Place	Stranraer: Town Kirk
Stranraer: Old	Stranraer: Town Kirk
Stranraer: St Andrew's	Stranraer: Town Kirk
Stranraer: St Margaret's	Stranraer: High
Stranraer: St Mark's	Stranraer: Town Kirk
Strathconon	Contin
Strathdeveron	Mortlach and Cabrach
Strathdon	Upper Donside
Stratherrick	Dores and Boleskine
Strathgarve	Contin
Strathglass	Kilmorack and Erchless
Strathmartine (C of S)	Dundee: Mains
Strathy	The North Coast Parish
Strowan	Comrie
Suddie	Knockbain
Tarfside	Edzell Lethnot Glenesk
Tarland	Cromar
Tarvit	Cupar: Old and St Michael of Tarvit
Temple	Gorebridge
Thankerton	Cairngryffe
The Bass	North Berwick: St Andrew Blackadder
Tighnabruaich	Kyles
Tongland	Tarff and Twynholm

Name no longer used	Present name of parish
Torphins	Mid Deeside
Torrance	East Kilbride: Old
Towie	Upper Donside
Trailflat	Kirkmichael, Tinwald and Torthorwald
Trailtrow	Cummertrees
Trefontaine	Kirk of Lammermuir and Langton and Polwarth
Trossachs	Callander
Trumisgarry	Berneray and Lochmaddy
Tullibole	Fossoway: St Serf's and Devonside
Tullich	Glenmuick
Tullichetil	Comrie
Tullynessle	Howe Trinity
Tummel	Foss and Rannoch
Tushielaw	Ettrick and Yarrow
Uddingston: Aitkenhead	Uddingston: Viewpark
Uddingston: Chalmers	Uddingston: Old
Uddingston: Trinity	Uddingston: Old
Uig	Snizort
Uphall: North	Strathbrock
Uyeasound	Unst
Walston	Black Mount
Wandel	Glencaple
Wanlockhead	Lowther
Waternish	Bracadale and Duirinish
Wauchope	Langholm, Eskdalemuir, Ewes and Westerkirk
Waulkmill	Insch-Leslie-Premnay-Oyne
Weisdale	Tingwall
West Kilbride: Barony	West Kilbride: St Andrew's
West Kilbride: St Bride's	West Kilbride: St Andrew's
Wheelkirk	Liddesdale
Whitehill	New Pitsligo
Whiteness	Tingwall
Whittingehame	Traprain
Wick: Central	Wick: Pulteneytown and Thrumster
Wick: Martyrs'	Wick: Pulteneytown and Thrumster
Wick: St Andrew's	Wick: Pulteneytown and Thrumster
Wilkieston	Edinburgh: Ratho
Wilsontown	Forth
Wishaw: Chalmers	Wishaw: South Wishaw
Wishaw: Thornlie	Wishaw: South Wishaw
Wiston	Glencaple
Wolfhill	Cargill Burrelton
Wolflee	Hobkirk and Southdean
Woomet	Newton
Ythan Wells	Auchaber United

INDEX OF SUBJECTS

Action of Churches Together in Scotland
(ACTS)   xviii, 30
Artistic Matters Committee   12
Assembly Arrangements Committee   17, 22
Associations (and Societies)   53
Auxiliary Ministry   284

Baptism   70
Bible Societies   56

Carberry   xviii
Central Services Committee   17, 22
Chaplains to HM Forces   9, 23, 285
Chaplains, Hospital   287
Chaplains, Industrial   295
Chaplains, Prison   295
Chaplains to the Queen   66
Chaplains, University and College   296
Charity Numbers   xviii, 333
Child protection   41
Christian Aid   xviii
Church of Scotland Guild   21
Church of Scotland Insurance Company   xviii, 33
Church of Scotland Investors Trust   25
Church of Scotland Offices   xviii
Church of Scotland Pension Trustees   26
Church of Scotland Societies   55
Church of Scotland Trust   26
Church and Society Commission (CEC)   29
Church and Society Council   4
Church music   68
Church Offices   xviii
Church Pastoral Aid Society   53
Church Without Walls Group   27
Churches, Overseas   45
Churches Together in Britain and Ireland   30
Churches in the United Kingdom, other   44
Committee on Church Art and Architecture   12, 27
Conference of European Churches   29
Congregational Contacts (Social Care Council)   17
Congregational Statistics   349
Council Education Committees,
Church Representatives on   326
Council of Assembly   3
Councils   3
Councils and Committees, Index   2
CrossReach   15

Deceased Ministers   331
Design Services   31
Diaconate, Membership of   297
Discontinued Parish and Congregational
Names   402
Divinity Faculties, Scottish   49
Doctrine, Panel on   14

Ecclesiastical buildings   33
Ecumenical Relations Committee   17, 27
Editorial   xxi
Education and Nurture Task Group   12, 30
Elder training   10
Endowment grants   7
European Churches, Conference of   29

Facilities Management Department   31
Forces registers   23
Fundraising and Marketing,
Social Care Council   16
Funds (and Trusts)   58
Funeral services: fees   75

General Assembly (2007)   98
Decisions of   99
Moderator of   98
Officials   98
General Assembly (2008), date of   xix
General Treasurer's Department   18, 31
General Trustees   32
Glasgow Lodging House Mission   xviii
Glebes   33
Guild, Church of Scotland   24

Healthcare Chaplaincies   287
Highland Theological College   53
HIV/AIDS Project   20
Holidays for Ministers   58
Hospital Chaplains   287
Housing and Loan Fund   9, 34
Human Resources Department   35

Index of Councils, Committees, Departments
and Agencies   2
Index of Discontinued Parish and
Congregational Names   402
Index of Former Parishes and Congregations   402
Index of Ministers   384
Index of Parishes and Places   396
Industrial Chaplains   295
Information Technology Department   35
Insurance   xviii, 33
Inter-Church Organisations   28, 53
Investors Trust, Church of Scotland   25
Israel, accommodation in   21

John Knox House and Museum   11
Jubilee Scotland   21

Kirk Care   xviii

Law Department   18, 36
Lay Agents, Retired   328

Legal Questions Committee   18, 36
Libraries of the Church   67
Life and Work   11, 14
Long Service Certificates   67
Lord High Commissioners (list)   64

Marriage   71
Marriage Services, conduct of   73
Media Relations Unit (Press Office)   xviii
Ministers deceased   331
Ministers having resigned Membership of
    Presbytery   301
Ministers holding Practising Certificates   303
Ministers ordained sixty years and upwards   328
Ministries and Mission allocation   31, 350
Ministries Council   5
Mission and Discipleship Council   xviii, 10
Mission and Evangelism Task Group   13, 37
Moderator of the General Assembly
    (see General Assembly)   xvi, xx
Moderators of the General Assembly (list)   65

Netherbow, The   xviii, ii
Nomination Committee   37

Office Manager (121 George Street)   xviii
Offices of the Church   xviii
Overseas appointments   21
Overseas Churches   45
Overseas locations   306
Overseas Resigned and Retired Mission
    Partners   21, 310
Overseas vacancies   20

Panel on Doctrine   14
Panel on Review and Reform   37
Panel on Worship   14
Parish Appraisal Committee   38
Parish Assistants and Project Workers   314
Parish Development Fund   38
Parliamentary Office (Scottish Churches)   xviii, 41
Pension Trustees   26
Personnel Department (Human Resources)   35
Practising Certificates   303
Precedence   66
Presbytery Advisers   306
Presbytery lists   105
Press Office (Media Relations Unit)   xviii
Principal Clerk's Department   18, 38

Prison Chaplains   295
Project workers   314
Properties   33
Publishing Committee   11, 14, 39
Pulpit Supply   xviii, 9

Queen's Chaplains   66

Readers   314
Records of the Church   68
Regional Development Officers   10

Safeguarding Office   41
Saint Andrew Press   11, 14
Schools of Divinity   49
Scottish Charity Numbers   xviii, 333
Scottish Churches House   30
Scottish Churches Parliamentary Office   xviii, 41
Scottish Storytelling Centre   11
Social Care Council   xviii, 15
Societies (and Associations)   53
Statistics, Congregational   349
Statistics, summary   350
Stewardship and Finance Committee   18, 39
Stewardship Programmes   40
Stipend   7
Support and Services Council   17

Travelling expenses   7
Trusts (and Funds)   58

University Chaplains   296

Vacancies overseas   20
Vacancy procedure   76
Vacancy schedules   90

Well Asian Information and Advice Centre   11
Wills   76
World Alliance of Reformed Churches   29
World Council of Churches   28
World Day of Prayer   55
World Exchange   54
World Mission Council   19
Worship, Panel on   14
Worship and Doctrine Task Group   14, 41

Year Book, Information on   xviii, xix

INDEX OF ADVERTISERS

BOOKSHOPS
SPCK... xv
Wesley Owen .... OBC

CAR HIRE
Zenith Executive Drive 104

CAR SALES
Autosave... 42

CHURCH CLOCKS
James Ritchie & Son Ltd 426

CHURCH FURNISHINGS
Hayes & Finch Ltd 348

CHURCH MAINTENANCE
Davis Duncan Architects xiv
Fleming Muir Architects 426
K2 Specialist Services 96
Richardson & Starling 332

CHURCH SIGNS
Greenbarnes Ltd..................................... i

CLERICAL TAILORS
J & M Sewing Service 348
Wippell's xii

EQUIPMENT
Capital Solutions.................................... IBC
Concept Group....................................... ix

FUNDRAISING
Erskine Hospital....................................
Royal Blind Asylum ....

MUSICAL SUPPLIES
Allen Organs.. x

PUBLICITY
Contact Publicity.................................... 387

PUBLISHERS
Life and Work .... IFC

REGULAR GIVING ENVELOPES
Church Finance Supplies Ltd 332
Donation Envelopes Ltd vii

SILVERSMITHS
Eleanor Macdougall............................... 391

SOCIAL WORKS
Christian Aid Scotland........................... v
CrossReach xiii
Housing and Loan Fund vi
Scottish Bible Society............................ iv
Stewardship and Finance ii

STAINED GLASS
H&R Developments................................ viii
Roland Mitton 385

STONEMASONS
Arlington Stone...................................... 389